CLINTON HEYLIN

Described by the *New York Times* as 'the only Dylanologist worth reading', Clinton Heylin is the author of the acclaimed *Bob Dylan: Behind the Shades* (1991; revised 2001) and over two dozen other books on music and popular culture, including biographies of Sandy Denny, Van Morrison and Orson Welles, and the two classic studies of punk's origins, *From the Velvets to the Voidoids* and *Anarchy in the Year Zero*. The first volume of this definitive biography, *The Double Life of Bob Dylan*, was published in 2021. An ex-pupil of Manchester Grammar School, and with two degrees in History, he has been a full-time historian and critic for three decades. He lives in Somerset.

ALSO BY CLINTON HEYLIN

On Bob Dylan:

Bob Dylan Behind The Shades (3 editions)
Dylan Day By Day: A Life In Stolen Moments
Dylan: The Recording Sessions 1960–94
Judas! – From Forest Hills To The Free Trade Hall:
A Historical View Of The Big Boo
No One Else Could Play That Tune:
The Making And Unmaking Of Dylan's 1974 Masterpiece
Revolution In The Air: The Songs Of Bob Dylan 1957–1973
Still On The Road: The Songs Of Bob Dylan 1974–2008
Trouble In Mind: Bob Dylan's Gospel Years
The Double Life of Bob Dylan:
Volume I: 1941–66: A Restless, Hungry Feeling
The Double Life of Bob Dylan: Volume 2: 1966–2021: Far Away from Myself

On Popular Music:

All Yesterday's Parties: The Velvet Underground In Print 1966–71 (editor)
The Penguin Book Of Rock & Roll Writing (editor)
The Act You've Known For All These Years: A Year In The Life Of
Sgt Pepper & Friends
All The Madmen: A Journey To The Dark Side Of British Rock
Anarchy In The Year Zero: The Sex Pistols, The Clash And The Class Of '76
Babylon's Burning: From Punk To Grunge
Bootleg! – The Rise & Fall Of The Secret Recording Industry
Can You Feel The Silence? – Van Morrison: A New Biography
Dylan's Daemon Lover: The Tangled Tale Of A 450-Year-Old Pop Ballad
E Street Shuffle: The Glory Days Of Bruce Springsteen & The E Street Band
From The Velvets To The Voidoids: A Pre-Punk History For A Post-Punk World
It's One For The Money: The Song Snatchers Who Carved Up A Century Of Pop
Joy Division: Form & Substance (with Craig Wood)
Never Mind The Bollocks, Here's The Sex Pistols (Schirmer Classic Rock Albums)
No More Sad Refrains: The Life & Times Of Sandy Denny
Rise/Fall: The Story Of Public Image Limited
What We Did Instead Of Holidays: Fairport Convention & Its Extended
Folk-Rock Family

On Pop Culture:

Despite The System: Orson Welles vs. The Hollywood Studios
So Long As Men Can Breathe: The Untold Story Of Shakespeare's Sonnets

CLINTON HEYLIN

The Double Life of Bob Dylan

Volume 2: 1966–2021
Far Away from Myself

VINTAGE

1 3 5 7 9 10 8 6 4 2

Vintage is part of the Penguin Random House group of companies whose addresses can be found at global.penguinrandomhouse.com

Penguin
Random House
UK

First published in Vintage in 2024
First published in hardback by The Bodley Head in 2023

For permission to quote from unpublished correspondence, interviews and diaries, grateful thanks are extended to Bruce Springsteen, Justin Martell (on behalf of the Estate of Tiny Tim), Marcia Stehr (on behalf of the Estate of Geno Foreman), Sharyn Felder (on behalf of the Estate of Doc Pomus), Beverly Martin, Robert Polito and James Ostrow

penguin.co.uk/vintage

Printed and bound in Great Britain by Clays Ltd, Elcograf S.p.A.

The authorised representative in the EEA is Penguin Random House Ireland, Morrison Chambers, 32 Nassau Street, Dublin D02 YH68

A CIP catalogue record for this book is available from the British Library

ISBN 9781529923797

Penguin Random House is committed to a sustainable future for our business, our readers and our planet. This book is made from Forest Stewardship Council® certified paper.

Dedicated to Dr. Peter Heylyn (1599–1662),
who was 'Unfriended' by Thomas Fuller in 1659
for 'Telling It Right Like It Is'.

Contents

Three Distinctly Different Amnesiacs

(a.k.a. I Forgot To Remember To Forget)

Of course, all life is a process of breaking down, but . . . the big sudden blows that come, or seem to come, from outside – the ones you remember and blame things on – . . . don't show their effect all at once. There is another sort of blow that comes from within – that you don't feel until it's too late to do anything about it, until you realize with finality that in some regard you will never be as good a man again. The first sort of breakage seems to happen quick – the second kind happens almost without your knowing it.

F. Scott Fitzgerald, 'The Crack-Up', *Esquire*, 1936.

Most of the time I do feel like I'm an amnesiac. It's good for me to feel that way, so I can block out the past.

Bob Dylan, to Pete Oppel, October 1978.

★

The first 'crack-up' – or as Dylan called it, 'the amnesia' – came late. Historians and fans alike look for epiphanies; a proclivity the late, great cartoonist Ray Lowry sedulously satirised when he drew his 1974 cartoon of Dylan sailing over the handlebars on July 29th, 1966, as a light bulb came on, 'Country Rock!' Actually, as Dylan himself explained to Jonathan Cott in September 1978, his own post-accident crack-up belatedly snuck up on him without him knowing, 'One day [in Woodstock] *I was half-stepping, and the lights went out.* And since that point, I more or less had amnesia.'

How did I become Another in that moment? This was a question with which Dylan would wrestle all through what he appositely called 'the amnesia', even mocking himself in the opening line of 1971's 'Watching The River Flow', 'What's the matter with me, I don't have much to say.' Only when the amnesia subsided in early 1974, did he find the words of a poet to encapsulate what he had been through in a single couplet, written in blood:

> Till he started into dealing with slaves,
> And something inside of him died.

By the time he wrote those lines, in the spring of 1974, one must assume he'd read, or cast a glance at the letters Arthur Rimbaud wrote from Abyssinia in the years when he was allegedly 'dealing with slaves'. These mundane documents have not a whiff of the 16-year-old thief of fire who wrote to Paul Demeny in May 1871 expounding his own unique variant on the Blakean creed that the road of excess inexorably led to the palace of wisdom. When the shattered symbolist crossed the Mediterranean, 'something inside of him' really had 'died'.

So, how did Dylan come out the other side, and other contemporaries did not? It's not like he was alone in an era when self-discovery and prodigious drug use went hand in hand. Indeed, the motorcycle accident – *that* fabled motorcycle accident – comes at almost the exact mid-point between two of the more spectacular crack-ups on the Sixties pop scene, both in sleepy London town. One, in May 1965 claimed Brit-rocker Vince Taylor – and almost claimed Dylan himself. The other came in August 1967 and turned Pink Floyd's Syd Barrett from being a one-man epicentre of the psychedelic scene into a laughing madcap, first; a vegetable man, second. Both were the result of a conscious disordering of the senses (*dérèglement de tous les sens*') brought on by the hallucinogens a Hollywood-based Huxley once unwisely suggested opened the doors of perception.*

If Taylor had just been at the wrong place, Dylan's Savoy suite – at the wrong time, an impromptu party – to be 'dosed' by person or persons unknown, Barrett was a confirmed pot smoker by the time this self-confessed Dylan nut's life was changed by the May 1964 Festival Hall show, the night the American debuted 'Mr Tambourine Man', a

---

* Actually, he didn't say anything of the sort, but he might as well have, such was the book's influence.

song widely taken to be a drug song, but actually a homage to the Rimbaudian seer.

Syd then called his first significant composition 'Bob Dylan Blues'. Composing it shortly after that Festival Hall show, it had one couplet which hinted at the later scatter-brained Barrett, 'My clothes and my hair's in a mess/ But you know, I just couldn't care less.' After August 1967, he really 'couldn't care less', and Rock music had lost the one pop poet who could have become Britain's Bob Dylan. Neither Taylor nor Barrett would ever quite be the same again. Both eventually subsided into silence, the call of their muse put on permanent hold, to be joined there by other Sixties casualties like The Beach Boys' Brian Wilson, Fleetwood Mac's Peter Green, Atomic Rooster's Vincent Crane and Nick Drake.*

It would take a sixty-something Dylan to encapsulate the curse that consumed the above gifted souls in verse: 'You can always come back/ But you can't come back all the way.' Yet for Dylan, that first crack-up had come only *after* the most creative eighteen months of his career – not the eighteen months before his accident, the eighteen months after it.

By then, he knew he had been one of the lucky ones, even after something similar happened a second time. That second 'amnesia' would come after he decided to retire from the road and regroup, in 1981, after pushing his voice to the limit to get his message across, and still losing half his audience. Finally, he was forced to conclude, 'They don't want me around/ because I believe in You.' How ironic that many former followers had already decided it was his conversion to Christianity that represented his second crack-up, not its post-fundamentalist aftermath.

Again, the actual amnesia – a combination of writer's block and a fear of performing – took a while to appear, and longer still to abate. In the immediate aftermath of his second retirement from the road – one that save for a brief tour of Europe lasted four and a half years – he came up with *Infidels*, which should have been his best album since *Blood on the Tracks*. (He certainly had the songs to make it so.) And even after the 1984 European tour, which at times resembled a man going through the motions, he still found the inspiration to (co-)write one of

---

* I refer interested readers to my book on the subject, *All The Madmen: A Journey To The Dark Side of British Rock* (Constable-Robinson, 2012).

his most epic creations, 'New Danville Girl', before the fog descended for a second time.

For the next three years, the songs refused to come – Dylan often resorting to recording instrumentals and songs with dummy lyrics, hoping inspiration would later dawn – while most of the shows he gave with Tom Petty & the Heartbreakers and The Grateful Dead smacked of a man caught in the spotlight, showing all the signs of stage fright and/or a few draughts 'of vintage' too many.*

For the second – and last – time, he would use the word 'amnesia' to describe what had happened, telling the trusted Robert Hilburn in December 1997, 'I was going on my name for a long time . . . I had sort of fallen into an *amnesia* spell . . . I didn't feel I knew who I was on stage.' Not just onstage. Witchy women were giving him trouble, nothing but trouble, throughout most of the Eighties (see chapter 5.3). He was as emotionally adrift as he was creatively shot.

Thankfully, having escaped the asylum of amnesiacs before, he did so again, rediscovering his muse in time to make *Oh Mercy* (1989), *under the red sky* (1990) and *Time Out of Mind* (1997) – the first and third of which were widely acclaimed, while the second has gone unjustly underappreciated – before the clouds rolled in again.

Or did they? When Dylan took a business card he'd been given some time in 1999 and jotted on its back a single line, 'I'm trying to get as far away from myself as I can,'† was this an amnesiac fearing a third amnesia, or was this a man self-consciously looking to separate his twinned Selves, Artist and Man? Had a man who for decades referred to 'Bob Dylan' in the third person finally decided to make the separation as real as could be; the same man who at the height of the second amnesia in June 1987 once almost signed a note to his eldest son, 'Bob Dylan' and only just remembered in time, scratching it out, and writing, 'Dad'?

Almost immediately after writing that line, he took a leaf from Michael Douglas's professor in *Wonder Boys*, dumping everything from

---

* The video feed of the opening Dylan-Dead show in Foxborough on July 4th, 1987 provides all the proof required.

† Appropriately, the line would trigger a song about a man suffering a seven-year long writer's block. 'Things Have Changed', the theme song to Curtis Hanson's magnificent movie of Michael Chabon's *Wonder Boys*, would win Dylan an Oscar, a rare instance of the Academy recognising genius in its midst.

the memoir he had been working on for the past eighteen months in the river and starting again, explicating a new credo. It would no longer be the work of a man who lived outside the law. It would be 'A Liar's Autobiography', a work that laughed behind its authorial hand at those who couldn't tell truth from fiction, lies from fact.

But it wasn't just his book – still filed under non-fiction, down the shelf from Patti Smith's *Just Kids* – which took liberties with every turn of the page. Dylan's songs no longer addressed the life he once led. Instead, they now interweaved a mosaic of intercultural references with imaginary lives, convincing would-be Dylan scholars to become Sherlocks, as they followed the trail of clues without ever asking themselves, Is this man still doing pretty good stuff?

And still the ex-Pop idol turned Pied Piper played the tune in his forgetful heart – through albums imperceptibly different in technique, style, reference-points or aesthetic, yet each invariably greeted as the twenty-second coming – until fifty years on from the night he went half-stepping, he told a Martin Scorsese interviewing him for the *Rolling Thunder Revue* film, 'I don't remember a damn thing!' Though he seemed to think his audience might believe him, it was the one line at the NFT premiere in 2019 in London where the whole audience burst out laughing.

By then, Dylan had been a third-term amnesiac by sheer force of will for nigh on two decades. But perhaps what he'd really done was carefully create the persona of an amnesiac from the bits he remembered when he had been a *genuine* amnesiac. Like the Ronald Colman character in *Random Harvest* (1942) – who only became a writer *after* he lost his memory, and stopped being one when he got it back (a neat reversal) – Dylan gained the world's confidence only when he knew he was stringing it along.

Unlike Colman, he has not been saved by the love of a good woman. No Greer Garson, as far as we know, has led a life of sacrifice, waiting for him to come back at least some of the way. Even 'his' Sara, who endured the entire first crack-up for the love of her man, has long passed out of his life. No wonder he reached the point where he was 'sick of love', and in his sixth decade on earth decided to write of it no more.

The work that has followed this third epiphany has been of a different hue; indeed, has come from an entirely 'different point of view'.

Mortality has trumped the power of Women. It rather smacks of that hard left turn just before the last hairpin curve. But is this work as worthy as what came before? Can it still divide the word of truth? Or is it 'just the price you pay for the chains you refuse'? Let's wait and see. We've got a long way to go, the shadows are lengthening, and the sign on the window says, 'Lost time is not found again.'

Read on, rave on, rock on,

Clinton Heylin, April 2022.

Prelude

July 29th, 1966:
Bound Upon The Wheel

At that time I deserved to crash, 'cause I certainly couldn't have gone on.
                        Bob Dylan, to Matt Damsker, 15th September 1978.

New York, Tuesday [9/8/66] – Bob Dylan is reported to have broken several neck vertebrae and suffered concussion as a result of his motorcycle accident last week. The accident occurred near the home of his manager, Al Grossman, at Woodstock, New York. Dylan was riding the machine to a garage for repairs when the rear wheel locked and threw the motorcycle out of control. He was tossed over the handlebars . . . His doctors say he must recuperate for at least two months . . . There is a veil of secrecy over where Dylan is . . . In fact, news of the accident itself took three days to leak out to the press.
                        Ren Grevatt, *Melody Maker* 13th August 1966.

*

Grevatt, the man who had previously 'broken' the story of Dylan's marriage to Sara back in December was at it again, and seemed to have the scoop on *Time* magazine, who merely reported that Dylan had 'severe face and back cuts'. Three days after he filed his report, Dylan's editor at Macmillan, Bob Markel, was telling his staff a different tale:

'I must advise you that the publication date for Dylan's book TARAN-TULA must [now] be considered 'indefinite'. As you know, Dylan has been spending every bit of his time in past weeks holed up at his manager's place in the country revising his galleys. He was not satisfied with the book the way it stood in galleys. As he told me, 'I want this to be a real book, not just something that people will buy because it's got my name on it.' On Friday, July 29th, Dylan hopped on his motorcycle for a short ride to town. The front wheel locked on him, there was a crash and the result was a concussion and a fractured vertebra of the neck. I have been told that the first thing he said to his manager when they brought him to the hospital was: 'Holy [shit]! What the hell am I gonna tell Bob Markel and the MacMillan Company?'

Spinning one version to the press and another to Dylan's own would-be publisher, the singer, Grossman and whoever else cooked up this motorcycle nitemare couldn't even stick to a version of events consistent in every detail. Was it the front or back wheel that locked? Was he taken to hospital, or wasn't he? Did he 'fracture' a single vertebra or break 'several neck vertebrae'?

If these two contemporary accounts have more holes than Butch Cassidy and the Sundance Kid, Sally Grossman eventually confirmed a growing suspicion that this was a story planted in the press, much like his March 1965 *Village Voice* 'press conference' and March 1966 *Playboy* 'interview'. She recalled him leaving 'her house in Bearsville that morning [and] . . . returning a few minutes later,' under his own steam.

Yet, within a matter of weeks, he had convinced TV executives, publishers and record company lawyers alike that he was laid up, and laying low. Even after he had time to formulate a set narrative, Dylan would take journalists for a ride, telling the first pressman to track and chase him down, Michael Iachetta, the following May that 'the back wheel locked . . . I lost control, swerving from left to right. Next thing I know I was in some place I never heard of – Middletown, I think – with my face cut up . . . and my neck busted up pretty good . . . New X-rays should be comin' through any day now.'

Despite his best efforts, though, an alternative narrative soon started to form, one that questioned the severity (and even the veracity) of the accident. At the Isle of Wight press conference in August 1969 one impertinent scribe even asked him to 'tell us *exactly* what happened when you suffered an accident a while ago'. Dylan visibly blanched and turned to festival MC Rikki Farr, with whom he had a pre-agreed signal to bring proceedings to a close if things got too personal, only to find he wasn't there and he'd have to come up with a response. The reply he managed was as monosyllabic as most of that afternoon's answers,

'It's true I suffered a broken neck. It's awful hard to explain. I have to take it easy sometimes.'

The question still would not go away. Craig McGregor asked him straight out on his next tour of Australia, 'Did you have a motorbike accident at all?' When Dylan replied in the affirmative, McGregor raised the ante, 'It wasn't just a cover-up?' almost prompting a man always on the run from the truth to be honest: 'It wasn't that the crash was so bad. I couldn't handle the fall. I was just too spaced out. So, it took me a while to get my senses back . . . It was almost as if I had *amnesia*. I just couldn't connect for a long, long time.'

By 1986, when it was playwright-actor Sam Shepard asking Dylan *if* he 'had a crash', such was the mythology swirling around the motorcycle accident that Dylan knew anything he said would merely compound the myth-making. Not that he wasn't happy to oblige. His reply reads like a lost section from their contemporary co-composition, 'Brownsville Girl', further proof that the 'liar's autobiography' approach to his personal history was no latter-day whim:

[It happened] way back. Triumph 500 . . . It was real early in the morning on top of a hill near Woodstock. I can't even remember exactly how it happened. I was blinded by the sun for a second. This big orange sun was comin' up. I was driving right straight into the sun, and I looked up into it even though I remember someone telling me a long time ago when I was a kid never to look straight at the sun 'cause you'll get blinded. I forget who told me that . . . and, sure enough, I went blind for a second and I kind of panicked or something. I stomped down on the brake and the rear wheel locked up on me and I went flyin' . . . [My wife] was followin' me in a car. She picked me up. Spent a week in the hospital, then they moved me to this doctor's house in town. In his attic. Had a bed up there in the attic with a window lookin' out. Sara stayed there with me. I just remember how bad I wanted to see my kids [sic]. I started thinkin' about . . . how short life is. I'd just lay there listenin' to birds chirping.

The doctor in question, Dr Thaler, later recalled, 'Sara did not take Bob to the hospital. She drove Bob directly from the Grossman property to [my] house-cum-surgery in Middletown' – which was fully fifteen miles away. Given that Thaler was not remotely qualified to deal with the kind of injuries sustained in a serious motorcycle accident, this does rather suggest that Dylan's immediate injuries – if any – were minor, but that he had been in bad shape before the spill. It was this which was most in need of treatment. Dylan's relocation to Thaler's home also meant no-one could track him down to corroborate the press release. According to the doctor's wife, Selma, it was Dylan's idea, 'He didn't want to go to the hospital. So, we said, "You can stay here." '

I think we can be fairly certain he did not spend a week – or any time at all – in hospital. It seems equally unlikely that Sara, who was nursing their six-month-old son, Jesse, stayed at Dr Thaler's with Dylan. Indeed, a single verse to an unfinished lyric called 'Key To The Alley', which seems to date from the immediate post-accident period, contains a reference to 'sitting in my lonely room/ waiting for you to come.' For now, he was seeing no-one, and talking to no-one. Not even Bob Markel. The shutters had come down, internally and externally.

Part 3

Why Must I Always Be The Thief?

Turn on, tune in, drop out.

Timothy Leary, 1966.

There is a revolution coming. It will not be like revolutions of the past. It will originate with the individual and with culture, and it will change the political structure only as its final act.

Charles A. Reich, *The Greening of America*, 1970.

You sat behind a million pair of eyes and told them how they saw / Then we lost your train of thought, your paintings are all your own.

David Bowie, 'Song For Bob Dylan', 1971.

Do you hear the voices in the night, Bobby? They're crying for you.

Joan Baez, 'To Bobby', 1971.

I can't be the saint people dream of now. People want a . . . saint with a cowboy mouth. Somebody to get off on when they can't get off on themselves . . . [That's] what Bob Dylan seemed to be for a while. A sort of god in our image.

Patti Smith, *Cowboy Mouth*, 1971.

People shouldn't look to me for answers. I don't know what's going down on the campuses, what's in their heads. I have no contact with them, and I'm sorry they think I can give them answers. Because I can't.

Bob Dylan, to Anthony Scaduto, January 1971.

3.1

July 1966 to May 1967:
There Must Be Some Way
Out Of Here

[Any] kid [of mine] wouldn't open his eyes . . . until [he was] five or six years old. I wouldn't imagine I'd even be around by that time.

Bob Dylan, to Nat Hentoff, October 1965.

I don't know if Dylan can get on the stage a year from now. I don't think so. I mean, the phenomenon of Dylan will be so much that it will be dangerous.

Phil Ochs, October 1965.

I came to believe . . . that Dylan was sacrificing himself in his whole philosophy, his thinking. That he would eventually die or that something horrible would happen to him . . . Other people felt it [too].

Rosemary Gerrette, Australian actress.

I was never confident when I was riding on the backseat of his motorcycle . . . I remember one time he almost got creamed . . . We were waiting anxiously at a train stop, gunning our motorcycles. The train goes by, he guns it – only he didn't see the train coming in the opposite direction. He almost slipped down under the wheels.

John Bucklen, childhood friend.

I got a motorcycle . . . but unlike the last ones I had on south dakota an minnesota roads, this one's for the fields. so . . . I'm not really goin all that fast. you cant go too fast in the fields you know.

Letter from Bob Dylan to Lawrence Ferlinghetti, February 1964.

Each of Dylan's concerts this past year had had a way of arousing the same feeling. There was no sensation of his having performed somewhere the previous night or of a schedule that would take him away once the inevitable post-concert party was over. There was, instead, the familiar comparison with James Dean, at times explicit, at times unspoken, an impulsive awareness of his physical perishability. Catch him now, was the idea. Next week he might be mangled on a motorcycle . . .

Richard Fariña, 1964.

'You look very near death.'
  Remembering. 'He passed me last night. On Academe Avenue . . . Kind of a bald cat, looked like a teenager, though.'
  'You should have asked him in for a nightcap, save him the trouble of looking you up in a year or two.'
  Richard Fariña, *Been Down So Long It Looks Like Up To Me* (1966).

I could feel the steady thrust of death that had been constantly looking over its shoulder at me.

Bob Dylan, to Sam Shepard, August 1986.

*

The premonitions of death and disfigurement had been coming thick and fast in the first six months of 1966 as Dylan bound himself to the spinning wheel of fortune, wondering how to get off. What we don't know is when exactly he found out that his literary rival and former friend, Richard Fariña, had died in a motorcycle accident on wife Mimi's 21st birthday, April 30th; riding pillion without a helmet, after a well-attended launch party for his debut novel, *Been Down So Long It Looks Like Up To Me*.

Unbeknownst to Dylan, the Fariñas' last recording had been a new song of Richard's called 'Morgan The Pirate', the subject of which was unmistakeable, as was the bitterness: 'I appreciate your velvet helping hand, even though you never gave it / I am sure you had to save it, for the gestures of the friends you understand.' The song would not be released until 1968, by which point Dylan himself may have come to recognize the validity of Fariña's acerbic portrait if something he wrote in the summer of 1966 – part of an attempt to rework *Tarantula* perhaps – was autobiographical:

> famous most well respected artest (that whom is redeemed); [']the legendary public harmless' when once was great & suffered to conceive & starved & birth is unknown but public accepts him as kind madman as he is but still now [his] mysti[q]ue & that which radiates his name has been rewarded; he is blessed with many sex & success; the sacred rubies of his country at his feet; he is all fortune & quite [d]erive[d] . . . his name of basterd.

In David Hajdu's dual biography of the two writers, he suggests it took two decades for Dylan and Mimi to speak again, and that all Dylan offered at that point concerning Richard's death, was, 'Hey, that was a drag about Dick. It happened right around my thing, you know. Made me think.' In fact, not only did Dylan spend time with Mimi on the 1974 tour, she also attended a personal preview of the *Blood on the Tracks* material at Pete Rowan's house, the following summer. She had already written to Dylan, in 1968, offering him the lead role of Gnossos in the (never-to-be-made) movie of Richard's novel, a letter she signs off with a surprisingly heartfelt, 'I still do and always have loved you very much.' Clearly, whatever hard feelings he'd left behind had not sundered that particular bond.*

As for Dylan's claim that Richard's death 'made me think', the evidence is against him. A few days before Fariña went flying from a motorcycle, another beatnik buddy of Bob's, gentle giant Geno Foreman, had been knocked from his motorcycle in Rome by a misdirected football, doing enough damage to his back for him to consult a doctor in London, setting in motion a series of events that would see him graveyard-bound just six months later.

Dylan would hear Foreman's tale of woe first-hand, on touching down in Stockholm in late April. The fact that Foreman found himself there at all was entirely down to Dylan, who had summoned him to the Swedish capital to help him with his tour film, even sending him a

---

* In the recently published transcripts of Anthony Scaduto's interviews for his 1971 biography, Joan Baez says, 'He always loved Mimi. She always loved him, but she always picked on him, and she had the knack.'

thousand dollars advance and an airline ticket. Foreman, the son of civil rights activist Clark and a close friend of Baez, had been estranged from his friend and fellow traveller for over a year, after Dylan advised him *not* to marry his pregnant girlfriend, Marcia.

Geno had told Dylan he thought they needed to be legally married to stop their baby from being taken away by the government.* Shortly afterwards, the couple fled America, convinced they were about to be arrested by the CIA. Oddly enough, the lady Dylan was advising Geno not to marry, Marcia Stehr, was one of his oldest New York confidants, a close friend of Suze, and the former wife of Mark Spoelstra, whose 1962 wedding Suze and Bob had both attended.

And yet, when Geno informed Dylan that he had given the money he'd sent him to his wife, the singer responded, 'Hey man, if I had known you were going to give it to your old lady, I never would have sent it.' In fact, barely had Geno and Dylan resumed relations than the former was promptly dismissed – seemingly at Grossman's behest – for corrupting Bob's backing band with some powerful weed, as outlined in a letter he wrote to Marcia after high-tailing it to London:

Having [had] just one slim joint and strict orders from fat al the gross man NOT to hold anything, I met dylan, whose plane arrived twenty minutes after ours and climbed into a car driven by an obliging swede along with his lead guitarist and his runner and no sooner had we swung out on to the high way but ol' reliable had his rippity tip lit up and hangin on his lip plus passin it around to musicians and other humouns alike, this action being naturally accompanied by my marvellous musical admonishment that this was my last and only and then I was clean clean clean as it were, only to have an old and dear friend that very night lay a grandiose hunk of the old chocolate on me for safe combustion. well the next night was concert night and by [now] I was natch fast friends with all the musicians whom I sent to the stage in a rather righteous state of mind.

Clearly, the paranoia that had hovered over the tour since the

---

* Geno and Marcia were married on March 1st, 1965 at Rev. Gary Davis's New York apartment. Neither Dylan nor Baez attended. Eight months later, Dylan married his own heavily pregnant girlfriend, Sara Lownds.

Melbourne drug-bust was still rampant. Indeed, according to a hastily scribbled note to Mrs Foreman, Geno got his marching orders not because he shared his largesse but because he 'got Dylan and Grossman [so] paranoid . . . they gave me the gate.' Meanwhile, the old, dear friend who had given him said hunk of hash – undoubtedly Victor – remained in situ, distributing said chocolate bars far and wide.*

And it was not just the band who maintained 'a rather righteous state of mind' long after the tour finished. Photos taken by a European photographer just days before his own motorcycle spill show a sunken-cheeked, hollow-eyed 25-year-old ex-folksinger. Dylan later told Shelton said epiphany happened when he went out 'one morning after I'd been up for three days'. So much for rest and recuperation.

Robbie Robertson states he was in Toronto when Grossman called to tell him, 'Bob had flipped over on the bike and fractured his neck,' and that he 'had gone for treatment to a particular doctor in Middletown, New York, from whom he could receive private and intensive care.' Dylan later described Dr Thaler to Robertson as 'a miracle worker' (which he must have been if he treated him for fractured vertebrae from his *home*). He also supposedly told Robbie, 'Come up to Woodstock when you get back,' having now remembered the whole band were still on retainer and the meter was ticking.† Robbie wasn't the only person Dylan invited upstate to attend to outstanding business in the immediate aftermath. Donn Pennebaker was summoned, too:

> I saw him a couple of days later, walking around with a brace. He didn't appear very knocked out by the accident . . . But he was very pissed [off] . . . [] . . . I know he wasn't as sick as he made out. I was working on a television show with him then, and one of the things this provided was the basis of an excuse for delaying delivery of that show, which is what he wanted to do. But I know he [had been] at a doctor's. I went to see him a number of times [when] he was in a brace. When I heard he'd been hurt I was in California and I went right back and drove to Bearsville . . . and said, 'I heard about the accident.' And he said,

---

* Both Spitz and Sounes – paraphrasing the former without checking his facts, perchance? – suggest Geno was fired from the tour for asking Bob for money. Not true.
† They were due to resume performing just a fortnight later, an August 13th show at the Yale Bowl.

'Where'd you hear about it?' It was a very funny reaction, and I thought maybe there wasn't any accident . . . But then . . . I knew he'd been hurt in other ways, so either [way], what he was doing was recovering.

Other visitors who came to see him that August included Odetta – who found him at the Thalers, having come to visit the doctor herself for 'exhaustion'. She saw fellow Grossman client, Dylan, 'living in a spare room on the third floor . . . [and] well enough to complain about artists recording cover versions of his songs with mistakes in the lyrics.' Meanwhile, Allen Ginsberg 'brought him a box full of books of all kinds. All the modern poets I knew. Some ancient poets like Sir Thomas Wyatt, Campion, Dickinson, Rimbaud, Lorca, Apollinaire, Blake, Whitman.' Ginsberg would also be quoted in *World Journal Tribune* that October, suggesting, 'This accident may have been a good thing. It's forced him to slow down,' a view Dylan would come to share by the turn of the century, when he told father-confessor Jeff Rosen, 'I'd just about had it with the scene. Whether I knew it [or not], I was looking to quit for a while.'

In fact, the accident all but brought him to a dead stop, creating more mystery than your average crime writers' convention. One lyric from this period, possibly tied to the million dollar smash, reads:

> I went down to the graveyard & looked into the sun
> The hound dogs took a piece of my pants
> That old piece that was pulled from the wreck on the road.
> Begging for just one more chance.*

A month later, The Beatles joined him in semi-retirement, playing their final paying gig at San Francisco's Candlestick Park on August 29th, at which they played not a single song from their latest, most ornate studio concoction, *Revolver*. They were as sick of the touring treadmill as Dylan, albeit for different reasons, and felt no need to concoct a get-out clause to pull the plug. Perhaps seeing Dylan and The Hawks in full flight three months earlier had made them realize performance-art was not their forte and never would be.

---

* The last line of the verse has been cancelled with xxxxs on the typewriter, but is still legible.

Both Sixties trendsetters had made a conscious choice, one Dylan articulated to Ian Brady in 1969, 'When I was touring, that was my job. You have two choices – either go out and do it, or don't go and do it . . . I realize now that there must be another way of doing things . . . I don't want all *that* to happen again.' In another 1969 interview, Dylan almost let slip that maybe the accident was not 'real', even if the damage was: '[It was] at least a year after that [before] I realized that it was a *real* accident. I mean, I thought that I was just gonna get up and go back to doing what I was doing before.'

Time to find another path, something he addressed head-on in one of the more intriguing lyrical fragments of the period, bearing the evocative title, 'Stand Back From The Fire':

> When desolation
> falls on you
> what do you do?
> Do you walk around
> with your head bowed down
> saying it isn't true?
> Do you praise your perverted ways
> or do you look for something new?

These were the kind of questions that begun to consume him, even as his mind turned to what to do about the *Stage '66* film he was due to deliver. According to Pennebaker, he was already feeling the 'pressure on him to get the film ready for TV'. He, in turn, pressured Pennebaker and Neuwirth to make a rough cut of the film, to show to ABC. The result was, in Pennebaker's words, 'All guessing. We didn't figure out what to do with any of these things, we just stuck them together quickly as a kind of sketch to jump-start the editing process, because nothing was being done.'

Only after Pennebaker and Neuwirth delivered their forty-five-minute edit, to which they (and/or Dylan) gave the name *Something Is Happening Here*, did Dylan take a look at the rolls and rolls of film shot himself – 'all of it, including unused footage' – and came to the conclusion, 'It was garbage. It was miles and miles of garbage. That was my introduction to film.'

Actually, the film Pennebaker and Neuwirth compiled on his

behalf – now housed in the Tulsa Dylan archive – was perfectly fit for purpose, contractually at least. In many ways it is more akin to what ABC thought they'd contracted, nay expected. The excerpts from exchanges with John Lennon and Johnny Cash – the 'special guests' ABC had been promised – are wittier and wackier than those in the final film Dylan and Howard Alk produced. In this context, even a clear drug reference during his exchange with the Beatle would probably have slipped past ABC's censor:

> **John Lennon**: I hear you're backing the Mamas and the Papas.
> **Bob Dylan**: You're just interested in the big chick. She's got a hold on you, too.
> **JL**: Barry McGuire is a great war hero. He met me through you, Bobby . . . He looks so natural but he's really shaking . . . [interrupted]
> **BD**: Tell me about the Silkies? I've taken a few milligrams of Silkie once.
> **JL**: . . . Barry being on the bosom of the folk-rockin' boom.

The sequence where Dylan and Cash discuss how to sing 'I Still Miss Someone' together – something they still hadn't figured out by February 1969 – is also more complete. Cash offers to 'do it your way. It'll make you look better,' Dylan shooting back, 'I'm not noted for looking better. I haven't looked better up till now. Don't you dare! You didn't know I was a piano player, I bet.' Cash insists he heard him play piano 'at a session, in between songs', just before the film cuts to Dylan and Lennon in a car and the famous exchange:

> **JL**: Come, come, it's only a film.
> **BD**: Why don't I vomit into the camera. I've done just about everything else.
> **Tom Keylock** [at the wheel]: It'd be a nice ending.

It is almost the end. As Dylan bemoans, 'I wanna go back home. Baseball games. All night TV. I come from paradise, man,' the film cuts to him and Robbie working on 'I Can't Leave Her Behind' in the Glasgow hotel room, before the last four minutes of a live 'Like A Rolling Stone', some of it shot upside down, after which Dylan says, 'Thank you. You've been very nice to us. You've been the best audience.' And that is it. The end of *Something Is Happening Here*.

Though the film has none of the cut-cut-cutting Alk preferred, many of its tropes should be familiar to anyone who has watched *Eat the Document* more than once, albeit nothing like as 'fast on the eye'. It has Dylan talking to schoolkids and boy scouts; a close-up of an old man dining on a terrace; little scenarios played out with continental women in Scandinavia and Paris. Meanwhile, four sections of 'Tell Me Mama' (almost the entire song), a solid chunk of an animated 'Thin Man', and a manic 'Leopard-Skin Pill-Box Hat' collectively hit a better balance of music and midnight mayhem than *Eat the Document*.

All in all, it's hard to see why Dylan did not simply turn this over to ABC and collect that $200,000 check. After all, he was going to need it. The only explanation which springs to mind is that he not only didn't like the man he saw on the screen, but couldn't relate to him. As he wrote in another lost lyric that summer, 'Some do it for peanuts, others do it for cash/ Some do it just for the sake of reward . . . I do it on my own accord.'

Perhaps viewing the raw footage from Europe persuaded Dylan to reconsider his shoddy treatment of his friend Geno Foreman. If it did, Geno never knew. He died at home in Hammersmith on November 15th, 1966 from acute peritonitis, having been suffering abdominal pains for months, which he thought were the result of his own motorcycle accident. It turned out he had ulcerative colitis, which had eventually perforated. The doctors missed the tell-tale signs and sent him home, where he died a painful death four days later.*

This time, Dylan was certainly informed of the passing of one of his oldest friends, aged just 25 – Geno having been born a mere five days after Bob. His wife wrote to Marcia to offer her condolences two weeks later, and to ask if Bob could possibly have back the hat he had given to Geno. The fact that it was Sara, someone who never knew Geno and barely knew Marcia, who wrote such a letter – rather than the person who had been friends with both – says a great deal about how Dylan was cutting himself off from the milieu which had created the piratical Morgan, and all the denizens who had shared it.

He'd consciously changed from the creature he was, and anyone and everyone who spent time with him in the months after the crash would

---

* Again, Spitz and Sounes (plus Jonathan Taplin) cast aspersions on Geno, suggesting it was an overdose.

comment on it, starting with Sara's college roommate, who, having first met him in 1965, at the height of his amphetamine insanity, felt 'it wasn't until after his accident . . . that I really got to meet him as he is when he's not play-acting . . . There was a great change in him from what I'd seen of him before. He'd positively mellowed . . . Even Sara said he was . . . very reluctant to go back to anything approaching the hectic pace of the early years of their marriage.'

One of those who had known him well in those mercurial times, Michael Bloomfield, revealed in a 1968 *Hit Parader* article that he had visited him post-accident, and that he had 'his neck in a brace, [even though] he just got scraped up a little'. He apparently informed the guitarist, 'he just didn't want to go out in front of the kids any more . . . because the crowds would yell at anything. It didn't make sense to play any more.'

Dylan also informed Happy Traum, who had relocated to the Catskills too, 'I've got to get a normal life here and the only way I can do that is to shut everybody else out.' He should perhaps have consulted with the missus first. When *World Journal Tribune* reporter, Mike Pearl, found Dylan's hideaway that October, and was confronted by 'a young woman' – clearly Sara – 'she refused to produce Dylan'. Nonetheless, she told Pearl, 'It gets very lonely here. Very few friends have come up, and we never go to town.'

At least his ever-patient editor, Bob Markel, was unfazed by this new Dylan, finding him to be 'far more friendly, far less distracted. He was more grown-up and professional, easier to be with.' But he was still not about to countenance the book's release, telling Markel, 'He didn't know if he wanted the book published *at all*.'

Some of the material now housed at Tulsa suggests Dylan could have started an entirely different book, a mantra Macmillan were now spouting if the question came up. When Tony Glover asked at a local bookstore for the book – as related in a letter to Dylan that August – he was informed his friend was apparently 'rewriting it'. But if 'the trouble with it was it had no story' – as Dylan suggested in 1968 – the pieces he was typing on his new typewriter were hardly more linear or narrative in style than the galleys he had failed to correct. Rather than reading the volumes of the venerable poets Ginsberg had brought for him, it seems he had simply re-read 'Howl':

No longer Lambs of Pagan Blood
No longer St Maude Screaming now & FLY BUY NITE
No longer the sound of sound of
No more soun[d] of sound of the pseude
No longer Jezabelle, the bearded women, mak[ing] me march in the name
    of Anthem, George Anthem, around my rosy room
No longer now comes Jezebelle, the bearded vessel . . .
No longer any change in Winston Keef, the man who knows everything
    & never dies; no longer any elements of matter & no more stealing
    what's been stolen from the lesser decent men . . .

One near-insurmountable problem is dating this material.* Fortunately, on the back of one sheet is Dylan's letter to Ginsberg about the
1966 *Kaddish* album, which is almost certainly pre-accident, suggesting
he may have been reworking the book before the crash. He certainly
appears at times to be still trying to emulate Kenneth Patchen, even
down to the oblique chapter headings, familiar names and lyrical references (the steam engine in 10, below, is based on 'Casey Jones'):

1. ramona put our heads in gunny sacks, tied our hands & feet – & took
our clothes to another room – we then would vi[o]lently hop around,
always being aware not to make any noise – she'd come back, scream at
the top of lungs 'FREEZE!' & whoever was the last to freeze not only
[would] have to stay in his gunny sack but also be her lover for the
nite . . . the others would only have to come to breakfast naked

THE REST IS HISTORY . . .

10. NEW METHODS OF SELLING GREEN
Shelley said he had a dream world & three people volunteered. one was
a common laborer who maintained that the sun was feminine & the
moon was masculine. one was a brave volunteer & the other was Shelley's father-in-law. one was going downgrade & the other two were on

---

* Like a great deal of material from the immediate post-accident era, these papers
were collected and collated at a later date, at the instigation of Dylan's new lawyer/
manager, Naomi Saltzman.

the hill. Shelley was going upgrade. along came a steam engine &
bashed one's brains out – the other three were scalded to death by the
steam.

Already, he cannot get back there, no matter how hard he tries. In a
section called 'Take One Like Kafka' – a *Tarantula*-esque chapter heading, if ever there was one – he crosses John F. Kennedy's famous request
with the golden rule, 'ask not what I can do for you. ask what you can
do for me,' before revealing more of himself than anywhere in that
rejected galley: 'you cannot kill illusion . . . when you do/ you are
doing nothing more [than] killing yourself.'

This reads like a post-accident Bob on his way to meet John Wesley
Hardin, in the company of Frank. And it is hardly a single salvo. Among
two-dozen extant pages, insights into a mind in turmoil repeatedly flit
forth: 'i'm scared of reliving the past/ but i'm not afraid to die'; 'there
is no direction but the one for me now' (circled, and handwritten); 'does
this mean that grief is lonely & that man has no business imitating
nature?'; 'it don't do no good to stand up and laugh about it/ just like it
don't do no good to sit down and cry' (again handwritten).

Elsewhere, he has a bee in his bonnet about religious advocates whom
'we must convince . . . of our sincerity, these long-haired preachers/
whose jobs are to flog us until we confess that we're comfortable.'* He
also uses religious imagery to make a more Sartrean point:

> the flesh of the image is the sound (of vision), the bones and the soul of
>   the image is a VISUAL thing not heard
> there is no beginning and there is no end
> the key to the sound of image is vision
> there is no such thing as di-vision [–] as [in] no sound.

At times, he adopts a declamatory tone which could have come
straight out of the New Testament: 'we are now on the verge of
becoming religious leaders & serious politicians/ but let us not forget
that we are not unwanted; let us openly admit that/ we are not good
husbands, patient wives nor perfect children.'

On the other hand, much of the content is renouncing past

---

* This is from a section headed 'Last Words'.

certainty: 'no more Popular belief in people. no more, this Overthrow-
ing of all Order. no more imagining that We are all Brothers . . . like a
Church on fire, i'll Just stand here & let my enemy Defend me.'
Through it all is an ongoing search for a meaning as yet unrevealed to
the 'hairy beggar', a Christ-like figure who finds himself on the receiving end of man's inhumanity:

> what's the meaning do you suppose? what's the meaning of seeing a
> hairy beg[g]er not only being dragged into an iron cage & then exam-
> ined by the ancestors of children but then also watching them cut his
> wrists & lay him down upon a filthy anvil – cut his hair – & cook him
> like meat & then bite him with their teeth? what's the meaning of that?
> what's the meaning of when they hang him up to dry – shoot him full
> of holes & gamble for his wig . . . does this mean that money is the root
> of all evil? does this mean that war is bad & pease is good?

Remarkable stuff, though for how long did he continue down this
road? Not long, I suspect, before he remembered he was a songwriter,
first and last. However, the evidence would not be forthcoming until
2014, when – after nearly five decades without anything known to be
composed between August 1966 and April 1967, i.e., post-accident, pre-
basement tapes – it turns out he was writing up a storm, lyrically
anyway.

That year, no less than twenty songs from this period appeared on a
set called *Lost On The River: The New Basement Tapes*, followed shortly
afterwards by a two-hour *Showtime* documentary called *Lost Songs: The
Basement Tapes Continued*.* Dylan, though, contributed almost nothing
to either project – save the briefest of interviews, during which he
insisted, 'A lot of this stuff just fell by the wayside. I don't even know
where it was kept all these years. I have never seen these lyrics since the
day they were written,' thus reinventing where the basement tapes
began in the same month a genuine *Bootleg Series* (vol. 11) recalibrated

---

* My own ghostly presence hovers over the documentary, the director having decided
to use my disembodied voice from *filmed* interviews. What is never addressed is the
rather crucial point that these lyrics have *nothing* to do with the basement tapes.

where it ended. If such a productfest was decidedly Dylanesque, it came with a double-D for deconstruction and disinformation.*

Where he missed a trick was in not making the resultant artifact an audio-visual affair, with all the handwritten lyrics – and a veritable night school's worth of artistic doodlings – reproduced alongside the febrile 'reimaginings' of two-dozen lost Dylan songs circa 1966-67 per-petrated by the likes of Mumford & Sons, Rhiannon Giddens and Elvis Costello (who, frankly, should have known better). But that might have allowed the material to be seen by the sort of people who could smell snake oil at ten paces; the kind who knew in a heartbeat, this was *pre-basement* – and all the more important for it.

Here was that vital missing link, the answer to what kept Dylan's raging mind occupied in the nine months that separates the crash from the Big Pink basement, and probably what he was rambling on about when he told Michael Iachetta in May 1967, 'Songs are in my head like they always are, [but] they're not goin' to get written down until some things are evened up – not until some people come forth and make up for some of the things that have happened.'

Here was a theme of atonement and retribution also spattered across lines like: 'If I were you, I'd put it back what I took/ A Guilty man has got a Guilty look.' Old-Testament-style judgement also rains down in the following:

> From somewhere, out of the darkest night, the strangers came to throw
>   rocks and sticks at him.
> This, and this alone, is what ye pay for if ye so pass him.
> Do not go self-cent'red and ye shall soon forget him.

It seems 'Drifter's Escape' is beckoning. The olde-worlde morality invoked in such songs may well reflect recent reading matter, now he had time to catch up on some. A typed reference among latter-day *Tarantula* papers cites page 54 of the Hindu scripture, the Bhagavad Gita, which praises 'he who regards/ everyone as equal . . . the foe & the traitor/ the crippled & the wicked/ the man who arrested him/ &

---

* To further the disinformation, he told Bill Flanagan, 'They were found in an old trunk which came out of what people called the Big Pink house in Woodstock.' The one place they never could have been was Big Pink.

all those who judge him.' Another song from this period, 'The Return
Of The Wicked Messenger',* predates its non-returning namesake by
a good year, setting the stage for its compositional cousin as well as
'Quinn The Eskimo':

> The sky was dark and the cloud was in sight
> People were lining the streets in the night
> Gold neon signs and glittering lights
> Everyone had shut their shutters and turned in for the night . . .
>
> The people were lining the streets below
> When a voice sprang forth both loud and clear
> Say[ing], Everybody in trouble, dry your tears
> And lay your burden on the Lord.

Some of the more interesting lyrics in these two *pre*-basement folders would remain mere fragments, unsuitable for 21st century
desecration by ye heathens, going mercifully unreferenced by T-Bone
Burnett, the overseer of *Lost On The River*. These included lines like,
'I'm waiting for the one that's not from this world', 'If the devil looks
into you, can you expect god to look out,' and verses like, 'Now the
Lord looked down from a cloud on high/ and he set my people free/
The earth shook as he passed by/ And he set my people free,' and, 'Do
not curse the idle youth. sing him God-sent messages. Do not unto
Him but unto him as you would have him Do unto God,' a witty vari-
ant on the golden rule twelve years before 'Do Right To Me Baby'.

Mercy – the biblical kind – was once again on his mind. In fact, the
'holy slow train' he referenced in the *Highway 61* sleeve notes crops up
repeatedly, most notably on 'The Whistle Is Blowing'. Not that one
would know this from the traducing it received from Marcus Mumford
on *Lost On The River*, who decided to remove the plentiful hints in Dylan's
handwritten draft that the train in question is the train of salvation:

> The diesel is humming, there's another one coming
> I'm late already, I must not stay . . .

---

* He revisited the theme not once, but twice, writing a sequel to the *John Wesley Harding* track, called 'I Am That Wicked Messenger?' in 1968.

The whistle is [blowing, the train is] going
Has all my labor been in vain
A wild dust storm blows across the platform
It seems all my life I been trying to catch that train.

The reference to 'the diesel . . . humming' confirms Dylan is consciously evoking the spirit of Curtis Mayfield's 1965 45, 'People Get
Ready' – which contains the line, 'All you need is faith to hear those
diesels humming.' It's a song cogently captured at Big Pink the following year, and twice more in the studio, in 1975 and 1987.

Mumford preferred to make the song about 'that woman [who]'s
always right', an aspect of the original lyric f'sure, but only as a way for
Dylan to admit his most egregious former sin, 'a wandering eye', as he
stands on the platform awaiting Her, wondering whether he should get
on board: 'All of my possessions are loaded on board/That woman she
left me, she wouldn't accept me . . . The rain is falling, the engine's
crawling/All my life I been looking at that train.'

Another fragment suggests he has finally come to realize the hurt
his wanton ways have caused, and recognizes a need to atone, not so
much to God as to his significant other:

The tears of a lonely man are hidden within
As he moves from one woman to the next, his spirit grows thin
And when he falls in love with one, it's hard but it's true
But it's oh so much harder still when that woman is you.

One lost lyric hinting of promise even contains a symbolic renewal
of vows, aligned to the very covenant God made with His chosen
people:

I wanna tell you I love you / more than any man can
So come on/ take me to your Promised Land.
I wanna tell you a secret/ no-one else should know
I want you to take me where no *one else* [crossed out] can go
I wanna tell you I love you and give you a wedding band
So come on take me to your Promised Land.

Seemingly, she gave the songwriter in him religion, prompting this supplication: 'You hold my future, you hold my past/ You hold every-thing I do . . . Oh how I love you.' But the change in Dylan was not just on the inside. As Al Aronowitz noted, 'In the years following his motor-cycle accident, Bob acted like a romantic cornball when he was with [Sara]. More and more, he depended on her advice as if she were his astrologer, his oracle, his seer.'

Though some of these lyrics hint at the moralism of *John Wesley Harding*, others – like 'That Blue-Eyed Girl' (surely a conscious nod to Jimmie Rodgers's 'My Blue-Eyed Jane') – come from that 'romantic cornball'. This time the door is open and the one who is coming through is 'all that I can heed'; the one who will 'always do it'.

Dylan had made a conscious choice, one articulated in a rare moment of candour in *Chronicles*, 'I wanted to get out of the rat race. Having children changed my life and segregated me from just about everybody and everything that was going on.' The change both amazed and impressed someone who had known him at the very height of *le déréglement de tous les sens*:

> **D.A. Pennebaker**: He understood that . . . he had to get straight with his wife and family, and live a kind of personal life that was in fact evo-lutionary and made sense . . . That's something very few people thrown into that incredible [fame] thing can ever figure out.

Another occasional eyewitness to the new Dylan, local painter Bruce Dorfman, whom Dylan befriended hoping to learn some tricks of the trade, sensed 'he was trying to reclaim some way of incorporating his sense of family into his life. He had an idea about some kind of middle-class life, and the closeness and comfort of family,' one which undoubtedly derived from childhood, and parents from whom he had become estranged in the headlong rush into the abyss. Or so it seemed to the family man and son of Abraham, and to Dave Van Ronk, who felt he'd 'returned to being the middle-class Jewish kid'.

Dylan articulated all his mixed-up confusion in a long free-verse poem he wrote for himself, and perhaps his nearest and dearest. It was called, simply, 'A Quest'. It begins with him talking about the birth of 'an age of [self-]discovery', before delineating two forms of love – 'One love' and 'The other love'. Trying to learn to trust, he is consumed by 'a disbelief that it might be returned'. He admits to a 'desperate desire to please' but is consumed by a blend of emotions 'indefinable', the strong-est of which, tellingly, is revenge. But he knows if he perseveres he will come to know 'the real "kind" of love' – what he calls 'the other love'. This he groups with contentment, compassion, trust, unselfishness, even pleasure. He considers anyone who feels a need to please, blessed.

He insists he has only known the former; that he may have known contentment, self-assurance, compassion and pleasure fleetingly, but he has never known true trust. He feels that any man who reveals 'his limitations, his failings, his doubts' to a woman he loves is 'laid bare'. Any 'protective covering' he has is stripped away, leaving him mocking himself for such a display of 'weakness'. Only finally, painfully, does he come to accept that he must learn to trust someone else completely. If he fails, he can never 'love another completely'. Such is the quest, and when Dylan wrote this letter to himself, it had 'only just begun'.

How soon after the accident he wrote such a heartfelt poem is unclear, but now was evidently a time for confession. It was also time to relearn the craft of songwriting, in isolation, reflecting on new con-cerns that for all their mundanity were excitingly new to him, something as simple as seeing 'the children playing, their mother talk-ing'. It seems he really meant it when he wrote, 'Everyday I make a brand new start . . . When my true love and I aren't apart/ It's all I can do to go out of my head,' perhaps referencing their enforced separ-ation at Thaler's.

However, the old Bob is biding his time, still inclined to satirise the normality of such a life – as he would a year later, with the inspired 'Clothes Line Saga'. One song, 'Try A Little Muscatel', might even have found a home on *New Morning* with a little work:

> When the old weathervane is all rusty
> And that windmill just plows up and down
> And silly as it might seem, it's all dusty
> And anyway it's just driving a hole in the ground
> When that old hardware man comes a-calling
> And gives you that old hard sell
> Just keep both feet on the ground
> Don't let it get you down
> And try a little muscatel.

All of these new songs – finished and fragmentary – seem to have come relatively easily. There are certainly enough of them. Yet they are not a bridge to Big Pink. Though they lead within a matter of months into the hijinks and low ribaldry of the basements, hints of its rambunctious tone prove surprisingly thin on the ground, even if 'Eskimo Woman' employs a double entendre or two: 'Eskimo woman, my behind's in the bin/ Gimme some of that mouth, not only a grin,' and 'Eskimo woman, how 'bout a little chunk/ Come give me a kiss, gimme some of that funk/ I'm all saddled up and I'm ready to plunk.' Likewise, 'Bank Teller' threatens to become a proto-'Please, Mrs Henry'. Right now, though, he just needs a dime to ring his baby, not relieve himself:

> Bank teller, take me back to the backroom please.
> I just gotta make a phonecall. I'm on my bended knees.
> I'll ask you and I'll beg you 'cause I got to find a phone
> My baby's waiting patiently, she's waiting all alone.

The third verse of 'Card Shark', which just about survived Taylor Goldsmith's Attic Trax rendition on *Lost On The River*, benefits from a sip of its own bottle of bread, with a dash of 'Lo And Behold': 'Set 'em up Sambo and sit on it a while/ Toss in the towel and kick/ Stick it in the rear and roar for a bit/ And waddle down the road like a brick.' In a similar vein is another unresolved fragment, 'You gotta kick loose, turn on the juice, there's no excuse for more abuse this morning/ You gotta hold tight, see the light, save your might, and don't fight this warning/ For life is a puzzle, those who disagree are few/ So if you just promise to love me, little girl/ I'll promise to love you, too.'

His more lascivious self peeks over the parapet in lines like, 'My woman's got a mouth like a lighthouse on the sea/ Every time she smiles, she shines her light on me.' But wacky characters and non sequiturs remain in short supply, save for one snatch preceding 'Duncan And Jimmy': 'The king is sleeping, said Tiny Tim, but your secrets are safe with me.' Of course, Tiny Tim – unlike the cavalcade of characters to come – was a real person, someone Dylan spent time with in the winter of 1967 (as meticulously documented by Tim's own diaries).

Elsewhere, he flirts with traditional idioms in a way that almost presages his next LP, while tweaking the lines with a disconcerting modernity. In 'Spanish Mary', he returns to 'Kingston town, of high degree', in the company of 'the buffoon, the fool, the fairy'; in 'Duncan And Jimmy', unlike 'Duncan And Brady', they 'walk side by side/ Nobody walks between them.' In 'Santa Cruz', he enquires of a woman, 'Just where would [you] be going to, my dear sweet lovely swan?' only for her to inform him, 'I was just driving up to Santa Cruz . . . and then she commenced to yawn.' At this point the song unexpectedly morphs into something Chuck Berry might have penned, 'Now I'm not one to brag any but man did I hit that gas/ I tore right out of there so quick, her head nearly hit the glass/ Everything was in front of me that day but there was nothing I didn't pass/ And when we pulled into Santa Cruz, she said, "Boy, you sure got class." '

In one sense, the songs on – and contemporaneous with – *Lost On The River* resemble those songwriting exercises he'd scribbled on the table of Eve and Mac McKenzie back in 1961, just with a firmer grasp of songcraft and vernacular. Reaching for a branch on the tree of roots, nothing quite gels like it had the previous winter, or would, the following spring. Not so much *Lost On The River* as lost in the woods, looking for a successor to the brilliantine sheen of *Blonde on Blonde*.

These songs ain't that. Nor are they a bridge to the Babylonian basements. In fact, the main motif they share with this more mercurial material is an inner resentment and desire for retribution – a characteristic Dylan always kept well hid, save in song. Here, the male partner of Pirate Jenny shows his flickering face in lines like: 'There I sat with my eyes in my hand/ Contemplating killing a man/ For greed was one thing I just couldn't stand.'

He later alludes to such impulses when on the road to recovery, admitting there came a 'turning point . . . back in Woodstock, a little after the accident. Sitting around one night under a full moon, I looked out into the bleak woods and I said, "Something's gotta change." There was some business that had to be taken care of.' And the feeling would still be there in a 1984 interview, 'I woke up and caught my senses, I realized I was just workin' for all these leeches.' Such feelings prompted the following verse from a post-accident bank account blues:

> You don't have to turn your pockets inside out
> But I'm sure you can give me something
> You don't have to go into your bank account . . .

The 'Bank Teller', in Dylan's case, was near neighbour Albert Grossman, who continued to control the purse strings, an arrangement that had not previously caused the artist sleepless nights, but began to do so as contract negotiations with Columbia came off the rails, and Dylan began reading some of the contracts he'd signed in the years his manager had lined both their pockets.

What was concerning Dylan greatly was the way Columbia were running circles around his rottweiler manager regarding the terms for release from the slave contract he had signed in 1961 and reaffirmed in 1962. Evidence Columbia was spoiling for a fight can be found in an internal memo Jack Wiedenmann sent to corporate attorney Clive Davis on December 8th, 1966. In it, Wiedenmann breaks down all the studio recordings Dylan has made across the five annual terms of the contract by 78 rpm side – with both 'Desolation Row' and 'Sad-Eyed Lady Of The Lowlands' each being assigned a single 10" 78 (maximum playing time: two minutes 58 seconds), as Columbia sought to make the ludicrous argument that Dylan should 'maintain' the average number of 'sides' he had recorded for the label per annum, based on the 190 sides he recorded in the first four years, in the 'final' year of his contract.

Actually, Dylan had only once in those years released two studio albums in a single twelve-month period, having already delivered an album since March 1st, 1966, the contract's fifth anniversary – and a double-album at that.

Also – as Wiedenmann noted – the label had 'at least a two-record set from the 1966 concert [sic] recorded in England'. They were even threatening to bastardize Bobby's studio detritus to make up another album or two, after staff producer Dave Rubinson, who would go on to produce Moby Grape and precious little else of note, 'listened to the older material and . . . indicated that he feels some of the material would be very saleable if the tracks were musically sweetened in order to update the sound.'

Thus did Columbia lay bare its patent disregard for Dylan's artistic integrity. Here was the very label which in 1973 would release *Dylan*, widely regarded as an act of revenge on an artist who had given them ten years' loyal, lucrative service. They missed a trick by not simply getting Dylan to agree to release a double live album from Manchester, and leaving it at that – but such a deed would have required vision.

Wiedenmann, blessed with neither, advised 'a brief discussion to establish the number of sides we feel would be reasonable to request from Mr Dylan before the expiration of his contract'. The memo prompted an immediate response from Davis, in thrall to the same idea that a one-minute joke like 'Talkin' Hava Negeilah Blues' should share parity with the six-minute-plus songs Dylan had been writing and recording in the past year; an argument they could never have won in court. And yet, on December 13th, 1966, Clive Davis wrote to Dylan via Grossman 'requesting twenty-one sides to fulfill contract,' to prove he had a lot of nerve.

Grossman was almost entirely to blame for the situation in the first place for not advising Dylan to delay the Nashville *Blonde on Blonde* sessions for three more weeks, and for failing to tell his artist to go on strike until Columbia honoured a previous verbal agreement to 'bump' his royalty rate retrospectively. He now found himself between a rock and a rolling stone.

Dylan was anxious to resolve the matter, though not so anxious as to okay the release of a live album. The haste with which he had pressed the label to release the live 'Just Like Tom Thumb's Blues' stands in stark contrast to the silence that now ensued on the subject of that live album from the edge of forever.

Now, he just wanted out of Columbia. A brand spanking new, lucrative contract with MGM Records was sitting on the counter, just waiting to be signed. That contract was for $1.5 million, paid over ten years, though the contract only required product for the first five, with a mechanical royalty of 24 cents per album, a contract Columbia could not or would not match. To do so would have required the kind of foresight in perpetually short supply on Seventh Avenue.

Their own offer had been a $650,000 advance with $150,000 in re-adjusted royalties payable along with the advance, an open admission that they had been robbing him blind for the last five years. They would return what they had stolen in the first place – but only if it became part of a new deal. (Their mothers would have been so proud.) At the same time Davis set out to use sleight of hand to scupper the MGM deal in order to retain an artist the label had never understood and only recently prioritized.

First, he asked Dylan's producer if he had heard anything about the rival offer. On January 4th, 1967, Johnston replied, via Richard Asher, 'I have received no communication from Bob Dylan except by way of a publisher friend who advised me that a high exec. of MGM advised him that he was signed.' Davis sensed he needed to act fast. Two days later he wrote to his boss, Goddard Lieberson, 'We have been very reliably informed that he has received a guarantee offer of $1.5 million from MGM payable over ten years, and that unless an immediate counter-proposal is received from us, the deal will be signed.'

By then, Davis almost certainly knew what the MGM offer was, down to the last red cent, having in his possession a copy of the contract Dylan just needed to sign, courtesy of an advisor to the MGM board with whom he had just had lunch; an individual whom an English High Court judge, presiding over the dissolution of the world's biggest band three years later, would describe as having 'the flavour of dishonesty'. His name was Allen Klein, and according to Marc Eliot's wretched *Rockonomics* (Omnibus, 1989), he had already 'made a complete study of Dylan's finances, and considered wooing him away from his over-protective manager . . . [convinced] Grossman's rank amateurism was displayed nowhere more clearly than during . . . negotiations with MGM.'

Klein was, in Davis's words, 'obstreperously opposed [to] the [MGM] deal', and became doubly so after being fed Dylan's true sales figures by Davis, a clear breach of ethics. But it was as nothing to the one Klein breached when he gave Davis in return a copy of the MGM contract, which still sits in the Sony archives.* Convinced that the Dylan deal was a bad deal for MGM, Klein was determined to scupper it; code of ethics go hang.

As it happens, he was hopelessly wrong about Dylan's ongoing commerciality. Every single album he would deliver Columbia in his second term (1967-71) would outsell *all* the albums from the first. Dylan's retreat would make him a greater cultural icon, a point lost on someone who saw only the bottom-line: a bean-counter, and a crooked one at that.

What the MGM contract would have meant for Dylan's career had

---

* In case anyone thinks I am exaggerating the ethical breach, when MGM Records' then-president, Mort Nasatir, heard of the tête-à-tête between Davis and Klein – just that – he threatened to bring suit for conspiracy. If Davis's defence was that the figures he gave Klein were true, it was no defence.

he signed it, can only be speculation at this point, though some clauses suggest he still had some business lessons to learn. Having no doubt about his own ongoing fecundity, he was prepared to commit himself to twenty-four 'sides' a year for MGM for the next five years, knowing that should he fail to come up with the requisite number of tracks 'during any year of the term hereof, Artist agrees to repay to MGM upon demand, for each record side or equivalent thereof, not so recorded by Artist, the sum of $12,500'.

In return, he would receive that whopping 'mechanical copyright royalty of 24 cents per single-disc album and 48 cents for each double-disc album *which contains musical compositions written by Artist* and having a playing time of not less than thirty minutes per single-disc album and sixty minutes per double-disc album'. Yet, nowhere did it say that Dylan must record *only* his own songs. Perhaps he already intended to 'beef' up his output by recording covers. He certainly recorded enough of them in 1967.

The other unusual aspect of the MGM contract was Dylan's use of 'deferred payments', meaning that the substantive advance would be spread over a ten-year period to mitigate his personal tax liability. Not only that, but there were several long and complex clauses about how said money would be reinvested on Dylan's behalf by the record company. Such schemes were an innovation Klein had previously used to convince, among others, The Rolling Stones to use his services, a decision they continue to rue to this day. They would only benefit Dylan if he was planning to constrain his touring activities and other revenue streams in the same period. It seems he was.

But before he could put pen to paper, there was still the small matter of an outstanding commitment to Columbia, one that the label was using to bully him, beginning with a letter on February 9th notifying Dylan he was in breach of contract and 'that we have put into effect the suspension provisions of sub-paragraph fourteen' of a contract he signed as a minor, and affirmed without legal representation.

Even now he could have challenged them on the excessive length of that contract, and the fact that it was reaffirmed without due representation. Columbia knew this. Knowing that the matter might go to litigation – which they would almost certainly lose, while delaying Dylan's return – they made plans to raid the vaults. Richard Asher wrote to Walter Dean on March 16th, 'We have sufficient suitable unreleased Dylan material to make up two Dylan albums.' Eleven days later, Dylan signed a settlement agreement – with a remarkably child-like signature – that required him 'to render [his] services at recording sessions at our studios, at mutually agreeable times, for the purpose of making satisfactory master recordings which shall constitute a minimum of fifteen 78 rpm record sides, or their equivalent'.

The royalty on said record would remain a miserly 4%. Nor were Columbia content with their pound of flesh. They also wanted Dylan to acknowledge 'that we have validly exercised all our options to extend the term [of the original contract]. You also hereby acknowledge that you have made no written objections to any royalty accounting statements previously furnished to you . . . and you hereby affirm that all of said royalty accounting statements were properly prepared.' In other words, he was required to acknowledge that Columbia had been *legally* robbing him for the past five years. Welcome to the US labels' way of doing business, Bob, where bending over is never enough.

A week later, Grossman called Davis personally and 'begged that we reduce our demand to fourteen sides and said that we'd get them in about a month'. Davis agreed, hoping he might woo Dylan back to the label. Such was the state of play even unto the second week in May, when Grossman informed Dylan's UK publicist Ken Pitt that 'sometime in the near future Bob will be going into the recording studios in Nashville to cut fourteen songs for CBS to fulfil his contract with them'.*

By this time one must assume Dylan had heard about the death of Paul Clayton, proof that April really was 'the cruellest month'. Like Fariña and Foreman, Clayton had frequently behaved like he was immortal as he had spiralled downward, buffeted by, in Stephen Wilson's words, 'an endless prescription of Dexamyl from his college days. In the early years, Dexamyl and grass were the only medications in play. Later, there was some experimentation with LSD, but it was infrequent. [By April 1967,] he was living with a guy called John. John and

---

* The magical figure of fourteen has so enticed some online Dylan 'experts' they have convinced themselves these are the same fourteen songs as those that appeared on acetate from the Big Pink sessions with The Hawks. Those songs were copyrighted in two parts – and total fifteen songs, actually – six to nine months after the original settlement agreement. Sometimes a number is just a number.

David Lyle found him floating in the bath with a clock radio. I had managed to get an Emergency Psychiatrist to come to his apartment the day before. He was ruinously psychotic, but Clayton looked out the window and would not admit the stranger . . . That was his last social transaction.'

How many of these details Dylan heard at the time is unknown. He portrays Clayton in *Chronicles* as 'an intellectual, a scholar and a romantic', but he and Clayton had been estranged since that January 1965 copyright claim, and Dylan was by now far removed from the milieu which had fed and watered his own creativity and curtailed Clayton's. The folksingin' folklorist would not be the last lost soul to be found dead in strange circumstances in the years Dylan beat the retreat. Another old friend, Brian Jones, would be found floating upside down in a Surrey swimming pool in July 1969, in circumstances some still deem suspicious.

Dylan could not afford to dwell on these losses. As he told Liam Clancy in the 1990s – when, pint of Guinness in hand, the blunt Irishman asked whether he felt any responsibility for the tragic deaths of so many friends who had lived in his shadow – 'Man, how can I be responsible? . . . These people had to do what they did. If I were to dwell on that, become obsessed with it, I wouldn't get on with my life. I wouldn't create anything. I wouldn't write anything.' Nothing was more important than that, especially now he had to find fourteen songs from somewhere before he could be free and clear of the 'whores on Seventh Avenue'.*

---

* This line in Paul Simon's song, 'The Boxer', recorded by Dylan in 1970, has been widely interpreted as a reference to Columbia Records, to whom Simon signed in 1964. Dylan even riffs on that very line at the March 1970 session perhaps aware it has some hidden significance, having met Simon the previous summer.

February to December 1967:
A Bunch Of Basement Noise

Back then, Bob was one of the guys . . . He just wanted to ground himself . . . raising a family and coming over to Big Pink each day to make music.

Robbie Robertson, *The Times* 13th February 2021.

I'd retired . . . I was fulfilling my recording contracts, but outside of that I think I felt like I had retired from the cultural scene.

Bob Dylan, to Mikal Gilmore, 25th September 2001.

A gypsy-like figure in faded dungarees, lavender shirt with collar turned up to cover his neck and a purple-and-blue striped blazer, his sandy hair . . . longer and wilder than ever.

Michael Iachetta, describing the Dylan he interviewed in May 1967.

It's unnerving at times, but he can switch himself off as it were, and be completely withdrawn from what is going on around him. It gives him a misleading, unapproachable expression, bordering on coldness. It's almost impossible to tell what he's thinking or whether he's [being] serious or not. He makes the wildest statements and tells downright lies all with the same deadpan face. [But] when he can be bothered, he's a gifted conversationalist and speaks in a soft, cultured voice far removed from the popular hip hillbilly image so beloved of pressmen and public.

Sara's college roommate, describing Dylan, circa 1969.

Serious writers and serious composers are interested in speaking to their public through their writings and through their music. If they were interested in communicating with their public on a different basis, perhaps they would choose a different profession, and perhaps become a journalist or work for some sensational [sic] magazine. It is my firm belief that performers' personal lives . . . are their own.

> Albert Grossman, rebuffing three questions directed at Dylan by
> *Melody Maker* readers, *Melody Maker* 15th April 1967.

Albert's a beautiful guy. He really is a genius. His mind works in these weird circles. You have to get high to understand him, and [yet] he's completely straight.

> Bob Dylan, 17th July 1963.

Woodstock was a place you could go and get your thoughts together. It was an artists' colony. There were plenty of painters who lived in that area but very few musicians . . . Later there was, but when we were up there in the mid-sixties, we were pretty much by ourselves . . . The events of the day were happening [but] seemed to be a million miles away. We weren't really participating in any of that stuff. It was the summer of love, but we weren't there. We did our thing [and] wrote [songs like] 'Million Dollar Bash' [instead].

> Bob Dylan, *Lost Songs* DVD (2015).

*

In a life of contradictions, no year presents greater contradistinctions than 1967, whether it be the American artist or the son of Abraham showing his face, as a fast-burgeoning motorcycle-crash mythology swirls around in the mist. Remove the enigmatic wrapping paper, though, and two undeniable works of genius stand revealed: 'The Basement Tapes' – whatever that entails* – and *John Wesley Harding*, Dylan's eighth studio album, released two days after Christmas to

---

* The 1975 CBS double-album is certainly a travesty, comprising eight wholly unrelated Band songs and sixteen Dylan Big Pink recordings in mono, some with overdubs. The original 14-song acetate, assembled by Garth Hudson and released on vinyl in 2014, remains the one official artifact reflecting the original conceit.

bring seasonal cheer to discerning rock fans who prized songwriting over sound effects.

For the first two or three months of 1967, though, Dylan was doing a whole lot of nothing and seemed content doing so. The Hawks had now relocated upstate, seemingly under the mistaken impression – the recently-affianced Robbie excepted – that they would continue where they had left off in Europe, the previous May. Much to Robertson's chagrin, 'The other guys would go into town and pick up chicks and come back and party all night long.'

If the guitarist meant Woodstock, calling it a town in 1967 was a stretch. It was little more than a hamlet, and not yet a safe haven for hippies when the Canadian carousers rolled in, expecting to resume making music and mayhem with their main man. They discovered Dylan was more interested in making home movies with Howard and Jones Alk, the kind of home movies Pennebaker privately disdained:

> Howard Alk's concept of editing I found very destructive. I would never let Howard edit a film for me because he really likes the idea of undoing anything – bump, bump, bump – a kind of throwing things against the real time of a scene or a situation. Whatever it is, go against it. So what you get in the end looks to me like someone just being really smartass.

Nonetheless, Pennebaker agreed to loan Dylan some movie equipment so he could play the *auteur*, filming some test scenes for 'The Movie' he and Howard were going to make – one day. Meanwhile, the retained Hawks found themselves playing bit parts, even as Dylan drove his wife mad, leaving 'movie camera equipment all over the place . . . with leads and plugs ly[ing] around on chairs and tables.'

When he wasn't causing chaos and upsetting his pregnant wife, he would sometimes disappear for a few days, alone or with a single companion. Thus, on February 5th, 1967, two days after the eighth anniversary of Buddy Holly's unnecessary plane crash, he and Robbie Robertson flew all the way to Houston to watch Muhammad Ali fight Ernie Terrell in a private plane, in apparently atrocious weather.

Enter nightclub singer Tiny Tim who, due to start filming with Dylan the following week, felt compelled to write in his diary that day, 'I pray Mr Dylan and Mr Robertson's flight will be safe.' Two days earlier, he had thanked the Lord 'for a swell night at The Scene as I rehearsed with

Mr Bob Dylan's orchestra [!] for the movie on Tuesday'. Due to 'the blizzard', the original filming date for 'the movie' – which was not Dylan's, but one Peter Yarrow was making concurrently with Alk, *You Are What You Eat* – was rearranged.

Dylan had first seen Tiny Tim with Suze at the Living Theatre circa 1963, and what delighted him *and Suze* was that 'it made no difference to him if he was being ridiculed or appreciated. He revelled in both . . . He never stepped out of character.' His secret was safe. Dylan knew exactly how that felt. He even drove down to New York to see Tim play with The Hawks, before going to Texas to see Ali beat Terrell on points. He asked the falsetto singer if he would be interested in helping with his own film, prompting Tim to thank the Lord 'for letting me be . . . good friends with the greatest composer and personality of our day – as well as poet.'

A week later, Robbie phoned Tim to tell him, 'Dylan wants [you] to come up to his place next week for filming.' The following Monday he became 'one of the privileged few who stayed at Mr Bob Dylan's house – as well as having a chance to be playing [in] his upcoming television spectacular in April . . . Mr Ronnie drove me up to Mr Grossman's house and a handy man . . . then drove me to Mr Bob Dylan's real house. It has 26 rooms – [including] a big music room in which lies Mr Dylan's guitars, pianos, electric mandolin, etc . . . I chatted with him about Mr Rudy Vallee . . . I also sang for his beautiful wife and kids.'

Mostly, though, they discussed the film project, Tim's above comments suggesting Dylan was planning to add 'new scenes' to the unfinished *Stage '66* film, to make it something other than a tour documentary – something 'smartass', more like the film he described to John Cohen the following year, 'What [Alk and I] were trying to do was . . . to make a story which consisted of stars and starlets who were taking the roles of other people . . . [But] we were very limited because the film was not shot by us, but by "The Eye," and we had come upon this decision to do this only after everything else had failed.'

Not surprisingly, their idea hit a brick wall called ABC, who were quoted in an April 1967 *New York Times* article as saying the special had been cancelled because 'there was some disagreement over the format of the show'. Full house. Dylan was now in dispute with ABC, Columbia *and* MGM, while still contracted to deliver Macmillan a book. And still he chartered private planes.

Meanwhile, back in Woodstock, Dylan the moviemaker was going ahead with some tests on the third day Tiny Tim stayed with him, only to discover – as Tim's diary records – 'a leak in the camera . . . may have ruined everything we did today, as well as in the past . . . [But] Mr Dylan [still] wants me back.' Sure enough, on Sunday, February 26th, Tiny Tim travelled up to Woodstock again – this time staying at a motel – ahead of four more days of shooting. On the following Tuesday and Wednesday, Tim 'sang with Dylan, [and] heard him sing and play his guitar' before returning to New York on the Thursday with his $88 fee, 'thrill[ed] to [get to] act and sing with him. Also [had] a nice time with Mr Rick [Danko], Mr Rich[ard Manuel] and Mr Robertson.'

According to a notebook of Dylan's, the plan for Thursday had been to shoot a 'scene where Tiny plays a very tall man and [I] use box to stand on'. The following day, he had 'Richard leaning out [of a] window,' hoping to match it with a shot of a door frame. What they were shooting has not survived, but a reel of 'wild audio' has, in a most unexpected place – amongst a box of audio reels for *Dont Look Back* Pennebaker was keeping safe – as have some black-and-white photos Alk kept (see photo section).

One would love to know what D.A., the master of *cinéma vérité*, made of something so unscripted and chaotic, especially as Dylan had previously sketched out a couple of scenes – found among the *Lost On The River* papers – including one in a sandwich shop in which a policeman confronts the owner:

Policeman: Have you seen this man?
[**Man**]: What did he do?
[**Policeman**]: He stole a motor out of a car down at Louie Louie's, three nights ago. We got a lead on him from two ladies, just happened to see him go by.

The 32-minute audio reel contains no such scene, but begins with Dylan riffing on various ways to introduce a different kind of star: 'Here he comes now, that valiant Cornish knight, King Mark himself, [and] here comes his faithful servant, Curverknell . . . Here he comes now, that famous ringmaster.'* Instructing Mrs Alk, 'All right, Jones,

---

* 'Dylan was interested in doing a film, with a circus act. Tiny Tim was supposed to be the circus guy, with the hat and the whip.' –D.A. Pennebaker to Justin Martell, 2017.

enough of this,' he then breaks into an acoustic blues in a strong southern accent, 'Cruisin' with my baby last Wednesday morn/ with my
foghorn.' Cue shouts of 'Foghorn' from The Hawks.

Finally, after everyone calms down, he gets Tiny Tim to recite the
lyrics to 'Yesterday', à la Peter Sellers's *Richard III* 'Hard Day's Night'.
Dylan then suggests, 'Why don't you sing one,' and Tim counters, 'I'll
sing one with you,' prompting Dylan to again adopt a fake southern
accent. This lyric also barely gets off the ground, 'A thousand miles
from nowhere/ In my country shack . . .' Dylan then requests Henry
Burr's 1915 standard, 'Memories' – evoking, 'Childhood days, wild
wood days/ Among the birds and bees . . .' – and Tim obliges while
assorted Band members sing harmonies seemingly designed to drown
out the birds and bees. At this point the tape mercifully runs out.

Whether or not this was Alk's idea of 'throwing things against the real
time of a scene or a situation', ABC were never going to green light this
kinda thing. Nor were their executives likely to think much of Dylan's and/
or Alk's scattershot 'notes' on camera technique, which ran as follows:

> technique: (also but just one) during conversation of which circles
> around the crucial happening, dialogue being sometimes pert[ine]nt
> and needed for all moviegoers whom come in hop[ing] to watch the
> movie without speaking) case in point of which: A speaks to B & B is
> speaking to A. full convers[a]tion held perhaps in 5 or 6 [shots] or what-
> ever pleases. camera follows all time . . . cut inside of editing room.

Not surprisingly, this is as far as this film project ever got. A more
pressing matter now took precedence. As of March 27th, Dylan had
agreed he owed Columbia fourteen songs. And as of May 27th, *Disc* was
reporting he would 'in the near future . . . be going into the recording
studios in Nashville . . . to fulfil his contract with [Columbia],' even as
the first tentative steps to resolving his contract dispute were being
taken. A Columbia memo from Clive Davis, five days earlier, reported he
had 'just had lunch with [David] Braun . . . Assuming Grossman follows
Braun's advice on the other two points, this is the last remaining issue.'

Whatever could he mean? It meant Dylan and/or Grossman had
been getting cold feet about the MGM deal. Davis, in his 1974 memoir,
Clive, suggests Dylan had already signed the contract and it was merely
awaiting ratification by the MGM board. But that appears to be a form

of self-justification for his own actions in scuppering the deal. Dylan had not put pen to paper, and since MGM were currently stymied by his obligation to deliver an album to Columbia before they could proceed, the ball was very much in his court.

Davis's May 22nd memo makes it clear that Columbia's own counter negotiations with Dylan were by now well advanced. By June 16th – under a blanket of complete secrecy – a new contract had been drafted and sent to Braun. A fortnight later, it was ready for Dylan's signature. The following day, he put his normal signature to the document. Once again, he used 'deferred payments' to spread his tax liability, with, 'payments of more than $75,000 or $150,000 [in] any contract year [to be kept in] a separate Deferred Payment Account to which shall be credited all accrued royalties in excess of $75,000 or $150,000. Columbia will invest . . . the amount credited to the DPA as artist may direct.' Such provisions suggested a period of retrenchment was still in the offing.

Although Davis rather suggests it was down to his brilliant negotiating skills,* something more personal had led to a dramatic change of heart on Dylan's part. What was perhaps preying on his mind was the sheer amount of product the MGM deal committed him to – effectively two albums per annum for the next five years. He began to suspect he simply didn't have it in him.

He instead committed to just 'Eight Long Playing 33⅓ Record Sides (i.e. four albums) During The Term', which would run for five years. (He would deliver ten sides in that time.) He would in turn receive a $75,000 advance for any single album, double that for a double, considerably less than MGM were offering. Likewise, the royalty – though it doubled what it had been under the old contract – was still less than the MGM deal. But at least he finally got the royalties on back catalogue bumped up to 5% *retrospectively*. He also made sure Columbia would not release any of the bulging shelves of outtakes and live tapes they had been assiduously cataloguing for a rainy day or twelve.

Contrast this with the deal The Beatles had signed with EMI on January 27th, 1967 – at the height of Dylan's battle with Columbia – which was a nine-year deal, tying the band collectively and individually to the label until 1976 and requiring the group to deliver a minimum of

---

* Even in his 1974 memoir, Davis could not get the deal right, insisting it was for no advance and for five years.

seventy tracks by 1972, for only the same royalty rate Dylan was receiving. The EMI deal also allowed Brian Epstein – and / or his *beneficiaries* – to take 25% of all earnings for the full term of said contract, even though his own management contract was due to expire in a matter of months – along with the man himself, it transpired.

Dylan, by contrast, was already counting the days to the end of his association with Grossman, a prospect that probably helped to persuade him not to give his manager a huge wedge of any $1.5 million deal with MGM. The new Columbia contract also noted, 're the agreement dated March 27th, 1967, minimum of 14 78rpm sides – these recordings shall be deemed to have been recorded.' Dylan was free and clear of any immediate obligation. Maybe now was a good time to call a temporary halt on the regular home sessions he had been privately taping with The Hawks. After all, Sara was due to give birth to their second child any day now.

Because, unbeknownst to the world, by early July 1967 Dylan had recorded more than enough songs to have fulfilled his now obsolete get-out clause with Columbia. Had this ever been the intended purpose behind all this music-making? Did Dylan really resume recording with The Hawks in early spring just in case he needed some songs with which to fob Columbia off? As noted earlier, some would-be authorities have seized on fourteen – the number of songs he owed Columbia in March 1967 *and* the number of songs assembled on a Dwarf Music demo-tape in January 1968 – put two and two together, and come up with 3.14.

Which isn't to say that these 'home' sessions did not begin with a view to conjuring up the songs he owed the label. We know Dylan needed to work up some songs, and quickly, but had no intention of giving Columbia anything intended for the 'real' follow-up to *Blonde on Blonde*. Perhaps he would give them exactly what they asked for, fourteen 78 rpm sides, i.e. songs which lasted less than three minutes, pop songs like the ones Bobby from Hibbing dreamed of writing when all he had to do was dream.

Even for such an adept lyricist, the idea of writing a dozen or more pastiche pop songs on every subject from the scatological to the sacrilegious – all containing a catchy chorus – was an outrageous notion. Yet that is precisely the direction he now went in. Nothing in his career leads up to the basement tape songs and nothing leads away from them. It would be like a busman's holiday.*

Any songs he had been working on just prior to the start of these home sessions would go unrecorded, even one tellingly called 'You Can Change Your Name (But You Can't Run Away From Yourself)'. Was he saving this for some more rarefied purpose? Not if Al Aronowitz's contemporary eyewitness account of a home session is anything to go by:

> 'Dylan has been doing nothing, absolutely nothing,' said Jamie Robertson, Dylan's guitarist, to an inquiring reporter . . . But that was just a contribution to the Dylan mystery. Actually, Dylan was writing ten new songs a week, rehearsing them in his living room with Robertson's group, The Hawks, and trying to complete a one-hour film TV special for ABC, which said it couldn't use the programme because it was seven months late . . . He was sitting at an electric piano while a Japanese windchime played random melodies on the porch outside . . . He wore a beard now, and rimless Benjamin Franklin eye-glasses, and from behind his incognito he sang . . . 'You can change your name but you can't run away from yourself [twice].' 'Do you like that song?' he asked [me]. 'I think it's great.' . . . Dylan turned to Jamie Robertson. 'See,' Dylan said, 'We shouldn't keep any music critics around here. We just lost another song.'

Sure enough, the song is nowhere to be found among four pre-Big Pink reels recorded that spring with The Hawks, none of which were taped in a basement, or a garage. They were made in Dylan's 'big music room', the Red Room, part of what Aronowitz depicts as 'a rambling American chateau of mahogany-stained shingles that clung to a mountain top'.

I doubt the reason the song wasn't recorded was Aronowitz's familiar presence. Rather, as Dylan suggests in the 2015 *Showtime* documentary on these new 'basement tapes', 'I knew I wasn't gonna be writing anything about myself. I didn't have nothing to say about myself.' *This* song was very much about himself, as we now know because its lyrics have

---

* The *Lost On The River* songs have far more in common with *John Wesley Harding* than the songs on these ferric-shedding tapes, leading some to believe they date from after that album. I can't see it.

been serendipitously preserved in one of those small notebooks he continued to use to jot down song-ideas. No question, this was a song of self-analysis, designed to save money on a therapist:

> You can conquer everybody (anybody)
> But you can't conquer yourself [x2]
> You can judge yourself
> But you can't judge anyone else.
>
> Everyone asks you
> 'Where have you been?'
> Everyone will ask why and when
> are you going back again? . . .
>
> The times have changed
> Any fool can see that
> Everything is rearranged.

Although one must assume the notebook in question dates from around the time Dylan started the Red Room recordings, neither 'You Can Change Your Name' nor the other fragments of lyrics or song titles therein tally with anything found on these pre-Big Pink reels: not the song titles 'Cat Fever', 'You Can't Do No Wrong' and/or 'Three Redheads'; not the revelatory line, 'I'm gonna start out again, but this time I'm gonna know when to stop'; nor, 'A holy man is a man who doesn't mind the flies buzzing around his head'; or an entire verse hinting at a youth revisited:

> When I was 12, I invented the wheel,
> I could use it to run and it taught me to steal
> Janis the clown, she came from Green Lake
> She was filled with desire, and was quite a mistake
> She gave me a thrill and I paid her my wheel
> The next thing I knew, I was watching her kneel.

So, what exactly *was* Dylan recording in the Red Room? Was he, as he audibly suggests at one point, just 'wasting tape'? Or did he record some forty songs there, as asserted by ex-Long Ryder Sid Griffin in his revised edition of *Million Dollar Bash: Bob Dylan, The Band And The*

Basement Tapes (Jawbone, 2014)? As the de facto author of sleeve notes to the eleventh official Bootleg Series, *The Basement Tapes Complete*, he was privileged to hear all the tapes – including nine songs omitted from the 'complete' official edition. He should surely know.

But in this hastily-executed cash-in, confronted by recording dates where information was sketchy or in most cases non-existent, Griffin simply resorted to guesswork. Though he heard everything, he never consulted with the producers of the set nor bothered to reference the more edifying 'historical notes' that follow his essay in that 6-CD set. Those notes make it clear that of the original master reels, three were clearly marked 'Red Room', one of which – a crucial one, full of classic country covers – Griffin bizarrely assigned to Big Pink.*

When the correct order and sequence is used, the Red Room reels reveal a new Dylan emerging from its chrysalis, even if the process is neither instant, nor painless – for Dylan *or* latter-day listeners.[†] According to Garth Hudson, who was operating the reel-to-reel: 'We were doing seven, eight, ten, sometimes fifteen songs a day. Some were old ballads and traditional songs . . . Others Bob would make up as he went along . . . We'd play the melody, he'd sing a few words he'd written, and then make up some more, or else just mouth sounds or even syllables as he went along.'

Save for the part about 'old ballads and traditional songs' – which Dylan only starts to do on the final Red Room reel – Garth has it about right. Of the 'originals' on these reels, not one sounds composed. Rather, they remind one of Dylan's description to Ginsberg – from around this time – of a technique he'd used in late 1965: 'babbl[ing] into the microphone then rush[ing] into the control room and listen[ing] to what he said . . . arrang[ing] it a little bit, and then maybe rush[ing] back out in front and sing[ing] it [again].' The fact that a dozen such examples from these home sessions are now part of the official canon – and copyrighted accordingly – says much about the grip these sessions have on pop mythology.

---

* None of which has stopped Olof Björner from accepting Griffin's song assignments as gospel on his widely-referenced *Still on The Road* web resource, singularly failing to reference the more reliable 'historical notes'.
† The first two Red Room reels, recorded at 3¾ ips, suffer from distortion, the ostensible reason why most of these songs were shuttled across to the 'bonus' 6th CD on the 2014 set.

Dylan was just enjoying himself. As Robertson has said, 'There was no particular reason for it. We weren't making a record. We were just fooling around. The purpose was whatever comes into anybody's mind, we'll put it down on this little tape recorder. *Shitty* little tape recorder.' When Sally Grossman popped by to lend an ear, her response was dismissive, 'It sounded like throwaway stuff. Nonsense stuff. Bob and the guys were [just] hanging out, playing and having fun. The titles alone are enough of a clue.'

Though Sally is actually referring to the Big Pink songs, she might just as well have meant 'Edge Of The Ocean (Seagulls)', 'Northern Claim', 'On Blueberry Hill (I Am For You Baby)' – inexplicably omitted from the 'complete' 2014 boxed-set – 'King Of France', or 'I Can't Come In With A Broken Heart', five of the more realized improvisations recorded during those weeks in the Red Room. As Robertson rightly recalls, '[Bob']s ability to improvise on a basic idea was truly exceptional and a lot of fun to witness.' But there was never any question of this material being used, as is or reworked.

For now, whenever Dylan and the boys attempted authentic covers, they almost entirely eschewed the folk canon, the guys in the band remaining innately suspicious of the whole genre. As Robertson told Griffin, 'None of the guys in the band were about folk music. We were not from that side of the tracks. Folk music was from [the] coffee houses, where people sipped cappuccinos. Where we played as The Hawks, nobody was sipping cappuccinos, I'll tell ya [that]!'

Where these good ol' northern boys' tastes did coincide with the big boss man was Fifties rock'n'roll. So, it should come as no surprise that two of the earliest songs attempted in the Red Room were the 1954 Hank Ballard song Bobby had performed as his camp debut, 'Work With Me, Annie' (a.k.a. 'Annie Had A Baby'), and a song he cut to acetate on Christmas Eve 1956: 'Confidential'. Dylan also got The Hawks to cut one of his favourite Hank Williams songs, 'My Bucket's Got A Hole In It'. They also tried to capture 'Hey Good Lookin', before Garth rewound the tape and erased it, a common crime that spring.

Dylan really is returning to the starting point, retracing roots. He even adds the date (1956) to the title of 'I'm Not There', one of the highlights from these magnetic movements, captured before The Hawks lost some of their identity. Dylan lamented the loss, telling

Kurt Loder, 'What came out on record as The Band . . . was like night and day . . . They could cover songs great. They used to do Motown songs, and that, to me, is when I think of them as being at their best.'

If he was still feeling his way back to his good ol' used to be, Ian Bell noticed an inherent irony: 'Whenever Dylan delves . . . in[to] old music – and only a handful of basement songs sound other than ancient – he seems to wind up pointing to the future.' If the first two Red Room reels were mostly spent trying to twist raw ideas into song shapes, the last two show him returning to musical roots with which The Hawks were barely familiar:

Robbie Robertson: He would play songs . . . I'd never heard, and after we'd . . . played it, I would say, 'Did you write that?' and he would say, 'No, that's an old song by blah-blah-blah,' and frequently he would tell a little story . . . [about] what was behind the song. And that was interesting, learning some of these old-timey songs.

Though it is hard to believe that the Hawks would not already know 'You Win Again', a Hank standard, or the Sun-era Cash classics, 'Big River' and 'Folsom Prison Blues', Dylan sometimes left them fumbling for the light switch. He does so when, just before the Red Room sessions draw to a close, he pulls out six traditional songs, reflecting every aspect of Anglo-Americana: the hillbilly hokeyness of 'Cool Water'; the Irish drinking songs, 'Ol' Roison The Beau' and 'Johnny Todd'; two songs he used to sing in the clubs, 'Come All Ye Fair & Tender Ladies' and 'Poor Lazarus'; and, most gorgeous of all, Dominic Behan's quasi-traditional 'The Auld Triangle', a.k.a. 'The Banks Of The Royal Canal'.*

Robertson, for one, sensed there was some underlying method to such madness. The boss was gently leading the guys by the nose: 'Bob was educating us a little . . . He'd come up with something like "[The] Royal Canal," and you'd say, "This is so beautiful! The expression!" . . . But he remembered too much, remembered too many songs too well . . . He'd prepped for this . . . and then [he'd] come out here, to

---

* 'Young But Daily Growin', 'The Auld Triangle' and 'Big River' would all be pulled to the 'comp. master' reels from which Robertson and producer Rob Fraboni would compile the 1975 CBS album.

show us.' Sure enough, the lessons led somewhere The Hawks, if they chose to, could call home.

At some point that spring they left the Red Room and re-convened at The Hawks' newly-rented place in West Saugerties: a gaudy old country shack called Big Pink. One suspects Sara had a say in the relocation. If it wasn't camera equipment, it was 'Mr Dylan's guitars, pianos, electric mandolin, etc.'

This was when it all changed. As Robertson notes, 'There's the music from Bob's house, and there's the music from our house. The two houses *sure* are different.' For the first time, Dylan wasn't just prepping songs from his past, he was creating characters Lewis Carroll and Edward Lear might have jointly imagined after a night with Thomas De Quincey in the opium dens. The first of these were found in 'Tiny Montgomery', with his partners-in-crime Skinny Moo and T-Bone Frank. One still wonders how much of this was made up on the spot. Did Dylan really sit down and type 'Scratch your dad, do that bird, suck that pig and bring it on home'? According to the 2015 Dylan, he was simply watching too much TV:

> These songs weren't tailor made for anybody. I just wrote what I felt like writing . . . I had nothing else to do, so I started writing a bunch of songs. I'd write them in longhand and I'd write them on a typewriter. Whatever was handy. The TV would be on – *As The World Turns*, or *Dark Shadows*, or something [like that]. Just any old thing would create a beginning to a song. When China first exploded that hydrogen bomb, that kinda flashed across the headlines of the newspaper, so we [would] just go in and [do] 'Tears Of Rage'.* . . . Just one thing led to another. And after [I] got the lyrics down, we'd take the song to the basement.

Robertson challenges his former paymaster's take in his 2016 memoir, 'I never saw Bob write out lyrics longhand; he either typed them out or scratched a couple of words on a napkin.' According to Danko, their employer even sometimes used the typewriter as an alarm clock, 'If we were sleeping, he'd get us up. He'd make some noise or bang on

---

* The first Chinese nuclear test was in October 1964, three years before Dylan wrote 'Tears Of Rage'.

the typewriter on the coffee table,' but not before he had hammered out that day's excursion/s into what Greil Marcus would fondly christen, Weird Ol' America.

Yet so scant was Dylan's regard for the lyrics he was now producing like ticker-tape that not one of them appears among the Tulsa manuscripts, even though he retained the earlier, unrealized *Lost On The River* material and at least a smattering of drafts for *John Wesley Harding* songs. Nor has a working draft of a Big Pink song ever emerged on the lucrative manuscript market.

What happened to them? We know from co-author Richard Manuel, he saw the 'Tears Of Rage' typescript, which came about after Dylan went 'down to the basement with a piece of typewritten paper . . . It was typed out – in line form – and he just said, "Have you got any music for this?" . . . I just elaborated a bit, because I wasn't sure what the lyrics meant.' Presumably, Danko received something similar for 'This Wheel's On Fire', as the blessed recipient. Danko's handwritten lyric did later turn up in a Band-related archive, possibly hand-corrected by Dylan, but not the original typescript he was handed.

Otherwise, all we have to go on from this productive period is a single, incomplete typescript of 'I'm Not There', sent anonymously to Wanted Man, the Dylan Information Office, in 1990. Seemingly authentic, the absence of a couplet like, 'Now when I treat the lady I was born to love her/ But she knows that the kingdom weighs so high above her,' suggests it and others were improvised when the tape rolled. Yet the song was clearly always heading in this direction, as indicated by two unrealized thoughts at the bottom of the page: 'heaven knows the answer – don't call nobod[y]/ i go by the lord BEWARE BE[WARE].'

How long he worked at songs like this – minutes, hours or days – is mere conjecture. All we have are finished takes. But if 'Tiny Montgomery' really was the trigger, Dylan didn't empty the chamber just yet. He had three more reels of musical lessons he wanted to teach The Hawks before he felt they were tutored enough to sit their first serious 'studio' examination since January 27th, 1966.

This gave Garth the opportunity to fine-tune the audio set-up, to Dylan's visible delight. According to Robertson, 'When he saw the setup in the [Big Pink] basement, he scratched his chin, looking pleased. "This is great. Can you record *anything* here?" In response, Garth played back some experimental taping we had done.'* Everyone proceeded to make themselves comfortable:

> **Robbie Robertson**: Garth set up these microphones . . . Not a lot of people [were] doing recordings like this . . . [just] a little echo unit or something like that, and just getting a vibe . . . out of the . . . sound there . . . [We] would set up in a circle, so we could balance the instruments. No monitors, no nothing . . . If you played too loud you couldn't hear the vocal, and that meant you were playing too loud. Because we were sitting in a circle looking at one another . . . it became like, hey, this is the way to play music! Everybody was in on it . . . [It was] the idea of musicians near each other, making eye contact and reacting to the physical.

If Dylan remained in improv. mode for most of the first Big Pink reel – destined to yield the bacchanalian delights of 'See You Later Allen Ginsberg', 'The Spanish Song' and 'I'm Your Teenage Prayer' – by the third reel, the vamps and riffs take on a life of their own as Dylan begs and pleads, 'Baby, Won't You Be My Baby', 'Try Me, Little Girl' and 'Don't You Try Me Now', before laying down one last breathtaking trilogy from tradition: 'Young But Daily Growin', 'Bonnie Ship The Diamond' and 'Hills Of Mexico'. He will not revisit the past again till the fall. Instead, he uses up four 7" reels of tape – three Scotch and one Shamrock† – cutting nineteen original songs that for anyone else would be a career. For him, they were just footsteps in the sand.

Across the next four decades he would be pretty consistent about the underlying purpose – or the lack of one – insisting in 1975, 'It wasn't a record, it was just songs which we'd come to this basement and recorded – out in the woods,' and then in 2015, 'I had no intention of putting these songs out.' The fact remains, he cut eleven original songs, one after the other, in no more than two takes, while using up just two Big Pink reels. They include perennial favourites 'You Ain't Goin'

---

* Presumably, he means the truly awful 'Even If It's A Pig' which acquired legend status until it was heard.

† Shamrock was a notoriously low-grade tape-brand. As Robertson explains, 'We were always afraid of running out of tape and were too poor to buy extra, so we recorded on a slow speed, 7½ ips or maybe [even] 3¾ ips if we were running really low.' It never seems to have occurred to Dylan to order a box of blanks.

Nowhere', 'I Shall Be Released', 'This Wheel's On Fire' and 'Million Dollar Bash', all of them copyrighted by September 1967. All were cogent compositions, conceptually of a piece – the sublimely semi-coherent 'I'm Not There' excepted – as the musical faucet flowed unceasingly.

Hudson, for one, was 'amazed [by] his writing ability . . . How he could come in, sit down at the typewriter, and write a song? . . . Also, what was amazing was that almost every one of those songs was *funny*.' A riot, in fact. And they got funnier still when he recorded them. In one instance, 'You Ain't Going Nowhere', he recorded what are clearly dummy lyrics at the start of a session – the famous 'Ain't no head of lettuce' version – before returning later that day, or the next, with a set of *compos mentis* lyrics that served to provide the perfect summation of their activities, 'Strap yourself to a tree with a roots/ You ain't going nowhere.'

Whether his original impetus in writing such a cohesive set of songs was simply to get Columbia off his back or whether, as he claimed in 1978, 'They were written vaguely for other people,' these eleven songs were unlike anything anybody else was doing in 1967. As Dylan observed a decade later, 'At that time psychedelic rock was overtaking the universe and we were singing these homespun ballads.'

If he still thought he might have to give Columbia fourteen such songs, then the latest recording date for the first six Big Pink reels would be June – which could be the case. If the first ten 'basement' reels, four from the Red Room *and* six from Big Pink, were recorded between late March and June 1967, then the picture one can garner for this period is reasonably complete, rewound and erased snatches notwithstanding.*

Before sessions resume, though, there seems to have been a signifi-cant hiatus, perhaps coinciding with the birth to Sara of a daughter, on July 11th, Anna Lea; the visit of two delighted grandparents; and Dylan beginning to sketch out an entirely different brand of song for his eagerly-awaited seventh Columbia offering, now that contractual obli-gations receded into the distance.

---

* If the reel with 'Goin' To Acapulco', 'Gonna Get You Now' and a coupla Band instrumentals is the 'missing' Reel #6, then reels #1-10 have all survived. We are not so fortunate with reels #11-20.

Fatherhood had inextricably changed Dylan's view of many things, including his own father, prompting him to write in a post-accident folder, 'My daddy was a . . . good man. Very seldom did I ever see him raise his hand. To each of his children, he gave love and care.' When the more effusive Beattie also came to the house, she was delighted to find 'a huge Bible open on a stand in the middle of his study. Of all the books that crowd his house, overflow from his house, that Bible gets the most attention. He's continuously getting up and going over to refer to something.' She wasn't the only one to have noticed this new interest:

Al Aronowitz: Of course, Dylan had always used Bible imagery in his songs but that had nothing to do with his personal faith. But when I was spending time up in Woodstock with him, after the accident, it was different. He had a large Bible at home and he was reading it. It seemed to me like he was searching. Not for lyrics this time though, but for something else . . . He didn't say anything to me, but there was *something* going on.

The notebooks of the period bear out a revived interest in eschatology, with Dylan noting down chapter and verse from various parts of the Old Testament. He also left little doubt which edition he was referencing, writing 'KJV' – for King James Version – next to both 1 Chronicles 17:8 ('And I have been with thee whithersoever thou hast walked, and have cut off all thine enemies from before thee, and have made thee a name like the name of . . . great men that are in the earth') and Ecclesiastes 11:9-10 ('Rejoice, O young man, in thy youth; and let thy heart cheer thee in the days of thy youth . . . but know thou, that for all these things God will bring thee into judgment . . . for childhood and youth are vanity'). Both suggested a new-found gratitude for God's infinite mercy.

But the most surprising citation from the former apostate must be Hosea 13:4, a famous verse which twelve years later would assume especial resonance: 'Thou shalt know no God but me; for there is no saviour beside me.' In his notebook, Dylan prefaces this quote with the words of a preacher, 'For all those who speak of the savio[u]r, let them open their books . . . and read this.' And when an old friend came to call to preach the word of the Fab Four's latest 45, he was advised in no uncertain terms to expand his reading matter beyond the sleeve of *Sgt. Pepper*:

> **Noel Stookey**: After Bob had his motorcycle accident . . . a friend, [a DJ called Dave Dixon,] and I . . . wanted to go see Bobby . . . We felt that The Beatles' music . . . was now expanding the human psyche. So, I called Bob up in Woodstock . . . I said, 'Hey, I want to come up and talk to you.' He said, 'Okay, come up.' He was really gracious. What I was trying to say was that [I felt] The Beatles were talking about Love . . . I asked, 'What do you think The Beatles are trying to say? You've been writing a long time, where are *you* headed now?' And Bob said, 'Based on your questions, Noel, I think you're going to like my next album.' . . . Bobby also said, 'You should read The Bible, Noel.'

At least two Big Pink songs also contain passing references to the gospels. The freshly composed 'I Shall Be Released' inverted Matthews's prophecy, 'As the lightning comes from the east and shines as far as the west, so will be the coming of the Son of Man' [24:27], the imprisoned narrator seeing his own 'light come shining from the west down to the east'. While the most sublimely spiritual of the Big Pink songs – the seven-minute 'Sign On The Cross', recorded during the second phase of sessions – sees Dylan ponder the words nailed above Christ on the cross, 'This is Jesus, The King of the Jews' [Matthew 27:37]. Again, the song has a most unexpected moral:

> If that sign on the cross . . . begins to worry you
> Well, that's all right because you just sing a song
> And all your troubles will pass right on through.

He remained wary of the epithet Prophet, even when citing the most apocalyptic of Old Testament Cassandras, Jeremiah, 'Ye do not hearken unto the words/ Of the prophets who are prophesying to you, They are making you vain things.' [23:16] There are other clues in these notebooks of Dylan enjoying taking an irreverent attitude to Scripture. He describes Jonah as 'a selfish man – who burned his children at the stake', and referencing the deeds of another Judas, wonders, 'How much could the thirty pieces of silver weigh? . . . Was it enough money to buy a camel?'

However, nowhere in these notebooks does he cite the Book of Isaiah, from which he would soon take a verse prophesying the fall of Babylon – 'For thus hath the Lord said unto me, Go set a watchman, let him declare what he seeth. And he saw a chariot with a couple of horsemen' [21:6] – as the starting point for his most Apocalyptic song since 'When The Ship Comes In'. For the first time in a Dylan song the Thief of Fire, a.k.a. the Joker, converses with the Thief in The Night.

'All Along The Watchtower' could well have been one of the songs he played to Bob Johnston when he came to Woodstock in September to hear some works in progress. But aside from playing him some new songs – none of them from Big Pink – Dylan had little to say. Johnston later recalled, 'My old lady Joey and Sara talked for a couple of hours while Bob and I sat and watched the fire. He never said a word, and neither did I.'

Another possible sounding board for the new songs was banjo player Happy Traum, another former Village stalwart who'd relocated upstate. Traum has described this as 'the time we knew Bob best. It was very family-oriented – dinners together, hanging out and playing a lot of music. He would come down to our house and say, "Hey, you wanna hear this new song I wrote?" . . . I [particularly] remember some of the songs from *John Wesley Harding*. Very few people were let in to that world.' Not even Ginsberg was so blessed, though he remembered Dylan at this time 'telling me how he was writing shorter lines, with every line meaning something . . . No wasted language, no wasted breath.'

Such was certainly the case with four new songs. Two small notebooks from the second half of 1967 contain rudimentary drafts of 'I Dreamed I Saw St Augustine', recorded at the first *JWH* session on October 17th, 'I Am A Lonesome Hobo' and 'As I Went Out One Morning', both cut at the second (November 6th), and 'Dear Landlord', recorded on the third and last (November 29th).*

This suggests Dylan might have had much of the album sketched out in his head before he recorded a single song – 'sketched out' being the operative phrase. 'I Dreamed I Saw St Augustine' just has the lines, 'Oh I awoke in agony with no place to stand or hide / I put my fingers against the glass and bowed --- cried,' which is how he sings it on the

---

* These remain the only extant draft lyrics from this landmark album housed in Tulsa.

first take, released in 2019. 'As I Went Out One Morning' also contains just the germ of the idea: 'Until I soon lost all resistance/ Pity me, Tom Paine, I said/ (Twas then I turned to my long lost soul) . . . Who took me over the field and the mountain.'

There's more of 'I Am The Lonesome Hobo', but rather than serving time 'for ev'rything', the hobo has 'never stolen from a thief', and once had 'a sweetheart'. It is unclear whether a stray verse in the notebook served as its early bridge: 'How much does a man need/ Before his need turns to greed/ Before his want turns into lust/ Before his bones turn into dust.'

Wherever the verse went – and it could have belonged to either the lonesome hobo or a morally dissolute landlord – it is the early draft of 'Dear Landlord' which provides the greater revelation. Any doubts that the song is 'about' Albert Grossman – as has been long rumoured – fly out the window with the very first couplet: 'Dear Landlord, please don't put a price on this soul/ I'll pay you the debt just as soon as I can get out of this hole.' And the tone only becomes more ominous. The not-so-cryptic ending to the first verse reads, 'I told you before and I'll tell you again/ Everything's soon going to change, just as soon as I'm able,' while the third verse peels back the layers yet further: 'I've heard all the stories they've told about you/ And I've never believed one to be true.' Finally, an impending comeuppance is explicated with the final line, 'You'll get everything that's coming to you.'

Its inclusion in these notebooks suggests he could have done the song at the first *JWH* session. Something stopped him – perhaps the actual presence of Albert Grossman, who can be heard after a long breakdown on the opening song, 'Drifter's Escape', saying, 'Bob, Charlie can do the turn around on one of the other tracks, if you're satisfied with the other track.' To which Dylan replies, 'I'll get through it another time,' already eschewing any unnecessary overdubs on the multitrack.

Perhaps Grossman thought that attending the session was one way of stopping his client writing and recording songs directed at him. If so, he was sorely mistaken. Possibly, he had already been tipped off that Dylan was writing about himself again. In 2014, Sally Grossman recalled an evening at Big Pink where the couple had been invited to 'hear some [new] material' recorded in situ. One of the Hawks' girlfriends had baked a cake, but as 'they played the tape . . . almost immediately Albert looks at me and says, "We gotta go." He was allergic to the buckwheat flour in the cake . . . They thought Albert hated the music so much, he'd got up and split.'

It may not have been the cake. Another new Dylan original, 'Nothing Was Delivered', references someone who 'must provide some answers/ For what you sell [that] has not been received,' and is asked to explain 'just what you had in mind/ When you made ev'rybody pay.' 'Nothing Was Delivered' was one of four new songs recorded on a single reel [#10], the contents of which were now added to the ten previous Dwarf demos. The others were 'Quinn The Eskimo', 'Open The Door Homer' and 'Tears Of Rage', all top-drawer Dylan, all with choruses and unchained melodies, if darker in tone than the songs previously captured that summer.*

The fact that he could shuttle styles so effortlessly, while simultaneously sketching out his first concept album, still beggars belief. But for others in a tight inner circle, the growing tension between Dylan and his personal manager was proving wearing. Pennebaker recalled, 'Towards the end, both were telling me different stories about things, and they [simply] didn't agree,' while Aronowitz lamented, 'If Albert wasn't managing Dylan anymore, he was still managing The Band, and Robbie was caught in the middle, just as I was.'

One thing was for sure. By the time a second Nashville session was booked, the first week in November, Grossman was *persona non grata*. The first session had resulted in 'Drifter's Escape', 'I Dreamed I Saw St Augustine' – from which Dylan dropped a lovely harmonica intro after two takes – and his own reimagining of the kind of laconic ballad he'd rediscovered in the Red Room, 'The Ballad Of Frankie Lee And Judas Priest'; proof positive his kaleidoscopic imagination remained intact, even if he now spoke more like Luke The Drifter than Bobby the Poet. Musicians McCoy and Buttrey were as prepped as ever:

Charlie McCoy: When we did *John Wesley Harding*, I didn't have any information prior to going in about what it was going to be like. But [us] Nashville studio musicians . . . usually never [know] what we're going to be doing. We hear the music the first time we walk into the studio.

---

* *Melody Maker* journalist Nick Jones, son of Max, heard two of these songs in London in late October, so the songs date from no later than mid-October.

By the second session, McCoy and Buttrey realized the days of all-night sessions were long gone. Dylan was looking to cut these songs in double-quick time. If the session logs can be believed, he cut five songs on November 6th between six and nine in the evening, beginning with 'All Along The Watchtower', which save for a fluffed ending, he nailed on the first take. After a second take where Buttrey – thinking he'd got the hang of it – gets a little carried away, Dylan does the unthinkable and simply records a new coda, which he tags onto take one and moves on.*

Once again venturing into the unknowable region, Dylan's focus proves unerring. The contrast with the next set of Nashville sessions in February 1969 – where he merely embellished the same rhythm section – could not be starker. Not only do these complex songs have original arrangements, they also have real tunes, something not immediately obvious because of the stripped-down acoustic guitar-bass-drums set-up. If there is a lead instrument, it is the harmonica, which Dylan wields with judicious precision.

He can even allow himself to cast aside a decent original tune for 'I Pity The Poor Immigrant'. After recording it with the now-familiar tune and a great harp intro., and having pushed his voice as far as it can go, he tells Johnston, 'Don't take this,' and proceeds to teach the musicians a different tune. The next take starts with Dylan telling them, 'Yeah, the melody changed.' Still not satisfied, he attempts a synthesis of the two, capturing it by take four. The tune the memory man ended up using was one he learnt from Jean Redpath in the Village, Scottish folksong, 'Tramps & Hawkers'.

By the end of this second session, *John Wesley Harding* was all but in the bag. What now became apparent is that he was making a concept album. Not a *Sgt. Pepper* 'we'll stick with the concept for three songs, put a pointless coda on the end and call it a concept' album, but a cohesive piece of work with a narrative arc, which achieves resolution.† As Ian Bell notes, 'There is a formal unity to this collection

---

* The *John Wesley Harding* take information in Michael Krogsgaard's sessionography, used verbatim on Olof Björner's website, is pure fantasy. By fall 1967, logging false starts had become anathema at Columbia.
† For a fuller explication on *Sgt. Pepper*'s merits and demerits, I refer interested readers to my 2007 volume, *The Act You've Known For All These Years* (Canongate).

[that] is unlike anything Dylan had attempted previously.' It also has a moral, the same one offered at the end of 'Sign On The Cross'. Dylan was deliberately making *his* statement without studio jiggery-pokery, later rebuking The Beatles for all the goings-on at Abbey Road through the first half of 1967, 'I didn't think all that production was necessary.'

Dylan was able to do this because for the first time he had a clause to his new contract – one that was only added on September 18th, ten weeks after he signed on the dotted line. It read, 'Dylan has the right to approve positioning of master recordings on albums.' From hereon, it would be his sequence, and his alone. With this in mind, he completed his carefully-conceived narrative arc on November 29th with a six-hour session (6-12 p.m.) that gave him the album's last three tracks: the moralistic 'Wicked Messenger', and the bucolic 'I'll Be Your Baby Tonight' and 'Down Along The Cove'; as well as a song he'd mused over for a while, 'Dear Landlord' – his very own 'Take A Message To Albert'.*

The album was done and dusted. For those paying attention, everything about it sounded original, even the use of pedal-steel on the last two tracks of a folk-rock album. The player responsible, Pete Drake, notes, 'It opened the door for the pedal-steel guitar, because then everybody wanted to use one. I was getting calls from all over the world. One day my secretary buzzed me [to say], "George Harrison wants you on the phone."'

Yet Dylan would later claim, 'I didn't intentionally come out with some kind of mellow sound. I would have liked . . . more steel guitar, more piano, more music . . . I didn't sit down and plan that sound.' If Robbie Robertson can be believed, the two of them even 'talk[ed] about doing some overdubbing on it, but I really liked it when I heard it, and I couldn't really think right about overdubbing on it'.

Any such conversation – like life – would have been brief. The album was in the shops within four weeks of that third and final session. There was not even time to arrange a proper photo-session for the cover. Instead, Dylan asked Columbia's art-director, John Berg, with whom he had clashed on previous covers, to come up to Woodstock

---

* Only the completed masters from the final *John Wesley Harding* session remain in the Sony vaults. The session-tapes seem to have been lost or stolen, as the November 6th tapes were, before being bought back.

and snap a Polaroid of him wearing his *Blonde on Blonde* jacket, just to prove he hadn't changed, he was the same man.

He would be flanked on either side by some visiting folk musicians, Indian cultural ambassadors, the Bengali Bauls. After taking half a dozen photos, Berg spread them out on Dylan's dining-room table, and Dylan picked out the one he liked, which was ever so slightly blurred and in black and white (though some colour shots were apparently taken). He told Berg he wanted something that 'looks like a snapshot'.

Some post-production would still be needed. As soon as the album appeared as a belated Christmas present, observant fans began claiming all four Beatles had been super-imposed in the tree behind, something Berg admitted was true, 'but was reluctant to talk about', when *Rolling Stone* approached him two months after the album appeared for a news story called 'Dylan Record Puts Beatles Up In A Tree'. He also let on that 'the hand of God . . . was nestling along the right-hand side of the tree.'

Further proof that Dylan had not lost his sense of humour could be found on the rear sleeve, which featured the story of Three Kings, Frank (the key to the album) and Terry Shute. This parody of a parable confirmed his immersion in the 'King James' while sending up the very idea that the album had a 'key', and it allowed Dylan to cast himself as a modern John Bunyan, talking in riddles, challenging the listener to discern the word of truth.

It was a narrative style, sadly, he never revisited, but one he had evidently been playing around with for months, writing in one contemporary notebook: 'The man who wins the lookalike contest looked exactly like the president except for a small mole beneath the nose and a scar which he would not say how he received. "I'm a peaceful man," he said as he accepted the bronze plate.'

If Three Kings suggested he had become a moderate man, the whole premise had as its precursor an unused section of the *Tarantula* ms. dating from March 1965, which included a reference to 'three wise constipated kings: Hobble, Jobble an Jerry' who are looking for a 'young mountain climber', having brought along 'a bag full of games'.

Dylan had his sleeve, and his album. And what an impressive piece of work it was, even if the *auteur* in him would prove slightly dismissive of the results in later life, telling Cameron Crowe it was 'just a bunch of songs, really,' and indicating to Matt Damsker that he had originally 'figured [the basement tapes] was just the kind of stuff I wanted to do on my record . . . But then I went back and wrote just real simple songs . . . I knew it wasn't where I was gonna stay very long, but I had to explore that territory.'

Now he just needed to wait and see what the folks back home made of a work that comprised largely 'homespun ballads', sure in the knowledge that he had at the very least found his own moral compass for this brave new world.

3.3

October 1967 to February 1969:
When The Lights Went Out

Robert Love: In a period around 1966, you went into seclusion for more than a year, and there was much speculation about your motives. It was to protect your family, wasn't it?

Bob Dylan: That's right . . . I gave up my art to do that.

RL: And was that painful?

BD: Totally frustrating and painful, of course, because that intuitive gift – which for me went musically – had carried me so far . . . and it hurt to have to do it. But I didn't have a choice.

[2015]

There was a very strong middle-class or lower-middle-class ethic lurking with him all the time. You could really see it when he was around his mother or when he talked about his brother . . . I remember him sitting in the studio and dwelling on his notoriety and the inner tension that came from it. He'd sit there and say, 'I can't understand it – all I am is an entertainer.' I think he really believed that.

Bruce Dorfman, painter.

Woodstock is a very womb-like place . . . and people who go to Woodstock are transformed; people who live there, that is.

Elliott Landy, photographer.

I could never reach him directly, for he guards his privacy very carefully. The technique was to call his secretary Naomi, who would call him; then, if he chose to, he would call back.

Clive Davis.

In the early years everything had been like a magic carpet ride for me –
and then all at once it was over . . . Suddenly, I didn't feel I could do it
anymore.

> Bob Dylan, to John Preston, 26th September 2004.

*

If Dylan had taken a fair few liberties with the cover material he and
the Hawks had recorded in the Red Room the previous spring, it was
as nothing to the ones he now took with the first song recorded at Big
Pink that fall, Bobby Bare's 'All-American Boy'. Originally recorded by
Bare as a demo for Bill Parsons in December 1958, and mistakenly
released as a Parsons original, the song – intended as a comic talkin'
blues about the recently enlisted Elvis Presley – went all the way to
number two.

Dylan clearly remembered the gist of it, but once he begins to riff
on some of the lines there is no stopping him: 'Pickin' hot licks . . .
showin' off,' becomes, 'Kicking a hot storm up over the ocean/ He
took himself a notion/ He got some lotion/ And he put it on his guitar.' 'Impressin' the girls,' turns into a lascivious reverie as he begins to
imagine, 'makin' 'em little girlies giggle . . . makin' 'em all just jump
up an' down an' wiggle/ Empty their socks in their britches.' Everyone
in the high-flying band joins in with the festivities. Likewise, the portrait of 'a man with a big cigar/ [who] said . . . I'm gonna make you a
star,' was rendered more relevant, nay apposite, as Dylan replaced Colonel Tom with Uncle Albert:

> Well, sooner or later a man's gonna come
> He gonna take a look at you, look at your drum
> He'd be a man and he'll take you home
> Yeah, he'll take you out to his farm
> He'll give you a good one, he'll give it to ya.
> Well, sooner or later you're bound to meet his wife
> And you'll come in 'n' have the time of your life.

Grossman wouldn't hear the song in real time; indeed, not until his
business relationship with Dylan was severed in 1971. Imagine his surprise when a tape consisting of eleven Dylan originals and a traditional

arrangement ('900 Miles') arrived on his desk, sent it seems from Columbia, where it had been lodged for safe-keeping. The songs had been compiled from at least four of Garth's 1967 reels, all recorded after the previously copyrighted demos, some recorded at 3¾ ips, some at 7½ ips; with 'Sign On The Cross' and 'All-American Boy' tagged on last, but almost certainly recorded first. If 'All-American Boy' was meant to be a joke at Albert's expense, it didn't stop Grossman copyrighting the song – to Dylan, and Dylan alone* – one of five belated additions to the ever-expanding catalogue of Dwarf demos from the Big Pink treasure trove.

Even if one was tempted to think his reimagining of 'All-American Boy' was a spur of the moment exegesis on Dylan's part – a recording nobody was ever going to hear – it's not so easy to explain the inflammatory rewrites he made to the song sometime between August 4th, 1971 – when he was sent a typed transcript of the 1967 recording to correct for copyright purposes – and June 15th, 1973 when he returned the corrected lyrics, with handwritten amendments.†

By the time Dylan rewrote these lines he had entirely extricated himself from Grossman's commercial clutches. Yet the animosity evidently still ran deep. At a time when he was struggling to write anything from scratch, Dylan seemed to have no trouble immersing himself in a vat of Big Pink again, adding a couplet like, 'There was a holy cow and a medicine man/ And a sacred cow and an iron jaw that wouldn't break,' and another where the Mephisthophelean manager proffers a poisoned chalice, 'Drink that sonny, it comes in a cup/ Yeah, he'll take you out to his farm/ Where he's fixin' it up.'

There could be some truth to Dylan's implied *j'accuse* – that Grossman actively encouraged his clients' addictions – if one attaches credence to two remarks made to Barney Hoskyns for his history of the Woodstock music scene, *Small Town Talk*; one from ex-Fug Ed Sanders: 'Too many of [Grossman's] artists were junkies, and I think it's possible he used their addiction as a way of controlling them'; the other, offered anonymously and all the more unguarded for it: 'If Bob

---

* Perhaps a righteous response to Bare claiming a half-copyright to Hedy West's '500 Miles From Home', the title-track of his 1963 album.
† Dylan's amendments probably date from the summer of 1972, when he was also sent transcriptions for other songs found on the same reel (see chapter 3.6).

had been my client, I would have put road people on who made sure he didn't get any drugs, or certainly wouldn't have supplied them to him. Albert made sure to do exactly the opposite.'

Dylan himself only came to share such suspicions after he stopped drinking from Grossman's cup, which definitely happened by autumn 1967, by which time his animosity had become obvious enough for Aronowitz to notice, 'My first hint of bad blood boiling between Albert and Bob came when Bob started sneering at the very mention of Albert's name, muttering angry words about a mysterious incident concerning somebody's wife' – probably the very one who had offered the all-American boy 'the time of your life', having disappeared with him for three hours on her wedding day back in 1964.

Others less observant took longer to recognize the festering animosity. Levon Helm only noticed 'Bob and Albert weren't speaking to each other' at a benefit concert in January 1968. After a sabbatical on an oil rig, Levon had returned to the fold in early November, probably while Grossman was still in England, and just after Dylan and The Hawks cut the last of the home reels [#13] to be accessed by Sixties bootleggers.

'Get Your Rocks Off' – the one song on this reel copyrighted in January 1968 – again shows him enjoying making the girls giggle. But Dylan was also looking to rock out. 'Odds And Ends' is the most raucous thing he'd recorded in a year and a bit, delighting Helm when he heard it, though he did not play on it. Equally catchy was 'Apple Suckling Tree', which sees Dylan take to the piano for a parting glass of largely spontaneous ribaldry.

This last pre-Helm reel draws a line in the sand. Gone is the pop sensibility of the fourteen 'acetate' songs the others recorded between May and September, even if pastiche remains the order of the day. The satirical send-up 'Clothes Line Saga' – originally named 'Answer To Ode' – does for Bobbie Gentry's recent number one single, 'Ode To Billy Jo', what he'd done to Bare's 'All-American Boy' a matter of days before.

Yet Dylan continued to demo songs with his retained friends. Between this reel and the 'final' basement reel [#20] in early 1968 – featuring Dylan's one genuine nod to Harry Smith's *Anthology of American Folk Music* on these tapes, country-rock renditions of 'Wildwood Flower' and 'See That My Grave Is Kept Clean' – there are still plenty of joys to behold. But no-one, it seems, can agree on when the material was recorded or on what 'basement' songs the returning Helm plays. Sid Griffin has him playing on 'Silent Weekend', but not on any of the other dozen songs on the same reel, a faintly ludicrous assertion; especially as Robertson vividly describes Helm's playing on 'Santa Fe', from the same reel, as 'a bit rusty and tentative from just getting back, and still a little unfamiliar with the clubhouse groove'.

Maybe this rustiness explains the unembellished playing on these songs. Or perhaps Helm had simply figured out the boss liked drummers who just kept the beat. A greater issue is the twenty songs which cannot be assigned to any given reel, or to a specific period – though all are from post-September '67 'home' sessions. (Some are evidently from Wittenberg Road, where The Band moved in late November.) They include songs as important as 'Sign On The Cross', 'Wild Wolf' and 'All You Have To Do Is Dream', three enticing avenues Dylan could have gone down.*

'Wild Wolf' and 'All You Have To Do Is Dream' take on particular importance because both appear to be post-*John Wesley Harding*, and each contain lyrics that are, at times, 'authentic frontier gibberish', to quote Mel Brooks. The copyrighted transcript of the former reads like the work of a slightly deaf Edward Lear. All we know about 'Wild Wolf' is that he's 'gonna howl his way from morning', is 'still bubbling under', and he had something to do with the destruction of 'the Pharaoh and his armies'. Its one performance is as enigmatic and unfathomable as Blind Willie Johnson's 'Dark Was The Night'.

Destruction also rears its head in 'All You Have To Do Is Dream', as something which 'causes damage; and damage causes lust', to which the narrator himself seems to have succumbed, as on the very next line he asks some 'little girl' to 'come . . . blow this horn, hard as any horn I've seen.'

In both cases, the tapes would take years to appear, the originals having been mislaid by Garth. 'All You Have To Do Is Dream' would emerge on a fabled 1986 four-LP bootleg set, while 'Wild Wolf' would

---

* Of the second ten 'basement' reels, only #13 and #20 are numbered. The gaps suggest lost tapes and more Band-only recordings like the 'This Wheel's On Fire' and 'We Can Talk' demos.

not be heard until 2014's official round-up of the source tapes.* As such, the evidence they offer of Dylan's mindset post-*John Wesley Harding* remained under wraps until well after he emerged from that first 'amnesia'.

Also on this reel, surely with Helm *in situ*, are 'Ain't No More Cane' and 'Don't Ya Tell Henry' – both songs Helm later sang with The Band. Each receives a raucous Dylan vocal, as do two songs from Dylan's 1961 repertoire, '900 Miles' and 'Satisfied Mind', and full-blooded electric arrangements of 'Blowin' In The Wind', 'One Too Many Mornings' and 'It Ain't Me, Babe', the first time in eighteen months he had acknowledged the existence of a pre-accident canon. These are worked-up performances, too. There is a purpose to them, vouchsafed by the fact that they were captured on the same reel – in the case of 'Blowin' In The Wind' at 7½ ips – as 'Don't Ya Tell Henry' and the Mardi Gras mayhem of 'Bourbon Street'.

One possibility is that Dylan was thinking of doing one (or more) of his own songs at a tribute concert for Woody Guthrie at Carnegie Hall on January 20th, 1968. He certainly intended to bring along the band – now called The Crackers – whatever he elected to do, a decision that made others nervous. As Robertson recalls, 'I felt like a bit of an intruder in this setting, but the responsibility for inviting us along fell on Bob's shoulders.' Also intruding backstage between sets were Michael Bloomfield and Ramblin' Jack Elliott, who claimed the two of them ended up 'playing . . . guitar for two hours backstage . . . We were just making up shit, just like when we used to be together.'

In the end, Dylan did three Guthrie songs, in a way that showed he had fully assimilated Woody's most important lesson, 'Be yourself.' He wasn't about to give such a respectful audience what they expected, pulling off – in rock critic Ellen Willis's words – another 'of his brilliant reversals: having had the nerve to use only acoustic instruments on *John Wesley Harding*, he now came on in the middle of a memorial to the quintessential folkster with a four-man electric band and three rousing country-rock arrangements'. Guthrie, who had died the

---

* Sid Griffin fondly imagined he heard two takes, as opposed to two dubs of the same 'Wild Wolf'.

previous October, finally succumbing to Huntington's, would have approved.*

It was a crackerjack performance from The Band, too, even if it was also a symbolic parting of the ways. Ten days earlier, they had entered A&R Studios, the very studio where Dylan had recorded his first six albums, Columbia's old Studio A. They were going to record their own *Music from Big Pink*, including two songs with Dylan lyrics and Band tunes, 'Tears Of Rage' and 'This Wheel's On Fire'. Indeed, a demo of the latter in mile-wide stereo is the final song on the 'Wild Wolf' reel. This time it's a Danko vocal and a Band arrangement.

These floorbirds were about ready to spread their wings, and they knew they had better hurry up and choose which of Dylan's discards they wanted before they all disappeared. As of January 16th, when Dwarf Music copyrighted the last four songs for the fabled 'acetate', there was an unseemly rush to record all fourteen songs, generating Dylan's – and Grossman's – primary revenue stream for the foreseeable.

At some point in October 1967 Garth Hudson had set about compiling a mono 7½ ips reel from the master reels at Grossman's behest.† Quite probably the impetus for this was Albert's imminent visit to the UK. We know he took with him at least some Big Pink songs because his British publisher promptly played seven of them – including the not-yet-copyrighted 'Tears Of Rage' and 'Quinn The Eskimo' – to *Melody Maker*'s Nick Jones.

The tapes soon found their way to the likes of Manfred Mann (who successfully covered 'Mighty Quinn', as they decided to call it) and Julie Driscoll, Brian Auger & The Trinity (who had a number one with 'This Wheel's On Fire'), as Dylan covers once again filled the airwaves. He might even have had a third Top Ten from these tapes if Hendrix hadn't decided to release his stunning interpretation of 'All Along The Watchtower', rather than the 'Tears Of Rage' he demoed at this time. But no

---

* Many assumed Guthrie was already dead, notably the punter who heckled Dylan in Liverpool in May 1966, 'Woody Guthrie would turn in his grave.' Dylan evidently knew something of the state his mentor was in because when Alan Price asked about him in 1966, he replied, 'He's alive, if you call that alive. He's breathing.'
† Robertson claims *he* and Garth put the tape together 'for Albert to pass on to the music-publishing people'. Perhaps he could therefore explain why he omitted three of its key performances from the 1975 CBS LP.

matter how much energy Grossman exerted spreading the word, these seminal recordings were destined to become the last administered by him on Dylan's behalf.

A bitter war for the reversion of Dylan's copyrights was about to commence and Dylan, who knew his enemy and had come to know himself, was fully prepared to fight dirty, if required. The first shot across the bows came on March 28th, 1968, when Columbia Business Affairs received the following letter from Dylan's new legal secretary, Naomi Saltzman:

> Gentlemen: Please be advised that . . . Mr Dylan, requests that all checks and original statements forthcoming to him under the [July 1st, 1967] agreement be hereafter addressed as follows: Mr Bob Dylan, P.O. Box 36, Prince Station, New York 10012. Copies of all statements should be sent to Mr Albert B. Grossman.

Evidently, Dylan had finally got around to reading all his contracts. Sara, who remained friends with Sally even as she was forced to take sides (and deliver any messages Dylan had for the Grossmans, after he cut off all other lines of communication), confided in Bruce Dorfman that her husband 'was thinking of changing managers. [He felt] that he shouldn't have had to read the contract, which . . . a lot of artists would say: they feel they shouldn't have to. They should be able to trust people.' Trust and betrayal lay at the very heart of the matter. As Dylan later said, in deposition, when asked how long he had known Grossman, 'Well, I don't think I've ever known the man.'

It was primarily Grossman's double-dipping on Dylan's publishing that had made him take a long hard look in the mirror. How and when he came to discover Uncle Albert was guilty of this practice is not documented. Sounes suggests it was after a brief discussion with David Braun – his *and* Grossman's lawyer – in Dylan's car, after Braun explained the real terms of the contract he had signed in April 1966 setting up Dwarf Music. In response, Dylan apparently convened a meeting at Naomi Saltzman's house with her, Braun and a forensic accountant.

Former road manager, Jonathan Taplin, in his 2021 memoir claims it was Saltzman who first stirred the pot: '[Dylan] had an accountant [sic] named Naomi Saltzman, who was constantly reminding him how much he was paying Albert Grossman, and she'd gotten him so worked up about money that Bob proposed they renegotiate their publishing deal. Albert . . . was [not happy about] the same tactic [he'd used repeatedly] being applied to his share of Bob's music publishing.' Once Braun joined the Dylan team, Taplin sensed it was all over for Albert, 'They essentially got Bob to feel that Albert was taking way too much of the music-publishing revenue. Once Bob began to believe that Albert was screwing him, it was all downhill.'

Both Sounes and Taplin imply Dylan *needed* to be told the truth; that he had to be brought to the realization he'd been screwed. I don't necessarily buy that. But whatever the truth, recruiting Saltzman and Braun, thus turning his ex-manager's poachers into gatekeepers, was a masterstroke. Between them, they knew where most of the bodies were buried. It gave Dylan an edge he could use, and evidently did, because by the end of 1968 he had renegotiated his publishing arrangements with Grossman, who agreed to set up a new company, Big Sky, even though the Dwarf Music contract had *seven* years left to run. Under the terms of a new agreement, new songs would be lodged with Big Sky and Saltzman would be in charge of its administration.

It meant that Grossman was reliant on Dylan to receive his cut, not the other way round. Grossman still shared net profits on Big Sky songs in the same 50/50 proportion as Dwarf Music but only until June 1971, when the new Columbia deal was also due to expire. Such a deal can only have been agreed because Dylan had found the smoking gun and threatened to use it. The feared negotiator had been outmanoeuvred by his protégé.

If, in this instance, Saltzman already knew the name of the beast, her next adversary, ABC, was an entirely different creature. Her brief was to extract Dylan from his ABC contract and the *Stage '66* deal with a minimum of upfront costs, while retaining maximum control. ABC had already commenced an action against Dylan's production company, Rangoon, in New York's Supreme Court, so time was of the essence. Naomi promptly proved her mettle by negotiating an agreement (dated February 1968) which, for an upfront payment of $10,000, ensured the problem went away. Under the agreement, duly ratified by both parties in May, Rangoon became the 'sole owner of film and program', and was 'not obligated to complete or release film'.

In theory, the agreement meant ABC were entitled to receive half of the net receipts the film generated up to $100,000, but it was not beholden on Dylan to do anything with the film. Given the fate of the basement tapes and *Tarantula*, such a clause should have given ABC cause to pause. By now, though, they just wanted shot of the whole sorry project. Yet the film had not actually been abandoned by Dylan or Alk. Indeed, the day after the ABC settlement Alk forwarded Naomi an estimate of the cost of completing the film – $38,493 – and a request to 'know what the release situation is [with] Lennon, Spencer Davis, Johnny Cash &c.' The film now had its title and an aesthetic, or as Pennebaker suggests, an anti-aesthetic:

> Dylan [and Alk] made this film from the outtakes of the rough cut Bobby [Neuwirth] and I had put together. They took these pieces of footage and jammed them together. They were trying to make a point by doing that. It was a . . . put-down of documentaries . . . The title is Al Aronowitz's. He said, 'Documentary? Eat the document!'

There was even a proposal drawn up, supposedly designed to sell the film to distributors, though it would be ten years before Dylan and Alk released any movie, and when they did, it would be entirely self-financed. Evidently, Pennebaker was not alone in disavowing Alk's schtick. According to the proposal, probably jointly composed by Aronowitz and Dylan:

> [EAT THE] DOCUMENT [is] based on the Novel, 'Document' by Alfred Aronowitz [and is] to star Bob Dylan. music & the abstraction of the condition of the music to illustrate the Prolonged Mind destroyed & re-created thru the process of previous experience. this is not an easy feat, but to plant the seeds of both motion & stability has not always been an easy challenge. mr dylan will sing six or seven songs of Lore. nine if necessary to show the power of a Passive Universe . . . The songs themselves shall then, too, dissolve when the Monumental Failure of both Disappearance & Investigation cease to become entrapped in the suggestion & not the probability of the song itself.

The film described here bore no evident relationship to *Something Is Happening Here*, or indeed any film made before or since, even as it gave Dylan and Alk breathing space to make a film according to their joint vision. They certainly proceeded apace because John Cohen saw what Dylan called 'a rough work print' the following month, when he came to Dylan's house to interview him for a *Sing Out!* cover-story.

Dylan seemed keen to talk about this 'new method . . . [where] we tried to . . . construct a stage and an environment, taking it out and putting it together like a puzzle.' He also claimed to Cohen that 'the reason it didn't get seen [originally] was that the program folded, and by the time we handed it in, they had already [started] a state-wide search . . . to confiscate the film,' something of an exaggeration. Dylan also showed it to George Harrison when he visited in November, Harrison later writing him an exuberant note, 'The film was too much, and all the gang here would love to see it someday.' Yet still Dylan did nothing to secure releases from the likes of Lennon and Cash as *Eat the Document* became one more project lost on the river of no return.*

Meanwhile, Cohen had an interview (or three) to conduct, Dylan's first major interviews since the accident; the first of which came just days after he returned from Hibbing and his father's funeral. On May 29th, the 56-year-old Abram Zimmerman had died of a heart attack. Dylan, now a family man himself, expecting a third child, was in shock; so much so that when café owner Bernard Paturel drove him all the way to JFK airport, he never even mentioned the reason he was flying home.

After the funeral, Dylan had driven around Hibbing with his brother, David, and leafed through old records, tapes and books at the family home. It seemed like another lifetime; like he had been maybe born to the wrong parents. He stayed five days before playing the pregnancy card, flying back to be by his wife's side when their second son arrived. The boy was late, not arriving till July 30th, by which time Dylan had received Cohen's transcript of their conversations for his approval. He and Sara called their new addition Samuel Abram, after the grandfather he never knew.

Cohen had found the interviews, whenever they departed from music or Dylan's film, hard work, so much so that he eventually asked Happy Traum to join them. It only made things worse. As Traum

---

* It would eventually be screened at the Whitney Museum in 1971, then on local PBS-TV in 1979, from which it was readily, and widely, bootlegged on videotape (and eventually DVD). It remains officially unreleased.

recalled, 'The Vietnam War was on . . . and I really wanted him to say something about that. I was trying to get Bob to make some definitive statement about where he stood. But he . . . was just talking about this stone-mason he knew.'

Traum pushed as far as he dared, at one stage asking, 'Do you foresee a time when you're going to have to take some kind of a position?' 'No,' was Dylan's monosyllabic reply. Happy also tried to get his near neighbour to discuss why people felt the need to 'analyze and pull apart' his songs. Initially, Dylan seemed willing to engage, 'It's not everybody does that – just a certain kind of mind. Most people I come in contact with don't have questions – maybe scholarly minds . . . they take everything apart now, not only music – paintings, movies [as well]. The aspect of just letting it happen to you, to take you out of your thoughts at the moment, I don't know what's happened to that [idea].' However, on seeing Cohen's transcript, he deleted everything after 'questions' and, despite Cohen calling these comments 'the fulcrum of this interview for me', he declined to reinstate them.

As for Vietnam, he sedulously avoided the subject for another decade, before making a passing reference in 1978's 'Legionnaire's Disease'. That he had an opinion is clear from a late Nineties draft of *Chronicles* which draws parallels with 1962's *The Manchurian Candidate,* using the word 'debriefed' to describe those soldiers who returned without 'compassion for life itself'; a view he reiterates in his own celluloid 'state of the nation' address, *Masked and Anonymous* (2003). In all three cases, he suggests that the true battle was fought back in America and it was one that the nation collectively lost, a stark assessment of a collective national folly.

Yet the sense of displacement from everything going on in the outside world, writ large in that lengthy 1968 interview, was no put-on. As Aronowitz remarked, 'In Woodstock, Bob's lifestyle became very country squire-ish. In addition to painting, writing songs, working on a book and editing his tour films into a one-hour TV special, he would sometimes drop into the drug store for toothpaste, go to a movie in one of the nearby towns, visit with neighbours or attend antique auctions with Sara.'

If the couple wanted to go to Manhattan, Aronowitz would usually pick them up in his station wagon and drop them off at the luxury high-rise in the Village where Naomi Saltzman lived with her husband,

Ben. During this sustained period of retrenchment, Aronowitz saw another side of the man, 'I've never seen him treat another human as civilly, as respectfully, as lovingly and as humanly as he treated Sara in the years following his motorcycle accident.' Sara admitted as much to her old college roommate, telling her, 'He's positively mellowed . . . He's human lately and very reluctant to go back to anything approaching the hectic pace of the early years of our marriage.'

He knew he had some rebuilding work to do on their relationship, and for now that took priority. Yet one exchange recorded in a 'Tulsa' notebook, presumably reflective of a real conversation, suggested the couple were still having the odd communication problem: ' "You have often felt like walking away," she said many times. [I replied,] "I have. But this time I'm gonna stay right here and FIX IT." '

Sara also informed her ex-roommate of how he would go off for long periods of time, and when he did, 'she doesn't know exactly where he is'. But when he was around, the centre of Dylan's universe was his family, so much so that on her visits to see her friend said roommate rarely saw 'him during the day without a child attached like an extra limb'; a change that delighted his widowed mother:

> The kids are always around, climbing all over [his] shoulders and boun-
> cing to the music . . . they love the music, sleep right through the
> piano . . . and Jesse has his own harmonica, follows Bob in the woods
> with a little pad and pencil, jots things down . . . These are the things
> Bob feels are important . . . and this is the way he's chosen to live his life.

How much solace the shut-down son proffered to a grieving mother that summer is the lost text of another mystery play. But Beattie was welcomed into the home of the Dylans through the end of August, while the two brothers organized the sale of their childhood home. Beattie found it, as she gamely admitted, 'a constant struggle to try to get through the day without my wonderful husband, Abe, [after] two years of courtship and thirty-four years of honeymooning'. But she would overcome, remarrying in March 1970, to a relative of a former band-member of Bob's, Joe Rutman. Small world.

Unfortunately for a Dylan who hoped he might continue to hold reality at hand's length, Woodstock was not really far enough away from the bright lights, big city to dissuade deranged disciples from searching out, and sometimes finding, the man who once 'sat behind a million pair of eyes and told them how they saw' (as David Bowie phrased it on their behalf in 1971's 'Song For Bob Dylan').

Bowie was not the only singer-songwriter who felt a need to call on Dylan to return to the fray. The same year, Baez would write 'To Bobby', perhaps feeling she couldn't get through to him any other way. Maybe she couldn't. Dick Weissman recalls his friend, Artie Traum, taking 'care of one of two houses that Bob Dylan owned in Wood-stock . . . [and] people would come by to visit uninvited and calls would come in from all corners of the world. Artie was instructed not to give out Dylan's phone number to *any* caller. The first caller was Joan Baez . . . Artie followed [his] instructions.'

By 1968, the Dylans had developed something of a siege mentality, the husband confiding in Robbie, 'Strange people just show up at my door anytime – night or day. It's really upsetting for Sara, and I don't know who these people are, or what they want. It makes me angry dealing with all this shit all the time. You move up to the country for some quiet peace of mind, and they come [to] my doorstep . . . I don't want to live like *that*.' One day he snapped – and Bruce Dorfman was there to witness it, 'He asked me to come up to the house because he'd heard some noises in there. So we went in and roused a couple out of his and Sara's bed. He went to get his gun, and it wasn't a *conversation*.'

His view of these days would subsequently turn sourer still, so much so that whenever Never Ending Tour band-member, Larry Campbell, who moved upstate in the Nineties, broached the subject, he was met with short shrift: 'There were never any conversations with him where he reminisced fondly about [Woodstock]. With Bob it always seemed like, "Well, I did that and now I don't do that anymore." I do remember asking what he was doing up here, and he put it very simply. He said, "I was raising a family. That's all I was interested in at the time."'

In a vain attempt to stem the tide of humanity invading his space, Dylan bought eighty-three acres of woodland around his property. But still they came, and still they wrote – as Dick Weissman duly dis-covered. On paying a visit to see Artie, he found a whole room full of 'sacks and sacks of [fan-]mail. We randomly read a half-dozen of the letters. The one that I remember came from a female fan in North

Dakota. She had been to a Dylan concert and reminded him that they had met [and] plaintively added that if he didn't remember her, then maybe one of the members of Dylan's group, The Band, would.' Rather than simply bin them, Dylan evidently read some. According to Sara's ex-roommate, he kept his two favourite fan letters behind a jug, in the house. They read:

'Sir, you are an abomination on the face of this country and the sole cause of my son growing his hair down his back. He worships you, but I say you must be dirty and your hair harboring ticks – his does. – Ethel M. Linfield.'

'Dear Mr Dylan, Please let me know if you are really dead. My brother says you are and I want to burn candles for you if it is true. I love you. Alice Duquesne, Age 11.'

For all his protestations, the Dylan who once loved to verbally joust with his fans hoping to interact and instruct was still inside the man in him, and only he could bring that person back to life. But it would be a long haul. As he said, in 1978, 'What I survived after that [accident] was even harder to survive than the motorcycle crash. That was just a physical crash.' The mental crash left him adrift for a long, long time, trying to learn how 'to do consciously what I used to be able to do unconsciously'.

Thus, the most revealing line in a late Sixties notebook pertains not to any song. It is a message to himself, handwritten in capital letters: 'I AM NOT DONE/ I HAVE NOT EVEN BEGUN.' His travails started some time in 1968, when his muse flipped a switch and the lights went out. For now, Dylan gamely struggled on, jotting down song-ideas like always, thinking up song titles like 'Big Tough Woman', 'Going To Savanna', 'Rear View Mirror' and 'Dump Truck'. But this time around, they went nowhere. The one verse he managed for 'Dump Truck' just about summed it up: 'Got nowhere to Go/ Got nothing to do/ Gotta Drive As Slow as I Can/ In my dump truck.'

At least these notebooks suggest he was continuing to use The Bible as something that could be bent to an ulterior purpose. 'Arise oh Satan and take back your thieves,' sounds biblical, but is not. Likewise, the line, 'I will own the gate of MY ENEMIES', is a reworking of, 'Thy seed shall possess the gate of his enemies' [Genesis 22:17], a line spoken by God to Abraham. Now, though, such ideas were staying still-born as he allowed himself to be consumed by the idea of revenge – a subtext of his last album – on some unspecified person, whom he addresses with the lines, 'Take back your flattering tongue . . . I'm not going to get up every day and go to work for some other man.'

Continuing in this vein, another unrealized post-*JWH* song warns potential listeners not to emulate someone's malevolence, 'You gotta stay away from his ways/ Lest you meet his fate.' Someone else, it seems, is already on his trail, 'The judge of his deceit has left his [?sons]/ to seek out the wicked man/ and to break his arms and legs,' while a greater judgement awaits, 'A wicked man does not live forever – he suddenly get[s] sick and dies. All his dreams/ [and] plans shall go floating down the river.' This greater judgement to come awaits everyone, even Quinn the Eskimo, the Joker and the Thief:

> It's gonna rain on the captain who commands the ships
> It's gonna rain on the lady with the great big hips.
> Nobody's now gonna get their mail
> It's gonna rain rocks, and it's gonna rain hail.

The only person seemingly immune from judgement is a witchy woman, 'Miss Lucy', who 'sleeps in the bed of fine silk/ She keeps her own cows, she drinks her own milk.'

Dylan's own musical faucet may have temporarily run dry, but his Canadian protégés had stumbled on their own river of song. One day in June, Dylan broke his self-enforced embargo on visits to the Grossmans to hear an acetate of the album 'his' Band had been making while he sat watching the Hudson flow. He went over there with Sara and Aronowitz, and according to Robertson: 'When "The Weight" came on, he . . . slapped me on the arm and said, "Damn! You wrote that song?" [And] at the end of the album he stood up and said, "You did it, man, you did it."'

It sounds a tad effusive for Dylan. And yet, his appreciation of 'The Weight' tallies with other comments. Here was a song that captured the Big Pink spirit in a jar. He even requested it to be included alongside his *Sing Out!* interview that fall, prefacing it with, 'My good friend Jamie Robbie Robertson composed this fine song.' Twenty years later, he would join Levon Helm at the Lone Star Cafe to sing a rousing rendition of the one Band song he ever returned the favour on.

Dylan had good reason to love the song; he was taking a share of the publishing, it being assigned to Dwarf Music along with the rest of *Music from Big Pink*. Robertson later claimed he specifically asked Grossman to 'publish all our Big Pink and basement songs with Bob's publishing company, Dwarf Music'. It is hard to imagine that a man who once worked for the notorious Morris Levy would have been naive enough to think Dwarf was 'Bob's publishing company'. Nor is it likely that Grossman didn't strongarm his new clients, The Band, into using *his* publishing arm. One hopes Dylan appreciated the gesture, even if it left the five members of The Band splitting 50% of the songs five ways. (Robertson would eventually relieve the others of any such burden.)

Meanwhile, Dylan had transferred most of his creative urges to painting, so much so that he offered to do the cover to The Band's debut LP, due out in July. The painting – supposedly 'of an American Indian looking straight ahead, while in the background an Indian woman . . . rides away on the back of a horse with a cowboy' – Robertson felt 'hinted at a story'. He was hardly about to turn down visual proof of the closeness of their association, whatever story the cover painting itself would offer.

Big Pink, for all its enduring influence, would need all the help it could get, only peaking at number thirty in the *Billboard* 200, whereas Dylan's *John Wesley Harding* – even without a single to generate AM airplay – had peaked at two, selling nearly three-quarters of a million copies domestically by September 1973 (when Dylan demanded Columbia account for all his record sales to date), 300,000 more than *Highway 61 Revisited*. So much for a failure to tour or release a single – two marketing no-nos – amounting to commercial suicide. It was almost like the reclusive Dylan was more attuned to his audience than the city dudes tasked with selling his records.

No matter how much Columbia wanted a follow-up, though, Dylan was free of all contractual obligations. Having put his business affairs in order, he took up his easel instead. He began taking some informal painting lessons with Dorfman, who was worried Dylan might be trying to run before he could walk. When the novice said he wanted to paint in the style of Vermeer, Dorfman remarked, 'Are you *sure* this is where you want to start?' Then he asked to paint something like Monet: 'Same deal. An hour, a mess.'

Finally, one day he appeared with a book of Chagall paintings: 'You had all these multilayered images – things flying, things walking, clocks flying, rabbits with green faces. It was all there. Chagall was it. He made the connection.' Dylan had recently returned from a Chagall/ Redon exhibition at the Guggenheim, which he attended with Beat poet, Michael McClure. According to McClure, 'Bob wouldn't look at the Redons. He had eyes for nothing but the Chagall. Chagall was the meaningful world to him.'*

But when Dylan's next painting received a public airing, on the cover of *Sing Out!* – a study of a man sitting playing a guitar while his alter-ego, in a top hat, peered through the window – it came out closer to Tony Hancock's *The Rebel* than the American Gothic Cubism he sought. Dorfman was a little put out, 'When I saw the thing on *Sing Out!* magazine, I was almost annoyed . . . He should have said some-thing.' Bruce didn't think much of the end result, and evidently neither did other folk Dylan confided in. But he had been bitten by the paint-ing bug and he would not be dissuaded. It was just like learning to play the harmonica all over again; he didn't give a shit what others thought – even when they thought, what is this shit?

By summer's end, though, Woodstock was really starting to become oppressive and when Bob and Sara's favourite journalist suggested they head out to Fire Island, a popular summer resort, after all the weekenders went back to work, Dylan decided to risk it – only to immediately regret it:

Al Aronowitz: I finally talked Bob and Sara into sharing a summer beach house on Fire Island . . . I picked up Bob and Sara at their place in the Village and started out on our drive, about two hours long . . . We hadn't even escaped the city limits when we were stopped dead in bumper-to-bumper traffic and Bob had a tantrum. 'Shit! Fuck! How'd I get talked into this? You sure this is the only way to get there? I bet you took the wrong road, dammit!' . . . With traffic at a standstill, he

---

* Odilon Redon seems a strange choice to share a joint exhibit with Chagall. They were not contemporaries, nor was he a major influence. But there really was such an exhibition: 'Rousseau, Redon and Fantasy'.

suddenly opened the car door in a burst of anger and walked out in a huff. 'Where are you going?' Sara called pleasantly after him, 'Do you plan on walking there? Maybe you think you're going to catch a cab.' . . . When it came to Bob's moodiness, Sara was as good as a Paxil. [He sheepishly got back in.] I'd arranged to meet David Amram at the ferry dock in Fire Island's Davis Park . . . David knew . . . Hank Baumeister, a ferryboat captain and a trumpet player. We stayed that weekend at Baumeister's Davis Park house.

Dave Amram: I went to the ferry and Bob got off with all these kids and his wife Sara, whom I had known before Bob met her, [through] her husband [sic] Hans Lowndes . . . it was so great to see her, because [the last] time [I'd seen her] she and her husband had split up, she was with a little baby and struggling. And [now] she looked terrific. She looked happy and beautiful and she had these beautiful children with her . . . It was in September, after Labor Day. [They] all stayed for the weekend and they had a wonderful time. I talked to him a little about Jack Kerouac . . . I told him what it was like for Jack [Kerouac] when he suddenly became a worldwide celebrity overnight [with *On The Road*], and how devastating it was for him – he just wanted people to read his books.

The experience ultimately proved a rewarding one, and Dylan even began to think about returning the following summer, this time maybe renting a place to stay. He had greatly enjoyed Amram's company. A loquacious man, who had known both Kerouac and Guthrie, he was an authority on jazz, and had written the powerful score for *The Manchurian Candidate*, a movie that fully accorded with Dylan's own paranoiac vision.

Once back in Woodstock, though, he seemed increasingly preoccupied, and what was worrying him most was his muse staying *schtum*. Of the seven song titles he wrote down in his latest notebook, three had gone the way of the dodo, 'How Dare You Woman', 'High Taxation Blues' and 'Take A Little Trip With Me', leaving not a trace. The last of them suggested, 'You don't have to be a visionary to count up to ten,' which was a stroke of luck because further visions resolutely refused to come.

Instead, mundane matters crowded in, like the amount of tax a millionaire like him was expected to pay, prompting him to complain he's 'got the high taxation blues', and bemoaning the IRS 'leeching me for money', like a latter-day Van Morrison. It was almost like he had become someone whose mind 'multiplied the smallest matter'. Intrigued by the persona of the Wicked Messenger, he even began only his second-ever sequel song:

> I am that wicked messenger
> That you all have heard about
> But [I'd] just like to tell you my side of the story
> So your minds will be free [of] any doubt.

He never completed this reimagining, just as he never completed the sequel to 'Mr Tambourine Man'. Instead, the last line of 'The Wicked Messenger' – 'If you cannot bring good news, then don't bring any' – became the springboard for songs like 'To Be Alone With You', 'One More Night' and 'Lay Lady Lay', all ones he begun that fall. At the same time, he abandoned each and every song-idea from the past half-year which had a point of view, after telling Aronowitz, 'The kind of song I [now] like is the kind that, when you hear it . . . makes you want to do good things.'

In the one interview he gave to promote the resultant album, he would claim such 'songs reflect more of the inner me than the songs of the past'. In fact, they reflected *nothing* of 'the inner me', being merely songwriting exercises – ostensibly resembling the Dwarf Music demos, but minus the strata of subtexts. For the first time in his life, he was asking himself, whither now? It would be another decade before he admitted to himself – and a handy reporter – 'I was trying to grasp [for] something that would lead me on to where I thought I should be. [But] it didn't go nowhere – it just went down, down, down.'

After his ninth Columbia album appeared, he would suggest it had never been his intention to complete *John Wesley Harding Vol. 2* (even after he test-ran the 'new' voice on Garth's last home reel, the previous February). Rather, he 'was waiting for people to tell me what they had in mind, what direction they wanted me to take, but nobody did. So I just went ahead and cut [this],' indicating a lack of creative direction entirely new to him and his fans.

A brief visit from Columbia president Goddard Lieberson in early October hadn't left him any clearer about a possible direction, offering almost nothing finished he could play for him. At least by the time his next guest arrived, with his gorgeous wife Pattie, Dylan had completed the most promising of the seven songs with which he had been tinkering, 'I Threw It All Away'. Even then, it took a fraught couple of days getting reacquainted before he would play it to George Harrison. The experience prompted the Beatle to recall, 'He seemed very nervous and I felt a little uncomfortable – it seemed strange, especially as he was in his own house.'

It was even more tortuous for Pattie, who shared with her husband a genuine love for her host's work, 'God, it was absolute agony. He just wouldn't talk. He certainly had no social graces whatsoever. I don't know whether it was because he was shy of George or what the story was, but it was agonisingly difficult.' Finally, at Harrison's suggestion, 'On the third day we got the guitars out, and then things loosened up.'

The new song Harrison heard that day had begun life as 'I Gave It All Away', hinting at how close he had come to losing Sara. He decided even this track was a little too close to home, electing to remove the one couplet that cut to the quick, 'I treated her cold, I had treasure untold / I gave it all away.' What was left, although it wouldn't have been out of place on a Hank Snow album, was still the best song he had written in a while. If he was hiding his real self in song, he was also trying to keep it from George's wife:

Pattie Boyd: There's a touch of cruelty in [his songs], against women, I think. [But] he wouldn't talk in Woodstock. And he was wearing brand-new jeans. I knew they were brand-new jeans because the label was still stuck on the back pocket. That's when we stayed with them . . . We were in Bob's house for a long time. And we must have stayed with Albert Grossman and his wife, 'cause we had breakfast there. Very chic. To be with really great, cool musicians [like The Band] was great. And they really loved George . . . I thought Sara was really fabulous – very feminine and very womanly. I thought she was finding it quite difficult, 'cause she had two [sic] children by then. So she was under pressure. To have children on top of [living with such a] manic man, very difficult.

Dylan confided to George that he was finding it hard to come up with new songs – the reverse of the problem Harrison himself had. *He couldn't get all the quality songs he was now writing onto a Beatles* album. The Scouser suggested they write something together. The result was two decent songs, 'I'd Have You Anytime' and 'I Don't Want To Do It'; the latter of which – unreleased until 1985 – almost broke through still waters by tapping into the past, 'To go back on the hill beside a track, and try to concentrate/ On all the places that I want to go.'

Meanwhile, a bridge Dylan came up with for the former song – 'All I have is yours/ All you see is mine/ And I'm glad to hold you in my arms/ I'd have you anytime' – sacrificed a set of platitudes he might have put to good use on his own album. The co-authored song became a rare outing for the salacious writer previously present at Big Pink, perhaps persuading him to tap into the same sensibility on 'Lay Lady Lay', also written that fall and the most commercially successful song from the whole 'amnesia'.* Though he later suggested, 'On *Nashville Skyline* you had to read between the lines,' here was one song which left little to the imagination. Rather than send it to Hank Snow, he went backstage at an Everly Brothers reunion concert at The Bitter End on February 1st, 1969 and offered it to Phil and Don. They foolishly demurred.

The same night, uptown at Carnegie Hall, the likes of Leonard Cohen, Graham Nash and promoter Harold Leventhal were lauding a landmark concert by Joni Mitchell, after which the party adjourned downtown to Colby's club, even as Dylan kept himself at a remove. Nash recalls, 'Bob was being Bob. Very hard to penetrate his aura. What do you say to him anyway?' For now, words failed them all, even the triumphant songstress.

Twelve days later, Dylan flew to Nashville to record his second album since re-signing. By then, Dylan already knew that for the first time songs as good as 'Lay Lady Lay' were in short supply. He didn't have enough for an album half as good or half as long as *John Wesley Harding*. And yet, he continued to give away songs which did not fit the conceit in his increasingly reactionary head. Having 'felt everyone expected me to be a poet' on its predecessor, he recorded a set of songs

---

* A contentious handwritten ms. of this song emerged circa 2013, on Atlantic Lumber Company notepaper, with some nice touches, such as rhyming 'You can have your cake and eat it too,' with, 'Why wait for the sky to turn blue?' It ends, unconvincingly, with the narrator having 'the heartbreaking blues, and they're all for you'.

almost good enough to constitute a Sixties Elvis film soundtrack. In the process, he discarded 'Wanted Man', an updated 'Outlaw Blues' with verses to spare:

> Now I find my [way] to Frisco, take my time and smile nice,
> Hoping not to get sh[anghaid] while I shoot somebody's dice . . .
> I'm just about to collect my winnings . . . every nickel, every dime,
> But someone always recognizes me before it's time.
>
> I might be in Colorado, or maybe Tennessee
> Working for some man who may not know who I might be . . .
> Now I plot my destination by the lamp inside the can
> That is how it is, boys, when you're a wanted man.

He never even recorded it, giving the song to his old friend Johnny Cash, who had recently been stuck in Folsom prison – playing a concert. Neither did he run down a solo version of 'Champaign, Illinois', a song he co-wrote with another hero from Sun's Fifties heyday: Carl Perkins, of 'Blue Suede Shoes' and 'Matchbox' fame. Perkins ended up joining Dylan and Cash one February afternoon (the 18th) in Music City USA, after some bright spark – clearly not anyone who had seen the Dylan/Cash sequence in *Eat the Document* – came up with the harebrained idea of recording an album of Dylan/Cash duets.

In the four days before he committed himself to this cockamamie concept, Dylan had already recorded eight throwaway songs in arrangements the A-crew could have recorded while still playing cards. Once again, he recalled Buttrey and McCoy, along with Wayne Moss and Hargus 'Pig' Robins. All four had played on *Blonde on Blonde* three years earlier, and must have thought Dylan had been kidnapped by Martians, who returned him to earth with an intermittent southern twang as a joke at humanity's expense.* Charlie Daniels, the one musician new to this, found the sessions a breeze:

> We recorded [the album] in three sessions. They had a lot of sessions booked that they didn't use. They had a rent-a-cop outside the door all

---

* As Aronowitz later remarked, '[When] hanging out at home, he seemed to lose a lot of his Oklahoma twang.'

the time, but . . . everything came together beautifully . . . With most of
the things, after they'd got the balance, we just went straight into [it]
and did them in one or two takes.

It sounds like it is Daniels who suggests an extra bridge on 'I Threw
It All Away'. The singer responds, 'You talkin' 'bout a turnaround?'
Recognising a hit in the making, Daniels replies, 'I just want to hear
more of it.' But the well is dry: 'Well, I don't know how to get anymore
of it in there. There aren't any more verses, and there's no more
bridge.' And this from a man who three years earlier *to the day* recorded
a song which took up a whole LP side in the same studio, with the
same producer and most of the same musicians!

As of now that rock'n'roller was in cold, cold storage. A semi-
improvised blues, 'Goin' To Chicago', on the 13th, fooled no-one, even
a fool such as him. When the inconsequential 'To Be Alone With You'
starts out with a Perkinsesque blast of country-rock, Dylan suggests
they're 'pushing it a little bit'. After a stuttering take three, another
musician wonders aloud if they shouldn't 'bring [in] another tempo'.
Dylan's response is simply, 'Let's just go till we find it.' Contrast this
with fifteen months earlier, when he was brimming with ideas, tunes
filled his head, and almost nothing ended up on the cutting-room
floor.

Further proof that this was not the first *John Wesley Harding* session:
of the four songs done on that first afternoon, the most promising – 'Lay
Lady Lay' – would require a remake the following day, at a session that
would yield three more tunes 'by numbers', plus a realized 'Lay Lady
Lay'. If he'd almost got enough for a fair-to-middling side A, to Dylan's
mind he almost had an album. Having pretty much shot his wad song-
wise, no amount of candy or cocaine was going to enable him to step
up and produce an album of stature.

All he had was a two-day recess, while he waited for his friend Johnny
to hit town. In that time Dylan did come up with 'Tonight I'll Be Staying Here With You', a mirror image of 'I'll Be Your Baby Tonight' even
down to Drake's pedal-steel. But with this single shot of inspiration, he
was done. Unfortunately for him, they had stopped making ten-inch
albums in the Fifties.

Needing more of the same, all he could do was leaf through some
back pages. On the 17th, Dylan countrified an old Mexican rag tune he

had toyed with once before, at a 1963 session,* and dispatched a brisk and breezy 'Tonight I'll Be Staying Here With You' with the ink not even dry. The rest of the session – with Cash now on hand – was devoted to excruciating re-recordings of three other songs from the early Sixties, one by Cash ('I Still Miss Someone' – again) and two of Dylan's.

The once sacrosanct 'One Too Many Mornings' and 'Don't Think Twice, It's All Right' – on which Dylan suggests Cash sings 'Understand Your Man', which has the same tune – are given the treatment, not only with tape rolling, but video tape, too. A documentary crew (there for Cash, not Dylan) filmed the pair trying – and failing – to keep straight faces listening back to too many bum notes on 'One Too Many Mornings'. What they didn't film was an exchange on an earlier take, during which Dylan jokes, 'I was a few miles behind.' Producer Bob Johnston asks if he wants to hear it back. Speaking for his loyal fans, Dylan replies, 'Don't matter to me.'

The chastening experience failed to dissuade these old friends from repeating the exercise the following afternoon, on a grander scale. This time they ran down (or over) just about any song either cared to call out. If Dylan had taken the lead on songs like 'Mystery Train', 'That's Alright, Mama' or 'Matchbox', it might have worked – and Cash does his level best to cajole Dylan into stepping up – but their voices don't so much mesh as turn everything they try to mush.

The 'amnesia' also seems to have affected his prodigious memory; he can barely remember the words to songs he sang word-perfect in the Red Room. The one song they take semi-seriously on the 18th, 'Girl From The North Country', would become the opening cut on *Nashville Skyline*, a gesture guaranteed to raise his core audience's hackles. The one song it really needed, 'Wanted Man', they ran through just once at the end of the afternoon, having figured out alternating verses was the way to go. The will to work up a proper take just wasn't there, and they soon resumed ransacking the past.

Hearing of the collaboration, the record company execs. initially thought a Dylan/Cash album might offer a two-for-one synergy of fan bases – until they heard it. As Johnston informed Robert Hilburn,

---

* 'Suze (The Cough Song)', recorded in October 1963 was released on *The Bootleg Series 1-3* (1991).

'They cringed. The only thing they could hear was [them] laughing in the middle of some songs, or [when they] didn't come out exactly together at the end of others. Maybe Columbia was just trying to protect their stars; they didn't want to let people hear them like this.' Columbia's instincts tallied with Cash himself, who sensed that Dylan 'was embarrassed over that and I don't blame him'.

If neither of them came out smelling of roses, Dylan got the better of the deal as Richard Asher at Columbia got them both to confirm that 'you perform a duet with the other on one song to be included in the other's next album'. Actually, Cash recorded 'Wanted Man' solo, in prison, where it served as the perfect jailhouse party piece, unveiled to a hall of San Quentin internees who knew just how that felt.

But if ideas for original songs remained in short supply, Dylan still had the Midas touch whenever others sang his songs. Having blessed two of the most acclaimed albums of 1968 – The Band's debut and The Byrds' *Sweetheart of the Rodeo* – with the best of Big Pink, and after Hendrix reinvented rock with his 'All Along The Watchtower', both the song he gave to Cash that February and the one he co-wrote with Harrison the previous November would open albums which went straight to number one, making the cash registers ring and Big Sky Music solvent.

He had less success in the singles market himself. Having finally acceded to Clive Davis's request for a lead single, he picked the best of the bunch, 'I Threw It All Away', hoping the resultant album might actually reach this landmark, too. After all, he'd removed every element that had ever set folks' teeth on edge: those wordy lyrics, six-minute-plus songs, that barbed-wire voice. Only he knew for sure whether he was consciously 'shilling the rubes',* having for the first time delivered an album that 'didn't go nowhere – it just went down, down, down'.

---

* This expression, supposedly a circus term denigrating country folk, was the working title for David Bowie's 1975 album, *Young Americans*, another fall from grace of epic proportions, with one decent single to sustain it.

3.4

March 1969 to February 1970: Town & Country

He was so changed by his accident that he had become religious; he had become a family man; he'd stopped smoking. You know, there'd been a total change in his personality.

Happy Traum.

Back then, [Sara] was with me through thick and thin . . . It just wasn't the kind of life that she had ever envisioned for herself.

Bob Dylan, to Ed Bradley, 19th November 2004.

Maybe it's just that I [have become] so used to [the crazies]. I mean, we get a Christ every six months coming up to our house. Even the kids are used to it. We even got a John The Baptist last year.

Sara Dylan, 1975.

I only knew him from the pictures and he didn't look anything like he was supposed to look. He just looked like a normal Jewish guy. Somebody said to me afterwards, 'That was Bob'. I said, 'You're kiddin' me.'

Van Morrison, on running into Dylan in Woodstock.

He loves to play [music], but in the highly competitive world of rock'n'roll that he was thrust into . . . that wasn't [necessarily] part of the picture . . . Bob used to talk about . . . how he just wanted to play music and, even though he wanted to be appreciated, how hard it was sometimes to be . . . treated like some kind of a person from out of space when all he wanted to do was tell his stories through songs.

Dave Amram, to author.

> [The English] live on an island. That does something to your mind.
>
> Bob Dylan, to Michael Braun, May 1966.

★

The twelve months after the February 1969 *Nashville Skyline* sessions would be a period of intense inactivity for the man who could still do no wrong, commercially. Just three days in the studio, two concerts (one a surprise guest appearance, the other to nearly a quarter of a million people on a small island off the south coast of England) and a single TV show would be the sum schedule for a year in which he continued to insist he was just a song and dance man.

And yet, the coffers continued to bulge. Al Aronowitz in his February 1968 review of *John Wesley Harding* had already let the cat out of the bag, 'Dylan's albums began to sell better than ever . . . in the year following his accident. . . earning him three [more] gold records' in those twelve months.

'Twas all true. On its April 1969 release, *Nashville Skyline* defied all logic – and some rather mixed reviews – outselling every album to date, despite offering barely half an hour of Dylan Lite. It even got a second shot in the arm when Columbia issued a follow-up single, 'Lay Lady Lay', in July, which far outstripped 'I Threw It All Away' sales-wise on both sides of the pond, giving Dylan his first AM hit of the post-accident era.

He seemed briefly galvanized, returning to Nashville just two months after the failed covers album, to repeat the experiment (minus Cash) doing other folks' songs, and to do Cash a favour by appearing on his new network television show, *The Johnny Cash Show*, as a special guest, playing his latest single, 'I Threw It All Away' and the next projected single, 'Living The Blues'.

If he had seemed to drive off a cliff creatively at those February sessions, the recordings from late April and early May suggested he still had a long way to fall. Three days of sessions either side of the TV recording resulted in eleven cuts, ten of them covers. They included two seminal Johnny Cash songs, 'Folsom Prison Blues' and 'Ring Of Fire', mercilessly mangled and then thankfully discarded.*

---

* The 1969 *Copyright Collection* – released in a very limited edition in 2019 – has now hoovered up all the outtakes from that year's sessions, save for April 26th and May 3rd, whose session-tapes have gone astray.

Even when he hit on a promising arrangement, as he did on a slow, flamenco-flavoured 'Spanish Is the Loving Tongue', halfway through the take he changed his mind, producing a kitchen-sink arrangement and backing singers whose heads should have been stuck under a tap, preferably in mid-take. Rewarding versions at these sessions were few and far between, though a beautiful 'Let It Be Me' bucked the trend, and showed the Everlys what he could do with one of theirs. Otherwise, the sessions seemed to suggest Dylan was wondering how far he could venture in this new direction without entirely losing his audience.

Absurd as it sounds, 'losing his audience' had a certain perverse appeal to the befuddled amnesiac, the idea lingering long enough for him to later claim the album on which six of these songs ended up 'was put out . . . [because] at that time . . . I didn't like the attention I was getting. I [had] never been a person that wanted attention. And at that time I was getting the wrong kind of attention, for doing things I'd never done. So, we released that [material] to get people off my back.'

Could career suicide really have been at the back of his mind? If so, he was going about it the right way. *Rolling Stone*'s Bill Reed played 'Blue Moon' to some friends months before its release. One of them 'became so enraged he stormed out of the room'. Meanwhile, the tapes sat on the shelf all year while Dylan chewed the cud. He even changed his mind about making 'Living The Blues', a marginal rewrite of Guy Mitchell's 'Singing The Blues', his next 45, wisely releasing 'Lay Lady Lay' instead.

Still in town, Dylan didn't just stay tight-lipped about his plans for these eleven b-sides. Al Clayton, the official Columbia photographer at the sessions, recalls, 'I tried to talk to him but whenever I would bring up a topic, he would say, "I don't know anything about that." He was completely withdrawn and very unto himself.' That he had doubts about what he was doing is apparent from a single comment he made before a second attempt to commit blue murder to 'Blue Moon', 'I don't know if I can do it this way.'

Only after he returned to Cash's house after a session was he reminded that 'the way to do a recording [is] in a peaceful, relaxed setting . . . with the windows open and a dog lying on the floor.' Johnny (and June) had arranged 'a dinner at our house with Nashville song-writers to meet Bob Dylan. We all sat around and sang songs together.

The guitar was passed from one to another.' An attendant Bob Johnston remembered the guest-list including Earl Scruggs and the great
Nashville songwriter, Boudleaux Bryant, co-author of 'Take A Message To Mary' – a song Dylan would record a few days later. Such
esteemed company perhaps gave Dylan cause to pause:

> **Bob Johnston**: When it came to Dylan, he really didn't want to play, but
> everyone coaxed him and so he took it and sang 'These Working
> Hands' . . . an old country song. Well, he just screwed every one of us
> up, with the result that someone took the guitar and hung it on the wall,
> 'cause nobody could follow that.*

The exercise was repeated a couple of days later. This time two contemporaries, Joni Mitchell and Graham Nash, were the honoured
guests, Joni and Bob having just recorded their slots for the first *Johnny
Cash Show*. According to Nash in 2009, '[Dylan] and his wife, Sara, were
sitting on the stairway – a stairway that led up to the second floor of
Johnny's house off the main dining room – and he didn't play until the
end of the evening. I actually got up first . . . I'd just recorded "Mar-
rakesh Express," so I played it.' This time, Dylan did songs of his own,
perhaps sensing a competitive spirit which was never far away when
Joni was in the room (witness the footage of her playing him 'Coyote'
in *Rolling Thunder Revue* [2019]). According to Nash, a riveting 'Don't
Think Twice' moved Dylan's wife to tears.

If these two performances featured a relaxed song and dance man,
the same could not be said when the cameras had rolled earlier in the
day. Those close at hand included musician Doug Kershaw, who soon
'realize[d] that he's afraid. Deathly afraid'. Joni, waiting to record her
big TV break, offered her own, unguarded explanation, 'When he was
younger . . . he would . . . diminish you if he thought your questions
were stupid or inartistic. Now, he knows he can't be an angry young
kid any more . . . Instead, he stays silent and explodes inside.'

The show's producer, Bill Carruthers, was under no illusion as to
why Dylan was putting himself through this, and what he was fighting

---

* It is possible that Kris Kristofferson and/or Shel Silverstein were also there. Cash
suggested they were, during a 1985 TV interview. He may well have been conflating
two separate evenings of socialising.

against, 'He [i]s the center of attraction, and he hates it – just hates it. And [so] the string is very taut at the moment regarding Bob Dylan even doing the show . . . He's on the edge. But he's sticking it out because of Johnny.' Stick it out he did, though his three-song perform- ance rather resembled a rabbit caught in the headlights until Cash took his mind off lesser concerns by treating a joint 'Girl From The North Country' with more crude insensitivity than he ever managed.

Dylan and Sara had enjoyed their time with Johnny and June. Cash even tried to persuade him to buy property down south, offering him a piece of his own land by the lake. But even when it came to buying property, he seemed incapable of making a definitive decision. A previ- ous change of mind over some land he'd considered buying in Woodstock the previous June had already resulted in legal threats, and ultimately a 1971 lawsuit.

Only when he wanted to stop something in its tracks or make a past problem go away did he act with alacrity. So, when Pete Fonda and Dennis Hopper asked to use 'It's Alright Ma' in their new biker movie, *Easy Rider*, Dylan declined.* When they got Roger McGuinn to re- record the song, hoping to use the first part in the movie, Dylan still proved intransigent.

George Lee at Warner's, who loved the smell of dollars in the morn- ing, considered giving Witmark's consent on Dylan's behalf until an April 28th telegram from Dylan's lawyer, David Braun, set him straight: 'If the synchronisation and performance license is granted by your company in direct violation of Mr Dylan's rights and wishes, you may be certain that appropriate legal action will be initiated by Mr Dylan, action which may well jeopardize your company's rights to the entire catalog of musical compositions written by Mr Dylan . . . administered by you.'

Oddly enough, Dylan had already anonymously contributed one of the more poignant moments in the entire movie, writing the plaintive bridge to the song which plays over the titles, for which he had taken no credit. 'The Ballad Of Easy Rider' as published was a solo McGuinn composition, even though 'The river flows, flows to the sea / Wherever the river flows, that's where I want to be' came from Dylan, offering a fair summation of his current worldview.

---

* He told the pair he was unhappy with the film's downbeat ending.

Three days before Braun fired off his legalistic volley to Lee, Dylan had paid Jean Ritchie, the great traditional singer, $6,500 on the understanding that she drop her suit for copyright infringement on 'Masters Of War'. The lady had already written in a pointed preface to a 1965 songbook about 'recent developments in the field of folk music [making] it necessary to copyright many of the Ritchie family songs'. She had finally gone after Dylan for using her unique arrangement of 'Nottamun Town'. She would have had a far better case against Davy Graham, Bert Jansch or Fairport Convention, all of whom directly lifted her arrangement, but none of them sold what Dylan sold.

It was a salutary lesson for this former 'thief of thoughts' and it was one he might have discussed with Paul Simon that summer. Back in 1967, Simon had reached a whole new audience with 'his' arrangement of 'Scarborough Fair', a repeating motif throughout the Oscar-winning *The Graduate*. Except it was essentially Martin Carthy's arrangement, and Dylan – of all people – knew it, having learnt the same arrangement from the same man eighteen months before Simon; when he had been a scuffling folksinger himself.

If by 1969, both Dylan and Simon were riding the crest of their own respective commercial waves, Simon felt he had never received the critical recognition Dylan enjoyed. And he never would, largely because the Brill Building had left its indelible mark on him. Still, he continued bugging Aronowitz to arrange an introduction. When both songsters found themselves on Fire Island that summer, Al made it happen:

> Paul and I [had] got friendly through a *Saturday Evening Post* colleague of mine . . . This was in the days when . . . Bob said I should open an office to just introduce people . . . Did Paul become a friend of mine as a way of getting to Dylan? I prefer not to be paranoid about it . . . But Paul kept coming after me. He kept trying to pin me down. He wanted to meet Dylan. Finally, I caught Bob in a mellow mood on the beach and he said, 'Yeah, bring him over. But you should charge him a commission.'

Once again, the Aronowitzes tagged along, while Dave Amram continued to come by most days. Dylan – who had been true to his word to Amram, returning to Fire Island with the family for a second summer break, renting another house that Hank Baumeister owned in Bayberry Dunes, a mile east of Davis Park – recognized Simon straight away from the chip on his shoulder.

Amram, there to run interference, also got to jam with Dylan and Simon: 'There was one night we stayed up till dawn playing music, just the three of us. I brought only my flutes and my horn. I didn't want to impinge on their guitars. [But] they treated each other so respectfully, taking turns playing behind each other.' Whether or not Simon realized it, this was one of Dylan's favourite ways to test contemporaries, famous or otherwise. In fact, he preferred to play with the latter, as Amram was privileged to witness:

> I used to go down almost every day and hang out with him and Sara and the kids . . . At that point . . . he'd just stopped for a while . . . Then he used to come down to my little part of the beach. He would leave Sara and the kids, and he'd just come down, different people would just come by to play music and just jam and, whatever they would play, I would play with them. One time we had an electrician named Jack Lovinger [who was] a very good drummer and he was playing on pots and pans, and they were really having fun and we played for about three hours and Bob was having a ball. So, I walked him back home up the beach, and we were walking in silence and he turned to me and said, 'Boy, you really enjoy doing this, don't you?'

Simon failed to establish a strong bond with the man he had satirised in 'A Simply Desultory Philippic'. Continuing to consider himself a peer among equals, he told *Rolling Stone* before the latter's 1974 comeback, 'Dylan was great, I gotta say he was great. [But] I don't feel that at the moment,' a criticism that drew this incendiary retort from Dylan, 'What's Paul Simon ever written that means anything to *anyone*?'

While Simon remained desperate for commensurate critical recognition, Dylan by 1969 was looking to disappear before unknowing eyes. And it turned out, he had something of a gift for it. It helped that he had changed so much, physically, that even those who once claimed to know him well walked on by. In a November 1968 *Saturday Evening Post* Dylan cover-story, Aronowitz related one occasion, two months before the release of *John Wesley Harding*, when the pair had been walking

through the Village and walked right past Izzy Young: ' "He didn't recognize you!" I gasped. "He never recognized me before," Bob answered,
"Why should he recognize me now?" ' The acid tongue still worked, it
seemed.

The feature did not identify Izzy, but Happy Traum told everyone
who it was. Young was cut to the quick, writing to Dylan, 'Why didn't
you greet me? We're supposed to be friends. Don't you think that I
own feelings, too?' Dylan kept the letter, but never responded. Meanwhile, in old Woodstock, a more inspirational songwriter than Simon,
Van Morrison – who was hiding out upstate, not so much drying out as
waiting for Bert Berns's Italian chum, Carmine, to stop looking for
him – had much the same experience as Young (see opening quote).
Not that Dylan's chameleon capabilities were anything new. As Maymudes liked to observe, 'Bob can walk and look *unlike* Bob. He hunches
over, he softens his body, curls his shoulders and walks so innocuously
that you don't pay attention to him . . . Nobody would ever recognize
him.'

He still liked his anonymity. Sometime in late July, he drove Sara's
ex-roommate to visit her grandmother in hospital in Pennsylvania. On
the long drive, she found him 'surprisingly easy to talk with', as long as
she stuck to general topics: '[He] even bought me a meal at a diner.
Nobody recognized him . . . Maybe people simply don't expect to see
Bob Dylan in a drive-in Pizza restaurant.' So, when the following spring
it came time to do the sleeve for the album he'd begun on April 24th,
1969, he called up John Cohen – the first New Yorker to photograph
him back in 1961 – to shoot a cover:

[He] requested that I bring a camera which could take pictures from a
block away . . . I rented a telephoto lens for the day. Although he never
talked about it, I realized his thought was to show that he could walk
unrecognized through the streets in the city . . . The photos were composed spontaneously, careful focus was out of the question. He
sometimes appeared carrying a drum. Walking the streets alone,
nobody paid attention to him. He was unnoticed, unrecognized. There
was no event, no critical moment, no celebrity, no photographer in his
face. He crossed Houston Street, looked at a baby in a carriage, faded
into the city landscape, hidden in plain view.

He yearned to be just another face in the crowd.* And yet, the previous August, he had unexpectedly turned up for his tenth annual high school reunion, to which he brought his radiant jewel of a wife, and basked in the afterglow of a boy done good. Here was someone who still sometimes caught himself 'looking back upon my youth/ The time I always knew the truth.'† The 1969 notebooks confirm a newfound nostalgia for his lost 'youth', especially Duluth, as evoked in an unfinished song from this period:

> I remember as if it was yesterday
> Sitting on the hilltop, looking [down] below
> To Lake Superior, in the iron grey morning (when)
> fog (was) on the bottom and lights in the snow.
> Just the sad lonesome sound of the big beat horns blowing
> Twisting its echo through the wandering mist
> And me with my knapsack [and] school books . . .
> Before I'd been anywhere.

Nor did this insidious nostalgia confine itself to the days and wonder of his youth. When Maria Muldaur and her husband Geoff moved to Woodstock, Dylan and his wife would 'once in a while . . . come over'. Maria was delighted to find Sara 'gorgeous, serene, elegant, and very good for him'. One evening in 1969, though, he came over alone:

> Our friends Betsy and Bob Siggins . . . were in Woodstock from Cambridge, and . . . [they and] Jim Rooney, a bluegrass singer, came over for dinner. Everyone was sitting around. We heard a knock on the door and there's Bob, wearing one of those little Russian fur hats with the flaps down, [saying,] 'Jim Rooney told me Bob and Betsy [Siggins] were here. Can I come in?' . . . [] . . . He wanted to touch base with his old friends, who knew him before he was a big famous rock star . . . We went . . . next door and sang Hank Williams songs.

---

* 'People have one great blessing – obscurity.' – Dylan, *Playboy* interview March 1966.
† The lines come from a song he wrote with George Harrison the previous fall, 'I Don't Want To Do It'.

His love for the music he had heard in the cellars and bars of New York and Boston retained its enduring appeal; it remained to his mind 'the only true valid death you can feel today'. On March 17th, 1969, he undertook a two-hundred mile round trip to White Plains simply to see the Clancys play a St Patrick's Day show at the Community Center, and to say hello. Tom Clancy felt he came 'across very much as a guy who has gone through the mill coming back to himself, very sensible, looking for a way to begin again'.

Likewise, when the Northumbrian traditional singer, future Clancy and woman, Louis Killen, came to play a small coffeehouse in Woodstock that year, 'Dylan turned up disguised in dark glasses. [He] revealed afterwards . . . that one of the reasons he had hidden himself away had been not so much the trauma of folkdom's refusal to accept his electric experiments as [others'] later, overenthusiastic move from acoustic to electric music . . . He [said he] had been pursuing a personal vision, not charting a recommended course of action for his peers.'

Nor was he so removed from the local music scene as to be unaware that the British folk guitarist-singer John Martyn and his ravishing wife Beverley were recording an album in Woodstock that summer, with the help of Levon Helm and Harvey Brooks. The album, a cult classic called *Stormbringer!*, was being produced by Joe Boyd, who had made a name for himself as *the* folk-rock producer in the years since Newport. (He was just months away from defining the genre for all time with Fairport Convention's *Liege & Lief*.)

Taking a break from the sessions, the Martyns agreed to play a charity gig at the Woodstock Playhouse on July 20th, in aid of Pete Seeger's Clearwater Project, which aimed to clean up the Hudson River. (Fat chance.) After their performance concluded – 'to thunderous applause and wolf whistles' – Beverley recollected:

Everyone gathered in the foyer, and somehow John and I got split up. I was wondering what to do when I see this character walking through the door. It was Bob Dylan. He was tiny, gazelle-like, wearing a black frock coat and a white shirt. He looked like a yeshiva boy in his gold spectacles, a student of the Talmud . . . Here was my idol standing talking to my husband. And then I saw that the man himself was looking at me. He began walking towards me. I was wracking my brains to think

what I could say . . . 'I'm really pleased to meet you,' he said. 'Oh, you
can't possibly know what it's like to meet you,' I gurgled back and he
laughed and took my hand, pulling me towards him so I could kiss him
on the cheek. I thought for a moment he was staring at my breasts, but
I quickly realized he had his eye fixed on this horned pendant hanging
round my neck, a present from John . . . I felt Dylan was looking into
my soul . . . Then he noticed that one of my moccasins was unlaced and
for a moment I [thought] he was going to kneel down and lace it up for
me. But at that moment John marched over and pulled us apart . . . I
heard Dylan say something like, 'Don't hurt her, man. She's only saying
hello to me.' And then John snarled at me to get into the car . . . I never
did get to meet Dylan again, but on the Monday after the gig . . . I had
to walk down to the supermarket in the village to get supplies. As I was
carrying the groceries home, a car pulled up behind me [and] this man
came up to me . . . He said he was Dylan's pianist. He told me I was a
great singer and that Dylan thought I didn't like him because we hadn't
turned up for tea at his house on the Sunday . . . This was the first I'd
heard about it. John had obviously been too jealous to tell me we'd been
invited.

This Sephardic beauty, a match even for Sara at this time, never got
to hear first-hand about the four-song set Dylan had played just six days
earlier at an open-air festival in Edwardsville, Illinois. He had been the
surprise guest during a Band gig in front of legions of stunned fans,
performing two songs from his 1961 club set, 'Ain't Got No Home' and
'In The Pines', both given a *Big Pink*-style makeover by The Band.*
Returning to Fire Island, Amram asked him, 'How was it?' He replied,
'Man, there was something like 30,000 people [there], and they didn't
forget me . . . It was a good feeling. [But] it's good to be back here, at
the beach, in silence.'

The surprise guest appearance was not just some whim on Dylan's
part, more like a trial run. He wanted to see if he still had an audience
and had what it took, before signing up to play to five times that number off the south coast of England on August Bank Holiday for a high
five-figure sum to a six-figure audience, drawn largely from his most

---

* According to *Zimmerman Blues*, the set was taped at the desk but Dylan nabbed the
tape afterwards.

loyal fan base. Nine days later, the deal was done – and just in time. Plastered across that week's *Melody Maker* was the headline, 'Dylan Here In August' – with not a question-mark in sight.

Bizarrely, Dylan was essentially volunteering to play to a hundred thousand-plus fans to *get away* from two to three hundred thousand fans trampling through his backyard in the once-idyllic backwater in which he lived. Much to his all-consuming chagrin, a local promoter was trying to organize a mid-August weekend festival in – or, as it turned out, seventy miles from – Woodstock, with the express intent of enticing Dylan into endorsing and/or appearing at 'Three Days of Peace & Music' in that order.

Festival promoter, Michael Lang, tried every trick in the book to get a pow-wow with the reclusive rock star. Having found out going through Grossman was a non-starter, he signed up The Band, hoping that might secure at least a guest appearance. Finally, he resorted to asking local photographer Elliott Landy, who'd snapped the only authorized shots of the man in the past eighteen months, to suggest Dylan turn up unannounced. Ever the optimist, Lang hoped that if he 'simply invited him to come along . . . if he wasn't advertised, he wouldn't be under any sort of pressure.' Dylan curtly informed Landy, 'You'd have to bring guns.'

As of July 23rd, it wasn't even an option. By signing to do the Isle of Wight, he agreed no other public performance would occur before-hand. The closest Lang came to his wish was when The Band devoted a third of their dozen-song Woodstock set to Dylan covers against intermittent shouts of, 'Where's Dylan?' The answer was, anywhere but here.

It was no coincidence that negotiations, which had begun shortly after Christmas, had been going nowhere until June 28th, when Bert Block phoned Ray Foulk, one of two brothers who'd promoted the 1968 Isle of Wight Festival, to report, 'Bob is interested.' At this stage, the Woodstock festival, booked to happen at Wallkill's Mills, really was too close for comfort.

Testing the Foulks' resolve, Dylan was asking for $50,000 for himself, $20,000 for The Band and all expenses to be paid by the Foulks. They readily agreed.* He also insisted on a clause prohibiting filming 'of any

---

* By comparison Hendrix, the highest paid of the acts at Woodstock, was paid $18,000.

kind', while making provisions for a possible official live album, for which the promoters would receive a flat $2000 (which they received in 2013). By July 16th, Bert Block, working out of Grossman's office, cabled Dylan's acceptance, but only if the Foulks came to New York, the following Tuesday: 'Bob wants to meet you!'

The auspicious meeting took place at the Drake Hotel, where the Foulks were staying. Ray Foulk recalls, 'Grossman was not there . . . I discovered later that he and Dylan . . . [had] fall[en] out.' Once Dylan saw the whites of the eyes and the colour of their money, the deal was done. However, on August 14th, the day before the 'Woodstock' Festival came to Bethel, disaster struck. As Dylan's whole family was boarding the QE2, Jesse fell and struck his head. When a doctor refused to confirm he was safe to travel, the Dylans disembarked. So much for a family vacation. Not that they were about to return to Woodstock, where the ravening hoards were already descending.*

Instead, Dylan and Sara arranged to fly to London eleven days later, minus the children, with Aronowitz as designated companion of the road. It was Sara, though, who took 'charge of pushing the luggage cart up to the customs inspector, who at first waved her through, but . . . realizing the luggage was also Dylan's, called her back.' Seeing her heavily pregnant state, the inspector fondly imagined he knew a drug mule when he saw one. Actually, that was Al's job. They finally made it to the Isle of Wight, arriving at the farm that would be their island hideaway for the duration in the wee small hours of the 26th.

What Dylan had expected is unclear, but he was quoted as saying on his arrival, 'I thought the island would be kinda derelict, with sandy beaches. But this is just like a normal country.' Fire Island, it was not. Dylan would remain attentive to his expectant wife throughout their brief stay, as Aronowitz saw them acting 'like a pair of lovebirds. At Forelands Farm, they'd hold hands or put their arms around each other and go for long walks along the chalk cliffs.' The housekeeper at Forelands, Judy Lewis, 'suggested [they] go to Quarry Abbey to hear the monks chanting. He and Sara enjoyed that.'

The farm itself was both secluded and well away from the festival

---

* Dylan gave vent to his feelings about the whole event to Jim Jerome in 1975: 'I felt they exploited the shit out of that [Woodstock thing], going up there and getting fifteen million people all in the same spot.'

site. And as Ray Foulk had promised, there was 'a swimming pool, tennis court, lovely walled gardens and a . . . refurbished stone barn, ideal for rehearsals,' something 'Block had added to Dylan and The Band's list of requirements.' Lucky that he did. Boy, did they need it. Unbeknownst to the Foulks, whose own houses were on the line if the festival flopped, Bob and the boys had barely rehearsed their set. It was Friar's Tavern, all over again.

Meantime, the level of expectation was going through the farm roof, with early reports of a three-hour set compounded by talk of an all-star jam-session finale. Reading his latest *Melody Maker*, Dylan discovered, 'Blind Faith are flying in from Honolulu after asking if they could appear [with Dylan] . . . The Rolling Stones – except for Mick Jagger, who is filming in Australia – are staying on Keith Richards's yacht off the island, and it is understood they also . . . wish to take the stage with Dylan after his performance.'*

Three of the fast-imploding Beatles also formed part of a British Invasion of this island outpost, led by genial George, who arrived on the 26th with some necessary supplies for the musicians and The Journalist, who remembers he drove 'all the way to Portsmouth with his wife, Patti, in a blue Italian sports car . . . George felt safer making the trip by auto because he was muling Ringo's marijuana stash for delivery as a care package for Bob, The Band and me.'

The personal dynamic between Dylan and Harrison fascinated a starstruck housekeeper, who thought 'Harrison was in awe of Dylan. They got on very well, but I got the impression that Dylan felt Harrison was a bit pushy . . . He didn't seem to be allowed to [go] off with his wife on his own as much as he [wanted].' In fact, Sara was delighted to see George and Pattie again, and they were soon all playing a new kind of tennis at Dylan's behest:

Pattie Boyd: We all stayed with them in a rented house and it had a tennis court. And I was mad about tennis, so I said, 'Let's play tennis!' And so Bob took [my suggestion] literally – *everyone* was to play tennis. It must have been six-a-side. It was great fun. No tennis etiquette whatsoever – whatever you're wearing.

---

* Blind Faith were surplus to requirements, but said band was the brainchild of two of Dylan's favourite English Sixties performers, Eric Clapton and Stevie Winwood.

The Harrisons were enjoying themselves, especially George. Away from the other singing Scousers, he basked in his famous friend's company. He even became a little loose-tongued. When Ray Foulk came to check all was okay, he found Harrison 'candidly discuss[ing] the difficulties . . . within the group . . . [He] freely complained about John and Paul never allowing him more than two of his own compositions on their albums.'

The Dylans had heard it all before. What they had not heard was the new Beatles album, *Abbey Road* – featuring two of Harrison's finest compositions, 'Something' and 'Here Comes The Sun', both songs Dylan would attempt in concert – which was not out for another month. A proud George had brought an acetate and proceeded to play it through the rehearsal barn speakers for the assembled party.

The song suite on the second side alone had more song-ideas than Dylan had mustered in a year or more. Conceptually and composition-ally, it was autobahns ahead of his own recent offering. But if he was impressed, he cast his mind back to the Warwick, and did not show it. Aronowitz's 'own mind *was* blown . . . [but] if I detected any sentiment at all [from Bob], it was envy.' Anyway, he preferred making music to listening to it. Judy the housekeeper's 'happiest memories [of that week was] listening to Bob and George and The Band trying out their new songs on their guitars. Sitting around the table after supper, they'd always swap a few songs on their acoustic [guitar]s.'

Even as the pair hid their mutual love of song away, the island was filling up, thanks in no small part to the many stickers the Foulks had had printed up, asking fans to 'Help Bob Dylan Sink the Isle of Wight'. If they thought Dylan would be amused by the idea, they were soon disabused. When he saw the stickers on the windscreen of the Triumph Herald that had picked them up from the hovercraft, he tried to remove them and when he failed, lost his temper, 'Damn these stupid labels, they're everywhere!'

It was the second time Dylan and the Foulks had not seen eye to eye on promotion. The first had come when his factotum, Bert Block, had visited the festival office and seen the eye-catching poster they had designed for the festival, using a classic Dylan '66 shot: Behind The Shades Incarnate. Block told Foulk straight, 'That's wrong, that placard . . . That's the old Dylan.' A less eye-catching poster, a homage to *King Kong* of all things, was hastily substituted.

No matter how much Dylan tried to shut the pop world out, though, it was beating a path to his door in double-quick time. After one impertinent tabloid reporter gate-crashed Forelands, he reluctantly agreed to do a press conference at the Halland Hotel on the Wednesday afternoon, hoping this would satiate the Fourth Estate. In fact, as an exercise in incomprehension, it was not far behind the one at London's Mayfair three years earlier. At least it proved he had not entirely lost his sense of comic timing. The funniest exchange came when he was asked for his view on drugs and in his best cowpoke accent, he gee-shucked the following reply, 'I don't have any of those views . . . I wish I did. I'd be glad to share them with you.'

A disbelieving *Guardian* scribe would report, 'The questions [seem to] completely puzzle him. He seems genuine when to each one he says he doesn't understand what the reporter wants to know.' Predictably, when asked for his main message, he came up with, 'Take it easy and do your job well.' When one particularly persistent pressman asked, 'What exactly is your position on politics and music?' Dylan turned to Rikki Farr and said, 'I think I've answered enough questions.'

Actually, he had yet to answer a single one. The one time he gave an honest response was when he was asked whether he'd changed since 1966: 'That stuff was all for publicity. I don't do that kind of thing anymore.' The experience, not immediately rewarding, would later unlock a song called simply, 'Interview', a dry run at 'Day Of The Locusts':

> The joint was packed and the flash bulbs popped
> I wished I was back in bed
> Some crank yelled from the corner of the room
> Speak up, we can't hear what you said.
>
> Outside the sea was blowing up a storm
> And sailboats were on top of the wall
> While inside the hotel, an interview was taking place . . .

The song concludes with Dylan leaving 'in a hurry', still not sure 'what the whole thing was about'. The whole lyric comes across as remarkably matter-of-fact, save for a dig at his manager, standing 'over there in the wings . . . Somebody told him to fly a kite.' That somebody was Dylan.

As of August 19th, Grossman was no longer Dylan's manager and no longer entitled to commission from such crosswind jamborees.* He wisely didn't show up at the press conference, nor at Forelands. Instead, he went directly to the festival site in the somewhat provocative company of Michael Lang. If the erstwhile manager was not quite sure what to expect, nor did anybody else, despite Dylan assuring the pressmen, 'Everything we will do is on record. I'm not going to sing anything new. [It will be] things you will have heard before, but with new arrangements.'

Albert knew only too well, this could cover a multitude of sins, and Dylan had done little to dampen expectations at the Halland by saying, 'I love the Beatles and I think it . . . a good idea to do a jam session,' even though jamming was hardly the forte of either The Beatles or The Band. As for the provisional set-list, it contained at least three songs *not* 'on record', one of which was down as an encore, something that as the Sunday evening wore on seemed less and less likely.

Dylan had arrived backstage to a scene of complete chaos, with the VIP section at the front overrun with liggers and chancers, and the sound up cripple creek. Chris Colley, the man who had driven Dylan and his wife around the island, was standing nearby as he went into full-blown meltdown mode, à la Paris '66:

He was all ready to go on, with an acoustic guitar around his neck. It was a wide stage with two ramps. He was walking up and down there, with Sara hanging on to him, strumming his guitar in a manic and tuneless fashion. He seemed really anxious and Sara was comforting him, 'Bob it's gonna be alright. They want to hear you. Really, you're gonna be great.' Sara had her arm around him.

Part of the delay before The Band's own set – which ran to well over *two* hours – was down to the decision to record a live album. As Ray Foulk later remarked, 'Pye's mobile studio was commissioned, and the set-up for the recording had to take place during the break between Richie Havens and The Band. Hence the additional mikes, and the additional chaos as technicians from Pye worked around The Band's

---

* He made $16,000 in commission from this one concert, something Dylan perhaps could have avoided had he signed the contract after August 20th.

roadies to get everything perfect before the artists came on. All of this was under the supervision of Elliot Mazer, whom Dylan had personally sent over from New York for [this] purpose.'*

It was Sheffield '66 all over again. Rikki Farr tried to calm the crowd, telling them, 'Cool it, people. You've waited three days. Be cool and wait another five minutes and you'll have the sound 100% perfect.' 150,000 people sensed he was stalling, while Dylan took it out on Aronowitz, berating his favourite verbal punching-bag, 'This is spoiling everything . . . that I came here to do, everything I wanted to accomplish.'

The Band finally took to the stage for a truncated nine-song set, which featured not a single song from their imminent second album, itself fully the equal of *Abbey Road*. According to Robertson, 'We couldn't hear one another very well on stage, so I just put my head down and plowed straight ahead.' They continued this 'heads down' approach even after Dylan joined them onstage, breaking quickly into 'She Belongs To Me', one of only three songs retained from the 1966 set.

It was hard to tell if the sound just got worse, but Dylan's vocals now became only intermittently audible out in the night. In fact, he only really started to make himself heard after The Band took a four-song respite, and he began to play solo for the first time since the Albert Hall. A riveting rendition of Scottish folksong, 'Will Ye Go, Lassie', was an exquisite reminder of why he had an audience in the first place. But the next three songs – 'It Ain't Me, Babe', 'To Ramona' and 'Mr Tambourine Man' – were nothing short of disastrous; all rushed, lacking in intensity and bowdlerized. (He got through all three wordy works in less than ten minutes.)

As Dylan's performance turned tepid before unknowing eyes, parts of the audience started drifting towards the shore. Even the return of The Band for a respectable 'Lay Lady Lay' failed to revive spirits. It took a rousing rendition of 'Highway 61 Revisited' – the tenth song of the evening – for The Band to throw Dylan a lifeline. Finally, he pensioned off the *Skyline* voice – one he could only maintain if he stuck to mid-range and mid-tempo – as The Band threw in the kind of vocal harmonies that could rouse a rabble, if not quite raise the dead. At last

---

* Mazer, who would end up becoming Neil Young's producer, had been doing some work for Albert Grossman, including compiling the famous 15 ips 'safety reel' of the basement tapes.

Dylan began stretching himself vocally, closing the main set with a singalong 'Mighty Quinn' and encoring with the unfamiliar 'Minstrel Boy', a lost basement original from early 1968 he sang with real gusto, hinting at what his set could have been.*

But the hour was getting late, and they barely had time to resurrect 'Rainy Day Women' before calling it a night. Fittingly, the last line Dylan sang to the islanders was, 'They'll stone you when you're singing at the mike' – which is precisely what happened. Reviews were almost universally lukewarm. Even his so-called friend, Lennon, damned him with faint praise, 'He gave a reasonable, albeit slightly flat performance, but everyone was expecting Godot or Jesus to appear,' a fortnight before his own performance at a Toronto rock'n'roll festival ended in boos and catcalls.

One of the IOW organizers, surely Farr, informed *Disc*, 'We expected him to be on stage a good bit longer than an hour. I don't know whether we would want to rebook him,' while a sour Ronnie Foulk told *The Times* he had expected 'Dylan to sing for a bit longer, but he fulfilled his contract.' At least Sara enjoyed it. According to Aronowitz, she was 'unable to take her eyes off Bob . . . as she watched his performance from the wings.'

If Dylan sensed another night of the big letdown, he did not let on. Tom Paxton, who had been added to the IOW bill at Dylan's insistence, travelled 'with him and The Beatles to the farmhouse, where he was clearly in a merry mood, because he had felt it had gone so well'. However, the morning after the night before, the Dylans couldn't wait to leave the island, visiting Weybridge long enough to hear Lennon's harrowing new single, 'Cold Turkey', and staying with the Harrisons overnight, before boarding a flight back to JFK, where he told waiting reporters, 'They make too much of singers over there.'

Only in the weeks ahead did it become apparent just how unhappy Dylan was about events overseas, so much so that Sara's ex-roommate learnt, 'The Isle of Wight fiasco has made him determined to see heads roll . . . Even mentioning it causes him to go off into rages beyond belief. All kinds of hell broke loose when he came back . . . There were all manner of side payments, playing time clauses and agreements drawn up that he knew nothing about.'

---

* Clearly chosen for its burden, 'Who's gonna throw the minstrel boy a coin,' the song was copyrighted to Big Sky, not Dwarf, presumably because it had new lyrics.

According to Sara, he soon headed for New York on a kind of witch-hunt. In fact, he had recently taken an apartment in the city, where he continued his brooding alone, save when cheering on the Mets from the box seats at Shea Stadium, in the company of John Hammond Snr, as they smashed hot favourites, the Orioles, 4-1 in the 1969 World Series. He had finally decided to quit Woodstock for good. Already that summer, he had bellyached to Aronowitz, 'The motor from my pump broke down and I haven't had any running water for three days. I'm ready to sell this whole place to the land developers. My children need water. We buy a lot of food in this town and we pay a lot of taxes. We expect better service than this.'*

In one of his notebooks he wrote of other concerns, closer to home. Afraid for his children, he told unnamed strangers to 'go slow for there are children on this road', warning those who did not that they would 'live to regret it'. He also addressed unspecified ladies and gentlemen – a tad hypocritically – to watch out for 'a reel strange fellow' who is pushing pot, as the counter-culture's guru turned father of night. Dylan had become convinced some intangible force, a psychic magnetic field, was keeping him there. His wife shared his conviction, mentioning it to family friend Bob Finkbine in 1972, after they had temporarily fled west:

> Bob and Sara [made] comments on their previous home in Woodstock, New York . . . They had heard the legend, an ancient Indian curse had been placed on their land when it was usurped by white men in the 1600s. A lot of strange things happened there. One mist-filled morning they looked out their window and saw Puritan-clad figures moving through the woods . . . They felt that the land had a mysterious attraction, a power over local inhabitants. They knew several couples who had been trying to move and, for some unknown reason, could not pull themselves away. According to Bob and Sara, it took them well over a year to move once they had made a firm decision to leave.

The original typewritten draft of Dylan's 1975 love song, 'Sara', also included a decidedly unromantic image of the two of them 'living in

---

* Dylan may well be referring to just such an occurrence in the winter 1968 composition, 'Goin' To Acapulco': 'Now, every time you know when the well breaks down/ I just go pump on it some.'

Woodstock in a house full of flies'. As late as 2004 he would complain, 'Woodstock had turned into a nightmare, a place of chaos . . . [So, I] moved to New York City for a while . . . [still] hop[ing] to demolish my identity.' But as he ruefully reflected in 1989, 'The worst times of my life were when I tried to find something in the past. Like when I went back to New York for the second time.' While trying 'to find something in the past', almost his first stop on his return to the Village was the Van Ronks' apartment, where Terri Thal still resided:

> Bob came over to visit me at the end of 1969, right after he got back to the Village . . . He wanted to see some of his things that I still have, like his corduroy cap . . . I showed him a colouring book that I still have. I bought it the day David and I had the blood tests we needed to get married, and we all coloured in it, including Bobby, and he looked at it like he was looking into the old times . . . He told me, 'I'm completely uptight. Got all this money and don't know what to do with myself. Got a great wife, great kids, but don't know what to do. Can't perform any more. I hate performing in front of big audiences. But I guess I'll have to, 'cause I don't have anything else to do. Ain't done any writing in a while. Can't seem to write.' . . . He was looking for a piece of his past.

Also there that evening, or another evening when he came back, were Van Ronk and Barry Kornfeld, who both had very different takes on the dude they encountered. The former expressed the view, 'He's now looking for safety because he's scared – not scared of America and its monstrosities; that poor kid is scared of himself,' whereas the latter, who had not seen him since the fateful night he broke up with Suze, found him 'much more cordial and relaxed. And [he was the same when] I subsequently ran into him [at] a party at Clive Davis's . . . He just seemed . . . a little easier to communicate with, a little less of that constant obfuscation that he always had going on.'

If he was searching for his lost muse, though, She continued to prove recalcitrant. As he had told Ian Brady before the Isle of Wight, 'I don't strain to write. A song just comes out . . . something may trigger it off, I might hear a phrase or a word and a song comes out.' Perhaps he needed to push things along a little if he was planning to pen some more of 'the type of songs that I always felt like writing when I've been alone'. After all, it had been seven long months since *Nashville Skyline* and the sum total of new originals was 'Living The Blues', hardly a candidate for the Country Music Hall of Fame.

It was at this juncture that he was approached to collaborate on 'a ballad play' based on the 1936 Stephen Benét short story, 'The Devil and Daniel Webster', by esteemed American poet, Archibald MacLeish;* a collaboration about which almost nothing was known prior to the 'New Morning' section in *Chronicles* – and even less was known after it. As the play's producer, Stuart Ostrow, would write in *his* 2006 memoir, *Present At The Creation*, '[When] I read . . . Dylan's version of his experience with *Scratch* . . . I discovered Mr Dylan had . . . reinvented all the facts, egregiously.' Ostrow would follow suit.

Dylan began his own account with a letter he supposedly got from the 76-year-old MacLeish, having 'just returned . . . from my father's funeral', i.e. in June 1968. Actually, it was October 1969 before the pair made any contact, and it was at the instigation of Ostrow, who had been introduced to Dylan by Clive Davis.

Ostrow was looking to straddle the two literary generations, a notion MacLeish initially found 'preposterous'. Things moved quickly once Ostrow read the playwright's first outline of the as-yet-untitled play on September 9th, 1969. MacLeish said he envisaged the play as four scenes: 'a ballad prologue, a ballad epilogue and two acted scenes between, in which the ballad singer (and his combo?) play the part of the chorus and "orchestra." ' The role of the ballad singer was clearly crucial, MacLeish explaining to Ostrow: 'He will do what the old ballad-makers always did: he will "set the stage" for the play . . . However, our singer will do something more than define the situation. He will be poet as well as ballad-singer. He will "invent the metaphor." '

By October 1st, the elder poet, bustling with ideas, was suggesting 'we should now talk . . . with Dylan'. By the following Monday, Ostrow had received Dylan's first contribution to the project, 'The Ballad Of Jabez Stone' – typed out on Ostrow's own Theatre 28 Company stationery. An eight-verse ballad about the farmer the Devil is looking to tempt, the song contained enough flashes of Bob the balladeer to excite producer and poet:

---

* Though Benét's story is best known from the 1941 film adaptation, Benét himself had previously produced a 'folk opera' based upon the original story.

The land was good, it was soft and brown
From father to son it was handed down . . .
Finally Jabez Stone's turn came
To run the land and do the same
But the farm failed and the land went sour
And things got worse by the hour . . .

Oh yes he wished to be a comfortable man
His farm was too hard to work by hand
He wanted a machine in place of his plow
And he wanted steam heat instead of a cow.
Yes he wanted all these things and more
(He woke up each morning and paced the floor)
He carried no work and dug no hole
Would a man like that sell his soul? . . .

Dylan later claimed he had 'taken the songs [sic] up to [Ostrow's] office in the Brill Building in New York and recorded them. He then sent the acetates to Archie.' An enticing but chimerical thought. Only the above lyric remains. It was enough for Ostrow to arrange a meeting involving Dylan, MacLeish and director Peter Hunt, at MacLeish's Massachusetts home on October 17th. Ostrow's description of that fateful meeting, written less than two years after Dylan's, took equal liberties with the facts:

It was strange enough driving four hours with Bob Dylan to Conway without his saying a word, but nothing compared to the seven hours that followed. The MacLeishs' home was a charming 18th century saltbox . . . Into this harmony of past and perfect I brought America's troubadour and he freaked. [We all] spent the afternoon watching Dylan drink the house brandy as quickly as MacLeish could refill his snifter. He never once responded to any question nor joined the conversation regarding the musical's dramatic problems, but kept belting the brandy down, so by the time we reached Act Two he was asleep.

In fact, the meeting seems to have been a success. The project proceeded full steam ahead.* By the following month, MacLeish was

---

* The Chronicler claims he 'told MacLeish [he] would think about it'.

writing to Dylan via Ostrow, responding to questions he'd raised about the role of the balladeer, and informing Ostrow that Dylan had already forgiven him 'in advance for taking a crack at the beginning of the Master Ballad'.*

In answering Dylan's question, MacLeish showed himself to be from the 'classic impersonality' school of Milman Parry and Albert B. Lord, seeing the ballad-singer merely as 'a vehicle for the ballad'. He ended by informing the singer-songwriter, 'It is the ballads which are important, not the singer,' an idea that probably sat uneasily with a Dylan becalmed.

Still, the songs would not come. In December, Ostrow even wrote to MacLeish to inform him he had spoken to Tom Paxton (lined up as a possible replacement if the amnesia endured), but for now he 'was continuing with Dylan'. He also suggested they 'meet with Dylan again and encourage him to ask questions'. The songwriter had just a single song-idea at this stage, another sad complaint:

> The snow is piled high but the plow's lost its blade
> Oh heavens, can't you see thru my cool masquerade? . . .
> When the hill gets steep and it's hard to make the grade
> Just think about it in your cool masquerade.

Meanwhile, MacLeish continued wrestling with the question, 'Who is our balladeer?' Trying to make Dylan feel more comfortable in the role, he explained in a letter dated January 26th, 1970, he is 'a balladeer of our epoch. He is the youngster with the guitar and fashionable hairdo whose attitude toward his country and his time is precisely the attitude we want, . . . deeply concerned . . . with the human misery which flourishes in both.' If the letter made Dylan feel better about his role, the same intractable problem remained: an ongoing inability to come up with appropriate songs relevant to the story. After much cajoling, Ostrow finally got one more song:

Bob Dylan whined . . . at me to quit pushing him one afternoon while working in my Pound Ridge studio; [saying] something like, 'If it comes,

---

* A reference to a ballad about Daniel Webster, the lawyer who defends Jabez Stone, which he never completes.

it comes, if it won't, it won't; if it rhymes, it rhymes, if it don't, it don't.'
Too bad it wasn't a finished song for . . . the ballad musical . . . 'How's
this?' he asked, handing me a verse and chorus scrawled on a foolscap
pad. It was illegible. 'Sing it to me Bob, I can't read Sanskrit,' I replied . . .
hoping to get him to use the guitar he brought each week, yet never
played. Dylan mumbled something, then picked up his guitar and sang
'Father of Night' with his signature nasal-monotone assurance.

Ostrow's constant imprecations by February 1970 would generate two
more songs. One used one of MacLeish's suggested song titles, 'The
Man In Me'. The other would close the first act, in a section MacLeish
called 'The Next Morning'. What Dylan wrote was 'New Morning', but
by the third verse he was already wandering from his brief:

> Can't you hear the rooster crowing
> Can't fool the naked eye.
> I needed something, and she was right there
> So I took her by the hand and led her from that sleepy town.

Having already started another song concerning a visit to see 'the
gypsy', the two briefly entwined,* the central idea of the earlier 'Ballad
Of Jabez Stone' being transposed to 'Went To See The Gypsy'. Dylan
later told guitarist Ron Cornelius, as they set out to record the song, it
'was about going to see Elvis in Las Vegas'.† The song was really about

---

* The line in 'Went To See The Gypsy' has the singer watching the sun 'rising from
that little Minnesota town'.
† The timeline fits almost exactly. Presley played his third Vegas residency, his first
since his 1969 comeback, in January/ February 1970. Yet forty years later, Dylan suggested he never met Elvis – 'because I didn't want to meet Elvis . . . I wanted to see the
powerful, mystical Elvis that had crash-landed from a burning star . . . And that Elvis
was gone, [he] had left the building.' He told an equally tall tale to Lauren Bacall in 1986:
'My mother and my aunt met Elvis. They went to Vegas once and Elvis was playing
there so they go see him and afterwards my aunt Etta pulls my mother around to the
stage door and insists on meeting the King . . . They are led backstage past the cables
and drum kits, past the gospel singers and stage hands . . . Elvis is seated in his boxing
robe, "So, are you Bob Dylan's mother?" he asks rising. "Yes" ' says his mother ' "Bob
Dylan is just his stage name, like Elvis Presley. His real name is Robert Zimmerman."
"Oh no, ma'am," says the King. "Elvis is my real name, as God is my witness." ' The
truth remains obscure.

'breaking through the mirror', an idea he almost certainly took from Hermann Hesse's *Steppenwolf*, and transferred initially to the end of the aforementioned ballad: 'Oh many times I've often wondered, does success last? Is it a thing of tomorrow? Or a thing of a past?/ Will I know it when I see it? Can I hold it while it's near/ Many times, I've often wondered, will I find it in the mirror.'

Unbeknownst to Ostrow and MacLeish, this would mark the end of Dylan's interest in the ballad play (now called *Scratch*). He had other songs he wanted to record, and a project he was finally ready to complete. As for the Isle of Wight album, *Rolling Stone*'s 'Random Notes' for November 15th, 1969 reported that 'Bob Dylan has refused to allow Columbia to release tapes of his Isle of Wight performance ... Meanwhile, his very unofficial new album, *Great White Wonder*, is still being bootlegged around the country.'

This passing mention should have given Dylan cause to pause. The birth of the rock bootleg album the previous summer – inextricably bound up with the wide dissemination of those basement tapes Dylan had refused to release – meant his wishes regarding the Isle of Wight concert were unlikely to be respected by other labels to whom he now unwittingly lent his music; labels like Peace Records, who in the early months of 1970 would release their own *Isle of Wight* album, an artifact which, if Dylan ever got to hear it, surely prompted him to exclaim, 'What is this shit?'

March 1970 to March 1971:
A Different Village

Bob had held his creativity back for quite some time in Woodstock. He got into painting and stuff, but that was just a pastime. It wasn't a substitute for his music and never could be, so inevitably he became restless. Also, because Bob was so famous there was massive added pressure. Even if he could manage to split his Self between his music and his family, the time he had with his family was often intruded upon by his fans . . . Sara couldn't cope with this. He would withdraw from the world.

Faridi McFree, a girlfriend.

He often goes away for weeks on end, without bothering to say where he is or what he's doing.

Sara Dylan, to her college roommate, 1970.

I never know where his head's at . . . It can really be upsetting when somebody doesn't talk. Hell, he doesn't even talk to his old lady . . . for weeks – according to her.

Kris Kristofferson, 1973.

When I told Pete [Townshend], Bob wanted to meet him . . . he [thought] Bob meant to honour him with recognition, for what he had accomplished with his so-called 'pop opera'. But when I brought Peter to Bob's table at Max's [Kansas City], Bob . . . [was] waiting to ambush him . . . [His] reaction to *Tommy* was to exclaim that Peter should be run out of town on a rail.

Al Aronowitz.

★

By the start of 1970, a general suspicion that the rock scene was passing Dylan by was palpable. If he refused to be impressed by *Abbey Road* or *Tommy*, he was certainly out of step with his core audience, who bought both albums in their droves. And the thought that former fans might prefer to spend their hard-earned cash on bootleg albums like *Troubled Troubadour* (the Big Pink demos), *Stealin'* (with its 1965 outtakes) and/ or *In 1966 There Was* (the original bootleg of Manchester '66), rather than his latest Columbia offering, clearly annoyed him greatly.*

When his former music publisher, Witmark, sent out a nine-track LP of demos in January 1970, trying to generate interest (and revenue) in his early, unreleased songs, George Lee received another terse missive from Braun, to which Lee replied, 'Please be advised that we only made a total of twenty dubs, which were sent to A&R men at major record companies for the purpose of obtaining recordings.' Twenty copies still proved enough for the bootleggers to get their hands on one, and release it as *The Demo Tapes*.†

And it wasn't just bootleg *albums* filling the void in Dylan product at a time of unprecedented demand. There was also a steady stream of Dylan booklegs – especially in Europe: *Tarantula*, the lyrics to his albums, his early sleeve notes; so much so that one morning in early 1970 Macmillan editor Bob Markel was sat in his office when his 'secretary came into my office, and . . . whispers, "It's Bob Dylan on the telephone!" . . . I picked up the phone . . . He said, "Why don't we publish the book?" I said, . . . "You don't really feel that you wanna do [some changes]?" He said, "No. That's what I wrote. That's the way it is."'

Perhaps when Dylan had told John Cohen in 1968, 'I do have a book in me,' he truly believed he did. But talk of writing a different book had by now entirely receded, even if he continued trying his hand at prose. The phrase, 'Tarantula/ "Somebody Else's Story,"' appears in the notebooks, along with a fine short story called 'Porky Morgan', which even features a tarantula. Could it have been a provisional set of sleeve notes for *New Morning*–à la *John Wesley Harding*? It was certainly something he worked at:

---

* Dylan would challenge Tony Glover 'to explain [how the Hotel Tape leaked] . . . It really pissed him off – he thought I was making a buck or something.' The tape formed a constituent part of *Great White Wonder*, the album which gave birth to the rock bootleg (qv. my history of the subject: *Bootleg!* [Omnibus Press, 2000]).

† On the promo LP was a piano demo of 'I'll Keep It With Mine' which would otherwise not be extant, the original tape having been lost.

Porky Morgan didn't like Russo and instead of waiting at Lucy's where the tarantula dwelt, he waited instead at Point Ram. This is where he first heard the gunshot in his mind . . . 'No man writes the truth about anything else, except himself.' That's what Seed would say when confronted by . . . writers who write for newspapers and books . . . Eventually Russo would get up and leave . . . Seed would then explain his position, having to go into the story of his entire lifetime . . . As he would begin to tell his story, a bargirl would begin to weep. Then someone else from upstairs would sob. The whole place turned into [a] bunch of dancing Lunitics. Ladders were carried in and out by normal men with no hair and no clue whatsoever as to what they were doing and where they were going. Books were forced out of people, and chains were beaten on their heads. Ants crawled down from the mountain . . . Brains were being eaten by Charlie's worms and not a soul in the place to stand up and be sympathetic. This is what Russo missed.

In November 1970, a fortnight after *New Morning*'s release, *Tarantula* finally made its official appearance after a half-life in the netherworld of pirate publishing, just like those other pirated cult classics, *Candy* and *Lord of the Rings*. He could have done the same with the bootleg albums if there weren't already too many of them.

He could always release his own bootleg. And perhaps he had. When his first official album that year appeared, on June 8th, Greil Marcus suggested, '*Self-Portrait* most closely resembles the Dylan album that preceded it: *Great White Wonder* [sic]. The album is a two-record set masterfully assembled from . . . mostly indifferent recordings made over the course of the last year, complete with alternate takes, chopped endings, loose beginnings, side comments [sic] and all sorts of mistakes.'

Dylan almost admitted to the charge in *Chronicles*, referring to 'one album (a double one) where I just threw everything I could think of at the wall and whatever stuck, released it, and then went back and scooped up everything that didn't stick and released that, too'.* However, assuming Isle of Wight chauffeur Chris Colley remembers an August 1969 conversation right, this arch-cynic had yet to emerge:

---

* Surely, a reference to *Dylan* (1973), a wholly unauthorized artifact.

George [Harrison] and Bob were talking about *[The]* *Beatles* double-album. George said, 'It seems when you are as famous as us you can bring out any old stuff and people will buy it.' Dylan turned on him. [He] was really put out and shocked, saying, 'What the hell are you talking about, man? These are our fans – we owe them.'

In an early draft of *Chronicles*, Dylan would write about 'a country album' – presumably *Nashville Skyline* – that, to his mind came out, 'pretty bridled and housebroken,' only for 'mudslingers and backseat drivers . . . [to] wonder aloud, "whatever happened to the old him. who is this guy?"' He also suggested elsewhere annoyance as a motive for releasing *Self Portrait*, 'At that time I was getting the wrong kind of attention, for doing things I'd never done. So we released that album to get people off my back.' If so, the plan blew up in his face.*

It also fails to explain why he put so much work into sequencing the album in question. Acetates were repeatedly ferried back and forth between Nashville and New York as Dylan asked Bob Johnston to EQ a track differently, or change the sequence. Johnston later confirmed, 'He'd listen and say, "Could you put [a] couple of drumbeats on there?" . . . He passed everything I did, mixing-wise. [But] everything had to go through him.' At the same time, Dylan was jotting down new lyrics on acetate sleeves, including this *New Morning*-esque couplet, 'The sky turn[s] yellow, birds fly away / The earth's so mellow, what more is there to say?' – an indication something might be stirring.†

He'd actually been planning to make an album of covers for some time, quite possibly since his 1967 Columbia contract. Indeed, ten months before *Self Portrait* appeared, he told Ian Brady, 'If it wasn't for my recording contract, I don't know if I'd ever write another song. The contract requires me to make a certain amount of records, so I have to. I don't mind if I have to record other people's numbers. They don't have to be mine. I didn't [originally] want to make *John Wesley Harding* . . . I planned to do an album of other people's songs.'

Shortly afterwards, he sounded out Clive Davis about the idea. Davis

---

* *Self Portrait* still went on to outsell *Blonde on Blonde*. Stateside sales, up to Sept. 1973: 379,527 vs. 312,656.

† We know all this because 149 acetates from 1970 were acquired by US record dealer Jeff Gold, in 2014.

claims, in his 1974 memoir, he already 'knew he'd been having some difficulty coming up with his own material . . . so I encouraged him.' Dylan even seemingly anticipated the controversy to come, writing an imaginary Q&A in one of his 1969-70 notebooks: 'Why are you recording other people's songs and not your own?' 'Because I don't need as much money as I used to and other people write good songs.' None of which exactly tallies with the material he later issued from three days at Columbia's New York Studio B, in March 1970 [3rd-5th], which was largely traditional songs he could claim copyright on (and did).

Actually, work had been scheduled to start on March 2nd, with Dylan intending to use a folk-rock combo who had just finished recording a live album of their own at the Felt Forum. The Byrds owed him, but seemed to think not. Head Byrd, Roger McGuinn, was mortified when the rest of the band flew west instead, leaving him to carry the can:

> I [had] got[ten] a call from Clive Davis, saying, 'How would you like to work with Dylan?' . . . I said, 'Sure thing . . . Just tell me when and where.' So I called Dylan and he wasn't there, but he returned the call . . . I said, 'I don't know what we'd do. Do you have any ideas?' And he said, . . . 'Maybe if you come in with some of the old stuff and I do, too, that'll be all right.' I think he meant some of his old stuff, so it would be all his publishing. I [just] said, 'Well, the only thing we could do is go into the studio and see what happens, right?' And I asked him if he had any material to spare and he said, no, that he . . . hadn't been writing as much as he used to, and I mentioned that we all get fat and lazy, and he laughed . . . So [The Byrds] got to New York and did a couple of gigs [at] Felt Forum . . . By Monday we were still in town, waiting for some kind of word. Finally, the guys took a 12:00 plane back to the Coast. And at 1:00 I got a call from Billie Washington . . . at Columbia, and she said that the session was in Studio B at 2:30 . . . He was pissed off that we didn't have the courtesy to sit around and wait for his phone call . . . [But] I'm just glad that we didn't get on this particular album . . . because it was poorly prepared . . . He came into the studio prepared to use a lot of outtakes from *Nashville Skyline* [sic].

Although McGuinn did his best to shrug off the snafu, he duly revealed Dylan phoned him one or two days later: 'He was [still] kinda angry.' He wasn't the only one. Clive Davis – whose idea it was – had been made to look bad, having unwittingly 'called Dylan at the studio on East 52nd Street. He was boiling [mad]; he no longer wanted to work with the group . . . [He] finally called Al Kooper, who put together a group of local New York musicians, including David Bromberg.'

For the foreseeable future, Dylan would work with musicians he could call up on a few hours' notice, like Kooper and Bromberg, who were both summoned to Studio B the following afternoon. Kooper was a no-brainer – doing A&R at Columbia at this point – while Bromberg was someone who had been on Dylan's radar since coming to New York the previous summer, the pair having met through a familiar conduit:

> Al Aronowitz introduced us . . . He showed up . . . when I was playing with [Tom] Paxton at the Bitter End . . . I was playing with all kinds of people [then] – Jerry [Jeff Walker], Paxton, Doug Kershaw [&c.] . . . but he showed up once a week every time I was there . . . At one point he said he'd like to get me in a studio some time, but . . . I didn't really want to believe it until it happened . . . One afternoon he came up to my house . . . We played all afternoon . . . We talked about music and his records, about what he wanted to do . . . It was really fascinating to see how straight he was . . . [after] expect[ing] the guy to be some kind of Sphinx who speaks in riddles. After that, I didn't hear from him for about a month and then he called me up about two o'clock in the afternoon and asked me what I was doing . . . He said he was going to test out these studios and would I like to come along . . . We had to be in the studio in half an hour.

It was a lot more than just a test! On day one, Dylan would record seventeen songs; on day two, eleven more, before adding another eight on day three. Of these, twelve would appear on *Self Portrait* – two ('Alberta' and 'Little Sadie') in two-fold incarnations. Two were Dylan's own tunes: 'Woogie Boogie' and 'All The Tired Horses' (which actually has a two-line lyric, repeated by backing singers); the rest were covers. Bromberg, for one, was taken aback by the informality of it all:

> [Sometimes] it was just Bob and me . . . sitting across from each other playing and trying things . . . [But] Dylan's very together, studio-wise . . . Al Kooper played on [those sessions], too. I was very impressed with him. He helps a lot . . . He really knows his way around a studio . . . Bob Johnston

and Dylan [also] have a great relationship. Bob always says, 'I just let the
tape run,' . . . but he produces a lot . . . [in] the mixing and the editing.

These three days are like no other Dylan Columbia sessions. Their
closest point of reference would be the cover sessions at Big Pink, with
Dylan doing most songs in single takes. This time, though, he wasn't
trying to fool Bromberg or Kooper into believing 'he'd prepped for
this'. As Kooper said in 2013, 'The first day I walked into the studio, Bob
had a pile of *Sing Out!* magazines [sic] . . . and he was going through
them; songs that he'd known in the past. He was using the magazines
to remind himself of them . . . [But] as the week went on, Bob's choices
got stranger and stranger.'

He wasn't playing songs *from* magazines. Bromberg promptly set
the record straight, '*Sing Out!* published a couple of songbooks, and I
remember that Bob had one or two of those. But he knew those songs.'
Dylan had brought along *The Collected Reprints from Sing Out! Vols. 1-2.*
However, he couldn't – and still can't – read music. He would have to
already know the tunes. What is stranger than strange is that he should
re-record 'The House Carpenter' and sing the *Sing Out!* version, a
straight copy of the so-called De Marsan broadside, not the far more
traditional version he cut back in 1961. In this instance, the new
version – issued on *Another Self Portrait* (2013) – really does sound like
an amnesiac reaching for a lost self. Most of the time, though, he seems
to be enjoying himself, playing the music he loved while leafing through
the back pages of his Village tutelage, talking between takes.

After a glorious 'Copper Kettle' (v2, p149) – the highlight of the
sessions – he calls out, 'Here's one called "The Old Rebel Soldier". D'ya
ever see that?' and he starts to recite it, breaking off as he has come
across 'Hick's Farewell', a 19th century preacher's polemic at man's
folly, which prompts Dylan to note, 'Wow, there's some songs in here
that are really [out there].' He begins reciting: 'Let persecutions rage
around/ Let Antichrist appear . . .,' but although he probably knew
Doc Watson's version, he doesn't attempt a take. Instead, he reels off
four composed songs one after the other, in single takes: 'These Hands',
'It Hurts Me Too', 'The Boxer' and 'Spanish Is The Loving Tongue'.*

---

* 'These Hands' was surely done for Bob Johnston, who'd still not forgotten the performance at Cash's house.

Sometimes Dylan can't decide which voice to adopt, but generally he sticks to his 'real' voice. Occasionally, he ladles on a little country syrup, notably for 'Spanish Is The Loving Tongue', an extraordinary five-minute tour-de-force on which Bromberg's flamenco flourishes embellish Dylan's piano-playing.* Though Bromberg rightly notes at take's end, 'We both had a couple of clams in there,' it is mystifying why they don't attempt a more realized take.

Such is the *modus operandi* at all three sessions. Every single track from New York on *Self Portrait* will be a first take (or re-take). Only 'Pretty Saro', the song which opens the first session – which he is clearly doing for his wife, who is audibly present – is really worked on, Dylan attempting five takes before admitting, 'I think I'm about Pretty Saro'd out.' He also perseveres with his own 'Went To See The Gypsy', a song he tries at all three sessions, and Eric Andersen's 'Thirsty Boots', both of which seem to be already earmarked for a separate project.

As for the rest, as Bromberg recalled, 'There was not a whole lot of discussion or direction . . . He listened to the results, and what he really liked, he used.' Or, in the case of 'The Boxer', abused. Having dis-patched the Paul Simon song – which was less than a year old – using his 'new' voice, Dylan said to Johnston, 'Wouldn't it be fun to put a harmony [vocal] on.' The producer had 'never known him to overdub before, but he just put the cans on and sang. He heard the playback; said, "Yeah, that's okay, put it on." And that was that.'† The original take, where he 'played it straight out', sounded like a genuine tribute to another contemporary songwriter, one of a number so honoured at these sessions. Whereas the double-tracked released version was a trav-esty, the one obvious act of self-sabotage on *Self Portrait*.

His intent on entering Studio B on March 3rd may have been to partly acknowledge such peers – on this occasion attempting Tom Pax-ton's 'Can't Help But Wonder Where I'm Bound', Ian Tyson's 'The French Girl', Buffy Sainte-Marie's 'Universal Soldier' and Andersen's 'Thirsty Boots'. But only a mangled 'The Boxer' made it onto *Self*

---

* If this doesn't sound remotely like the version on *Another Self Portrait*, credited to March 3rd, 1970, there's a reason. That version is actually from June 2nd. This one finally appeared on *The 1970 Copyright Collection*.
† When exactly he did this overdub is unknown. There is no reference to it, or any alternate vocal, on the logs.

Portrait. And everything else he used from the first session was copyrighted to him.* He may have recognized that 'other people write good songs', but it would count for naught after Saltzman reminded him that if he stuck to traditional or public domain songs, he could copyright them to himself and keep the money.

Throughout the remaining two days he stuck almost exclusively to traditional songs like 'Tattle O'Day', 'Railroad Bill', 'Days of '49', 'Alberta', 'Little Moses' and 'Things 'Bout Coming My Way', a song he whimsically identified to the engineer as 'My Previous Life'.† Just two copyrighted songs from these sessions would make the album, Gordon Lightfoot's 'Early Morning Rain' and Paul Clayton's 'Gotta Travel On', both of which he would later perform in concert.

Otherwise, his approach remained largely the same: stick to single takes and then either drop it or use it. If he had a conceit in mind, it revolved around getting musicians' first impressions. Or perhaps he simply couldn't be bothered to interact with a band, one of Michael Bloomfield's earlier criticisms: 'He never really gets with the band . . . so that we can groove together.'

At no point, it seems, did he intend to release the results 'as is'. After bringing 'Copper Kettle' to the boil, he tells Johnston, 'Put a little note on that. Add some, er, put everything on that one. Bass, big piano, strings – do the whole thing.' Even on a performance this powerful, he refused to leave well alone.‡ At the end of that marathon session, with some terrific performances in the can, he informed Johnston, 'I guess we can come in tomorrow, add some bass. We could probably take a few of those things and make *something* of them.'

The following day, he continued sending up the whole process. After a promising 'Little Moses' fizzles out, he says to Johnston, 'That's the place for the horns. [Pause] Could use a dog barking, too.' For the final March session, he brought in a rhythm-section but barely used them, spending the final hour or so coaxing the three backing singers to add vocals to 'Went To See The Gypsy', hum along to a really nice

---

* Even 'It Hurts Me Too', which he surely knew was a Tampa Red original.
† Nothing in the original song, as recorded by the Mississippi Sheiks, pertains to the title Dylan gave it.
‡ The untainted, undubbed version appears on *Another Self Portrait*.

instrumental (simply logged as 'New Song #2') and record an a cappella 'All The Tired Horses'.*

He had lost the thread again. Three weeks later, *Rolling Stone*'s 'Random Notes' was reporting, 'Having put down mostly commercial folky stuff by other writers, plus a few originals . . . Dylan wasn't at all happy, and just might split to Memphis and do the whole thing over in April.'†
In the end, he did nothing of the sort. Instead, he picked songs he wanted overdubbed and dispatched Charlie Daniels to Nashville with three eight-track tapes, which were then dubbed onto 16-track reels, over which Nashville's A-Team were requested to overdub 'everything . . . bass, big piano, strings.' Charlie McCoy, for one, didn't think much of what he was asked to play on:

> [Johnston] asked Kenny and me to overdub bass and drums. And that was difficult, because Dylan's tempos [were off] on those tapes . . . [] . . . The tape was mostly other people's songs and it sounded like he was experimenting with them. The tempos didn't really hold together real well, and he wasn't real steady with his guitar . . . I assumed . . . it was just stuff he'd thrown together for the heck of it.

Buttrey had already recorded his parts when McCoy entered the studio. He turned to his friend before heading home for a stiff drink, 'You're not gonna believe this.' To add insult to injury, the arranger Bill Walker dolloped strings over everything he could, while doing his darnedest, to 'get rid of a lot of the things that he played'.

Whatever his original conceit, by the time the tapes left Nashville Dylan had constructed an album guaranteed to get 'the wrong kind of attention', especially as he decided to call it *Self Portrait*. With this in mind, he asked John Cohen to take the cover photos, even consciously 'reprising a photo session I did with him . . . in 1962 on the roof of my loft', a reference no-one but photographer or artist would have got.

Nor did he leave it at that: 'A week later [he came to] my farm in

---

* 'New Song #2' is credited by Krogsgaard – and therefore Björner – as 'Time Passes Slowly'. Not so.

† This appears to be when Dylan planned to do a session with Jim Dickinson's band, The Dixie Flyers, by 1970 based at Criteria Studios. According to Dickinson in 1997, 'The Dixie Flyers were supposed to record with Dylan when we were down in Miami . . . In fact, we didn't know the session was cancelled until the Monday.'

upstate New York, about fifty miles from the city [for another photo session]. We had a couple of hours together . . . play[ing] my guitar and . . . talk[ing] about music . . . and he's suddenly just laid-back and in the country.' As far as Cohen was concerned, 'These country photographs . . . were one more simple disguise for him . . . On the album . . . he sang other people's songs, creating a picture of himself defined by the musical world around him. And [now] he used my place as a stand-in for his own.' So, decidedly *not* a self-portrait.

Even as the resultant album was fast-tracked by a label who had given up second-guessing Dylan's commercial instincts – at the exact moment they should have expressed concern – he was phoning up Clive Davis 'directly – no longer through his secretary. He couldn't wait for the album to come out.' It was 1966 again, when he and Hentoff concocted their 'spoof' interview for *Playboy*, and Dylan was bugging the reporter every few days, 'When is it coming out?' There was one difference, though. That gag was funny.

Davis hadn't encountered this Dylan before, someone who would constantly 'change his mind about the design or the title, holding things up for weeks at a time . . . [Finally,] he called the day the artwork was supposed to be printed and said that he'd decided to do his own cover. I liked the idea – a painting of himself – but [it meant] the album was delayed a month.' Which meant it came out the same week he was hard at work on the *real* follow-up to *Nashville Skyline*. By then, the joke was on him. While Columbia tried telling its reps, 'Reaction to this recording is stronger than any of his previous albums,' the reviews were unsparing. *Rolling Stone* gave it to Greil Marcus, who wrote a thoughtful piece which hardly anyone remembers, save for its provocative first line, 'What is this shit?'

Dylan was now shuttling between Byrdcliffe and a Manhattan apartment he was renting while searching for a house in the city for the whole Dylan clan. If two dated notebook sketches confirm he was in Byrdcliffe in February, a drawing from March 29th is of an apartment door left symbolically open. A contemporary lyrical scrap also implies a restless, hungry feeling was eating at him, while a wanderlust gnawed: 'Got a ticket on a western train/ Leaving in the driving rain/ Going where the wind blows [on my] face.'

Recognising the signs, Sara grew increasingly concerned he might be slipping back into bad habits, fuelled by this two-stage relocation. He was also spending time with an old flame, Barbara Rubin. Thankfully, Rubin was no longer the romantic threat she had once been, having become engaged to a devout, orthodox Jew.* Nonetheless, after Rubin and Wendy Clarke opened the House of Seraphim store in February 1970, Clarke recalls, 'Dylan would come all the time. I knew . . . that they had been boyfriend/girlfriend, so I wasn't surprised. They would be sitting in front of the store, having these intense talks about Judaism.'

The ever-questing Dylan was again exploring his own relationship with his father's faith, confirmed by another lyrical scrap from 1970: 'I've got faith! I don't care who knows it! I'm not ashamed!' But life in the city wasn't all philosophical discussions. Someone from Saltzman's office 'distinctly remember[s] being in Naomi's apartment and there was a girl measuring him for a costume. They were in there with the door closed, and I knew they were fooling around.'

An unfinished 1970 lyric even suggests the birth of the couple's fourth child – a boy, Jakob, born December 9th, 1969 – was making Dylan feel like an outsider in his own home, with the new baby 'taking up all of her time', leaving him 'in the background'. However, he still preferred to eschew confrontation, even when Sara visited the new apartment one time with her ex-roommate and all hell broke loose:

> It was when [Sara] went into one of the bedrooms and found a very expensive fur coat that the trouble started. She tackled him the minute he came through the door, 'Whose is this?' and tossed it at him. 'Yours?' he asked brightly. Then the fun started. He denied all knowledge of it, said he hadn't been there the night before, which led to, Where had he goddamn been then, and who had he been with? I just got out . . . Sara came to find me [later] . . . Cool as ice she was, and when I asked if it was all settled, she said, 'Oh, yes. He's coming home tonight.'

According to Bruce Dorfman, the New York apartment was almost a bachelor's pad, 'It was pretty much Bob and his pinball machine in the living room. I can't imagine how Sara even stayed in the place.' Sara's friend was equally uncomplimentary, 'Horribly impersonal, although the picture of Raquel Welch used as a dartboard offered a

---

* When Rubin was married in New York on March 2nd, 1971, both Bob and Sara attended, as did Allen Ginsberg and Al Aronowitz.

homely touch.' If Dylan was theoretically coming into the city to stimulate his wayward muse, one song which got as far as a notebook, 'Off The Deep End', was a curious reimagining of the great murder ballad, 'Frankie & Johnny'. In it, another lovestruck pair were meeting up again, one last time:

> Becky and Albert were buddies
> Lordy, how they could kiss
> They swore they were thru with each other
> Except for one more night of bliss
> He was her man, but that was over now . . .

Even if he allowed himself to be tempted by the fruit of another, he continued to cling to the idea of Sara as the one person who could 'bring something out in me that's hidden deep within/ . . . And every time you do it, it tells me where I've been/ And shows me where I'm going, and pulls me out of the hole,' lines from another unfinished lyric of the period.

More importantly, his wife was the inspiration for a memorable new song he *did* finish, 'If Not For You', one of three panegyrics to a life he'd left behind, completed in time for a May Day return to Studio B. Of the others, 'Time Passes Slowly' seemed like a rhapsody to the joys of torpor, 'Ain't no reason to go into town . . . Ain't no reason to go anywhere,' while 'Sign On The Window' – his best song since 'I Threw It All Away' – consciously concluded, 'Have a bunch of kids who call me Pa/ That must be what it's all about.' Had he at last found peace? Or was the key line the first: 'Sign on the window says, Lonely'?

While *Self Portrait* was being readied for release, he was already beginning work on an album of original (or mostly original) songs with a friend who had just gone solo. Having just (re-)recorded his response to the continual battle he had waged to get *his* songs on Beatles' albums – the scathing 'I Me Mine' – George Harrison found out Dylan had made his own way through the mirror. Dylan seemed to feel the session with Harrison had gone well, pulling versions of all three new originals to master. Less satisfactory to his mind was another single-take 'Went To See The Gypsy' – featuring its fiercest-ever vocal – and 'Working On A Guru', another nonsense song searching for a Big Pink feel which he left at the starting-gate.

Having booked the studio for the day and got five originals under his belt in a single afternoon, a jam session of epic shambolicness ensued. For bassist Charlie Daniels, 'It was a day I'll never forget . . . It was [just] four guys in the studio making music . . . Anything you threw at [Bob], he could sing . . . hour after hour.' Throughout this marathon musicfest Dylan led the others a merry dance across twenty songs, half of them his; three others more reflective of Harrison's taste – two Carl Perkins songs and an Everly Brothers standard they had last sung together, 'singing close harmony,' at Forelands Farm.

No such luck this time around. 'All You Have To Do Is Dream' was a sleepwalk through the song, as were most tracks. Exceptions included a surprisingly heartfelt 'Song To Woody' straight out of the traps and a semi-convincing 'It Ain't Me, Babe' at one-thirty in the morning, a performance found on a coupla *New Morning* comp. reels. The real travesty was McCartney's 'Yesterday', Harrison sarcastically suggesting they 'dub some cellos on'. If the tapes were no worse than those Harrison included as a 'bonus' disc on his next album, *All Things Must Pass*, Dylan wisely filed them with the Cash sessions in the cupboard marked, D.N.U.

At least he now knew he had a handful of quality originals for his next contractual obligation, which – according to some handwritten notes, designated 'My Album' – would feature 'three or more songs other than mine', as well as 'one long electric one, long acoustic song and the rest short songs'. Peter Orlovsky, Ginsberg's longtime partner, had suggested a title Dylan discounted. The apposite title for this antidote to *Self Portrait* had been staring him in the face for months, one of three songs left over from the MacLeish project, *New Morning*.

The intention to record an album partly comprising covers, partly original, lingered. Indeed, draft lyrics to the three MacLeish songs, plus a new original, 'One More Weekend', appear in a notebook of the period alongside handwritten lyrics to five old favourites: 'Mary Ann', 'Alligator Man', 'Sara Jane', 'Bay Of Mexico' and 'Lily Of The West', three of which he had recorded on the May 1960 St Paul tape! All four originals and four of the covers would be recorded for *New Morning*, 'Bay Of Mexico' being the one absentee.

His abiding intention to work up more covers was evident the minute sessions resumed, a month to the day after Harrison's third audition tape. A June 1st session at CBS's Studio E was spent solely on covers, specifically 'Mary Ann', 'Alligator Man' – given both a 'country' and a 'rock' incarnation – and 'Sara Jane', as well as single-take versions of Peter LaFarge's 'Ballad Of Ira Hayes' and Don Gibson's 'Oh Lonesome Me'.*

If there was a purpose, it was probably the one Dylan later suggested to Cameron Crowe as the rationale behind the already-completed *Self Portrait*: 'We did that stuff to get a (studio) sound. To open up, we'd do two or three songs, just to get things right and then we'd go on and do what we were going to do.' Not on day one, they didn't. Ron Cornelius – the electric guitarist Dylan had recruited for these sessions – concluded that on the 'first day we were just feeling out each other's playing'.

The second day offered more of the same, save for a brief detour to redo 'If Not For You' and 'Time Passes Slowly', suggesting Dylan felt the Harrison takes were no longer up to scratch.† This would become something of a pattern. 'Mary Ann', an innocuous arrangement of a traditional favourite, scuppered by the overbearing backing singers, wasted tape for a second day running. And yet, 'Mary Ann' – as well as 'Ira Hayes' and 'Mr Bojangles' from those first two sessions – appeared on early sequences of the album.

Unlike the March sessions, Dylan stuck at it, working on these songs with a full five-piece featuring Kooper on organ, Bromberg on guitar and dobro, Cornelius on electric, and Russ Kunkel and Charlie Daniels,

---

* The information in Krogsgaard's sessionography on the June sessions can't be corroborated, and is hard to credit. Thirteen consecutive long false starts on 'Time Passes Slowly', a song he'd already 'pulled to master'? Really? The session-tapes no longer exist. All the 'usable' tracks were pulled to 'comp.' reels with titles like '16 Track Rejects' and 'Complete Takes But Not Masters'. Not in dispute are the songs they recorded. All the extant takes were referenced for 2013's *Another Self Portrait*, and those omitted from that set were included on *1970 Copyright Collection*. These include three songs absent from said sessionography: 'Harmonica Blues', a 'Harmonica Instrumental', with band, and a solo electric piano take of 'Went To See The Gypsy'.

† Early press reports suggested the May 1st version of 'If Not For You' was slated for inclusion on *New Morning*. Kooper was quoted in September 1970 as saying, 'Harrison is on at least one cut.' Sounes claims, 'The [Harrison] tracks did not officially appear on an album . . . because he did not have a U.S. work permit, but copies of the tapes soon passed into the hands of bootleggers.' Total rot. It took over two decades for the session to be bootlegged, by which time the Harrison 'If Not For You' had appeared officially on *The Bootleg Series*.

the rhythm-section. If Bromberg was delighted to be working with Kunkel, having 'always [been] a huge fan of the way he plays', Cornelius was less enamoured with Bromberg's contribution, frustrated that he tried playing 'on everything. [In fact,] it was a question of how to stop him playing. There were a few times when it needed a bit of silence to let Dylan come through.' But he had nothing but admiration for the authoritative way Dylan went about his work:

> It was just five guys in the studio for a week. We did about twenty-seven tunes, and it was pretty loose. Dylan knows exactly what he wants in the studio, and if he doesn't get it, he moves on to something else. There was no rehearsing. It was all, 'Okay, this is how it goes, let's do it.' If it fouled up real bad then he might do it a second time, and if that was bad, just possibly a third. But . . . I don't know anyone who's so certain about his direction.

A remarkable visual document of the June 3rd session, shot on open-reel video, confirms the perspicacity of Cornelius's contemporary recall. We see Dylan working up a full-blooded arrangement of 'Long Black Veil' that turns it into a seven-minute jam. During a rehearsal Kooper plays piano, before Dylan switches Kooper to organ à la 'Rolling Stone', leaving him to pound away at the black keys himself.

This would become something of a pattern, much to Cornelius's amusement, 'You fall over laughing the first time you see [him play piano], because his hands start at opposite ends of the keyboard, then sorta collide in the middle. He does that all the time, but the way he plays just knocks me out.' Kooper concurred, 'He's the weirdest piano player of all time, but . . . nobody can play like that.'

'Long Black Veil' was just one manifestation of Dylan's determination to rock out at these sessions, perhaps trying to prove to himself he still could. Yet it is one aspect almost wholly absent from the resultant album. Putting the band through its paces from the very first track, 'Alligator Man', some songs were stretched out just for fun (including 'Sarah Jane', savagely edited for the *Dylan* album).

Wearing shades most of the time, Dylan tended to discard them only when briefing the musicians. Refusing to use headphones or allow baffles, he directed the musicians with his eyes, or the briefest of comments, 'No lyrics. Just the girls.' Songs were suggested; some were tried, some – 'Sitting On Top Of The World' for one – were not. If the leakage on the resultant tapes made overdubbing nigh on impossible, Dylan could still be heard at the end of a stirring 'Can't Help Falling In Love', asking the other Bob, 'D'ya wanna overdub?' Johnston, adrift in a sea of chaos, just went with the flow; only for Dylan to impertinently blame *him* for the hit'n'miss results in *Chronicles*: 'He's thinking that everything I'm recording is fantastic. He always does . . . On the contrary, nothing was ever together . . . even after a song had been finished and recorded.'

The Nashville man was probably just waiting for 'Bob' to get serious. Which took until the fifth and final day. Despite claiming, in a draft version of *Chronicles,* that he 'started with the songs I wrote for the play & then added to them', Dylan did anything but. It took until late on the 4th, after an evening spent making a mockery of Joni Mitchell's 'Big Yellow Taxi', for him to finally scratch that itch, cutting 'New Morning' in just two takes.

By the next day, something fundamental had changed. Perhaps it was the bassist, Harvey Brooks being brought in. According to his 2020 memoir, Brooks had got the call because they 'still hadn't gotten the tunes the way Bob wanted them . . . There was a lot of burnt-out emotion in the studio when I got there, and I couldn't miss the frustration that Bob and Al were going through. The room was like sitting in a pressure cooker that was ready to blow! It took a while for everyone to settle into a groove.'

The recall of Brooks wasn't as impromptu as it seems. The pair had spent some time together that spring, playing chess and swapping unflattering stories about their ex-manager, Uncle Albert. The singer admitted his 'falling out centered on management fees and publishing', whereas the bassist had stopped working for Grossman because he never came up with a contract or wanted to pay the going rate. Dylan was temporarily enthused with a book he'd been reading called *The Death Ship* by the pseudonymous author, B. Traven (best known for *The Treasure of Sierra Madre*). The book told of a seaman who had lost his passport and papers and could not find work or assert his legal rights. He ends up being repeatedly deported because the officials 'do not want to be bothered with helping or jailing him'.

A few weeks later, Brooks got the call from Kooper asking him to come to Studio E. It was time to get down to business. Perhaps negative feedback Dylan was getting about *Self Portrait*, released that week, concentrated his mind. Whatever the case, after four days spent recording mostly covers, Dylan now cut six originals and an impromptu instrumental in six hours. Suddenly, he had another album.

Though he later alleged, in *Chronicles*, 'I didn't care what I was doing at that point,' he clearly did care. Listening to the June 5th takes, one can hear an album unfold. There is barely a let-up. He even squeezes in a slice of Sun-era Elvis, 'I Forgot To Remember To Forget', between 'Winterlude' and 'The Man In Me'. Otherwise, he focused on his own songs. He even completed 'Father Of Night', before allowing himself to revisit 'Lily Of The West' – first attempted two days earlier – a circle-completing end to proceedings.

All this he achieved while one of his sons crawled around the studio and his wife listened on patiently and, one presumes, proudly. He even introduces 'The Man In Me' as his 'Broadway play song', on a first take which retains something of its original premise, 'Temptation circles all around my door.'* A grinning Dylan stretches the song to five minutes, after which one musician opines, 'That sounds like the last track on the album.' Dylan had his 'one long electric one'.

The 'long acoustic song' he had had in mind all along could well be 'Sign On The Window', which started out that day with just Dylan on piano, backed by the odd 'ooh ooh' from the girls, a performance that, if anything, is even more touching than the exquisite ensemble performance on the album.

Also sprung on the musicians on the 5th was 'Winterlude', whose lyrics he hadn't quite finished. Again, it came easily. Even a mid-session instrumental interlude – given the title, 'Ahoooah' – showed Dylan taking control, calling out, 'Okay. Let's get this one. There's nothing to this. David, you take a ride. Hey Al, you wanna take a ride on this?'

At session's end he had an album, and not one which needed bolstering with covers. And yet, initially that's precisely what he planned to do. An early sequence opened with 'Mr Bojangles' and 'Ira Hayes' and even found room for a lovely, anachronistic 'Tomorrow Is A Long Time', with some cracked country inflection. At this stage, 'The Man In Me' was retained in its full five-minute pomp, leaving no room for

---

* This version is absent from *The 1970 Copyright Collection*, as is all the material captured on open-reel video.

'If Not For You'. An acetate of this version Dylan took back to 124 West Houston Street, played once and left there to be found in a closet when the owner died in 2014, in a box marked Old Records.

At some point in July, he turned the tapes over to Al Kooper, hoping he might come up with a suggested sequence. The result was even less commercial, 'New Morning' and 'If Not For You' making way for the unmemorable 'Mary Ann'. How much of this was Dylan's idea and how much Kooper's is unclear, but Kooper was growing increasingly exasperated: 'When I finished that album I never wanted to speak to him again . . . He just changed his mind every three seconds, so I just ended up doing the work of three albums . . . We'd get a side order and we'd go in and master it and he'd say, "No, no, no. I want to do this" . . . [or,] "Let's go in and cut this." '

By the time he started shuffling assorted sequences, Dylan was in receipt of a letter from a frustrated MacLeish, dated Independence Day, asking his supposed collaborator to stick to his Broadway brief. He starts out by complimenting Dylan on 'New Morning', which he felt 'marries the opening as though they'd been intended for each other by the queen of Chinese marriage brokers'. After the soft-soap, he proceeds to ask Dylan to look again at 'Father Of Night', which he hopes will bring similar weight to the trial scene, but only 'if we can straighten out the words. As I recall them . . . they belong to the father of day as well as to the father of night. But Scratch, who will sing them, is, of course, night without day.'

He quotes the very lines from the play that Dylan quotes in *Chronicles*, 'I know there's evil in the world. Essential evil. Not the opposite of good or the defect of good, but something to which good itself is an irrelevance, a fantasy.' MacLeish reminds Dylan that *this* is the singer of 'Father Of Night', even rewriting a verse to explicate his point, which is presumably what Dylan dimly recalled when he wrote, '[MacLeish] wondered why the songs weren't darker than they were, and he made suggestions . . . [He] explained [that] the main character was, among other things, envious, slanderous . . . and that should be brought out more.'

The ever-optimistic MacLeish, in signing off, offered Dylan his 'highest regard'. However, in the copy he sent to Ostrow, he added a note explaining 'that my letter to Dylan is the result of considerable time and thought and . . . says what I think has to be said at this point.' This one last pitch fell on stony ground. The author of 'All Along The Watchtower' now knew the play had 'an apocalyptic message . . . and I didn't want to know.'

In fact, as MacLeish informed his literary editor, he had already 'decided . . . to use old songs of Dylan's . . . For one thing, the old songs are more to our purpose, since Dylan has now entered advanced middle age . . . For another, they are far better than anything he is now doing.' When Ostrow himself wrote to Dylan, on September 22nd, there would be none of MacLeish's supplicatory tone from producer to poet:

> Out of respect for a year's work, I'm writing to explain why the songs I have chosen, [all old Dylan songs], are the ones that will work in *Scratch*. Please consider seriously the theatre objective and tell me if it is accept-able. If it is not, I assume I'm free to go on without you . . . I don't see any possibility of using the songs you suggested. They have to do with a love relationship between man and woman. This Play is not about that. Maybe next time we can groove.

Ostrow signs off by hoping Dylan will look on his request to use old songs favourably, but 'if not, all you did was waste some of my pre-cious time'. A chastened Dylan declined to do the decent thing. The play, which finally opened (and closed) the following May, thus became a conventional play, not 'a ballad play'. That MacLeish was as bitter as Ostrow is apparent from a letter he sent the following January, clearing the producer of any blame for the debacle: 'Your instinct about this play was right – that rock-singing balladeer we imagined was just the boy to raise the Devil. The device failed us because Dylan failed us (and himself).'

By July 1970, the trio of songs with 'banal words and [a] bumping beat' which Dylan had previously scratched together for MacLeish – two of which addressed 'a love relationship between man and woman' – had been assimilated into his second album of the year. Not that he was done. Dylan went back into the studio on August 12th to recut two songs and add another. He still felt he was a couple of songs shy of an eleventh Columbia album.

One of the songs he recut, 'If Not For You', had only just got back from Nashville, having had pedal-steel and violin overdubbed to its

June form. Overdubs were also applied to a solo piano 'Spanish Is The Loving Tongue' and a solo electric piano 'Went To See The Gypsy', both probably from the June 2nd session,* an indication he was still looking for that 'long acoustic song'. The overdubs could well have been at Kooper's suggestion, as he looked to take over the reins:

> In the middle of [New Morning], Bob Johnston just disappeared, and so for the second half of the record, I was actually producing it. I also had some arrangement ideas. Not that Bob always agreed with them . . . I did an arrangement where I put a horn section on ['New Morning'] and [on] 'Sign on The Window', I added strings, a piccolo and a harp . . . while he wasn't there . . . But when I played them back for him, he didn't like them . . . He [just] kept one little part of each of them. [2013]

At the time, as a concession perhaps to Columbia's internal politics, Kooper was more circumspect, suggesting he simply 'helped with the mixing . . . I wanted to try out this technique . . . The trick is not to go over the red line . . . It has a different style to anything else he's done.' Meanwhile, Dylan kept his options open, one of which was to consider releasing a more baroque album. The 'horns' and 'strings' overdubs on 'New Morning' and 'Sign On The Window' both made it to the 16-track master reel, suggesting the decision to use Kooper's overdubs more sparingly was only made at the mixing stage.

Still uncertain how much Rock he wanted on there, Dylan gave both 'If Not For You' and 'Time Passes Slowly' on August 12th the bellow of the blast. The latter was even logged as 'Mad Dogs & Englishmen version', a nod to the Joe Cocker-led travelling revue which had made a pit-stop at the Fillmore on March 27th, a show Dylan caught. Though Dylan refrained from calling up Cocker's drummer – Sandy Konikoff – Billy Mundi attacked the drums with similar gusto, before Dylan wisely dropped the 'Mad Dogs' intro to 'Time Passes Slowly'[†] and curtailed 'Day Of The Locusts' before the big band jam out.[‡]

---

* The solo 'Gypsy' is certainly not from the same session (June 5th) the album take comes from.

† Krogsgaard has the official take of 'Time Passes Slowly' as take three. It's the eighth & last take.

‡ Something he would also do to the June takes of 'The Man In Me' and 'Went To See The Gypsy'. Both tracks are again 'intact' on the 16-track master reel, the former

Logged as the 'Locust Song', this new composition was a thinly-veiled account of his receiving an honorary doctorate from Princeton University on June 9th, what he later called 'a strange day', for which he had written a strange song whose surreal coda about a man's head exploding jarred with its prosaic preamble.*

At least the album was finally done. Mixing and trimming of the songs could begin. Dylan was determined to use *all* the original songs he had, and *none* of the covers, chastened perhaps by *Self Portrait*'s reception – not that he would ever admit he had made a foolish move. Instead, he would disingenuously inform Larry Sloman in 1975, 'It just happened coincidentally that one came out and then the other one did as soon as it did. The *Self Portrait* LP laid around for . . . a year. We were working on *New Morning* when the *Self Portrait* album got put together.' Perhaps, but only half-heartedly.

When Ralph J. Gleason trumpeted, 'We've Got Dylan Back Again!', in *Rolling Stone,* Dylan may even have believed he had pulled it off. By *Chronicles*, though, he joked, '*New Morning* . . . was heralded as a come-back album & of course it was . . . the first of many.' He was treading water and he knew it, even if its release sparked a brief flicker of inter-est for getting back on the road, an itch he continued to scratch. In his one conversation with Van Morrison before escaping Woodstock for good, the Belfast cowboy recalled Dylan 'talking about a revue, sort of like the [1975] Rolling Thunder . . . He said he was thinking about hav-ing different singers come out with him.'

Harvey Brooks also recollects, 'We talked a little bit about playing shows, but it didn't get very far down the line. We did have a few rehearsals at a place, a studio on Houston Street where he did a lot of painting . . . and we tried out a few different combinations of musicians, but it just didn't click.'† The rehearsals at his Houston St. studio were low-key affairs, as was every move he made upto the end of his second 'New York' phase.

Dylan was looking to clear the decks. As he wrote in a 1970

---

running to 4.49, the latter – which also includes a prescient spoken intro, 'I figure if we're ever gonna get it, we're gonna get it now' – to 3.33.

* The most authoritative account of the ceremony is by Sean Wilentz in the *Princeton University Library Chronicle* Vol. 78, No. 1 (Autumn 2020), pp. 12–21.

† In December 1970, *Rolling Stone* reported, 'Until just a month ago, Dylan was in rehearsal with a couple of the musicians . . . on *New Morning*, along with members of Brethren. But then [he] changed his mind.' Brethren's drummer was Rick Marotta.

notebook, 'I guess this is called taking care of business, facing up to my karma. I'm looking forward to the day when it'll be unloaded, [and] this mess will be cleaned up,' presumably a reference to the ongoing negotiations aimed at extracting himself from Grossman's grasp. And as of July 17th, it seems he had succeeded, both parties agreeing to (i) terminate the Management Agreement, reserving to Grossman his right to royalties on works created during the management period; (ii) confirm Grossman's rights under the Witmark Partnership (i.e. Dwarf Music) and Joint Venture (i.e. Big Sky) Agreements; and, (iii) shift the control and administration of the Partnership and Joint Venture catalogues from Grossman to Dylan.

Once the Big Sky 'joint venture' expired in June 1971, they'd be done. Dylan was methodically extricating himself from everything and everybody in his previous life, as if preparing for things coming his way. He had fulfilled his four-year contract with Columbia by delivering *New Morning* and Bob Johnston, for one, sensed his association with his most important client was at an end, telling *Melody Maker* in September 1971, 'He's got a little studio with an organ and mikes, [which] is big enough for him to do an album in.'

A month later, Dylan was telling biographer Anthony Scaduto, 'I don't have a studio anymore.' According to Scaduto, the reason was that 'even that studio hideout began to make too many demands on his time and his head. The phone number had a way of getting around, and friends who wouldn't dream of knocking at his door at home would knock on the studio door.' He continued to find reasons not to get down to work. The few verses which appear scattershot in his 1970-71 sketchbooks, one of which could have sat securely on *John Wesley Harding*, convey a need for atonement and doing the right thing:

I don't wanna offend nobody, I'm just a-passing through
So just let me know before I go if there's anything I can do
If you'd like me to say goodbye to someone or if you'd like me to say hello
It's all the same to me. I'll do it, if you just let me know.

These post-*New Morning* lyrics abound with admonishments to himself, thus: 'Blind men never see just what's in front and/ If you take a look around, you'll see/ You've got what you want.' It was like he said to Scaduto, about how just 'before [making] *John Wesley Harding* . . . I discovered that when I used words like "he" and "they" . . . I was really talking about nobody but me.' Equally suggestive of someone who 'stays silent and explodes inside' was a lyric written sometime after mid-November, offering a whole new take on 'The Water Is Wide'. In it, he admonishes the listener to 'cross that lonesome water' by themselves, 'cause no-one is going to do it on their behalf:

We were walking by the gatehouse just as happy as can be
And to whom should we come upon while passing by the door
But a young man who'd been grieving for forty years or more . . .
A strap was on his ankle and a clasp was on his head
As we passed him by so cautiously, this is what he said . . .

Another song scrawled on the back of an envelope two weeks after the final *New Morning* session, called 'Shirley's Room', hinted at a ding-dong relationship – perhaps with his wife, whose real name was Shirley. Starting out in Dylanesque fashion, 'It had been a long blind night, lot of heavy drinking . . . until dawn/ Bongos played [across] the street from the hotel/ Where lonesome men were holed up in Shirley's room,' by the end the narrator is back on the gypsy trail, 'I grabbed my rucksack and headed out of town.'

However, the most telling passage in those contemporary notebooks housed in Tulsa's Dylan Center is not a forlorn attempt at new songs. Rather, it is the prosaic admission that he feels devoid of inspiration. He even compares himself with French Dadaist Marcel Duchamp, someone who, he writes, 'quit painting at 30 to become a chess player. He's got one year on me (the poet) already. Obstruction all around me. Got to clean the board!' In all likelihood, it was an exhibition at MoMA in March 1971 that triggered his interest in Duchamp, a fascination that would endure,* even as Dylan considered following his example by taking early retirement (for a third time), lamenting the fact that he 'used to sing songs that would make 'm stand on their heads scratching the floor with their eyes'. As of now, he just wanted to go get drunk, and forget all about music. If only he could.

---

* Perhaps the Marcel in 1977's 'Where Are You Tonight?' – a strong man 'belittled by doubt' – is Duchamp.

3.6

January 1971 to February 1973:
Escaping On The Run

I couldn't be anybody but myself, [but] at that point I didn't know it or want to know it. I was convinced I wasn't going to do anything else.

Bob Dylan, to Jonathan Cott, 17th September 1978.

When I stopped working, that's when the trouble started. Then I was no longer a spokesman for anybody . . . When[ever] you stop working, they want more – those people always want more. It's not what have you done for me yesterday, but what can you do for me today . . . I['d] got sick if it by that time.

Bob Dylan, to Pete Oppel, October 1978.

Woven into his character, except in unique moments, was an air of guardedness, a protective shell around the man. He seemed to create part of his mystique by surrounding himself with an aura of mystery.

Bob Finkbine, referring to time spent together in 1972.

Dylan had been in hiding – meditating or something – since his motorcycle accident and he came down with his tall Indian hat and his little moustache. Very strange cat . . . He was like quicksilver. You could never put your finger on Bobby.

James Coburn.

I was playing with David Bromberg and Steve Goodman, but I needed a harmonica player. I asked if there was anyone around . . . He had brought a harmonica and . . . about two people were clapping. No one believed it. They thought Dylan was either dead or on Mount Fuji.

John Prine.

★

Throughout 1971–72, Dylan's attempts to 'clean the board' and unblock 'the melody line' would make little difference. The songs were now only coming through in dribs and drabs. Just six completed songs date from these two years, only three of which would be released in real time, all in 1971. Yet the idea of becoming just another 'oldies act' remained abhorrent to him, a determination reinforced by events on October 15th, 1971, when he attended a Rock'n'Roll Spectacular at Madison Square Garden to see, amongst others, the great Ricky Nelson, an experience he waited until 2022's *The Philosophy of Modern Song* to describe:

> They [had] tried to relegate Ricky to the oldies circuit. Ricky wasn't having it. In 1971, Richard Nader tried to book Ricky for a rock and roll oldies show. Ricky agreed to appear [provided he was] billed as Rick, not Ricky Nelson . . . Bo Diddley, Chuck Berry, The Coasters . . . They were all good, did their hits. Rick was the only one out there trying to do new material . . . People booed. Later he wrote a song about it, called "Garden Party", and took that song into the Top Ten. The people who came and saw him again didn't even recognize themselves in that song.

Nowhere in the three paragraphs he devotes to this story does Dylan mention the fact that not only was he there, but is directly referenced in the song Nelson wrote about the experience: 'Mr Hughes hid in Dylan's shoes, wearing his disguise/ But it's all right now, I learned my lesson well/ You see, ya can't please everyone, so ya got to please yourself.' Nor does he mention that Nelson's 1970 countrified cover version of an old song of *his*, 'She Belongs To Me', had sparked a mini-revival in his fortunes that had led to him joining the star-studded bill.

While Dylan's own contemporary work made almost no impression, his influence on contemporaries had never been greater. This was the heyday of the singer-songwriter – the era of *Harvest, Blue, Sandy, Tapestry, Tupelo Honey, Hunky Dory, Tumbleweed Connection, Pink Moon, Blue River, Tea for The Tillerman* and John Prine's and Paul Simon's eponymous debuts – all albums where Dylan's presence looms large. It was also a period when fine debuts by Bruce Springsteen (*Greetings From Asbury Park*), Willis Alan Ramsey, Elliott Murphy and Jesse Winchester were all heralded as the work of the 'next' Dylan. Indeed, when Dylan first met Springsteen in New Haven in 1975, his first line to the young pretender was supposedly, 'I hear you're the new me.'

Not that Dylan was about to readily embrace the kind of confessional songwriting this new decade spawned. When his old friend Lennon released his first solo album, *Plastic Ono Band,* the product of Primal Scream therapy, he distanced himself from it: 'I don't write those kind of songs . . . He wrote one song, "Mother you had me . . ." [which] is a very personal kind of song . . . I can't even relate to it.'

As long as he remained in the city, and as long as young colts dared play Paul Colby's Bitter End, he could continue to check the competition out in person. Shortly after he finally relocated the whole family to a townhouse on MacDougal Street in spring 1970, Colby was approached by a familiar face, Al Aronowitz, who 'came running up to me on Bleecker one day . . . "Bob Dylan wants to come to the club." "So let him come. I'll give him a good table." . . . But that was no longer the way Bob worked. That night Al brought Dylan . . . Bunky and Jake were playing.'*

From this point forward, Colby made sure he was always made to feel welcome. However, Colby himself did not feel quite so welcome when he and Kris Kristofferson – a regular at the club – paid Dylan an impromptu visit at the new homestead:

One day Kris said, 'Let's go see Bob Dylan.' Now I knew Dylan, of course, but you never knew how well you knew him. I may have had a drink or two that night. Kris had more than two, which was his way back then. It was the apartment on MacDougal Street. We knocked, and Dylan's wife came to the door. [It was like] we were in a spy movie. 'We want to see Bob Dylan.' . . . 'Who wants to see Bob Dylan.' So Kris said, 'Kris Kristofferson and Paul Colby.' Well, she locked the door and went away. By now Kris and I were not sure what to do. About five minutes later she came back, unlocked the door and we went inside. Whenever I hung out with Kris, it was always a blast . . . But not tonight. The conversation was a little about music, but Dylan's wife was there. I felt like we were old people all of a sudden. Out came the tea set. Here was Dylan, but he was very subdued . . . [It was like,] *At Home With The Dylans.* 'Do come again. Don't forget to call before you come.' That kind of thing.

---

* Jake & The Family Jewels were long-standing local favourites on the Village folk-rock scene.

The compartmentalizing of Dylan's life was such that Sara never accompanied him to the End, just in case she reminded him that this was his good ol' used-to-be. When an old Minnesotan friend reconnected with Dylan in 1972, the three of them were walking around the Village when, passing an old theatre, Sara teased her husband, 'Your friend Neil Diamond is playing here right now.' According to the friend, 'He smiled cryptically and motioned for us to keep on walking.'

So, imagine the surprise when the great Chicagoan, John Prine, made his New York debut at the End the first week in November 1971, and Dylan got up to play harmonica, having been given a copy of the ex-mailman's impressive debut by either Bromberg or Steve Goodman. According to Colby, Dylan was playing 'little grace notes at first until he picked up the melody, and then he started to wail. John turned around when [he] finished, pointed . . . and said, "Dylan!" ' The song was 'Sam Stone', Prine's most powerful piece at the time, about a VietVet who returned home a junkie. It evidently spoke to Dylan, and still spoke to him in 2009, when he described Prine's work as, 'Midwestern mindtrips to the nth degree . . . All that stuff about "Sam Stone," the soldier junkie daddy, and "Donald and Lydia," where people make love from ten miles away. Nobody but Prine could write like that.'

Jackson Browne, who'd just signed to Elektra, was not so lucky when he came to the End. He asked to meet Dylan, and Colby obliged. According to the club-owner, 'They talked. [Then] Jackson took the stage. After the first two songs Dylan got up and left. Poor Jackson said, "There goes my career." '

It was 'Tomorrow Never Knows' all over again. Though Browne had once been part of Nico's nocturnal downtown demi-monde, Dylan now saw Browne as one of the Ladies and Gentlemen of Laurel Canyon, the new home of singer-songwriting, a clique of whom Dylan was not entirely enamoured, especially after turning on the radio the following spring and hearing the break-out single from Neil Young's *Harvest*:

The only time it bothered me that someone sounded like me was . . . about '72 and the big song at the time was 'Heart of Gold'. I used to hate it when it came on the radio. I always liked Neil Young, but it bothered me every time I listened to [it]. It was . . . number one for a long time, and I'd say, 'Shit, that's me. If it sounds like me, it should as well be me.'[1985]

Dylan seemed to prefer his singer-songwriters to come from Chicago, Nashville, New York, Oklahoma, or even, at a pinch, Pinner, Middlesex. Elton John – the new hot songsmith from England – came to the Fillmore East in November 1970. This was before the showman wholly subsumed a serious songmaker, and Dylan was so impressed he returned the following evening with his wife to check him out again, visiting the unprepossessing piano-player backstage.

Having fallen back in love with the piano himself, receiving deserved plaudits for his playing on *New Morning*, Dylan was knocked out by Elton's dynamic performance. It was like he became another person. (Now there's an idea.) Dylan's return the following night was not entirely about Elton, though. John was sharing the bill with a piano-player whom Dylan had long admired, whose work he knew well, and who had already recorded 'Girl From The North Country' (as part of *Mad Dogs & Englishmen*) and 'Masters Of War'; the originator of the Tulsa Sound, Leon Russell.

It was Russell whom Dylan called up when he wanted to try a new sound and a new studio (Blue Rock), in March 1971; his first non-Columbia recordings since Big Pink, and an assertion of independence which should have sent a clear signal to the suits on Seventh Avenue.

Appropriately, the only original Dylan brought to the sessions was 'When I Paint My Masterpiece' – with 'when' serving as shorthand for 'if and when'. It was a song he'd already offered to Robertson for the fourth Band album, *Cahoots*, after the guitarist admitted his own well-spring had run dry: 'We needed one more. I didn't go into too much detail, but I implied that it was a bit rough going [this time] . . . He picked up my guitar and sang what he had so far on 'When I Paint My Masterpiece' . . . [We] recorded the song the next day.'

Robbie says he had just received an acetate of Elton John's 'Levon', which wasn't recorded until February 27th, so their meeting must have been close to the first Blue Rock session on March 16th. Yet the lyrics Dylan gave Robertson were quite different. The song including a bridge – 'Sailin' around the world in a dirty gondola/ Oh, to be back in the land of Coca Cola!' – absent from the Blue Rock version Dylan released later that year. It turns out there were two sets of lyrics with significant variations, landing in Brussels 'with a picture of a tall oak tree by my side'* in one; 'On a plane ride so bumpy that I almost cried' on the other. Saltzman duly copyrighted it in both guises.

Meanwhile, Dylan proceeded to record the song with and without a bridge at Blue Rock, beginning with two solo piano takes featuring a bridge that rhymed 'Victrola' with 'rock'n'roller', before running down an instrumental version with the band, and half a dozen ensemble takes, from which he chose a bridge-less version for *Greatest Hits Vol. 2*.† An outtakes reel for the double-album shows that the earlier piano version and a 'full band version' were both short-listed. It was an important song, bristling with potent images and seeming to hint of a returning muse. Only Dylan knew if it was anything of the sort, having insisted to Anthony Scaduto two months earlier, 'I still have a lot of talent left. I can still do it. None of it has left me.'

Proceedings at Blue Rock had actually started with a series of 'Russell-Dylan jams', using the studio band which had just cut Russell's second album, *Leon Russell and the Shelter People*, and featuring two musicians destined to work extensively with Dylan in the future, uber-beatmeister Jim Keltner and Muscle Shoals pianist, Barry Beckett.

That first day's work was the June 1st *New Morning* session revisited, even down to Dylan doing a great Don Gibson cover, 'I'd Just Be Fool Enough (To Fall)', along with worthy stabs at 'Blood Red River' – surely learnt from Sonny & Terry – the traditional 'Alabama Bound', and a never-completed 'Spanish Harlem', which prompts Dylan to ask, 'You don't remember the lyrics for that, do ya?'

It wasn't the only lyric at Blue Rock that required Dylan raid his memory banks. *Rolling Stone*'s session-report quoted a new song featuring the couplet, 'What am I to do when a fence needs mending?/ Can't stand around here picking more flowers.' The lines actually come from a semi-improvised verse Dylan threw into 'That Lucky Old Sun', after another rewrite, 'Up in the morning, working on my horse/ Riding the range every hour . . .'

Indeed, *Rolling Stone* proved remarkably well-informed about the

---

* Could this refer to 'Leaf By Niggle', a Tolkien short-story about a man who obsesses about painting a tree?
† The LP was called *More Greatest Hits* in Europe, presumably to distinguish it from the three greatest hits already issued in various territories.

way these sessions came together, describing 'Watching The River Flow' as *written and cut* during the Russell-Dylan jams at Dylan's New York studios . . . Russell [had] followed up on a meeting with Dylan last year by sending him an acetate of Leon and the Tulsa Tops doing three [Dylan] songs . . . Soon enough, Leon got the call from Bob.' All true.

In 2008, Keltner recalled Dylan 'writing . . . songs on the spot in the studio, or finishing them up.' In the case of 'Watching The River Flow' he had started the song back in 1965, and just never known it. The three interpretations of old Dylan songs Russell had sent him – all from *Bringing It All Back Home* – included an arrangement of 'Love Minus Zero' that's a dead ringer for 'Watching The River Flow', hence presumably Russell's claim:*

> With 'Watching The River Flow', I made the track; it didn't have any words or melody, and he wrote the song and sang it on top of the track. It took him about ten minutes! He really does write like that; he even types like that, most of the time! He's very prolific, he writes tons. He told me one time that when he was singing by himself, he would write four or five songs, sing them at night, and never sing them again.

How quickly they cut the song itself is unknown – any alternates are lost – but it sure sounds like a first or second take; that delicious jump-start – 'What's the matter with me/ I don't have much to say . . .' – offering a single-line summation of the subject-matter of 'Masterpiece'. If he held back the latter, he considered 'Watching The River Flow' exuberant enough to release it as a non-album single, with a sublime solo 'Spanish Is The Loving Tongue' from the previous June on the flipside. Surprisingly, the single didn't even dent the Top Forty, proof – were it needed – that Dylan was now officially an 'FM artist' and the divide between AM and FM was so wide, he couldn't cross over.

By the time the 45 appeared, on June 3rd, 1971, Dylan was returning from the land of his forefathers, Israel. Though he later denied there was any 'great significance to that visit', he also admitted, 'I'm

---

* The other two songs, which appear as bonus tracks on the expanded 1989 CD of *Leon Russell and the Shelter People*, are 'It's All Over Now, Baby Blue' and 'She Belongs To Me'.

interested in what and who a Jew is.' And here he was, caught at Jerusalem's Wailing Wall by a sharp-eyed photographer on his thirtieth birthday no less. According to *Chronicles*, 'the image was transmitted worldwide and . . . changed me *from a revolutionary insubordinate* into a Zionist overnight.'*

He later complained, privately, that 'he and Sara [had] tried to honeymoon [t]here in the seventies and the hungry Israeli reporters . . . ruined any chance the couple might have [had] for romance.' The 'hungry Israeli reporters' actually amounted to a single female *Jerusalem Post* journalist who engaged him on the beach in a ten-minute chat. And it was hardly his first interview of the year. Rather, it was his fifth, though none save a taped phone conversation with A.J. Weberman had made it to print as yet.

He had given two to journalists who were threatening to publish biographies – ex-crime reporter Anthony Scaduto, who did so before the year was out, and Robert Shelton, who took fifteen more years to prove in print the task was always beyond him. In both cases, Dylan feared the worst, having had a hard time recognising himself in another selfless portrait recently put into print. A young student of New Journalism, Toby Thompson, had embarked on his own odyssey to the north country, to investigate Dylan's Minnesotan roots. The results, published first as a series of articles and then as *Positively Main Street*, appalled their subject:

> I was over at someone's place and there was a book there called *Positively Main Street*. I started reading it, and it just made me crazed . . . I was having a hard time separating me from the person I was reading about . . . I just felt like another person; it was like Doctor Jekyll and Mr Hyde. [1986]

But his most sustained concession to the interview treadmill he'd stepped off in 1969 was a series of sit-down conversations with his old friend, Tony Glover, in late March, for an intended cover-feature in *Esquire* magazine. Surrounded by 'amplifiers, instruments and several of Dylan's paintings', Glover prodded and Dylan parried his way through three and a half hours of chat; this after Dylan had informed

---

* The italicised phrase was deleted from the final, published text.

his old friend, 'I don't know what we'd talk about. It'd be kinda like a fake interview.' For much of the time, little was really revealed, though for an amnesiac Dylan's memory remained remarkable. He had total recall of Chris Welles, who wrote a 1964 *Life* feature; the circumstances behind the notorious 1966 *Playboy* interview; and the girl who assaulted him in Glasgow in 1966. But the only time he really opened up was when he was asked what it was like making records then *and* now:

TG: Why did you make records?
BD: At that time they were like a document. *Also, I wanted to be famous . . .*
TG: Do you remember how you felt when you recorded [those] old albums?
BD: I was all wired up . . . *I was up for days at a time* . . . Those albums spooked me out. You don't sing songs like that and live a normal life. In order to be that strong on one level, you have to give up a lot in other ways . . . leaving nothing for your life at all . . . [Now] I know what I'm doing as far as music goes, and I feel I have a right to go and make a record any time I want, and . . . put on that record anything I want.*

In the end, *Esquire* decided not enough was on show and passed on Glover's world exclusive. And no matter how much Dylan sought to control the narrative of his own luminous past, some old friends still seemed intent on lecturing him about a supposed abnegation of his 'responsibilities'. Having become less assiduous at reading reviews after *New Morning*, he initially missed an interview by Roger McGuinn in a May 1971 *Melody Maker*, in which the Byrd lambasted the man who'd made him a star:

Does a performer have an obligation to the public? If so, [Dylan] has shook that obligation. I find it disappointing to see someone who was so brilliant, come down to such a mediocre show. After *Self Portrait*, I thought that was sufficient to pull him together, I thought the next was going to be great. Yes, like you, I regarded him as a brother, I wanted to protect him from criticism. But somehow that feeling has gone . . . I

---

* The italicised comments are handwritten additions Dylan made to Glover's typed transcript.

don't think [The Byrds] owe anything. He owes me something. Somehow, he doesn't appreciate what we did for him . . . 'Tambourine Man'
was a big asset for him, and when we continued recording his stuff, it
gave him a real boost.

It is an astonishing outburst from a man who hadn't made a decent
record since he drove the last pukka songwriter – Gram Parsons – from
'his' band in 1968; someone who owed Dylan 'everything, always'.*
The Byrd-brain didn't have to wait long to find out what the man he'd
traduced thought. In September, Dylan entered Columbia's studios
again, to record four old songs for a second greatest hits his label
wanted for the Christmas market.

This time Dylan had decided to get hands-on – really hands on –
selecting the tracks and adding a number of unreleased recordings.
Lucky he did – a double-album *Greatest Hits* from a man who had
enjoyed exactly one big hit, 'Lay Lady Lay', since the last greatest hits
was rather subverting the format.†

Unhappy with how the basement tapes sounded, he decided to re-
record three of its most era-defining songs – 'I Shall Be Released',
'Down In The Flood' and 'You Ain't Going Nowhere' – as well as 'Only
A Hobo' from 1963.‡ He evidently had a stripped-down sound in mind
even before arriving at Columbia on September 24th for his first acoustic session since January 1965; there to await his only accompanist,
Happy Traum:

> I got a call from Bob . . . asking me if I'd like record some songs with
> him . . . Could I do it tomorrow, and would I bring my guitar and banjo.
> I was fairly casual about the whole thing . . . As neighbours in Wood-
> stock, we often picked together informally, so it wasn't a great leap to
> take what we had been doing in the living room into the studio. So,
> laden with all sorts of instruments, I took the bus from Woodstock to
> New York City . . . To my surprise, the entire session consisted of just

---

* *'All of us will owe him everything, always.'* – Jean-Luc Godard, referring to Orson
Welles.
† It still managed to outsell all of his pukka albums to date, save *Nashville Skyline*.
‡ He had originally planned to include 'Who Killed Davey Moore?', when it was just a
single album. Also deleted from the final album at the last minute was a stereo 'Can
You Please Crawl Out Your Window?'.

Bob and me and the engineer in the big, nearly-empty studio. The first song Bob suggested was 'Only a Hobo', one of the tunes he had recorded eight years earlier as Blind Boy Grunt . . . After two takes it was obvious that it wasn't coming together, so Bob dropped the song. Fortunately, the next one, 'I Shall Be Released', immediately caught the right spirit and we relaxed into the music . . . I joined in singing on the chorus, and before I knew it, Bob was grinning and we were on to the next song . . . I had heard 'Down in the Flood' in bits and pieces during the Basement Tapes sessions, but the version that we did at this recording was totally impromptu . . . Again, Bob was strumming the rhythm with his flatpick, so I just tried to complement his singing with some sliding licks and bluesy, fingerstyle fills . . . The whole thing went by so fast that I didn't realize it was a take until we played it back. Finally, we cut . . . 'You Ain't Going Nowhere'. Bob set the pace with a strong rhythmic strum, and I tried to give the tune a rollicking, joyous feel with a frailing banjo part . . . We nailed it in two takes. [1999]

In fact, Dylan recorded 'You Ain't Going Nowhere' immediately after 'Only A Hobo', in five takes, four complete. As he well knew, it was one of the tracks with which The Byrds had 'invented' country-rock a year too late, back in 1968. All of the takes had an opening verse that now ended, clear as day, 'Pack up your money, put up your tent, McGuinn/ You ain't going nowhere.'* The session was a delight. All three Big Pink tracks were used on the well-received double-album, without coming close to the Big Pink originals.

As the Isle of Wight had previously proven, Dylan could connect to these songs even when the night was dark and the ground cold. And just to prove it was no fluke, on New Year's Eve 1971 he made a surprise appearance at the final Academy of Music show by The Band – recording their defining double-album, *Rock of Ages* – and blew the horn section off the stage. Of the four songs he did, two were basement-based, 'Down In The Flood' and 'Don't Ya Tell Henry', both good enough to be released. But when the album appeared the following August, Robbie the spokesman explained, 'Four songs with

---

* I say clear as day, but not apparently to the inept transcriber responsible for the version in the gargantuan, annotated, 'Ricks' edition of *Lyrics* (2014), who has: 'Pack up your mind, put up your tent in the wind.'

Dylan . . . is a lot [for a] record. Like, it wasn't the Band / Bob Dylan Concert. He came to watch and got up there like a friend. But I would have liked to [include] 'Down in The Flood'. . . . It's a shame we couldn't use it.'

The question is, why not? Dylan was out of contract with Columbia by the time the album appeared, and they didn't own the original recording. Because the bootleggers also missed the show, it was thirty years before the full four-song encore was released on a Deluxe *Rock of Ages*, including a truncated 'Don't Ya Tell Henry' – that is to say, Dylan omitted the following verse he had sung back in 1967:

> Now I went down to the whorehouse the other night,
> I was looking around, I was out of sight.
> I looked high and low for that big ol' tree
> I looked upstairs but I didn't see nobody but me.

Pure basement mettle. Yet Dylan, it seems, now wanted to rework seven basement songs found on a stray reel in March 1971, starting with 'Don't Ya Tell Henry' – which he cleaned up – and 'Sign On The Cross' – which he rendered nonsensical. Both were copyrighted in August, in time for McGuinness Flint to cover them on an LP of unreleased Dylan, the Manfred Mann-produced *Lo & Behold* (1972) and, more tellingly, for an edition of his collected lyrics.

A collected edition of his lyrics, provisionally called *Words* – designed to supersede European bookleg bestsellers like *Words To His Songs* – prompted him to finally copyright some songs the bootleg brigands had stumbled upon, like 'I Wanna Be Your Lover' and 'She's Your Lover Now'. He also drafted an extra verse for 'Minstrel Boy', beginning, 'The sky turned yellow on Cajun Nell/ Making her a promise is a heavy load'; while in 'Apple Suckling Tree', 'The forty-nine of you go burn in hell,' became, 'The forty-nine of you like bats out of hell.'

He would work on his collected lyrics through 1971-72, even as he set aside time to tinker with the likes of 'Bourbon Street', 'Santa Fe' and 'All-American Boy', none of which were under consideration for *Writings & Drawings* (as *Words* became). He still felt like 'completing' them, which was more than could be said for the songs in his 1971-72 notebooks, some of which would form the endpapers to the 1973 edition of

Writings & Drawings, with titles like 'Bowling Alley Blues' and 'Field Mouse From Nebraska'.

Were these meant to be indicative of what he was writing now? There was no way of knowing. He wasn't recording any new songs and the original typed sheets were cut-up on the page. Oh, and the two most telling lines, at the bottom of the first endpaper – 'singsomething-safe' [sic] and 'is it right to think about what [one] can do or is it right to think about what one has done?' – actually date from 1964-65, proving that Lennon wasn't the only one playing *Mind Games* in 1973.

Even the contemporary lyrics were cut up, Dylan deleting the best verse from a song about a telephone girl: 'I love a switchboard operator/ She's the one that I adore/ I wear shoes made out of alligator/ When I take her dancing across the floor.' Also removed was a song with the intriguing notion, 'I walked into the store where they were selling trained serpents . . .' Nor did he use, 'Oh brother can't you see it now/ Egypt is burning and they're all wondering how/ Oh sister can you not see/ Egypt is burning so mysteriously.' These all remained fragments, some petering out after a couple of lines, others – like the one below – lasting a couple of exploratory verses before hitting a brick wall:

> As I walked back from the boarding house
> I looked to my rear
> Two strangers were talking and another one was near
> One could not help but overhear them say
> I got good reason to be here
> And I need you right by my side
> Breathing down my neck/ poor forgotten stranger
> I am just a Falstaff Rambler . . .

He proceeds to profess a love for her 'sweet meat', which has brought him to her door 'thru rain, thick and cold'. But by now the amnesia was real, and it was remorseless. Hence, perhaps, a note to himself in one 1971 notebook, 'People I never knew ten years ago come up and say, Hey, remember me, and I don't.' The past was a foreign country and, like the sailor in *The Death Ship*, he'd lost his passport. He even joked in one lyric that he 'had some roses with me when I came/ but I can't for the life of me remember/ Just what I did with them or what month it is/ Perhaps it is September.' He wondered to himself why his 'poems don't rhyme anymore . . . I can't remember if they ever did.'

Only when he put words to images did they seem to connect up; hence, the decision to change *Words* into *Writings & Drawings*, and to create an alter-ego called Morris Zollar who drew some surprisingly literal drawings to accompany the lyrics – five of them in the basement tapes section alone. The funniest of them, weirdly enough, related to an instrumental from his most successful album, and so was hardly likely to feature in a collected lyrics. It was attached to a self-portrait of Dylan singing the first line of 'My Back Pages':

MORRIS ZOLLAR "WANTS TO KNOW".
About the Nashville Skyline Rag.

What does he "want to know?"
Does he want 2 no
If it cleans good
Yes, will it shine his windows?
YOU BETCHA!

In an aside to the above, he has written two words in capital letters – DISREGARD THIS – alongside two arrows pointing to the following: 'What was that, that Henry Miller said about artists in America? Yes he said America first classifies, then attempts to ossify him, that America is no place for an artist, that a cornfed hog enjoys a better life. Where did he say that?'*

In the end, the drawings were used without reference to Zollar. His only appearance in *Writings & Drawings* would be on the final page, when he asks how far it is to the nearest tatoo parlour. In draft form, Morris is told he ' "can't git no" TATOO', while on the published page he is informed 'the secret is out'. Presumably, that secret was that Dylan didn't have much to say and was content to watch the river flow, or would be, the second he got out of the city.

Writings & Drawings didn't appear until 1973. As its editor, Robert Gottlieb, remarked on publication, 'I know it wasn't a rushed,

---

* It comes from the 1944 monograph, *The Plight Of The Creative Artist In The United States Of America*.

overnight piece of hysteria because too many books happen that way and I can recognize the signs. There was nothing sloppy or careless or rushed . . . about this.'* It also closed the book on Big Sky. Dylan and Grosssman's joint publishing agreement expired quietly in June 1971, leaving the singer-songwriter free and clear to start again – or put his feet up.

He did the latter, though he wasn't about to tell the courts that, insisting in a sworn statement in September 1971 relating to a vexatious legal dispute about a piece of Woodstock property he almost bought in June 1968, 'that in view of my professional commitments, [I ask] reasonable latitude be given in fixing the time and place of any depositions'. What commitments, pray tell?

To celebrate his new-found independence, he agreed to appear alongside his new friend Leon Russell, his old friend George Harrison, and the man looking to steal his best friend's wife, Eric Clapton, at a concert for Bangladesh, where floods had destroyed crops to leave millions starving.

Harrison was still trying to extract himself from Allen Klein's clutches when he and Dylan ventured onstage at Madison Square Garden on July 31st to soundcheck 'If Not For You'. Suddenly, to Harrison's consternation, his friend began to get cold feet, 'He saw all these cameras and microphones and this huge place. He [started] saying, "Hey man, this isn't my scene, I can't make this." . . . I was just tired of trying to organize the whole thing, and he was saying, "Got to get back to Long Island, got a lot of business." ' In the end, Dylan did honour his obligation to a good friend, playing two five-song sets drawn wholly from before the crash. It had been touch and go.

Dylan graciously let Apple release his entire evening set on a three-LP boxed-set of the concert and, according to Braun, without 'getting a penny', using as leverage with his own label the fact that his 'contract comes up for renewal shortly'.† Though Columbia had been pushing

---

* What a shame the same cannot be said about the three subsequent editions of Dylan's collected Lyrics.

† Officially, Columbia was the only label to take a small cut for Dylan's services – 25 cents profit on each set. Capitol claimed a huge amount of expenses, but backed down and did the distribution, etc., for cost, after Harrison shamed them on The Dick Cavett Show. In theory, Apple weren't taking a penny from the project, beyond costs. But they were being looked after by Allen Klein, and the general consensus is that he

Dylan to re-sign for some months, he continued to keep them at arm's length. The fact that the tracks with Traum were part of a separate contract, dated October 26th, should perhaps have clued in Columbia that this wasn't going to be easy.

And yet, a month later a draft contract was sent to Dylan, via Braun, for his signature. It was due to run for five years from July 1st, 1972, and would pay Dylan a $666,500 per album advance for the first three albums, $250,000 for a third *Greatest Hits* and would allow him to appoint 'an independent producer'. It even acknowledged that the days of recording at Columbia's behest were past, one clause spelling out the way the wind was blowing: 'In furnishing the services of the Producer hereunder, you shall have the status of an independent contractor and nothing herein contained shall contemplate or constitute you and/ or the Producer as our employee or agent.'

Like a number of other twice-shy artists, he was now licensing the label his work – for seven years – after which 'we shall, subject to [the advances being recouped], assign to you all of our rights in such master recordings'. Nor could they do anything with any leftover tracks, having promised, 'during the three-year interval immediately succeeding the expiration of the term hereof . . . not [to] employ any master recording . . . unless such master recording is approved by you for such purposes.' Finally, 'after the tenth anniversary date of the expiration of the term of the 1971 Agreement, [Columbia shall] . . . assign to you all of our rights in each master recording recorded under the pre-1971 Agreement before the date November 29, 1971.' He was clawing back his recordings, track by track. Or he would have been, if he had *signed* the contract.

In fact, as Columbia attorney Elliott Goldman advised his new boss in June 1973, 'Although final contracts were prepared, signed by us and sent to his attorney, they were never counter-signed by Dylan.' It had been Goldman's former boss, Clive Davis, who had 'negotiated [the] contract with David Braun . . . and had it prepared for Dylan's signature. Everything seemed fine. But then Dylan decided not to sign

---

ended up taking his own cut as the project's 'manager'. *New York* magazine did an investigation at the time (28/2/72), and reckoned that there was as much as $1.14 unaccounted for on each set sold, and the suspicion remains, Klein took it. (Thanks to Peter Doggett for the above info.)

it. He said he just wasn't able to make a commitment to *anyone* for that long a time . . . [He said] he simply was emotionally unwilling to be tied down.' In so doing, he left the door open for an album like *Dylan*, Columbia's bottom-of-the-barrel retort when he later jumped labels.

For now, Dylan would keep them guessing. As late as July 1972, internal CBS memos were suggesting they still thought he might sign. But by then Dylan had decided 'he wouldn't take shit from no one/ he wouldn't bow down or kneel,' lines he'd sung on his last offering for the label, ten years to the month after he made his first. Nor was he about to let 'em bleep out what was just a four-letter word, putting the song on both sides of the single, released eight days after he recorded it on November 4th, to stop DJs flipping the single.

The song was called 'George Jackson' and it eulogized a man who, in the words of one website, 'was little more than a crook, a petty thug and ultimately a murderer'.* Fittingly, Jackson was gunned down whilst trying to orchestrate a jail breakout. Five hostages – three guards and two white prisoners – were afterwards found dead in his cell. Though Dylan had a long history of seeing criminals as victims, never before had he written something this trite ('Sometimes I think this whole world is one big prison yard/ Some of us are prisoners, the rest of us are guards.'), about someone so contemptible.

On both fronts, he was shadowing an old friend. John Lennon had been writing turgid pro-IRA, pro-black power polemics for his latest platter – the commercially catastrophic *Some Time in New York City* – when he invited Dylan to a session he was producing at Record Plant with local protest singer and pot smoker, David Peel. Lennon had previously sent Dylan a signed copy of his *Plastic Ono Band* album with an arrow pointing to the circled words 'I don't believe in Zimmerman'. When Peel began singing 'The Ballad Of Bob Dylan', which asked, 'Who is Robert Zimmerman, where does he belong?', Dylan walked out.

When 'George Jackson' appeared, elements of the press accused him of doing it just to get the 'Protesty people' off his back; as did Joan Baez, who had written something equally yearning weeks earlier. Called, 'To Bobby', it begged him to (re)join The Cause (see section

---

* Funnily enough, Jackson's woke-like Wikipedia entry describes him as 'an African-American author'.

heading). In *Chronicles*, Dylan describes Baez's 'song call[ing] out to me from the radio like a public service announcement'. In fact, it hadn't even been released, merely quoted in a *New York Times Magazine* cover-story by Anthony Scaduto. The article prompted Baez to write and explain herself, impolitically point out that they were both now thirty and 'that in some strange way I'll always remain very close to you'. Just to prove some telepathic contact endured, Dylan phoned her just as she was finishing the letter, something she described in a P.S. as 'quite an experience'.

If Scaduto's article inadvertently put the two ex-lovers back in touch, it burnt any bridges which remained between him and 'Bobby'; so much so that the following February Dylan stopped by the *Village Voice* offices to find out why they had not printed a letter he had written about his biographer. According to 'Random Notes', 'The letter, rejected by [the] editors as being malicious and "full of slanderous statements," was a severe castigation of . . . Scaduto and anyone else who questioned Bob's motives in writing and singing "George Jackson."'

Like many before and after him, Scaduto had fallen into the trap of thinking he could be Dylan's sounding board and an independent critic at the same time. It wasn't like he hadn't been warned by Dylan. The first time they met in January 1971 to discuss the biography he had just completed, he'd been told, 'Six months from now I won't care any more. But now I want to help you.'

That help came at a price – he wanted to see what Scaduto had written – and for a reason. A.J. Weberman, a self-styled Dylanologist who'd been rifling through Dylan's bins since shortly after he moved to MacDougal, had told the singer the book was some kinda exposé. Dylan soon learnt he had far more to fear from Weberman, whom Tony Glover had warned him about as far back as October 1970, asking if he knew 'this psycho named A.J. Weberman? I met him recently, and man is he sick? He brags about going thru your garbage cans to get clues.' After initially engaging with Weberman in person and by phone, trying to gauge his motives, Dylan extracted from him a promise to stop searching his rubbish looking for clues as to his 'Current Bag', a pledge he did not keep.

Meanwhile, Scaduto's book served as a timely reminder that he'd once threatened to write his own book about 'the simple years'. As he told the reporter in their last conversation, 'I never thought of the past. Now I sometimes do. I think back sometimes to all those people I once did know. It's an incredible story'; remarkable enough for Scaduto's collection of first-hand Village anecdotes to make the *New York Times*'s bestseller list. The book Dylan was planning to write, though, would be more fiction than fact.* As he told Glover in one of their March conversations, 'I got a lot of stuff I want to tell . . . but I don't want to tell it the old cornball way. A real writer knows how to hold it all up – he can then place the facts wherever he feels like it.'

Dylan hoped by looking back, he might find a way forward. As he wrote in a 1971 notebook, 'Got to get back to Minnesota, got to see where I'm coming from.' Instead, he continued trying to convince himself MacDougal Street was his home, even accepting an invite to a neighbour's cocktail party, to which he brought Dave Amram:

[Myself,] Sara and [Bob] . . . were looking through the window and I said, 'Man, I'm glad to be with you guys, this looks like a pretty weird scene.' . . . They were older people, very well dressed, beautiful Village townhouse, everybody drinking cocktails, and I was trying to read everybody's body language, and [they] looked like a bunch of really tense people . . . not . . . hanging out, just relaxing, sitting on the floor, drinking a glass of wine and rapping, the usual scenes we enjoyed. And Bob said, 'I don't know what kind of a scene it is, but after I've been there, it's gonna change.' And he laughed. So we walked in there and all these successful, established people – when they suddenly saw Bob Dylan walk in – completely freaked out and became like gawking high-school students . . . I said, 'My God, man, what it must be like to have to deal with that all the time.'

The mind-guard role was one Amram assumed on another occasion that fall, after Dylan called him up to say Allen Ginsberg and Gregory Corso, his two favourite beat poets, were doing a reading at NYU's Loeb Student Center, did he wanna come? Sure:

---

* In April 2022, the University of Minnesota Press published *The Dylan Tapes*, a partial set of transcripts from the interviews Scaduto did. They include his first conversation with Dylan, where he discusses his own memoir.

Bob came over and played the piano a little bit . . . Then we got up and
went over to Loeb . . . And Gregory was in top form! . . . During intermission, we went up to say hi to them. . . . Allen was thrilled. He said in
a surreptitious whisper, 'D'ya think you could get Bob to come over to
my place afterwards? I'm working on some music and stuff.'

Dylan proved surprisingly amenable when Ginsberg started ped-
dling the idea of setting improvised poetry to music, an idea which had
always appealed to him. But no sooner had he picked up a guitar in
Ginsberg's 10th Street apartment to tune it, Amram caught sight of,
'Allen push[ing] down a button on a tape-recorder, which he had . . .
plugged in, ready to start taping us. Bob looked over and said, "Turn
that goddamn thing off." . . . I thought Dylan was gonna walk out.'
Thankfully, his paranoid visions of beat-poet turned bootlegger
soon passed. By evening's end, Dylan got so enthused by the idea that
he turned to Ginsberg and said, 'Why don't we go over to the studio
and do this?' Encouraged, Ginsberg used his friendship with Lennon to
secure state-of-the-art studio, The Record Plant, for two days in
November, looking to produce a largely spontaneous set of songs (save
for the epic 'September On Jessore Road', penned for the occasion).
Amram was again on hand to witness, 'Ginsberg attempt[ing] to coax
Dylan into improvising some lines of his own. He all but clammed up,
asking leading questions of Allen [like], "What are we doing? What
exactly is this?" '*
They would be Dylan's last studio sessions for a while. He was tired
of the city and though he wasn't planning on getting 'back to Minnesota', he now made a gesture to that past self, Just Bob, by inviting
childhood chum, Louie Kemp, to come visit. Now a successful seafood
importer, and a regular traveller, Kemp got the message through
Dylan's Minnesotan social secretary, Beattie, 'If you're coming to New
York, he'd like to see you.'
It was a surreal experience for them both. Kemp, who saw a lot of
Dylan in the ten days he was in town, sensed his restlessness. One
afternoon, when they were 'sat in the apartment building's small courtyard, Bobby gestured toward the fence, through which we could see

---

* Dylan does sing on two songs, 'Put My Money Down' and 'For You, Oh Babe For
You', both later bootlegged.

the building's garbage cans . . . Apparently . . . people rifled through them regularly, he told me, to find out more about the mysterious Bob Dylan. When I realized he wasn't joking, I said, "Well, . . . I guess that means you've arrived!" Bobby laughed, but there was a strange expression on his face – part resignation, part irritation.'

Kemp didn't stick around long enough to see the 'Who Threw The Fucking Glass' Dylan, a month or two later, when Weberman resumed rifling through the rubbish to impress an Associated Press reporter. Sara, seeing him there, freaked out. Dylan went looking for him and when he found him – on nearby Elizabeth Street – became a white George Jackson, pounding his head on the pavement until 'some hippies came along and broke it up'. He had had enough of Weberman, and all those who intruded on his privacy.

He even tried to erect a stucco wall to section off his part of the back garden from his neighbours, in what was a communal area for *all* the residents on that block. He was told by the tenants association's Bob Rubin, in no uncertain terms, that the wall would have to come down. Dylan's response was a letter which showed the man who wrote 'Positively 4th Street' was alive and kicking, in which he threatened to turn his expensive townhouse into 'a zombie monastery opened to drugged out, fagged out . . . jaded dregs', and to turn over a set of keys for the garden to the same folk, in order that they may interact with the well-to-do residents in the communal square that was their exclusive play area. He signed off, sarcastically, 'In your good graces, Bobby.' One neighbour simply took matters into his own hands, with calamitous consequences. Waiting until the Dylans headed out of town, he attacked the wall with a sledgehammer with such gusto he collapsed from a heart attack.

Unbeknownst to the cocktail crowd, the Dylans hadn't simply taken a vacation, they had temporarily relocated to Arizona, trying, in Dylan's words, 'to cool out for a while. New York was a heavy place . . . I needed to lay back for a while, forget about things, myself included.' Scottsdale, the posh part of Phoenix even then, seemed like the perfect retreat. His mother even connected him with an old family friend, Bob Finkbine, who was already resident and could be relied on not to invade his space, being a regular guy who just happened to like his music:

> Unknown to most Valley residents, Bob [Dylan], the ex-model Sara who was then his wife, and their children had secretly moved to Scottsdale

that [spring]. They had come down to see his mother, Bea, who wintered there, and decided to stay on. The Dylans rented a roomy ranch house on the northeast corner of Scottsdale Road and Lincoln Drive . . . My wife's grandmother had been a close friend of Dylan's grandmother, Anna Zimmerman, [and] his mother and my mother-in-law, Mary Chessen, had known each other as little girls in Duluth. Bob enjoyed Scottsdale. Here he was able to be just another person. He and Sara were, for the most part, unrecognized and unbothered. They went shopping, [went] out to eat or to the movies without the burden of fame.

Try as he might, though, Dylan couldn't escape reminders of his good ol' used-to-be coming through on the radio – notably 'Heart Of Soddin' Gold'. Even his wife couldn't stop herself from twisting the blade. Finkbine remembers one occasion when he was 'sitting in Dylan's kitchen drinking coffee one afternoon, [and] I asked him, "Bob, did you ever have a time when you had trouble writing?" Sara turned from fixing sandwiches at the counter and quipped, "Try the last two years." ' So much for speaking 'like silence'.

Stung to the quick, Dylan picked up the guitar, 'Actually, I've been tinkering around with a new song . . . I wrote it for Jesse,' the most boisterous of his children. He proceeded to play, 'Forever Young', his first song of note in a year, though not the only song he'd recently written about a childlike person. The other one was not quite so hymnal: 'What's day is day and what's night is night/ It takes a lot of strength to see the light/ And our differences must be reconciled/ Although you're a stubborn child.' Was this about a child or a woman? He wasn't about to say.

The thirty-something Dylan remained belittled by doubt, and the song was never finished. As he admitted to Randy Anderson in 1978, 'Insecurity in the area of being able to write and perform? I had that for a while . . . around '72, '73. I wasn't sure what I was gonna do and didn't really feel much like singin' and playin' – or writing.' And yet, he proved perfectly willing to sing and play for Finkbine and his friends, knowing the pressure was off:

In late spring ['72], Dylan joined me on several float trips down the lower Salt River . . . One trip was especially memorable. We put Bob in the HMS Fink with a gifted Arcadia graduate and folk singer, Craig Stromme, and a buddy of Craig's named Ray Sohm . . . In with the three performers and their guitars we packed the ice chest of beer. Then we were off, the guys wanging and singing away, and the rest of us floating alongside . . . It was a floating Dylan concert . . . [Then] unexpectedly, someone in the boat shifted his weight and it capsized . . . Bob, Craig and Ray [were] treading water like crazy, feet churning and guitars held high over their heads [till] we hit shallow water.

What had been an enjoyable couple of months had left Dylan refreshed and reinvigorated. But he knew there was some business he needed to attend to in New York, some decisions he was required to make. As the days ticked down on his Columbia contract, he arranged to meet with Mo Ostin and Joe Smith, point men for Columbia's west coast rivals, Warner's:

Joe Smith: He wanted to meet us and find out where we were at, personally. He was interested in the differences between companies, how records are distributed and marketed . . . But he was indefinite about what he wanted to do. He was bored, and he didn't want to, or seem able to, get it together for an album at the time . . . But we didn't talk terms or anything . . . We just told him if he wanted to talk further, we'd be prepared to talk.

Warner's was not about to leave it at that. Dylan was still the big fish in the singer-songwriter pool of talent, and they were hoping to reel him in. In October, Dylan got a letter from old friend Mary Martin, now working with Lenny Waronker at Warner's. She was writing on behalf of 'the good folk of Warner Bros. . . . [whose] talents bloom in the studio with Arlo, Randy, Gordon and Van, and to be honest, they were just a little shy.' Despite her offering 'visiting privileges' for his former cat, now named Rolling Stone, Dylan did not rise to the bait.

He did, at least, resume experiencing live music that summer, catching Elvis at Madison Square Garden in June, and attending the Mariposa Folk Festival on Toronto's Central Island in mid-July, where the likes of David Bromberg, Louis Killen, Jean Ritchie, Mike Seeger, Hazel Dickens & Alice Gerrard, Gordon Lightfoot, John Prine and Taj Mahal – a veritable who's who of his favourite folk performers – were all performing. On the Saturday afternoon there was even a workshop hosted by Dave Bromberg, called 'the influences on Bob Dylan'.

Fellow attendee John Cohen noted, 'He was disguised as a hippy and had on a red bandanna,' and for most of the three-day festival he wandered around unrecognized, sans shades, sporting a curly mop and a moustache. But when he was finally spotted and the crowd closed in, Cohen sensed 'they wanted to take him apart. It's a very inhuman relationship to do that to somebody . . . to gang around him like he was a queen bee.' Dylan headed for the waterfront where the pretty Sue Kawalerski was standing, camera in hand. He asked her, 'Why aren't you listening to the music?' She replied, 'Because everybody's running from stage to stage hearing applause and thinking it's you!' before asking if she could take his photo. What she got was that rare thing, an unmasked man (see photo section).

A week later, he was just another rock star at Mick Jagger's post-MSG birthday party, in the company of Sara. The show he had just seen was the post-*Exile* Rolling Stones at their rollicking best. Arthur Rosato, who would become Dylan's assistant on his next tour, thinks the show 'had a big influence on him. That was the biggest thing going and Bob's a major rock & roll fan.' Yet, no sooner had he vacated the building than he was heading for a reunion with Bob Finkbine 'and friends' in their own private Idaho:

Having [been there] the summer before, I convinced Bob to meet us in Ketchum in August of '72 . . . Weekends were spent in the majestic Sawtooth and White Cloud mountains, and weekdays in Ketchum. We crashed at our friend Don Petelle's house . . . I loved our daily in-town schedule. We woke to a noon breakfast, played a no-holds-barred game of basketball on the little court across the street, then our four singers [Craig, Ray, Mark and Terry] and Bobby D. jammed and sipped wine in Petelle's backyard for the rest of the afternoon. They started each session by singing 'Ride Me High' [sic] . . . After supper, and a drink or two and pool game at the Casino, we drifted over to the Alpine . . . [Then] when everyone was shoved out into the night, our group – Dylan, the band and its few customers – would make our way to Don's house and jam the rest of the night. Bobby D. would join in; a wiry guy named Hambone would slap his thighs and body in time to the music and we drank and sang the night away . . . Bob, a guarded man, was content to hang out with us because we treated him as a non-celebrity, just another guy to elbow on the basketball court, hit in football games, tell jokes and jive with. We never, but never, asked him about his music.

Such was his surprising willingness to be one of the boys, Dylan even allowed Finkbine to take holiday snaps of him sat around the camp fire playing guitar, bare-chested playing basketball, or hiking through the woods and fishing. It was almost like he thought he really 'could be happy being a blacksmith. I would still write and sing,' as he would insist in 1976. Who exactly was kidding who? As one Nineties girlfriend retorted, when he suggested they 'run away together, somewhere far away, [and] raise llamas', 'Yeah, I see you not getting bored with that for about all of two hours.'

Back in New York City by September, the restless, hungry feeling still gnawed away at him even as he maintained a hand's-length relationship with most musicians. He made an exception for Jerry Garcia and Leon Russell – introducing the two, taking 'Jerry G. up to the magician's place, [which] was unrewarding, maybe because of the pot.' Garcia told *Rolling Stone*, 'We just sat around and talked and picked . . . He wants to get out of the music world. He says he doesn't think it's right to go pick on a stage and get paid for it . . . He's in a house now with five kids in it. [He] has no time to write, no solitude.'

Fifteen years later, Dylan admitted he had always struggled to pull off this particular balancing act: 'You have to have the isolation to write. . . . There was a time when nobody cared, and that was one of the most productive times – when nobody gave a shit who I was – . . . [But as] you get older, you start having to get more family-oriented.'

Dylan summed up his mindset in real time in two sentences from a 1972 notebook, 'I'm cooling it! Too much rendezvousing, no sense of reunion.' When he sat in for a few days on some Doug Sahm sessions that October, he did so because, in Garcia's opinion, 'With Sir Doug, he didn't have to do a Bob Dylan trip.' He even bequeathed the Texas Tornado an original song, 'Wallflower', which had been lying around for almost a year.

But the most intriguing remark from Garcia concerning Dylan's plans was an aside, 'Anyway, he's into movies [now].' Sure enough, he had been in discussions with a novelist he knew through Bert Block, Rudy Wurlitzer, about appearing in a movie Rudy had been writing about Billy the Kid, in which he says he 'wrote the role of Billy with Bob in mind'. (They do share a physical resemblance.)

As befitted the author of *Nog*, Wurlitzer had his own conceit, telling film historian Paul Seydor he wanted 'to explore some parallels between the lifestyles and careers of rock stars and outlaw heroes of the Old West, specifically what it must be like to live your life to its fullest very early . . . climaxing "at one incandescent point, then it's over." '

Did he share this intent with Dylan? Probably not. But when MGM producer Gordon Carroll came on board, Wurlitzer continued pushing for an acting role for Dylan. As the project grew nearer to realization, Wurlitzer's 'conception . . . changed [and] I thought of Dylan more as Alias. Alias is an observer. He, more than anyone else in the film, is *aware* of Billy's legend.'

On October 18th, with discussions well advanced, Rudy sent Bob a note, 'If you have any questions, feel free to call any time.' Shooting was now scheduled to begin on November 13th, in Durango, with the combustible Sam Peckinpah – riding high on a critical wave of praise for *The Wild Bunch* – directing. Meantime, Dylan ran across an old acquaintance who had made the switch from photography to cinematography, Jerry Schatzberg:

> We caught up at a friend's wedding. I knew he was always interested in making films, in some capacity. By that point I had made three films, [so] he was like an interrogator; he wanted to know how I was able to make three films, how I knew how to make them, etc. I knew someday he would end up in some capacity in film.

Dylan also seems to have consulted the man cast to play Billy, Kris Kristofferson, before accepting the role of Alias. Like Schatzberg, the actor-songwriter realized, 'he wanted to learn about movies, even though he wasn't too wild about acting . . . He was also interested in Sam. He screened *The Wild Bunch*, and got so jazzed between that and [Rudy's] script that he wrote that [title] song.'

The song in question was a nine-verse ballad about Billy the Kid, a subject Dylan hardly had 'dibs' on. In it, he consciously alludes to the traditional ballad, where, 'Fair Mexican maidens play guitars and sing/ A song about Billy, their boy-bandit king.' Once again, he used a ballad to pass an audition. This time, though, he went straight to the director, turning up in Durango on November 23rd to woo Peckinpah, who after a largely liquid dinner, turned to the superstar, 'Okay kid, let's see what you got. You bring your guitar with you?!' By the third tune he was convinced: 'Who is that kid? Sign him up.' And so began Dylan's hellish sojourn in Durango, one that lasted through to the following January,* from which he would emerge with just one thought, 'I learned by working in *Pat Garrett* that there is no way you can make a really creative movie in Hollywood.'

What he didn't cope well with – and never could – was the downtime. As he opined on the set, 'The roughest thing about film making is the waiting between takes. I never realized it was such painstaking work . . . like a recording session' – one that lasted two and a half months. Or it did when Peckinpah was in charge and determined to do things his way. As the producer, Gordon Carroll, later noted, 'The picture was . . . a battleground from two to three weeks before we started shooting to thirteen weeks after we finished.' When Carroll refused to allow some scenes shot with an out-of-focus camera to be reshot, Peckinpah simply went behind his back.

Second unit director Gordon Dawson reports, 'Sam would tell me to set up a scene. Carroll would veto it, because it wasn't authorized. Then there'd be a race to see if I could get a wrap before they could rip it out.' Caught in the crossfire, Dylan confided in Kristofferson his growing concerns: 'He came up to me one day and said, "How important to you is it that I finish this picture?" And I said, "I don't care if I finish it." Then I realized he was serious and said, "Bob, it's important," and that son-of-a-gun stayed [for] the whole picture.'

If Dylan had hoped the experience might unlock his muse, the pipeline remained blocked. He even joined the cast during its own peyote-like ritual, telling a girlfriend in 1976, 'When I was in Mexico making *Pat Garrett & Billy the Kid*, everybody was eating [magic] mushrooms . . . They would all be tripping, but I'd barely get a buzz. Drugs don't do it for me anymore . . . You know how people on acid see a tree come alive? . . . That's how I see things all the time.'

To keep Dylan's spirits up, Kristofferson's girlfriend, singer Rita Coolidge, would duet with him 'until three or four in the morning'. At

---

* A brief Christmas stay at the Harrisons in Henley-on-Thames would be the one welcome respite.

some point, Wurlitzer – who was having almost as rough a time of it as Dylan, having been reluctantly 'drafted into being a witness to the actual filming' – told his girlfriend he was 'desperate to avoid the usual lingering involvement'. Left in limbo, the pair began writing their own film, based on a Truffaut classic Dylan had first seen with Suze:*

> Bob was really bored out of his mind 'cause you have to wait such a long time before being called, because Bob didn't have such a big part. So, he'd come to wherever my little scribbly shack was and was like, 'Alright, let's do something. What about [rewriting] *Shoot the Piano Player?*' It never got finished, we just started. I think if we had continued to work on it, it would have turned into *Shoot the Director.*

Part of the problem was that Dylan was no actor. Even after Rudy rewrote scenes to remove Alias's stutter, as soon as cameras rolled it was out of his hands. As he told Seydor, 'I wrote some scenes in Mexico, mostly about Alias . . . but by then Sam had taken over.' Dylan would later claim, 'I tried to play whoever it was in the story. But . . . there was nobody in that story that was the character I played.' Actually, Alias *was* based on an historical character, whom Rudy did his best to flesh out.

Kristofferson recalled one such occasion on set, when 'Rudy came in here . . . and asked me, could I help him with [the new Dylan scene]? He said, "You got to help me. My mind is blown, I feel like a TV hack. I been rewriting these scenes and nobody knows what we want." So we wrote one and Sam liked it. Dylan hasn't had anything to say and I wanted to get into some close relating things with him. Usually we're on a horse or something and he's so worried about hitting a mark, he's not even looking up at me. Bob's so down by now, he'll do anything.'

Just when it seemed things couldn't get any worse, a flu epidemic hit the set, devastating the crew. Almost everyone – including at least one of Dylan's children – contracted it. As did the director. Dave Marsh, down in Durango on assignment for *Creem*, described the situation he encountered as 'unhinged. Peckinpah was so sick that most mornings

---

* Producer Gordon Carroll's wife, Jean, captured some of the mood on the set in her diary (published in 1982), 'Rudy Wurlitzer . . . says Peckinpah is rewriting the picture with the help of his old TV scripts . . . Dylan's unhappy . . . Rita Coolidge says all that remains of her role thanks to MGM is that of "a groupie." '

it was all he could do to drag himself onto the set; there were a few mornings when he couldn't even do that . . . The project was both over schedule and over budget and MGM head James Aubrey is not known for his tolerance of *auterist* excesses.' By January 13th, when Dylan was scheduled to fly to Mexico City to start work on the film soundtrack, everyone who was anyone wanted to tag along. Marsh would soon hear about this lost weekend:

> The weekend before I arrived, Dylan and the rock'n'roll members of the cast headed for Mexico City to try to record the title song. With them went Coburn, screenwriter Rudy Wurlitzer, editor Roger Spottiswoode and a number of others. This intrusion on Peckinpah's domain wouldn't have been welcome under any circumstances, but it was an especial insult on this occasion: Sam had scheduled Saturday evening for a screening of his latest, *The Getaway* . . . Since nothing productive came out of the Mexico City session, the kind of brouhaha that has made Peckinpah famous seemed to be brewing. Peckinpah wasn't on the set until noon Monday. That was his way of getting back, someone said, 'for picking their movie over his.'

Peckinpah wasn't the only one pissed off at Dylan that weekend. The studio engineer foolishly tried getting him to retake 'Billy' because he kept hitting the mike. This was not 1963 though. Dylan merely snorted, 'Mmmm, too bad.' Kristofferson had brought along his band to accompany Dylan, seemingly unaware of how he worked: 'He was barely showing them something, they would almost learn it, and he'd move on to the next one. And they were trying to be so perfect for Dylan! But he wanted their first impressions. He's like a certain kind of painter . . . I thought he was just fuckin' with my band.'

At least Dylan got something out of the session, a way of working that steadily stripped the sound down to its core elements. A version of 'Billy 4' with just Terry Paul on bass would give him an idea of how to record his next but one album. The paucity of other usable material, though, made him realize that Jerry Fielding – hired to score the film, about whom Dylan audibly opines, '[He']s gonna shit when he hears this!' – was right when he 'asked that he write at least one other piece of music, because you cannot possibly hope to deal with an entire picture on the basis of . . . one ballad.'

If Fielding hadn't expected an ingénue, for once Dylan did as he was told, sketching out a gospel-infused song to augment (and ultimately replace) 'Goodbye Holly'. He brought it to Fielding, who shit himself a second time: 'He brought to the dubbing session another piece of music – "Knock-knock-knockin' on Heaven's Door." Everybody loved it. It was shit. That was the end for me.' The haunting simplicity of that all-time classic may have been lost on Fielding, but it wasn't on Peckinpah, who was one of those who 'loved it'.

Another manuscript in Dylan's hand, on TWA notepaper, emerged circa 2010, and tried to suggest he wrote some other verses, about putting guns on the wall 'before I lose them all', and asking someone to take 'these bells from [my] ears, I can't listen to them anymore'. They don't fit, and the two verses he did end up using were probably all there ever were. They were certainly all that was required – even if Carroll's edit, the one put on general release, used an instrumental version.

With the end in sight, Dylan finally started to relax a little and learn to enjoy a country he had long mythologised but never visited; a country his childhood friend, Larry Kegan – whom he had barely seen since their Minneapolis days – had made his home. After talking about possibly heading to Texas to play some dates with Doug Sahm, Dylan instead called up Kemp and asked if he'd like to come down to Durango – and to bring Larry, too:

Louie Kemp: So, one cold February morning, I gladly departed Minnesota yet again, this time for Mexico, where I was picked up by Larry and his Mexican assistant, Alfonso. Both of them had lived in Mexico for years and knew more about it than anyone on any Hollywood movie set. Soon we were skimming our way across the desert in Larry's trusted van, on the dusty road to Durango . . . I knew Bobby had deliberately waited until things were beginning to wrap up so he'd have some time to spend with us, and it worked out perfectly . . . Larry, Bobby, Harry Dean [Stanton], and I hopped in Larry's van and took off for Mazatlán. We stayed at a funky little hotel on the beach, where my three amigos jammed together and drank tequila, and I drank a hell of a lot of orange juice. At one point, Larry asked Bobby to sing one of his well-known songs; I can't remember which one. To my surprise – because who could deny Larry anything? – Bobby said no . . . After a few days, Bobby was starting to get recognized. [So] we hopped in Larry's trusty van and headed over to Guadalajara, where Larry had lived for a long time and run a facility for the disabled. We met a lot of friendly Mexicans, none of whom had ever heard of Bob Dylan but all of whom knew and loved Larry. Larry was enjoying being the star for a change.

In Kegan's company, 'Bobby' once again became that busking guitar-player singing for his supper. In Guadalajara itself, they frequented Toni Verling's pizza joint, where Kegan cautioned a local reporter, Carlos Nuno, not to try and get too chummy, 'He's been my friend for fifteen years and he comes here on condition that there is no trouble with the press. He doesn't want any camera[s] . . . He feels everything. [So] say hello, [but] don't talk too much. He's very smart, he will know what you've got on your mind and he will [just] leave.' Nuno did as he was told and was rewarded with an impromptu singing session insti-gated by actor Harry Dean Stanton, fresh from his own bit-part in Peckinpah's movie, who began declaiming some favourite Spanish songs, followed by the café owner. Finally, Dylan took hold of one of the guitars, much to Nuno's delight:

> At first he accompanied Larry and that's when he smiled the most. I suppose that those songs brought back memories of the times when they sang them together in Minnesota . . . Then the master gratified us with four covers, three of his own compositions and a Spanish version of 'Adelita'* . . . He said that the [original] songs he had just played . . . were brand new compositions.

Maybe there was life in the old dog yet. A three-song home tape made by Kegan at a party for Billy Vargas contains one new song, 'Stormy Weather'.† One presumes another of those he played at Toni's contained the memorable refrain, 'Knock-knock-knockin' on heaven's door.' Mean-while, back in L.A., a restless, angry Fielding was tossing and turning, unable to get that damned three-chord tune out of his head . . .

---

* Dylan would allow Harry Dean Stanton to cut 'Adelita' at the *Planet Waves* sessions, and would drunkenly tackle it himself during Eric Clapton's March 1976 *No Reason To Cry* sessions.
† Also on the tape is a song by Looking Glass called 'Brandy (You're A Fine Girl)', another song he hadn't been able to escape on the radio the previous spring.

3·7

March 1973 to February 1974: Bobby, You're So Far Away From Home

Who would want to live in a place [like L.A.], where the only cultural advantage is that you can turn right on a red light.

Woody Allen.

I was pretty spread out a few years ago, trying to do this and do that, and it didn't make much sense to me, I didn't get anything much out of it.

Bob Dylan, to Craig McGregor, March 1978.

The Kid always looks like the most endearing kind of guy. He's got a certain impish quality to him but he also looks like a Billy Budd type. The Kid was born with a halo. He beams with innocence. He can do no wrong. He can tell any kind of lie and everybody will always believe him. Nobody ever wants to suspect anything ill of The Kid. He can get away with all sorts of cons and he usually does.

Al Aronowitz.

Billy the Kid died at twenty-one, Jesus thirty-three, I've outlived both of 'em, but it's taken a toll on me. I wonder sometimes about the will to succeed, if it's worth it to go on.

Bob Dylan, January 1974.

He's not 'The Kid' anymore – so what can he be now?

Nat Hentoff's wife, on leaving Madison Square Garden,
30th January 1974.

If you play the song twice [in the studio] and you learn it, that isn't the best it's gonna be *to me*. But Bob doesn't want to mess with it anymore, and if it's got the essence there, then it's fine.

> Robbie Robertson, discussing *Planet Waves*, 1975.

★

Dylan had got out of Durango just in time. The first rough cut of *Pat Garrett & Billy The Kid* was supposed to be finished by February 13th. Unfortunately, the last few days' dailies didn't arrive back from L.A. – where they had been sent because the studio wanted to know what the hell was going on down there – until a week later.

As late as 2011, Rudy Wurlitzer still took the view that 'they had[n't] planned to take the film away from [Peckinpah]. But certainly that was the cause and effect . . . He had been going to war with them repeatedly, and it all culminated when a producer came down to look at the footage and Sam got up and peed on the screen.' Dylan was evidently still in Durango when this showdown happened, because Kristofferson, sat next to him, remembers, 'Bob turning and looking at me with the most perfect reaction: "What the hell have we gotten ourselves into?" ' What, indeed?

Not that there was ever any question in Kristofferson's mind that Dylan was on the director's side, 'Bob thought [Peckinpah] was an artist, and he respected him, [whereas] he always felt that the producer put [him] in the movie for his name value.' Dylan confirmed as much in a note he wrote after seeing the film, 'Regardless of its flaws, Sam Peckinpah's *Pat Garrett & Billy The Kid* is THE Billy The Kid movie.' He admired the director, who had taken a story 'where everyone knows the outcome' from the outset and produced something monumental.

Dylan even put his name to an extraordinary document Peckinpah sent to the studio in February. By now Peckinpah – and Dylan – were back in Los Angeles, where Sam 'staged a scene depicting himself on a hospital gurney looking as if he's being administered Johnny Walker intravenously, his middle finger raised to the camera, the gurney surrounded by several members of the crew. [Below the photo,] the memo read, "Sirs: With reference to the rumors that seem to be spreading around Hollywood, that on numerous occasions Sam Peckinpah has been carried off the set taken with drink, this is to inform you that those rumors are totally unfounded. However, there have been mornings . . ."'

The memo was signed not just by 'Alias', but by Coburn, Kristofferson, Dean Stanton and John Beck. Far from keeping it as an insider's prank, Peckinpah paid for a full page in the *Hollywood Reporter*, where it appeared on the morning of February 13th, the day the first cut was supposed to have been delivered. It was a declaration of war. Perhaps Peckinpah had overplayed his hand. The studio held all the cards. As Gordon Carroll's wife, Jean, noted in her diary:

> *Pat Garrett & Billy The Kid* is brought in twenty days over schedule and $1.5 million over budget. MGM needs cash. The studio moves the release date up and gives Peckinpah only two and a half months to edit. On the sly, MGM duplicates the work print and employs another cutter. Peckinpah's version runs between 122 and 126 minutes. The studio's runs 106.*

The film was now taken away from Peckinpah, a move which appalled Dylan: 'I saw it in a movie house one cut away from his and I could tell that it had been chopped to pieces . . . The music seemed to be scattered, and used in every other place but the scenes in which we did it for – except for "[Knockin' On] Heaven's Door."'

Dylan was not used to having his music used cavalierly, especially after he had gone to the trouble of arranging to (re-)record 'Knockin' On Heaven's Door' and yet more manifestations of 'Billy' in L.A., where he and his family had relocated after his Mexican jaunt. He even recalled bassist Terry Paul, forgave Roger McGuinn and remembered Jim Keltner, who all assembled at Burbank Studios, along with a bevy of backing singers, primed to capture a moment Keltner remembers to this day:

> ['Knockin' On Heaven's Door'] was a perfect example of a beautiful session and how Bob works. We went in, we heard Bob play the song maybe once or twice. He played, we played, and that was it . . . [] . . .

---

* Peckinpah's own 'preview' version would be released in 1988, replacing the studio cut, now almost impossible to find, although a new Criterion edition is reportedly imminent, and should include both.

In those days you were on a big soundstage, and you had this massive screen that you can see on the wall, [with] the scene . . . running when you're playing. I cried through[out 'Knockin' On Heaven's Door' from] . . . the combination of the words, Bob's voice, the actual music itself, the changes, and seeing the screen.*

Dylan was clearly relieved to be back in the studio, even breaking into an impromptu jam on the traditional 'Amarillo' and busking one of those inspired Big Pink-style 'improvs.', 'Rock Me Mama', riffing imagery assimilated from Arthur Crudup and/or Big Bill Broonzy. It was only a moment in time, and never meant to be more than that.

However, an intrepid collector – who would later work for Dylan – chanced on the session-tapes in 1994, and sent them underground.[†] 'Rock Me Mama' was duly singled out by the legendary Scorpio label for inclusion on their own *Genuine Bootleg Series*, which is where it came to the attention of Ketch Secor of the Old Crow Medicine Show, who added a couple of verses and rechristened it 'Wagon Wheel'.

The song was recorded by Secor's band in 2001 and subsequently by Darius Rucker, whose 2013 recording went triple platinum. Dylan's 50% share of 'Wagon Wheel's publishing, ended up netting him close to seven figures, pretty much demolishing the argument that bootlegs cost the artist money, even if Dylan continued to claim 'bootleg records . . . are outrageous . . . It's like the phone is tapped . . . and then it appears . . . with a cover that's got a picture of you that was taken from underneath your bed and it's got a striptease type title and cost[s] $30.'

If, by 1973, Dylan held bootleggers in little regard, he held rock critics in even less. But even he did not expect his first soundtrack album, when it appeared on July 13th, to be described as 'Merely Awful', by Jon Landau, in *Rolling Stone*. Landau went further, depicting the album as 'an extension of its myth-destroying predecessor *Self-Portrait*, a record

---

* Booker T, in his unreliable 2019 memoir, *Time Is Tight*, remembers 'there was Kris Kristofferson up on the screen' while they recorded 'Knockin' On Heaven's Door'. He wasn't on that session, playing on the second Burbank session, when 'Billy' and 'Turkey Chase' were on the menu.

† Thankfully, as the session-tapes never reached Sony. Dylan provides a suspiciously vivid recollection in a 2017 interview, 'I did record ["Wagon Wheel"]. It's on one of my old bootleg records. [It] just had a different title.'

which further eliminates the possibility of anyone placing Bob Dylan on a pedestal. It is every bit as inept, amateurish and embarrassing as the earlier album.'

Here was an astonishing attack from an unexpected quarter, and though Landau later admitted his comments 'were rooted in a complete lack of understanding of the album', it prompted Dylan to write something in his notebook, ostensibly about the critical reaction to the film itself, but smacking more of a retort to Rolling Stone, damning those who criticize what they don't understand. Dylan dismisses such critiques as mere 'foliage', put there merely to 'confuse the public and feed off the artist' until the sound and the fury they generate fades away 'in the mist of the incoming drum'.

The album in question, and the break-out single, 'Knockin' On Heaven's Door', had both appeared bearing the CBS label, despite the one man who had any understanding of Dylan there – president of the record division Clive Davis – having been unceremoniously fired on May 29th, accused of financial malfeasance.* According to Davis, he had been on the brink of concluding 'a new contract with Bob [that] was limited to a commitment for two more albums, plus the Billy the Kid soundtrack album – there was no time period involved . . . the guarantee was . . . $400,000 per album – . . . [But] Columbia [then] backed out of the deal after I left.'

The man who took over from Davis, Irwin Siegelstein, was not a music man at all; he was a bottom-line bean-counter. In fact, almost the first thing he asked to see was Dylan's sales figures, which required some working stiff to explain to both him and CBS president Arthur Taylor, by memo, 'Dylan's sales have typically been far below those of other so-called "superstars," but nevertheless it was felt that his image was sufficiently important to justify a royalty rate as high or higher than that paid to the top pop artists on the label.'

What the TV exec. failed to take account of was that these figures were for domestic sales only. But Dylan was a worldwide brand, who sold as well or better in other key territories like Germany, Japan and Britain, and CBS made more money from those territories because, in

---

* The sums involved, around $70,000 in expenses, came as Davis in three years turned the label into a money-making machine. This was a corporate coup, not a financial crackdown. Davis later sued the label, and Dylan testified on his behalf.

keeping with longstanding US corporate (mal)practice, they paid a substantially lower royalty (usually half) on overseas sales, despite invariably owning their subsidiaries outright in the more lucrative territories.

The figures also showed that Dylan's most recent release, the expensive and largely redundant second *Greatest Hits,* had sold close to a million copies domestically. Someone needed to spell it out to Siegelstein before Dylan jumped ship and went to one of their equally rapacious rivals. The well-informed in-house attorney, Elliot Goodman, tried to do just that, three days after Davis left the building:

> Dylan . . . has over the past year been in recordings by various artists as a sideman and also in the new film just released, *Pat Garrett & Billy The Kid.* He has also established a close relationship with Jerry Wexler of Atlantic Records and has received substantial offers from all the major record companies. These offers range anywhere from RCA's obviously 'loss leader' offer of $1 million per album plus $1.25 per album in royalty, to a $750,000 per album 95 cents per album [royalty] offer from Warner Bros.

Siegelstein saw units, not cultural artifacts. He was even toying with the idea of passing on the *Pat Garrett* soundtrack, to which the label had already committed. Only after Braun threatened legal action was a contract hastily agreed, and signed on June 19th. Had Dylan ever seriously considered signing Davis's previous deal, the trail was now cold. In fact, he instructed Saltzman to go after the label for outstanding royalties, conducting the audit Grossman should have called for back in 1967. Surprise, surprise, Columbia had miscalculated his royalties for the period 1967 through 1972 to the tune of more than $300,000. An agreement both parties drew up on October 26th, 1973, settling the dispute and paying Dylan in full, saw a chastened CBS admit:

> (i) that the CBS packaging cost deductions were improperly calculated.
> (ii) that the so-called "distribution discounts" were improper . . .
> (iv) that the method utilized by CBS in computing the wholesale price for royalty base purposes was incorrect.
> (v) that additional royalties were due because of assumed errors based on Dylan's inability to check unit calculations.

In other words, even after 1967 the label had relied 'on [an] inability to check' royalties against sales to orchestrate financial malfeasance on a corporate scale. And Dylan was finally calling them to account. But at what cost? If he thought that the bootleggers made some pretty bad stuff, anything they might do, CBS could trump. Within a week of the above settlement, Columbia announced they would be releasing an album called *Dylan*, 'consist[ing] of material recorded during 1969-70, the period of *Self Portrait* and *New Morning*. All the tracks, apart from "Mr Bojangles," are Dylan originals.'

It was obvious at a single glance that *none* of the tracks on the album – which according to *Melody Maker* had been 'assembled and remixed by one Mark Spector' – were 'Dylan originals'.* Even on the original sequence, which featured 'Running' and 'Alligator Man' as opposed to 'Big Yellow Taxi' and 'Can't Help Falling In Love', there were just three traditional songs Dylan could copyright to himself – 'Sarah Jane', 'Mary Ann' and 'Lily Of The West' – all from the *New Morning* sessions. The others were already spoken for.

A single listen confirmed the album was a turkey, minus the chase. Nor were Columbia's motives lost on industry insiders. One of them, David Geffen, who was actively courting Dylan, was prepared to call a digging tool a spade in print: 'It was blackmail,' he told *Melody Maker*'s Michael Watts, 'Columbia . . . wanted to re-sign him and were threatening the release of an album of three-year-old tracks as a [form of] inducement.' It only served to alienate the chess player further. He even considered taking legal action, instructing Braun to look into the possibility.

But when Braun hired the expert Joe Santora to advise on the likelihood of success, he was informed his client's chances were slim: 'From the facts before me, even assuming Dylan is not prevented from seeking an injunction by the agreements [he signed], he would have little chance of obtaining one unless the records to be released were blatantly distorted or so inferior as to suggest a design to intentionally injure him.'

This was exactly the intent, from a label which had the complete Manchester 1966 show sitting in its vaults, but knew full well that the

---

* I asked the only Mark Spector still in the Music Biz, Joan Baez's manager, about the album. He responded, 'No comment'.

moral rights the Berne Convention provided artists in every other civ-
ilized country did not apply Stateside. Watts didn't candy coat his own
view in *Melody Maker*, 'The release damns Columbia Records . . . as
money-grabbers, determined to grab their pound of flesh without specific regard for showing the artist at his best.' Bullseye.

Even the uncredited remix by Spector (in name only) seemed
designed to distort the original sound of the sessions, with the girlsingers no longer backing Dylan so much as drowning him out. That the
album went Top Ten on its release that December merely proved that
for all of Siegelstein's fabled bottom-line, even barrel-scraping detritus
by Dylan sold. On top of the worldwide success of 'Knockin' On Heav-
en's Door', it suggested Columbia had let an artist who in the eyes of
his audience never made a foolish move, slip through their grasping
hands – and into Geffen's.

Clive Davis, for one, had seen it coming, writing the following year,
'Irwin Siegelstein came from television, and couldn't be expected to
have a knowledgeable opinion.' He was soon struggling to compre-
hend how twelve million North Americans – nearly 4% of the
population – were prepared to pay top dollar to see this ex-CBS artist
in concert.

Dylan had not been idle in the months since relocating the family,
lock, stock and barrel to L.A., even drawing up grandiose plans for the
Malibu property he acquired in June from local sports writer, Jim Murray. As he would tell Craig McGregor, 'I found a man who was pretty
much like me in a lot of ways . . . He was a contractor, and he didn't
have hardly anything going . . . and he said, "Well you can do anything!
You just draw it up and we can do it." ' The problem with Point Dume,
as architect Dave C. Towbin later remarked, was that, 'asking Bob
Dylan if he's happy with [the plans], you never come up with a simple
answer . . . The dome [he wanted] was originally going to be an eagle's
nest; you know, just a little hideaway. Then it was going to be a [whale
watching] observatory, then something else.'

Initially, the move proved propitious. As the singer recalled, when
still considering covering this period in *Chronicles*, the Dylans were living nearby in a rented house when they heard Murray was selling up.
By the time Dylan had taken over his work studio, he was itching to
start work, so much so, he suggested he 'immediately wrote about
twelve or fifteen songs in about three days'.

Only two songs are actually known from the early months in L.A., though contemporary notebooks (and the back of business cards) contain a fair share of pithy little aphorisms, like, 'When they say that Christ walked on water, they meant he walked on a mirror, a reflection of his own self,' and/or, 'A poet is someone who writes but never reads what he writes.' He even references the ritual murder of 'Sir Hugh of Lincoln' which inspired a famous Child ballad: 'Just because 35 jews pounced on a little christian boy and killed him and mixed his blood in their stew.' A contemporary list containing (italicised) song titles provided further evidence he was re-exploring tradition:

> *Blackjack* / *Duncan* + *Brady* have their faces lifted
> Ragitty rag – Spanish-American / throttle /
> Williamsburg / *St James Hospital* / Vacuum
> Cowboy voodoo / Abduction / Venge[a]nce
> *Ella Speed* / *Charles Giteau*
> Chain Gang Dance / Shakespeare lynched
> Voltaire – Lucille / Tom Cat.

Meanwhile, Dylan struck a vein of musical gold in Malibu. 'Never Say Goodbye' and 'Nobody 'Cept You' were both demoed acoustically that June, along with 'Forever Young' (issued on *Biograph* in 1985). The first of these he had previously played to McGuinn, who was back in his good graces after 'he came over to my house and looked through my record collection. You know, he'll look at your books first, and then your records. [It's his way of] checking you out.'

Jolly ol' Roger was one of the few musicians in L.A. he already knew well. They even ended up trying to write a song together after McGuinn 'asked him if he had anything. He said he had one that he started, but he was probably gonna use it himself.' McGuinn told *Rolling Stone* that, although the songwriting session was a bust, Dylan did agree to play harp on a song the ex-Byrd had written which spoke to him, 'I'm So Restless'.

If 'Never Say Goodbye' was first in a series of love songs to his wife that would form the core of his 'comeback' album, *Planet Waves,* 'Nobody 'Cept You' would fall at the last hurdle.* It wasn't the only

---

* According to producer-engineer, Rob Fraboni, the song *was* mixed for possible inclusion on *Planet Waves.*

song he left unfinished as the plethora of song titles in the *Planet Waves*
notepads confirm. Stray fragments are everywhere. Connecting a title
to a set of lyrics soon becomes a game in itself. One such opening suggests they're looking to impeach the President and send him 'to an
island off France'. Said fragment concludes with a couplet that hints at
'Tangled Up In Blue': 'I was offered a job in the White House/ Running cargo to the baggage claim . . .'*

Other song-titles like 'Flagpole Renegade', 'Digger's Lament', 'Matinee Idol' and 'Rockin' Blues (Battle Zone)' – perhaps ideas he worked
on in Murray's 'abandoned work studio' – stayed as fragments. Other
ideas given block capitals in the notebooks included 'I'M A MAN, NOT
AN IDEA' and 'PRETEND NO MORE IT'S WHAT USED TO BE' (a
nod to the 'Wedding Song' theme perhaps). Meanwhile, 'Martha' –
later the dedicatee for 'Dirge' – was at this point an actual song with
the subtitle '(Down By The Canal)' and eleven verses. Another, 'Ruling
Kisses', used an idea which would blossom into 'Simple Twist Of Fate':

> It was just a simple romance, it was a casual love affair
> He was a bum on the Bowery, she was a college square.
> She came down to do a story on the town after dark
> He said he would talk to her, and they went to sit in the park.

The song-titles 'Street Angel' a.k.a. 'Warsaw Reunion', 'All & Everything (Stranger's Song)', 'Medicine Song' and 'Whirlwind (You Arouse
Me)' would soon mutate into 'Tough Mama', 'Nobody 'Cept You',
'Wedding Song' and 'Something There Is About You', respectively.
In 'Whirlwind's case, though, he would first jettison the notion of
'working in a leather store/ Making clothes that were tailor
made/ When she came in one day, closed the door/ . . . I pulled down
the shade,' the sort of scenario relocated to 1974's cast-aside masterpiece, 'Up To Me'.

He was hoping to build a bridge to a brighter future, without all the
parts yet to hand. For now, Dylan was content to work with what he
had and get to know the L.A. singer-songwriting scene – which had

---

* The initial Watergate hearings were held between May and August 1973. In the early
version of 'Tangled Up In Blue', the narrator would find himself 'loading cargo onto
a truck'.

overtaken New York's – centred as it was on the Troubadour, a legend-ary west coast nightclub and natural successor to the Whisky. Geffen offered to be his guide. Despite being gay, he was living with the boyish Cher, whom Dylan had known in New York back in the day, when she and Sonny were riding his folk-rock coat tails. But Dylan remained wary.

Also making a pitch for the son Allen Klein never had was that other survivor of the folk-rock wars, Robbie Robertson, who had moved west himself, tired of the upstate torpor that had enveloped the other members of The Band, most of whom had co-dependent junkie part-ners and were as such happy to play the odd festival and live off the proceeds till the next payday came round.

No sooner had Robbie relocated than Geffen invited him to his house for dinner, where he brazenly asked him, before the port was even passed around, 'What's Bob Dylan doing these days?' Robertson deflected, 'He's very involved with his family. He keeps having kids, so all you can do is get out of the way.' Geffen would not be blown off-course. He had an agenda and he aimed to stick at it. At another wine'n'dine a few days later, he suggested, 'You should get the other guys to . . . join you out here. We should put something together with Bob Dylan and The Band. It could be historic . . . You guys could make a lot of money.'

According to Robertson, the carrot Geffen offered was that he 'was willing to help put the tour together for free, if he thought he could get the live album or a new [Dylan] record on Asylum'. Geffen remembers it differently, insisting this discussion involved Dylan, too: 'Sometime during the summer, me, Robbie Robertson and Dylan were sitting around and thinking how great it was back in the Sixties and how dead and dull it is now, and I said, if they went out that would be what was happening. Bob said if it could be worked out without hassles, he'[d] do it . . . You see, Bob has been waiting for so long for somebody else to pick up the ball he threw down.'

In his memoir, Robertson claims he had already warned Dylan, '[Geffen] comes from the streets . . . You might want to go slowly and be careful what you wish for.' Dylan's unpublished account of these discussions, intended for Chronicles, rather suggests it was Robbie who tried to persuade him to work with Geffen, portraying the man as 'some kind of artists' friend'. A sceptical Dylan apparently snorted, 'So what!'

At this juncture, Robertson laid his cards on the table: he suggested they did a national tour, recording and releasing it on Geffen's label and perhaps even giving him 'a record of new unreleased songs'. Dylan supposedly responded, 'Sure, why not?' But according to Jonathan Taplin, former road manager to Bob and The Band, a savvy Dylan saw Geffen coming, and already had his eye on the lion's share: 'Robbie introduced David to Bob, and David just put on this push . . . [He assured Dylan,] All the perks would be there but . . . Bob would get to keep most of the revenue . . . Bob really liked that. The last time Bob had been out on tour, the promoter had paid him and kept all the rest.'

It seems the runes were once again aligned, as Geffen succeeded where others, including Jerry Wexler – with whom Dylan spent five days in August, recording at the fabled Muscle Shoals Sound Studio – failed. Wexler was a real music man; something to which Geffen only ever played lip service. His own motto was, 'Money – fuck, yeah.' Warner's insider Stan Cornyn described their tussle thus:

> Wexler assumed that the Courtship of Bob Dylan would be played: slowly, stately, a polite wooing like the ones upper-class boys . . . of Victorian England played out . . . kicking one another's shins, but with manners . . . Not [really] Geffen's game . . . David didn't look at artists' deal points, he looked into their eyes. Night and day. Geffen got home phone numbers. He'd call at ten-thirty at night to get an update or deliver one. It was like David was suddenly . . . woven into your life.

Wexler had recently agreed to sign Dylan's friend, Barry Goldberg – with whom he last shared a stage at Newport, during an electrical storm – to a one-album deal with ATCO on condition that the two of them co-produce the record. Dylan not only agreed, but went through all the material Goldberg had, some thirty songs, picking fifteen to record with Wexler. They included two instantly commercial songs Goldberg had written with Gerry Goffin, 'It's Not The Spotlight' and 'I've Got To Use My Imagination'. Dylan drove all the way to Alabama in his van, where he was as hands-off as he thought other producers should be:*

---

* Goldberg may have snuck a sly tribute to his friend onto the former, singing 'It *Ain't* The Spotlight'.

Barry Goldberg: He let me basically do what I wanted, putting absolutely no pressure on me. I'd have to ask him, 'Is this cool?' and he'd say,
'Yeah, man. [But] what if we did it a little more like this?' . . . Bob would
come out and say, 'Let's get this kind of feel on it,' and he'd play a riff
on the guitar . . . and he would make it better. In a song like 'Dusty
Country' . . . Bob would start playing it, and I'd play a more delta-type
style and Bob would add a folk-rock touch . . . Dylan didn't even want
to . . . sing on the album, because he didn't want people to say that [it's]
good only because he was singing on it.

Working with Barry Beckett again, and with Wexler for the first
time, Dylan stored away the experience for when the holy slow train
pulled in. Although the two Goldberg-Goffin songs became big hits for
Gladys Knight and Rod Stewart respectively, the resultant album
remains something of a lost treasure, albeit not for want of trying
from all concerned.

When Dylan finally began his own album of new songs, on November 2nd, he was back in L.A., and the sound was strictly country-rock – at
least on the finished artifact it was. Before that, he felt he needed
peace and quiet to finish up a handful of songs, and so he went to the
noisiest city in America, New York, for a coupla weeks in September,
still unable to reconcile family life with the need to work on new
songs.

Despite recent experiences, New York was where he still looked to
be inspired. This time it worked, even if the only song we can specifically locate and date to NYC is 'Tough Mama'* which Dylan states, in
his unused album notes, he wrote 'during HEAT WAVE & festival of
San Gennero, vengeance in the air, on a night where everything was
too correct.' Searching for the loft of the late ice-hockey player, Harvey
'Busher' Jackson, he instead 'saw the Temple of Madness, the Pawnee,
the Arapahoe, the Pueblo and the Apache.' The date for San Gennaro
was September 19th, and at this stage 'Tough Mama' made 'Dirge' read
like a love poem:

---

* Two separate drafts of these notes suggest he wrote two versions of 'Going Going
Gone' – subtitled 'Ben's Song' at this stage – one in California and one at Victor
Hugo's house in Paris. He did visit Paris at this time.

[2.] Primma Donna, sucking on the milk of bygone time
Why you wanna stand in front of a mountain they can't climb.
The cowboy's gone, he's up where the eagle flies*
He's riding with the lone wolf in them (dark) lofty skies . . .

[5.] Tough Mama, the world of illusion is at the door
I ain't gonna open my mouth & plead with you no more.
The balcony is falling, the Big Cats are in sight.
I'm packing up my belongings, I've lost my appetite.

Across multiple drafts, the song would veer between bitterness and regret. By the time it returned to earth, it had become a more yearning creature, '(Blue) birds of desperation are flyin' thru the skies/ Dark Beauty, I can see the sunrise in yr eyes.' Though in the interim he'd 'picked up some table manners', he still lacked an appetite. For what, pray tell? The will to succeed? Certainly not her body, for which his need had never been greater.

'Wedding Song' originally had the more ambiguous title, 'Wedding Song, Medicine Song', and more of a double-edge, containing lines like: 'My thoughts of you don't ever rest, they would kill me if I lie/ You put a strain on me sometimes, but I'll need you 'til I die.' Entering the confessional, he admits, 'When I was down and dwelt in poverty, you taught me to forgive,' perhaps referring to immediately after the accident, when he turned his back on the man he found lying at the side of the road.

Determined to avoid another *Another Side*, he was soon second-guessing some of the more personal lines in these songs, deleting both, 'You . . . made me know what is mine to give,' and the cryptic, 'Man chooses his own army, from whom even he can recruit,' from 'Wedding Song'. Also wisely dropped was a double entendre from the opening track, 'On a night like this, it's the proper time for love/ Come next to me, pretty miss, put your hand inside my glove.' He then removed a reference to 'a struggle deep inside' between faithfulness and creativity from 'Something There Is About You'. Dylan instead

---

* The cowboy, presumably another alter-ego, is a recurring motif in the drafts, appearing in the third verse as someone who 'stole the Golden Prize' and was 'riding in disguise'. An early manifestation of 'the Jack of Hearts'?

reserved his darker feelings for 'Dirge', a song that was originally some-thing of a parting glass:

> I'm going far, I'm going wide, I'm going by myself.
> I still hate myself for loving you, but that just can't be helped . . .
> [So] sing you praise of progress & of the Doom Machine
> Strong medicine is still taboo, if you know just what I mean
> The bandits (ghost riders) in the sky will tell you where I'm at
> I hate myself for loving you but I'll get over that.

The cathartic nature of both recorded dirges – one solo; the other piano/guitar – suggests it was always an intensely personal song to his mind. Certainly, the animosity sounds personal. But in his provisional album notes, Dylan suggests this dramaturgy was 'for Dying America, the dream gone sour, cold blue steel-eyed morning of death, visible from the rising ashes of tumult, black Angola, Tombstone vapor, bloody tears of Chicago . . . Julius + Ethel, 4 Dead in Oh-High-Oh,' perhaps suggesting a conscious debt to Allen Ginsberg's most recent collection of poems, *Fall of America*.

If the intent was to personalise the panoramic, he still couldn't quite manage it. He was still months – two of them on a national tour – away from 'Idiot Wind', which would do exactly that. But at least he was acknowledging what some of his poetic contemporaries were doing. It is Leonard Cohen, another respected poet, who sings 'of Birds and Man Forever Stripped' in the early drafts of 'Dirge', a song which comes closest to the spirit of *Planet Waves'* successor, and would have come closer still if he had used the acoustic original, as he first intended.

Even after paying a stipend to his self-censoring self, he left New York with an album's worth of sustainable songs for the first time in six years. A sense of gratitude spills forth in the notes he planned to include with the album, in which he thanked his wife for sticking with him.* She also seems to be on his mind when he playfully suggests 'Wedding Song' 'could be about anybody, but it's not'. 'Tough Mama', on the other hand, supposedly came about when he was 'thinking about my father and the holy spirit'.

More convincing is his suggestion that 'Something There Is About

---

* The album itself he dedicates to Sam Peckinpah, in a handwritten amendment.

You', 'could be [about] lost youth', while the notes to 'Hazel' allude to a spiritual sister with whom he could have 'caught a bus to the void, or joined a traveling circus'. Just one note hints at an underlying emotional anguish, and it is for the hymnal 'Forever Young', the centrepiece of the album and the song with the least amount of angst: 'Got the jolt of this Anthem in Mexico, camping off of Cho[l]la Bay . . . I started crying out loud & tore myself loose from East to West. Began to feel no attachment to anything . . . Comfort kills.'

The oldest song on the collection, 'Forever Young' was also the one he had the most trouble recording, becoming *Planet Waves'* 'Went To See The Gypsy'. He tried it every which way – fast, slow, acoustic, electric, country, rock, and even, according to the session notes, in a 'gospel/cajun' version – attempting it at five of the seven recording sessions.* None of which was down to The Band, who remained on their game throughout. For them, everything came with relative ease, impressing engineer Rob Fraboni, the co-owner of Village Recording Studio and producer in all but name:

> Robbie is the one who gives a lot of direction . . . [We] all had to be ready to go because . . . when [Bob] starts playing, there's nothing else happening but that, as far as he's concerned. I don't think I've seen anyone who performs with such conviction . . . Bob would just run it down, and they'd play it [through] once. Then they'd come in to the control room and listen . . . to what they should do, and then they would go out into the studio. That would usually be the take, or the one following.

Dylan appreciated Fraboni's willingness to just roll tape and apparent desire to please the paymaster, even confiding to him the problems he was having with the centrepiece, 'I been carrying ['Forever Young'] around in my head for five years and I never wrote it down, and now I come to record it, I just can't decide how to do it.'

At least four versions were 'pulled to master', including one from the Helm-less first session, when Manuel's scattershot drumming put the kibosh on an otherwise exemplary rendition. Perhaps this is what

---

* Krogsgaard's sessionography for *Planet Waves* is a mess, full of incorrect dates and LP takes incorrectly assigned. The session dates were November 2nd, 5th, 6th, 9th, 10th and 14th, plus an undated seventh session.

Robertson meant when he later wrote, 'We played it straight . . . [and] Bob just sang it to pieces – it gave you goose bumps . . . but Rob kept pushing for the emotional take.' In the end, the phantom engineer got what he wanted at the fourth (and supposedly 'final') session, Friday the 9th. His relief proved short-lived:*

> Lou Kemp was dating a girl [called Stephanie] from North Beach Leather, a shop on Sunset and LaCieniga. Lou brought her by Village Recorders when we were cutting *Planet Waves*. We only did one take of the slow version of 'Forever Young'. This take was so riveting, it was so powerful, so immediate, [but then] she said, 'C'mon, Bob, what! Are you getting mushy in your old age?'

If Fraboni was mortified, Kemp insisted to me, 'Stephanie was very outgoing, and she wasn't at all taken aback [by Dylan's fame]. She was just flipping to Bob. But he's [the one] asking my date for an opinion, [even as] Rob was like, "Oh my God." ' In his memoir, Louie suggests Dylan's initial reaction to her comment was to laugh, before asking, 'What do you think, Louie?' His childhood friend replied, 'I think it's one of the best songs you've ever written,' which it wasn't, by a long chalk.[†]

Whatever its merits, Dylan ended up brooding on the lady's comment. Perhaps he should have asked the infinitely more qualified Jackie DeShannon and Donna Weiss, who both paid a visit to the Village that night, and apparently left so inspired they returned to the former's home and wrote that most Dylanesque of DeShannon hits, 'Bette Davis Eyes'. Fraboni himself still couldn't get over a 'Forever Young' he'd been waiting for all week:

---

* 'Nobody 'Cept You' and two instrumentals, 'Crosswind Jamboree' and the five-minute 'March To The Dinner Table', were all recorded on the 2nd, and pulled to master. There may well have been an album of sorts by Friday the 9th. The reels from the 9th were dated the 8th, then corrected. Fraboni said at the time, 'We took two days off, then . . . came in Friday.' The AFM sheets Krogsgaard relies on for some of his info are pure fiction.

† Stephanie had her allies in the press, *NME*'s Nick Kent describing the song as having 'a schmaltz count so high it could kill a diabetic'.

When we were assembling the master reel [the next day] I was getting
ready to put that [take] on the master reel. I didn't even ask. And Bob
said, 'What're you doing with that? We're not gonna use that.' And I
jumped up and said, 'What do you mean you're not gonna use that?!
You're crazy!' . . . It was based on her comment that he wanted to leave
[that version] off the record . . . which I protested against [until he
relented.]

Nor was it the only potential calamity, said lady's presence created.
The jacket she had brought Dylan from her store as a present is the one
whose Antler buttons can be heard click-clacking against the back of
his Martin on 'Wedding Song', cut solo the day after the 'slow' 'Forever
Young', in a studio free of all carping critics. As Fraboni remembers it:

We were assembling [the album] . . . around noon. Bob said, 'I've got a
song I want to record later. I'll tell you when.' We were doing what we
were doing, and all of a sudden, he came up and said, 'Let's record.' So, he
went out in the studio, and that was 'Wedding Song' . . . Usually he
wouldn't sing unless we were recording. That's the way he was. You
couldn't get him to go out and just sing, unless he was running something
down with The Band . . . [This time] he asked, 'Is the tape rolling? Why
don't you just roll it?' So, I did, and he started singing, and there was no
way in the world I could have stopped him to say, 'Go back to the top.' It
was such an intense performance. If you listen to the record, you can hear
noises from the buttons on his jacket. But he didn't . . . care.*

At the death, Dylan was suddenly starting to add acoustic performances to the album, as if he intended to complete the task alone. On
Saturday the 10th he not only recorded the solo 'Wedding Song', but
also cut an acoustic 'Forever Young', with Harry Dean Stanton on
backing vocals, also 'pulled to master'. And at another 'final' session on
the 14th, he not only worked up a 'fast' version of 'Forever Young' –
which ultimately made the album – but cut a savage solo 'Dirge' that
came from nowhere. Chillingly intense, he needed just one false start
and one take to render lines that seemed bound to enter the lexicon,

---

* The unreliable AFM sheets suggest a full Band version was recorded on Nov. 2nd. If
so, the tape is lost.

notably, 'When hatred runs against itself, love is bound to win/ In the chamber of the golden deep, you might say angels play with sin.'

He had unwittingly tapped into his bloodiest track in years. With this 'Dirge For Martha' – as it was logged – they started compiling a third *and last* master reel for the album. On it, he placed the fast 'Forever Young', 'Dirge', 'Wedding Song' and a single-verse jam version of 'House Of The Rising Sun' from the first session on the 2nd which, as Fraboni says, had been intended simply 'to get set up and get a feel for the studio . . . Levon was supposed to show up, but he didn't . . . When he didn't, it was like, Let's just do something. They just started playing. It was just a jam session for a few hours. Then Bob said, Let's try this, and we did "Nobody 'Cept You," "Never Say Goodbye" and "Forever Young." '*

Dylan, though, was not done tampering. It was *New Morning* all over again, with 'the final recording happening,' in Fraboni's words, 'during the mixing. We had mixed about two or three songs and Bob . . . went out and played the piano while we were mixing. All of a sudden, he came in and said, "I'd like to try 'Dirge' on the piano." ' He wanted it to sound different from the rest of the record: 'He wanted a kind of barroom sound from the piano . . . rather than a majestic sound. He also wanted a raunchy vocal sound . . . That's the kind of stuff he was sensitive to . . . [as] more important to him than the sound quality.'

Accompanied by Robertson, the one Band member pro-active in the album production, the new 'Dirge' if anything ramped up the song's intensity, thanks in no small part to a starker tune and some razor-sharp rewrites, presumably penned the night before, possibly post-session, Dylan being known to sometimes return to the studio after everyone left to rewrite lyrics.

If recording a song from scratch during mixing was a sign of things to come, so was Dylan finally – and ever so reluctantly – embracing the vocal overdub. This was not something Fraboni was expecting, having been told by Robbie on day one, 'There are going to be no overdubs. We're doing it live. This is it, what's happening here is *it*.' So, how

---

* The other two master reels were compiled on the 10th. They comprise #1: You Angel You; Hazel; Tough Mama; Something There Is About You [all from the 5th or 6th]; #2: Going Going Gone; On A Night Like This; Forever Young (slow); Never Say Goodbye [all from the 2nd, 5th and 9th].

come the multitracks reveal not just the bootlegged 'Going Going Gone' guitar/ vocal overdub, but also another vocal overdub on the same multitrack?:

Rob Fraboni: It was made such a big issue that Bob didn't overdub vocals, [from] the day we were setting up. [So,] when we did 'Going Going Gone', he started to try and do an overdub without the guitar, and he got a certain way through and said, I can't do this without a guitar, and he got the guitar and went out and did it again. But when he gets to the bridge, he stops playing, and then he comes back in . . . Richard Manuel was sitting on the couch [next to] the console and . . . when he walked into the control room [afterwards], Richard looked up at him and said, 'How come you always sing sharp?' And Bob looked [back] and said, 'Because I want to.'

He kept going, too, doing four complete vocal overdubs on 'On A Night Like This' and one on 'Never Say Goodbye' (none of which were used), despite audibly sighing at the end of 'Going Going Gone' on the multitrack, 'I could spend all day doing this, and I don't even know if it's the right thing to do.' He sounds exhausted – and all the better for it.

Perhaps this was the night he and Kemp visited Geffen's house, 'where Joni Mitchell happened to be staying . . . She was [also] recording for his label . . . Bobby and Joni got absorbed in talking shop; she had just finished recording *Court and Spark* and he was up to his eyeballs in *Planet Waves*. After a while, Joni offered to play us a few of the songs from the new album . . . [and] Bobby fell asleep.'

Leaping to his chum's defense, Kemp would later insist, 'He had been in the studio for days. He was genuinely tired.' It didn't stop Joni airing her keen sense of resentment in conversation with *Rolling Stone*, suggesting that 'there was all this fussing over Bobby's project, 'cause he was new to the label, [whereas] *Court and Spark* – which was a big breakthrough for me – was being entirely and almost rudely dismissed . . . Dylan played his album, and everybody went, "Oh, wow." I played mine, and everybody talked and Bobby fell asleep . . . I think Bobby was just being cute.' This isn't what she told a long-time confidant, Joel Bernstein, at the time. She very much considered it a deliberate snub. Maybe it was; perhaps Dylan heard 'Free Man In Paris' and sensed that hers was the real deal, whereas his was but a stepping stone back to greatness, a halfway house to bringing it all back home.

Ever hedging his bets, Geffen released both albums on the same day – January 17th, 1974 – on the same label. And while the reviews for Joni's were her best since *Blue*, the Dylan reviews were a mixed bag, with *NME*'s Nick Kent playing lead Doubting Thomas, back to his offensive best:

> If Dylan really thinks this work is worthy of superlatives, then both he and his ever-expectant audience better pack up the tent and forget about any future projects, because I can't think of anything more tragic than Bob Dylan trying too hard to be Bob Dylan and consequently falling flat on his Jewish-caretaker's mug every time out.

By mid-January, all attempts to hype the release of *Planet Waves* were being drowned out by the tsunami of chatter about Dylan's comeback tour, a forty-date *schlep* across North America that had begun a fortnight earlier – which is when *Planet Waves* was *supposed* to have hit the shops, as opposed to 'as soon as we can get it out', which was what one exasperated Asylum staffer gave *Rolling Stone* as its official release date.

Even Robertson admitted, three years later, '[We] were preoccupied with the tour, [so] the album really took a back seat.' But even after a week of mixing, Dylan and Fraboni weren't done. As Fraboni noted at the time, 'We spent more time than it took to record or mix just to *sequence* the record. Bob wanted to live with a few different sequences.'

Sure enough, it was December 5th – three weeks after the last session – before Dylan approved a 'final' sequence, a ten-track album which began with 'Tough Mama' – a terrific opener – placed the slow 'Forever Young' at the end of side one, and began side two with 'On A Night Like This'.

But before Geffen could fire up the presses, Dylan changed his mind again. Two days later, it became an eleven-track album, with both a fast and slow 'Forever Young' (but without a 'House Of The Rising Sun' coda). He couldn't even make up his mind about the title, originally *Ceremonies of the Horsemen*, a nod to Sara and his own back pages, before it became *Planet Waves*, perhaps a reference to Ginsberg's 1968 collection, *Planet News*.

Nor was a phlegmatic Geffen out of the woods yet. Having worked on his notes to the songs extensively, Dylan decided to scrap them and pen instead an impressionistic, free-form poem, which suggested 'the ole days are gone forever and the new ones not far behind', a line straight out of Booth Tarkington. Oh, and he wanted one of his drawings as the cover, after cover art and cover shot had already been approved, à la *Self Portrait*.

He didn't finish these new notes until New Year's Eve, making a release date of January 3rd out of the question. Even a release on the 17th required the label to wrap a loose-leaf sheet with the poem printed on it around the first pressing. For Dylan, it may have been a case of 'one step at a time', but his endless second-guessing meant the album thus appeared mid-tour, probably wiping a couple of hundred thousand sales from the total* and driving Geffen to despair.

The new notes read almost like a coda to 'Wedding Song', a way of Dylan psyching himself up for the task ahead. The day he completed the notes, he reminded himself, 'When the Lord speaks, the oceans move.' Finally, as far as he was concerned the album was done and pawned. Yet, on the day the album was finally shipped, he played exactly two songs ('Something There Is About You' and 'Forever Young') in an eighteen-song set, as he settled into a mindset that led him to largely disregard the new album, and most of his post-accident work, on this 'comeback' concert-tour.

Within a week of the start, the more interesting songs began to drop like grouse on the Glorious Twelfth. The first to bite the dust was the opener in Chicago both nights. 'Hero Blues' was not only officially unreleased, but unrecognisable, even to those who had TMQ's *While The Establishment Burns*. On one verse he appears to be singing, 'Don't you remember, I told you once before / That nickel and dime shit just ain't gonna work around here anymore'; in another, 'I got one foot on the highway and the other foot in the grave.' He signs off: 'Watch her move sideways, until the early dawn / You can write on my tombstone, been here and gone.'†

---

* Dylan didn't learn his lesson. He later released both *Desire* – his best-selling album ever – and *Shot of Love* – one of his worst – *after* the relevant tour, an industry no-no. On the other hand, Pink Floyd released *Dark Side of The Moon* fifteen months after they started touring it, and that seemed to do okay.

† Thankfully two-track board tapes of both Chicago shows reside in the Tulsa archive, because the audience tapes are hard work. Let us hope they shall be released.

During the initial rehearsals, 'Hero Blues' wasn't the only oft-bootlegged song he was considering performing on what was shaping up to be the most bootlegged tour in rock history. Also run down were 'Who Killed Davey Moore?', 'Mama You Been On My Mind', 'Tiny Montgomery' and 'Long Distance Operator'. But for whatever reason, the surprises all but ended after the second show in Toronto, one week in: a terrific, full-blooded Band arrangement of 'As I Went Out One Morning'.

Despite harbouring real doubts about the wisdom of touring, concerned that 'maybe I wouldn't feel like singing them anymore', he tried telling himself 'they still felt right'. Writing in his private tour diary after the first two Philly shows, he suggested this might be his last tour; that 'there may be the big retirement coming' as he got 'into something else . . . change[d] directions entirely.'

In Toronto, he felt he'd been dragging his heels, yet the paper 'says fantastic, so who knows'. The audience reaction certainly seemed out of all proportion to the merits of the shows, which were workmanlike at best. Nor has hindsight made them sound any better, or convinced him to appreciate such lung-bursting vocals. As he said in 1989, 'We were playing at that point three, four nights at Madison Square Garden and three, four nights at the Boston Garden. But what justified that? We hadn't made any records. When we were playing out there earlier in the era, we weren't drawing crowds like that.'

For once, it seems he succumbed to the pressure of meeting peoples' expectations as to what they *thought* they were paying to see. Robertson later suggested as much to Cameron Crowe, 'We were hoping to do an extremely different kind of show. But we . . . eventually settled on a show that wasn't dissimilar from our last tour.' Such a sea-change was reflected in the later set-lists,* even if Dylan didn't address this temporary loss of artistic surefootedness until 1978, when he admitted:

The problem was that everyone had his own idea of what that tour was about. Everybody had a piece of the action. The publicity people. The

---

* He still sprang the occasional surprise: a 'Desolation Row' in St Louis, a 'Visions Of Johanna' in Denver, both pretty wretched, and a lovely band arrangement of 'Mr Tambourine Man' at the final show in L.A.

promoters. I had no control over what was going on . . . . I don't like to feel controlled by others. I choose people . . . My work is my life. [So,] I choose people who can help me in my work.*

Dylan had asked Louie Kemp to come on tour, because 'I was someone . . . who was his friend. So, I was there [for him]. Everyone else – aside from The Band – were all unknown to him.' But the first that tour managers Bill Graham and Barry Imhoff knew of this arrangement was when the limo pulled up at the private jet they'd hired for the tour and Dylan got out and said, 'This is my friend, Louie. He'll be coming along on the tour.' He needed his own sidekick because, as he told Barbara Kerr, 'I knew that going through with the tour would be the hardest thing I had ever done.' Kemp described the experience to Robert Greenfield as 'like going into a vacuum or a bubble . . . They would just pick us up and put us down and bring us everything . . . It was not a normal life.'

Indicative of a resultant sense of detachment was the absence of interviews after Washington (Jan 15th), when a reporter from the *Post* was warned not to ask political questions. So, his first question was about Richard Nixon, which Dylan assiduously sidestepped, 'I'm not really into presidents, I prefer kings and queens.'†

The night before, in Boston, Mimi Fariña had come to see him and brought some friends, which Dylan felt 'didn't work too well'. He was missing Sara, who waited three weeks before flying to Houston and spending the night. Dylan also spent time with a banker's niece in St Louis, as bad habits reared their head again. At least by Denver (February 6th), he felt he had discovered 'the backbeat, the heartbeat'.

It had taken five weeks to get there, and the tapes suggest he was mistaken, as he later admitted: 'There was nothing other than just force behind that . . . It's a very fine line you have to walk to stay in touch with something once you've created it.' His own, lone state of mind, only grew more wretched as L.A. on Valentine's Day – for the

---

* The one person on the tour he never worked with again was Geffen. Draw your own conclusions.

† Such was the veil of secrecy around Dylan's whereabouts that tour publicist Paul Wasserman was, by his own admission, 'put in a separate hotel from the group so that when the press would try to find me, they wouldn't find Dylan . . . My job as tour publicist was to keep them *away* from Dylan.'

final two shows – loomed into view. Naturally, they brought a mobile truck in to record these shows for the much-vaunted live album, though the bootleggers again beat them to the punch.

Geffen, in particular, was anxious to ensure it all came together. All of his hopes were riding on getting that live album. But on the final night in L.A., he was suddenly made aware of how little Dylan thought about him. At the show's end, the song and dance man walked back out and thanked Barry Imhoff, the crew and especially Bill Graham for putting 'this whole tour together. Without [them], this thing would never have happened.' But no mention of David, who was still con-vinced it was his idea.

Robertson, who had a lot riding on a fair deal going down, 'called Bob the next morning and said we should go over to David's . . . and tell him how appreciative we were.' Dylan admits to making such a trip in his diary. He found Geffen 'dispirited . . . Who would've thought?' Certainly not him. He had always considered Geffen a money-man. It apparently had not occurred to Geffen that Dylan might be a money-man, too, and one who had learnt to be wary of label-heads bearing gifts. Geffen was shocked to find an artist who liked money as much as him:

> Most of the artists [back then] were trying to make a living, trying to get laid, trying to figure out who they were. They weren't trying to change the world. That's what other people put on them. I knew all those people . . . intimately and well. [And] I would say that Bob Dylan is as interested in money as any person I've known in my life. That's just the truth.

Having to deal with someone (else) who saw all the angles just wasn't on. Geffen never saw it coming, either, having not dealt with Dylan on a day-to-day basis – unlike Dylan's new assistant, Arthur Rosato, who *had* realized 'by the end of that tour . . . Bob was kinda figuring out what he wanted to do.' Perhaps this is something he raised with fellow poet-of-song Leonard Cohen after the first L.A. show, when Leonard brought a Greek chanteuse along whom Dylan had long admired, only to end up hogging Dylan's attention himself:*

---

* Cohen had already taken Dylan to a Nana Mouskouri concert. Dylan cautioned Nana he would be leaving before the intermission, but then showed up in her

Nana Mouskouri: You should have seen Leonard and Bob together! Neither of them is what you would call a talker, so when they had a conversation, it was like watching a game of chess. Everything happened very slowly and each word had so much meaning. They would always talk about music, asking each other about certain songs and lyrics.

In this brave new world the returning Dylan was starting to concoct, there would be no place for Geffen. Nor, as it happens, for Sara. Yes, he was soon back home with his wife, 'still in a semi-daze', with the horses whinnying and the wind blowing. But he was also thinking about a lady he'd met in Oakland three days before L.A., at a party organized on his behalf. Her name was Ellen Bernstein, and she worked in A&R at his old label:

Bill Graham had a party at the Trident for Bob – I had lived with Bill for, like, a year and a half – The Trident was the quintessential flower-child restaurant, all these beautiful waitresses, everybody was beautiful. There were more beautiful women there than I've ever seen at any party, every gorgeous woman in Marin County was there. I remember getting a little bit drunk, not like plastered, and he kinda appeared, sitting next to me. And I was a little out of it . . . I wasn't so out of it that it didn't dawn on me that this was Dylan. The next thing that happened we were walking up to my house, which was up the hill, and we stayed up all night playing backgammon. He was much funnier than I thought he would be, a really good backgammon player, I was a single 24-year old girl. The attention was very flattering. The next day was the concert at Oakland, and we['d] literally stayed up all night, so I couldn't figure out how he was going to play a concert, but he said, 'You should come. Be with me at the show tonight.' It was fantastic, and I can't remember the hotel, but I went back there. They left the next day.

At the afternoon Oakland show, Dylan would play 'Wedding Song' for the very last time. By the evening show, it had been replaced with 'It's Alright Ma (I'm Only Bleeding)', a switch pregnant with symbolism, albeit one lost on those fans waiting for the line, 'Even the

---

dressing-room both in the break and after the show. The three of them then adjourned to a restaurant 'and talked the night away, comparing notes on favourite singers'.

president of the United States sometimes must have to stand naked,' which brought the usual roars of affirmation as Nixon stood on the cusp of impeachment.

Dylan had an idea for a song with a similar panoramic sweep, Dirge's bitter twin, even jotting down, 'Idiot Wind – shake your head/ change your ways,' in a notebook. Within a few weeks, he would be writing another new song, called 'Don't Want No Married Woman', which seemed to suggest a life of domesticity had lost its allure:

> Don't want no married woman, digging thru my clothes
> Going thru my pockets, peaking up my nose . . .
> I don't want no married [woman], breathing down my neck . . .
> Cooking me my breakfast, reading through my mail . . .*

So much for 'a love that doesn't bend'. The years of connubial 'bliss' were at an end. It was time to go back in the rain. And to hell with the consequences.

---

* 'Don't Want No Married Woman' is one of seven lyrics Dylan included in the fair copy 'little red notebook' in the summer of 1974, but never recorded. A near-complete, ever-so-slightly out of focus facsimile of said notebook was reproduced in the Deluxe edition of the 2018 *Bootleg Series Vol. 14*. A wasted opportunity.

3.8

March 1974 to January 1975:
Into Dealing With Slaves

That tour with The Band was . . . a heavy burden . . . I had to step into Bob Dylan's shoes.

Bob Dylan, to Toby Creswell, 1986.

Do not think that I have become a slave trader.

Arthur Rimbaud, to his family, 3rd December 1885.

I haven't come to the place that Rimbaud came to when he decided to stop writing and run guns in Africa.

Bob Dylan, to Ron Rosenbaum, November 1977.

He'll do stuff to [deliberately] send people off on the wrong trail.

Rob Fraboni.

I think that he's always in some measure of pain, being that creative. That kind of artistic genius goes hand in hand with demons . . . [But then,] I think he is generally uncomfortable in his own skin.

Ellen Bernstein.

When I'm listening to 'Subterranean Homesick Blues', I'm grooving along just like [everyone else]. But when I'm listening to *Blood on the Tracks*, that's about my *parents*.

Jakob Dylan, son of Bob and Sara.

I read that ['You're A Big Girl Now'] was supposed to be about my wife.
I wish somebody would ask me first before they go ahead and print stuff
like that . . . I don't write confessional songs.

Bob Dylan, to Cameron Crowe, 1985.

*

It wasn't just his wife who would never know the hurt he suffered. The
audiences on the 1974 tour heard not the thunder on the mountain, as
Dylan roared his way through songs that continued to define the decade just past. As he later said, 'We were cleaning up, but it was an
emotionless trip.' Although 'it was a highly acclaimed tour; artistically,
I'm not sure what it was all about'. He 'wasn't comfortable and [he]
wasn't happy'.

By the time he got to the west coast, the second week in February,
he certainly wasn't thinking of introducing anything new into the set;
he was too busy shedding songs from the Seventies. Even when he
wrote the natural sequel to 'Wedding Song', it stayed unheard even by
Sara, to whom it was clearly addressed, cast as 'the big girl now', a.k.a.
Mother Confessor.

What no-one knew until Dylan's papers were deposited in Tulsa was
that 'You're A Big Girl Now' was the first lyric completed after *Planet
Waves*. It evidently dates from the tour itself, possibly written after an
intense evening in Houston spent thrashing 'some things out, feelings
& so forth'. Its memorable opening couplet, 'Our conversation was
short and sweet/ It nearly swept [me] back off my feet', rather suggests so. He wrote it out as an *aide-memoire* on a double-sided sheet,
alongside possible additions to the set,* and the rewrite of 'Knockin'
On Heaven's Door' he was performing.

So, 'Big Girl' clearly came to Dylan as is, when he still had Her –
which means it's no longer a plea to return, as its position on Dylan's
'break-up' album would suggest, but rather a continuation of the conversation he began with 'Wedding Song'. In this context, the tour is

---

* Some of them sound mouth-watering – 'Sad-Eyed Lady', 'You Ain't Going Nowhere'
and '4th Time Around' – though perhaps not if what he did to '4th Time Around' in
Memphis (January 23rd) is any indication.

what he means to 'make it through', and 'the road' is what he's on
when 'back in the rain'.

Ever the prophet, by the time he recorded the song eight months
later all the fears it expressed have come to pass. Indeed, it is *that* realization which inhabits the recorded song and makes it so raw and
real – too raw and real, it seems, because Dylan would end up replacing that searing September song with a pale Sound 80 shadow. But the
sense of clinging to somebody already slipping through his fingers is
there from the outset, as it was in a brief prose-piece he wrote that
winter, looking back on a love so simple:

> For a short time, I found you and you found me. Those were the best
> days. Days of youth. (Days of glory, of inner struggle.) A time when we
> didn't know or care who we were. We walked in the woods, in a world
> of our own. I was the child and you were the Madonna. It would be a
> while before the Man and the [Madman] would enter, before the struc-
> tured roles would change our beings. How did it happen? . . . Where are
> we that we are so far apart from ourselves, from what we used to be?

A tour that was like a bookend to the Sixties – to his mind – had seen
him reimagining the past, again inhabiting a time when 'revolution
was in the air'. Sure enough, immediately after the above reverie, he
jots down a verse to a song it will take him months to finish. But when
he does, it restarts his very own wheel of fortune:

> I lived with them on Montague St.
> For about a year, maybe less.
> We listened a lot to Coltrane
> Tried to find happiness.
> Suddenly they changed on me
> And the revolution never came . . .*

Here is the big bang in blue and white, a song he doesn't even have
a name for yet, just a handful of cinematic images, one of which, 'He

---

* Also in the same notebook – discarded soon after he began writing these songs, only
to return to it in the fall – is the 'too busy, too stoned' verse from 'Tangled Up In Blue'
which survived all the way to the New York sessions.

got into dealing with slaves and burning the midnight oil', conjured up the ghost of Rimbaud in Abyssinia.* But unlike Rimbaud – stuck in diamond hell, crippled and dying – this 32-year-old poet has been unleashed. Ideas begin to gush out of him like a geyser in the weeks after the tour, so much so that he can barely keep them in their appointed place.

Even as he imagines another episode from this tangled travelogue – in which a figure much like Hermann Hesse's Hermine in *Steppenwolf,* 'moved in a little bit closer/ and studied the lines of my face' – the narrator finds himself walking 'about the city block/ Like a skeleton that can hardly talk/ And waits for her by the clocks,' in the grip of a familiar twist of fate.

Completing a trio of song-sketches on which the next album will pivot, he again felt the breeze from that idiot wind. In fact, as the Watergate scandal came to the boil that spring, he had the perfect backdrop for another song of star-crossed lovers as resentful as 'Dirge', as vengeful as 'One Of Us Must Know'. The 'L.A. notebook' contains images of an idiot wind blowing from the Grand Coulee Dam to Omaha. Again, his original notion contains two songs in one; its offshoot, a western adventure yet to assume an identity of its own:

> You had to leave Tombstone in a flash . . . to leave that mess behind
> Guess you thought hooking up with me was gonna buy you piece of mind . . .
> Now you play for pennies and dance for kings
> When the curtain falls, I'll still be waiting in the wings.[†]

If revenge still sat in his soul, at this stage it was directed not at the one he loved the most, but more macrocosmic manifestations of Mammon: 'I'll kiss the howling beast goodbye and roll the dice/ While trumpets blow and imitators steal me blind.' As he writes in the same notebook, looking back on his career to date, it had 'only served to

---

* It is a surprising misinterpretation of a letter to a friend by the eminent Enid Starkie in her acclaimed biography of Rimbaud which forms the basis of the suggestion that Arthur was a slave trader. He was not.
† The second couplet remains part of 'Idiot Wind' for some months, appearing in the little red notebook.

take me across the desert. ok now let's get back to life.' And life continued tracking him down, demanding he got down to business. Even
with his long-absent muse and/or mistress banging at the door, he had
matters he needed to address here and now, the most pressing of which
was the live album – his first.

Though there was no shortage of material to sift through, from
New York, Seattle, Oakland and Los Angeles, time itself was short.
Some delegating was required. The engineer responsible for the west
coast recordings, Phil Ramone, found out Dylan wanted him to select
and 'play him the best recordings, [so he could] choose the best from
that. Rob Fraboni . . . was there all the time, so . . . Dylan will get ideas
from him.' Which is perhaps why just one song from the superior New
York shows (which Ramone did *not* engineer) – a decent 'Knockin' On
Heaven's Door' – ended up being used.

Almost immediately, another issue arose. According to Robbie Robertson, 'After I [sic] got four or five songs mixed, I went to play them for
Bob . . . [but] I could see he was bothered about something.' Dylan
duly informed him, 'I don't think I want to do this Asylum Records
deal with Geffen. It doesn't feel right to me.' Robertson insists he
appealed to David Braun, who was doing the negotiations, that there
was a moral obligation involved, Braun told him, 'A man has a right to
change his mind.' Dylan was doing exactly what Geffen had done a
million times, looking after number one.

Geffen – ever the paranoiac – thought the whole thing was Robertson's idea, telling him to his face, 'You're the only one of those guys
smart enough to have come up with this scheme.' He may have had a
point. In a draft section for *Chronicles*, Dylan describes a meeting
between him and The Band in which he reports it *was* Robertson who
told the others Clive Davis would give them more money for the live
album. Davis flew into Beverly Hills and made his pitch, which Dylan
promptly used to help Geffen 'decide if he wants to pay more than he
said he would', and thus save face.

Geffen was thus obliged to recompense Dylan with a substantive
royalty hike for what the latter already saw as the commercial failure
of *Planet Waves*. Although it had been Dylan's first-ever US number
one, it had sold disappointingly. Indeed, *Billboard* reported in August,
'Dylan was extremely displeased with total sales tallies of . . . *Planet
Waves*, due to heavy returns after an unprecedented publicity wave for

his spring tour comeback with The Band petered out.' The same report suggested Dylan had also 'apparently expressed displeasure about the spate of media stories hailing . . . Geffen as a genius.' Dylan did not 'like to feel controlled by others', and Geffen, who prided himself on his reading of people, should have known that, even as their business association ran its course in less than six months.

Before The Flood, when it appeared in June, did go Top Ten, which was impressive for a live record – and a double at that – but Dylan still found this hard to equate with the unprecedented demand for tickets. In truth, the record as released was a hard sell: it was from the wrong end of the tour; it had a side and a half of perfunctory Band performances less than two years after *Rock of Ages*; and Dylan did nothing to promote it, either in the way of TV appearances or by making himself available for interviews. He was more concerned about spending time with the new love of his life, who had not had to wait long for him to come running:

> **Ellen Bernstein**: I heard from him fairly quickly, about a week or so later. He would come up [to San Francisco] and visit me. I would come down and visit him . . . . I would come up there for long weekends and then I would leave. I did say I was planning a trip to Hawaii.

Dylan turned the possibility of that trip to Hawaii into a timeless classic about the inevitability of loss, penning a song 'for her' called 'You're Gonna Make Me Miss You When You Go'. Like 'You're A Big Girl Now', the song's vantage point was not what it seemed. It still came almost as easily as 'Big Girl'.

From this point on, almost every stage of the writing process is covered by two notebooks for *Blood on the Tracks*, whose existence was unknown before 2016. If the first, 'L.A.' notebook (circa February-March 1974) contains just a few flickerings of inspiration, the jam-packed 'San Francisco & New York' [S.F./NY] notebook (March thru July) is bathed by full-on illumination.*

A third notebook (the so-called 'little red notebook'), its existence known of since the mid-Nineties, is now lodged at New York's Morgan

---

* Both these notebooks are housed at the Tulsa Bob Dylan Archive, along with digital scans of same.

Library. Reproduced in facsimile in the *More Blood, More Tracks* set, it is essentially a 'fair copy' notebook made when he thought he had conceptualised the album, only for a final wave of inspiration to hit, resulting in rewrites of 'Idiot Wind' and 'Up To Me' and the addition of 'Buckets Of Rain'.

Only the 'S.F./NY' notebook – chock-full of lyrics, realized and unrealized – really reveals the many dead-ends and no-through roads he had to travel down to get back home. Thus, in the first draft of 'You're Gonna Make Me Lonesome' he complains, 'Up till now the road's been steep.' Mostly, though, the song is one of thankfulness, a one-on-one communique in which he admits, 'I feel no remorse,' and that he's 'changed ever since you said hello.'

He feels young again, younger even than Ellen: 'Being with you is easy, hon/ The easiest thing I ever done/ You make me feel like a child.' But mostly, he feels gratitude for rediscovering that 'voice . . . deep inside . . . you speak to so direct.' The bridge co-opts an image from another discarded lyric ('You Were Good To Me'), jumping between past – 'No strings attached/ Everything about it seemed to match . . . I kissed you 'neath a yellow dog moon/ And held you for eternity' – and present: 'I'll play all night for you if I know the song/ I'll do what I can do to make it last real long.'

Thankfully, the songs are coming so thick and fast, he need not linger on ones which don't readily click. By the time he leaves for New York in mid-April, he has already abandoned 'Blind Alley', 'Blazing Star', 'Horse Thief', 'Selfish Child', 'The Pouring Down Rain' – which does have the promising couplet, 'I been to the circus and was almost baptized/ With robes on my flesh and tears in my eyes' – and 'Little Tiger (Night In The Dark Swamp)', in which he tells some young tyke to 'stop that growl, stop your mind and rest/ Little Tiger, little tiger, stop beating your brother up.'

Meanwhile, the title of 'Fishing On A Muddy Bank' is something of a red herring. The song in question will donate one promising image to 'Idiot Wind': 'Imitators follow me thru the hall of mirrors/ As if they think I'm blind . . .' Already, he can see this song – an epic tale of love, loss and larceny – as the album's centrepiece, just as soon as he connects two images from the 'L.A.' notebook – 'buttons of our coat/ letters that we wrote', and, 'It was destiny which got us together and destiny pulled us apart.'

Destiny, the first cousin of Fate, will be a key motif in all the tab-
leaus to come. Initially, though, he is in 'Plain D' mode, lashing out in
all directions: at imitators who have 'stolen . . . so much . . . from me';
at 'Husbands from the Sixth Brigade [who] have cashed their blue chips
in for change'; and more pertinently, at 'her': 'She never bothered to
notice me/ Until I took off the mask she wore.' Here is the self-same
person who makes the transition into second-person for the surprisingly graphic, 'I just heard yesterday . . . you like to brag about the
time you saw the general on his knees.' Nor is there much doubt which
rhyme he intends to use after the couplet, 'You hurt the ones that I love
best/ And fly away like a witch . . .' He hasn't yet got her lying in a
ditch. Instead he tells her, 'Don't apologize to me, and put your arm
around my back/ Don't look at me with that foolish grin, why don't
you go lay down on the track.'

Here was a song 'about marriage' that would make 'Wedding Song'
blush and would take almost as long to write as Leonard Cohen's 'Hallelujah', another song about adultery and marriage. Initially, he even
questions the institution of marriage itself: 'What do I want a wife
for?/ To take to parties and show off her pretty face?' But just as he is
building up a head of self-righteous steam, he puts it aside.

With so many ideas blowing around his skull, some fly off and form
part of its twin song. 'Up To Me' begins life with a couplet that could
easily have slotted into 'Idiot Wind', sections of which encircle it:
'Everything has gone from bad to worse, Money didn't change a thing/
You still got the same old thoughts and I still feel the same old sting . . .'
He would return to both quests.* For now, though, it is time to return
to another break-up song; perhaps the greatest song he will ever write
about the inevitability of loss, 'Simple Twist Of Fate'.

As always, when he thought of the great losses in his life, he thought
of Suze. It had been a long time, but that spring, while visiting New
York, he called her. As Suze later recalled, 'He was with Lillian and
Mell Bailey, old friends of both Bob and me. As I remember, Mell was

---

* In the case of 'Up To Me', the burden never features in the L.A. notebook but he
does pen thirteen rhymes for the phrase: be, by degree, free, flee, he, she, good
naturedly, naturally, knee, plea, see, sea, we; proof he had finally bought himself a
rhyming dictionary. He also writes down twelve rhymes for 'fate' and sixteen rhymes
for 'blue': 'jew – who – few – clue – do – flew – grew – new – rue – sue – too –
you – zoo – shoe – glue – view.'

annoyed with Bob for calling me up again, "Leave her alone, she's married." I felt nervous, he wanted to see me. I would have liked to see him, but I was uncomfortable for my husband's sake.'

Rebuffed, he poured himself into this song about clocks and docks, for which he had already found a hook: 'Maybe she'll pick him out again/ Among the many other men/ It'll be worth the wait . . .' He does not complete the thought, leaving potential listeners hanging on the fate of the hooker who provided solace, 'She'd gone back to the streets/ Forgot about a simple . . .'. Although it is set against the backdrop of his true love sailing away in the morning, when he returns to the docks he meets a lady of the night, the first time such a figure has appeared in a song of his own since those bawdy basement tapes.

In the process he removes passages that address that lost love directly, including one which perhaps alluded to the phone conversation they'd just had: 'The person that I tried to be, who failed you to the core . . . Won't bother you again, or wait at your door/ He'll pass right by the gate.' He also discards a revealing coda that strips much of the romance from a life well-travelled: 'A lifetime of roads and wives/ Empty rooms and false desires/ And burning hope that never tires.'

That springtime trip to New York also saw him connect with another old friend from the Village whom he hadn't spoken to since December 1965, when he had tossed him out of his limo. It was April 26th, and Dylan was at The Bottom Line to see Buffy Sainte-Marie, having paid for his own ticket, when he ran into Phil Ochs and foolishly asked, 'What's happening?' Having downed a few already and well on the way to his later mania, Ochs took this as his cue, 'I'll tell you what's happening . . . Remember that song you wrote, where it said, "It's much cheaper down in South American towns/ Where the miners work almost for nothing?"* Well, how d'ya like to work for nothing and sing that one song for this goddamn rally [I'm doing]?'

Eventually, Dylan gleaned that the well-oiled Ochs had arranged a benefit for Chilean agitators at the Felt Forum on May 11th, but lacked a headliner who would shift all the tickets. Ever a sucker for a hard luck story, Dylan agreed to appear, as long as there was plenty of wine

---

* The song is 'North Country Blues', which Dylan does perform, pissed, at the Friends of Chile concert.

backstage. The result was a PR triumph and Dylan's most inebriated performance since January 12th, 1963.

In the interim, Dylan continued searching for a way to tune into his inner eye. For this, he would need to pick up a paintbrush and contact a man who might be able to teach him how to use it – or so he'd heard. That man was Norman Raeben, and Dylan described his idea of tutoring in 1978, 'He would tell me about myself when I was . . . drawing something . . . It wasn't [about] art or painting. It was a course in something else . . . [] . . . He taught you [about] putting your head and your mind and your eye together . . . He looked into you and told you what you were . . . My mind and my hand and my eye were not connected up . . . Needless to say it changed me. I went home after that and my wife never did understand me ever since that day.' Which put another way may be Dylanspeak for, I began sleeping around. Even Ellen was not enough, it seems. According to another student's son, in a 2021 essay called 'The Silent Type':

> One day, Bob Dylan showed up [at Raeben's class] unannounced. They were painting abstracts at the time, and when it was my mother's turn to comment on Dylan's work she just shrugged . . . One evening, after a particularly long session, Dylan abruptly asked my mother whether she wouldn't mind hosting a party . . . He came to her apartment in red cowboy boots. People . . . left around 2 a.m. Dylan closed the door behind the last guest . . . So began a year of what she would . . . politely refer to as 'dating'. . . . They painted and read poetry, and talked very little about the fact that he was married. He often called at odd hours to play the music he was assembling . . . Once, she read him Petrarch while they smoked, which is the only time she seems to have made it into his lyrics. Eventually, . . . she just changed her phone number and stopped responding to his letters.

In the idealized portrait Dylan painted of Raeben in various 1978 interviews, the teacher had made 'his living boxing . . . In the thirties in France he roomed with Soutine, the painter, [and] knew people like Modigliani intimately' – none of which was true. Yet he made no mention of the fact that his father was the well-known Yiddish writer, Sholem Aleichem (né Rabinovich), whose stories formed the basis for the hugely popular stage-show, *Fiddler On The Roof.*

Though Dylan recognized a 'former' self in Raeben's own reinvention, it seems he never knew the real Norman, even as he dutifully attended his classes on the eleventh floor of Carnegie Hall, where the maverick teacher indulged in a reign of terror on students. As one contemporary of Dylan's recalls: 'He'd flick his cigar into your palette – he always had a cigar stuck between his teeth. If you were a favourite student, you'd leave with black and blue marks because he'd poke your shoulder: You understand? You understand? *You don't understand anything!*'

The classes themselves were small, no more than half a dozen pupils, all of whom stood at their easels, not allowed to sit down. It wasn't like Dylan hadn't been warned by his friends, the ones who spoke of 'truth and love and beauty, and all these words I had heard for years, and they had 'em all defined'. When he asked how come, they told him *all* about Raeben. Dylan subsequently told Claudia Carr (later, wife to Jacques Levy), who attended classes on his recommendation, 'He will destroy you.' For Carr – as much as Dylan – the experience was like a revelation:

> All of your assumptions about what art was or what you were trying to do or how you inhabited your skin, Norman would turn on its ear . . . He used to say that nothing exists without the dark and the light. You can't have form, if you don't have dark . . . Feeling is superior [to emotion]. Emotion is a reaction, but feeling is an exploration. It came from your depths, you had to understand that feeling . . . If you were trying to do something and make it look good, you weren't being real . . . It had to come from your soul . . . [But] Raeben was a brutal taskmaster. He'd say, 'You didn't see that! Are you trying to tell me you saw that? That isn't there. Look at it again and then look at it again, and then maybe you'll see it.' . . . Norman would call you an idiot. He would tell you all the time, You're an idiot! You could take it as an insult, but he'd say, 'Don't worry – I'm an idiot, too. We're all idiots.'

Dylan already knew the world was full of idiots, even if he hadn't quite realized he was one of us. Although the classes didn't turn him into a first-class painter, they did help him see the world afresh and to apply his palette to a vinyl album. Indeed, he later told Elliot Mintz, the resultant record was 'like taking a brush, and painting those songs onto a canvas'. Equally evocatively, he described the process in another interview as one which 'allowed me to do consciously what I unconsciously felt. [Because] I didn't [yet] know how to pull it off. I wasn't sure it could be done in songs.' The song he first tried this approach on was one he had started immediately after the 1974 tour, but was as yet merely a series of vignettes:

> 'Tangled Up in Blue' . . . was another one of those things where I was trying to do something that I didn't think had ever been done before . . . I was trying to be somebody in the present time, while conjuring up a lot of past images. I was trying to do it in a conscious way . . . I wanted to defy time, so that the story took place in the present and the past at the same time . . . I wanted that song to be like a painting. [1985]

During his early tinkerings, its kinship to 'Simple Twist Of Fate' remained. In that song, one potential love was a prostitute. In this one, 'She was dancing in a topless place . . . I just couldn't make that scene, too much of a fuss/ As a couple of lovers walked away, I couldn't help but think about us.' All of this postdates Raeben recommending that Dylan check out the French wartime *cineaste* favourite, Marcel Carné's *Les Enfants du Paradis*, about four men in love with the same mercurial woman. It had a profound impact on the poet in him – and the *cineaste* in him.*

He now returned to the scene of the crime – on the road again: 'I was holding up a sign saying California or bust/ Watch[ing] lovers pass us by, couldn't help but think of us.' Having not yet realized that 'chance is the fool's name for fate',† and failing to find her, no matter how hard he tried, he lamented, 'The way we covered our past, it's hard to find the traces/ I wish we'd tied the knot just like I tied the laces/ Of my shoe . . .' Again, though, he puts the song aside to play around with other song-ideas about some fellow idiots.

In one of these, called 'WHITE SONG GHETTO MONEY', he asks

---

* In his 2021 memoir, Jonathan Taplin suggests Robbie Robertson screened the movie for Dylan back in 1969, in Woodstock. Where would he have got a print, let alone the equipment to do so?
† The tag-line on which hangs the plot to *The Gay Divorcee*, the second Astaire-Rogers movie alluded to in verse two of 'Tangled Up In Blue' ('She was married . . .').

someone to 'remember when you burned me'; another, called 'Parting Shot', is directed at someone he's 'leaving . . . behind . . . I'm tired of making deals. I can't be bought/ I'm tired of being a fish you thought you caught.' Two others will make it as far as the 'little red notebook' compiled in August: 'It's Breakin' Me Up' and 'Ain't It Funny'. The subject-matter of the former is about as unambiguous as can be, as is its timeline – 'Was it really 12 years ago? Well, it seems like just the other day/ We took the vow to stay together and now we both are going away . . . We built a world, a world that ya just can't buy/ And it hurts me so to hear ya say that it was all a lie.' – rather suggesting a reference-point near the Catskills, shortly after the fall. The bitterness spills over into 'Ain't It Funny', which begins as a requiem on the acquisitive society:

Ain't it funny how they take everything real good and twist it into shit.
To ruin the very earth we love takes a certain talent I must admit.
They're draining out the fountain of youth, taken it to town and bottled it . . .

As May turned to June, Raeben's influence started to tell as Dylan's writing went into overdrive. In double-quick time, he put the finishing touches to 'Simple Twist Of Fate' and 'Tangled Up In Blue' – after rejecting 'Dusty Sweatbox Blues' and 'Blue Carnation Blues' as possible titles for the latter – and begins to get the measure of 'Idiot Wind'. He also pens the first rough outline of another epic travelogue, at this stage called 'Lily And The Ace' (as in, 'Nothing would ever come between Lily and the Ace'):*

The cabaret was empty, a sign said closed for repairs
A light rain was falling on Lily's golden hair
The queen struck pay dirt which was paid for her with her soul
The king was in the graveyard, the Ace was in the hole.

He also found that memorable opening for 'Tangled Up In Blue',

---

* The idea had been percolating a while. Twenty-four pages earlier, Dylan had written the couplet: 'Dolores was standing with the Ace of Spades/ She opened the window and I climbed up on her braids.'

'One morning the sun was shining, I was layin' in bed/ Wondering about that dear [???], if her hair's still red/ I certainly did my best for her, but boy she treated me rough . . .' He's off and running, even if the narrator currently works in a furniture store, where 'they treated me like a kid/ I surely would've wound up in jail if I didn't leave when I did.' Mere details await their slot. Meanwhile, he finds an ending for 'Simple Twist Of Fate' which has all the right words, just not necessarily in the right order:

> He skipped out, couldn't have been very long -
> When he got back, she was gone,
> Leaving him a note upon the dresser by his coat
> Goodbye was all she wrote.
> To which he could not relate . . .

But the real tipping point for this album of genuine 'cast-iron songs & torch ballads' came on June 22nd, when Dylan awoke to find he was newsworthy again, and not in a good way. Syndicated gossipmonger Earl Wilson had seen fit to air Dylan's dirty linen in public, and had got it all wrong, reporting that, 'Bob Dylan and wife Sara (parents of five) [have] separated. He is friendly with Laurie [sic] Sebastian, ex-wife of John Sebastian of The Lovin' Spoonful.'

The story even made it to CBS-TV news and *Rolling Stone*, prompting a swift rebuttal from a livid Lorey, who denied any involvement with Dylan, and an even swifter rebuttal from Dylan in song. Initially, he made a joke out of it, 'Well now, there's a story floating around/ That I made it with a camel late last week, someplace in Jerusalem.' But the man who wrote 'Restless Farewell' was never going to leave it at that. And nor did he:

> Somebody's got it in for me (setting me up)
> They['re] planting stories in the press . . .
> They're so confused by what they've read
> They think I'm someone I'm supposed to be.
> People all have a different idea
> Of who I am but . . . none of them know what I'm really like . . .
> They never really look at me
> I don't know what they're looking at

But an idea of what I'm supposed to be
Well, there's no way I can play to that.

It was just like Dylan once said, to his west-coast promotion man,
'When people meet me, they think they're meeting the lyrics.' For
now, he preferred spending time with his favourite west-coast A&R
woman at her place in Mill Valley, while he wrote and rewrote his most
ambitious narrative in a decade, a western ballad whose characters
came not from Zane Grey but from a deck of cards, Arthur Edward
Waite's infamous Tarot pack.

'The Magician', surrounded by the rose and lily in Waite's pack, is
represented in Dylan's song by the Jack of Hearts. 'The Queen and
the King and [the] Ace in the Hole', all present in an early draft, are
soon replaced by Lily ('a princess . . . fair-skinned and precious'),
Rosemary ('a queen without a crown') and Big Jim ('no one's fool'),
who was fool enough to believe 'nobody would ever come between
her and the King/ . . . 'cept maybe the Jack of Hearts.' All these characters act in accordance with the Jack of Hearts' desires: Rosemary
sees herself 'riding on the Jack of Hearts'; Lily has 'a little penknife for
an ace in the hole/ Nobody noticed when she slipped it to the jack of
hearts'; even Big Jim, who is 'used to dealing from the bottom', finds
he keeps 'coming up with . . . the Jack of Hearts.' Whatever could it
mean?

Dylan knew all the characters' personal histories, enabling him to
write this epic ballad in reverse, penning the first and last verses and
then filling in the blanks. He even writes a note to himself to adopt 'a
neo-realistic point of view', as a seemingly unconnected couplet, 'I'm
looking for beauty, I find it everywhere/ I'm looking for an angel, to go
with the jack of hearts,' leads him back to the starting point:

> He stood in the floodlight a-tearing everybody up with his smile
> The festival was over and the tables had been turned
> Everything without any purpose had been burned
> He stood in the doorway looking like the Jack of Hearts . . .

Ellen, with whom he shared all the songs as they took shape, asking
her what she thought, was amazed: 'It was always different, every time.
He would just change it and change it and change it. You definitely had

this sense of a mind that never stopped.' The end result took her breath away. How could it not?

The other major song started in San Francisco was 'Shelter From The Storm', which began with a single image, lifted from 'There Ain't Gonna Be Any Next Time': 'You never knew she could understand your tune . . . better'n'you do/ When cruelty is the message, the crown is one [of] thorns.' But in 'There Ain't Gonna Be Any Next Time' he addresses his own mortality, at the tender age of thirty-three:

> You thought you had it covered
> You never wanted to get in too deep
> But now you've sadly discovered
> That the nights are long and you can hardly sleep.
> It's now or never, and while she's here and close to you
> You'd better decide what means the most to you . . .

Initially, he would spend two pages reworking the 'crown of thorns' image, telling himself to 'hold her, kiss her, love her while you're still alive', still thinking he was working on the former song, shuttling between a lost love – 'You were always thinking about her/ But she slipped away and you lost her trail' – and what he has now, until it abruptly turns into a re-examination of a marriage turned sour: 'Suddenly I looked around and she was standing there/ With silver rings on her fingers and wild flowers in her hair/ She walked up to me so gracefully and took my crown of thorns . . .'

'Shelter From The Storm', a song about a man who has lost everything, came quickly. Initially sung by someone who's 'been moved out from the factory and stranded in the leaves/ It's a holy sin, but a man must pay for everything he believes,' it ends not on the hopeful note of someone 'bound to cross the line', but rather someone who'd 'bargained for infinity and she gave me a lethal dose'.

The self-same sense of loss permeates 'It's Breakin' Me Up' – 'Something is missing, I wish I knew what it was/ We both took a vow to stay together, and now both of us are going away' – and a song called 'Blood On The Ice', which gave 'Idiot Wind' its central image after giving up the ghost: '[Now] that the veil has lifted from his eyes, the bitterness is gone/ The pleasure of his days with her still lingers on.' Meanwhile in 'Don't Want No Conversation', he admonishes himself for 'living in a suitcase too far away too long/ Got some kind of occupation but I'd sell it for a song.'

In 'Belltower Blues', he lifted a motif or two from 'Good Morning Schoolgirl': 'Waiting round the school yard, honey, woncha ring my bell/ I think you might like me some, but oh, it's hard to really tell.' Was the 24-year-old Ellen really making him feel old? Certainly a nagging sense of his own mortality had reared up by the time he got to the last page of the S.F./NY 1974 notebook, where he penned 'Death Is Inside Of Me':

> Death is inside of me, heroes fall by the way
> Pushing the walls to the limit while seconds keep ticking [away?] . . .
> Life is inside of me – fighting to breath[e] and create
> The mountains beyond me are dark and oh so foreboding . . .*

All in all, the weeks he spent in San Francisco – across at least two visits – proved highly productive, even if it ended on a sour note when he lost the acoustic Martin on which he had conceived these defining songs. As Ellen recalls, 'The guitar was stolen from his van when it was parked in front of my house in Mill Valley . . . We went around town putting up notes asking people to call if they knew anything about the whereabouts of the guitar, [which] I believe David Bromberg had given him . . . He was truly upset to lose [it].'

Perhaps his saving grace was telling Dylan he might be done with these songs. He later suggested he had sub-consciously 'left [the guitar] behind. I'd squeezed it dry'. Fortunately, he had at least an album's worth of songs already, as he proved on July 22nd, when he pulled up at the St Paul Hilton after a Crosby, Stills, Nash and Young show to play Stephen Stills and bassist Tim Drummond his new songs.

The experience prompted Drummond to enthuse to *Rolling Stone*, 'Dylan's got an album. It's great . . . it's gutsy, bluesy, so authentic. I heard eight or nine new songs, and . . . liked everything I heard.' A jealous Stills was far less effusive, much to Drummond's mortification, 'At one point Stephen said something to him about the songs not being

---

* Surely a reference to the traditional ending for 'The House Carpenter': 'Oh what mountain is yon, she said/ That looks so dark to me?/ O yon is the mountain of hell, he said/ Where you and I shall be.'

good. I was so goddamn embarrassed. He was probably coked out. Dylan, being the . . . man that he was, said, "Well, Stephen, play me one of your songs." . . . Stephen couldn't even find one string from another at that point.' Also there was Kemp, who concurs that Stills 'was obviously loaded . . . When Bobby sang "Idiot Wind," he became paranoid and very agitated. "You wrote that song about me! . . . Why did you write that song about me?" '

He wouldn't be the last person to think this song – one of three cornerstones for the album in Dylan's head – was about them. But Dylan was not done. Taking no more chances, in mid-July he packed a different acoustic guitar and headed for the Minnesotan farm he'd purchased the previous year as a family hideaway. If, as *Melody Maker* reported, he was 'showing his three older children his old Hibbing home, the Mesabi Range and other memories,' he was also spending some quality time with Ellen:

> He wanted me to come to Minnesota . . . He was at his best there, at his most comfortable, with his brother's house down the road. He had a painting studio out in the field, and the house was far from fancy, out in the middle of nowhere . . . He would do his writing early in the morning and then kinda materialize around midday, come downstairs and eventually, during the day, share what he had written.

Considering she was sleeping with the enemy, Ellen's employer was giving her a fair bit of time off. Actually, he was coming home in more ways than one. As early as February 14th, David Braun had written to Naomi Saltzman to say, 'I feel that it would not be wise to put Bob in an adversary position with CBS at the moment.' It seems their boss was already exploring his options. By July 2nd, even those not on the inside track at the label had heard whispers, with Richard Asher from CBS-UK writing to Elliot Goldman:

> I understand that negotiations with Dylan are currently taking place. This may give you an appropriate opportunity to raise the question of obtaining permission for us to release an LP of the 1965 Dylan Royal Albert Hall Concert . . . Bootleg LPs of this concert have been sold extensively here and in the US . . . and the music press here constantly asks when we will release it . . . Although we know CBS recorded the

concert, we do not know where the tapes are located, but presume they are in New York.

A key UK executive didn't even know that the show the music press was clamouring for was from 1966! Nonetheless, Dylan was soon telling New York staff 'that he felt far more comfortable dealing with personnel whom he'd known for over a decade'. By the first week in August, there was only one major sticking point – unreleased masters. Dylan was determined to ensure there would be no more *Dylans*. Goldman was obliged to inform his boss, Don Biederman, the jig was up:

> Braun and Naomi Saltzman very strongly resisted my position that any extra recordings made by Dylan while recording an album be owned by us, even though we could not use them . . . I have yielded this point. In essence, Dylan will retain ownership of any outtakes recorded in conjunction with an album he is recording for delivery to us. However, Dylan cannot deal with those recordings during our period of exclusivity with him.

As it happens, CBS had jumped the gun. The week before, at their annual record convention in L.A., the label proclaimed they had signed Dylan and Barbara Streisand to long-term contracts.* According to a *Billboard* report, the former was 'reported to have a number of songs ready for his next album, although studio dates and producer assignment are not yet set'.

Leaving Braun to dot the i's and cross the check, Dylan stayed north by mid-west making a 'fair copy' notebook of all the songs under consideration for a return to CBS, including another new song, 'If You See Her, Say Hello', which emerged from the embers of 'There Ain't Gonna Be Any Next Time', via two 'trigger' phrases: 'So kiss her nice and say hello/ And hold her tight and don't let her go,' and, 'I respect her tho' for what she did/ Tho' the emptiness still lingers . . .' By mid-August, he had inspiringly recast such sentiments:

---

* Actually, Dylan had only signed a three-album deal, which he would complete by the end of 1976.

If you're making love to her, kiss her for the kid,
Who could never express his love and kept his feelings hid
He respects her for what she's done, it lifted up the veil
The veil that covered up his eyes and kept his mind in jail.

Also entered in this 'fair copy' notebook was a major new song he'd
been carrying around in his head since page five of the S.F./NY notebook. He had begun 'Up To Me' shortly after writing a short prose
vignette in said notebook that, just like 'Tangled Up In Blue' and 'Simple Twist Of Fate', was about brief encounters and fated lovers:

I am not a person who thinks highly of love. In fact, I've gone to
extremes to avoid it. But let me tell you about her. She was different.
She came in to mail a package one day and woke me up. I was just about
to get turned loose anyway . . . The only reason I was there in the
first place was that my superior was my sister's husband. But wait, let's
get back to the point. I was daydreaming and she snapped me out of
it . . . The next time of real import was at the corner cafe. I was drinking
at the bar when she came in and sat at a table of men philosophers,
poets, agents from some place out of the question . . .*

The ideas were coming thick and fast. On the last page of the S.F./
NY notebook, after a set of directions to the new farm, were three
traditional song-titles, including 'Betty And Dupree'. Sure enough, in
verse nine of 'Up To Me', 'Dupree came pimpin' tonight to the Thun-
derbird Cafe . . .' He had distilled another movie script down to a
six-minute song.

He already had more than he could use – which is why seven songs
from the 'little red notebook' wouldn't even get a test run at the forthcoming sessions: 'There Ain't Gonna Be Any Next Time', 'Belltower
Blues', 'Where Do You Turn?', 'It's Breakin' Me Up', 'Don't Want No
Married Woman', 'Ain't It Funny' and 'Little Bit Of Rain'. Instead, he
spent the last few back pages rewriting 'Idiot Wind' and 'Up To Me',
both clearly earmarked for the LP.

He now set about deciding what to record the way he used to, before

---

* Verse seven of 'Up To Me' opens with, 'The only decent thing I did when I worked
as a postal clerk . . .'

fame took him away from the Village store of traditional lore; playing the songs to people whose opinions he respected. Ellen believes, 'As he played them for people, the sequencing decided itself.' Those people included the great country songwriter Shel Silverstein, who lived on a houseboat in Sausalito. It was the only time Ellen accompanied him on this mini-tour of the Bay Area, playing these stunning songs to interested parties.*

Altogether more non-plussed by the experience was Michael Bloomfield, who was living in town and thought Dylan wanted him to play along, as he had when first he heard 'Like A Rolling Stone', a decade earlier. Instead, Dylan 'took out his guitar . . . tuned to open D tuning, and . . . started playing the songs nonstop . . . I was saying, "No man, don't sing the whole thing, just sing one chorus and if it's not gonna change, let me write it down so I can play with you." [But] he didn't. He just kept on playing . . . one after another, and I got lost. They all began to sound the same to me, they were all in the same key, they were all long. It was one of the strangest experiences of my life . . . [And] he was sort of pissed [off] that I didn't pick it up.' In one dispiriting sense, the experience would serve as a dry run for the New York sessions, sessions on which he intended to take no prisoners.

An equally intriguing private preview took place at bluegrass pioneer Pete Rowan's house. The last time their paths had crossed, Dylan had been recording *Blonde on Blonde* (with two drummers). This time he was looking not for a guitarist, but for a guitar, only to unexpectedly encounter an old flame:

Peter Rowan: I got a call from Seatrain lyricist, Jim Roberts, over in Bolinas. Bob Dylan had shown up at his door. [He] must have been on a walkabout from life as a rock and roller! Jim said that Bob was looking to replace his favourite guitar, which had been stolen. I had my treasured 1936 Martin 000 Sunburst guitar and [he wanted to know,] did I maybe want to sell it to Bob? Well, Bob got on the line and we talked. I

---

* Ellen did get to witness another preview, in Brooklyn, when Dylan went to visit a Hasidic Jew he knew in Crown Heights for dinner. When they arrived, his friend's sister was there, whose husband was Ellen's cousin. She recalls, 'After the meal we went out in the backyard and he played the songs for . . . this group of Hasidic Jews. It was wonderful . . . But it was a real unusual experience to have before recording the album.'

still thought it was a hoax . . . I gave Bob directions how to find my place . . . [on] Stinson Beach . . . I watched the blue van pull up. Out stepped a man in brown corduroy clothes and cap. I watched him find his way and listened to his footsteps on the wooden stairs. In the room was my partner Leslie, and Milan and Mimi Melvin [neé Baez], just returned from Tibet . . . We waited. Only Bob's nose entered the doorway, sensing like radar the vibes! I went to greet him, he seemed taller than expected, wearing shades. 'Someplace we can go?' he asked quietly. We went downstairs to the empty front room with ocean light filling it . . . I took the old Martin 000 out of the case and handed it to him . . . He took the guitar and started to sing all the material from the unreleased *Blood on the Tracks*. We sat there for hours trading songs . . . It grew dark, and still the songs came . . . and still he wore his shades.

Though a sequence was already forming in Dylan's head, there was a slight problem. He couldn't stop writing songs. Two more boarded the midnight train from Minneapolis to New York, where Dylan and Ellen arrived the second week in September. 'Buckets Of Rain' emerged from a snatch of lyric written on the final page of that 'fair copy' notebook – 'Little red wagon, little red bike / I ain't no monkey but I know what I like.' While 'Meet Me In The Morning', which had been gestating since page one of the S.F. / NY notebook, came to him so late it never even made it to a notebook already full of the blues:

My grandfather had a farm but all he ever raised was the dead,
He had the keys to the kingdom, but all he ever opened was his head
Meet me in the morning, it's the brightest day you ever saw
We could be in Kansas by the time the snow begins to thaw.

One of the 'red notebook' blues songs was 'Don't Want No Married Woman', from which he co-opted the couplet – 'Look at the sun sinking like a ship / Ain't it just like my heart when . . .' Why Dylan felt the need to write another blues lyric and apply it to the tune he already had for 'Call Letter Blues' is one more for his therapist. Yet, it clearly filled some conceptual need, becoming one of ten songs Dylan cut on September 16th, his first day back at the studio where he had consistently made magic between November 1961 to January 1966, the old Columbia Studio A – now renamed A&R Studios. The 'R' stood for co-owner

Phil Ramone, the engineer who had worked on *Before the Flood*. Ramone immediately knew what it was about A&R that appealed to Dylan:

> [He] had an incredible love for this room, which had been sold by Columbia. A group of us, including me, ended up buying the studio, and we made a few changes, but not too many. It was a big room, just like a church, with a huge, high ceiling.

Ramone had done his cause no harm when, during a March 1974 *Melody Maker* interview, he rejected the term 'producer' for 'guys like Dylan and Paul Simon – who . . . [just] need a close friend in the control room . . . I think the title needs redefining.' Dylan had no intention of letting anyone else *produce* these songs (not that this would stop Ramone from implying he did in later interviews). As Ellen notes, Bob 'knew his vision for these songs [which] was very pure and very unadorned, and you don't need a producer if your vision is that personal'. What he needed was to capture the sound of himself 'sitting in a room singing', something his last album had singularly failed to do:

> I played acoustical songs on that Band tour in '74, but I pushed too hard . . . And for my type of style I can't really afford to push too hard, because I lose the reason behind the song. If you heard me sittin' in a room singing, I wouldn't be pushing too hard. [1978]

The very afternoon he arrived at A&R, Dylan shared this aesthetic with an old friend who knew his methodology well: 'I want to lay down a whole bunch of tracks. I don't want to overdub. I want it easy and natural.' It was John Hammond Snr. Yet Hammond was slightly baffled by Dylan's choice of recording date, pointing out to his former protégé, 'This is a strange day to start recording . . . It is Rosh Hashanah, and it is hard to get musicians.' Dylan was unfazed, 'Why not today? It's the new year, isn't it?'

Such was his impatience to get started that A&R's assistant engineer, Glenn Berger, found himself scurrying to set up the mikes, 'We had no idea what he was going to do, so we had to be ready for anything . . . As I ran around the studio tweaking mic positions, he called off a tune.'

That tune was 'If You See Her, Say Hello' and from take one, a five-minutes-plus performance with four swooping harmonica breaks, he stepped up to the plate.* Ramone soon realized this was 'a very . . . deliberate letting out of the inside of him. Emotionally, he was in a state of revealing his life,' something Ellen already knew.

Despite Ramone barely noticing the A&R lady – later insisting 'the only people in the studio [that first day], other than the musicians, were Columbia's Don DeVito, John Hammond and me' – it was Ellen, not this Phil, who would be Dylan's primary sounding board, the one he would bounce ideas for songs off. We hear her voice for the first time after take two of song three that afternoon, 'That was great.' It was 'Simple Twist Of Fate', and once again the take – another five-minute vocal/harmonica tour de force – took her breath away. It was the first song that day pulled to master, *and* mixed. He was word-perfect again, perhaps because, as Ellen suggests, the songs were fully internalized:

> He was totally and completely immersed in the creation of this album, and if that's where you're coming from . . . it's not a matter of remembering the words, because he was living the creation of it and it was a part of him in every way imaginable. It flowed through him. He never needed to look at that little red notebook when . . . recording a track. By that time, he had absorbed the words.

As if to demonstrate this self-evident truth, Dylan – after briefly returning to 'Big Girl Now' – promptly recorded in single takes, two of his wordiest, wittiest songs, 'Up To Me' and 'Lily, Rosemary And The Jack Of Hearts' (after a long false start). The latter he prefaces with an off-mike comment, '[Hope] I'm gonna get through this one.' Both tracks will be pulled to master, and in the latter's case, he will not return to it again until he applies some mid-western swing during a bleak mid-winter.

In a single afternoon, he had rattled off five of his most emotive songs. Thankfully, this was no *Another Side*. His focus was unerring. Or at least it was until some other musicians arrived at A&R to break the

---

* I have no idea why the first fifty seconds of the harp intro. have been lopped off the version included on *More Blood, More Tracks*, which cuts in as Dylan is about to start singing. It certainly isn't a false start.

spell. Each of them had been summoned there at Dylan's behest. Some even had messengers sent to their door, including Barry Kornfeld, who had seen little of his old friend since the singer last had his heart broken:

> For some reason, Dylan was doing this album [on the hoof]. It's already the night and I'm teaching at [the] Guitar Study Center. [Don] DeVito comes into the class and says, 'Grab your mandolin.' What I had was a metal body, National mandolin. I said, 'This is not [really a mandolin!]' 'Never mind, just bring it.' He actually came to the school, drove me down to my apartment. [I] grabbed a couple of instruments and we took off.

Somewhere in the midst of all this, Kornfeld found time to phone Stephen Wilson, who remembers Barry telling him, ' "Bob is trying to recapture the feeling of yesteryear and he'd like some of the old crowd at the session." Barry was there when I got there. [Bob] was very proud of "Lily, Rosemary." He asked me, "Did you follow the timeline?" ' Kornfeld and Wilson hung around all night, though as the former says, 'We never did find out what it was that I was supposed to do.'

The same could be said of Eric Weissberg's band Deliverance, who would be credited on the LP-sleeve, though they played on just a single track. Dylan first summoned banjoist Weissberg, whom he'd met in Madison back in January 1961. Eric 'asked him who [else] he got. He said he tried everyone but it was too short notice.' He told him, 'I got a band.' When they duly arrived, Dylan seemed to have no clear idea what to do with them all, prompting Weissberg to later recall:

> Bob came into A&R Studio A-1 and called us to the center of the room, where he began playing and singing . . . We scrambled for paper and pencils to try and scribble down the changes . . . I don't know which song it was, but it had a lot of verses [sic] . . . I think we ran it down once, maybe twice, and Bob asked Phil if he was ready to record . . . We did our first take. Bob asked for a playback . . . [and] during [it, he] . . . started to run down the next song.

Actually, Deliverance first worked on an electric arrangement to 'Big Girl' which went unrecorded. Only then did Dylan teach them 'Simple Twist Of Fate' and 'You're Gonna Make Me Lonesome When You Go', neither of which really worked, as Dylan knew instantly, along with Ellen: 'He knew as soon as he heard something whether or not it was what he was going for. It never took him more than one time to know.'

What the musicians failed to realize was that he was only interested in their first impressions. Guitarist Charlie Brown III was the first to figure it out, and even he 'didn't get the message until about three-quarters of the way through the first day . . . Then I thought, "Oh, I know what he's doing. He just wants to hear whatever comes out."' He informed the first reporter to write about these sessions, *Rolling Stone's* Larry Sloman, that Dylan's 'whole concept of making an album seemed to be to go ahead and play it and whichever way it comes out, well, that's the way it is'. Drummer Richard Crooks also soon realized this was someone who didn't *want* the musicians to 'lock in on it too much. He likes that loose, unpredictable feel' – almost as if he knew what he wanted:

Richard Crooks: I [had] never thought of Dylan as much of a musician, but . . . this guy was unbelievable. As well as having a phenomenal memory for lyrics, he had a [really] good grasp of musical technique. He would say, 'Ah, I don't like it in that key,' and change to another, but he never capo'd anything on the guitar. He would barre-chord the changes. We probably went through six or seven different keys on just one song, and he never capo'd anything. He had all the transpositions right there, bang, bang, bang.

The most forlorn figure at A&R was probably Weissberg, who unfairly accused Dylan of being 'ill at ease in the studio, as if he wanted to get it over with'. In fact, he just wanted to capture things while fresh, which he managed to do twice. By doing two versions of the same electric blues, he got 'the immediacy of the moment', securing 'Meet Me In The Morning' and 'Call Letter Blues' – with the same tune and arrangement – in consecutive takes, without even telling the band they were different songs.

Only when an attempt was made on 'You're Gonna Make Me Lonesome', did things go pear-shaped. After seven false dawns, Dylan finally cut the drums and turned up the organ. Berger looked on aghast: 'Everyone there had been incredibly excited to be playing with this guy . . . but it was becoming apparent to each musician, as they were summarily dismissed, that this was not likely to happen . . . We all stole looks at each other . . . You could see it in the musicians' eyes, as they sat silently behind their instruments, forced not to play by the mercurial whim of the guy painting his masterpiece.' At the end of the session, Dylan decided to revisit 'Billy 4' on another ballad, 'Tangled Up In Blue', accompanied by just Tony Brown's bass and his own guitar.

When Berger counted the takes pulled to master that day, he realized there were eight, five of them from the solo afternoon session. He was stunned: 'We [had] cut the entire album in one day like that. Now that blew my mind . . . The style of the time was set by guys like Paul Simon, who would take weeks recording a guitar part, only to throw it away.'

Dylan also now knew for sure the sound he wanted, the one he'd captured on an epic 'Idiot Wind' mid-session and that final 'Tangled Up In Blue'. The following afternoon, Brown – and Brown alone – 'got a call . . . from a woman, who . . . worked for Columbia, telling me to come in for that evening's session. I remember asking her if she had called Eric . . . and she replied . . . "No, Bob just wants you" ':

Glenn Berger: [Having] cut the whole thing in six hours on a Monday night . . . [Dylan] came back in on Tuesday, and recorded most of the album again. This time he had [Tony Brown and] Paul Griffin, the keyboard player . . . That seemed to work, but [again] it turned out not.

Actually, Dylan thought he was just tidying up loose ends at this second session, as he successfully nabbed versions of 'You're Gonna Make Me Lonesome', 'You're A Big Girl Now' – both accompanied by his old sidekick, pianist Paul Griffin – and 'Tangled Up In Blue', as well as the two songs he'd not tackled on Monday: 'Buckets Of Rain' and 'Shelter From The Storm'. Once again, one take of each was pulled to master, save for 'You're Gonna Make Me Lonesome', which generated both a fast and a slow version, the latter recorded at session's end with just Brown playing tag.

Bassist Brown had started to get the hang of things: 'He was using an open tuning, so I had to rely on my ear rather than read the chord changes off his hand. [But,] unlike the previous day . . . I was sitting right next to him, so I could actually hear his lyrics and voice . . . That helped me get into it.' At the end of the evening, Ramone created three master reels, comprising fourteen takes of twelve songs. They would start assembling the album the following evening, after a few overdubs. Anyway, that was the plan.

However, when Deliverance's Richard Crooks popped by on the 18th – not to play, but to listen in – he found a Dylan 'so bombed you'd think he wouldn't be able to play. [Yet] he was still going through the changes smoothly.' The sloshed singer was attempting a retake of 'Buckets Of Rain', but kept stumbling over the ending. Ramone suggested, 'Get more wine,' to which Dylan responded, 'I might have had too much [already]. I'll try one more . . .' Finally, he came clean, 'I just don't feel like it.' Abandoning the song, he turned to the New Riders of the Purple Sage's Buddy Cage, an act Ellen A&R'd.

Cage had been brought in to apply pedal-steel, à la Pete Drake: 'Bob played [me] the tapes . . . and said, . . . "Play on whatever tracks you want."' Again, he was looking for 'first impressions'. Cage applied a few light brushstrokes to 'Big Girl' and 'Meet Me In The Morning' before Dylan left Ramone to do some rough mixes, while he and Ellen went in search of the Rock'n'Roll Doctor at The Bottom Line.

When he returned the following night, he was stone-cold sober as a matter of fact. Again, as Berger reports, he seemed to want to 'record the album for a third time, this time just with the bass'. Like *Planet Waves*, he was stripping the sound down in stages. And what had seemed two days earlier to be the finishing end was merely the starting point.

The final New York session on September 19th would run from 7 p.m. to 3:30 a.m., Dylan racking up thirty-seven takes of eight songs. This time, Ellen made her feelings known more often than the previous three sessions put together, perhaps sensing that tonight, of all nights, he needed some reassurance. Thus, after a bluesy, acoustic 'Meet Me In The Morning', she hits the talkback to offer, 'Hey Bob, I think you're a little out of tune.' And when he finally nails 'Buckets Of Rain' on the fourth take, she tells him, 'That was good.'

That Dylan needed some reassurance became clear from his own comment before 'Buckets Of Rain', 'This is hard. You gotta keep three or four things going at the same time – *just like life!*' Its immediate successor – a single-take 'If You See Her, Say Hello' – even prompted him to ask his muse, 'Whaddya think? Was it dramatic enough?' Ellen reassured him, 'It was real good,' ticking off another track for the album-to-be. But even her cajoling didn't always do the trick. When he asked her if a retake of 'Up To Me' was 'better', she said, encouragingly, 'I thought it was great.' Dylan refused to buy it: 'What was the matter with it?' 'Nothing that I could hear.' But to his razor-sharp ears something wasn't right, prompting him to attack the six-minute song no less than eight times that evening.

When he finally captured lightning in a bottle on a clattering 'Tangled Up In Blue', Phil Ramone simply bit his tongue and remembered the golden rule, 'You can't discard when you're working with Bob Dylan,' while Ellen took his side, '[Sure,] you can hear the sound of his fingernails on the guitar – that didn't matter to him [or me]. What was important was the overall emotional weight of the song.'

Though Dylan surpassed that 'Tangled Up In Blue' on the final take of the evening, this was the take he chose to open the album; almost as if he was toying with his audience, knowing the last sound listeners had heard on his previous album was the clatter of buttons. He also chose an 'Idiot Wind' from the 19th over the one from the first night, even though, by his own A&R-based admission, 'We fucked up a lot.'

After capturing 'Buckets Of Rain', 'If You See Her, Say Hello' and 'Tangled Up In Blue' in quick succession, it seems like he was starting to believe he had the Midas touch. A disastrous series of retakes followed, all songs he got right first time around – 'Simple Twist Of Fate', 'Big Girl', 'Meet Me In The Morning' – until Dylan enquired of Ramone, after a remake of 'Big Girl', 'Is this paying off at all?' All Ramone can say is, 'It's pretty, man.' Trying it again, Dylan finally remembered he had already nailed it, 'We must have had it on that other one . . . We ain't gonna do it better. I just keep hearing that organ.' But still, he keeps rolling tape, doing one last, surprisingly resplendent 'Tangled Up In Blue', the album's starting point and now, hopefully, its finishing end.

It was time to retire to Shel Silverstein's West Village apartment with Ellen and Mick Jagger, who had been mixing Rolling Stones live tapes all week in the adjoining studio. Ellen thinks 'we stayed up most of the night talking, and drinking Kahlúa and cream . . . I ran into Mick years later, and he remembered me as . . . the girl in the control room with a giant stopwatch around her neck.'

The stopwatch was needed because the album Dylan completed that night threatened to be the longest album ever to hit the *Billboard*

200. Even after jettisoning 'Call Letter Blues', the eleven-track album Dylan, Bernstein and Ramone assembled the following Monday clocked in at an eye-watering 61.30, only five minutes shorter than the Stones' 1972 classic, *Exile on Main Street* – and that was a double-album. One of the long songs would have to go. Given that he had two album-closers, 'Buckets Of Rain' and 'Up To Me' – one short, one long – the latter became that necessary sacrifice.

It would still take Dylan another fortnight to approve a final sequence, as it had with *Planet Waves*, making a provisional release date of November 1st, his third album of the year, a non-starter. Part of the delay was down to Dylan insisting on acetates being cut for each potential sequence. As Ellen recalls, 'We played around with different sequences, and then listened to them to see how they felt.'*

Eventually, on October 8th, the album mix was approved and a listening party arranged – theoretically, the final preview before heading for the presses. But when Dylan heard the final product it sounded different, prompting him to approach Rich Blakin, who had taken over as assistant engineer for the last two sessions, while Berger worked with Jagger:

> There was music, conversation, and milling around. Suddenly, Bob seemed to be meandering his way, drink in hand, shades on, toward me. He stopped four inches from my face. He was about eye-high. 'What did you do different?' he said . . . This was the last thing in the world I would have expected to be asked . . . See, I had mixed a few of the songs, Phil had mixed the rest . . . I said the first thing that came to mind, 'More reverb.' There was a pause, followed by the head gesture for okay, and he drifted away, back into the crowd.

Reverb was something of a Ramone trademark, and this album had it in digging implements. It also had a sustained intensity lacking in every LP since *John Wesley Harding*. Dylan still wasn't sure, and began playing an actual acetate to those whose opinion he respected, like Robbie Robertson – who thought it 'more powerfully personal than anything I'd heard him do in a long time' – and George Harrison, who

---

* Fortunately, Ellen had the presence of mind to keep some of the acetates, see Appendix IV in my *No One Else Could Play That Tune* (Route, 2018).

was just blown away by 'Tangled Up In Blue'. Once again, though, the opinion that hit the mark was the only negative one that came his way. And it came from a most unlikely quarter – his brother, David, who told him, flat out, 'You know this isn't going to be a radio record unless you do something to it.' So he did 'do something to it': he fucked it up royally.

Meanwhile, the one external voice who had been keeping him on the artistic straight and narrow for nine months was being edged out of the picture, and she knew not why: 'He was down here [in L.A.], I was up there [in San Francisco], and he wasn't terribly communicative, and I was left to do a lot of guessing. But it was definitely on a down[ward] swing.'

This was probably because Dylan was simultaneously working his way back into his wife's good graces. When he called to interrogate Ellen about the source of press reports on the sessions, she remembers him 'not coming directly out and saying: "Did you give this information out?" But he was trying to find out, without asking me, and I remember thinking, this is really weird . . . It was just too hard . . . and I didn't know what was going on.' In fact, it was Dylan himself who 'confirmed some details of the sessions' by phone, Larry Sloman recalls. What *really* was bothering Dylan were stories that appeared in the gossip columns in October suggesting he might be getting married again.

The subject never came up, even as he played the acetate one last time. As he told Cameron Crowe in 1985, 'I hadn't listened to it for a couple of months . . . [and] I thought the songs could have sounded different, better.' This time he turned for reassurance not to Ellen but to the album's technical overseer, Phil Ramone, as Berger listened in, 'We'd be in the control room recording, and the phone would ring . . . I'd hear Phil say, "Bob, it's amazing. Really. Probably your best album ever. Don't worry. It's great." Phil and I would [then] look at each other and shake our heads in disbelief.'

Meanwhile, Dylan had slipped into New York to confer with CBS execs on the album cover,* after which he dropped in on an old flame, Dana Gillespie, who was playing at Reno Sweeney's, where he got to

---

* The album cover was originally intended to be 'a shot of a huge red rose on a white background'.

meet her Trilby, David Bowie, no longer the latest new Dylan. And still, he was plagued by doubts, as his thoughts turned to re-recording part of the album, which had become something of a habit since *New Morning*.

He asked his brother if he could put together a band of local Minneapolis musicians to, as *Rolling Stone* later put it, lend 'a hand with the album's corrective surgery'. Ellen, for one, 'had absolutely no idea that he had any intention of re-recording any of the tracks. I thought it was as close to a perfect musical creation as had ever been recorded.'

That 'corrective surgery' could conceivably have left only a couple of minor scars. Musician Chris Weber, who arrived at the first Sound 80 session on December 27th with a Martin acoustic guitar Dylan was interested in, was the first to find out, 'He wasn't too happy with the original recording of the album, and wanted to have different takes of [some] tunes, so that he could decide which cuts he liked the best.'

Unfortunately, Dylan was now a man of wayward instincts. Predictably, everything he now cut, he used. He seemed particularly intent on reworking 'Idiot Wind', but couldn't make up his mind whether to howl or whisper, before taking a calypso cudgel to 'You're A Big Girl Now'. Neither had much to recommend them, but Dylan still departed with a 7½ ips reel of rough mixes 'to consider at his leisure'.

On the evidence of the tape he took with him, he was intent on stripping every ounce of subtlety from both songs. As Kevin Odegard, a participant at the sessions, noted, 'He overdubbed that organ [on 'Idiot Wind'] himself . . . He knew . . . how he wanted it to sound – he turned on the Leslie speaker and overdubbed it.' What Odegard didn't know – it wasn't revealed until the multitrack was accessed in 2018 – was that he also overdubbed his own vocal, and this time he used it. The mix was also rougher than a bear's backside, after engineer Paul Martinson discovered Dylan wanted it to sound like the 'rough mix' he'd taken away with him:

Paul Martinson: We started mixing, [and] as engineers do, I started cleaning things up, working the guitars, separating things out . . . Bob said, 'I really don't like this.' . . . 'What do you want to hear, [then]?' He pulled out a copy I had made for him of the rough studio mix we had done the night of the session, and said, 'I want it to sound like *this!*' . . .

Having proven that not much is really sacred – even when it came to his own work – three days later Dylan returned to rework 'Tangled Up In Blue', 'Lily, Rosemary And The Jack Of Hearts' and 'If You See Her, Say Hello', all of which he gave the Sound 80 sound, with thankfully better results. A take of 'Tangled Up In Blue' gave him 'a radio record' and 'Lily, Rosemary' took its share of musical liberties while still raising a smile.

But if he imagined that anyone privileged to hear the 'New York version' of the album was going to share his belief that this was better, he was quickly disabused. When he turned up at Shangri-La, the new studio home of The Band, to play the two Robs this new version, Fraboni remembers, 'Robbie and I look[ed] at each other, [as if] to say, "What the hell happened?" We loved that other record. Robbie said [after Bob left], "Leave it to Bob. He makes these kinds of choices."'

Joni Mitchell would also later accuse him of acting in character: 'He took the vulnerability out of [*Blood on the Tracks*], and in the process he took the depth out. The New York sessions were touching. [On] the Minnesota sessions . . . he reasserted himself again as a man.' West coast promotion man, 'Rap' Rappaport – an early recipient of the 'New York' version – had to tell himself, 'Well, some of these new versions are good. They're not *bad*. It's still an amazing record. It's just not what it was.'

It was the new 'Idiot Wind' which seemed to particularly upset those who had heard it in all its A&R glory, Glenn Berger describing the new version, a tad unfairly, as 'this searing, wrenching, bloody song turned into a happy little jingle'. Tony Brown also felt 'that what Paul Griffin and I did was far superior to what was used on the final album. Nothing can touch our version of "Idiot Wind."'

Inevitably, the original New York versions were promptly bootlegged, and Ellen, for one, was delighted: '[It meant] everyone could experience what . . . I still believe was one of the epic creations of his legendary career.' But for most folk, the appearance in the shops of the recalibrated *Blood on the Tracks* on January 20th – just a year and three days after *Planet Waves* – was still a cause for unbridled celebration. They had no point of comparison, knew nothing of the pain he had not so much risen above as masked over, and would not for a while.

This time, it wasn't just Ralph J. Gleason who felt he had got Dylan back again.* It was just about anyone who wielded a critical pen, including those to whom Dylan had once given the time of day: 'good critic' Paul Nelson described it as 'vital and alive, its despair tempered throughout with the joy of being a survivor,' while Paul Williams – no longer at *Crawdaddy* – advised 'every singer currently working the rock circuit . . . to shut up for a year and just listen to . . . Dylan's diction on this album.'

Nick Kent, Britain's own archdeacon of rock critics and a fierce critic of Dylan's last offering, thought the album, 'Despite its manifold flaws, makes statements that overshadow anything currently being put out in the rot of the medium.' Greil Marcus, at *Rolling Stone*, simply stated, 'No one else in rock & roll could make a record like this,' while Michael Gray – the author of the first serious book-length study of Dylan's work, *Song & Dance Man* – considered 'the sum of these parts [to be] a greater whole than either the Dylan of the sixties, or any artist since, [has] ever brought to rock'.

Only blood brothers Dave Marsh and Jon Landau carped at Dylan's achievement, making themselves look irredeemably stupid into the bargain, Landau foolishly dismissing it as an album which 'will only sound like a great album for a while' (an even dumber critique than his take on *Pat Garrett*). By the time *Rolling Stone* convened a symposium of critics to review the album in their March 13th issue, *Blood on the Tracks* was number one on both sides of the pond. The fans all agreed: They had got *their* Dylan back again.

And so had Sara. A month earlier, to the day, 'Random Notes' turned gossipmonger to report that 'Dylan's mid-30s romantic lurchings seem to have ended. Months ago rumors flew of an imminent marriage breakup. But Bob is back with Sarah [sic] and the kids.' That, apparently, was that. On March 23rd, 1975 he was a special guest at a benefit concert in San Francisco – Ellen's hometown. Very publicly present on his arm that day was Sara. The circle, it seemed, was complete.

But he had come back from New York a changed man, and try as he might, 'that's when our marriage started breaking up. She never knew what I was talking about, what I was thinking about, and I couldn't

---

* Gleason would join the clamour, using his regular column in *Rolling Stone* to laud the album in a piece called 'The Blood of a Poet', a Cocteau reference Dylan doubtless enjoyed.

possibly explain it.' He would not see Ellen again until May 1976, but when he did, he was performing with a pick-up band on the second Rolling Thunder Revue a set-list that included 'You're Gonna Make Me Lonesome When You Go', 'Tangled Up In Blue', 'Simple Twist Of Fate' and an incandescent 'Idiot Wind'. Turns out Raeben called it right. He was still an idiot.

Winterlude #3

May 1975:
Lost In France

Now, suddenly, here's this startlingly exposed figure standing in the sunlight. Could this be the real Bob Dylan? We still can't know. But we do know there's something profoundly different about this album. We don't know what change has come about in Dylan's life. Maybe even he doesn't. In any case, he isn't saying . . .

CBS ad for Blood on the Tracks, Rolling Stone 13th March 1975.

Bob Dylan: I haven't been able to spend as much time with my wife as I would like to.
Jim Jerome: Are you living with your wife?
Bob Dylan: When I have to, when I need to.

People Weekly 10th November 1975.

I can see the turning of the screw / I've spent too much time avoiding you.

An early draft of 'Abandoned Love', June 1975.

*

In July 1981, Dylan finally played his first shows in the south of France, generating a great deal of publicity and excitement, especially for the final, open-air show of his European Tour, in Avignon on the 25th. As far as most non-readers of *Libération* knew, this was his first time he'd ventured outside of Paris. Sure, in 1978 Dylan had talked about 'recently' visiting the King of Gypsies in southern France on his birthday, but as the man himself almost said, if you want somebody you can trust, trust someone else.

Now came evidence he might have been telling the truth: a feature in the esteemed left-of-centre French newspaper two days before the Avignon gig; an interview with the painter David Oppenheim, under the headline, 'I Could Have Kidnapped Dylan', in which Oppenheim (seemingly) revealed where Dylan had been in the spring of 1975, and what he had been doing:

At that time I had just built myself a house in Savoie . . . He arrived at two in the morning. We stayed together for two months [sic] . . . Two of us together here, alone. To see this bloke completely despairing, isolated, lost – I didn't want to be like him . . . He was having problems with his wife. She was supposed to have come with him but she hadn't arrived. He phoned her every day . . . We lived an adventurous life. No complications. We screwed women, we drank, we ate . . .

Two days later, in the foyer of the Hotel de l'Europe, the two men would be reunited for the first time in six years. It never occurred to Oppenheim that Dylan – who constantly insisted he never read the press, and couldn't read French – might have seen the article. But there he is with a copy of *Libération* under his arm, which he unfolds and points to the line, 'We screwed women, we drank, we ate . . .'

Over the intervening years Dylan had evidently forgotten the unapologetic character of his host from long ago. Oppenheim bristled at the *j'accuse*, 'You're going to believe this shitty reporter! I said that as a joke, in the middle of a conversation. Listen, if you don't like it, I'm leaving.' Never one who liked tables being turned on his staged acts of confrontation, Dylan indicated it was not important, and the painter agreed to stay. That night Dylan would dedicate a song to his 'great friend, the French painter, David Oppenheim'. Now a Christian, the dedication came after 'Slow Train', the song of a penitent who might have recognized the portrait Oppenheim had recently painted in words about the man who shared his food and drink in spring '75:

Pathetic and superb at the same time, Dylan is a bloke who invents everything. He's the most egotistical person I know. That's what makes him an incredible person – his amazing self-confidence . . . When I got him to understand that he was completely mad, he would grow pale in the face, and that made me feel good because I identified with the person that I thought he was in those moments of inner understanding . . . This bloke who talked of nothing but love was very, very much on his own.

If Oppenheim reached this assessment of his guest while Dylan slept in his house, he had done so in double-quick time. The 'two months' they spent together was in reality a fortnight at most, hence the title of a slim monograph self-published in 2018 by former student of Fine Arts Robert Martin, *Dix Jours Avec Bob Dylan*. Martin, at twenty-two, had been hired by Oppenheim to wire up his barn in exchange for some art lessons. Imagine Martin's surprise then, when on May 22nd, 1975 their guest arrived, almost alone.*

Oppenheim was already unamused by the flurry of mutually-contradictory telegrams which had preceded his guest: 'One day it was, Mr Dylan will come with his wife, Sara, then the next day, "he won't come," "he's coming tomorrow," "in a month['s time]." I was fed up.' In fact, Sara's absence would cast a shadow over the whole fortnight, as Dylan ate up his francs making daily long-distance calls to his recently-reconciled wife. Not that this was how it came across to Oppenheim:

> When he arrived at my place in Savoie, I thought he was going to stay for three or four days and then I realized why he had come. His wife didn't want to see him anymore, and in his head he thought that I was going to bring him something fresh, an inspiration, to live experiences. With me, he was safe from his fame.

On one amusing occasion, when Oppenheim was in the room as Dylan was talking into the phone, 'He hands [it to] me. It was Sara. We talk for a couple of minutes, Dylan stands there with his arms crossed, staring at me. She asks me how it's going. I tell her, "Don't worry, he's well fed." She laughed. I felt like I was talking about a child.'

Even an ocean away, it seems the songwriter could not stop himself mooning over his own white goddess. And as Oppenheim confirms, he was always 'clutching his notebook. He would write down everything

---

* Actually, Dylan brought a female translator with him, Yannick, arranged at CBS's behest.

he saw all day.' So, this could be when he began a song he wrote 'for the only woman I ever married, before I got to know her'. It seems he never completed the song in question, but in the same notebook he refers to 'a place I remember/ That I can't get back in', and 'a beautiful woman/ Standing (equal to me).' In fact, he had never felt equal to his muse, whom he knew had been the inspiration for all men down the ages, and her name was Anatha, Ishtar, Eurydice . . .

The night the American poet arrived, Oppenheim told an excited Dylan about the annual pilgrimage of the gypsies to the Saintes Maries de la Mer, which was taking place May 24-25th, when Saint Sara 'The Black', the protector of gypsies, was celebrated. Oppenheim 'saw in his eyes that it echoed'. Dylan wanted to go there and see. According to an onstage rap with which he prefaced 'One More Cup Of Coffee' in the fall of 1978, that's exactly what they now did:

A few years ago I went over to the South of France. The day I was born, it happens to be a high holy gypsy holiday. The gypsies all get together on that particular day and they have a party for about a week. It's like Christmas time. [So,] I went . . . and checked it out. And I was fortunate enough to meet the King of the Gypsies over there. A young man with sixteen wives and 125 children, I swear. And a lot of girlfriends too. Anyway, he took me under his wing, and I stayed with them about a week and partied with them.

This version of events, though – one Dylan assiduously embroidered over the years and reiterated in Martin Scorsese's 2019 mockumentary, *Rolling Thunder Revue* – Oppenheim rather shot down in a November 2018 interview:

There are gypsy kings on every street corner! . . . I went to see [this gypsy king] alone, telling him that I was with a very rich American singer who could buy [from] him objects in his flea market. He didn't want to meet Dylan, and didn't even know who he was. Dylan didn't even get out of the car.

To further debunk the legend, it turns out the King of Gypsies was actually a scrap-metal dealer, who lived 'behind a . . . vast field full of carcasses and scrap metal, [with] barking dogs tied to chains, [in] a

house surrounded by an iron terrace – neither fortune teller nor flamenco dancer . . . [and] scrap metal as far as the eye can see.'

After the gypsy festival, Dylan convinced Oppenheim, Martin and
Yannick that a few days in Corsica would be 'very nice'. While there,
he shared a room with Oppenheim, to whom he showed some song-
ideas, one of which was a song about Marseille – the setting for the
sequel to *The French Connection*, which had opened the week before.
Oppenheim 'told him it was a bad idea, it didn't sound right, it sounded
like he was talking about bouillabaisse!' By now, Oppenheim had realized they were hardly kindred spirits and presumed Dylan wouldn't
take the slightest notice:

> Not once did he ask me how I earned my living . . . He had lost touch
> with reality . . . I was fed up with it, I thought I would be calm once [he
> went off] the continent. But no, it had to last longer . . . He was sleeping
> dressed next to me, with his boots on and everything. To piss him off, I
> used to put his hat on his head . . . I tried to get him involved in all sorts
> of things, just to make him understand that he didn't know anything
> about anything.

He had a shock when he heard Dylan's next album, and discovered
the singer had simply substituted Mozambique – a place he doesn't seem
to have actually visited – for Marseille. Of course, Oppenheim's increas-
ing annoyance with Dylan could have been partly down to his obvious
success with women; in stark contrast to his own, near-disastrous
attempt at a dangerous liaison. While in Corsica, Oppenheim unwisely
began flirting with a young, pretty brunette who was already spoken for.
When a rather drunk Oppenheim, in a fit of fantasy, suggests he'd like to
marry her in the village church, 'the brunette's boyfriend, a guy from
Cervione, [threaten]ed to kill' him. Fortunately, one of his friends, a
wealthy local who lived in a castle, talked the suitor down.

On the other hand, when Dylan took a fancy to another 'little brunette, a secretary' in Marseille, who may or may not have known who
he was, he simply asked Oppenheim to introduce them, and took it
from there. Even on the last night, in Paris, before returning to New
York, a dog-tired Dylan almost scored at the home of Baba Limousin,
a decorator and friend of David's. Baba, who lived with her sister on
the rue de Milan, in the ninth arrondissement, later recalled:

They both arrived around 9pm. We didn't have much to eat, just boiled potatoes. He was quite taciturn, I didn't even realize it was him at first, it didn't make me hot or cold . . . My sister made him listen to tango, Astor Piazzolla, I remember he loved it. He had drawn something on a small napkin, but I lost it. He also wanted to know why I lived here, in Paris, and not on a farm . . . [My sister spent the night with him, but] almost nothing happened, he was stoned, tired, and [then she] took him the next day for a walk in Saint-Germain-Dès-Prés.

After this one last liaison, Oppenheim finally said goodbye to the rock star. He could get back to his painting, and willing obscurity. Not for him a monograph on his *Ten Days With Dylan*. In fact, he wished he'd never opened his mouth as to where Dylan had been holed up when he turned thirty-four.

Meanwhile, his famous guest had another idea for a song, and this one he would later say was on a 'subject so large it might be an entire album'. Throughout his stay, Dylan had been carrying around a book called *The Sixteenth Round*, about an imprisoned ex-boxer called 'Hurricane Carter'. Asked about it by his host, Dylan had explained it was about 'a black boxer sentenced to life for a murder of which he proclaims his innocence for nine years'. He had found another cause to champion, and even if he only had the boxer's word that he was innocent, Dylan's commitment was for now steadfast. So long, Saintes Maries de la Mer – howdy, Patterson, New Jersey . . .

Part 4

Like A Thief In The Night

Behold, I am coming like a thief! Blessed is the one who stays awake.

Revelation 16:15.

It happens to everybody – . . . periods when people . . . lose it and have to regain it, or lose it and gain something else.

Dylan, to Jonathan Cott, 17th September 1978.

Our [group's] singer is called Josephine. Anyone who has not heard her does not know the power of song . . . Among intimates we admit freely to one another that Josephine's singing, as singing, is nothing out of the ordinary. Is it in fact singing at all? . . . Josephine's alleged vocal skill might be [easily] disproved. But that would merely clear the ground for the real mystery which needs solving – the enormous influence she has . . . She [herself] denies any connection between her art and ordinary piping . . . For those who hold the contrary opinion she has only contempt . . . She believes . . . she is singing to deaf ears; there is no lack of enthusiasm and applause, but she has long learned not to expect real understanding.

'Josephine The Singer', Franz Kafka, 1924.*

---

* The Kafka short-story is cited by Michael McClure in his 1974 article on Dylan, 'The Poet's Poet'.

I can tell you that it doesn't mean anything to [Dylan] that people might not like what he is doing. Him still do it. And that is the most important thing. Him still do it.

Bob Marley.

An artist is a creature driven by demons . . . He is completely amoral in that he will rob, borrow, beg or steal from anybody and everybody to get the work done.

William Faulkner.

To speak about Bob is usually to try and pin him down in some kind of way.

Jim Keltner, to Damien Love, 2018.

June to December 1975: Rolling With The Thunder

Bill Flanagan: Why didn't you try to sustain what you'd tapped into with *Blood on the Tracks*? Why not try to keep it going?
Bob Dylan: I guess I never intended to keep that going. It was an experiment that came off.

March 1985.

He's alchemized a lot of the hang-ups of his past. Like his insecurity, which has now become an acceptance of and an ability to work with continuous change.

Allen Ginsberg, to Nat Hentoff, November 1975.

My son got where he is today not because of his father and me. He was born to us, but then he went away and he did this on his own.

Beattie Zimmerman, to Larry Sloman, November 1975.

There was a Rolling Thunder energy, which was his invention.

Joan Baez, *Rolling Thunder Revue* (2019).

Behind the Rolling Thunder's hang-loose spontaneity, Bob was choreographing all of it.

Ken Regan, RTR photographer, *All Access.*

He's really brilliant, but sometimes he acts . . . like there are gaps in his perception and if you fill in the spots for him, he really freaks out.

Roger McGuinn, 1975.

Louie [Kemp] and some of the other guys I met from Minnesota . . .
they're all a little bit awed by him. [They] seem to have a relationship
[with each other] similar to the guys I grew up with, a lot of put-down
humour, a lot of irony, a certain kind of toughness that city kids get.
[But] I think that Dylan . . . is cut off from those kind of roots.

Mel Howard, 1975.

Bob had been through several lifetimes by the time Rolling Thunder
happened and he brought people together – people he'd just met,
people he'd found on the street, old friends he'd been travelling with for
decades . . . [It] taught me how to pace a show; how to make a movie;
how to write a poem . . . It was a master class in art and show
business.

T-Bone Burnett, 2019.

★

Between March and June 1975, the chameleon poet had fully lived up to
his name, blending into the scenery and disappearing into the woodwork. Then, starting on June 25th – with a surprise appearance in the
audience at a Patti Smith concert – he was rarely out of the limelight
for the remainder of the year, riding the crest of a critical wave of
approval. But for a few weeks after his return from Corsica via France,
he seemed content to scout the East Village, rediscovering the well-
spring that had inspired him a decade and a half earlier. Revolution, it
seems, was still in the air as he encountered another muse at the café
of an Italian poet from the fourteenth century:

Claudia Levy: I met Bob in the Dánte Caffé, where I was working as a
waitress, in late May / early June '75. When he came in, I said, 'You look
very familiar to me.' . . . He thought that was very funny. My graduate
degree was [in] Poetry, so I said, 'Oh, are you a poet?' He said, 'Well, I
like to write.' So, we talked a lot about poetry. He asked me what I did,
and I said I was going to go study painting at the Brooklyn Museum
School. He said, 'Don't do that . . . You go study with this guy, and he'll
change your life.' And he sent me to Norman Raeben, [who] became
my teacher. . . . The third day he was sitting [in the café], the light was
coming in in a certain way and you could see the light through his hair.

I [realized], 'Oh my God. I've just been sitting here casually chatting with Bob Dylan!' I was so flustered. I said, 'I know who you are.' And he said, 'Does that mean you're not going to talk to me anymore?' [2020]

While becoming ever more friendly with Claudia, he continued to attend to business, awaiting the next wave of inspiration to hit. Back in the early spring, he had popped by Malibu's Shangri-La Studios to see how the two Robs – Fraboni and Robertson – were getting on with setting up their new home away from home, as the rest of The Band slowly set about upping sticks and leaving the Catskills for la-la-land. According to Robertson, it had been Dylan who had given them something to do by bringing up the subject of the basement tapes, irked by another piratical piece of product:

While we were chatting, he mentioned another bootleg of our basement tapes coming out, and how it really annoyed him . . . I suggested going back to the original tapes to see if there were some tracks we could release properly. We didn't want to put out music that was sonically unacceptable, but with the technology of the time, I thought maybe Rob . . . and I could reduce some of the hiss and improve the sound quality. Bob agreed . . . Anyway, we did all that was possible at the time to make the music . . . less like a field recording.

Not content with reducing the basement tapes from mile-wide stereo to mono, Robbie overdubbed instruments on a couple of tracks and added two 'fake' Band tracks to the 24-track double-album. Despite Dylan telling Mary Travers back in March he wanted it released 'so people could hear it in its entirety', it featured just sixteen Dylan cuts (somehow omitting 'Quinn The Eskimo' and the sublime 'I Shall Be Released') and six genuine Band *Big Pink*-era recordings.

But it was another payday bonanza for the perpetually hard-up Band members, just a year after *Before the Flood*, after Dylan put his name to a six-figure contract to 'transfer and assign to CBS all right, title and interest in and to certain master recordings embodied on the double LP phonograph album entitled *The Basement Tapes*' on June 9th, providing a welcome reminder of a period when Dylan found collaboration a really good way to write songs.

For now, though, he had only a few scraps in his lyrical locker, and a single completed song – the tasty 'One More Cup Of Coffee' – suitable for *Blood on the Tracks'* much-awaited successor. As he told *Rolling Stone* reporter Larry Sloman, later that summer, 'I certainly wasn't thinking of making a record album . . . [All] I had [was] bits and pieces of some songs I was working on.'

He did, however, have a yen to write his first protest song in four years, having finished reading *The Sixteenth Round*, the first-person account of the plight of Rubin Carter, who had been indicted and convicted of the murder of a barman and two customers late at night in a New Jersey bar, back in June 1966, based largely on the unreliable testimony of two convicted burglars, Bello and Bradley.

The way Dylan described his first, early June visit to the incarcerated Carter to Sloman, that auspicious meeting was almost the first thing he did after returning Stateside: 'I had come back from overseas and I hadn't [really] talked with anybody for a long time . . . I took notes because I wasn't aware of all the facts. I thought that maybe some time I could . . . condense it down and put it into a song . . . The intention was just to keep the facts straight.' But sticking to the facts had never been Dylan's m.o. when he felt like protestin', and this was no exception. Even before he found a collaborator who could help tell 'the story of the Hurricane' in song, he was already taking liberties with the events that dark, sad night, suggesting it was gangsters who did the deed and Arthur Bradley – who wasn't even there – was riffling through the corpses:

> Two gangsters entered a barroom
> The bartender grabbed a bottle, heaved it at one of 'em
> Then the gangsters opened up and left 3 people dead . . .
> Now you might ask why they['re] doing this to him and not you
> 'Cause you don't speak your mind out, that's why,
> Arthur heard shots down the street and he went over to investigate
> And, arriving first on the scene, he robbed the dead bodies . . .

Having got this far, and no further, he turned his mind instead to 'a song about marriage' he was also struggling to formalise. This one was strictly at the idea stage, Dylan envisaging a three-tiered narrative which somehow involved robbing a corpse, but also punishing one's brother, who is 'an assassin [of] one's mother, to avenge one's father'.

In the end, the narrator is obliged to 'surrender the corp[s]e', and await 'rescue by friends'. By the time it became 'Isis' – as I presume it did – little remained of its original allegorical conceit or the ritualized murder of Horus.

He was still mulling over the twin themes of crime and punishment when he caught Patti Smith, a rising star in the downtown firmament, at Paul Colby's new club, The Other End. It was night one of a five-night residency for Clive Davis's latest signing to Arista, and according to Colby, Smith was 'doing a cover version of a Rolling Stones song ["Time Is On My Side"] when he came in. They locked onto each other immediately. She said something to him from the stage like, "Don't think you can park your car next to my meter."' Dylan immediately recognized a kindred spirit:

> **Patti Smith**: He started getting really turned on by the idea of the band – my guys – . . . pushing me and not faltering, or wondering about what musical changes to go into . . . Bob started going up on stage, jamming with these [Village] people . . . getting attracted to certain people – Rob Stoner, Bobby Neuwirth – it was great to see him and Bob back together . . . He was thinking about improvisation, about extending himself language-wise. In the talks that we had, there was something that he admired about me that was difficult [for me] to comprehend.

He desired his own band of brothers; something different from Robbie's renegades or Patti's patsies. Though he had never toured with anyone but The Band, their sound no longer synched with the one inside a head which was no longer coursing with wild mercury. Instead, he heard gypsy violins. So, when, four days after the Patti epiphany, he saw a gypsy-like woman walking through the Village with a violin case, he couldn't help but ask her who she was, and where she was going. The lady in question was Scarlet Rivera. The man who'd accosted her in the street needed no introduction.

Sensing a villager with her own aura, Dylan did the only thing he could do: he invited her to a small rehearsal studio to jam. Even though Scarlet in 1990 could not recall any specific songs he asked her to play that day, save for 'One More Cup Of Coffee', she instinctively realized it was some kind of test, 'I'm sure [he] consciously didn't play anything that he had recorded before, so that I couldn't have a head start on knowing how it sounded, or how to play it. [But] after playing a few songs . . . there was a little half smile.' He could hear a key turning.

Duly inspired, he completed his first American song since he left his own blood all over the tracks on last year's Columbia comeback. Three days later, he got up at The Other End, vacated by Patti in time for the return of Ramblin' Jack Elliott – whom Dylan had first met at Woody's bedside on January 26th, 1961. He had already told Colby, 'he wanted to get onstage so bad he could taste it, but he was worried, "These are new songs. I just want to make sure I'm not recorded." . . . Sure enough, there was a girl at one of the back tables with a tape recorder and her pocketbook open . . . [So,] I took the tape recorder.' It was a pyrrhic victory. A more covert Boston-based Springsteen nut was rolling tape, capturing Dylan on a roll, singing an untitled song which suggested any reconciliation with Sara had come with strings. If the lyrics he sang that night were classic Dylan, in the original manuscript one could hear an idiot wind blowing through:

> I can read the writing on the wall
> I've been deceived by my good friends, one and all
> My Patron Saint is dancing on a train
> Something is telling me I wear the ball and chain.*

He now had two songs worthy of a successor to *Blood* – plus 'Golden Loom' – but still wasn't thinking about another album. All that changed the night he met up – a second time – with Jacques Levy, a musical director who had written lyrics with Roger McGuinn. Again, it was at The Bitter End, probably on July 5th. Within ten days, he would have enough of 'these movies [in song] that take place in eight-to-ten minutes, yet seem as full or fuller than regular movies' – Levy's own description of Dylan's balladic *métier* – to make an album. Their collaboration was not entirely spur of the moment. Dylan broached the idea the previous May, while still engrossed in songs too personal to share:

---

* The song became 'Abandoned Love', the second couplet of which he revised, to: 'My patron saint is dancing on a train/ My friends have gone their way, while I remain,' and then at The Other End, 'My patron saint is fighting with a ghost/ He's always off somewhere when I need him most.'

Jacques Levy: Bob and McGuinn have known each other for years, of course, and Bob knew all the things I'd written for McGuinn. Two years ago [sic], we met for the first time on the street here. He was walking one way and I was walking the other, and we both knew who each other was, so we stopped and talked. We spent the evening together, agreed to meet again and maybe work together, and left it at that.

The time was ripe, the tide was high. They adjourned to Levy's Village apartment to talk and imbibe some more. The first song-idea they discussed was the story of the 'Hurricane'. Dylan himself would write in abandoned sleeve notes for *Desire*: 'That's the song I wanted to write, but the subject [was] so large it might be an entire album, instead of a song.' It didn't happen that night because, as Levy later recalled, 'Bob didn't have a guitar with him. I didn't have a guitar either, but I had a piano and "Isis" was the one song that he had started to write on the piano. It was so slow . . . it would have taken a whole side of the album.'

It was a propitious choice, as the stars aligned. As Levy told *Melody Maker*'s Chris Charlesworth, 'By the following morning it was finished. We did it together, going back and forth and trying things out on each other . . . He had [had] the general feeling of the song when he came around here, but he hadn't got [any] further.' By the time Dylan left, he felt 'we had this song which was out there'. Out there enough to contain a coda, which was still there on a July 10th work-tape the pair made at Levy's apartment:

> True love never goes wrong
> Body to body, it's always the same
> So never say no when you hear a love song
> It's always on purpose and part of God's game.

Otherwise, it was the song Dylan would record twenty days later (save for the lovers' final exchange, which on the work-tape was, 'I said that's okay/ And she asked me to stay'). Suddenly, they were hanging out at The Other End every night, and retiring to Levy's apartment in the wee small hours to write more songs – as you do. Dylan even shared some of the results with his fellow barflies, Levy recalling one occasion when Dylan announced 'to these people sitting there that we had just written a new song, "Did [they] want to hear it?" Everybody, of course, says, "Sure, sure." He doesn't sing the song. He opens up the piece of paper and he reads it to them, like . . . a poem.' He hadn't done that since September 1962. The man was enjoying himself:

> **Paul Colby**: He was comfortable. He saw people he hadn't seen in years . . . More and more people began stopping by the club. Cindy Bullens, Ronee Blakley, Allen Ginsberg, Eric Katz, Logan English . . . As Logan walked past him, Dylan said, 'Is that you, Logan? I thought you were dead.' Logan said, 'I heard the same thing about you a couple of times.'

One night he invited Claudia down from the Caffé Dánte to the club, (re)introducing her to Jacques. They were soon a couple, and then husband-wife, 'Isis' redacted into real life. Another July evening, McGuinn walked in to find 'Bob and Jacques Levy sitting at a small table in the back room, drinking brandy. Bob yelled, "[Hey,] McGuinn, we were just talking about you!"' The only night the pair went elsewhere, they broke bread at some friends of Levy's, the Orbachs, who spent the evening regaling their esteemed guests with stories about the late Joey Gallo, a New York gangster.

Far from being appalled by the carnage 'Crazy Joe' left in his bloody wake, Dylan decided, 'He retained a certain amount of his freedom and he went out the way he had to.' They returned to Levy's apartment and wrote 'The Ballad Of Joey Gallo', an eleven-minute movie-in-song whose subject-matter would rattle some cages. Unfazed, the pair continued to write about subjects 'so large [they] might be an entire album'.

During that heady week, they even began rewriting 'Hurricane', the first verse of which read like a movie screenplay, 'Pistol shots ring out in a barroom night. Enter Patty Valentine . . . Roll credits: This is the story of the Hurricane . . .' At this juncture, 'Isis' was nearly nine minutes, 'Hurricane' and 'Joey' were both over ten. They already had an album with the two Dylan solo originals and a ribald verbal riff about Rita Mae Brown, author of *Rubyfruit Jungle*. Indeed, so immersed was Dylan in the moment he convened a session at Columbia just nine days after he and Levy started writing songs to record some of their output to date.

From not even thinking about an album on Independence Day, he found himself starting work on one on Bastille Day. He wasn't just seizing the day, he was wringing it dry. Nor was he cowed by the complexity or length of the songs he and Jacques had written. When a nine-piece band – Scarlet, five members of the Dave Mason Band and a trio of girlsingers – convened at Columbia at 7 p.m. on July 14th, Dylan may have fondly imagined he might capture all that he had. As it is, he cut just 'Joey' in seven takes (the last of which is preceded by the engineer calling out, 'Okay, this is lucky take seven') and 'Rita Mae'. In the guise of wailing mourners, the girlsingers slotted in easily on 'Joey', but were too much of an in-joke on 'Rita Mae'. They all called it a night at 3:30 a.m., not knowing if the 'big band' experiment was abandoned or merely on hold.

Dylan felt he needed a few more songs in his back pocket, even though he had an album's worth already. He suggested to Levy they adjourn to a place he had out in the Hamptons and provide themselves with more options. As Levy noted, 'Nobody was around, and the two of us were just there for three weeks.' Actually, it was ten days. Levy was equally inflationary with the number of songs they wrote there, suggesting it was fourteen. It was no more than half a dozen, including two fantasy travelogues, 'Black Diamond Bay' and 'Romance In Durango' – in both of which the protagonists meet their Maker – plus a song Dylan considered too personal to share.

Levy remembered his co-lyricist 'had been fooling with ["Sara"] . . . for a long time. He'd got the choruses down, but the verses were actually written out at this place on Long Island . . . [with] the dunes and beach and all that stuff . . . [mentioned] in the song.' Save for an early draft of 'Hurricane' it is the only handwritten *Desire* draft in the Tulsa archive.* And like the *Planet Waves* songs he'd directed at 'her', it seemed to lose some of its edge in the rewriting. Originally Dylan remembered her 'unbuttoned on the lawn', a pet frog called Flamingo and them at a Forest Hills shooting gallery, before earnestly enquiring, 'Whatever happened to that side of you?'

The ninth and final verse of this pre-Hamptons draft seemed to suggest any imminent return to him might not be a given – 'The North Atlantic is calling for you/ I left the door open and I hope you come

---

* One must assume Levy wrote out lyrics on which they collaborated, hence their absence from the archive.

through.' That she retained her position on a pedestal was seemingly affirmed by a long list of female personae on the reverse side of the 'Sara' lyric, including Empress, White Goddess, Queen Bee, Lady of the Lake, Mother Supreme, Scarlet Angel and Bright Prophetess. Would he even dare to record such an autobiographical aria? Too personal to collaborate on, it was certainly too personal to share with the two-dozen musicians present at Columbia Studio E on June 28th, there to help him complete his third album in twenty months.

This wrecking crew included his old friend, Eric Clapton, who was shocked to find, 'like, twenty-four musicians in the studio, all playing these incredibly incongruous instruments – accordion, violin – and it didn't really work. He was after a large sound, but the songs were so personal.' Another attendee informed Dylan's old friend, Michael Bloomfield, he'd been asked to play 'some acoustic guitar at that session [but] . . . it was crazy, insanity reigned . . . twenty guitar players playing at once; no one knowing what was supposed to happen.'

Another soul struggling to make sense of the tsunami of sound was a young Emmylou Harris, fresh from making her first solo album, brought in to sing harmony with Dylan on songs she didn't know and hadn't been given time to learn: 'I just watched his mouth and watched what he was saying. That's where all that humming comes from. You can hear me humming on some of those tracks . . . I didn't even know I was supposed to come in and had to jump fast.'

Unfortunately, it's probably too late to fully document these two 'big band' sessions (July 28th-29th). Sony Music have mislaid most of the session-tapes, though only after a Dylan scholar ('that be me') xeroxed all the multitrack sheets in the mid-Nineties.* So, at least we have documentary evidence of the kind of instrumentation producer Don DeVito piled high on 16-track, 'big band' versions of 'Hurricane', 'One More Cup Of Coffee' and 'Oh, Sister'. But that is all. In a rather sick joke at posterity's expense, we instead have multiple versions of 'Catfish' and 'Money Blues' from *both* days perfectly preserved on tape. Neither really warranted official release, then or now.†

---

* The complete multitrack sheets for the album are reproduced in my *Dylan: Behind Closed Doors* (1996).
† Krogsgaard attributes the 'Catfish' on *The Bootleg Series Vols. 1-3* (1991) to the 29th. It is from the 28th.

As of 2022, the only 'big band' versions *of the album tracks* definitely extant comprise 'Romance In Durango' (the master take), from the 28th; the seven-minute 'Black Diamond Bay' (takes 1-12; takes 1, 4, 8, 11 and 12 complete) and 'Mozambique' (takes 4-7, takes 4 and 7 complete). These merely confirm the recollection of one anonymous soul, who told Sloman, 'Sometimes it sound[ed] like two different songs recorded at the same time.' Dylan's 1978 memory of these sessions also reflects a rising frustration: 'We tried it with a lot of different people in the studio, a lot of different types of sound and I even had back-up singers on that album for two or three days, a lot of percussion, a lot going on . . . I couldn't sleep.'

'Mozambique' certainly sounds at times like two different songs, with a recording of a train-wreck in the middle, while 'Black Diamond Bay' meanders like a boat without a sail across five full takes of a song more intricate – musically and lyrically – than 95% of the Dylan canon.

Everyone there seemed to want to play on everything. The one exception was Rob Stoner, whom Dylan first met when the bassist was playing with John Herald back in 1972. When Bob heard him backing Ramblin' Jack in early July, he said, 'Hey man. Let's do something someday.' Stoner thought this 'is basically what people in his position say to every musician they meet'. But Dylan meant it. The subsequently summoned Stoner arrived at Studio E, and was appalled by what he saw and heard, 'I mean, they had a buffet table . . . it was like a backstage reception thing after a gig more than a recording session . . . and there was no room for me to jump in on any of these tunes . . . I mean, I wanted no part of this when I saw [what was] going on.' Finally, late on the 29th, after the others retired to the End, a despairing DeVito asked Rob Stoner what he thought. He gave it to him straight, no pussyfooting:

> I told him that I thought it was not a likely way to get a productive project out of Bob Dylan, that it was too crowded, it was too confusing, it was inefficient. Bob's music really is dependent on catching a moment . . . So, DeVito asked me what I would suggest. I said, 'Why don't you come in with a tiny band . . . no girlfriends, no wives, no nothing!'

With English pub-rockers Kokomo – never a good fit – splitting the scene, never to return, Dylan had need of a new drummer. Stoner knew the perfect foil – Howie Wyeth, who, when he wasn't playing boogie-woogie piano in bars, played drums like a metronome with a heart.

The next night Dylan returned to Studio E, with just Stoner, Wyeth, Scarlet and Emmylou in tow. The buffet was gone, as were the hangers on, and in one night this quintet recorded nine songs – two of them ten minutes-plus; another couple nudging eight. Almost everything, perhaps everything, would be captured on its first full take.* And Stoner knew why, 'We could get that first-take spontaneity because we didn't have to keep going over and over things to show them to all these musicians who were faking it . . . His music is *in the moment*. And all you need to get is one take without mistakes – without terrible mistakes, I should say, because there are plenty of mistakes on Dylan records.' Even the evening's first take, a 'test run' on 'Golden Loom', was a keeper – though the new drummer assumed it was a bust:

> **Howie Wyeth**: The first song we started to do – I had just barely met him – I think they were recording . . . we played the song and we sort of fumbled the ending . . . He said, 'Okay we're gonna do that again.' – and I said, 'Bob, are we gonna end this or is it gonna be a fade?' And he went into such a lengthy explanation, he went on and on, that everybody got so confused, it ended up we didn't even do the song [again]. He said, 'Let's not even do it.' And Stoner said, 'Don't ask him anything. Just play.'

After that first playback, Stoner recalls, 'We just went back into the studio and started running through tunes, bam, bam, bam, just getting every complete take. Every complete tune was a take . . . just like that . . . I think we were still doing takes as late as five, six a.m.' Dylan simply rode roughshod over any mistakes, inserting a new intro. to 'Joey' but otherwise leaving well alone. 'Oh, Sister', after two false starts, was got in one, only for an embarrassed Emmylou to confess, 'I fucked it up on the chorus.' Dylan didn't agree, and it became the

---

* Attributions in Krogsgaard's sessionography of false starts and full takes are wholly unreliable. He also mis-assigns songs to the 30th which were recorded on the 31st.

album cut.* Stoner sensed Dylan's harmonic shadow was finding the going tough, 'Emmylou's pitch was amazing, but [Bob's] phrasing, you can hear her struggling to match.' Dylan reveled in her wayward vocals, especially on 'One More Cup Of Coffee', also cut in one go, after the briefest of (recorded) rehearsals.

He had been around long enough to know nights like this came around once in a very blue moon, and he rode his muse's tail all night long. By night's end, he knew he had an album. And yet, the two best performances that night – 'Hurricane' and 'Isis' – have yet to appear officially. In the former instance, Dylan's lax attitude to the facts would make Columbia nervous; the latter – a gorgeous eight-minute 'Isis', slow and stately, with Dylan on acoustic guitar and Scarlet and Emmylou wailing like a pair of banshees – would be superseded by an equally great piano-led take the following evening.

That version also trimmed ninety seconds off the song, which was becoming as much of an issue on *Desire* as on *Blood on the Tracks*. The songs just kept piling up, especially after the quartet (minus Emmylou, who had to be elsewhere) resumed work on the 31st, adding two more 'keepers' to the mix, along with yet more 'Money Blues', a throwaway song Dylan refused to let die a natural death. He also got around to 'Abandoned Love', first with Stoner in the Harris role, then with a solo vocal and a harp intro. One of them should have made the album, even with Dylan's delivery being far more self-conscious than at The Other End. Perhaps it was because the one who really did wear 'the ball and chain', Sara herself, was there.

According to Stoner, Dylan warned the band, 'We're gonna do a song for her tonight. So, be on your best behaviour.' He didn't mean 'Abandoned Love'. He meant the song completed in the Hamptons without the Levy levy. Jacques, still an interested party, was there that July night. He believed she had come to town 'to see if there would be some kind of a getting back together . . . I know it was in his mind, [too].' It sounds it. Levy, sat in the control room with the muse herself, saw 'her face change . . . when Dylan sang the line, "When the children were babies and played on the beach." . . . And when he got to the very

---

* Emmylou's self-directed rebuke appears on both the quadraphonic mix of the LP and the official Eighties cassette.

last line – "Don't ever leave me/ don't ever go" – well, you could hear a pin drop.'

Nor was Dylan done with the marriage battleground, switching to piano in order to tell his muse, 'What drives me to you is what drives me insane.' Still, he wasn't done. Before wrapping things up, he got DeVito to run tape on something called 'You Go And I'll Stay', elements of which would carry over to the live arrangement of 'One More Cup Of Coffee', after which the other attendees were asked to reconvene the following evening to select master takes for an album that, while hardly as heart-wrenching as its esteemed predecessor, was a quantum leap in form and substance. Finally, Bob and Sara could now catch up in private.

The others were entirely unprepared for the person who greeted them the following evening. Gone were the unerring instincts Dylan displayed when recording, as he quickly rejected 'Abandoned Love' as a candidate (as well as 'Golden Loom', 'Catfish' and 'Money Blues'). 'Rita Mae' hung on, making it to an early side one sequence. It made the album ridiculously long.

Even without it, but with the ten-minute take of 'Hurricane' from the 30th, it ran to over fifty-eight minutes. Still, he refused to cut the off-key 'Mozambique' or recut the sluggish 'big band' version of 'Romance In Durango'. In a toss-up between guitar and piano versions of 'Isis', he went with the latter, but point-blank refused to lose 'Joey', which would have brought the album down to forty-five minutes in a single stroke. He wanted it out there, and the various factual faux pas were neither here nor there. Gallo was dead. Can't libel the dead. But Bello and Bradley were very much alive, meaning there would still be trouble ahead.

It was now August, high time he was back on the farm. But first he needed to prep Levy about the show he wanted to take on the road, built around these songs: 'Just before Bob left New York at the end of the summer . . . we sat down and talked about what kind of show it would be and who would be in it . . . Bob had very little to do with putting the Revue together. He left all that to me . . . He really just wanted to be part of the whole.'

One pressing issue box-office Bob needed to address if a US tour loomed was what to do about the songs from his last album, number-one worldwide. Fans would expect to hear 'em. It had not even been a year since he wrote down fifteen songs in his little red notebook. But already he felt removed from the material, so much so that he set about rewriting three of them: 'Simple Twist Of Fate', 'Tangled Up In Blue' and 'If You See Her, Say Hello'.

The first of these he would debut to a national TV audience alongside two *Desire* songs, on a September PBS tribute to John Hammond Snr. The third of them, he would break into at his next studio session, for the benefit of the *Rolling Stone* journalist who first reported on *Blood on the Tracks*. But this time he was singing of 'a knockdown fight, broken glass and chairs,' unsure if he wanted her back. Thankfully, no divorce lawyers were there to take notes. The Bob/ Sara relationship was still teetering on the brink. When he turned up to his cousin Linda's wedding at the end of August, to sing 'Forever Young', Sara was nowhere to be seen. Far from spending all his time down on the farm retying his marital bonds, he was busy setting up a tour like no other tour and putting in place the apparatus to make the road movie he had been planning ever since he buried 1966 tour documentary, *Eat the Document*, in 1968.

The tour he was planning was one he'd already talked at length about to fellow Sixties survivor, Robbie Robertson: 'This thing . . . Bob's been talking about for years . . . He's always wanted to have that kind of gypsy caravan situation happening where it was loose, and different people could get up and do different things at different times.'

Dylan was determined to ensure the new tour was unlike last year's comeback tour in every conceivable way. Bill Graham was nowhere to be seen. Instead, he asked '74 sidekick, Louie Kemp, to take a sabbatical from the fish business and become tour manager for six weeks. For now, though, he kept one secret from his boyhood chum: 'The movie was not part of his original pitch. It was maybe late September when he said he'd like to shoot a movie . . . And then he told me about Howard Alk . . . Howard put together the rest of the film crew.'

And then there was the band, now that he had decided to tour without The Band. Even Dylan knew the trio who'd just made their TV debut could not carry a whole show. He would need more textures, more interplay, more musicians, prompting him to return to New York, and take up where those afterhours July jam sessions left off, as he remembered the band old sidekick Bobby Neuwirth had assembled for his own Village residency that summer, featuring alpha-male musicians like David Mansfield, Stephen Soles and T-Bone Burnett:

David Mansfield: Most of the people who'd played with Bobby [Neu-wirth] ended up playing with Bob Dylan. The stage at The Bitter End was so crowded you could barely find a place to stand . . . This crazy, swirling thing that was the Rolling Thunder Revue was what Neu-wirth was at the time, and what he did when he went onstage at The Bitter End. He was getting paid something by Paul Colby, [but] he immediately starts sending friends plane-tickets . . . [all] to create this scene.

Both Bobbies yearned to take the spirit of Greenwich Village in the Sixties on the road, hoping to save the Seventies from itself. But first, Dylan had another *Freewheelin'* on his hands. It was time to lose another 'libellous' lyric. Sure 'nuff, as the Revue got down to rehearsals at Studio Instrument Rentals [S.I.R.] in Gramercy the third week in October, Stoner noticed 'all these suits from CBS come in, and they're all talking about this "Hurricane" controversy, saying, "Look the band is here . . . Let's go across town and do another version of it now, so at least we got an alternate one."' Oh, and can we lose the line about robbing bodies? Which is how Dylan and the nascent Revue spent the evening of the 24th recutting 'Hurricane', while two journalists, Larry Sloman and Jim Jerome from *People Weekly*, jotted down notes.

By the time the latter arrived, DeVito was doing his level best to keep Dylan's spirits up: ' "Just hold that tempo, Bobby," he encouraged from the control room, "That last take was startin' to smoke." The star leaned into his mike and responded: "We're gonna get it, man, I know we are. Let's get this thing in the can and out on the streets."' The smarter Sloman had arrived in time to see the real Dylan warm up with 'some old country tunes', including an 'I Still Miss Someone' on which they ran tape (perhaps to erase the memory of the execrable Dylan/Cash duet from 1969).

But as the night wore on, Dylan's mood turned darker and his focus dimmer. He finally called it quits after putting ten takes on tape, none of them satisfactory, offering this parting shot to Don, 'Let 'em sue. CBS'll drown him. Hey, my vision is going. I'm seeing double . . . Pick a good one.' DeVito spliced takes two and six together, but everyone knew the new 'Hurricane' lacked that July moon dust. Had Dylan been thinking straight, he'd have overdubbed a new vocal onto the July 30th backing track, as he'd done with 'Idiot Wind' at Sound 80 the previous

December, or simply used the version recorded at the Halloween show at Plymouth Rock. He did neither.

But when Columbia president Irwin Siegelstein turned up in Brandeis, a month later, to see Dylan, it was Blind Boy Grunt who greeted him. As for the July 30th, 1975 version of 'Hurricane', Dylan had no problem using it in his 1977 movie, *Renaldo & Clara*, even though Patty Valentine had by then filed suit for libel – a suit she duly lost.*

Dylan also recorded the Halloween show, using its opening track as the opening sequence for his road film, the ironic, not-yet-iconic 'When I Paint My Masterpiece'. He was determined to ensure that the Rolling Thunder Revue would be one of the best documented tours of the era. And not just on film. He wanted it photographed, and memorialised in print. When it came to the former, he got Barry Imhoff to ring up the snap happy Ken Regan, and hand him the phone:

> An instantly recognizable voice got on [and said,] 'This is Bob Dylan.' [He] said he'd love [for] me to come down to S.I.R. rehearsal studio the next day . . . 'And . . . bring your portfolio just to have a meeting with me, Barry and Louis, and talk about this tour. I'd really like you to do it.' . . . At one point during the next day's hour-long discussion, Bob said, 'I'm a very private person, [but] if I hire you, you're going to have total freedom and access. I want you to document every single thing. My kids and my wife might come along . . . You can photograph them, but do not release anything of my family.' . . . I never betrayed that trust . . . I shot 13,750 pictures on Rolling Thunder, and Bob . . . went over the contacts with a loupe, again and again, marking frames and asking, 'What do you think about this?'

A couple of days later, he invited Larry Sloman to join in. This time strings attached themselves: 'Bob invited me on the tour. He said, "There's got to be a journalist covering the tour." . . . I was [already] friends with . . . half the band . . . [But] then once I get on [the road], all of a sudden there's the whole protective structure around him.' It was Pete Karman in 1964 all over again. Unlike Karman, though,

---

* In his sessionography, Krogsgaard suggests the vocal tracks for the 30th July 1975 'Hurricane' were erased in December 1976. Absolute rubbish. Dylan subsequently used said vocal track in *Renaldo & Clara*.

Sloman stuck at it and refused to be belittled. The result would be one of the great rock chronicles, *On the Road with Bob Dylan* (Bantam, 1978).

Sloman was not the only writer Dylan invited along, or the only one to end up with a book deal. Dylan also wanted someone to help him write a script of sorts for the tour film. Patti Smith suggested her ex-beau, Sam Shepard, knowing that, 'Sam was an accomplished playwright and had written the script for the film *Zabriskie Point* for Michelangelo Antonioni.'

Worryingly for the unholy Shepard, at his own pre-tour meeting with the singer, Dylan's first words were, 'We don't have to make any connections. None of this has to connect.' Whatever did he mean? He proceeded to ask Shepard if he had ever seen Marcel Carné's *Les Enfants du Paradis* or François Truffaut's *Shoot the Piano Player*, both films made in trying circumstances, neither of them road movies. If the former had been a recent Raeben recommendation, Dylan had been carrying the Truffaut film in his head since 1962.*

When Alk and his camera crew started filming, around October 21st, the footage was as unscripted as could be. It certainly failed to impress the experienced cameraman, Mel Howard: 'To me, a lot of the stuff that we were shooting in New York . . . was conventional [*cinéma vérité*] and worse than that . . . You want to believe in what's happening, but I thought the stuff was home movies . . . and I said [as much].' He was assured things would change once they hit the road. And at least the cameras were rolling at S.I.R. witnessing the musicians jam, audition and despair in roughly equal measures, especially English glam-rock axeman Mick Ronson, whom Dylan had met while hanging out with ex-Mott The Hoople frontman Ian Hunter in clubland:

> It wasn't really a rehearsal; it was like a jam. There were like six or seven guitarists there, so I didn't think I'd be on the tour . . . I'd never even heard half of the numbers they were playin'. Two days we were there. That first day we must have got through . . . 150 songs . . . It was fuckin' madness . . . I wasn't comfortable at all . . . Dylan never said what he wanted from you . . . He wanted you to do your thing and see if it wouldn't fit with him.

---

* As he said at a 1997 press conference, 'Everything about that movie I identified with. Everything.'

Even Stoner, who was fast establishing himself as de facto band-leader, had 'no idea what the purpose for these jams was, except we were being invited to jam . . . So, we're up there jamming, and it turns out what we're really doing is rehearsing.' Part of the problem, as multi-instrumentalist Mansfield soon realized, was that any given song 'might be [one] that you were gonna be rehearsing for the tour, [or] it might be something like ["People Get Ready"], where you're playing it just to play.' The highlights at these initial rehearsals were invariably the latter, songs like doo-wop classic 'Mountain Of Love', the traditional 'These Hands' or the first Hank Williams song Dylan ever learnt to play, 'Kaw-Liga'. Meanwhile, cameras rolled and the band played.

On the 23rd, the day before 'Hurricane' revisited, rehearsals ended early because everyone adjourned to Gerde's Folk City to celebrate the birthday of Mike Porco, the man who gave Dylan his first professional gig. Again, the camera crew tagged along, capturing Patti Smith free-rapping a song with Eric Andersen, Dylan sharing a stage with Joan Baez for the first time in ten years, and apparently – according to Dylan's handwritten film notes – 'The best tit shot ever made.' Baez had arrived direct from the airport, still not quite sure whether she wanted to do the tour, or what terms were even on offer.

The symbolism was not lost on others there that night, including a *Rolling Stone* photographer and Bette Midler, who had recorded a ribald rewrite of 'Buckets Of Rain' with Dylan a coupla nights earlier. According to Midler, 'He absolutely charmed the pants off me . . . Actually, I tried to charm the pants off him.' The running-tape of the session suggests Dylan was a willing participant. When Midler asks him, 'Are you a one-take guy?', he insists, 'I can last *all* night.' He would later say, 'I was lucky to get out of there.'

The one discordant note struck at Gerde's was provided by that casualty of the folk-rock wars, Phil Ochs, who had *not* been asked to join the tour, and was visibly hurting. By then, everyone knew Ochs was on a downward spiral, including Paul Colby, whom Dylan thought 'was being cruel to Phil because I was short with him . . . He was a mess, and I told him that I would buy him no more booze. I didn't want to encourage him. [But] Dylan told me to buy him a bottle of wine, which I did. I couldn't sit Bob down and explain to him that Phil was going off his rocker. [He] would come around and bad-mouth Dylan; then Bobby would show up, [and] they would be best buddies.'

Ochs's schizophrenia at this point led him to record a tape one evening with artist-archivist Harry Smith in the persona of Luke Train,
which caught him imagining in his disintegrating mind's eye that he
has just 'kill[ed] Ochs in the Chelsea Hotel . . . walks out the hotel and
coincidentally there stands Bob Dylan, Ochs' friend, enemy, jealousy
figure, rival in poetry and, in Ochs' opinion, sell-out.'

Days later, a resurrected Ochs mounted the Gerde's stage, only to
see a 'drunk in the second row' with a knife. He glares at him and says,
'You better use it or I will.' A genuinely concerned Neuwirth shouts
out, 'C'mon, Phil, we're not making a snuff film,' unaware that 'the
drunk in the second row' was a half-Indian musician named Roland
Moussa, an old friend of Dave Amram's, and the knife Ochs was eyeing
up was one he himself had concealed between two cushions in his
dressing-room. Finding it there, Moussa had taken it upon himself to
remove it, unsure whether Ochs intended to use it on himself or his
'jealousy figure', making the tour film more *L'Age D'Or* than *Les Enfants
du Paradis*. Not surprisingly, Ochs's behaviour that night failed to convince Dylan he should invite him on tour, or even to Allen Ginsberg's
house party, three nights later, on the eve of everyone else's departure
for New England.

The press was already reporting that this 'secret tour' was a wholly
ad hoc affair, despite Dylan telling its semi-official chronicler before
they left, 'We got a big show so we're gonna have to . . . play some big
halls.' The day before Ginsberg's shindig, tickets had gone on sale for
two shows at the spacious Civic Center in Providence, Rhode Island.
But like Ochs, the media wanted to believe Dylan the purist had sold
out. Otherwise, where's the story?

A better story was that Dylan and Baez were together again, and it
was just like old times – no rehearsing until they hit the road, only then
working up duets of 'Tears Of Rage' (which Baez had recorded on *Any
Day Now*) and Child ballad 'Mary Hamilton', neither of which they
would sing together onstage. Nonetheless, on opening night, October
30th, in Plymouth, Mass., there was an audible gasp from the cheap
seats when Baez joined Dylan, to sing 'The Times They Are A-
Changin', 'Hattie Carroll' and two covers.

This was the last concession he made to the lady. As Mansfield
recalls, 'He would do that Appalachian phrasing thing to the nth degree
and give you no cues, [but Baez] would stick to him like glue. I seem to

recall once or twice he would do that to her, and she would kick him in the pants.' She had the proximity and the history to get away with such a deed. For someone like Mick Ronson, used to jamming with Weird and Gilly, sticking to his new paymaster like glue was not an option, 'He'd just wander off somewhere, expecting us to follow him . . . Plus, he never played anything the same way twice.'

At the third stop in Lowell, rather than trying to find out why Dylan was performing in whiteface, Baez simply came onstage in whiteface, too – much to Dylan's surprise. Others – like Ken Regan – enquired of him, 'What's with the whiteface?' only to be told, 'Well, I'm playing these halls and it's really dark. I want the people way in the back to be able to see my eyes.' Yeah, right. Sloman also enquired, and got a different explanation, 'You ever see those Italian troupes . . . *Commedia dell'arte*. Well, it's just an extension of that, only musically.' Perhaps the closest Dylan came to admitting its true purpose was to Bruce Springsteen's pretty girlfriend, Karen Darvin, who asked him about it backstage in New Haven. Dylan self-consciously mumbled, 'I saw it once in a movie.'*

The luminous paint Dylan applied to his face nightly was not the only white powder that freely flowed on these November nights. If Goodtime Charlie was the musicians' Secret Santa, he did not stay secret for long. By tour's end, Joni Mitchell – who joined late, and stayed – was performing a powerful new song called 'Coyote', in which the singer admitted, 'I'm just a prisoner of white lines.' Nor did she indulge alone; hence her description of her fellow performers 'tak[ing] their temporary lovers, and their pills and their powders, to get them through this passion play'.

She later told biographer David Yaffe that she ended up requesting, 'Pay me in cocaine – because everybody was [already] out of their minds. I was the only straight person. Try being the only straight person [on that tour]. So, I thought I might as well bite the bullet . . . It made me so aggressive, the next thing I knew, I was ripping off [badges from] cops.'

Being paid 'in cocaine' was not as hard as it sounds. As Wyeth told me, 'There was a guy carrying duffel bags full of coke on the tour and

---

* One presumes he means *Les Enfants du Paradis*. Other guests who attended in New Haven included Patti Smith, and Sally and Albert Grossman.

you could buy grams for $25, and just get 'em written off to your *per diem*.' In Joni's case, it made her paranoid enough to convince herself 'Joan Baez would have broken my leg[s] if she could.' Others also took to the white stuff like the proverbial duck to water:

> **David Mansfield**: Mick Ronson was young, but not a kid. I don't think he had really tried cocaine before . . . I saw [very quickly] how much he learned to love that leisure activity . . . [But] while people were getting wasted out of their minds, doing all kinds of crazy stuff, there were also kids and grandparents around.

No question, either, Dylan himself was a full participant in the revelries, and not just 'from the well-stacked bar at the front of the bus'. As RTR publicist Chris O'Dell witnessed, the post-gig bus rides saw 'everyone talk[ing] too fast, laugh[ing] too loud'. As the tour progressed they also sometimes played too fast and too loud. The 2019 Scorsese film, *Rolling Thunder Revue*, almost provides its own contact high, such is the intensity with which everyone is playing by mid-November. The razor-sharp Dylan is back, snapping into his lines, bending the words to breaking point. But even he seems to occasionally hammer the message home, especially on 'Hurricane'.

The mind games were also back, so much so that when the Teflon-coated Mitchell 'got on the bus . . . I thought, God . . . they're cruel people, being cruel to each other . . . [So] the manifestation of multiple personalities was almost a necessity.' At least, they waited for her. Joe Cocker was not so lucky:

> **Ken Regan**: At one point Joe Cocker hopped on the tour bus, invited to join the Revue for one Connecticut gig. But when the bus driver stopped at a light, Joe told him, 'Hey, I'll be right back.' He got off the bus, and the driver waited, [but] then nobody wanted to wait anymore, so we left.

By mid-November, the tour may have found its good-time groove but the film was nowhere. Even Dylan's perpetual cheerleader, Ginsberg, noted in his tour diary, the film 'requires discreet scenes . . . with thematic relation but no need story line plot.' Cameraman Larry Johnson had come to feel it 'was a journey that had a mission, but . . . you never quite knew what it was . . . At that point . . . Dylan really [just] wanted to be the jester-mixer.'

The project needed a kick-start. Finally, fearing another still-born film, Howard *and* Alk began pushing Dylan in a particular direction. Howard had made a film called *Snapshots* back in 1972, which 'purported to be real, but was actually fictionalised . . . [and] Dylan was attracted to the form . . . [so Alk] and I decided to invite Sara on the tour and see how much of this [tension] he would permit to be on film.' Howard knew Sara from her pre-Dylan, single-mother days. This undoubtedly helped. Sure enough, Mrs Dylan wafted in at Niagara Falls, captivating all, without ever quite engaging with 'this passion play':

> **Chris O'Dell**: [Sara] had the same aura and elusiveness [as Bob]. When she was talking to you, you felt that she was right there with you – like Bob. But when she wandered off, you kept your distance . . . Her boundaries were clear and firm, just like Bob's.

Sara was delighted to see her performing husband again blazing a trail, and was not ashamed to be seen loving it. As Sloman notes, 'There's a great Ken Regan photo . . . looking from behind Bob, and you see the back of his legs and you see beyond the stage, [to] the orchestra pit, [and] looking up at Bob, transfixed, [are] Joni Mitchell and Sara Dylan.' Another, altogether more intimate Regan shot caught Dylan and Sara back in the rain, fresh from a spin in the *Maid of The Mist*, eyes locked on each other.*

Sara's arrival finally gave Dylan the central theme for his film, providing him with his own Oja Kodar to put the F in Fake, and the M in Muse. Almost immediately, Howard recalled, 'There was this scene in Niagara Falls where Sara played this kind of witch-goddess creature and she set tasks for [Dylan] to fulfil.' In another scene, Dylan had 'Sara reading aloud from a book of magic.' And in another, 'Sara [had] to play a ragamuffin hitchhiker on an old dirt country road, picked up by Dylan in the luxury car.'

So, when Sara told rolling reporter 'Ratso', 'I have no real function

---

* The photo appears in the original 1978 edition of Sam Shepard's *Rolling Thunder Logbook* (Viking).

here. Back home, I have the kids,' she is being slightly disingenuous. She was saving the film, while keeping an eye on her man with the wandering eye, knowing what happened last time. According to Howard, before her arrival old girlfriends had been 'coming out of the woodwork . . . [and] some of them travelled with Bob.' Not now. Not surprisingly, the dynamics of Bob and Sara's decade-old, seesaw relationship spilled over into some of the film's improvised dialogue, impressing one cameraman with the unswerving candour Dylan brought to his art:

> **Larry Johnson**: At some point you feel that you're invading . . . people's lives . . . Is this real, or is this not real? Where is the line here? What's going on here? I remember feeling . . . there was a lot of personal stuff going on, of which I didn't know the undercurrent . . . He was a brave man, to put his wife and his ex-girlfriend and all these people . . . everything, [in the movie]; all . . . were fair ground for us to film.

In another new scene, Dylan talked about switching from following the rodeo to tightrope walking; an exasperated Sara sighs, 'I want a normal life. You don't want to be responsible for anything – for *me*.' Dylan's character proceeds to selfishly insist, 'I need you to perform certain magical things with me.' Mel Howard was delighted by the turn of events, convinced they finally were shooting a film worth making:

> We [now] had a whole subplot, all of the women in the film, black magic and white magic, and the different powers of women and men, and the focus of all this was Dylan himself . . . The thing that started to evolve as a general theme was Dylan, Sara and Joan. Sara and Joan as opposing forces, in different mythological guises, Joan as a certain kind of energy, Sara as a different kind of energy, and Dylan in between, attracted to both.

Sara was not so convinced, making an injudicious remark to an old friend – Nat Hentoff – forgetting he was on the clock, writing for *Rolling Stone*, 'After all that talk about goddesses, we wound up being whores.' For all the talk between husband and wife about invoking the White Goddess in her triple guises – Virgin-Lover-Mother – it seems she temporarily forgot said archetypal Muse was not just 'the virgin of Guadalupe, the patron saint of Mexico, [who] stands on the crescent moon'.

She soon threw herself into the role of the Madame in a brothel, previously kidnapped at fourteen by a rich man from her mother, herself a famous whore, now bellyaching, 'Business isn't what it should be. They all like certain things, but they're embarrassed to say what it is.' She then engages Baez, a more reluctant courtesan, in a discussion about men not getting it up, while the buxom Anne Waldman sits, reading Dante. Originally, a torrid Dylan duet with Stoner on 'House Of The Rising Sun' was meant to precede the whorehouse scene. Predictably, the conversation soon turned to a man both women once knew:

> **Joan**: One time I was involved with somebody and I think he was involved with you. Did he pay you? Did he give you jewelry?
> **Sara**: They all give me jewelry.
> **Joan**: Time is hardly on our side.
> *[They] discuss what men want.*
> **Sara**: They want our silence.
> **Joan**: May God strike them dead at [the] dinner table.

At the bottom of the notes to this scene – which didn't make the final movie – is the following couplet, in Dylan's hand, 'Whores are there to save your soul/ To move you on down the line.' Baez thought the whole project an indulgence, and convinced herself Sara felt the same. Her 1986 autobiography describes one scene where 'Bob was playing an unknown musician who'd come to pitch his songs to Bob Dylan, and I was playing Bob Dylan and being rude to the unknown musician. Sara wandered into the room, cocked her head and then shook it and laughed.'

If Sara shared some of her reservations, the lady who spoke like silence rarely let her feelings show, throwing herself into the bordello scene, while Baez held back. It prompted a note in Dylan's hand that read, 'Who is Joan Baez? She is a little girl pulling at the strings of sad enlightenment,' perhaps already sensing she was one of those 'people who didn't understand what we were doing . . . and weren't willing to go along with us.'

Long before Dylan made the above remark, Joan confided to Nat Hentoff her belief that 'the movie needs a director. The sense I get of it so far is that that movie is a giant mess of a home movie'. This didn't stop her trying to score points off her former paramour when the opportunity arose during a scene at The Dream Away Lodge, the owner of which, an old Jew called 'Mama', had given her something:

> **Ken Regan**: Mama rummaged through an ancient [tramp] steamer trunk and lifted out her wedding dress . . . She held it up against Joan, . . . 'I want you to have it.' On Joan it looked as if it had actually been fitted by a designer. Then Joan came down to the bar and sat next to Bob, who did a double take. They started to talk about their own relationship – how it had gone wrong years earlier, and why. It actually got very tense and emotional, [but it made] for a great sequence in the movie.

It did, but said scene only appeared in Scorsese's 2019 mockumentary. Others just went with the flow. So, when Dylan told Ronnie Hawkins, former frontman of The Hawks, 'I want you to be a rock'n'roller trying to convince this girl to be your companion for a six-week tour . . . Say whatever you want, but be sure to mention the following things: God, marriage, Daddy, rock'n'roll, good times and the end of the world.' Hawkins followed the brief perfectly, giving the film crew one of the best scenes in *Renaldo & Clara*.

Likewise, Sloman was handed a piece of paper in a hotel lobby and told, 'The secrets are only a foot away. Take this with you, don't let anybody see you, carry it, show it to the man at the front desk.' A disconsolate Sam Shepard could only look on as another scene was shot without his scriptwriting input, bemoaning out of Dylan's earshot, 'Making a movie isn't like writing a song – it needs more planning and more scripting.'

By the time they got to Canada in early December, Dylan had at least come up with his denouement, a scene involving his character (at this juncture called Rinaldo), Sara's character (Clara) and Baez's alter-ego (The Woman in White). In the film notes, it is simply labelled 'Threesome', Baez entering to find her rival's arms entwined around Rinaldo. In those notes, Sara acts more catty and Joan admits defeat more readily:

[**Joan**:] I came a long distance – I have a note.

Sara: I didn't know you could write . . .

[to Dylan] You always did prefer to be alone. I finally did leave you alone. I know her. We're like sisters.

[**Dylan**:] I'm a brother to you both.

[**Sara**:] So then we'll all be a family.

Joan: We can work [out] some arrangements . . . Bet we could try on each other's clothes.

Dylan: Where's the[re] to go?

Joan exits. Puts rose in mouth.

The Montreal show (Dec. 4th), was the apotheosis of the fall tour, musically, spiritually, and cinematically. One of the great Dylan shows, he was wired to the Canadian grid throughout. And with it, the filming was all but done. It was time to return to base – New York – via Clinton, New Jersey, and a photo op. for the Carter cause which was as dubious as the cause itself.* As Sloman observed, 'Clinton [Correctional Institute] was like a country club compared to most prisons. [So,] they had to pull down a cafeteria-like safety gate and put it between Rubin and Bob for that famous picture, so the public could get the impression that Rubin was suffering behind "bars".'

The following night was The Night of The Hurricane at Madison Square Garden, the only sell-out that the papers by this stage could legitimately report. Even though Dylan had been sandpapering his voice for the past five weeks – and it was starting to show – the tour had been a triumph. But Dylan wasn't taken in for a second by the papers' plaudits. He knew, deep inside, he was back. And that was all that mattered:

When I finally did get back up to a place where I could express myself again, it surprised a lot of people . . . I didn't get back into doing what it was – with everything blocked out of the way – until maybe the end of the first Rolling Thunder tour. [1978]

---

* After all the hoop-lah, Carter and his co-defendant Artes were both found guilty at a second trial, and were only freed after a third trial on a technicality. As the Scottish would say, the case went 'Unproven'.

4.2

January 1976 to March 1977: Gulf Coast Highway

This tour may not end as all other tours have. There is some desire among us to have a kind of permanent community, and Dylan is stepping very, very slowly to find out if that can work.

Allen Ginsberg, to Nat Hentoff, November 1975.

He [told me] that what he really wanted was the kind of tour that would last forever. He would start it off and then he would be able to go home and two months later, if he was bored, he could call up and find out where it was and take a plane and join it.

Farir Bouhafa, Columbia A&R, 1975.

On the second [Rolling Thunder tour], I don't know what was going on. The flowers had gone away and the scarves had disappeared and there were headwraps, and it just wasn't as glorious.

Joan Baez, 2019.

He did the first [Rolling Thunder] for his own reasons. The second one was like the Hollywood version of a sequel.

Arthur Rosato, RTR road manager.

Yves Bigot: Would you wish to do another tour just like the Rolling Thunder Revue . . .
Bob Dylan: No, you won't see that again . . . Things just couldn't go on that way.

12th June 1981.

*

If many Dylan fans consider the tours of 1966, 1975 and 1979 the verit-able peak of his performance-art, more adventurous types have a hankering for Rolling Thunder 1976, the Fall 1980 'Retrospective' and 1987's Temples in Flames, all tours that at times resemble a roller-coaster about to crash. For '66, '75 and '79 the sets are pretty much set in stone. Yet Dylan makes every night come alive – hence the two sub-stantive boxed-sets issued in the last few years covering the former two tours. Whereas in '76, '80 and '87 Dylan rips up the set-list night after night, throwing the band curveball after curveball, by sheer force of will determined to prevail.

The one common component all six tours share is a crack band, whether it be The Band, Guam (the RTR band's adopted moniker), the 'gospel era' band or Tom Petty & The Heartbreakers. Yet each tour is defined by Ingredient X: Dylan's mood. In 1976 – and, indeed, 1987 – he was in a filthy mood and a bad place, on the run from the power of Women; determined to pour his inner frustrations into his music and, when offstage, to play the bad boy, making his time onstage truly cathartic.

Riding high in the charts all winter, after the January 1976 release of *Desire* – his all-time best-selling album – Dylan's atypical response was to drop those songs from the set, save for the wholly disposable 'Mozambique', and return to the precipice. No matter how hard he tried, though, he could not convince the FM stations to play 'Hurri-cane' instead of 'Sara', the obvious second single and therefore the one he refused to release, heavy rotation airplay notwithstanding.

Even the news of a new trial, and a second Night of the Hurricane at the Houston Astrodome on January 25th, couldn't get DJs to spin Dylan's eight-minute shit-stirring summation for the defence. As for the Texan show, it was something of a disaster, critically and financially (it netted barely $50,000 for Carter's defence fund). Two days of rehears-als proved insufficient for Dylan to readily integrate the likes of 'One Too Many Mornings' and 'Positively 4th Street', two songs last played back in 1966, when incomprehension was the norm. For 'Sara', Hous-ton was its live swansong.

He also broke the mould by allowing Stephen Stills and Stevie Won-der to bring their own bands to this half-a-million-dollar-bash. A wiser Joni Mitchell was nowhere to be seen, wanting nothing to do with another Carter fundraiser. She had started to believe Hurricane was a destructive individual who might be innocent of this particular crime, but was not an innocent man. Undeterred, Dylan showed up at one of her own concerts in Austin, two days later, looking a little worse for wear, catching her by surprise:

> He was acting really weird. He showed up onstage like a crazy person. He wandered around through the amps. He made it very apparent to the audience that he was there, but he never came forward. He just got on the stage and wandered around. We didn't sing anything together.

Not quite true. Dylan attempted to duet on 'Both Sides Now', though the jury remains out on whether he succeeded. One thing was for sure, he had lost his ball and chain. Whether simply happy to see Joni, or being back in the rain, he seemed disinclined to go back home. Even when he returned to Point Dume, he was looking for the quickest way out, and when Rob Fraboni, Eric Clapton and Ron Wood rolled up at Shangri-La, Malibu's latest studio, in late March to start work on Clapton's successor to *There's One in Every Crowd*, he had a reason to roam. The last Dylan album Fraboni had worked on was *The Basement Tapes*, and at times these sessions almost resemble those, at least when it came to libations and bacchanalian cover versions:

> **Ron Wood**: This [one] session went on for a couple of days solid. There was a point where we stopped the master-tape, and just ran a two-track . . . One night I went to creep off to my room and there were no bedclothes at all, and the window was wide open, and I looked out and I could see this tent in the distance, right in the middle of this big field. And Bob had made off with this girl, but she was in a plaster cast . . . It was like *Invasion of the Zombies*.

Consumed by that familiar restless, hungry feeling, Dylan even donated a couple of his discards to the two Brit-pickers: 'Sign Language' (an idea dating back to *Desire*, about a breakdown in communication between two lovers) to Clapton, and 'Seven Days' (about a returning 'beautiful comrade from the north') to Wood. Also indicative of his current mindset was a jam session on Clapton's birthday (March 30th) when he attempted the song that would become a nightly motif for the impending return to Rolling Thunder – 'Idiot Wind'.

Plans were already afoot to reassemble the Revue for a swing through the southern Gulf states, where he fondly imagined he had a following similar to the ones he had on the eastern seaboard. He did not. At least this time he was prepared to put in more than a couple of days' rehearsal time. Starting on April 8th, always a propitious day, the Revue gathered at the Pool Studio at Clearwater's Bellevue Biltmore Hotel, to begin a new chapter.

Spirits were high – at least they were among those who had gotten the call. Absent was a despairing Ramblin' Jack, who finally phoned Dylan direct, 'I was . . . willing to go out again. [Bob] was embarrassed . . . They weren't planning to take me. He said, "I don't have anything to do with who gets to go,"' a patent untruth from a man who preferred using his lyrics to speak his mind, not the phone. The sultry Ronee Blakley was also scratched from the list, perhaps at Baez's behest. Instead, Kinky Friedman supplemented the bill, presumably because Dylan really did want Kinky to know how much he liked 'Asshole From El Paso' and 'They Ain't Making Jews Like Jesus Anymore'.

But if Kinky was brought along to lighten the mood, he barely had time to do so before the vibe turned dark, and Dylan saw the black dog. After a productive three days rehearsing at the Pool Studio, they were due to move to the larger Starlight Room for a further week of rehearsals prior to a one-hour TV special in the same room on the 22nd, when Dylan heard that Phil Ochs had taken his own life, nine years (almost to the day) after Paul Clayton took the easy way out.

Dylan was bereft. Scarlet Rivera remembers 'sitting at the [dinner] table [with him], when he got the word about that. And he was really upset and angry that he had done that to himself . . . A couple of days went by when he was missing.' Mansfield also recalls 'him not attending rehearsals for a while . . . I remember how black his mood was, [but at least] he didn't do the kind of haranguing I've heard that he's done with other bands.'

When he did resume rehearsals, he was invariably uncommunicative, especially to his new guitar-tech, Joel Bernstein, who didn't know what to make of it, 'It seemed a very strange way to proceed with rehearsals . . . He would just give [everyone] these looks . . . Usually rehearsals began around noon, [but] Bob wouldn't show up until two or so . . . [He'd] just pick up a guitar and play a song.'

Stoner stepped into the breach, keeping the others focused while Dylan worked through his rage and grief. Finally, on April 15th, the singer summoned the original *Desire* trio to the Pool Studio late at night and roared through two hours of songs, mostly his, a couple not. If a one-off rendition of Elmore James's 'The Sun Is Shining' – 'the sun is shining, although it's raining in my heart' – perhaps came closest to expressing how Dylan felt, he also ran through five *Desire* songs, plus 'Rita Mae' (which would receive two outings on the tour). But it was the two *Blood on the Tracks* songs – 'Shelter From The Storm' and 'Idiot Wind' – which indicated a shift in mindset and a darkness descending. Not just their inclusion, but his intense interpretations.

Sure enough, on opening night in Lakeland on the 18th, the *Blood* ballads beat out *Desire*'s detritus three to one, beginning with the second instalment in a two-song acoustic opener immediately after Kinky tested the Floridian water with 'Asshole From El Paso': 'It went over extremely well, the crowd were laughing . . . At [just] that moment Bob chose to weave his way out onto the stage, wearing this weird turban, singing "Visions of Johanna".'

It was a stunning juxtaposition, and only the second time Dylan had sung his greatest song live since the Royal Albert Hall, ten years earlier. If the audience weren't sure what to make of it, Dylan followed it up by telling a half-full Civic Center, 'I'm supposed to announce a bomb scare. I don't know why *anyone* would want to bomb this building, but if any of you want to leave, you're supposed to do it now.' Preferring to die in his footsteps, he launched into a barely recognisable version of 'If You See Her, Say Hello' – and not because he was in his cups but because that once tender, wistful love song now made 'Idiot Wind' sound conciliatory, with an opening couplet that set the tone – 'If you see her say hello, she might be in outer space / She left here in a hurry, I forgot what took place,' as the gloves came off:

> Sundown, silver moon, shining on the gate
> My heart don't understand no more what my head don't tolerate
> I know she'll be back some day, of that there is no doubt
> And when that moment comes, dear Lord, give me the strength to keep her out.

As if this wasn't disorienting enough, Dylan proceeded to introduce

the largely unknown Bobby Neuwirth to the Lakelanders, before the
two Bobbies set about revisiting the '61 Indian Neck Festival with a
raucous duet on Hank Williams's 'Weary Blues From Waitin'. Dylan
was just getting warmed up as rewrites of 'One Too Many Mornings',
'I Threw It All Away', 'Lay Lady Lay' – now a 'get in bed' command –
and 'Going Going Gone' suggested his muse preferred he tinker with
his back pages to turning over a new leaf. A furious finale of 'Idiot
Wind', a semi-improvised 'Knockin' On Heaven's Door' and the late
Paul Clayton's folk standard, 'Gotta Travel On', wrapped up a show
that proved Dylan was not standing on ceremony or standing still,
even as a bemused semi-savvy audience shuffled off to get themselves
some sun.

For those who had also been there on opening night in 1974 – like
Zimmerman Blues editor Brian Stybal – there was no cause for concern.
After Chicago '74, things soon settled down as audiences got their way,
and fan favourites reappeared. Not in 1976, they didn't – even if fans of
Blood on the Tracks invariably got their fill. Over the course of the next
five weeks, those who followed the Gulf Coast tour heard him perm
from eight of the ten tracks on that near-perfect platter; in the case of
'Tangled Up In Blue', in both solo guise and as a raging, glorified punk
anthem as epic and angry as a nightly 'Idiot Wind'.

Even the bittersweet 'You're Gonna Make Me Lonesome When You
Go' gingerly joined in and stayed on, surely in part because its inspiration, Ellen Bernstein, briefly joined the Revue, ostensibly checking up
on her own A&R act, Roger McGuinn, whom she had recently convinced to give 'Up To Me' its own Revue-style arrangement.* If the
flame that warmed these former lovers had not quite burnt out, this
time she – and Sara – had some competition, Dylan having given up
any pretence he was a one-woman man:

> **Howie Wyeth**: [There was] the tight-rope walker . . . There was a real
> tall chick that was also a magician . . . There was a faith-healer too,
> though she was real innocent . . . a really nice lady from Vermont, into
> all sorts of weird foods.

---

* This fine version appears on McGuinn's 1976 album, *Cardiff Rose*, backed by assorted
Rolling Thunder folk.

Susan Green: Dylan invited me to become the tour herbalist, adding –
prophetically – that people are going to be getting sick.

Stephanie Buffington: [It] was like a travelling Peyton Place . . . All
Bob's girlfriends were jumping ship and I was asked not to leave . . . He
just said, 'Oh, my wife is coming,' and at that moment I remembered
that I had met her before . . . [But] as far as I knew, he [had been] separated from her for four months and free to do whatever he wanted to. He
certainly did whatever he wanted to.

Both Ellen and Sara had decided they should go to Houston for
Dylan's return on May 8th. This time, though, it was not Ellen that
Sara ended up pointing the finger at; it was Ms Buffington, who had
sold her some Tibetan artifacts a few years before, and was now surprised to be told, 'I thought it would be you!' Ellen didn't stick around,
and neither did Sara, who could see the writing on the wall. Meanwhile, Dylan decided to see if Stephanie's writings could have the same
edge as his own brand of poison-pen poems:

Bob one time told me that he didn't think women *could* be poets . . .
He'd say, 'You write the nastiest thing you can write, and then I'll write
the nastiest thing I can write.' . . . We'd just have these little games, writing things back and forth . . . [It was like], 'Okay, [Bob], what is this thing
that women can't experience, or write about, or verbalize, or put on
paper? What is this place?'

He wasn't just a poet. He was also a prophet, as Revue folk – himself
included – grew increasingly sick as the tour wound its way towards
the Louisiana hinterlands. By May Day, Susan Green recalls, 'Dylan
was sick again. Even after drinking my tea his condition . . . hadn't
improved by showtime. Unfortunately, members of the tour began
slipping him various other remedies . . . Nonetheless, Dylan gave a terrific performance.' He certainly did, reaching into his divided self that
night in Hattiesburg for an acoustic 'Simple Twist Of Fate' that put all
'75 versions to shame; a 'You're Gonna Make Me Lonesome' that went
down to the valley below, and a coruscating 'You're A Big Girl Now'
which made listeners long to hear Scarlet overdub all of *Blood on the
Tracks*.

But it wasn't just the *Blood* songs that were getting the treatment. Dylan wanted to show Scarlet off to a national TV audience, filming versions of 'Oh, Sister' and 'One More Cup Of Coffee' that were almost Hebraic incantations, Scarlet's violin vying with Dylan's flamenco flourishes for a TV special he filmed over an afternoon and evening at the hotel they had made their early base. But barely had he filmed the afternoon set than he got into an argument with the TV producer, Bert Sugarman, whom he rightly realized had the soul of a salmon, and in front of Howie Wyeth at dinner, said, 'No! We're not doing it. Fuck it!'

Filming was completed, but the project was doomed. He decided he didn't need Sugarman; he had Howard Alk, cameraman/editor extraordinaire. The TV special would now be both a representation of the Revue and a masterclass in how to shoot 'in your face' footage, eschewing the usual series of audience reaction shots. Not that the brilliance of most post-Clearwater shows was greatly improving his mood. When Mr and Mrs Levy flew in to see how the tour was progressing, Claudia got the cold shoulder:

> I was backstage and it hadn't been a good performance. And Bob . . . was wiping his face [with a towel] . . . And I said something about it being a really interesting performance. He looked at me and said, 'Ya think so?' And then he . . . took a chair and moved it away from everybody, and sat by himself. Nobody would talk to him and he didn't want anybody near him.

She knew not to take it personally. As did others who knew him well, like Dylan's right-hand man, Arthur Rosato, who remembers he didn't say 'two words to [me] on the whole tour . . . He didn't wanna be there, and he let everybody know about it.' Arthur smartly kept his head down when Dylan decided he was now an electric guitar-player, even though Rosato already knew, from the previous two tours, 'He is really a great acoustic guitar player. But . . . [when] you listen to his electric guitar playing [then], and you listen to it now, it's exactly the same – there is no improvement.'

In 1976, he was wielding a white National guitar that looked great but, as Rosato put it, gave Dylan 'that scrub-board style that grates through everything'. It left Mick Ronson wondering why he was even there. But at least when Dylan strapped on the National, it seemed like he was enjoying himself, perhaps picturing himself back at Bonnie Beecher's sorority house trying to master another unfamiliar instrument.

By mid-May, the tour had found an even keel of sorts – just in time. As everyone knew, the Wally Heider mobile-truck was due in Fort Worth on the 16th, to record a live album. Despite recording half a dozen shows the previous fall on multitrack, this was the first opportunity to capture this altogether more ramshackle version of the Revue in all its wayward glory.

Feeling that one last run-through might be needed, Dylan agreed to do a free show at the Gatesville State School for Boys the day before, providing an educational experience for one and all, including two refugees from the previous Revue, Joni Mitchell and childhood friend Larry Kegan, who showed up to lend a hand and lighten Dylan's load. The wheelchair-bound Kegan even got to share their mutual teenage fantasy, singing one of their favourite teenage laments, 'Framed', before the crew shipped everything to the Convention Center for a make-or-break show that would provide half of Dylan's second live album in two years, *Hard Rain*.

The soundtrack element would be added, a week later, after the Revue rolled into Colorado's Fort Collins for an open-air show Dylan (and Alk) intended to use to film that aborted TV special. Unfortunately, a change in the weather proved extreme enough to require consecutive postponements across two days, leaving everyone, Dylan included, kicking their heels:

> **Rob Stoner**: Bob was really hitting the bottle that weekend. That was a terrible fuckin' weekend . . . We were supposed to do the gig [on] two or three consecutive days – each time the [alternate] 'rain date' was supposed to be the next day – but it was pouring for days and days. Meanwhile, it's costing Bob a lot of bread. Everybody's holed up in this little hotel up in the mountains in the middle of nowhere, with nothing to do except get drunk . . . Here's the last gig [sic], and it's taking forever to do it. [Meanwhile,] the boss is getting in a progressively shittier mood.

By May 23rd, the sands of time had run out. Though it continued raining in Colorado – and Dylan's heart – Guam had no choice but to give a 'now or never' performance in conditions that tested the resolve

With Howard Alk, preparing to eat the document, winter 1967.

'That valiant Cornish knight, King Mark, with his faithful servant, Curverknell', winter 1967.

With Sara, the Seegers and Mr Shankar, 1968.

Guess who's coming to dinner. It's Ravi, 1968.

With Sara, fleeing to the Isle of Wight, August 1969.

Dr Dylan at Princeton, praying the pieces don't fall on him, June 1970.

Wearing a disguise at the Mariposa Folk Festival, July 1972.

A buttoned-up Bob shooting another scrapped album-cover, 1973.

A smile for his muse, with Ellen Bernstein, 1974.

'I have my friends but Los Angeles doesn't have the same tradition of hanging out as New York', March 1977.

of even these hardy pioneering folk. The rain was still, well, biblical, leaving Dylan to wonder if he'd done something to offend the gods. Maybe not, but he had certainly done enough to offend his nearest and dearest, as he admitted ten years after, telling another lovestruck lady, 'I knew I'd done wrong. You see, there's just women you have to fuck because they demand it.'

It was not an argument likely to hold much truck with a triple Scorpio. Sara stormed into the hotel the day of the gig to be met by former rival, Joan Baez, who knew exactly how she felt, 'She greeted me with a reserved hello and talked distantly about nothing in particular, all the while eyeing the closed door to the ballroom.' Dylan was ensconced within, presumably with one of those 'women you have to fuck because they demand it'.

A row in the parking lot with the missus before his biggest show of the year did not exactly improve Dylan's mood. Nor did the fact that when they arrived at the open-air stadium, his bandleader informed him, 'Everybody's soaked; the canopy's leaking; the musicians are getting shocks from the water on the stage [and] the instruments are going out of tune because of the humidity.' Fortunately, Dylan rose to the occasion. Usually at his best when up against it, these conditions were near perfect for a peerless performer determined to spit at the gods of Fate. As Stoner rightly notes, 'Everybody is playing and singing for their lives, and that is the spirit that you hear on that record.'

The record in question, *Hard Rain*, was a different document to the fifty-minute TV film of the same name, broadcast that September to a somewhat bemused international TV audience. On the record, fans heard not only raging versions of 'Shelter From The Storm' and 'Idiot Wind' that he would never better – while Sara stood three feet away in a pit of despair, watching her husband deconstruct their entire marriage before unknowing eyes – but also a 'Big Girl Now' that really did rise above the pain and the rain.

What wasn't used on either artifact was the full-blooded arrangement of 'Tangled Up In Blue' Dylan unleashed when rain really was falling on his shoes. Sadly, a Dylan/ Baez duet of 'Lily, Rosemary And The Jack Of Hearts' the pair had rehearsed at the hotel went unperformed until two nights later, in Salt Lake City, in what proved to be the final show of the grand experiment that was Rolling Thunder.

Arthur Rosato's abiding image of the flight back to L.A. was of Joan

Baez attempting a communal version of 'Happy birthday, dear shit-head'. (Oh, what a wag!) Dylan was already thinking of his next heist. He had a film to complete before he even thought about making another album, and with this in mind he had instructed his lawyer, David Braun, to 'confirm with CBS that the parties have agreed to treat *Hard Rain* as the third and final album under Bob Dylan's current recording agreement with CBS Records'. This they duly did, on December 2nd, 1976, before all the sales figures were in; i.e. before the label realized that a man whose last three studio albums had gone to number one was not about to make the next *Frampton Comes Alive*, or even *Bob Marley & The Wailers Live*.

Barely had Dylan landed in L.A. than he was heading to the Santa Monica Civic to check the real competition out, witnessing Marley in his pomp after partaking of some ganja backstage with another Bob the Poet, to get in the mood before heading for Mexico and a tequila sunrise or two at the home of photographer Lisa Law.

In November, Dylan also became an essential component of the most impressive rock bill this side of Bangladesh – a Winterland fare-well concert for The Band, who were trying to pretend they had spent the last sixteen years on the road – and the resulting triple-album. By the time Dylan found out they were planning to film the event, he was already hard at work on his own road movie and not at all inclined to let Robbie and his new buddy, Martin Scorsese, have dibs on a short-but-sweet Dylan set:

> **Robbie Robertson**: When Bob came to Shangri-La [to rehearse for *The Last Waltz*], he [said he] thought we should do a couple of tunes from *Planet Waves* . . . [and] maybe one of the tracks we used to do when we first hooked up, like 'Baby Let Me Follow You Down' . . . We played through a few songs once and left it at that. Afterward . . . Bob asked, 'What's this filming business everybody's talking about for the concert?'

What all interested parties – including Dylan's ex-road manager turned film producer, Jonathan Taplin – didn't seem to realize was that Bob didn't give a damn that they 'had a lot of money invested in this thing', or that, 'Without Bob in the film, it was certainly a lot less valu-able than with Bob.' Neither Robertson nor Taplin seemed to seriously consider the possibility that Dylan might not let them film his entire set until the night of the concert when, much to Taplin's ever-rising despair, 'The intermission was expiring and he *still* hadn't said okay. Finally, it was about five minutes before he had to go on and he said, "Okay, you can film me for the last two numbers."'

All Dylan was concerned about was his own film. By not signing the release permitting his performance to appear in *The Last Waltz* until his own film was ready for release, he ensured he got his out first. As it is, he need not have worried. The amount of post-production *The Last Waltz* required, and the industrial quantities of cocaine consumed during the editing, put paid to any preemptive release of what was hardly anybody's finest (half an) hour, Dylan included. The footage he had for his own film was vastly superior to anything Scorsese had to work with in 1977, as the esteemed director of *Taxi Driver* and *After Hours* would discover first-hand when he got to do the resurrection shuffle with the fall 1975 footage, forty years on.

Although Alk and Dylan had been hard at work on their own road odyssey for much of the second half of 1976, they were, in the words of Alk, 'interrupted . . . by the television show.' They didn't really get down to business till after Dylan gave Robbie a route into film. Even then, there was a delay because Dylan seemed to feel the need for a crash-course in arty film-making. Alk was happy to oblige. According to assistant Lynn Davis, the pair seemed to spend most of their time screening Fassbinder's *The Bitter Tears of Petra von Kant*. And if Dylan the film promotion man can be believed, he was also wont to check out Godard's cinematic debut, *Breathless*, or anything by his 'favourite director', Luis Buñuel, presumably including his latest, *That Obscure Object of Desire*, the female lead of which changed identity halfway through, just like The Woman In White.*

If muddying his muse's identity was a conscious choice on Dylan's part, it was also a thread blurred further in the editing. As he told the *L.A. Times*, 'We started out with a simple love triangle story. But the more deeply involved I got, I realized most of it happens all in the mind . . . And what I was trying to capture was what the inner mind was going through.' Mel Howard was not convinced this was his primary motivation, believing that 'Dylan obscured a lot of the personal

---

* In Buñuel's case, the original actress quit part way through filming, whereas Dylan always seems to have intended to interchange the role.

revelations in the editing process. I *know* that he left out some of the most revealing material with Sara and Joan.'

Not that Dylan or Alk knew what they had in the can when they started editing. According to Larry Johnson, 'Howard and he would call me up to ask if we got this and that – because they never knew what we were shooting till they saw it.' Dylan was at least prepared to discuss his conceit with Allen Ginsberg, who spent three days with Bob before taking to the airwaves to explain the film on its release to the masses:

> It's built in a very interesting way. You'd have to study it like *Finnegan's Wake,* or Cézanne, to discern the texture, the composition of the tapestry. He shot about 110 hours of film . . . and he looked at all the scenes. Then he put all the scenes on index cards, according to some preconceptions he had when he was directing the shooting; namely, themes [like] God, rock'n'roll, art, poetry, marriage, women, sex, Bob Dylan, poets, death – maybe eighteen or twenty thematic preoccupations . . . The idea was not to have a 'plot', but to have a composition of those themes . . . It's a painter's film, and was composed like that.

Just like *Eat the Document,* the nature of the footage shot dictated the narrative arc, Dylan never quite dispelling an ineffable sense that the film's so-called internal logic was something the two editors constructed *after the fact,* from footage assembled on the hoof. He was still delighted with the result when he first screened it for his children's art teacher, who had by now taken the place of his wife in his bed:

> **Faridi McFree:** I entered Bob's life when he was editing his film, *Renaldo & Clara.* It was virtually completed and he was very excited about it. The first time Bob screened it for me, he was like a child showing his girlfriend a new toy.

He should perhaps have been more concerned with how Sara might react when she saw the film. She was, after all, playing the title role of Clara (and, occasionally, The Woman In White). She was also, as of March 1st, 1977, suing him for divorce, claiming in her affidavit, 'My five children are greatly disturbed by my husband's behaviour, and his bizarre lifestyle.' Actually, it was *her* who was 'greatly disturbed', especially when she heard second-hand that her husband had been talking to the gregarious Lisa Law at her Mexican home about their relationship. According to Victor Maymudes, 'Ever the record keeper of history, Lisa relayed the [contents] to our very close friends.' Having given Sara the ammunition, Dylan now gave her the smoking gun she needed to raid the bank accounts of the ladies' man she'd lived with for twelve long years.

Once again, he had taken to fleeing the home for the sanctuary of the studio, and someone else's album, watching in wide-eyed wonder as Phil Spector made a hash of Leonard Cohen's latest, *Death of A Ladies' Man*, on which, according to Dylan, he 'had me and Allen Ginsberg and Ronee Blakley singing into one microphone and I was ten feet behind them two, [yet] when I heard the record it was all me'. Something of an exaggeration, though the message of the song was probably one he should have heeded: 'Don't Go Home With A Hard-On'.

What he did, instead, was return home with a poetess and confidant of Leonard's, Malka Marom, whom Joni had introduced to Dylan in December 1975 with the immortal words, 'Bobby, I want to introduce you to the only person I know who doesn't want to meet you.' Imagine Sara's surprise when she came down to breakfast one morning in late February and there was her husband and Malka having breakfast with the children.*

Was there ever anything between Dylan and Malka? The jury is still out. But if there was, perhaps it was her on his mind when penning a lyrical fragment within days of their breakfast club: 'You love me madly, I know it's true/ I don't wanna make the wrong impression on you/ But I can't give you back the love, the way you['d] like me to.' Not that there was any shortage of other candidates throwing themselves in his direction. As his next girlfriend told me, 'The women were especially nauseating.'

Dylan told Craig McGregor the following March, 'In [my] kind of situation, you meet a lot of people that are attracted to you, and also you become attracted to quite a few people, and . . . you just have to let the situation run its course.' Well, Sara was no longer prepared to

---

* Fifteen years later, Dylan insisted to a girlfriend the 'breakfast' episode never took place, and that he would never have done that to his kids. I'm inclined to believe him. Malka refuses to discuss the incident.

allow him to do just that. She started asking around for a good divorce lawyer and the ever-obliging David Geffen, still smarting from Dylan outsmarting him over the live LP, recommended self-publicist Marvin Mitchelson, who at their first meeting found Sara to be in a 'feisty' mood: 'She loved Bob Dylan – no question about it – but he chose to spend his time elsewhere and took up new relationships, and that all became part of the case.' Actually, it was the whole of the case, and the whole of the law.

Despite later claiming privately that the divorce 'broke him', Dylan did little to prevent it happening. In fact, according to David Hajdu (who could only have got such intel. from Baez herself), 'When they separated after twelve years of marriage and four children, Bob turned to Joan and lived with her again for a few weeks.' It was perhaps at Baez's place that he got back to doing what he did best – writing songs.

Though nothing came of the songs he wrote that spring, he would tell Robert Hilburn the following May, 'I had some songs last year which . . . dealt with that period as I was going through it . . . Some people around town heard them . . . but I had no interest in recording them.' The one piece of anecdotal evidence that such songs existed, prior to the 2022 opening of the Bob Dylan Center, came from Alpha musician Steven Soles, who told Jon Kanis (and, subsequently, Sounes), that Dylan had come over 'unannounced' to his apartment in early spring. T-Bone was in situ, too, 'and [he] played us, I don't know, ten, twelve songs . . . to get our take on [them]. And, of course, it just completely floored us . . . They were all very tough . . . dark songs. None of those saw the light of day . . . They got discarded because I think they were too strong . . . more [from] the angry side of that conflict . . . [One in particular], 'I'm Cold' . . . would bring a chill to your bones.'

Such a lyric resides in one of the many undated Tulsa notebooks, called simply 'Cold'. Bearing the burden, 'I don't like to be controlled – I'm cold', in one verse he rhymes it with, 'I can't go to sleep until my story's told'; in another, 'I been treading on a wheel where the armies of the night have rolled.' Another couplet seemingly intended for the same berth went, 'I don't question anyone, I don't care what they know/ You can change the course of rivers, but you can't stop the flow.'* Another

---

* The line about changing the course of rivers would reappear on 1983's 'Neighborhood Bully'.

'song title' on the same page was called 'Visitation Rights'. Although nothing in it obviously pertains to real life, said notebook is crammed full of verses directly addressing witchy women, at least one of whom seemed to want to call him to account:

> It was there on the border, she spit on the ground
> She had a list of grievances as long as the world be round
> She laid down beside me (like she did in my youth)
> (We didn't come up with any answers, but we wrestled with the truth).

Another, similar couplet, 'You tried to love a woman, you tried to fulfil her needs/ But her mind was darkened by the memories of any evil deeds,' appears alongside editing notes for *Renaldo & Clara*. He even seems to be frequenting the same bordello/s as the celluloid Sara and Joan on occasion: 'Leaning out the window I could hear the [taxi] roar/ And the moaning of the steeple and the blessings of the whore.'

Elsewhere is a song called either 'Mary And Joseph' and/or 'Possessive Eyes', which he worked on extensively. It promised much, as he alludes to searching 'for her in the whorehouse, in the schoolyard and in the church'. Neither Mary nor Joseph bear little resemblance to their Biblical namesakes: 'Mary called for Volunteers to fight the battles raging in her mirrors/And Joseph nailed a shield into the image of the Goddess in the field . . . /Mary sailed away upon a sea of mystery pursued by slaves reaching for the end/ . . . And a dark cloud rose over Joseph's head as he staggered into Leningrad.'

Nor are these the only potentially Biblical figures namechecked herein. Both song and notebook contain a smattering of references to Jesus and the Devil, caught up in a battle between good and evil. It suggests he was again searching for answers in a well-thumbed copy of the good book. Another snatch found among film-editing notes references both Old and New Testament:

> Treat him like Jacob treated you know who
> Use Jesus as your advocate
> 'Cause Jesus knows all
> You answer _____ killed
> Is the [beat] in the heart of the bottomless pit.

Next to this intriguing fragment Dylan has written, 'If a man remains Alone, he considers himself a God.' Whoever could he mean? The point where he flicked the switch on *Street-Legal*, signalling a major lyrical breakthrough, would come in the final draft of 'Possessive Eyes', when he references Satan and Robert Johnson in a single couplet, and hints of a time he almost boarded the 'holy slow train': 'I met an old man . . . caught the first smoking train . . . I said hello to the Devil, I said Goodbye to Love In Vain.'

It seems he really has started to worry that one or more of these witchy women may be in league with the Devil: 'She'll take you down to the gates of Hell/ And introduce you to the master sinner.' Both the old man and the smoking train are destined to reappear in a long, rambling rap with which Dylan would introduce 'Señor (Tales of Yankee Power)' nightly on the US leg of the 1978 tour, when he really was groping in the Descartian dark, fumbling for the light switch:

> I was riding on a train one time to Mexico coming to Torreón. In the evening hours there was nobody on this car that I was on and a full moon was shining. So, we made one stop, I think it was near Monterrey. This old man got on the train, he had a blanket . . . [] . . . It was dark outside, I was looking through the window, like a mirror, I saw him come and sit over at the other side of the aisle from me. So, I turned around and looked at him and both his eyes were on fire. And the smoke was coming out of his nostrils. Anyway, this old man, I just wanted to ask him everything, but I didn't know where to begin.

Other spring '77 lyric drafts, like 'Cross The Line' ('There's no place to run/ You might as well sit in the sun') and 'Let Me Taste It, Crystal Queen' ('She uncrossed her legs from around my back/ She went into the kitchen to make herself a snack'), came with guitar chords, suggesting he fully intended to develop these snatches further. Even if the majority would be left unfinished, occasional flashes confirm Soles's assertion that these songs came from 'the angry side of that conflict': 'You been wearing out my patience, trying to get me where I live/ When you learned to forget the consequences, did you learn how to forgive?' for one; 'Spent too many years walking hand in hand/ With a crazy woman who never meant me any good,' being another.

But perhaps the most personally revealing 'lyric' from these months is a litany of 'women troubles' composed in the form of a long poem (one he wrote out at least twice). In it, he jokingly lists all the girls he has ever loved – running to double figures – and where he went wrong in each case. The poem may have little basis in fact, but he seems to enjoy poking fun at his former selves. Thus, the fourth time it happened, it was a Thursday 'and the girl's name was Eileen/ she was 21, I was 16.' The fifth time it happened, he took her from a relieved best buddy, only for her to tell him, 'She didn't care for my style or my code/ She gave me a bathrobe and told me to get on the road.' And so on.

It would have made for an amusing set of sleeve notes, à la 'Eleven Outlined Epitaphs', if it had not been quietly forgotten, as he re-evaluated his lifestyle choices, fresh from being an eyewitness to *Death of A Ladies' Man*, and concluding that the life of a Hollywood party animal was not for him. As he confided in a woman journalist the following February:

I have my friends, but Los Angeles doesn't have the same tradition of hanging out as does New York or Chicago. People are less accessible here. I find generally that I'm more lonely when I'm out than when I'm at home. Why go out and sit around waiting for someone to talk to you?

As it happens, his next great love was about to come his way, having wakened from a dream convinced that he needed her help, and that she must go to him now, even at the expense of her friendship and working relationship with the man's ex-wife. And this time, Sara could wait at the gate and fume as much as she liked. He was a free man in Malibu – or so he thought.

4.3

March 1977 to June 1978:
Her Version Of Jealousy

I wasn't a very good husband.

Bob Dylan, to Craig McGregor, March 1978.

He can't lead a normal life. He goes to a party, he hides in the bushes . . .
'cause if he comes out of the bushes, everybody gawks. I mean, he can't
just stand around and talk to people.

Ronee Blakley, 1975.

Bob walks into a room and every eye in the place is on him. There are
eyes on Bob even when he's hiding. All that has probably not been easy
for him.

Joan Baez, to Nat Hentoff, November 1975.

There are people that he lets in to a certain degree. He's let me in pretty
close in certain ways. And yet he will act like we never have met the next
day.

Joni Mitchell.

If you just talk to him like a normal guy . . . and have a burger and onion
rings with him . . . he's very funny. He keeps up with politics and everything else, so there's never a lack of things to talk about. It only skews
itself . . . when you get into a room and people suddenly start treating
him like some idol.

Dan Fiala, tour manager 1978–80.

People don't talk straight to him. He's always gotta weigh and measure what everyone says because everyone's out to impress him, win him, sell him, whatever.

> Mel Howard, filmmaker, to Larry Sloman.

I feel the [man] is . . . future-shocked. It would take a huge amount of debriefing . . . to get him back to normal again, to put that character armour down.

> Michael Bloomfield, 1975.

Bob Dylan: [My film] is about the essence of man being alienated from himself and how, in order to free himself, to be *reborn*, he has to go outside himself . . .
Ron Rosenbaum: What are his needs?
BD: A good guitar and a dark street.
RR: The guitar because he loves music, but why the dark street?
BD: Mostly because he needs to hide . . . from the demon within. [Pause] But we all know you can't hide . . . from the demon within.

> *Playboy*, March 1978.

★

When the news came through of Dylan's imminent divorce, in early March 1977, the English music papers seemed particularly delighted at the prospect of another *Blood on the Tracks*, and sod any personal pain. *NME* even had one of their cartoonists, Benyon, come up with a drawing of a forlorn Dylan staring out, saying, 'Go 'way from half my window . . .' But an older, wiser Dylan was not yet ready to unburden himself on record, and wouldn't be for a year or more.

If *Another Side* was written and recorded in the heat of the moment – when the break-up with Suze was still raw – he would ruminate on, rewrite and rework the songs of *Street-Legal* for *months* before even showing them to the band with whom he planned to tour the world for a whole year. The one adult eyewitness to that tortuous writing process would be this year's Ellen, a lady who rushed to his side as the pain became so intense it passed through the ether:

Faridi McFree: I fell out of bed. I mean it was so intense, this loneliness . . . And then I had this pain again in my heart all day. I [thought], I can't stand it [and] I picked up the phone and I said, 'Bob, this is Faridi. I work with Sara and the children. I'm the children's art teacher. Are you okay?' And he said, 'No, I'm not okay.' So, I said, 'I had this strong feeling that I should call you.' . . . He said, 'Why don't you come over? I really, really need to talk to someone . . . You know, Faridi, [with] all the friends I have, *nobody* called me to see how I felt. Nobody!'

They both knew this was a recipe for trouble. Nonetheless, Faridi got in her car and started driving ninety miles an hour towards Dylan's dead-end drive. When she got there, she almost changed her mind, 'I was scared, because there are all these bodyguards . . . And then Bob came towards the light and . . . he looked like he was crazed . . . But he came to the car, and he drove with me to the house, and we just never stopped talking . . . We just talked into the night. I don't think we stopped talking until four or five o'clock in the morning. He just poured and poured and poured out his heart. All these grievances that he was feeling, grief and everything else . . . He was suffering when I met him. He was in a bad way. I brought him back to life. He was practically dead . . . This guy was shot emotionally.'

Whenever he felt this way, he would look for a sympathetic woman to listen to him, and pour soothing balm on his sea of troubles. The simple fact remains, as a later muse put it, 'Music is the constant core of his life. He lives for it . . . [But] he loves being with women and remains delighted at the marvels of interaction with them. Not just for sex, but when he needs support or direction or clarification for the ideas and feelings bouncing around his brain and body, he'll call a woman friend . . . He claims [to believe] in marriage, but not monogamy.' It would take Faridi some time to realize all of this. But she knew from day one how Sara would respond to the news – as and when she returned from a restorative holiday in Hawaii:

Faridi McFree: By the time Sara returned to the colony in Malibu, Bob and I were living together. Naturally, Sara was upset . . . Just as I had suspected, she felt I had betrayed her . . . She had [previously] told me all these stories about all these women that would use her to get to him . . . [And] when we were together, I noticed how obsequious people were, when they were in Bob's presence ... Therefore, Bob never really trusted anyone. Maria, Bob's oldest daughter, used to tell me that of all the people Bob knew, I was the only one he trusted. And that finally faded, too.

If Faridi didn't yet realize how green-eyed Sara's inner Scorpio could be, her new lover knew only too well. He actually seems to be anticipating all that was to come in one of those spring '77 songs, 'Crystal Queen': 'You pay in blood for what you believe/ But she's a powerful child and you're ni-eve[sic]/ And I won't allow her to destroy you.' Faridi soon learnt she was playing with fire, 'Bob's lawyers . . . [were] warn[ing] Bob to get rid of me. They said, "Let her go. She shouldn't be around you, 'cause you'll lose the [custody] case." And he just wouldn't. So I used to go into hiding when[ever] they came over.'

By late spring, the uncontested divorce was a *fait accompli*. What mattered now was joint custody of the children, and Sara was prepared to go to war to ensure Faridi played no part of their future, despite having been an important part of their immediate past.

When her former husband insisted on taking the children with him to the farm for their annual summer sojourn, Sara must have thought it was Ellen all over again. But this time, the children already had a strong bond with their father's latest mother-figure, through her affirmative art-healing, the reason Sara had first brought her into the fold. McFree even encouraged Dylan to share in the healing properties of painting, 'I enjoyed Bob's art, although he didn't [rate it]. As the art teacher to his children, I encouraged Bob to be kinder to himself and not to be so critical of his creative expressions. But [his] real joy was to watch me and the children . . . creating images with pretty colours and affirmations to heal the mind.'

Away from it all, on the Minnesotan farm, Faridi saw the real Bob begin to re-emerge at last, 'The farm was really where he got back up on his feet again.' Had Sara ever been privy to the many photos Bob and Faridi snapped that summer – some now in the hands of a major Dylan collector – seeing the children laughing and playing with the maternal Faridi while Dylan let his hair grow down to the ground (see the photo section), she'd have hit the roof of her Bel-Air bolt-hole.

For Faridi, the one dark night of the soul that summer was 'the night Presley died [August 16th] . . . He really took it very bad. He didn't speak for a couple of days. He was really grieving. He said that if it wasn't for [Elvis] he would never have gotten started. That he opened the door.' If Elvis would always be, to Dylan's mind, 'the incendiary atomic musical firebrand', he was also someone who had been burnt alive by the flame of fame. Dylan was determined that would not happen to him. The songs he was now writing on the farm – using 'memo' notepads he had printed for the children, rather than his usual pocket notebooks – may have had the same musical roots as Elvis, but lyrically, they were 'torn between Jupiter and Apollo'.

'Twas time to get serious about songwriting again. That summer of '77 – while the music world rocked to the sound of white men frequenting the Hammersmith Palais – Dylan took stray strands from the spring song-hoard and began to weave a familiar spell. One couplet in 'Possessive Eyes', in particular, was calling to him: 'Hey Bonny Jean – woncha tell me true/ Is that a dangerous train, or is your love in vain?'

That 'dangerous train' would remain in the sidings for a while yet. For now, he was concentrating on a song about vain love – asking of (himself and) her, 'Are you willing to take the risk?', while secretly admitting, 'I've grown to like solitude.' Perhaps Faridi was making him rethink the kind of woman he tended to desire. As he told Barbara Kerr the following February, 'Give me a woman who can cook and sew, and I'll take that over passion any day.' But even his constant companion didn't always seem to know when to give him creative space; hence, perhaps, a single sentence written on the back of a note to Christy's Editorial Film Supply, Burbank – presumably while co-editing *Renaldo & Clara* – 'I care more about you than anybody, but you just always wanna know what I'm thinking.'

If the lyric he began now would prove a tad too honest for the politically-correct creed of critic, he was unabashed to Kerr, 'Women use romance and passion to sweeten you up,' while also setting Jonathan Cott straight, 'When a man's looking for a woman, he ain't looking for a woman who's an airplane pilot.' It was a clear dig at fellow *Rolling Stone* scribe, Greil Marcus, for his mile-wide critique of 'Is Your Love In Vain?' in that once-esteemed journal, already rendered redundant by punk.

A Dylan laying bare real feelings, as he does in 'Is Your Love In Vain?', was familiar enough – he just wasn't usually this upfront. Leaving it unfinished, the lyricist turned the sheet over and began something completely different, determined to prove he warranted the soubriquet, Poet. Its working title – 'Her Version Of Jealousy' – referenced in conversation with Craig McGregor in March 1978, suggests a common theme. But any similarities end there. This was as allegorical as it was ambitious.

It also affirmed time in Paris the previous February had not been wasted. One of the *objets d'art* he had evidently picked up there was a copy of the Grimaud Tarot card deck, dating back to 1898. In it, the Pope card had been replaced by Jupiter; the Strength card – alluded to in 1981's 'Angelina' – was also featured. Confirmation he was using this deck in 1977 is provided by a detailed list of cards and their attributes in Dylan's hand, e.g. 'Priest/ Justified Suspicion (Eight of Swords)', #55 in the Grimaud Tarot deck.

Sidelined for now was the Waites deck utilised when depicting the Jack of Hearts as the Magician, lily and rose to hand; replaced by the Traitor who's been paid off, but is marked for death. Dylan sketched out a shorthand version of the new song next to lines from 'Sara' (presumably relating to the film he was working on contiguously), though barely a word from this sketch would tread the path to *Street-Legal*:

> Eyes – that sparkle and glow
> Ties – that go deep with the flow
> Swords – that come out of the past
>> To unravel the last
>> bit of pain that is cast
>> thru (ah) window
> Signs – that tell you care
> Hearts – tell tale heart
>> to create or destroy
> sexism, escapism, feminism, [humanism], patriotism,
> the worst is journalism.

His first overt lyrical reference to Poe, the suit of Swords and a litany of -isms betray the direction he's heading in. But it would be some time before he got as far as 'Queen's Robe Blues', 'No Time To Think's second working title. Once there, he embarked on a search for rhymes to go with its burden, 'no time to think': exemplified by a draft of verse three, where the narrator has 'surrendered to [her] charms & fell into her arms/ hung up in the body of nite . . . Like a virgin she's perched in the bowels of the church/ Like the plague *with a dangerous wink*,' and a fifth in which, 'There's a lookout man leaving, [as] she's tearfully weaving/ A spider's web next to you *as you drink* . . .'

In both couplets, his life seems in peril, and there is no mistaking the sex of his enemy, 'The wenches of sorrow & queens of tomorrow were pressing yr flesh to Her gate/ And now there's a vacuum, where you wept in the backroom, with wounds that the winds penetrate.' This Empress of Grimaud is dealing from the bottom of the deck – using those mid-line rhymes (sorrow/ tomorrow; vacuum/ backroom) which are such a feature of the finished song. Only in the final verse of draft #2 does he finally reveal the excessive road which has brought him here: '[Knowledge] enlightens you, Freedom frightens you/ There's many paths to the same place.'

Maybe I'm reading too much into it. It has been known. One should certainly be wary – as Michael Gray in 1981's *The Art of Bob Dylan* was not – of seeing a Dylan already treading the road to conversion. But something is happening, or why is he trying to incorporate the image, 'Jesus in a petticoat', handwritten at the bottom of one typed draft, into this song. Something inside also prompted him to type: 'SLOW TRAIN/ FROM TYRANNY/ RIVALRY AMONG DIPLOMATS/ HONOR AMONG THIEVES,' one more fragment found among the *Street-Legal* papers, just below a song with the working title, 'Spell-bound Magician', and the lines 'Peace at last . . . Idol Will Fall . . . Keepin' all hope alive between Shadow & [Sword].'

He has the poetical pivot for another important song, 'Changing Of The Guards', and another redemptive travelogue Dylan needed no-one's help to complete – just the time and solitude required to scrap the original title and find the core message he needed to convey, all of which he managed to achieve down on the farm:

> Gentlemen, he said, I'm on my way to glory . . .
> Peace will come with tranquility & splendor, in a shining cloak . . .
> Baby be still, she said, can you spare me a moment's passion
> Can I shine yr shoes, print yr money or mark yr cards
> What frozen/false truths can yr brave souls imagine
> Does yr hearts have the courage for the changing of the guards.

The ideas were pouring out of him, just as they had during another rural retreat three years earlier. He could barely contain himself, even as he sidelined a song that proclaimed, 'I don't wanna convert you/ I don't wanna hurt you/ I would rather desert you' – what later became 'We'd Better Talk This Over' – in favour of 'a long lonesome train . . . drizzling rain . . . tears – woman touch – drifting/ neon lights – cows – lonesome bell tones – bathed/ prince, convinced / upward, heart – ashes & dust/ he predicted to us – dreams apart/ babe in the arms – golden haired stripper on stage – wind back.'

A shorthand version of 'Where Are You Tonight?', the eventual album-closer, had come to him in code, one he was still trying to break the following April, when he was still rewriting the last three verses at the sessions themselves. Such was the discipline he had developed in his mid-thirties. For now, he kept the songs close to his chest, waiting until the following March to inform one Australian journalist he was 'usually writing most of the time, just fragments of songs . . . [which] I try to finish it up some place along the way,' and to another antipodean, 'I wrote a bunch of [songs] in the fall . . . I'll be writing a few more on this trip, [and] I'll record them when I get back to the States in April.'

Thankfully, this also gave him time to ditch some ideas that came to him that summer, like the couplet, 'Notify yr new advisor/ That yr not greedy & I'm not a miser,' found in an early draft of 'We'd Better Talk This Over'. Like *Blood on the Tracks*, he was building an album around three or four major songs, in this case all ones conceptualised on the farm. The last of them reimagined the old man and the smoking train. It would be called 'Señor', but was invariably introduced in concert by its subtitle, 'Tales Of Yankee Power'. If the old man was there from the start, Dylan wisely jettisoned Merlin along the way:

> Señor, Señor. This ain't the stopping point, or is it?
> Will we be here long or will it just be a short visit, Señor.
> Lemme help you with yr baggage there . . .
> I was in the deep end of a magnetic field
> A broken jawed wizard eating an ice cream cone
> Tipped his (pointed) hat, smiled a blissful smile, [and] said
> 'Son, yr in this dream alone.'

Here was someone who knew what he wanted to say, and just

needed to find the right sign language. As to who would get to release the results of a busy summer, that was still up for grabs, as it had been in 1974. CBS, with a new contract on the table, had continued making the same accounting 'errors' they had back in 1967 and 1971, and as of September 9th, an internal CBS memo was reporting, 'Dylan [is] demanding payment of all deferred royalties prior to signing new record agreement.'*

He knew now not to trust his record company. And he sure-as-hell didn't trust any of the major film studios, to whom he had been trying to sell his latest film, a four-hour technicolour dream from the febrile imagination of alter-ego Renaldo, in vain: 'We took the movie to one of the major studios . . . They thought it should run for one and a half hours, and that it had to be all music.' But, as he told *Playboy*'s emissary that November, 'I knew I couldn't . . . betray my vision on a little piece of paper in hopes of getting some money from somebody.' He already knew enough to know 'there's no way you can make a really creative movie in a system that breeds so much discontent'.

He decided he would distribute and promote the film himself, not quite realizing that films made outside the system rarely get an even break, or a fair hearing, especially when their *auteur* went so far as to admit, 'This was a movie done without a script. There were ideas from the beginning, but a lot of this film developed as we were doing it. Quite a bit was improvised . . . within certain rules.'

A remark like this was bound to be seized on and deliberately mis-construed, until he was obliged to spell it out to one particularly dense reporter, '[Of course] there was an outline for this movie. I mean, we didn't just all get together and say, "Go do whatever you want."' He was pissing in the idiot wind, even as he gamely tried to explain his intentions. Only Allen Ginsberg took a statement like, 'Regardless of what [the film]'s about . . . – a guy selling a horse, a guy singing on a stage or fighting with a man – whatever it is, we have stopped Time,' at face value. And only Jonathan Cott from *Rolling Stone* and Ron Rosen-baum at *Playboy* seemed prepared to give him the benefit of the doubt

---

* As the lawyer who oversaw Dylan's 1962 Witmark contract once remarked in print, no miscalculation of royalties in the history of the world ever disadvantaged a record company. How so?

when he suggested, 'The Woman in White . . . was a manifestation of the past,' not Joan Baez playing herself.

The unforgiving incomprehension of other interviewers did not sit well with Dylan, whose mood wasn't greatly improved by a protracted custody battle which continued draining his psychic energies through the fall. When Faridi tried to intervene on his behalf, she discovered the courts weren't about to take account of her art-healing powers, '[Despite being] the Surrogate Mother in the Dylan v. Dylan custody case, the art and affirmations that the children and I did during those hard and difficult times was rejected by the courts as evidence of my [right to] participation in this case.'

Sara, on the other hand, was apparently perfectly within her rights to declare to the court, in a public hearing the *L.A. Times* reported, that her ex-husband 'and Frieda [sic] McFree . . . are attempting to brainwash the minor children,' an outrageous assertion. Matters came to a head when, according to Faridi, the enraged ex-wife attempted some strongarm tactics of her own, 'Sara had armed herself with a few burly men and entered the children's classroom without permission . . . The children resisted the men and their mother. The more they resisted, the more force was used.'

Sara had counted on the children coming quietly. They did not. Unexpectedly, the least inclined to see Sara's side of things was Maria, who was not even Dylan's daughter, save in a legal sense. It drove a wedge between her and her mother that has endured. As Jakob later recalled, 'I can honestly say that day is the most sensitive [in] my life, [and] I remember it more vividly than almost any other day.'

Before things got entirely out of hand, Sara was obliged to admit to a charge of assault on the children's teacher, while Dylan finally agreed to cut Faridi loose, enabling the emotional heat to go out of the situation and the custody issue to be resolved – and just in time. He was leaving for a tour designed largely to refill his much-depleted coffers.

Meanwhile, the press acted as lynch-mob to Dylan the cattle-rustler, stringing *Renaldo & Clara* up to the nearest gallow's pole, and letting any benefit of the doubt go hang. Faridi, who was now holed up in Dylan's old Village townhouse, 'read the first reviews to him on the phone. They were awful, especially the *Village Voice*'s review. I said, "Bob, they actually really wish you were dead." But Bob's reaction to that dreadful statement was, "Faridi, there are all kinds of myths about me. I've gotten used to it." My heart bled for him, but the negative reviews seemed to roll off his back.' Perhaps because he'd learnt long ago that he couldn't afford to be too sensitive. They'd think he was going soft.

Only when well away from America did he give vent to his true feelings, telling Aussie journo Helen Thomas, 'We shouldn't have shown it to . . . intellectual people who sit around at parties and coffee tables . . . We're going to pull this film off the market and just show it to people who aren't going to worry so [much] . . . These people with logical minds . . . have to have everything explained to them, and I don't have time for that.'

Even before this, as he was preparing to depart for alien shores, he stoically expressed the forlorn hope that 'enough people see [the film] so that we get our money back. But if not, then we'll know it just wasn't meant to be.' The film never even made it to general release. When a US distributor offered to circulate a two-hour version, Dylan candidly admitted, '[We] just took it and . . . hacked it up . . . It only took us a day or two . . . The long version is the movie.' Overseas, the movie fared better, the proper version regularly screened in 'rep.' cinemas across Europe for the next half a decade.

Nor was *Renaldo & Clara* the only artistic statement he released that year to receive dumb incomprehension in the land of Puritans. Thankfully, the band he began assembling in December from the ruins of the Rolling Thunder Revue – due to include core constituents Soles, Mansfield, Stoner and Wyeth – would go all around the world with his new sound and grandiose arrangements for six months before American critics got a second chance to bury its greatest living songwriter 'neath the dust of rumour.

On December 21st, 1977, the hardier elements of Guam – led again by the redoubtable Rob Stoner – reassembled at a rehearsal studio in Santa Monica, after Dylan on a whim and a prayer had taken a five-year lease, thus inaugurating the Rundown Era. There to help him christen the place and keep him warm while the band warmed up was an old flame, a nemesis Sara couldn't keep away or chain down:

Ellen Bernstein: I wouldn't say [I] became reinvolved with him, but we did spend time together when he was rehearsing . . . in this building on

Main Street in Santa Monica. He had his own room set up upstairs, so I
would go and visit him at the rehearsals and then stay afterwards.

To welcome Ellen back, Dylan even rehearsed a new arrangement
of 'You're Gonna Make Me Lonesome When You Go' (which went
unused), and developed a fine waltzin' rewrite of 'If You See Her, Say
Hello' ('I know that she'll be back some day/ Most likely I'll be
gone . . .') which made it as far as Japan. On day one, he also attempted
'Tonight I'll Be Staying Here With You' and an otherwise lost song
called 'Woman In The Rain'.

A matter of days earlier, Dylan had told *Playboy*, 'I find myself [ven-
turing] into territory that has more percussion in it and rhythms of the
soul . . . The next move for me is to have a permanent band.' However,
when Stoner 'brought this weird band out [west] with me . . . Bob kept
us sitting around for a week.' When the frontman did show up, his
appointed bandleader found him 'always bummed out. He was chain
smoking and he was really in a bad mood.'

Only when three girlsingers augmented the musicians, did Stoner
finally see the boss begin to focus on the job in hand: 'He starts inviting
all these chicks to come down and sing . . . They weren't professional
singers . . . [but] the first time he shows up to do anything serious, it's
'cause he's got these chicks around.' The 'chicks' included Katey Sagal,
later a successful TV actress, who remembered, 'He'd have three girls
all sing a part that was not in our range, [but] we were too terrified to
say anything.' Yet Dylan persevered with the original trio of singers for
weeks, before accepting he'd have to hire some proper backing singers,
recruiting the young, gifted and brown-skinned Helena Springs, as
well as Jo Ann Harris and Debbie Dye.

He also began raiding his little black book, inviting every available,
able-bodied L.A. musician to audition for the gig, especially drummers. After two weeks of rehearsal, Howie Wyeth had reluctantly
surrendered the drum-stool when he found out they were heading for
Japan, a country with a strict no-drugs code, 'I realized I was either
gonna get busted or I'd end up being tortured to death. So, I literally
had to just tell Bob one night, "I can't do it." . . . [Although] he had his
own problems . . . he called me up when I got back to New York and
said, "Are you sure?" '

The search for a replacement drummer led Dylan down some

unexpected byways. To date, he'd toured with Levon Helm, Mickey Jones and Howie Wyeth. Luck like that couldn't hold forever. The returning Rosato recalls, 'There was one drummer, he was black, really strong backbeat but he played it through all the songs. Bob loved that. I said, "Bob, he's playing the same thing for everything."' Dylan demurred, only to invite down Mickey Jones, who'd abandoned drumming for an acting career playing the ubiquitous heavy.

Bruce Gary also auditioned, even though he was supposed to be getting The Knack, as did ex-Wings stickman, Denny Seiwell, who had to bail when McCartney's drug bust in Japan precluded him from getting a visa. Ex-King Crimson drummer Ian Wallace eventually snagged the stool, even though Stoner always thought he 'had a beat like a cop'. Organist Alan Pasqua, who had passed his own audition, was a witness to the daily games of musical chairs. He couldn't quite believe his eyes:

> There were . . . two or three drummers, three keyboard players. David Mansfield was there, Steven Soles, Billy Cross was there . . . Rob, of course, Steve Douglas . . . Bob showed up and we just started jamming. We weren't really playing any specific songs . . . A couple of days later . . . there were two keyboard players and two drummers . . . [Finally,] the band solidified and we got it down to me, Ian Wallace on drums, Rob on bass, Billy Cross, Soles, Mansfield, Steve Douglas, Bobbye Hall on percussion, they brought in three background singers, and then we started working on tunes . . . He asked me one day if I knew 'Positively 4th Street'. . . . I just looked at him and said, 'No, man, but I'll learn.' He looked at me and started laughing.

On the fifth day of rehearsals, Dylan allowed almost everyone to drift away before complaining to Stoner, a tad prematurely, 'I can't spring anything new on this band.' Trusting in Stoner, he proceeded to sit down at the piano and preview all the songs he had for *Street-Legal*, save for 'Changing Of The Guards'. As Joel Bernstein slyly turned on a tape-recorder, Stoner heard the core of an album he wouldn't hang around to play on. Though Dylan specifically asked Bernstein *not* to tape this historic moment, this modern Max Brod did the decent thing, knowing that the rehearsals themselves were all being recorded.

As Bernstein says, 'Not only was everything taped but he would have the band stay over after rehearsals finished and he would have me play back particular performances.' The Rundown Era (1977-81) would become not only Dylan's most productive period since 1967, but also the most well-documented.

This being Dylan, though, the fact that he was auditioning musicians in no way stopped him from playing songs they barely knew, or couldn't know. It was Scarlet Rivera all over again on December 30th, when a young silver-haired Swedish guitarist, Billy Cross, nervously made his way to Santa Monica to try and fill Mick Ronson's shoes. From the off, Dylan was testing his mettle, starting with a *Nashville Skyline* song he'd never played live, not even at the Isle of Wight, 'To Be Alone With You'. Next up was a song he used to play live, in 1961, the deeply traditional 'Wayfaring Stranger'. For the first time at Rundown, Dylan was going for all the notes and holding his breath three times as long as Caruso, while Cross plucked away and prayed to Clapton. A stunning moment.

But Cross hadn't got the gig yet. After expecting Cross to somehow emulate the Scarlet of 'One More Cup Of Coffee', Dylan began a piano tune which he wanted Stoner to 'teach . . . to everybody.' When Stoner asked, 'What is it?' Dylan helpfully told him, 'It's a new one.' In fact, Stoner had already heard it on the 26th. It was 'Is Your Love In Vain?', and they would return to it at the end of the session, after which Dylan informed the band, 'That's one of the new ones I wrote. We'll get to that stuff.' Not for months, they wouldn't. Though they would work up any number of new blues, this was the only *Street-Legal* preview the other musicians were getting anytime soon.

Meanwhile, Dylan continued springing surprises on Cross and co. After 'Is Your Love In Vain?', he launched into 'Hellhound On My Trail', the first of several Robert Johnson songs he would test-run throughout the 1978 rehearsals. Having put his own hellhound temporarily to flight, he tells Stoner he has a song called 'Joking', which begins, 'Left you after so many years/ Had no trouble with any tears/ I wasn't joking.' It's the last we hear of this potentially promising idea. Six days later he pulls another one out of his pocket. Again, Stoner asks him what it's called. Again, he stonewalls Stoner, 'It's a new song. I haven't finished it.' All he has is, 'Love you to the end/ Sundown, moon shine over me/ Do I go or shall I stay?'

By this point Stoner is starting to wonder whether Dylan will ever get down to the matter in hand: putting together a two-hour-plus show for his first non-English speaking audiences since Paris '66 – and we know how that went. Mr Bassman was convinced, 'We had blown our time having all these jam reunion things. But Bob had no relationship with that band. He wasn't hanging out.'

The big boss man could still produce blues with a feeling, though. The second day of 1978, he produced one called 'I'll Be There In The Morning', whose lyrics fit perfectly the big fat band sound he heard in his head: 'She rides in a Cadillac car / Big girl, she does the same / My girl rides in a hog and a mule / But gets there just the same.' It would be one of five such songs pulled to a copyright tape at the end of the month, along with '$64 Question', 'Woman In Iberia' ('I got a woman in New Iberia, and one up the water coast [x2] / I can't help but wonder which woman I love the most'), 'First To Say Goodbye' ('Before you give me trouble, baby / I swear I'll be the first to say goodbye') – a song he'd already played at the *Street-Legal* piano preview* – and 'Repossession Blues', a blues that could easily have been called 'No Money Blues' – with its opening line, 'I ain't got no money, I'm gonna lose everything I own . . .' – had he not let Bernstein name it.

The most promising of the bunch, and the only one to make the live set, 'Repossession Blues' was a sly dig at those cynics who were already calling this The Alimony Tour. Uncharacteristically, he gave a Canadian journalist a tape of the February 1st rehearsal version, and a month later recorded it for a Japanese live album – both great. Yet Stoner, for one, never made the connection with his first-ever Dylan studio experience, the 'big band' *Desire* discard, 'Money Blues'.

By the end of February Dylan had ditched it in favour of a rewrite of the Charley Patton / Son House standard, 'Pony Blues', as he reimmersed himself in the Mississippi Delta. As he'd recently informed Ron Rosenbaum, 'I still listen to the same old black-and-blue blues. Tommy McClennan, Lightnin' Hopkins, the Carter Family . . . Robert Johnson . . . I like Memphis Minnie a whole lot. Blind Willie McTell.' At the end of May he added to the list in conversation with Robert Hilburn, 'My music comes from two places: white hillbilly music – Roscoe Holcomb, stuff like that – and black blues – people like Son

---

* Without ever hearing said tape, Olof Björner decided this was a cover of a Gladys Knight song.

House, Charley Patton, Robert Johnson,' the first time he'd ever name-checked people like Charley Patton and Tommy McClennan.

The list could easily have been twice as long, and more rooted in the Delta. Tampa Red and Elmore James were just two names from the plantations' pantheon whose songs he rehearsed that January, the former's 'Love Her With A Feeling' becoming the regular opener through July, while the latter's 'The Sky Is Falling' never made it out of the Santa Monica parking lot. Another blues standard, Ernest 'Buddy' Wilson's 'Lonesome Bedroom', would open the first few Jap shows before being put to sleep.

Even some of his own songs were given a good shake. Bernstein looked on, as he asked the band 'to play certain songs . . . in one key and then another key and then half-time, then country, then reggae, then rocked up.' Some lyrics also underwent a revamp, notably 'Going Going Gone' ('I've just reached a place where I can't stay awake . . .') and 'Something There Is About You' ('Coming back from China, I saw you walking on your hands . . .'), both from the oft-overlooked *Planet Waves*.

Just as the Far East tour was promising to become another rip-up-the-set-list affair, Stoner saw that 'a telegram [had] arrived from the Japanese promoter, and in it he had a manifest of the songs he expected Bob to do on this tour'. The old Dylan might well have told him which creek he could jump in, but this Dylan needed the kinda payday a lucrative tour of Japan, Australia and New Zealand offered, especially when there was a proviso for a Japan-only live album, following in the wake of Deep Purple. When that album, *At Budokan*, became the best-selling import album of all time in the UK, Dylan was obliged to point out, 'I never meant for it to be any type of representation of my stuff, or my band,' even as he trousered the substantial advance.

When CBS begged him to let them release the double-album world-wide, at the conclusion of the world tour, Dylan insisted it become 'one of the five albums he was required to deliver under his February 1st, 1978 recording contract'. Dylan was no longer the greenhorn who had signed his first Columbia contract, having learnt the hard way not to trust a single word the label didn't put in writing. Which is why one of the provisos in his five-album recording contract, signed at the end of January 1978, was a non-recoupable $100,000 'if he plays at least twenty dates in Europe in first year of new contract'.

They had finally succeeded in tying their man to a long-term contract, knowing he was set to record his follow-up to *Desire* the minute he returned from the Far East. He just needed the last couple of songs to fulfil his own personal brief. In fact, he couldn't stop writing new songs or tinkering with the ones already earmarked. A Japanese rehearsal, after the second night of the 115-date tour, saw him revisit 'Woman In Iberia' (now called 'Woman In Florida') and attempt something then called 'Pony Boy', sandwiched between Tom Paxton's 'If I Pass This Way Again' and Paul Butterfield's 'Ain't No Need To Go Any Further'.

Soon he would have a ten-verse song he was calling 'New Pony Blues', presumably to distinguish it from earlier Charley Patton and Son House templates. Any non-generic debt lay largely in the direction of House, starting with verse one: 'Got a new pony, she loves it when I pull her reins/ She got big hind legs and a long black curly mane.' By verse seven, though, the gal had morphed into a close cousin of the witchy women who'd been haunting Dylan since the divorce: 'If you see Miss X, hold your tongue and walk away/ She gives all my money to a conman who beats her every night and day.' A second draft, on Christchurch hotel notepaper, suggested she's a blabbermouth, too: 'She hung my dirty laundry out the window for everyone to see.'

Finally, he had a blues song that fit the overarching theme he wanted for *Street-Legal* – beware of witchy women – even as he discarded some other promising material, including a song on Melbourne Hilton notepaper that envisaged a 'red river flowing thru a city of gold/ Bridges keep on burning/ Drunk man – slippery as ice/ Hanging in the balance.' As if this didn't contain enough allusions to songs he was two years away from writing, he began another called 'Long Time Train', which had him 'waiting for that train . . . smoking up the track.' He had found another woman who could read him like a book:

> They say that I'm a spokesman for some new age philosophy
> But I don't have to tell you, I don't speak for no-one but me.
> Sometimes I'm a legend, sometimes a back door man,
> But I'd never be able to fool you, girl, I'm sure you understand.

But it was the memory of a woman he used to know – 'I once had a woman friend, but she was too much of a responsibility/ She'd walk

thru the wind & rain, she'd outrace a train just to be with me . . .' –
who inspired a pop anthem which might not have had quite the same
impact worldwide had he gone with its original refrain, 'Don't jack me
off.' 'Baby please stop crying, stop crying' – as it became – was a marginal rewrite of Robert Johnson's 'Stop breaking down, baby, please
stop breaking down,' but at least it had the virtue of being able to be
played on the radio.

Equally radio-friendly were a couple of songs he penned with backing singer Helena Springs, one evening in Brisbane, mid-March. Springs
recalled, 'He was playing on the guitar and we were just goofing
around . . . I started to sing, just making up lyrics. And he'd make up
stuff, and that was when we got "If I Don't Be There By Morning" and
"Walk Out In The Rain."' Both would end up on an album which went
gold worldwide – just not a Bob Dylan album.* It was the beginning of
a beautiful, if brief, friendship, as for the first time Dylan wrote a
tranche of tunes with someone he was sleeping with.

If he was delighted to find a musical muse on the tour bus, bandleader Rob Stoner was not so happy, 'and Bob knew this – my not being
happy meant that I was fucking every chick on the bus, and I was getting a little wild'. Barely had the band taken a brief sabbatical after the
April 1st Sydney show than Stoner was telling Dylan he wanted out.

With gigging due to resume in two months, and an album to record
in the interim, this was not what Dylan wanted to hear. He had made
a longstanding plan, and Stoner was the only musician he'd entrusted
with precious previews of the songs he planned to record. When he
found out Stoner was joining Link Wray in Robert Gordon's rockabilly
band, not simply taking the cash, he had to admit to a sneaking admiration for the man, but he never used him again. He always set a high
store on loyalty.

Already baulking at comparisons with Elvis's Vegas bands, the
recruitment of Jerry Scheff – presumably at saxophonist Steve Douglas's suggestion – was hardly about to debunk them. Not that he was
about to give the veteran bassist an easy ride. At his April 10th audition,
Dylan threw two new originals at him: 'We'd Better Talk This Over',

---

* The album in question was Eric Clapton's *Backless*, which charted at eight Stateside,
eighteen in the UK.

not as yet nailed down lyrically, and a beautiful torch-ballad he'd written with Helena, 'Coming From The Heart'.

In fact, ever since that night in Brisbane, the pair had been writing
songs for fun with titles like 'Tell Me The Truth One Time', a 'kettle telling the pot' song with the narrator for once on the receiving end: 'Tell
me why you grin every time I ask where you've been/ Tell me what
trouble you've been in/ Tell me the truth one time, then you lie again.'

Having conceptualised an ambitious new album nine months earlier, would he now find room for such late-comers? It seemed not, even
as he seemingly considered slotting in some 'public domain' blues covers instead. Everything remained up for grabs as he spent the first
couple of 'album' rehearsals doing 'Depression Blues', 'It Hurts Me
Too', 'Love Her With A Feeling', 'Eyesight To The Blind' and two
lesser-known Robert Johnson songs, 'Steady Rollin' Man' (already
played once in Melbourne) and 'Little Queen Of Spades'.

Even the three new originals were all blues-based: 'Stop Now' (written with Helena), 'Baby Stop Crying' ('Woman, you better stop crying
or you're gonna blow away your mind') and 'New Pony' ('You're burning my mind up, you're scrambling my brain like an egg/ You could
make a millionaire get down upon his bended knees and beg'). It was
April 13th before Dylan finally cleared the deck and got down to business. The mobile truck booked to record the album was due at
Rundown on the 25th. Before that, he wanted to spend a week rehearsing the nine or so songs he planned to record.

But he still hadn't extracted himself entirely from the black muddy
Delta. He even gave 'Where Are You Tonight?' a blue-ish hue, before
jumping all over 'Stop Now' and grasping hold of another song-idea,
an archetypal 'Woke Up This Morning' blues with a 'trouble in this
world' theme: 'There must be trouble brewing somewhere/ I can feel
it in my bones/ It might be in South East Asia/ Or somewhere closer
to home.' Somewhere in the distance a train whistle was blowing,
smoking down the track.

Even when he stopped writing new songs, he continued to write
and rewrite those he had already. On 'We'd Better Talk This Over' he
began by reminding the recipient, 'Blood is thicker than water/ Oh
babe, you must be the devil's daughter.' If Scheff was starting to wonder if he had unwittingly joined a blues band, Dylan might have had his
own doubts as to Scheff's suitability. On the 21st, he ran down almost

the whole album plus 'Coming From The Heart' – a fabulous piano-driven performance that, frankly, should have ensured its inclusion on *Street-Legal* – and 'If I Don't Be There By Morning'. The cassette inlay card reads, 'bass – Tim Drummond': the man 'from Jericho', who would become his bandleader the following year.

It seems Dylan was simply keeping his options open, even as he called it a day on rehearsals, much to the relief of musicians like Mansfield who felt, 'We [had already] rehearsed [the songs] enough that we had things well in hand by the time the mobile truck came.' Or perhaps not. When his boss wrote out a test sequence for side one, it included a thing called 'Going To Chicago Blues', whatever that was.

Thankfully, by the time Wally Heider's truck pulled up, Scheff was back and Dylan was ready to record nine originals in six days: seven from '77, two from '78. Again, he was determined to cut 'em live, as if those first three *Desire* sessions had never happened. He even recalled DeVito as ostensible overseer, only to inform Hilburn, '[I] couldn't find the right producer, but it was necessary to do it. So, we just brought in the remote truck and cut it, [and] went for a live sound.'

As he'd revealed in another recent interview, his album aesthetic remained unchanged, his determination undimmed, 'My songs are done live in the studio; they always have been and they always will be done that way. That's why they're alive . . . I'm not doing [this] to see how good I can sound . . . or how intricate the details can be woven . . . I don't care about those things.' Such was the case, even when using a rehearsal space as a recording studio:

Alan Pasqua: [Rundown] was just a big open room with a linoleum floor. It was not a recording studio by any means . . . We spent a lot of time just trying to get it to sound good . . . We were in a highly reflective environment with low ceilings. That's not necessarily the greatest place to record.

David Mansfield: The recording crew were just having to scramble to get mikes into place, and get something on tape, while we were playing the thing the few times we were gonna play it . . . But that stuff sounded marvellous in the room . . . Arthur [Rosato] was tending [to the sound] mostly, so there was no sophistication, like having outboard equipment, and compressing and EQing.

Rosato began to realize his boss's vaulting ambition to make more genre-defining records in the era of endless overdubs was still waging an unceasing war with the young rocker who grew up in the Fifties, and had never quite got over the impact those records had on him:

> Bob was actually listening to a lot of Phil Spector [in 1977-78]. The sound of a Phil Spector production is something that is uniquely his. What I was hearing in the studio and [during] rehearsals was maybe Bob's interpretation of the Phil Spector sound . . . [] . . . [But] if all the sound in the world came through a transistor radio, [Bob] would be happy . . . We would record something and put it on cassette, and he would go sit out in his car and listen to it and then say, 'Okay, yeah, that's a take.' Or he would listen to it in the pool room [at Rundown]. There was a little boom box [there], and he'd listen on that . . . We'd never listen to it on playback through the studio speakers.

This perhaps explains all the cassette dubs of alternate takes and sequences from these sessions now housed in Tulsa. And unless someone turns up the missing multis, they may well be all that remains from these sessions, the master takes excepted. Not that there was much left to resolve by the time Wally sent his best truck. Dylan just needed to finish 'Where Are You Tonight?', which on the (i.m.h.o., superior) alternate version that almost made the album had even more of an edge:

> I fought with my twin, that enemy within
> No two brothers have the same name
> These uncertainties are killing me by degrees
> I've been tested, I've tasted the flame.
>
> Your partner in crime hit me up for nickels and dimes
> This guy you were lovin' was a mystery
> It felt outta place, my foot in his face
> But you know it was you who took advantage of me.

It was not just 'a new day', but 'a new way' the singer was determined to follow. Perhaps he already sensed a change was gonna come. For now, he had an album he could be proud of, one that has grown in stature over the years, aided in time by a 2000 remix from its equally proud producer, Don DeVito. And with the truck not due back till the second, Dylan took the opportunity to demo four Dylan-Springs songs he had heartlessly discarded, hoping Naomi in New York could find them a suitable home.

The band had earned themselves a three-week break, while Dylan allowed himself some downtime to muse upon the last time he toured Europe, a mere twelve years ago. If CBS were prepared to pay him a six-figure sum just to play some shows there, perhaps there really was a certain pent-up demand a-brewing. Maybe this time his label actually had their finger on the *pulse*. After all, CBS-UK had signed two of the best English punk bands going, The Clash and The Only Ones, both fronted by fanatical Dylan fans, Joe Strummer and Peter Perrett,* even if Dylan himself was no longer some young punk – more like a Godfather.

---

* The first time I met Strummer was at photographer Bob Gruen's New York apartment. He was intently listening to a bootleg CD of the December 1961 'Minneapolis Hotel Tape'. That is a proper fan. The last time I saw Perrett, he asked for a dub of the Royal Festival Hall 1964.

4.4

June 1978 to January 1979: More Than Flesh & Blood Can Bear

I had another dream the other day about music critics. They were small and rodent-like with padlocked ears, as if they had stepped out of a painting by Goya.

Igor Stravinsky.

Matt Damsker: I'm a critic, Bob. I've had to criticise your stuff . . .
Bob Dylan: Well, that's fine. A lot of the things I've done need to be criticised . . .
MD: Do you find that you have gotten insights from criticism?
BD: No, I don't think so. But . . . I've done a lot of things which I criticise myself.

15th September 1978.

I don't like to feel controlled by others. I choose people. They don't choose me.

Bob Dylan, to Barbara Kerr, February 1978.

I'm excited by those kind of principles on life, and moral codes, that are part of any religion. They get to me. But as far as organised religion goes, I don't see myself as partaking.

Bob Dylan, to Craig McGregor, March 1978.

If he . . . feels strongly about something, he's just immovable and unstoppable.

Carolyn Dennis, backing singer 1978-81.

I've always felt an unseen presence . . . ever since I was small.

> Bob Dylan, to Edna Gundersen, September 1997.

[A] Christian: One who follows the teachings of Christ in so far as they are not inconsistent with a life of sin.

> Ambrose Bierce, *The Devil's Dictionary*.

★

When Dylan flew into London the morning of June 13th, 1978, it was once again the epicentre of Rock, as it had been in 1966, the last time he played Handsome Molly's hometown. Product was pouring out weekly from indie labels still wearing diapers, while the 'major' labels' response was to release less, not more. Having released – or seen released – six new Dylan albums, two of them doubles, between November 1973 and January 1976, all of them Top Ten, three of them reaching number one, CBS decided to restrict Dylan to five albums in five years in his new contract, with delivery 'not [to be] more frequently than six months, nor less frequently than twelve months'.

It was like a publisher telling a writer how long a book should be. Like they'd know! This dumb-ass decision meant that albums Dylan could (and should) have recorded between *Street-Legal* and *Slow Train*, and between *Saved* and *Shot of Love*, never saw the light of day, going unrecorded, save in demo form.

Street-Legal wasn't even on the street when, on June 8th, the day after a sell-out, week-long L.A. residency at the Universal Amphitheater, Dylan set about recording another six-song demo-tape – redoing the four songs from May 2nd and adding two more Dylan-Springs compositions, 'Responsibility' and 'Without You'. The second of these was another witty send up of the torch-ballads he heard on the radio, not an expression of how he was feeling:

> How long till the maid comes in to clean up this mess
> I am so depressed . . . I think I'll take a match, set fire to this room
> And that will be that, and then I'll call the Police
> 'Cause I can't get no release, without you.

He certainly wasn't short of female companionship at this time. If anything, there were too many cooks invited to come on in his kitchen, so much so that Dylan's jocular nightly band introduction, interchanging the girlsingers as, respectively, his fiancée, his current girlfriend and his childhood sweetheart, became less a joke, more like a prophecy.

Debi Dye had already handed in her notice, in part because she was pregnant, but mainly because she 'could not get along with Helena'. Her replacement, Carolyn Dennis, was the suggestion of a non-singing girlfriend, Mary Alice Artes (credited as 'Queen Bee' on *Street-Legal*). She phoned Dennis and told her she'd heard her singing with Chile Wilkerson, that she was 'Bob's girlfriend' and that she was 'helping him put together a band'. The name was vaguely familiar, but it was the money which persuaded her to say, yes. Their first serious conversation came on the plane to London, when Dylan sat down next to her and began pumping her for information.

'Do you *really* not know anything about me or anything I've done?' he asked. 'Do I need to? . . . All I know right now is you're a guy named Robert and you've got your band and you're not sitting separated from us in first class; you're back here in coach with all of us. And you're wearing your lumberjack shirt and your jeans and your boots . . . Is there something that I need to know that's gonna make me feel differently about who you are?'

Landing in London, she started to glean just how famous this guy was. Photographers were out in force, as were the news crews. People had been sleeping out for seventy-two hours to ensure they got tickets for the six Earl's Court shows. Demand was through the ricocheting roof. On night one, his performance even made the *BBC Nine O'Clock News*. Unheard of, for a mere rock singer. Rave reviews of the show ran not just in England's four music weeklies, but in every daily, even the tabloids.

And it was two songs added at Rundown at the end of May that had fans with advance tickets tingling with anticipation. He'd come up with an arrangement of 'Tangled Up In Blue' 'with just electric guitar and a saxophone – . . . thinking that maybe if I did that to it, [it] would bring it out in an emotional way.' Didn't it just. The reviewers rhapsodised. The ever-perverse prince of folk-rock disagreed. By the time he returned to Britain a month later to play the biggest gig of his career, he'd replaced the song everyone wanted to hear with 'Girl From The North Country'.

The heavy-metal arrangement of 'Masters Of War' stayed, though, perhaps because Cross's metallic guitar solo allowed the singer a 'fag break'. Dylan professed to being delighted with how the whole combo was shaping up, telling Robert Shelton, 'A lot of blood has gone into this band.' At Earl's Court, they even dispelled the sonic demons that had previously made this venue something of a sonic graveyard for the likes of Bowie, Slade, Led Zeppelin and the Stones. The sound blew people away, as did the audacious new arrangements. 'Great to be here, sure is.'

He was not so enamoured of the venue he was booked to play with Eric Clapton as support on July 1st, the very stadium in Nuremberg where Hitler had held those Nazi rallies immortalised by Riefenstahl. Among the 70,000 attendant Germans were some neo-Nazis affronted by a Jew standing on the Fuhrer's stage, making history. His old friend Pattie Boyd, who was there with new husband Eric, 'felt weird – the vibes were still there, it was such a powerful thing,' while Alan Pasqua still vividly recalls 'some people in the audience . . . started throwing things on the stage. [These] rags soaked in paint were flying by.'

Equally horrified to see her boss in the line of fire – 'they're throwing rotten eggs and paint balls' – was Dennis, even if she wasn't quite sure why this was happening. But Dylan knew, prefacing a particularly furious 'Masters Of War' with, 'This is an old [song] . . . It gives me great pleasure to sing it in this place!' It was the only sour note on a tour that made Julius Caesar's triumphs look half-hearted. Nor was he standing still, as the set shifted to accommodate six *Street-Legal* songs. The Parisians not only enjoyed five nights wholly free of protracted tune-ups and broken guitars, the 135-minute shows also featured stellar arrangements of 'It's All Over Now, Baby Blue', 'The Man In Me' and 'I'll Be Your Baby Tonight', and from July 5th on, a first encore of 'Changing Of The Guards'.

Meanwhile, ticket sales for an open-air concert near Camberley, Surrey, in ten days' time was threatening to surpass even the Isle of Wight. Sure enough, Saturday, July 15th, dawned cloudless and sunny, as two-hundred thousand decamped from the city limits, including some friends from the simple years who struggled to get through the scrum:

Martin Carthy: It took me four hours to get backstage [at Blackbushe]. There were at least three levels of security and then his caravan. And he had no idea . . . He said, 'How's Anthea [Joseph]?' And I said . . . 'She's out in hospitality.' And he said, 'Why doesn't she come and see me?' I looked at him and said, 'Do you have any idea what the security is like here?' . . . There's a level of innocence about him that's really endearing. He didn't have a clue.

Dylan's thirty-one-song set would signal high summer for one of Pop's great years, and a commercial high watermark even this iconic singer would never hit again. The next six months would see the critical tide turn with a vengeance. A two-month respite from the road and its ubiquitous temptations was looming, even as Dylan banked his largest cheque to date.

Unfazed, he simply carried on writing new material, mostly reflecting an ongoing bee in his bonnet about the power of Women, one that prompted a surprisingly misogynistic remark from him the day of his next gig, 'I can't stand to run with women any more . . . I'd rather stand in front of a rolling train. But if you find a woman that is . . . also your sister, and your lover and your mother . . . you got a companion for life.' The songs he penned that summer suggested he had yet to find another sister-lover-mother like the discarded Sara – not even the African-American Mary Alice Artes, whom he'd first met when she was actress Sally Kirkland's roommate, and to whom he returned that summer:

David Mansfield: Mary Alice was one of these dynamic personalities that Bob's probably attracted to in general, and if they're black, so much the better . . . She could . . . dress really sexy, without ever exuding sex . . . [while] being one of those really competent mothers who would shower you with all this love and attention . . . tell you what you should do, and slap your bottom to get you off doing it . . . like the perfect Jewish wife.

Not even the companion on the road, with whom he was still writing songs in tandem, ticked all the boxes, although Helena still helped shape 'More Than Flesh And Blood', a major composition, and one he worked on tirelessly in rehearsals and soundchecks from August through November. With this song he really seemed to be on the brink of another breakthrough, creatively and philosophically, one he addressed in the last verse of the copyrighted version:

> I'm going down to find a church
> Try to understand
> I need new inspiration
> And you're only just a [wo]man.
> I quit the blackjack table
> I can't play another hand.
> The meat you cook for me is bloody rare,
> And that's more than flesh and blood can bear.

In fact, so much did Dylan tinker with it in the months before he took his first communion, it became more a series of song-sketches around a central idea – 'more than flesh and blood can bear' – than a single entity. In its early stages, pre-rehearsal, the narrator was some-one 'pretty indifferent . . . [to] captivating eyes/ till that green-eyed monster put a monkey on h[is] back.' But by the time he was teaching it to the band at the end of August, its narrator was searching for that 'holy slow train': 'Looking down the railroad tracks, all the way down the line/ There was the deaf leading the deaf, the blind leading the blind.'

These witchy women had become obstacles to his salvation. Hence, why he asks one such sinful soul – presumably the same woman whose 'shallow thoughts of matrimony' pierce him 'to the core' – 'Is the truth too much for you to share?' Having tied the knot, he found she was 'a whore'. This sounds like a man determined to throw some personal baggage overboard, but also increasingly convinced that time is short. The copyrighted version has a couplet that wouldn't have been out of place on 1979's 'Slow Train' – 'Country's being robbed/ foreign oil sw[am]ps the shores' – and another he could have held over till 1981's 'Angelina': 'There's a war in Italy, there's a war in Tel Aviv/ There'll be a war in the lobby of your hotel before you leave.'

The narrator no longer has any doubt that the lady who wants to torture him with mirrors and with pride, leaving him 'nothin' in this world but a prayer', is in league with the Devil, maybe even doing something more conjugal than that: 'You were sleeping with the devil at the Crowbar Hotel/ I was waiting in the room he kept beneath your lonely cell . . .'

It's all great stuff. Frustratingly, although the song appeared as a 'possible addition' on September US set-lists, it only ever made it to a string of soundchecks, despite it being a song the band loved to play. Given its refrain, that big sax sound and memorable burden, Dylan missed a trick when he didn't rework it *after* learning Satan was alive and well, and living on Planet Earth. But for now, he'd convinced himself that 'the Devil will go as deep as you let the Devil go . . . If you understand what that whole scene is about, you can easily step aside.' Only after he caught sight of the daemon lover's cloven hoof, would he change his way of thinking.

None of the four new originals he *did* debut on the US tour – which spanned some sixty-five gruelling arena gigs between September 15th and December 16th – unlocked his own secret history in quite the same way. 'I Must Love You Too Much', 'Coming From The Heart' and 'Am I Your Stepchild?' – a nightly highlight – were simply more of the same, powerful as the latter two were.

But it turned out, these were just the tip of an iceberg he would dissolve in brimstone. After another productive summer Dylan already had nearly enough for an album that really could have put those witchy women in their place, as became apparent the day Dylan spent rehearsing some more girlsingers (August 28th),* running down 'More Than Flesh And Blood', 'I Must Love You Too Much' and 'Am I Your Stepchild?', as well as 'This A-Way, That A-Way' (another 'road' song he soundchecked repeatedly, with the refrain, 'The road keeps turning this a-way, that a-way . . . straight to the one I love') and 'Pay As You Go' ('Ain't no difference, rain or snow/ Darling, you can pay as you go').

Two days later, he reassembled the full band at Rundown to 'prep.' them with the new songs, and to add a new opener in the 'blues' slot, Willie Dixon's 'I'm Ready', which contained its own message for US audiences, 'I'm ready for you/ I hope you're ready for me.' With a two-hour-plus show to knock into shape, he again allowed songs like 'This A-Way, That A-Way', 'But I Forgive You' ('Rocks in my pillow, stones in

---

* The girlsingers listed for this rehearsal are Vernetta [Venetta] Fields, Lois Brown, Alicia [Elisecia] Wright and Yolan [Yolanda] Howard.

my bed/ You had the nerve to tell me that you wish that I were dead/ But I forgive you') and 'You Don't Love Me No More' to preoccupy him initially. The last of these suggested his lifestyle was continuing to cause him some grief, as he repeatedly fell into traps of his own making. The song asked questions of the one who 'don't love me no more', he perhaps should have been asking himself:

> Did I drink too much? Did I create too much of a fuss?
> Did I think too much? Did I miss your bus?
> Did I create a situation? . . .
> Did I go out with someone you didn't like? . . .
> Did I do something wrong to someone else?

Despite insisting to the *L.A. Times*'s Robert Hilburn, 'You have to remember what your purpose is, and walk that thin line. You've got to guard against . . . things put [there] on the road to make you stumble or turn back,' he was lapsing into bad habits again, before he again turned for inspiration to the songs he knew and loved. When he said, some twenty years later – 'Those old songs are my lexicon and my prayer book. All my beliefs come out of those old songs, literally, anything from "Let Me Rest On That Peaceful Mountain" to "Keep On The Sunny Side." . . . I believe in Hank Williams singing "I Saw The Light" ' – he did not mean in some abstruse sense.

These songs spoke to him in a way other people imposing their philosophies did not. They did not feel a need preach. It was like someone wrote his story in a song. Merle Haggard, perhaps? And the song which probably reflected his state of mind most accurately that September was one of those traditional covers he sang in rehearsal like he was taking mass at the Eternal City, 'Lonesome Valley' ('You got to walk that lonesome valley by yourself').

Unlike Rolling Thunder, though, covers were soon firmly pushed into the background, save at soundchecks and rehearsals, as Dylan remembered he was meant to be prepping his returning standing band to play two-dozen of his own songs of faithlessness. Only at a final pre-tour rehearsal, on the seventh, did Dylan relax enough to blow the blues away with a stomping 'Look Over Yonder Wall' and a *de rigueur* nod to the King of the Delta Blues, 'Malted Milk'.

With a set-list to get ship-shape, some of his own songs he kept to himself. One song he worked on that summer, called 'Marching Out Of Time', contained clear allusions to a woman wielding a big black book in the narrator's direction: 'Well, won't you ramble down my way honey, with your chiseled face/ bring yr bible with you . . . Step down baby and come on back to me, to where you ought to be/ They're asking me to be a saint, when they're pulling my mama away and putting her on a transport ship.'

If this one never even got a test run at a soundcheck, a number of its kith and kin were taped at the desk, presumably for reference purposes. On October 5th, as the band pulled into Largo, just three weeks into a three-month tour, Dylan was feeling 'bout half-past dead. To revive his spirits, and keep the band on its toes, he decided now would be a good time to spring a few surprises on the band. The cassette of an epic soundcheck opens with Dylan singing an old Hank Williams song – but not 'I Saw The Light'. Rather, he sang an impassioned version of the altogether obscurer 'Help Me Understand', written from the viewpoint of a child seeing his parents' marriage disintegrate and asking God's help to understand ('A little girl prayed at the close of day/ 'Cause her Daddy had gone far away . . .'). The unmistakeable autobiographical subtext was not lost on the musicians.*

He was just getting warmed up. Another version of 'More Than Flesh And Blood' had a whole different take on this particular witchy woman leading him down to the pit: 'Oh child, you keep me down in the bottom of the well/ In the town of San Miguel/ Way above the electric chair/ Get down on your knees, girl/ Way down in despair, way more than forty below/ Down at the bottom . . .'

If lines like these were unlikely to get fans reaching for their rosaries, another line he dropped into the Largo version – 'Train pulled out at six o'clock, the hand of God upon it' – jes' might. He'd always written about trains, because as he would later reminisce in an onstage rap, 'When I was growing up, I used to watch the trains. They were always going somewhere . . . where I wanted to go.' But none of them had the hand of God on board, or were heading for the promised land. Whereas

---

* A similar moment occurs at the Carbondale and St Louis soundchecks [28th+29th Oct.] – both taped surreptitiously – Dylan putting heart'n'soul into Hazel Smith's cloying '(One More Year Of) Daddy's Little Girl'.

the above rap would be the spoken preface to a song played every night for three solid years, starting on November 1st, 1979.

That song was 'Slow Train', a song he began in October 1978. A verse in its earliest known full draft, on Executive Tower Inn notepaper, even suggests a connection to 'More Than Flesh And Blood': 'i got a woman/ down at the bottom/ she my salvation & cure for every sensation/ she love me even tho' she know[s] my situation.'

By the October 5th, 1978 soundcheck, Dylan already has a tune and an arrangement for the song, even if the words are a tad garbled. The one component it retained from Largo to Muscle Shoals was the refrain: 'an' there's a slow/ slow train comin'/ up around the bend.' The rest of the song in draft form gives a lie to the notion – propagated by Dylan himself, in a post-conversion chat with the trusted Hilburn – that he was 'doing fine':

A lot of people think that Jesus comes into a person's life only when they are either down and out, or are miserable or just old and withering away. That's not the way it was for me. I was doing fine. I had come a long way in just the year we were on the road. I was relatively content, but a very close friend of mine mentioned a couple of things to me, and one of them was Jesus.

Bullshit. An early draft of 'Slow Train' – reproduced in part in the *Trouble No More* booklet – tells it like it really was, that fall:

sometimes/ I feel so outnumbered/
i get weary from slings & arrows that I'm dodgin'
bridges burnin'/ i'm turnin' and tossin'/ . . .
I've seen snakes in the tall grass/ & the rulin' class
pass state laws in the men's room of the greyhound bus depot . . .
don't know if I can make [it] much further
on this pathway so blindin'/ with the steel rails hummin'.

I rest my case, M'lud. 'The steel rails hummin' is a conscious evocation of a song that was certainly part of his own lexicon. Dylan had already recorded Curtis Mayfield's 'People Get Ready' twice – in 1967 and 1975. A song about 'a train a-comin', it told all waverers, 'All you need is faith to hear the diesels hummin'/ Don't need no ticket, you just thank the Lord.'

An earlier, fragmentary 'Slow Train' confirmed it originally had a kinship with the woman in 'More Than Flesh And Blood', someone he was warned about by 'that gypsy lady up on broadway & first/ [who] said yr someone that I should [try to] forget.' Now, he finds 'he's down & not feeling well/ it ain't the time, gal, to get up & leave him.' Yet this is exactly what she had done, leaving his 'wounded heart . . . on the rack' and causing him to re-examine his lifestyle choices. That re-examination would, in the fullness of time, inspire a May 1980 rap to an Albany crowd, that sounded more like a recovering addict doing his first 'share': 'When you've exhausted everything else, when you have all the women you can possibly use, when you've drunk all you can drink, you can try Jesus.'

An inner pain he was feeling infects just about every song at that long Largo soundcheck. Even 'I Must Love You Too Much' had acquired a cryptic new couplet, 'You're gonna make me love my house and wife/ You got a protective shield around you, girl,' while the once-seductive 'Hazel' contains a plea for 'her' to come back, 'It's late, I don't think I can take it much longer/ You're looking for a man to hire, why not hire me?' before he completes a circle with Tim Hardin's 'If I Were A Carpenter', which famously asks, 'Would you marry me, any-way?'; the very question Dylan would recast in 1980's 'Caribbean Wind'.

Throughout the fall – and his longest-ever unbroken stint of shows – he continued using the *gratis* hotel notepaper to unburden himself of more teeming thoughts. Another lost song, seemingly addressing the lady wielding The Bible, asked, 'Is it the [Roman] times for which ya want to cling/ Tell me has Jesus been your boyfriend/ Is Buddah your King?' heralding the 'holy slow train' hoving into view. It is late Octo-ber, and Dylan is staying at the Kalamazoo Hilton Inn.

But he had yet to develop a monomania for saving souls, having spent the October 13th soundcheck getting the band to record a song not about the disease of conceit, but about a disease to which legion-naires were prone. His tongue seemed firmly in his cheek as he wondered aloud if 'it was the food they ate, either the salad dressing or the steak/ Some said . . . it came from the frosting on the cake.' The song was Dylan's first reference to the toll the war in Vietnam had taken on a generation: 'Uncle fought in Vietnam/ And then he fought a war all by himself.' A cassette of a soundcheck version later made its way into Billy Cross's haversack and back to Sweden, where it created a minor stir on his 1981 solo album.

Another lost song of the period that warrants release somewhere is a gorgeous solo performance from Dylan at the piano. 'Baby Give It Up', recorded around this time, was only preserved on a stand-alone cassette, labelled in Dylan's own handwriting and mistakenly copyrighted to Dylan-Springs.*

But Dylan was no longer staying up nights with Helena, writing songs. 'More Than Flesh And Blood', the finest of their joint efforts, he was apparently rewriting on his own. By now she was explicitly sleeping with the Devil, leaving 'forty men at the bottom of the well', the sort of riddling song reference he wouldn't really adopt wholesale until 1990's *under the red sky*.

On October 14th, he soundchecked another new song in Terre Haute, dispensing yet more advice to a witchy wanderer, in that admonitory tone which would become so familiar in a year or so: 'Look out for the one that looks out for you, and you surely won't miss/ Empty pockets won't be your guide . . . The spirit is willing and the heart can't resist/ Take it or leave it, one more time.' The song, presumably called 'Take It Or Leave It', became a staple at the soundchecks, one of them in Toledo a week later, even as he continued to wonder aloud if this was more than flesh and blood can bear.

But still he held back from testing any of this new material on the arena audiences he was playing to nightly, in marked contrast to the other major rock tour traversing North America that year, the one promoting *Darkness on the Edge of Town*, another CBS album that sold half what the label had been banking on.† Despite which, many US critics continued to champion Springsteen, somewhat prematurely, as the natural heir to Dylan's mantle, much to the elder singer's intense annoyance: 'People said I put a saxophone player in my band because

---

* The copyright was later revised to reflect the solo nature of the composition, see Tim Dunn's *Copyright Files*.
† Springsteen consistently introduced unreleased songs, some of which would ultimately appear on *The River*.

Bruce Springsteen has one.* I don't have *anybody* in my band copying *anybody*.'

Having seen this backlash appear on the horizon line, Dylan explained to Hilburn in May, 'In the '60s, *Time, Newsweek* – all those magazines . . . created this "mythical Bob Dylan" thing. So, now, the magazines must figure they made a mistake back then and they've gotta take [me] down some.' Sure enough, true to tradition, *Newsweek*, reviewing the opening show of the fall Tour, made a less than flattering comparison with Elvis in Vegas. A week later, Dylan rose again to the bait, asking Marc Rowland rhetorically, 'Is that a negative thing, Vegas? . . . [I guess,] if they're out to say something [negative] . . . there's very little you can [do] . . . unless you want to defend yourself against the wind.'

Newsweek had again succeeded in putting his back up, not enough to engender another 'Restless Farewell', but certainly enough for him to reiterate his incomparable credentials, 'I've probably heard more music than . . . anybody that I'm playing to . . . [And] I *know* what I'm doing . . . A lot of thought has gone into it . . . I don't know anybody else around who writes the kind of songs I write.' Such braggadocio was rare indeed, but he was angry as hell, and he wasn't going to take it anymore, certainly not from a bunch of self-appointed arbiters of what's real and what is not:

> People now listen to records on stereo sets worth ten grand . . . They listen to how it sounds rather than what it says . . . And those magazines; they write about the albums from . . . behind desks . . . In the '60s, they . . . just wrote . . . I'm not out [there] to bring back the '60s. They're over. I'm not nostalgic for those days.

There was nothing remotely nostalgic about the high energy, two-and-a-quarter hour show he was delivering to largely full arenas, whatever the set-list suggested. Songs like 'Mr Tambourine Man', 'It's All Over Now, Baby Blue' and 'I Don't Believe You' were now positively baroque, while neo-metal arrangements of 'Masters Of War', 'It's Alright Ma', 'Where Are You Tonight?' and 'Changing Of The

---

* Steve Douglas made his name playing sax with Duane Eddy, Dion, Aretha Franklin and Elvis long before Clarence Clemons paid the H.P. on his first shiny saxophone.

Guards' smack of Dylan raising a digit to those critics who heard Vegas and/or disco in the space between their ears. A still-fuming Dylan told Kurt Loder six years later, 'That band we assembled then, I don't think that will ever be duplicated. It was a big ensemble. And what did people say? . . . "Bruce Springsteen." Because there was a saxophone player! And "disco" – Well, there wasn't any "disco" in it.'

The result was a sound which stripped all the subtle textures from the arrangements that had wowed the Europeans and Antipodeans, making the experience even more in your face than 1974. He was also spitting out some lyrics, à la '74, which made for a particularly stark contrast to the earlier shows, represented now by the Japanese-only *At Budokan*, which was available on import, and widely reviewed.

Indeed, *Melody Maker*'s Richard Williams made a ludicrous comparison between a live '78 Dylan bootleg and recent radio broadcasts of Springsteen, saying, 'Betcha Dylan is still playing "It's Alright Ma" the same way in Denver this week that he played it in London five months ago.' It was a bet he would certainly have lost, even if Dylan himself may have been listening to those Springsteen radio shows, as he started to preface 'Thin Man', 'One More Cup Of Coffee' and, especially, 'Señor', with the kind of tall stories with which Bruce had peppered his shows for years.

The import of the travelling seer in 'Señor' had yet to be made explicit, as he refrained from performing either 'Slow Train' or 'More Than Flesh And Blood', let alone another new song, subtitled '(Message To A Jewish Girl)', the refrain of which ran, 'Gonna change my way of thinking/ Gonna ride a different set of stallions to the fair.' Sensing he needed to change in mid-stream, said lyric in its pre-Scriptural phase suggested he 'got beat up and didn't know it/ Like a drugged man, I didn't feel no pain,' further proof his later claim he was 'doing fine' was a case of him blowing smoke, like the character on the train to Monterey he described nightly prior to an increasingly powerful 'Señor'.

Something had recharged Dylan's batteries. Having run down a smoking 'Slow Train' in Nashville on December 2nd, prior to a show where cameras were rolling, the three songs from the show later shown on Italian TV – 'Mr Tambourine Man', 'Masters Of War' and 'Changing Of The Guards' – blew Bruce's recent performances out of the water.

The Nashville 'Changing Of The Guards', in particular, suggested not only that Eden was burning, but that his heart had finally found 'the courage for the changing of the guards'. He believed time was running out, and not just for the 37-year-old iconoclast. The following night, in another Hilton, this one in Birmingham, Alabama, he wrote a note to himself that put a whole new slant on Neil Diamond's 'I'm A Believer', declaring that he was a believer, too, and that 'The Messiah IS coming back – but HE'S coming thru the roof this time.' Somebody had made a believer of him, and not just of the teachings of Christ, but the whole End is Nigh *schtick*; no room for doubt.

He was no longer talking about the same religious figure he had described to Jonathan Cott, a year earlier, 'a healer [who] goes to India, finds out how to be a healer and becomes one,' an explicit disavowal of the Christ who rose from the dead.* Nor was Jesus merely 'the myth of the complete man . . . [whom] Renaldo is attempting to become . . . to step aside of himself,' as he suggested to Pierre Cotrell days before Cott pressed him on who exactly Jesus represented in his 1977 film.

One interviewer that year who encountered the Dylan who had 'all the women [he] can possibly use . . . [and] drunk all [he] can drink,' was Australian journalist Karen Hughes, who secured one of the better pre-conversion interviews he gave to working women. When she next met him in May 1980, he began to tell her how the Lord had 'always been calling me. Of course, how would I have ever known that? That it was Jesus calling me. I always thought it was some voice that would be more identifiable . . . [Now I know] there's a difference between knowing who Christ is and being a disciple of [that] Christ, and recognising Christ as a *personality*.'

The latter had been obliterated from Dylan's mind by the former in mid-November, a month from the end of this long, hard road. It all began at the November 17th San Diego show, as he related onstage the following year, playing the self-same town to a very different demographic:

Towards the end of the show somebody out of the crowd – they knew I wasn't feeling too well, I think they could sense that – and they threw

---

* The idea that Jesus survived the Crucifixion, and ultimately travelled to India, is found in oral tradition and features in a number of revisionist accounts, notably Robert Graves's *Jesus In Rome* (1957).

a silver cross on the stage. Now, usually I don't pick things up that are thrown on the front of the stage . . . But I looked down at this cross and I said, 'I got to pick that up.' . . . It was a silver cross, I think maybe 'bout so high . . . I brought it with me to the next town, which was off in Arizona [Tempe]. Anyway, when I got back there, I was feeling even worse than I had felt when I was in San Diego, and I said, 'Well, I really need something tonight . . . I never really had before.' I looked in my pocket and I had this cross that someone threw up on stage . . . And I put that cross on.

He was certainly seen wearing a large silver cross around his neck at the Fort Worth show a week later. By then, the woman in the café in 'Tangled Up In Blue' had stopped quoting Dante or Petrarch, and started quoting the Gospel According to Matthew. What prompted him to re-examine Matthew's account of the life of J.C. was a vision he had in his Tucson hotel room – not simply a vision, a physical assault, 'Jesus put his hand on me. It was a physical thing. I felt it. I felt it all over me. I felt my whole body tremble. The glory of the Lord knocked me down and picked me up.'

The location, Dylan later claimed, had no great significance, 'Some people say they just heard a voice on a lonesome road; other people say they were in the middle of a football game; some people were in the men's room of a Greyhound bus station. You don't have to be in any special situation' to hear Him calling.

But one does have to be in a receptive state of mind, and Dylan, for whom the blues – the 'Devil's music', as it was widely known – had been his lexicon for so long, knew now why Blind Willie Johnson was moaning when he recorded 'Dark Was The Night And Cold Was The Ground'. Like this 'other' Johnson, he no longer had any doubt he was 'going to see the King, bye and bye'. Dylan had seen the light shine on him: 'Jesus did appear to me as King of Kings, and Lord of Lords . . . They call it reborn . . . It changes everything.'

It irrevocably changed this son of Abraham, from a Jewish agnostic to an apostle who *believed* – exactly the kind of person Matthew wrote his gospel for; someone conversant with the Jewish Bible who *needed* to know that Jesus fulfilled all the Old Testament prophecies and was the One foretold. A fellow L.A. musician, Al Kasha, whose own religious epiphany came at this time, recalls how the post-tour 'Dylan would keep [me] up until three or four o'clock in the morning, asking . . . all kinds of questions, going from the Old Testament to the New Testament [and back again] . . . try[ing] to see consistencies [between Matthew and] Isaiah . . . He loved that book.' As he should, having played the Dylan song most overtly inspired by the Book of Isaiah – 'All Along The Watchtower' – at every 1978 show.

Only now the denarii had dropped, as he accepted Isaiah's prophecies had already come to pass. It prompted him to write another song inspired by the good book, this one taking as its fulcrum Matthew 7:12: 'All things, therefore, that you want men to do to you, you also must likewise do to them; this, in fact, is what the Law and the Prophets mean.' In Savannah, Georgia, on December 8th, he used the soundcheck to show the band his own take on the so-called golden rule.

The song was called 'Do Right To Me (Do Unto Others)', and as with 'More Than Flesh And Blood' and the pre-conversion 'Slow Train', it was a plea to a woman to do right by him; a shift not in subject-matter (the power of Women), but rather standpoint, from the songs written in the summertime. One of these, 'This A-Way, That A-Way', had also acquired a new couplet: 'Passed by my baby at the Baptist Church/ Voices are ringing out on the street, Halleluiah.' And at that evening's show, the Georgians heard a 'Señor' rap that had grown to Springsteen-esque proportions:

> I was riding on a train one time . . . from Monterey to San Diego. I'd fallen asleep and when I woke up this train was in [the yard] . . . An old man stepped up on the train. I was still in a daze . . . [but] I was watching it all through the window, which was looking like a big mirror . . . This old man . . . walked down the aisle, took a seat by me across the aisle, wearing nothing but a blanket. He must have been about 150 years old. Anyway, I . . . kept looking at him in the mirror. I felt this strange vibration so I turned to look at him . . . Both his eyes were burning. There was smoke coming out of his nostrils. I immediately turned away . . . The train pulled out of the station. [W]hen I turned to talk to him, he'd disappeared. I searched for him at the next town, but he was gone.

He now knew where he was heading. And it wasn't Lincoln County Road. According to David Mansfield, it coincided with the boss getting a second wind, 'When that year of touring ended, he didn't want to stop. He was having a ball . . . He [even] started talking to the audience all of a sudden.' The after-show shindigs were also fun, 'He'd hang out, he'd drink, he'd talk his head off, he'd play [guitar], total reverse of '76.'

In Jacksonville on the 13th, Big Joe Williams came to a show which opened with Tampa Red's 'She's Love Crazy', and they talked about Big Joe possibly taking Dylan 'around the south to visit bluesmen'. Not that he needed old bluesmen to quantify the amount of trouble women can bring. As Jo Ann Harris wryly remarked, years later, '[It] seemed . . . the [other] girls who were singing always had [something] going on with [Bob] . . . Carolyn and Helena almost had it out on stage one night, with me in the middle.'

The final show in Miami found him walking towards the Son, giving the first public indication that he'd added the New Testament to his hotel bedside reading: a live debut for 'Do Right To Me Baby'. However, in a slot previously reserved for 'All I Really Wanna Do', sandwiched between 'It's Alright Ma' and 'Forever Young', its import was not readily apparent to the Hollywood Sportatorium crowd. He merely seemed to be asking some woman not to judge him, deceive him, or hurt him.

The question now was, which woman? Mary Alice Artes was still a fixture, but according to Billy Cross, theirs was an increasingly rocky relationship, 'There were terrible scenes. I think [Bob] was lucky to escape without getting his eye blacked . . . Mary being larger than he was. [But] Bob . . . likes black women. He likes black music. He likes black style. When he asked for musical attitudes, they would always be black.'

If, on the other hand, it was mainly directed at Carolyn Dennis, he was laying out terms for a relationship that would cause her a great deal of heartache in the decade to come. Whereas Helena's Catholic upbringing would already have instilled an understanding of the *quid pro quo* arrangement. Both were back at the Miami hotel when Dylan joined the band for a post-tour party, talking animatedly about how he wanted to keep the show on the road. But it was Ms Dennis who found him outside her door at 3 a.m., making it blatantly obvious he wanted something more than a late-night chat.

That night's bonding session was the culmination of a sustained wooing campaign that had been going on for weeks, after Dylan told her she was the best singer he had ever had – during his first-ever tour with backing singers. Trapped in what she herself described as 'a failing marriage', to drummer Raymond Lee Pounds, Carolyn – like Helena – had been raised a Christian. However, like the unfortunate Springs, she had now fallen in love with this womanizer par excellence. She did not send him away from her room, nor did she tell him of a vision she had had a month earlier, of him onstage looking like he was going to fall, as she heard a voice saying, 'If Bob Dylan doesn't get it right, he could be responsible for leading millions of people to Hell.' When he informed her, 'I just received Jesus Christ as my personal saviour,' she interpreted this as a sign – not a warning. They spent the whole night together, Dylan leaving her room only when it was time to board the bus to the airport.

Now a believer, Dylan seemed strangely unconversant with the seventh commandment. Nor was it some momentary lapse on the new convert's part. Back in L.A., Dylan informed Dennis his relationships with both Springs and Artes were 'slowly diminishing'. In a series of heart-to-heart conversations with the singer, he told her that they had both grown frustrated as he became less intimate and more emotionally distant, especially Artes, who'd told everyone that she hoped to marry him.*

Dennis later remembered Dylan phoning her, 'like an excited child', after meeting with the self-same evangelists who had just converted Artes. They came from the local chapter of the Vineyard Fellowship – an evangelical sect who believed in the literal truth of The Bible and salvation by faith, not works. They explained to him what it meant to be born again. According to one of them, '[At] some time in the next few days, privately and on his own, Bob accepted Christ and believed that Jesus Christ is indeed the Messiah.' All very odd, given the note Dylan wrote in Birmingham, Alabama, making it crystal clear he had already accepted Christ as both Messiah and personal saviour in early December.

What seems indisputable is that it was Artes who proceeded to play a crucial role in bringing Dylan to this particular, Californian brand of Christianity, despite later claiming, 'I cannot lead anyone to the

---

* This contradicts press reports which suggested Artes had moved out of Dylan's home upon accepting Christ into her life.

Lord . . . I think that too many people wanna be glorifying themselves in a situation that really should not have any glory at all.'

If she thought this shared experience would bring them closer together, she was being a tad optimistic. Dylan was now telling Dennis that he had already discounted the very idea of marrying Mary Alice, 'much to her dismay', even as she continued to live in one of his many rental properties in town. With one of Dylan's 'main squeezes' making herself physically unavailable, if not quite getting herself to a nunnery, Dennis told the conflicted convert that despite her intense feelings for him, she thought they should henceforth refrain from 'express[ing] physical intimacy', lest it confuse the reborn Robert while he embraced all the teachings of Christ, and maybe even relearnt the Ten Commandments.

Already on the receiving end of tittle-tattle, Dylan now penned a brief devotional poem on the back of a letter from Howard Alk that New York office manager Jeff Rosen had forwarded to him that January. It ended with the couplet, 'Malicious tongue/ It's not your responsibility to repeat gossip.' It would be but a short step from here to, 'They look at me and frown/ They want to drive me from this town/ They don't want me around.' ('I Believe In You') He was already feeling the slings and arrows, even as he envisioned, 'Eternity staring up in the face [of the] Armor of God, the mind of Christ.'

It was time to express this new, profound faith in song, as only he knew how. Since he had already started a number of songs that spoke of the 'holy slow train', changing his way of thinking, and doing unto others as he'd have them do unto him, it was not a huge leap to apply the odd liturgical gloss to the concerns of a newly-repentant Old-School sinner. But he was still finding it hard to avoid the snares of the flesh. Indeed, at times he was finding it more than flesh and blood can bear. As Dennis later explained to Dylan scholar, Scott Marshall:

The apartment where I lived, at the end of the block was this church he was going to . . . He was coming to do the Bible studies, and it just happened to be almost across the street from where I was living . . . He said there were times when he would want to come [and] visit me, but something wouldn't let him ring the bell . . . So, he would call me [on the phone]. We'd talk about what was happening with him and what he was learning and how excited he was.

For now, these 'Bible studies' were keeping the former degenerate on the straight and narrow. But for how long? That, as any TV preacher might have said, was the $64,000 question now being asked by a million pair of eyes who, after the long 'amnesia', had thought they'd got *their* Dylan back, only to now lose him to the Lord. Lawdy, Lawd.

4.5

January to October 1979:
In The Lion's Den

Evangelist: A bearer of good tidings, particularly such as assure us of our own salvation and the damnation of our neighbors.

Ambrose Bierce, The Devil's Dictionary.

The whole press was printing the Christian [conversion] story and I said, 'I don't know how to handle it.' He said, 'Well, what's your problem?' . . . 'Well, Bob, are you a born-again Christian?' And he looked at me and said, 'What do you mean [by] born again?'

Paul Wasserman, Dylan's publicist, to Scott Marshall.

I . . . know I shouldn't deal with any current subject on an emotional level, because usually it won't last.

Bob Dylan, to Ron Rosenbaum, November 1977.

My thing was always to pull the mask off of whatever was going on.

Bob Dylan, to Robert Hilburn, 19th November 1980.

We were on [a] mission. Bob had a definite point of view . . . So, those of us in those bands . . . felt like we were participating in something historic.

Fred Tackett.

He's born on the twenty-fourth of May, [like] Queen Victoria. I always think that birth date is the day of the extreme moralist.

Joni Mitchell, Rolling Stone 30th May 1991.

> I wanted the songs out, but I didn't want to do it [myself], because I
> knew that it wouldn't be perceived in *that* way.
>
> Bob Dylan, 1984.

*

Ye shall be changed. That was the message of all the songs – and the
title of one – to consume the new convert in the first flush of faith.
And the songs continued to pour forth, as they had the previous year.
But unlike those from December 1977 through November 1978, only
two of which – both slight – would make it to vinyl, the outpouring
between December 1978 and November 1979 went direct to disc.

Two albums of faith would be the outcome, one recorded in May
1979, the other in February 1980, albums three and four of his newly-
negotiated CBS contract, neither of which was what the label was
expecting, or hoping for. Even more remarkably, seventeen of these
songs would form Dylan's entire live set for the foreseeable, spreading
alarm among the Dylan faithful and providing a whole host of anthems
for those preparing daily for Armageddon.

For those unsure when that might be, a man of the cloth-bound,
Hal Lindsey, had been churning out tracts giving the date, time and
location for the past decade, culminating in the ultimate proof that
there's one born every minute, million-seller, *The Late Great Planet
Earth*. And it seems Dylan, a brilliant man but an autodidact, bought
into Lindsey's counter-intuitive interpretation of St John the Divine's
Revelation like a long-term resident of Waco. It was exactly as McGuinn
once suggested to Sloman, 'There are gaps in his perception and if you
fill in the spots for him, he really freaks out.'

Lindsey's take on the prophecies of St John was not even that original. He began with the re-establishment of Israel – a common
starting point – before concocting a whole series of tenuous
connections that made Russia Gog and China Magog, and
concluded – Q.E.D. – that the battle of Armageddon was just
around the corner and America better wake up and 'strengthen the
things that remain'.

Like all tub-thumpin' tent-evangelists down the ages, the first thing
Lindsey required in order to sell his own brand of snake oil to the credulous was for them to stop reading other books, especially history

books, which carried annoying little facts that might cast doubt on (or, indeed, utterly demolish) his rickety thesis. For Dylan, who had been reading books on every subject under the sun all his adult life, perhaps it was a huge relief to find he only needed two, both of which were *literally* true.

Proof that Dylan had already dipped into *The Late Great Planet Earth* before those nice, well-dressed men from the Vineyard came a-callin' can be found in an early draft of 'When You Gonna Wake Up', which had not as yet taken its cue from Revelation 3:2 ('Be watchful, and strengthen the things which remain, that are ready to die: for I have not found thy works perfect before God'). At this stage he was simply berating unbelievers, 'when you gonna wake up & know the truth.' The song seems to have been one of the first he started penning – actually, typing – after he found a reason to believe. Already, he was looking to use his new-found faith to lay into familiar targets, specific-ally all those -isms and -ologies, because 'socio[lo]gy ain't gonna buy ya a ticket when ya decide to step back from the flame'.

Likewise, he warns one to be wary of any 'pied piper tryin' [to] sell . . . co[u]nterfeit philosophies.' Temporarily forgetting he was a multi-millionaire, the born-again singer set about metaphorically shak-ing the slumbering atheists of America, telling them he'd 'got wealth that you can't see & [a] dangerous friend that's just waitin' to play his part'. With Lindsey's looney tune in his head, a devout Dylan was building up a head of steam the like of which had not been seen since the battle of Fort Collins:

> the history books will just deceive
> in my opinion they ain't worth a dime
> if you say that He's coming they won't believe ya
> & that 2000 years is just a moment of His time
> Many people think that God is just an errand boy
> To help them in their wants & their desires
> With their barren wombs and mouths that make a lot of noise
> They're never sure about what He requires . . .

This reads like a man who had come to feel he has nothing to lose. Hence, perhaps, the line at the top of the earliest draft of the song: 'i don't care if i ever come thru these halls again.' He continued in much the same vein on the reverse page, now in the first person, avowing his faith and admonishing the faithless: 'lightnin' gonna strike on these balls & chains/ my spirit's gonna wake up & rise again/ you know I heard a [lot of] wise men, but I never have met one & [I] know the truth.'

The certitude that often comes to those who convert late had come to the wandering Jew, and this one had one weapon – a pen – that was mightier than the sword. He was determined to use it. Three Alpha Band converts to the same creed – Stephen Soles, David Mansfield and T-Bone Burnett – all recently returned from Miami, knew both Dylan and Artes, and though they all deny introducing either to Lindsey and/ or his works, someone did. Dylan broke bread with the man.

In that narrow window between the Tucson visitation and the Vineyard intervention – a period of two months at most – Dylan wrote or rewrote the likes of 'Do Right To Me Baby', 'When You Gonna Wake Up', 'Gonna Change My Way Of Thinking', 'Slow Train', 'Precious Angel', a song called 'Ain't Too Proud To Repent' and probably 'When He Returns', each of which came from the autodidact, not the future Sunday School pupil.

When Dylan's manager, Jeff Rosen, compiled the 2017 boxed-set *Trouble No More*, designed to highlight just how creative this period had been for his boss, he consciously incorporated into the accompanying book a whole series of lyrical drafts that are self-evidently pre-Vineyard. It was almost like he was making a point. Dylan may have been reading his Bible daily, but for now he was still using his own words to express himself. The message was the same, but the language was *his*. Thus, on the same page as an early draft of 'Precious Angel' was a fragment which provided a poetic summation of Lindsey's ahistorical standpoint:

> Armies of men marching into place
> The kings of the north & the kings of the south show their face
> & the night wind, restless as can be
> Some ruled by love, some ruled by the devil in the sea
> The battle between right & wrong, I know it won't be long.

Surely also written at this time was 'Ye Shall Be Changed', drawing on Lindsey's interpretation of a particularly contentious part of the

New Testament teachings, found in Corinthians 15:52: 'In a moment . . .
the trumpet shall sound, and the dead shall be raised incorruptible, and
we shall be changed.' Based largely on chapter 11 of *The Late Great
Planet Earth* – called, ironically, 'The Ultimate Trip' – this may well be
the song Dylan had in mind in 1984 when suggesting to fellow Christian Bono, 'The songs that I wrote for the *Slow Train* album . . . I didn't
plan to write . . . I didn't like writing them, I didn't want to write them.'

An early advocate of the so-called Rapture, Lindsey had sold Dylan
on the idea that 'in the twinkling of an eye, when the last trumpet
blows, ye shall be changed'. Thankfully, something inside Dylan that
smacked of career-preservation made him pull back from releasing, or
even performing, the track – maybe a real concern that people around
him would start reaching for the nearest strait-jacket.

Another song which fell by the wayside showed more of the gift he
couldn't deny, but 'Ain't Too Proud To Repent' ended up not even
being recorded (save for off-mike while auditioning a new guitarist).
Yet he wrote at least two complete drafts before putting on his school
uniform. In both drafts, the final verse reiterated that 'the devil has
already been defeated'. Whereas the first had Satan 'just playing out his
hand' – i.e. fulfilling the prophecies of St John, leading to his ultimate
defeat, while accruing as many sinners as he could to keep 'company
with him down below' – the other gave all the credit to Christ:

> . . . God sent his Son to take the rap for all mankind
> You can throw away your crutches – you been cheated
> They got a business selling eyeglasses to the blind.

The idea that Jesus had already taken 'the rap for all mankind' was
one Dylan expounded repeatedly in various spoken intros that graced
the livelier shows when he took his message 'for all mankind' across
America, explicitly telling a May Akron audience, 'The Devil's already
been defeated. All you gotta do is accept it, [and] be baptized with the
Holy Ghost. You will have the power.' For now, though, he was content to sing about having 'a home up yonder' on which he didn't have
to pay 'the rent' (a convenient rhyme for repent), while slipping in
some pre-(and post-) evangelical concerns regarding a society that
believed you could change yourself from the outside: 'You can even
change your sex & buy another face.'

Again, though, a seemingly unconnected line on the same page laid bare the root cause of his own despair with (51% of) humanity, 'Passion's blind and Romance is an Act.' Could it be that his own grand passion had brought him to this place, and the 'end' of his quest? He certainly seemed to suggest as much in the original 'Gonna Change My Way Of Thinking': 'Once you find the Lord is looking for you/ That's the day you give up your search.' The search was futile because, as he sang in 'Saved (By The Blood Of The Lamb)', he'd been 'blinded by the Devil/ Born already ruined.' Hence this original sinner's comment at a November 1979 show, prior to singing this very song: 'It's such a wonderful feeling when you've been delivered from that.'

And yet, when it came to dispensing credit for his conversion, he seemed to be suggesting the love of a good woman was largely responsible. He even began to pen a song of thanks, a hymn to this 'precious angel under the sun/ God sent you to me – you are the only one . . . you've saved me baby & [it] took some kind of nerve.'

If, as has long been thought, the subject of this supplication-in-song was Mary Alice Artes, he was playing fast and loose with the facts. The final lyrics refer to this precious angel 'talking to your husband, suffering under the Law', which can only refer to Carolyn Dennis. Also, by the time Artes brought her own brand of friendly fire to bear, he had already received a personal visitation from the Son of Man and had a firm foot on the running board of the 'holy slow train'.

Whichever lady he meant, it seems he was still consumed by more earthly desires, celebrated so sensually in the final lyric, 'You're the queen of my flesh, girl . . . and you torch up the night,' whereas in an earlier draft, he speaks only of the sincerity of his devotion – 'i just got to set my mind on you & i can make it thru another day' – and his wavering resistance to temptation, which 'springs up suddenly & thinks of me as easy prey'. The sensual world had become a snare, as had all non-believers, damned by the new Dylan in one withering couplet, 'You either got faith or you got unbelief/ And there ain't no neutral ground.' Even in the original 'Precious Angel', he contrasted her constancy with those so-called friends who have 'all turned me out – you'd think i'd [sic] have some kind of disease'.

Here was lyrical proof that even at this early stage in his journey there was no shortage of folk who hoped he'd return to the 'path thick beset wi' briers'. Certainly, there was a reaction from those who thought they knew Dylan well, including John Lennon, whom Elliot Mintz had phoned to tell him Dylan was a Christian, something he found hard to believe. He had two words for the man: 'Parking meter' (as in, 'Don't follow leaders/ watch the . . .'). Allen Ginsberg also gently chastised his fellow wordsmith in a postcard that spring, 'Christ or any "Absolute" reference point is projection of transitory Self -- spiritual reality's very tricky, don't get confused by the Final Projection -- Love, Allen.'

Dylan was a little taken aback. As he later told Hilburn, 'I did begin telling a few people after a couple of months and a lot of them got angry at me.' Over time he would learn to not 'talk about what I . . . became, because that sets people off.' By the time he admitted this – in 1985 – he had fully demonstrated that 'whatever it is that I am manifests itself through what I do'. The work would remain unequivocal for at least half a decade, but he would learn to stop talking about it to the press after the summer of 1981. For now, as he handwrote in the margin of an early version of 'When He Returns', he would continue browbeating 'those who say/ That God is dead . . . [They] are gonna eat their words.'

'When He Returns' could well be the last song he began while waiting on a visit from the Vineyard Fellowship, Artes's chosen advocates. Though, like 'Do Right To Me Baby', it took overt inspiration from a verse in the New Testament, Thessalonians 5:2, it was one referenced as far back as 'All Along The Watchtower': 'For yourselves know perfectly that the day of the Lord so cometh as a thief in the night.'

In its earliest draft form, it showed vestiges of the more jingoistic sections of Lindsey, as Rev. Gary Davis's ecumenical son poured scorn on all political systems as a manifestation of Mammon: 'the communists might be frightenin' you/ 'cause they only believe in man/ & the capitalists might be exploitin' you/ 'cause that's part of their plan.' The vision of the final battle – when, 'like a thief in the night/ He's gonna set the world right' – was pure Lindsey, just with a poetic sensibility the princely Hal lacked:

> The seas will shake, the earth will quake, when will you learn
> That there'll be no peace, & that the war won't cease, until He returns.

Like all that he had accrued to date, 'When He Returns' would only be bathed in direct biblical references after the Vineyard Fellowship entered the picture and imposed their vision of Christianity, subverting the poet, recasting him as a preacher man. The first link in that chain was Pastor Kenn Gulliksen, who was approached at the end of a fellowship meeting by Artes, who 'said that she wanted to rededicate her life to the Lord . . . Then she revealed that she was Bob Dylan's girlfriend and asked if a couple of the pastors would come, there and then[!], and talk to Bob.' Even if Gulliksen and his fellow pastors didn't expect him to tow the collective line as much as he would, they were confident their unholy brew of AA Addict-speak and King James English would win the day:

> **Bill Dwyer**: The thing that was going on with the Vineyard in those days was not in any way coercive, it was not ecstatic. Most of the people [who join the fellowship] . . . cry out to God, 'I need a Higher Power.' Most people come to that place because of a crisis in their life . . . [Our pastors] just talked with [Dylan], answered questions that he had. I think they gave him a Bible . . . It was very down to earth: Do you need help in your life? [Do] you have a sense of something more, [and want to] invite the Lord in? Are you aware that your own sins have created a lot of guilt and shame in your life, and [do] you want to get free of that?

The method was tried and tested. And when it comes to lapsed Jews, nothing works quite as well as a good guilt trip. What is more in doubt is whether, as Kenn Gulliksen has claimed, 'He responded by saying, yes, he did in fact want Christ in his life. And he prayed that day and received the Lord,' or whether, as Larry Myers asserts, 'Sometime in the next few days, privately and on his own, Bob accepted Christ,' which sounds more likely. After all Myers was there, as was Paul Emond. Gulliksen, something of a public spokesman for the sect, looking to extract maximum mileage from their latest 'celeb' convert, was not. Myers found someone open to The Word, 'There was no attempt to convince, manipulate or pressure the man into anything. But . . . God spoke through His Word, The Bible, to a man who had been seeking for many years.'

At some point in that initial, overwhelming rush of enthusiasm, perhaps on that first day, Dylan was told about the Vineyard's School of Discipleship. As Gulliksen was at pains to explain, 'It was an intensive course studying about the life of Jesus; principles of discipleship; the Sermon on the Mount; what it is to be a believer.' Never the keenest of pupils, Dylan initially refused to respond to the school bell, saying to himself, 'There's no way I can devote three months to this [Bible course]. I've got to be back on the road soon.' But the Lord, it seems, had other plans, 'I was sleeping one day and I just sat up in bed at seven in the morning and I was compelled to get dressed and drive over to the Bible school.'

Perhaps his chaste 'precious angel', Mary Alice, came and kicked him out of bed. For she, too, was devoting her time to (re)learning her catechisms. Davin Seay and Mary Neely describe in *Stairway to Heaven* (1986) how 'during class breaks, Dylan would often walk into the parking lot in back of the prefab building, dressed against the brisk morning air in a leather jacket and stocking cap, to smoke Marlboro cigarettes and talk with his girlfriend'. His presence there certainly didn't go unremarked by one of the pastors who was teaching there:

Bill Dwyer: He came to my class. He interacted with other students. But he was still Bob Dylan – he dressed like Bob Dylan. [I was almost tempted to say,] 'Take off the glasses, the leather jacket and the beret for a minute.' But he did all the assignments . . . All of our ministry at the Vineyard was based on Bible studies. That was a primary focal point. Every Sunday we taught The Bible, we told everybody carry your Bible, read your Bible every day. We started our actual Bible school, and [students] would go [there for] three, four hours in the morning. I taught one of the classes. Kenn taught one of the classes, Larry Myers taught one of the classes. It was intensive. The word of God is what we wanted to get across. The Bible class was usually about a dozen students, so it was very interactive . . . We would teach every book in The Bible from Genesis to Revelation. It was very Bible-based. At the same time, we weren't very fundamentalist . . . That [creed] was very black and white, very legalistic, very hard line. It was [more like], 'This is the Word of God and these words are to bring life to you.'

Another member of the fellowship who taught at the school, Terry Botwick, found Dylan something of a handful, in a good way, challenging the teacher to keep up with the pupil, 'He was a sincere and honest seeker trying to understand and learn. What struck me about

him was how deeply interested he was. My only frustration was keeping up with his questions. I'd go over five to six subjects each week, an
Old Testament book like Isaiah 28, and he would've read ahead to
chapter 43.' The singer evidently forgot to mention he already knew his
Book of Isaiah, even as he assiduously took notes, hoping, as had been
the case with the classes he took back in '74, it might inspire him. He
later suggested what he really learnt from three months of being a
morning-person was to live in the present:

> **Bob Dylan**: What I learned in Bible school was just . . . an extension of
> the same thing I believed in all along, but just couldn't verbalize or
> articulate. Whether you want to believe Jesus Christ is the Messiah is
> irrelevant, but . . . people who believe in the coming of the Messiah live
> their lives right now, as if He was here. [1985]

Living in the present was a lesson that lingered long. The pupil later
turned teacher to dispense his one-day-at-a-time philosophy to a Nineties' girlfriend, '[You see] these peaches. [They] look beautiful and as I
look at them, I'm thinking, I hope they'll taste as good as they look . . .
As I eat it, I think, Yup, it tastes really good, just as I thought it would.
But I don't sit here analyzing to myself – but why? – why does it taste
so good to me? Why do I like the taste of this peach? No. I just eat the
peach and enjoy it and appreciate the moment as it happens. I savour
the experience and then I move on to the next.'

For now, though, he was still waiting for the end of the world. Suddenly the songs of experience he was (re)writing sprang directly from
sections of the book he was being importuned to read every day. Thus,
'No Man Righteous' took its cue from Romans 3:10: 'As it is written,
there is none righteous, no, not one'; 'I Believe In You' drew its inspiration from Philippians 1:29, 'Unto you it is given in the behalf of Christ,
not only to believe on him, but also to suffer for his sake'; while 'Gotta
Serve Somebody' came about because someone – possibly Larry
Myers – brought Joshua 24:15 to his attention: 'And if it seem evil unto
you to serve the Lord, choose you this day whom ye will serve.'
(According to Gulliksen, 'Larry was often the backboard for Bob to
share the lyrics.')

At the same time, songs he'd previously sketched out were transformed. 'When You Gonna Wake Up' found a burden strong enough

to remain in Dylan's live set for the next three years. Meanwhile, the apocalyptic elements of 'When He Returns' fell into place. By the time he passed his discipleship course with flying colours, he had an album that had bolted the language of The Bible onto songs that were once sincerely his.

Such allusions, familiar to all educated men down the centuries, in a godless age were destined to go down less well. But the devotional Dylan simply couldn't wait to get in the studio the second his contract demanded, on April 30th. And this time he wasn't about to rely on God, or serendipity, to ensure the message emerged undiluted from the multitrack tape-boxes. He had received something of a shock when first hearing his last album blasting across the airwaves. It wasn't the record he thought he'd made:

I heard [*Street-Legal*] on the radio and it doesn't have . . . what I thought it did have, sound-wise . . . I didn't find out until . . . after the record was even out . . . that what they were getting in the truck wasn't what was happening in the room. [1978]

Perhaps someone a tad more technically-inclined than A&R man Don DeVito was required. Dylan finally pleaded guilty to an increasingly common charge conversing with Matt Damsker in September 1978, 'I could use a good producer, you know, I could make some well-produced records, 'cause my songs are good enough.' Amen. Actually, he had already taken steps to not stumble again at the final hurdle, turning up one summer '78 afternoon at L.A.'s Cherokee Studio to see an old friend (and co-producer) help the great torch-balladeer Etta James lose her chains and record her first comeback album, *Deep In The Night*:

Jerry Wexler: That afternoon in Cherokee, Bob told me he'd been writing on the piano. Since Dylan famously composed on guitar, I was intrigued . . . Back in New York a few weeks later, Bob asked me to produce his next album . . . Naturally, I wanted to do the album in Muscle Shoals – as Bob did – but we decided to prep it in L.A.

Wexler had all-but-invented southern soul in the melting heat of Sheffield, Alabama's one fairground attraction, Muscle Shoals Studio, with Aretha Franklin, after she fled the cloying commercialism of

Columbia and John Hammond Snr to testify that soul music was in need of some r-e-s-p-e-c-t. Wexler, though, hadn't seen his friend Bobby in a few months when he and his sidekick, Barry Beckett, one of the most musical engineers in the business, convened with the convert that April to hear his new songs. As he later, laughingly, recalled, 'I had no idea he was on this born-again Christian trip until he started to evangelize me.'

According to Beckett, '[Tim] Drummond was there, Mark Knopfler was there . . . Dylan was playing keyboards . . . He was writing in a different musical direction . . . The lyrics took on more of a blues phrasing.' If new waver Knopfler *was* there, it was after March 29th, the night Dylan checked out Dire Straits at The Roxy.

The idea of grafting the Strait-man's J.J. Cale-meets-John-Perry twin-tone onto the Shoals Sound was Wexler's, and it was an inspired one. Dylan, though, took some convincing, later going to some pains in a radio interview to make it clear it was 'Jerry [who] recommended him to play on that album . . . I went down to see him, and I thought he sounded sort of like me – not really, but a little bit.'

Dylan went along with Wexler, but bassist Tim Drummond – already on his radar – was *his* suggestion, as were a trio of black girl singers, an integral part of the sound he was hearing in his head. And he brooked no discussion on this matter. According to Carolyn Dennis: 'Jerry Wexler didn't want to use . . . me, or Helena, or Regina [Havis] . . . But Bob fought for us . . . He said, "You're going to use my girls." ' No neutral ground.

Dylan wanted Carolyn and Helena – both believers – to add their gospel-tinged inflections to the set of songs he had begun writing when he was still bed-hopping, even if their tense personal relationship left a bitter aftertaste for them. What mattered was the musical melting pot. Both backing singers found Beckett the more sympathetic co-producer, Dennis describing him as 'the one who really kind of guided us through our portion of the album. We had very little, if any, interaction with Mr Wexler.' Springs went further still, being greatly 'impressed [by] Barry Beckett's contribution to the album, [which] was much more than he ha[s] been given credit for. Actually, I think it was much more than Jerry Wexler's.'

If the co-production credit Beckett ultimately received seems to have been down to Dylan, they didn't always see eye-to-eye. Initially,

Beckett wasn't happy with the way Dylan's vocals and Knopfler's guitar meshed in the mix, at the expense of each party's paradigmatic texture. Eventually, he turned to Wexler for validation, 'We've got to do something about that guitar sound, and mix it [so] we can hear the *vocal.*'

Likewise, at the overdub phase Beckett remembers, 'There was this song we used horns on. The idea was to strengthen the guitars, not the use of horns per se. There was a sound I was looking for, just to help the overall tone of the guitars. And [Dylan] didn't understand. He thought I wanted to use horns for the sake of the sound itself.' Words were exchanged. An undeterred Beckett persevered, convincing him it would help sweeten the sound, as Kooper had on *New Morning*, before being permitted to add horns to 'Slow Train', 'When You Gonna Wake Up' and 'Gonna Change My Way Of Thinking'. Beckett's piano playing on 'When He Returns' also served as the perfect staccato backdrop to the album-closer, allowing Dylan to concentrate on one of his finest-ever studio vocals, having originally attempted a full band arrangement, before recognising sometimes less is more.

Things were not going smoothly on another, familiar front. Preferring to record like Aretha used to, Dylan spent the whole of the first day trying to get b-side 'Trouble In Mind'; the second, on the ultimately discarded 'No Man Righteous'. Wexler feared this was the way the whole set of sessions was gonna go down: 'First day . . . Bob was playing and singing on every [take]. I didn't know exactly what the protocol was gonna be, but we spent the whole day on one song! . . . [Eventually,] we sat down, had a little talk . . . I finally convinced him to hold off on the vocals until later, when the arrangements were in shape, and the players could play their licks around – not against – him.'

Dylan wasn't keen, confiding his concerns to Dennis, who had not worked on *Street-Legal*, and so didn't yet know he liked 'that just-the-band-in-one-room thing'. Wexler wanted to compartmentalize the musicians, as was the norm by the late-Seventies, at the cost of feel and chemistry and to the eternal detriment of a musical form that required both. A compromise was agreed, in which the musicians initially gathered in an unbroken circle:

Jerry Wexler: Bob [would] run it down on piano or guitar, just singing and playing the background until we had a rough shape in our minds, then the Muscle Shoals band would start to play it. In a very short time, they['d] find a pocket, they['d] hit a groove. We['d] stop that. We['d] send them all back into isolation [booths], isolate the amps, put the [head]phones back on and play back what they had just played. They played it a few times with the phones [on]. Then as soon as it sounded right, I took the track out of the phones . . . [and] Bob and the girls would start to sing. Take one.

Wexler claimed the effect was instant: 'We made four songs that [first] day. Did you ever hear of anything like that?!' Actually, the May 2nd session resulted in three songs, two keepers – 'When You Gonna Wake Up' and 'Gonna Change My Way Of Thinking' – and two distinctly different takes of 'Ye Shall Be Changed'. The following day, they revisited 'No Man Righteous', before capturing the title-track and 'I Believe In You'. Finally, on May 4th, Wexler got his four track day, including the album-closer.

Not that four songs in a day was unusual for Dylan sessions, no matter how hard Wexler convinced himself he'd broken the mould. Dylan kept his counsel and let him believe he had. Only when he returned to making records the way he always had, in 1981, did he make damn sure Wexler's replacement, L.A. producer Chuck Plotkin – fresh from working with Springsteen on an album that took *fourteen* months to complete – was aware he was gonna do it *his* way. After Plotkin informed him, he 'thought that *Slow Train [Coming]* was a great record', Bob replied, 'I felt uncomfortable making it. Because the first thing they did when I got down there was [make me] sit down and play them all the songs,' a reference to the circle game they started playing from the 2nd.

The experience gave Dylan a great deal of food for thought. As assistant engineer Scott Huffstetler observed: '[Whenever] they'd have a break on the sessions . . . he would . . . walk around. He wasn't a huge conversationalist but he would make comments and say things. To . . . walk out front and down to the river . . . was nothing for him.' He also happily chatted to the few fans who had made the pilgrimage.

Thankfully, not all of Wexler's suggestions set Dylan's teeth on edge. According to Dennis, Wexler was keen on 'Gotta Serve Somebody', whereas Dylan hadn't decided if he liked it that much. Returning to the house where he and the musicians were sharing bunks, after recording the song in four takes, he told Dennis, 'I don't think I like the song and I don't think I want to put it on the album . . . I don't like the way it's recorded and I don't like the way it sounds.' For once, she sided with Wexler – and the angels – telling her ex-beau, 'This song is going to cause people who have never listened to you before to be drawn to listen.'

He was persuaded, making it the album opener, even as he took the final song, 'When He Returns' – which he initially thought he'd ask the girls to sing – away from Carolyn and co. He had an album which didn't pull its punches, yet was as musically strong as anything he'd recorded in his second decade. So convincing was it that even Jann Wenner, the most politically correct of professional musos, used his own magazine, *Rolling Stone*, to acknowledge:

> At the urging of various personal friends, [Dylan] went to Bible-study classes led by a fundamentalist preacher. And, boy, without a doubt, this record is chapter and verse. The album's religious content is [all] perva-sive . . . [But,] musically, this is probably Dylan's finest record, a rare coming together of inspiration, desire and talent that completely fuse strength, vision and art.

Most other reviewers struggled to get beyond the 'chapter and verse' lyrics. It mattered not. The LP tapped into something they were putting in the water that year, *Slow Train Coming* almost matching his high watermark, sales-wise, *Desire*. It helped that the US single, 'Gotta Serve Somebody', proved once again that nobody sang Dylan like Dylan. Its August 1979 release, far from dampening the demand for a Dylan tour, merely stoked it. By then, a delighted Dylan was already assembling a band which could take the *Slow Train* sound on the road, minus Knopfler's trademark noodling, which drew an unjustified rebuke from Wenner, who accused him of playing 'licks . . . derived mainly from Albert King'. He was simply doing what he was told, the instruction having come from Wexler, 'Don't play Mark Knopfler, play Albert King!'

At least Wexler gave the Geordie boy *some kind* of instruction. It was more than Dylan would do when Fred Tackett, Rick Ruskin, John Pechizkjian and Wayne Perkins took turns auditioning for Knopfler's vacant berth, in mid-September. Remarkably, the largely unknown John Pechizkjian ended up in pole position after Dylan tried every

which way to trip the young tyke up – playing a song he never did finish, 'Ain't Too Proud To Repent', and at least three works in progress:
'Covenant Woman', 'Blessed Is The Name' and 'Hanging On To A
Solid Rock', all of which proved the singer had been leafing through
his 'King James' again.

'Blessed Is The Name' – the first encore through February 1980 –
took its remit and refrain from Daniel 2:20: 'Blessed be the name of
God for ever and ever: for wisdom and might are his,' while 'Covenant
Woman' clearly alluded to Jeremiah 31:31: 'Behold, the days come, saith
the Lord, that I will make a new covenant with the house of Israel, and
with the house of Judah,' the very verse emblazoned across the inner
sleeve of *Saved*.

Other songs that gushed forth that summer, as a divine inspiration
continued to hold Dylan in its vice-like grip, also drew on verses given
especial significance by his new teachers. While 1 Peter 1:23 gave 'In
The Garden' its *raison d'être* – 'Being born again, not of corruptible
seed, but of incorruptible, by the word of God' – 'Pressing On' was
triggered by Philippians 3:14: 'I press toward the mark for the prize of
the high calling of God in Christ Jesus.'

With *Slow Train Coming* barely in the shops, he already had another
LP's worth of songs in his backpack where the 'religious content is [all]
pervasive', though the angle of attack had changed. He was preaching
by example, having been saved by the blood of the lamb, guided by the
saving grace over him, inspired by the intervention of his covenant
woman, until all he could do was sing, what can I do for you? Yet barely
had he expressed his thanks than he was shedding verses at a rate of
knots, beginning with a particularly personal one from 'Saving Grace':
'All earthly riches can be stolen/ [But] you will never lose the gift which
is yours for free/ It ain't silver & gold which keeps me steady rolling/
It['s] the saving grace that's over me.'

Another verse dropped from 'Solid Rock' – 'One law for the flesh/
One law for the spirit/ No-one can drink from two cups/ No-one said,
it's easy not to slip up' – would inspire its own, rather ironic onstage
rap the following May to the Akronites, 'I know a lot of country and
western people sing very often, "You can put your shoes under my bed
anytime." And then they turn around and sing, "Oh Lord, just a closer
walk with thee." Well, I can't do that. That's right! You cannot serve
two masters. You gotta hate one and love the other. You can't drink out

of two cups.'* Did he really say this with a straight face? He certainly now knew its source, 1 Corinthians 10:21 – 'Ye cannot drink the cup of the Lord, and the cup of devils'.

Two weeks after the first guitar-audition, Dylan introduced the lucky winner to the rest of the band. As with the *Desire* combo, a trio had originally put all four guitarists through their paces – bassist Drummond, drummer Jim Keltner (whom Dylan had been trying to get to tour with him since December 1977) and Dylan on piano, sitting in for that stalwart of the Muscle Shoals sound, Spooner Oldham. 'Tim recommended me . . . I [ended up] rehearsing all these songs with those guys for about three weeks, and then Bob hired me to tour with them.' Fortunately for Tackett, appointed bandleader Drummond was a fan of his guitar-playing. Though Pechizkjian got the initial nod, Dylan changed his mind after a couple of days. Tackett was recalled and stayed.

Not that Tackett was told there was a tour, simply that Dylan 'was getting ready to be on *Saturday Night Live*', as indeed he was. Dylan had decided he wanted only the best, which meant a fair share of non-believers. Fortunately, he was no Linda McCartney,[†] even if he hired a personal assistant who was both a musician and a recent convert, and instructed him, 'Look, I need someone to talk to the guys, the crew and the band. Right now, I don't want to defend my faith; I don't want to have to explain to them what's going on. So, I want someone to be there and if need be, explain to them what's going on.'

Arthur Rosato was one of those Dylan specifically asked Dave Kelly to interact with, 'I would talk to him a bit about Dylan's faith.' Rosato, despite being wholly damned, was an increasingly trusted lieutenant who was now put in charge of the desk, rolling tape throughout rehearsals, 'whenever it seemed like an arrangement was close', and documenting all the shows, making 1979-81 a goldmine of great lost performances, none of them disinterred till 2017's *Trouble No More* eight-CD smorgasbord.

---

* A song with this title appears on a cassette inlay-card recorded during January 1980 rehearsals.

† Apparently, the lady, who insisted on employing fellow vegetarians, fired a soundman for eating a burger. He exacted his revenge by isolating her painfully off-key vocal on 'Hey Jude' live, and circulating the tape.

The band Dylan was taking on the road, returning to the theatres he'd played in the Sixties for the intimacy and intensity he needed to really get his message across, was as extravagant as the 1978 band, when he had been playing large arenas and even stadia. Having replenished the coffers, he was emptying them. It was a crack band, which came with belt and braces, including – he hoped – the two girlsingers who were an integral part of *Slow Train Coming*. Carolyn Dennis, though, declined to share the stage with Helena again, so Mona Lisa Young took her place.

From the second rehearsal on September 26th, these gospel-inspired girls were at the fulcrum of the sound. More surprisingly, given the personal nature of the new songs and Beckett's battle to get even a light brushing of brass on the album, there was a horn section, too, brought in for ten days from October 2nd, as they worked up horn arrangements on 'Slow Train', 'Gotta Serve Somebody' (both featured on *Trouble No More*), 'Gonna Change My Way Of Thinking' and 'When You Gonna Wake Up', as well as 'Covenant Woman', 'Pressing On', 'Solid Rock' and 'Blessed Is The Name' from the latest batch of brimstone ballads.

Dylan rather seems to have expected these professional players to vamp to the songs. Rosato looked on in wonder, 'When the horns appeared, he asked them to just play along. The horn players [we]re not used to doing that . . . Bob was a little disappointed that they just didn't [want to] jam.' Such a lack of flexibility, along with a word from accountant Marty Feldman, sealed their fate:

> **Dave Kelly**: It was about a week before we went on the road. He actually sat down on a sofa . . . and said, 'What do you think? The horns or the girls?' . . . [But] they tried lots of different things. Bob was really in charge of that. He'd get the [band] to change the tempo, the style . . . He was even telling the girls how to sing.

The really extraordinary thing about these rehearsals is the sheer ferocity and commitment in Dylan's singing. He had always sung, not busked, at rehearsals; in many ways they were his favourite part of the touring process. With no burden of expectation to meet, he could play what he wanted, how he wanted. Here, though, he seemed incapable of holding back. On the first day of rehearsals with the girls, he attacked

'Gotta Serve Somebody', 'When You Gonna Wake Up' and 'Slow Train' one after the other, like he was reliving that night in Tucson at the microphone.

But what made these rehearsals unique was that Dylan was bringing in new songs to teach the band with a refreshing regularity, not as a diversion but to build up a set of songs from the ground up. Kelly recalls, 'He did write an awful lot of [new] stuff and he did try them [all] out. There must have been twenty songs that he pooled from to do the tour . . . He'd go into his little room and come out with a new song.' A couple of these he only did once – 'I Hear Jesus Calling' and 'Stand By Faith' – the latter being unexpectedly copyrighted in its end-of-day rehearsal state.

Of the *Slow Train* discards, 'Ye Shall Be Changed', with new lyrics, was also worked on, but never took, while 'No Man Righteous' – for all its talk of perfection – was left imperfect. And the only time he attempted 'Trouble In Mind' – the b-side of his current single – was at Rick Ruskin's audition, when he also tried out 'Ain't Too Proud To Repent'. All these songs, less than six months old, were placed with the 'old things [that] are passed away'.

The last of the wholly new songs to make the live set was 'Saving Grace' (though, oddly enough, it was the first post-*Slow Train* song to be copyrighted). Hearing him run down the song for the first time was a spine-tingling moment that would go unacknowledged. The best of the bunch, though, was probably 'What Can I Do for You?', which took its cue from Job 5:7, 'Yet a man is born unto trouble, as the sparks fly upward.' First attempted at a couple of the September guitar-auditions with dummy lyrics – Dylan tentatively picking out the chords at the piano – the song was one he was keen to teach the band. (Reissue producer Jeff Rosen missed something of a trick using nothing – save for a couple of brass arrangements – from these revelatory rehearsals on the 2017 set.)

Enjoying the process, and adapting to every challenge – even the loss of the brass section – Dylan reluctantly called a temporary halt on proceedings in order to fly to New York, and debut three *Slow Train* songs on the smash-hit comedy show, *Saturday Night Live*. It meant four whole days away, and at least three preparatory run-throughs of songs they'd been rehearsing for the past three weeks, and knew like the back hand of God. But it had a huge weekly audience, a Dylan-friendly demographic, and on October 20th, a sympathetic host and confirmed Dylan fan, ex-Python Eric Idle.

It was the last time Idle hosted the show, and he found Dylan's behaviour curiouser and curiouser in the lead-up to the recording: 'He seemed very paranoid. He'd get off the elevator at the Essex House hotel on our floor, and then [would] stay with me while he asked [Idle's wife] Tania to go up one flight of stairs and make sure there was no-one outside his door. There never was . . . [But] he was highly aware of all that went on around him.' Perhaps he was hoping it was George Harrison, a close friend of both Idle and Dylan, whom Dylan thought he was meeting in New York for dinner. But for reasons unknown, Harrison had checked out of his hotel early, and Dylan seemed convinced, or so he informed Kelly, that it was some personal sleight on Harrison's part: 'The minute Bob checked in, George checked out!'

Maybe the misunderstanding added a cutting edge to the version of 'I Believe In You' Dylan sang that Saturday night, the highlight of a fifteen-minute performance that had none of the looseness of the rehearsals, but had all of the band's muscular musicality. Another ex-Beatle was sat at home, six blocks away, watching his old friend. Not knowing he himself would not grow old, he thought Dylan looked old. Lennon's damning verdict was fair, but actually poor. It was neither. Dylan just looked a little nervous, like he was playing with Johnny Cash again, and didn't know if his audience would ever forgive him.

Paranoid he might be, but Dylan had long known: just because one is paranoid, doesn't mean they aren't out to get you. A fan who stalked him until he secured his autograph just before the SNL filming bore an uncanny resemblance to another 'superfan', Mark Chapman, who a year later would ask Lennon for an autograph and instead of thanking him, gunned him down. It wasn't Chapman, but that didn't stop one English tabloid running the photo as a front-page story shortly after Chapman snuffed out Lennon's light, claiming that Dylan had been on Chapman's own, provisional hit-list. If so, his saving grace was still looking out for him.

The former New Yorker had not enjoyed his time in Manhattan, and was glad to get back to his Rundown refuge and the resumption of rehearsals, this time with a purpose he was prepared to share with the band: fourteen nights at the recently-refurbished Warfield Theatre in one of the seedier parts of Dirty Harry's domain. It was here Dylan intended to unveil the songs he had spent the past six months shaping to fit the rigid scriptural slant of a fellowship he barely knew, and was already starting to distance himself from. He was heading into another storm, with his own gang of angels to keep him company. Look out Arizona, and all points west of the Jordan.

4.6

November 1979 to May 1980:
A Man With A Message

Faith: Belief without evidence in what is told, by one who speaks without knowledge, of things without parallel.

Ambrose Bierce, *The Devil's Dictionary*.

God created the world, but it is the Devil who keeps it going.

Tristan Bernard.

When he went through his Christian period . . . he came up to me and said, 'Remember that time you asked me about God and the devil? Well, I'll tell you now,' and he launched into this fundamentalist [tirade]. I said, 'Bobby, be careful. All of that was written by poets like us; but this interpretation of yours seems a little brainwashed.'

Joni Mitchell, 1997.

A Last Judgment is Necessary because Fools Flourish.

William Blake, Gilchrist's *Life*, 1880 ed. vol. 2.

I said [to him] that . . . Blake's Christ was Forgiveness and Mercy, not Judgement and Wrath. And Dylan said, 'Sure, but He is coming to judge.' . . . He's saying that our evil has gotten so thick that it's going to come back on itself . . . His [new] songs are [all] about the End of Days.

Allen Ginsberg, 1980.

Check [out] Elijah the prophet. He could make rain. Isaiah the prophet, even Jeremiah, see if their brethren didn't want to bust their brains for telling it right like it is.

Bob Dylan, to Martin Keller, 5th July 1983.

Years ago, they used to say I was a prophet. I used to say, 'No I'm not a prophet.' They say, 'Yes, you are. You're a prophet.' I said . . . 'Not me.' . . . Now I come out and say Jesus Christ is the answer. They say, 'Bob Dylan's no prophet.'

Bob Dylan, onstage rap, January 1980.

Even preaching would be an extension of what I am and what I do and the music I play.

Bob Dylan, to Denise Worrell, November 1985.

I think he was trying to make a point and he made it – to himself.

Anonymous audience member, interviewed post-concert in Albuquerque, December 1979.

They were one degree short of buying fruit off the sidewalk and throwing it at him.

Tim Drummond.

★

It came without warning. Sure, the last album had sounded like a bulletin from a black-and-white world, but so had *John Wesley Harding*, an album from which he'd barely ever played anything – save 'Watchtower' – live. And there were no indications from Dylan or promoter Bill Graham that the fourteen shows at the Warfield would be more of the same. Only when the girlsingers walked on stage on November 1st, sans Dylan, and began their own six-song gospel set, did the first-night audience sense they might have inadvertently stumbled on a 'salvation ceremony'.

When Dylan finally did take the stage, he proceeded to play seven songs from *Slow Train Coming*, one after the other, ending the first half with a new song, 'Covenant Woman', about someone who 'got a contract with the Lord/ Way up yonder, great will be her reward.' Hardly a radical departure. After another gospel interlude from one of the girls, Dylan completed the *Slow Train* sequence, before debuting seven more new songs – previously, most Dylan fans' idea of manna from heaven – bearing titles like 'Hanging on To a Solid Rock Made Before The Foundation Of The World', 'Saved By The Blood Of The Lamb' and 'When They Came For Him In The Garden'. Even Pastor Larry Myers was taken aback by what he saw and heard:

> I have not been in the middle of anything quite like [that] before or since. The atmosphere . . . at the Warfield was charged with electricity that was palpable . . . As the [girls'] set progressed, some in the audience grew impatient and began yelling for Dylan to come on . . . [Then] the stage would go dark . . . Tim Drummond would count down – 3 -4 – and on the downbeat, the spots would come on and 'Gotta Serve Somebody' would start, and the power of the music [was] just unbelievable . . . Song after song, no in-between song patter, just the music . . . all new music. After a while, some would start yelling for their old favourites . . . Toward the end of the show I suppose a few walked out, but what I remembered most was seeing the audience sitting and listening intently.

If Myers's take on the show was bound to be sympathetic to the master of ceremonies, many of those who attended as interested observers felt there was an underlying 'Fuck You' to the choice of material and the unremitting nature of its presentation. City Books employee Raymond Foye, who had gone there with Dylan's old friend, Lawrence Ferlinghetti, found 'it . . . a disturbing experience because Dylan was so obviously possessed and his intensity definitely had an edge of hostility to it.' Joel Selvin, who had been sent there in his professional capacity as the *San Francisco Chronicle*'s rock critic, tapped into 'an undercurrent of hostility in the audience. I certainly picked up on that, and spoke for that element in my review. He was asking for it and he knew it.'

For those onstage, the experience was no less disorienting, even if a month of rehearsals meant that they, and they alone, knew what was coming. An experienced hand like Jim Keltner thought he knew his west coast audiences. But maybe not: 'They were all out there with their pot and ready to party, ready to rock & roll, [then] they would yell and scream. They'd holler at him, they'd curse.'

Many of those who did not holler and curse, simply walked out. Or so the reviewers would have their readers believe. According to Gail S. Tagashire of the *San Jose Mercury News*, 'There were loud boos . . . [and] over half the first-floor audience walked out.' And yet, Tagashire herself stayed, revelling in the intensity of Dylan's performance, '[He] is not some pained imitation of Neil Diamond, but a Dylan singing from a hurt in the heart . . . This one's for real. It's honest and true.'

Other so-called reporters interested only in 'good copy' simply read her and other reviews on the wire and honed in on the 'news' that Dylan fans had 'walked out'. Robert Hilburn, reviewing the following night's show, had already heard such stories, and vainly tried to correct them with his *L.A. Times* hat on, 'A few people did leave early, but there was no general uprising as was reported on opening night.' But even he could not turn back the wave of false reports, especially once they were picked up by the ever-eager *Newsweek* (December 17th), doing their usual hatchet-job, disguised as reporting.

Not surprisingly, Dylan was fuming, though his only comment the following night – the night Hilburn reviewed, after Bill Graham phoned and begged him to 'come up and see this' for himself, after 'the local papers killed the show' – came after 'someone in the audience shouted something affectionate at him', and Dylan responded, 'You'll be all right if you don't read the newspapers.'

Some months later, in Toronto, he would broaden his targets while narrowing his current reading-list down to one, 'I been reading all kinds of books my whole life, magazines, books, whatever I could get my hands on, and I never found any truth in any of them. But these things in The Bible they seem to uplift me and tell me the Truth.'

As the tour progressed, the verbal digs at the media would grow steadily more sarcastic. In Tempe, ten days after San Francisco, he talked about how 'we opened there about a month ago, [and] three or four people [sic] walked out because they didn't like the message. But we're still here now. Don't you walk out before you hear the message.' The following May, his first words to a Connecticut crowd were, 'Anybody left yet? They tell me everybody leaves at these shows. It's a little hard to see out there.' In Syracuse, too, he reaffirmed, 'All I read is The Bible, that's all I read. So, you can quote me on that if you want. Once in a while I look in the newspapers.'

In truth, he went out of his way to read all the reviews of the opening Warfield show, at a nearby greasy spoon diner, and in particular Joel Selvin's, going to the unheard-of lengths of phoning Selvin up and telling his wife, *in absentia*, that his reviewer credentials had been revoked. And there seems little doubt it was Selvin he had in mind when he told Scott Cohen in 1985, 'The man did not understand any of the concepts behind any part of the show, and he wrote an anti-Bob Dylan thing. He probably never liked me anyway . . . I don't mind being put down, but intense personal hatred is another thing. It was like an opening-night critic burying a show on Broadway. This particular review got picked up and printed in all the newspapers of the cities we were going to play.'

Actually, Selvin was a big Dylan fan, as were many of the reviewers, notably Leslie Goldberg, who summed up opening night in his *San Francisco Bay Guardian* review, thus: 'Jesus himself couldn't have looked more vulnerable, more lonely, more naked than Bob Dylan did onstage that night . . . It was as if Bob Dylan had already prepared a part for the audience and the audience, without actually realizing what they were doing, played it to the hilt. It was a good thing no one had thought to bring the rotten tomatoes.'

Dylan's old sparring-partner from the streets of Philadelphia, *Craw-daddy* founder Paul Williams, also attended that first night, thinking he might perhaps review it, and wrote touchingly about the moment when Dylan comes back for a second encore with barely half of the punters waiting to see when, or if, he returns:

> [Finally] he [came and] sat at the piano, almost out of sight, accompany-ing himself singing, 'I'm just pressing on to the higher calling of my Lord' . . . his best singing of the night, super – [then he] got up. We assumed he was walking off for the night, but he came around the piano and then made his way to the mike at the front of the stage. He beckoned, and other band-members started to come back on . . . He clapped his hands together a few times, and went on with the song.

Inspired by the experience, Williams (and his then-wife) came back half a dozen times more during the residency, gradually convinced that a mere review would not suffice; what was required was a book-length rebuttal of the reviews. What he wrote and effectively self-published was a monograph called *What Happened?*, that spoke from the heart of a non-believer about what a transformative experi-ence these shows were.* It must have hit the spot, because the convert

---

* The entire text of *What Happened?*, as well as Williams's 1980 companion mono-graph, *One Year Later*, can be found in the Omnibus Press anthology of his Dylan writings, *Watching The River Flow* (1997).

himself, via Howard Alk, purchased a box of books to give to other people who had 'tried to drive me from this town'.

This Dylan was pressing on. And nothing, not even the promoter's pleas, was going to knock him off-course. Tim Drummond would fondly remember 'standing right there with Bob when Bill [Graham] said, "Please, Bob, just sing one old song." And Dylan wouldn't.' Fred Tackett also recalls, 'Some people [at the Warfield] were very vocal about wanting to hear some old songs. I remember one guy had a sign that said, "Jesus Loves Your Old Songs Too."'

It made no difference. The show remained as set in stone as '66, save for the final night, the 16th – one of Dylan's finest-ever shows – which added a one-off performance of 'No Man Righteous', prefaced with a brief rap that proved Dylan hadn't lost his sense of humour, 'We're gonna do something right here that we haven't done before. This is a song that nobody knows. Nobody in this band even knows it – that's how I can tell who really wants to stick with me and who doesn't.'

Of course, the band *did* know it. They'd rehearsed it a number of times, Drummond and Oldham having both played on the original studio version. At least it showed a Dylan who, over the fortnight, had gradually relaxed into his righteous role, even cracking the odd un-PC joke. I doubt his remark, the previous night, that he had heard 'they won't [even] let the Iranian students into the whorehouses in Nevada now', would have gone down well with those who took him to task for alleged anti-Arab sentiments on 'Slow Train'.

Actually, he was simply responding to a section in *The Late Great Planet Earth* that advised those concerned by current events to 'keep your eyes on the Middle East. If this is the time that we believe it is, this area will become a constant source of tension . . . It will become so severe that only Christ or the Antichrist can solve it.' At the same time, Lindsey warned his fellow Americans that the domestic economy was on the brink of collapse and 'the only chance of slowing up this decline in America is a widespread spiritual awakening'. On that final night, Dylan flew the flag for the Lindsey plan in speech as well as song, prefacing 'Slow Train' with his longest rap to date:

> You know, we read in the newspaper every day, what a horrible situation this world is in. Now, 'God chooses the foolish things in this world to

confound the wise' [1 Corinthians 1:27]. Anyway, we know this world is
going to be destroyed, we know that. Christ will set up His kingdom in
Jerusalem for a thousand years, where the lion will lie down with the
lamb. Have you heard that before? I'm just curious to know, how many
believe that? [applause] All right. This is called 'Slow Train Coming'. It's
been coming a long time and it's picking up speed.

It was a defining moment, one that would be replicated a number of
times over the next six months, and it prefaces a 'Slow Train' that really
does seem bound for glory. Indeed, it's the version picked for the 2017
Trouble No More boxed-set – along with tonight's 'No Man Righteous'.
Yet neither included the rap that explicated and enhanced the ensuing
exegesis. Indeed, despite this transcendent evening being one of just
two complete shows captured by Rosato at the desk, it was not selected
as the one fall '79 gospel show to feature on said multi-disc set.* It
seems the revisionist Dylan would much rather rewrite history and/or
print the legend than re-examine his own religious mania. Often, in
the next six months, he would quote Scripture from an impressive
multiplicity of sources, confirming not only attendance but his own
studiousness at the Bible classes.

The pupil-turned-pulpiteer first emerged on November 10th, when
he prefaced 'Solid Rock' by quoting 1 Corinthians 1:18: 'For the preaching of the cross is to them that perish foolishness; but unto us which
are saved, it is the power of God.' Two shows later he was quoting 2
Timothy 3 – 'And the last days of perilous times shall be at hand and
men will become lovers of their own selves' – possibly a thinly-veiled
dig at those who took the tag, 'City of Brotherly Love' a tad literally. (If
so, it would not be the last.) On the penultimate night, he returned to
Corinthians to remind any recidivists in the cheap seats, 'If the gospel
is hid, it is hidden to those that are lost.' [2 Corinthians 4:3] It was
almost like he was prepping for his final exam: four charity shows at
the Santa Monica Civic Auditorium, beginning three days later.

He'd last played Santa Monica in 1965, when L.A. was not his hometown. This time, he knew the Vineyard Fellowship would be there to

---

* A rap-free, incomplete San Diego show would be the 'bonus' 2-CD set for those who
bought the set direct.

lend their support and bask in the reflective glow of their new proselyt-
izer. Robert Hilburn was also there, to review his second Dylan show
in sixteen days, and remembers 'people lifting their hands up – as a sign
of spiritual support or agreement – as he sang'. Indeed, on that first
night, when Dylan began to ask, 'How many of you know that Satan
has been defeated by the cross?' hundreds in the sold-out 3,200-seat
Civic Auditorium cheered. He smiled, looked at his vocal trio and said,
'Well, it doesn't look like we're alone tonight.'

Like a Trappist monk released from his vow of silence, the usually
taciturn performer soon couldn't shut up. At the second Santa Monica
show, after the usual band introductions, he gently admonished the
largely Christian audience to 'remember now, you wrestle not against
flesh and blood but against principalities and power – and the ruthless-
ness of the darkness of this world, spiritual wickedness in higher
places', thus demonstrating he knew even the little-read Book of Ephe-
sians [6:12]. But the most intense sermonising rap at that night's
revivalist meeting came before a frenetic 'Solid Rock', as Dylan imagined himself back in a Colorado tent in 1964:

> We're living in the last of the End times. I don't know if anybody's told
> you that before, but I'm telling ya . . . [But] we don't care about no atom
> bomb. 'Cause we know this world is going to be destroyed – there's no
> other way – and Christ will set up His kingdom in Jerusalem for a thou-
> sand years. When the lion lies down with the lamb, you know, the lion
> will eat straw on that day. Also, if a man doesn't live to be a hundred
> years old, he will be called accursed. [Isaiah 65:20] That's interesting,
> isn't it? . . . And if any man have not the spirit of Christ in him, he is a
> slave to bondage. [Romans 8:15] You know bondage? I know you *all*
> know bondage. So, you need something just a little bit tough to hang on
> to . . . This song is called, 'Hanging On To A Solid Rock Made Before
> The Foundation Of The World'. And if you don't have that to hang on
> to, you'd better look into it.

Backstage, though, Dylan was feeling increasingly uncomfortable,
surrounded as he was by jostling members of the fellowship. As someone who had previously always refused to join any club that would
have him, he was a reluctant conscript. At times Helena looked on

askance, '[They were] pressuring him a lot, about a lot of things . . . They were not allowing him to live. They were just . . . too much of a headache. One time [backstage] he said to me, "God, it's awfully tight [in here]." . . . Also, he found a lot of hypocrisy from those people . . . saying one thing and doing another . . . We had a lot of talks about [that].' At least out front they were with him all the way, making for some memorable shows in his adopted hometown after slightly disappointing gigs at the Inglewood Forum in 1974 and 1978.

Little did he know he was heading into a storm that would make the British 1966 shows look like a tea party on a summer's day. After L.A., there was a three-day respite, before Dylan book-ended four shows in Arizona: two in Tempe, two in Tucson, with double-headers in San Diego and Albuquerque, the last shows of a momentous year.

When he rolled into Tempe on the 25th, he was already going down the road feeling bad. But unlike the previous year, this time it was not any oppression of the spirit. According to the *Arizona Republic*, 'It was touch and go there for a while on Sunday. Bob Dylan had complained of a cold and made some noise like he might call off Sunday's show unless he could see a doctor. He was talked into taking the stage when he was assured a doctor would be waiting backstage to treat him.'

If he was feeling low before the show, the reception the girlsingers got when they began their six-song gospel set did not elevate his mood. As Regina McCrary recalled, '[The reaction in Arizona] really blew him away – [the fact] that it was a college crowd . . . Normally the audience would listen [to the story I told] and they would respond.* This crowd wanted Bob Dylan. They were real rowdy. Dylan was really disappointed.' Not so much disappointed, as angry; 'who threw that fucking glass' angry. He was still steaming mad six years later, when he told Cameron Crowe, 'College kids showed the most disrespect . . . where my so-called fans were. And all hell would break loose: [shouting:] "Take off that dress!" "We want rock'n'roll!"'

After a particularly poignant 'Precious Angel', Dylan finally had enough of one particularly persistent heckler and told the lighting man, 'Turn the light on that man over there.' Again asserting that Jesus

---

* The story, which she told at every show between November 1979 and June 1981, was about a poor sinner without a ticket to ride who Jesus nonetheless allows to board the train of salvation.

was 'the Lamb of God which taketh away the sins of the world', he wanted to know, 'How many of you understand that?' Dissatisfied with the response, he launched into a 'Slow Train' that didn't take long to pick up speed. But still the requests for pre-Christian songs kept a-comin'. In the end, as a bemused Dave Kelly looked on, 'He [simply] had to talk. I don't think they were walking out, but they were definitely heckling. They were insisting on the old songs.'

Before 'Solid Rock', he broke it to the students: they were wasting their time getting an education because 'the world as we know it now is being destroyed. I'm sorry to say it, but it's the truth. In a short time – maybe in three years, maybe five years, could be ten years – there's gonna be a war . . . called the battle of Armageddon.' Not surprisingly, there was no second encore as Dylan retired to his sick-bed, girding his loins for the following night's rematch.

With the next night's hecklers knowing what to expect, this time they resolutely refused to be silenced either by those around them or by the man they'd paid to see.* It didn't take long for them to make their feelings known. Just two songs in, Dylan was already calling them 'a pretty rude bunch' before launching into a five-minute tirade about 'the spirit of the Antichrist', interrupted repeatedly by shouts of 'rock'n'roll'. An exasperated Dylan rises to the bait, mid-rap, 'If you wanna rock'n'roll, you can go down and rock'n'roll. You can go see Kiss, and . . . rock'n'roll all your way down to the pit!'

Far from making the hecklers take stock or pick up their feet and walk, Dylan's retort merely lit a fire under them, forcing him to again tell the lighting man, 'Turn the lights on in here. I want to see these people. Turn some lights on. Give them some light.' Tackett recalls, 'We played a couple of songs with all the lights on. Somebody in the audience yelled, "Turn off the lights, Bobby," and Bob said, "No, I think we had better leave the lights on a little while." '

Refusing to change course, Dylan warns the crowd, 'There's many of these [false prophets] walking around. They might not come right out and say they're God, but they're just waiting for the opportunity. [But] there is only one God! Let me hear you say who that God is?

---

* Though there are beautiful soundboard tapes of both shows, the three known audience tapes perhaps give a better flavour of the polarized reaction out front.

[mixed shouts] *Their* God makes promises he doesn't keep.' Cue a 'When You Gonna Wake Up' fresh from the Free Trade Hall.

The cries of 'Rock'n'roll!' continued to reverberate, until Dylan declaimed, 'You still want to rock'n'roll?! [Well, lemme] tell you . . . there's only two kinds of people: There's saved people and there's *lost* people.' He warmed to his theme in the longest rap of the evening, between 'Do Right To Me Baby' and 'Solid Rock', unambiguously telling anyone who'd not been paying attention exactly who might be saved, and by whom:

> Jesus Christ is that solid rock. He's supposed to come two times. He came once already . . . Now, He's coming back again. You gotta be prepared for this. Because no matter what you read in the newspaper, that's all deceit. The real truth is that He's coming back . . . And Christ will set up His kingdom . . . and He'll rule it from Jerusalem. As far out as that might seem, this is what The Bible says.

Actually, it was what one specific, left-field interpretation of the last book in The Bible said. At this juncture, the more persistent hecklers changed tack. They began to ask for specific songs, only to be met with short shrift whether it was from 1963 – 'That's right. I told you the times they are a-changin' twenty years [sic] ago. And I don't believe I've ever lied to you. I don't think I said anything that's been a lie. I never told you to vote for nobody. Never told you to follow nobody' – or 1966: 'I'll tell you about getting stoned! What do you want to know about getting stoned?'

Rather than give the paying punters either song, he cut the set short, ending with 'In The Garden' – the first time since 1966 he'd refused to do an encore – which he prefaced with another memo to all unbelievers, 'Remember what I said, if you ever hear it some other time, that there is a truth and a life and a way.' It had been an evening of high drama, the like of which he had not experienced in thirteen years. If he failed to change many minds, the experience certainly changed him.

Less than four weeks into his mission, the rock'n'rollers were not about to leave him be. A delegation from The American Atheists were threatening to picket shows in Tucson in a fortnight's time, something brought to Dylan's attention by local DJ Bruce Heiman, who called him up at his hotel the night before he rode into Tucson to ask him about 'the music you're playing today and the different message you're trying to get across'. Dylan made it plain, 'I don't sing any song which hasn't been given to me by the Lord to sing . . . and whatever the old message was, The Bible says, "All things become new, old things are passed away." I guess this group doesn't believe that. Are they against the doctrine of Jesus Christ, or that He died on the cross or that man was born into sin? Just what exactly are they protesting [about]?'

Heiman – who was 'somewhat surprised that when we did chat, he was pleasant, personable and even complimentary of the initiative I employed to get through to him' – helpfully explained that 'the Atheists are against any sort of religion', at which point in the ten-minute inter-view Dylan delineates his position, 'Christ is no religion. We're not talking about religion . . . Jesus Christ is the way, the truth and the life.'

The local Atheists' chapter probably did not confine themselves to just picketing the two Tucson shows. A couple of unbelievers – who may have been at Tempe and thus knew how to push Dylan's button – snuck inside and began calling out for some rock'n'roll. They did not have to wait long for Dylan's response, 'I know all about rock'n'roll. I been rock'n'rolling when you w[ere] in diapers . . . Do you know about the end of times, though? I'm just curious. I know you know about rock'n'roll. But do you know about the end of times? The last days?'

These repeated cries of 'rock'n'roll' actually gave Dylan an idea; one he'd used at a previous pit-stop where unbelievers accused him of betraying Christ – the Free Trade Hall. He hired a crew to ask people leaving the show/s in Albuquerque their response to what they'd heard, intending to use the most trenchant in a radio ad promoting the next leg of the gospel tour from hell.

Sure enough, the crew captured one unhappy punter who com-plained, 'I was kinda disappointed. I wanted to hear rock'n'roll. Rock'n'roll!', the perfect introductory voice for a one-minute radio ad promoting the North-East shows in January that went on to suggest listeners decide for themselves. Most of the other responses, though, were not deemed fit for purpose, especially the more overtly hostile:

'I can tell you what I think. It was disgusting. Dylan wasn't here. He really should have put a bullet through his brain five years ago.'

'Tell me what you thought of the show?' 'No.'

'He acted like he was doing us a favour when he was singing the songs.'

'The music was great. [But] the message was a little redundant. It was twenty-five songs and one message.'

'I had no idea it was going to be like this. And it's really a drag. He wouldn't play any of his old songs. It was a total let down. I'm never gonna listen to Bob Dylan again.'

It was perhaps in response to comments like these that Dylan came out and said from the stage, the second night in Albuquerque, 'I was reading [sic] something somebody said [along the lines,] "I like the music, but I can't get the message." . . . That's like saying, "I like the eye, but the nose, I just can't quite place. The ears are okay, but the neck just don't work."' It made for a fraught end to the first leg of the gospel tour, made yet more fraught when one of his fellow soul-travellers got into it with him one night in the hotel:

Dave Kelly: Halfway through the tour one of the girl[singer]s disappears . . . They had a big row . . . [Their relationship] was only a rumour until the big split up, when it became pretty obvious . . . I remember her throwing things around the room and Bob [just] standing there.

Though it would signal the end for Bob and Helena, it was hardly the end of speculation about Dylan's penchant for black girlsingers. When a story broke in January 1980 that he had been seen buying a $25,000 engagement ring in a Seattle jeweller while playing three nights at the Paramount, Seattle journalist Patrick MacDonald contacted his office for a quote, only to be told, 'There are apparently several women involved. Nobody here knows who they are,' the first and last time anyone at the office ever broke the code of professed ignorance. His ostensible publicist, Paul Wasserman, muddied things further by telling a Toronto journalist, 'He has had a lot of women telling him a lot of things.'

The ring could conceivably have been for Helena's replacement, were it not that she was already married, as Carolyn Dennis returned to the band. Dylan still seemed inclined to bite into forbidden fruit. According to Dennis, Dylan was somewhat upset that his former lover chose not to rekindle their relationship, insisting to him they maintain 'only a professional, platonic relationship'. Indeed, her tenure with her fellow salvation singers would only last for a single leg of the gospel tour.

Her baptism was not one of fire, but of ice. The first show in Port-land, Oregon, on January 10th, had to be rearranged when a snowstorm of apocalyptic proportions blew in. Even the second night was in doubt. Spooner Oldham expected an empty hall, 'We were driving into the city that evening . . . the power was out on that side of town. It was total darkness, there was a lot of snow and the wind was howling . . . but that didn't seem to deter folks any. I was pretty amazed at that.' The set remained unchanged – despite working on a new song at rehearsals called, somewhat ironically given Dylan's carnal thoughts for Dennis, 'Drinkin' From Two Cups'.

At least for now Dylan reined in the raps, save for a single, salutary exception on night two: 'The deity of Jesus just drives people crazy sometimes . . . Some people hate Jesus and they throw toilet rolls at us. Jesus separates all people. [But] The Bible says, "If any man should preach you another gospel, let that man be accursed." ' [Galatians 1:8]

Remarkably, his commitment to the material stayed undimmed throughout a full month of shows, as did his vocal dexterity. After one particular display of vocal gymnastics – 'just doing incredible things, [like] back-phrasing, where he'll start to play a song and he won't start singing right away, he'll wait and start singing . . . catch up' – guitarist Tackett called him out, 'Bob, you were out on a ledge tonight.' He promptly 'did the exact same thing again . . . the very next night.'

He had rarely sung better, while the band stuck to him like Jeremi-ah's critics. As for Dylan's critics in the media, they were largely missing in action that winter, as Dylan, having warmed up in Oregon and Washington, steered clear of the east and west coasts and took his mes-sage to Middle America, a strategy Tackett considered 'very clever', playing 'places where people don't see Bob very often'.

He even returned to Colorado, where he had first experienced fire-brand tent-evangelism sixteen years earlier, playing three shows in Denver, close to the Naropa Institute where his old friend Ginsberg taught 'Poetics'. Sure enough, Allen brought along a cabal of inter-ested students to the final show, and seemed delighted to see Dylan 'trying to get out of himself – [to] transcend himself into something else – which I thought was healthy . . . It was [also] nice to hear Dylan being so outspoken.'

Backstage, though, he gently chastised the singer for not letting in the Christ of Forgiveness and Mercy (see chapter heading). Dylan wasn't listening. Within days he would write 'Are You Ready?', a turgid tirade at anyone who refused to ride the rails of redemption. Triggered by Luke 12:40 – 'Be ye therefore ready also for the Son of Man cometh at an hour when ye think not' – it would be the last Dylan song which took its cue, its language and its message, chapter and verse, hook, line and sinkhole, from the gospels.

At least the Denver faithful restrained themselves from requesting old songs. But at the next pit stop, in Omaha, Dylan responded to requests for 'Tambourine Man' and 'Rolling Stone' with a clear statement of intent, 'We're not going to do any old songs tonight, so if that's what you want, you can leave right now.' And when in Birmingham, Alabama, a particularly persistent soul kept calling for 'Lay Lady Lay', Dylan dismissed the request and seemingly the song itself, 'Ha, ha, I don't do that anymore. I don't even know why I did it in the first place.'

As Dylan and the band headed towards the places that first stirred the melting pot of modern music – Memphis, Knoxville, Birmingham, Charleston – he perhaps hoped it might prove an immersive experience. It was almost too immersive at one point. As Dylan, Drummond and the girlsingers were being driven by Muscle Shoals studio assistant, Dick Cooper, from Nashville to Sheffield, Cooper remembers them stopping 'for burgers in Pulaski, Tennessee, birthplace of the Klan. There we were, three white boys and three gorgeous black chicks in spandex and sequins. The white waitresses out front were outraged; the black cooks in the back were delighted.'

They were all returning to Muscle Shoals – three months ahead of schedule – to complete Dylan's gospel narrative with the same co-producers as *Slow Train Coming* and the touring band who'd taken that album's message to the people, hoping to record the second part of the show they'd been touring for the past three months over the same four days – with 'Are You Ready?' as the hammering album-closer.

Unfortunately, only two songs really rise above the muddy morass that is *Saved*: 'A Satisfied Mind', a song made famous by Porter Wagoner that Dylan knew back in 1961, and 'Pressing On', which required a whole new arrangement and was all the better for the thought that went into it. On the fifth day, according to Wexler, 'We reexamined everything we'd done and wound up recutting two songs . . . [and] did a little touching up.' Things only got progressively worse.

Despite his previous experience with *Street-Legal*, when the album was knocked into shape in rehearsal and then knocked out of shape across five days of recording, Dylan had convinced himself *Saved* would come free and easy. Others – notably Arthur Rosato, who had been here before – was not so sure: 'Muscle Shoals is as far away as you could possibly be from anything. It was tiring. And Wexler didn't really have a clue how to work with Bob.'

For Keltner, playing on his first Dylan session in seven years, Wexler was simply the wrong call: 'Jerry Wexler was one of my idols, [but] we got this sound that was so clean. I think that maybe they were trying to revisit the sound of *Slow Train Coming*. And you can't do that with Bob . . . It didn't want to be anything like *Slow Train*. It wanted to have a big, open, live, exciting sound to match the praise [in] the songs.'

One thing was for sure. Wexler wasn't about to get his way a second time when it came to stopping Dylan from cutting the thing live, or losing the headphones. As the producer gamely admitted, 'Whatever we did was live. Bob might run it down on piano or guitar, just singing and playing the background, until we had a rough shape in our minds . . . [But] as soon as it sounded right . . . we'd just keep recording . . . Bob knew what he wanted.'

Dylan *always* knew what he wanted. Getting it was the problem, and had been since the Minneapolis *Blood on the Tracks* sessions. Part of it was simply down to his disregard for the process. Tackett's description of the *Saved* sessions says it all, 'We recorded everything. There was very little overdubbing . . . We did this for a few days, and then we got in the bus and took off for the next bunch of shows [sic] . . . Bob said, "You guys mix it and send me a copy of it."' In that sense, *Saved* really was *Street-Legal* Mk. 2. And like that album, it would cut the ground away from him just as he seemed to be on another commercial high.

Having long ago wrestled back control of the sequencing of his albums and their artwork, CBS were powerless to stop him delivering the album he wanted, but as Dave Kelly recalls, 'CBS put a lot of pressure on him . . . By the second [gospel] album, they were like, "Oh no, you're going to continue this Jesus stuff?" . . . One of the things he said to me was, "They don't necessarily have to release it. But I'm going to record the album I want."' And he had.

Of course, a little self-sabotage never did any harm, and in this instance the album cover gave Dylan the opportunity to rub people's faces in it, and made the marketing of the album a real *merde*-fest. He had commissioned artist Tony Wright to realize a vision he had 'of Jesus, of the hand coming down and these hands reaching up. And he [told me] at the same time he had this vision, he saw the whole album.' When Wright showed him the finished artwork, Dylan told him he 'thought the cover was wonderful. In fact, we wanted to have it posted up on Sunset Boulevard . . . Big bloody hand reaching down.'

Wright was impressed at just how uncompromising his commissioner was prepared to be. But when the artist began to talk to the label, he was in for a shock, 'They were so rude, so nasty about Bob Dylan and said how they weren't going to promote this record.'

Even his first-ever Grammy Award, for Best Rock Vocal on 'Gotta Serve Somebody' (in truth, not even in the top three vocals on *Slow Train Coming*), failed to convince the label to keep the faith. And they weren't alone in shrugging off the performance Dylan gave at the Shrine Auditorium on February 27th, when he was at his blessed best, for once, on a live national TV broadcast. That riveting rendition came after an exchange of words at rehearsal the afternoon prior to the broadcast, witnessed by Spooner Oldham, 'Somebody in the production staff asked Dylan . . . would he cut the tune short for production purposes. In other words, it was like four minutes and they wanted it three. And he said no.'

In fact, he would give the anxious producer a performance that went on till the crack of doom. Just when it seemed the song must end, he stepped back to let Tackett take a lead, before locating a harmonica from somewhere inside the ill-fitting penguin-suit he was wearing, blasting the news straight on through. Still he found the time and energy for just one more chorus, spelling it out for them all – CBS executives, Grammy executives, the American Atheists et al – to hear: not 'it may be the Lord', but 'it can be the Lord'!

John Lennon, sitting in his Dakota belfry, couldn't help laughing to himself, even feeling inspired enough to deliver a belated riposte of sorts to Dylan's superior pastiche of 'Norwegian Wood' by sending up 'Gotta Serve Somebody' with the solipsistic 'Serve Yourself'. But if he thought that by doing so, he'd get under his nemesis's skin, he was sorely mistaken. A dozen years later, their mutual publicist, Elliot Mintz asked Dylan for his response to Lennon's 'reply' song, 'It didn't

bother me, it intrigued me. Why would ['Gotta Serve Somebody']
affect him [in] such a way? . . . It was just a song.'

And there were plenty more where that came from. When the band
reassembled at Rundown on April 9th for three days of rehearsals,
prior to rumbling close to the Combat Zone, Dylan already had three
more he was anxious to work on. The most straightforward of the trio
was 'I Will Love Him', a panegyric to someone he had 'thought . . .
was a storybook myth, but I was wrong.'

Determined to continue to 'serve Him [and] glorify His name', he
had also come up with two songs that were much more like the old
Dylan. The more cryptic of the two was called 'Cover Down (Pray It
Through)', though its in-concert lyric offered no reason for its title.
Only in draft form did Dylan hint at its meaning: 'cover down/ beautiful flowers covering over a wicked man's grave . . . [but] flowers can't
hide the smell/ flowers can't protect the soul once it's been enslaved.'
Leaving the girls to 'pray it through', a term reflecting the intensity
one brings to the act, Dylan concentrated on 'the Pharaoh's army
trampling through the mud' and 'the Hebrew children redeemed by
blood', signs he'd gone back to the Old Testament.

Not that he had stopped being a Jew for Jesus. In another song he
began on the same page as 'Cover Down', probably called '(Oh Yeah)
You Know Me', he attacked those who 'would change the truth of God
into a lie right before my eyes'. He was continuing to pursue that
higher calling, knowing, 'You have overcome the world & I know in
You there's victory/ i look to those things that can't be seen, 'stead of
what my eyes want me to see/ I know in You there is the truth.'

But it was the altogether unambiguous 'Ain't Gonna Go To Hell (For
Anybody)' that was the most refreshing indication he had turned
inward again, holding up a mirror to his divided self and calling his
other self out: 'I can manipulate people as well as anybody/ Twist 'em
and turn 'em/ divide 'em and burn 'em/ I can make believe I love
almost anybody . . .' Now that sounded like Dylan singing Dylan. He
wasn't gonna go to hell for *anybody*. Not even Robert Johnson. Aligned
with an exquisite melody, which he played for the band at the piano as
the arrangement slowly took shape, it was a sign he was moving out of
the shadow of the Vineyard, even as he continued pressing on.

If he spent most of the three days' rehearsals working on these new
songs – three of which were debuted in the first week of

shows – another song he had been working on did not make an appearance in rehearsal, though it did surface at a coupla soundchecks, without ever finding a concert berth. This time, what appeared to be a song about his relationship with Christ was also about his relationship with a largely agnostic audience. Called 'Talk About What He Did For Me', it spoke to that audience in reproachful tones:

> You can talk about me . . . talk about the things I done
> You can talk about me, say everything under the sun
> Say that you told me jokes and I never did laugh
> Say I tried to love somebody, say I was a trip and a half.
> But when you talk about me, talk about what He did for me,
> Say that He took my death upon Himself and He nailed it to a tree.

Sadly, the song never got further than soundchecks, as Dylan settled quickly into a familiar set with two supplements – 'Cover Down' and 'Ain't Gonna Go To Hell' – as he took his Good News message to the Canadians, playing four nights in Toronto and four in Montreal. A letter he wrote from Toronto to a fellow Christian who had sent him a King James Bible, just in case he needed one, suggested he still felt he was fighting a losing battle: 'The Spirit of the Lord is calling people here in their beautiful and clean city, but they are more interested in lining up for *Apocalypse Now* than to be baptized and filled with the Holy Ghost.'

Nonetheless, Dylan chose to record the last three Toronto shows on multitrack, and film the last two, for a possible live album and TV special, all on his own dime. Perhaps surprisingly, he even allowed himself to be filmed delivering a long, rambling rap about the famous Tempe showdown:

> [I was] someplace, it was a college campus, I forget exactly where, Arizona, I think . . . Anyway, I read The Bible a lot, you know, I mean it just happens I do and . . . it says certain things in The Bible that I wasn't really aware of until just recently . . . So I [told them], This country is gonna come down and attack, and all these people, there must have been 50,000 . . . [voice of band member: 'If there was one.'] [Okay,] there was . . . maybe 3,000. [But] they all just booed. You know, like they usually do. They just booed. I said Russia's gonna attack the Middle East

and they all went 'boo' . . . And a month later Russia moved their troops into Afghanistan, and the whole situation changed. I'm not saying this to tell you that they was wrong and I was right, or anything like that. But these things mentioned in The Bible I pay mighty close attention to. ['Cause] it does talk about [the] Antichrist. Now we've had a lot of previews of what the Antichrist could be like . . . But he will eventually be defeated, too. Supernaturally defeated.

Just as in 1966, he was intent on filming these shows in an authentic way, capturing them raw and real. He was also hoping to maintain control of the process. But when the local film crew he'd hired proved they were not up to the task, he called in Howard Alk to save the day. Alk hired a filmmaker he knew to shoot the two Buffalo shows from onstage. It was just like Rolling Thunder, all over again. He was even treading the same boards in places, as he ventured from Toronto and Montreal down to Worcester, Hartford and Providence. In Hartford, he even talked about the reaction when he had first played the Bushnell Memorial Hall, not in 1975 but back in 1965, proving he really did have an elephantine memory:

> I remember I was singing a song called 'Desolation Row'. You're clapping now, you weren't clapping then! . . . They did not understand what I was singing about . . . It took a while for 'Desolation Row', 'Maggie's Farm', 'Subterranean Homesick Blues', all that stuff to really catch on . . . So, I'm always prepared for adversity. I always have been . . . ['Cause, y'know,] walking with Jesus is no easy trip, but it's the only trip.

Also in Hartford, for the first time in a year and a half he allowed a journalist to come up to his room, the same one he had invited to join him for a bath in Sydney, two years earlier. This time he was a man with a message, informing a sympathetic Karen Hughes that the tour was 'a kind of public rehearsal for his backup band and, more importantly, an "off-Broadway" try-out of new, drastically different songs, some from Slow Train Coming, most from Saved, and still others yet to be recorded,' and that he would be 'taking the show to New York, London, Japan and Australia after one more album'. For now, though, he was 'adamant about remaining silent through all channels other than his music'. Not that he was entirely silent, or particularly right-on, the following night in Hartford, when he began to talk about places he had been and the judgement to come:

> Joshua went to Canaan land and God told him to destroy all the people; every man, women and children there . . . They was just all defiled. [But] then there was some cities he said, 'Don't go in there yet.' Joshua wondered why, and God said, 'Because their iniquity is not yet full.' So now, when we started out this tour, we started out in San Francisco. It's kind of a unique town . . . I think either one third or two-thirds of the population there are homosexuals. I guess they're working up to 100%. Anyway, it's a dwelling place for homosexuals. I mean, they have homosexual politics . . . I don't mean it's going on in somebody's closet, I mean it's political. You know what I'm talking about? . . . I guess the iniquity's not yet full.

Fortunately, Hughes, who was writing her piece for the most right-on paper in America, the *Village Voice*, did not stick around to hear Dylan condemn some of his oldest friends to damnation. Nor did she catch one of the raps Dylan reserved for some musical peers, as he tarred them with the same satanic brush.

Springsteen, who remained something of a target for Dylan – as he would for most of the coming decade – was first to get it in the neck in Syracuse: 'Bruce, he's born to run. And unless he finds something, he's gonna keep a running. And you'll be chasin' him. But you can't run and you can't hide.' He got a second pasting in Providence: 'Satan has infested the rock'n'roll world. Ol' Jackson Browne he's running on empty. Bob Seeger he's running up against the wind. Bruce Springsteen, he's born to run and still running.'

Dylan had less luck remembering the title of the opening track of *Beggars Banquet* in Montreal, 'The Rolling Stones had a song called Lucifer – [or] something like that . . . Anyway, he's . . . still around.' It was a theme to many raps on the third and final leg of the gospel tour: Satan is Real, and real dangerous, and the man who had unwittingly recorded his first song about the Devil at his first album sessions, wanted to send a warning to all married women: 'Sometimes [when] I go on and on, they say, "Bob, don't preach so much." . . . [But] we're talking about Satan now as a spiritual being. He's not somebody you can see, but he can possess you.' The underlying message was that music itself can be used for good or for evil, as he explicated one night in Syracuse:

> When I was growing up, I used to listen to Hank Williams, Little Richard, Gene Vincent, Wilbraham Brothers, all those people. They formed my style in one way or another. But I can't help this type of music I play. This is just the kind of type I've always played. I know a lot of other people who play this sort of music tell you some strange things. ['Cause] the Devil's taken rock'n'roll music and he's used it for his purposes.

Evidently, he felt it wasn't just Kiss's audience who were listening to music that could lead them down to the pit. In Albany, he was equally unambiguous about the danger facing us all, 'Satan's getting ready to weave his masterpiece and you got to have some strong faith coming up, [for] even the very elect will be deceived.' He was testing the waters nightly, invoking the name of the beast:

> I know that some people might not believe there is a Devil. I'm not talking about a Devil with a pitchfork . . . Are you listening to me? ['Yeah!'] Oh, good. Some of you might have heard about a Devil with a pitchfork and horns. That's not necessarily the Devil we know. We're talking about the Devil who was one time God's chosen servant, his right-hand man. Beautiful angel. We're talking about that Devil. He's a spiritual Devil and he's got to be overcome. He has been overcome by what Jesus did at the Cross. I just want to tell you that. Some of you may not have ever heard that. [But] we are living in the End times now . . . It's the midnight hour. God wants to know who his people are and who his people aren't. [Bible] says, 'Draw nigh to God, He will draw nigh to you.'

By now, he had developed an effective way of dealing with those who wanted to hear the old songs. He would inform them that they would hear nothing but Good News tonight: '[Even] in the middle of East Coast bondage, God is waiting to set you free. I know you don't hear too much about God these days, but we're gonna talk about Him all night. We're not gonna talk about no mysticism, no meditation, none of those Eastern religions. We're just gonna be talking about Jesus. The demons don't like that name. I'll tell right now, if you got demons inside you, they're not gonna like it.'

In Pittsburgh, on the first night, he had a personal message for some-one, delivered from onstage: 'Somebody out there called Zeke? . . . He wonders why I don't play no old songs . . . I love those old songs prob-ably more than you all do. And because I do love them so much, that's precisely why I don't do them . . . I'm not the same person who wrote those songs.'

On the third night at Pittsburgh's Stanley Theater, some optimistic fan shouted for 'Lay Lady Lay', and much to the crowd's audible delight Dylan began to strum the chords. But just as at Forest Hills, the Free Trade Hall, and other points inbetween, he just kept strumming the chords over and over again, before delivering the ultimate put-down, 'You want "Lay Lady Lay"? You sing it, we'll play it. Go on, sing it!'

And still the papers, the TV, the radio wanted to know, what gives? On night two, a local TV reporter, Pat Crosby, had tracked him down to the lobby of his hotel to ask him straight, 'Can you understand peo-ple's reaction to you when you come on stage and start singing about Jesus and they want the old stuff?' Dylan insisted he could. But – and it was a big but – 'The old stuff's not going to save them and I'm not going to save them. Neither is anybody else they follow. They can boo-gie all night, but it's not gonna work.'

Back in his hotel room, he put pen to Hilton Hotel notepaper to insist that he loved the old songs, but because he loved the old songs, he wouldn't sing them, going on to explain that what he was attempt-ing to do 'this year' was to 'let people know where I'm at'. Intriguingly, over the page he had written down another Biblical reference – Acts 18: 10 – 'I am with you, and no man shall set on you to hurt you: for I have much people in this city.'

Proof that this was at least partly true – he was not alone, and others *believed* – came in the very next city, Akron, Ohio, where on both nights he was welcomed with open arms. After a spirited 'Ain't Gonna Go To Hell', a delighted Dylan even crowed, 'What a friendly crowd. I'm not used to these friendly crowds no more. Usually the Devil's working all kinds of mischief in the crowds we visit.'

At all four of what proved to be the final gospel shows – in Akron, Columbus and Dayton, Ohio – the audiences gave the man a break and were rewarded with shows full of passion and playfulness. When it came time to introduce the girlsingers in Akron – including Carolyn Dennis's latest replacement, Clydie King – he remarked,

'Seems like I don't have to tell you about Jesus. Seems like you know all about Him.'

In fact, Clydie had now taken Carolyn's place in every sense of the word. As Fred Tackett put it, 'Bob just fell in love with her.' She would be his companion, lover and friend for the foreseeable, even as she saw him struggle to keep himself in line. It was a battle he had fought a number of times before and lost, perhaps because, as Sun Tzu wrote, 'If you know yourself but not the enemy, for every victory gained you will also suffer a defeat.'

It was time to get personal, and pull back from the pulpit. Not that Dylan would ever forget what the media did back in November 1979, telling Kathryn Baker in 1988: 'I've done tours before where people got real personal with their reviews . . . and for some reason all the towns that we were about to play, they'd like to pick these things up . . . intentionally telling people to stay away.'

What these easily-swayed folks missed were probably the best shows Dylan ever gave, delivered with a passion no-one can sustain, with a band that even he couldn't keep together forever. When he returned again to the Warfield, a year on, it would be with a different mindset, and a whole new set of songs. Songs about that old forbidden fruit.

4.7

June 1980 to April 1981:
A Voice In The Wilderness

Faith . . . heightens guilt, it does not prevent sin.

Cardinal Newman.

Guilt is an imperfect form of love.

Bob Dylan, to a girlfriend, 1990.

I don't adhere to rabbis, preachers, evangelists . . . The songs are my lexicon. I believe the songs.

Bob Dylan, to David Gates, September 1997.

He doesn't really take artistic direction from anyone. All you can do is provide him with technical and financial information.

Dan Fiala, tour manager (1979-80).

No matter what horrors befall the world, someone will still get up and sing to the moon and dance around the campfire.

Bob Dylan, to Barbara Kerr, February 1978.

I've made my statement and I don't think I could make it any better than in some of those songs [on *Slow Train* and *Saved*]. Once I've said what I need to say in a song, that's it. I don't want to repeat myself.

Bob Dylan, to Robert Hilburn, November 1980.

I can communicate all of my songs. I might not remember all the lyrics. But there aren't any in there I can't identify with on some level.

Bob Dylan, to Jim Jerome, *People Weekly* 10th November 1975.

Musically, *Saved* may be Dylan's most encouraging album since *Desire*, yet it's nowhere near as good as it might have been were its star not hobbled by the received wisdom of his gospel-propagating cronies.

Kurt Loder, *Rolling Stone* September 1980.

*

'Twas the time of his confession. Not that one would know this were it not for one of the crown jewels in Tulsa's Bob Dylan Archive, another blue notebook, this one a 'fair copy' set of lyrics from the summer of 1980; in its own way as important as the more famous 'little red notebook' from the summer of 1974. This one contains just eight songs, a rewrite of 'Cover Down' plus seven from an inspired summer, five of them epic enough to form the core of a classic album-length addition to the canon.

Unfortunately, his current contract with CBS specifically precluded him from starting such an album, stating unequivocally, 'No Album shall be delivered earlier than six months nor later than fifteen months after the delivery of the preceding Album.' So, the album that could have been his best since *Blood* . . . went the way of all flesh, with just a single salvo surviving to *Shot of Love*, the sublime 'Every Grain Of Sand'.

Meanwhile, CBS were busy sending out promotional copies of *Saved* – due to be released on June 23rd – in the LP equivalent of a brown paper bag, as if it was something from Olympia Press. Promotion man Paul Rappaport, 'Rap' to his friends, a diehard Dylan fan, thought he was doing the artist a favour, 'I might have sent that to radio [stations] without the cover – it's something I would have done, because I wanted people to hear the music first . . . I was adamant that Rock radio concentrate on the music and not get hung up with Bob's personal feelings or life's choices.'

Rolling Stone wasn't about to ride to Dylan's rescue this time, either. Kurt Loder's review was hardly the most abusive, and was positively tame by comparison with the English music weeklies, which were unsparingly savage. But Loder's remark about 'the received wisdom of his gospel-propagating cronies' (see above), was spot-on. What he didn't know was that Dylan had already moved on. 'Cover Down' and 'Ain't Gonna Go To Hell' – played at every show that spring – had signalled the end of the Vineyard marking his homework.

And by the summer, even these daisy-fresh ditties he was not content to leave well alone. The last song in the summer notebook would be 'Cover Down', or as it was listed here, 'Cover Down Pray Thru'. But now, there were no Pharaoh's army or Hebrew children. The threat was coming from new technology, 'Ain't no computer system that can take the place of your heart & your head,' and businessmen who, 'when you look [at their] deception, dishonor & disgrace/ They don't try to even hide it no more, they lie right to your face.' These characters, who all liked the odd glass of wine, had descended in a straight line from 'the leaders of religion' who, circa 30 CE, 'tried to finish Jesus, not wanting Him to survive,' not realizing, 'He'd be much more dangerous to them/ dead than he ever was when he was alive.'

Sadly, this is the last we hear of 'Cover Down', save for a one-minute instrumental snatch at the start of 'tour rehearsals' in September. But an apocalyptic edge didn't disappear from Dylan's work just because he'd uprooted the Vineyard.

'Ain't Gonna Go To Hell' – though absent from the notebook – fared a little better, undergoing a metamorphosis which must have delighted the lucky few at the November shows who heard the old Dylan at work again, even if the lyrics he sang nightly were the born again equivalent of 'Tell Me Mama'; seemingly garbled, and even when intelligible, hard to follow, let alone copyright. Proof there really was a proper set of rewritten lyrics is confirmed by a typed sheet from the early fall which set a vamp-like tramp at the centre of a Dylan song for the first time since 'More Than Flesh And Blood':

> In the twilight of glory, in a chrome blue dress, I can hear you say, Adios amigo,
> Now I'm calling out your black name (with that effortless smile)
> breathing hot smokestack flame (it amused me for a while)
> I can anticipate the dreaded downbeat of a battered ego
> of [the] sorrow & strife of a sexual life [crossed out] . . .
> Got to shut down that voice saying . . . to listen to my heart
> Even when you're walking away with your legs far apart.

Somebody had gotten a hold of his heart and given it a serious twist. But who? And why were feelings of animosity, bitterness and regret pouring out of the man with such a vengeance now that he was with Clydie? Because there is a tangible bitterness in almost all of the lyrics he wrote that summer. That first line could have been transplanted to 'Angelina', a song he would not write until the following March, but which depicted the same temptress, as could another couplet in the new 'Ain't Gonna Go To Hell': 'Men dying like animals not knowing which end is up/ Your mutilated face, so beautiful but corrupt.'

By the time he would begin 'Angelina', he had at least half a dozen songs 'about' this angel with two faces, including four songs in the summer 1980 notebook, one akin to 'She's Your Lover Now', but twice as bitter. Between them, they paint a picture of a woman who could 'run a whorehouse in Buenos Aires'; a friend of both bus-boys and presidents; a regular guest of the 'war-profiteer type'; someone prepared to 'put you on the path that leads to money and power', all the while turning 'virgins into merchandise'; someone who lives inside a 'mansion of hypocrisy', forever playing a role – sometimes that of a child, other times just like a woman – yet, also, a creature vulnerable to circumstance ('forsaken and beautiful, without any complaint'), desperately in need of saving from 'the End times'. This is the unmistakeable backdrop to three contemporary masterpieces: 'Caribbean Wind', 'The Groom's Still Waiting At The Altar' and 'Angelina'. That he failed to save her from the Enemy is clear, not just from the firing squad she faces at the end of 'Angelina', but from a sign-off verse he took out of 'Yonder Comes Sin':

> I['ll] be down the line when mornin' comes – just remember that I loved you best & that I pulled the hood up for ya, so you could get a real good look at your uninvited guest.

Though several references in these songs suggest she is black (the line, 'She had bells in her braids', for one), few of her characterisations fit with what we know about Helena or Carolyn. The assumption I make is that this character is a fictional version of Mary Alice Artes, if only because we know so little about how, when and why they broke up. It certainly seems to have ended badly; that rare instance of them failing to stay friends – something Dylan always tried to do.

References in both 'Caribbean Wind' and 'The Groom's Still Waiting' to an aborted marriage ceremony rather suggests 'she' could be the person Dylan bought an engagement ring for, in January 1980. Yet this is pure speculation, of a kind that Dylan very much dislikes. Which is, frankly, tough luck. One doesn't get to write three major songs, obviously telling a single narrative, with such poetic force, only to turn around and disparage biographers who get 'too personal, too probing' – not unless one lives in a 'mansion of hypocrisy'.

However, hard facts remain in short supply. Because even the summer notebook provides only fair copy versions of four core songs – 'The Groom Is Still Waiting', 'Yonder Comes Sin', 'Caribbean Wind' and 'Makin' A Liar Out Of Me'. So, there is no way of even sequencing them by composition date. Nor is the level of venom dispensed by Dylan an indicator. 'Yonder Comes Sin' and 'Makin' A Liar', probably written earlier than the others, pile on the dirt just as much.

The latter, in particular, contains some toe-curling images: 'i say that that ain't flesh and blood you're drinking . . . i say you'd never sacrifice my children to some false god of infidelity/ & that it's not the tower of Babel that you're building/ but you're makin' a liar out of me.' Even when he tries to see some good in 'her' – as in 'you're acquainted both with night and day' – lines like, 'I say there's nothing left of you worth hating/ & that your conscience's not been slain by conformity . . . but you're makin' a liar out of me,' cut the ground away. It feels very much like a post-conversion 'She's Your Lover Now', one he left equally unrealized and containing only the barest hint of regret: 'Now that you are gone, I got to wonder/ if you were ever here at all.'

Similar feelings of betrayal spill over unto 'Yonder Comes Sin', which suggests her conduct had been more than flesh and blood can bear:

> Yonder . . . it's a pleasure to meet ya
> 　　nice to have known ya
> Yonder . . . wantin' to kill ya – wantin' to own ya . . .
> Look at your hands, see what they been into
> Creepin' thru the needle of a pin YONDER COMES SIN.

Within this wide-ranging litany of Sin, loosely modelled on Ma Rainey's 'Yonder Come The Blues', he delivers perhaps the most damning indictment of this witchy woman, 'You've played upon my heart strings, honey, 'till they sounded just like chimes/ You've seen my eyes shining in your dark mirror, just like the signs of the times.' What a shame that couplet never even made it to the copyrighted version, derived from the one and only recording of its final arrangement, cut at Rundown on September 26th.

Both of these two terrific blasts of biblical bile became early casualties of that CBS clause, the former almost lost to posterity altogether. Until 2017, 'Makin' A Liar' was merely a title on one of Arthur Rosato's invaluable song-lists, just another lost song covered in the dust of rumour. Thankfully, there came a moment on the 26th when Dylan decided to figure out how to do both songs justice. By the end of September, though, he had removed them from the rehearsal set-list along with some of the unChristian sentiments expressed therein.

Of the two songs about 'her' that not only got copyrighted, but would make it to the album sessions, the following spring, only one would 'make' it to the album, albeit in a reconfigured form, four years after the fact. Before that, the seismic 'The Groom's Still Waiting' would go through almost as many changes as its greater first cousin, so much so that the three live versions at the November Warfield shows – all available as soundboard recordings – fail to stick to the same lyrical template. Nor do any of them retain the original notebook chorus, revealing the duality in her nature that ultimately drove them apart:

> Can't find her or forget her, can't remember or forgive her, and I can't
> fault her,
> Carnally she's nothing but talk, spiritually she['s] like the rock of
> Gibraltar.
> If you see her on Fannin Street, tell her I still think she's neat,
> And the groom's still waiting at the altar.

At this stage, her fate is as unambiguous – she ends up as a whore on the notorious Memphis thoroughfare immortalised by Leadbelly – as the couple's outlaw credentials: 'Never cared if we were loved, just wanted to be respected/ Among thieves and among children we were always accepted.' Dylan also dropped the reference to 'all kinds of hangers-on who would let the fruit go rotten' in a sustained rewrite that transformed the song into the most explosive moment at all three Warfield shows it featured in.

But the real breakthrough song that summer was unquestionably 'Caribbean Wind', one of his greatest and surely his most maddeningly unrealized. How early it was written is unclear, being prefaced in its one live appearance as 'a new song I wrote a while back'. In conversation with Paul Williams backstage, prior to that debut, he seemed to imply it was a song he'd carried with him a *long* time.

Though not a man who generally returns to song-ideas after discarding them, a lost song from winter 1977 contains the following lines: '*I felt the rattle of a snake*/ I was polishing my saddle/ when the battle broke loose/ *I heard children calling Daddy*, I saw dead men being seduced,' two lines of which he transplanted to 'Caribbean Wind'. There also seems to have been an intermediate (or spin-off) song called 'Somebody's Child', which he left in a similar transitory state:

> Was she a child or a woman, I really can't say
> But any one of those roles she could easily play.
> When a man[']s ways aren't right, he is destroyed
> It's just something that you'll have to avoid
> You can listen to the people with the crooked tongues
> Who live to be old, but who die young.

It would take the inspiration of nature to make Dylan set this love story of two converts ('Told her 'bout Jesus, told her 'bout the rain') in the End times, in a place where the 'Chimes Of Freedom' lashed against the ship coming in to save the worthy: 'And those distant ships of liberty on them iron waves so bold and free/ Bringing everything that's near to me nearer to the fire.' If that ship was mythical, the boat Dylan sailed the Caribbean with Clydie that summer was wholly real.

The *Water Pearl* was a schooner he had jointly purchased the previous year, and for eight years it would provide him with a way to sail the high seas, to escape L.A.'s landed gentry and groupies. Almost immediately, the experience gave him a title and chorus for this major new work: 'And that Caribbean Wind still swirls/ On a heart of gold and teeth of pearls/ Bringing into remembrance when the other world of

Heaven was living here.' Only later would he come to feel that he needed to broaden its scope so even that idiot wind paled in comparison: 'And that Caribbean Wind still howls, from Tokyo to the British Isles*/ From the circle of light to the furnace of desire.'

This was magnificent stuff, and Dylan knew it, which is presumably why it was almost the first song he began to rehearse when the band reassembled in September. At the very first Rundown rehearsal, on September 18th, Dylan was straight down to business, attempting to show the band 'The Groom's Still Waiting', 'Makin' A Liar', 'Yonder Comes Sin' ('now that Clydie's here'), 'Caribbean Wind' and something called 'Wild About You, Babe'. The following day, he returned to some of these, and added another new 'un, 'Let's Keep It Between Us'. The band were stunned. The magnificent 'Every Grain Of Sand' also reared its head in rehearsal immediately, Dylan playing it to the band that first day (he can be heard enquiring of someone, 'you like that one?'), teaching it them, then playing it with them, in the first week of rehearsals. But then, he didn't touch it again till the following March.

Unlike 'Caribbean Wind', it is one of those rare songs that had come to him whole, perhaps even in the fabled fifteen minutes he later said it took him to write 'I And I'. From the summer 'fair copy' notebook to the May 1st, 1981 *Shot of Love* version, 'Every Grain' only ever changed by four words; 'hanging in the balance of *a perfect, finished plan*' became the slightly clumsy, 'the reality of man'. Otherwise, its Blakean charm never wavered, at least not until its November '81 live debut, as Dylan finally tapped into his visionary self to express the profundity of his conversion experience, and again gave the lie to the notion he'd been doing just fine. Rather, J.C. came along, 'in the hour of my deepest need/ When the pool of tears beneath my feet flood every new-born seed.'

But barely had he begun showing them to the band before he was already looking to prune these End time poems. One of two love songs seemingly written for Clydie bit the dust after sixty seconds over Rundown. 'Wild About You, Babe' may sound like an innocuous title, but he was still dishing it out in spades:

---

* These are the furthest geographic points Dylan played on the 1978 world tour.

Some things in life you'd just as soon let be, but when you do, you get
   yourself criticized
They always answer you before they hear ya out, with raps that they got
   memorized
Always some new thing on the horizon to get everybody's attention
When the old values that Mom and Dad had don't even get [an] honor-
   able mention.

The other song 'to Clydie', 'Let's Keep It Between Us', fared better,
being rehearsed regularly and played nightly on the fall tour, before
Dylan donated the Rundown demo to Bonnie Raitt – married to his
old producer, Rob Fraboni – to craftily recraft. His own impassioned
live performances suggested some folk still wanted to drive him from
town, as he roared, 'Let's just move to the back of, the back of, the
bus!'* If what seemed to irk him most was 'these people meddling in
our affairs', another beef was people 'project[ing] on us their own
ungodly lust', a line he dropped from the song in rehearsal, perhaps
realizing he was the kettle in this scenario.

Not that he would know anything about 'ungodly lust', having
invited Carolyn Dennis to rejoin the band even as he was seen everywhere with Clydie by his side, including sharing the piano stool at
shows for a nightly duet as intimate as could be, and singing cheek
to cheek versions of 'Jesus Met A Woman At The Well', 'Abraham,
Martin And John' and 'Rise Again' in mid-October for a TV special he
still hoped to put together and sell to a Godless network one of these
days.

He certainly pulled out all the stops for the five songs filmed that
day, two weeks before finally deigning to catch a Springsteen show –
his first, it would appear – at the L.A. Sports Arena at the end of
October, the night after he and Clydie popped into Mark Knopfler's
L.A. hotel room to play him 'Caribbean Wind' and to tell him, 'We do
a lot of old songs now'; none quite as old as the 'Jesus Met A Woman
At The Well' Bob and Clydie serenaded him with that night. An English journalist fortunate enough to be keeping the Straitman company
described the new original as 'Dylan at his very best: enigmatic lyrics

---

* A reference to her colour, but also perhaps to the iconic ending of the 1967 film, *The
Graduate*.

which seem a lot more gritty than we've been hearing recently', whetting the appetite of *Melody Maker* readers, feeding the hope that they'd got Dylan back again after eighteen months in a fenced-in vineyard.

The next night, French journalist Yves Bigot saw him at the Springsteen show, and later suggested it looked like 'you were impressed'. Dylan claimed he 'sure was'. Yet Springsteen was increasingly producing shows of bluster and bombast, far removed from what the old Dylan was formulating back at Rundown. At least the elder statesman now knew he no longer had anything to fear from this New Dylan, even as he bumped into Robert Hilburn backstage, with his son. In fact, Dylan consciously steered himself toward the bemused journalist: '[He just] starts talking. You can imagine my surprise. When the intermission was over, he said he's going to be doing some gospel shows in San Francisco and I ought to come out and see a few of them.'

Just as he had the year before, once Dylan ran through all the new songs for the band – which he did by October 1st, when he recorded the 'Yonder Comes Sin' demo – he and the band got down to brass tacks, ostensibly rehearsing the songs he was intending to play at nineteen shows, the first twelve back at the Warfield. This time, the ads were telling the fans it was 'A Musical Retrospective'. The band, to a man, were delighted. As Fred Tackett says, 'We all wanted to play the old songs, too. But nobody in the band would say anything about it . . . I think it was just a business thing: to make people happy.' Dylan and the band even took a break from tour rehearsals on the 16th, to record a medley of 'hits' for a radio ad.

What the punters lining up at the ticket office didn't know was that he was back in January 1978 mode. As Tackett recalls: 'We'd rehearse all kinds of songs, but we wouldn't rehearse the songs we were going to do . . . He didn't want you to learn the songs real well. He wanted to have the spontaneity of it . . . So, he would . . . start playing something and we'd follow on . . . All kinds of interesting things would happen that way.'

Among the many interesting things that happened that month were a series of covers Dylan insisted on doing, proof he was not as cut off from mainstream radio – or modern movies – as others might have assumed. Cover versions of Willie Nelson's 'She's Not For You', Shel Silverstein's 'A Couple More Years' and Gordon Lightfoot's 'If You Could Read My Mind' on October 1st, offered familiar enough fare from this admirer of fellow songwriters. But Dave Mason's 'We Just Disagree', a 1977 hit; Bill LaBounty's 'This Night Won't Last Forever', a big hit when covered by Michael Johnson in 1979; 'Rainbow Connection' from 1979's *The Muppet Movie* (I kid you not); and 'Goin' On', to which he would return twice more during rehearsals, were not. The last of these was his first-ever cover of a Beach Boys song. It was also their most recent single, charting at a lowly 83 in the Hot Hundred. He even covered Neil Diamond. Not 'I'm A Believer' but rather 'Sweet Caroline', a dub of which he apparently sent a doubtless dazed and confused Diamond.*

But the song he really made his own that month was Dallas Holm's 1977 Christian rock ballad, 'Rise Again', which *personally* identified with the crucified Christ, perhaps suggesting a shift in Dylan's worldview. He even subtly improved on Holm's lyric:

> Go ahead, drive nails *through* My hands,
> Laugh at me where you stand.
> Go ahead, say it isn't Me,
> But the day will come, you will see.
> 'Cause I'll rise again,
> Ain't no power on earth can *turn* Me down!
> Yes, I'll rise again,
> Death can't keep Me *buried* in the ground.

And yet, when Dylan drew up a provisional set-list for the Warfield shows, three days before opening night, there were few pre-conversion songs and precious few covers. True to form, it did include an old Hank Williams song they hadn't even rehearsed and never actually played, the apposite 'I Saw The Light'. Also on said set-list was 'Caribbean Wind', which he continued to tinker with, but held back from performing.

The only new song in the seventeen-song set on opening night was 'Let's Keep It Between Us'; the only cover was a beautiful piano-duet with Clydie on 'Abraham, Martin And John'; the only pre-conversion songs were 'Like A Rolling Stone', 'Girl From The North Country',

---

* Dylan had travelled to San Francisco to see a Neil Diamond show in 1977, and apparently left very impressed.

'Just Like A Woman', 'Señor' and a gospel-tinged encore of 'Blowin' In The Wind'. The other ten tunes were all played in Portland, Maine six months earlier. More concerning was the sense that, as Paul Williams wrote at the time, 'Dylan [i]s sleepwalking through most of his Christian material (much more so than any of his other material) . . . [and] he [surely] can't be happy doing lacklustre performances of his "Jesus" songs just to keep them in the show.'

One presumes Williams refrained from sharing this view with the man himself when he and his wife went backstage before the show on the 11th. By then, Dylan had been at the Buck-u-Uppo, after being read the riot act by Bill Graham, who for a second year running found himself reading reviews of the first night that raked Dylan across the coals – this time, with due cause – still faced with another eleven nights' worth of tickets to shift.

Thankfully, Dylan took stock and by the third night was firing up all cylinders, having spent the afternoon talking candidly to Robert Hilburn in his hotel room about the moment he accepted Christ into his life, much to Hilburn's amazement: 'He opened the door himself and started talking about his religious experience before I even asked a question. He seemed to want to finally clarify things.'*

This cathartic experience seemed to galvanize Dylan, as he poured himself into most of the songs of faith he'd penned in the past two years, notably a 'Covenant Woman' that reaffirmed not only that 'contract with the Lord' but that two-decade-old contract with his audience; one he'd articulated to Jim Jerome some five years earlier: 'A songwriter tries to grasp a certain moment, write it down, sing it for that moment and then keep that experience within himself, so he can be able to sing the song years later.'

For now, the 'holy slow train' was back on track. The following night, Dylan arrived backstage to find a note from Paul Williams. The singer had uncharacteristically advised the writer the night before that if he wanted him to play him anything, to drop a note backstage. Williams took him at his word and asked for one of two new songs he'd talked up in the dressing-room, 'Caribbean Wind'. True to his word, Dylan played it. Not only that, he introduced it by saying 'there's someone important here tonight who wants to hear it'. And he didn't mean

---

* Their conversation, his first formal interview since 1978, was widely syndicated.

Greil Marcus. But before he began, he had another story he wanted to relate, a modern parable all about Leadbelly, the man who first inspired Dylan to become a folksinger:

> Leadbelly . . . was recorded by a man named Alan Lomax . . . [who] got Leadbelly out [of prison] and brought him up to New York . . . At first, he was just doing prison songs and stuff like that . . . He'd been out of prison for some time when he decided to do children's songs, and people said, 'Oh, why did Leadbelly change?' Some people liked the old ones, some people liked the new ones . . . But he didn't change, he was the same man!

The roar that greeted the punchline suggested he and his audience were back on the same wavelength. What ensues is one of the great moments in his (*and* rock) performance-art, finally released in 2017 from Rosato's soundboard tape after decades of circulation in collector circles from an average-sounding audience tape.

The way Dylan bends the couplet, 'Shadows moved closer as we touched on the floor / Prodigal son sitting next to the door . . .,' affirms, once and for all, that nobody sings Dylan like Dylan, coming as it does at the mid-point of perhaps his greatest-ever live vocal; a perfect example of what Tony Bennett meant when he said, 'He may not be able to sing, but he sure can *phrase.*' Yet Dylan seemed to think he'd been thrown from the bull at song's end, apologizing to the stunned punters, 'I don't know if you could get all of the lyrics. I don't know if we got that off, or not. [But] I know we can do this one,' launching into an impassioned 'In The Garden'.

He would not tackle the song live again, reserving the same vocal commitment for 'The Groom's Still Waiting' instead, which filled in some gaps in the same narrative and temporarily filled the void, being performed at the next three shows with different lead guitarists and nightly-changing lyrics, before also suffering the cruellest cut. Two of those performances – with Carlos Santana on the 13th and Michael Bloomfield on the 15th – have now been released. Bloomfield's, the best of the lot, would be his last live performance. (He would be found dead in a locked Mercury Marquis of a drug overdose the following February.) The third auditionee, from a band of local novices still learning to gel as a unit, blew his chance of joining Bob's band for good by overstaying his welcome:

Fred Tackett: Carlos played a song – thank you and left. Mike Bloomfield came out, played 'Like A Rolling Stone' – thank you – left. Jerry Garcia came out, played and stayed. The whole two-hour show. He didn't know any of the songs and he was higher than a kite. We finished . . . and Bob said, 'I'm never going to have anybody sit in with us again.' I said, 'Bob, you gotta do it after the whole show's done . . . Then you bring out Jerry Garcia and let him play. But you don't bring him out on the first song, 'cause he's liable to stay all night.'

At least Tackett's gig was safe. Whatever Dylan chose to throw at him, he coped with, even doing a fine pastiche of The Byrds' famous 12-string intro. to 'Mr Tambourine Man' when his boss introduced the residency's last guest, Roger McGuinn. The whole of that final show was again memorable – not the equal of the final '79 show, but with highlights galore: an uplifting 'Rise Again'; a gorgeous rewrite of 'Simple Twist Of Fate' where his great lost love seemed to adopt one of Claudette's traits, 'He looked at her, and she looked at him/ With that look that can manipulate'; and a version of 'Fever' that made Little Willie John's sound almost tepid.

He was also talking – not preaching – to his audience again, telling San Diego punters, 'In Tucson, there was a review in the newspaper that I'd like to get straight . . . [He said] this one here was about Jesus being born in a manger. Well, that's not entirely true. It's just an old Southern Mountain ballad about somebody dying in a snowstorm.' The song in question was 'Mary From The Wild Moor', an English broadside ballad he last played in 1961. No such review has ever been found. It matters not. The shows were a revelation, with set-lists full of surprises, the rearrangements and covers a consistent joy. Now would have been the time to take this superb band, primed and ready, into the studio. But the north country farm was calling Bob (and Clydie). As for the others, the check was in the post. Have a merry, merry Christmas!

The plan was to start up again in March, record an album in the usual week or less, rehearse a new set and tour Europe in June and July. But if ever there was a songwriter who needed less choices, not more, it was Dylan. The floodgates which had reopened back in the summer of '77 remained ajar, as Dylan continued to be pulled to and fro by each undertow. The result was six new songs – 'Dead Man, Dead Man', 'Need A Woman', 'You Changed My Life', 'Shot Of Love', 'Heart Of

Stone' (aka 'Property Of Jesus') and 'Angelina' – all of them perfectly worthy, all of them now potential contenders for an album he surely knew he already had in the bag.

The first two new songs he sprung on the band, on their second day back (March 4th), were 'Dead Man, Dead Man' and 'Need A Woman', the former of which he later claimed he wrote 'while looking into the mirror'. If so, he'd been staring at himself for a good two months, which is how long the song rode its lyrical rollercoaster, as Dylan returned to the 'Satan Is Real' theme for another demonic showdown:

> Don't talk about destruction, she said, it [will] only bring me down
> El Diablo'll wait on you. He'll bring your car around . . .
> if you want to find a thrill that's new, what you'll find is what he'll show ya
> but your own mother won't know ya when he gets thru with you . . .
> All of Babylon must fall & the gates of hell cannot prevail
> you'll watch it coming apart on TV & you'll hear about it in the jail.

None of these crackin' couplets would survive the endless rewrites. As for 'Need A Woman', it underwent so many lyrical changes, Dylan had to copyright two distinct sets of lyrics. Whatever version they were rehearsing or recording, there was little doubt he was baring his soul to one of his backing singers again, perhaps even overdoing the confessional stuff on occasion: 'need ya for a wife / don't need ya for a slave . . . Some men avoid marriage altogether – prefer prostitutes / don't know what kind of man i [can] be.'

Yet a sense of dislocation is never far away, as he admits he's 'tired of . . . finding myself in unfamiliar rooms at strange moments never knowing why I came.' One can't help but believe him. Again, the rewrites piled up while the theme stayed unchanged, until he had a seven-minute song when perhaps four would do.

The same could not be said of 'Heart Of Stone', a song Dylan showed the band a week after 'Dead Man, Dead Man', but barely touched after that. Seemingly written to show that just because he had rediscovered his poetic gifts, he wasn't about to stop praising the Lord, it poked unbelievers in the metaphorical ribs, telling them they 'got nothing to gain or lose but the chain / That is shackled to the inside of your mind,' while depicting himself as this martyr-like figure who'd been blind, but now could see:

Because he talks about man redeemed & of being set free
Keep him at arm's length/ Try not to let him see.
Because he's not up on the newest new[s], nor read[s] time magazine
nor sit[s] blank eyed & captive in front of a tv or movie screen.

'You Changed My Life', the weakest of the bunch, says much the
same thing less effectively, but it didn't stop Dylan working on the song
through the end of April, at the expense of 'Yonder Comes Sin', 'Ain't
Gonna Go To Hell' and 'Makin' A Liar', all of which were patently
superior, and thoroughly Dylanesque. On the same page the Poet
Within also penned a verse of an entirely different stature, introducing
an Antichrist with eyes that 'were two slits, make any snake proud',
and a woman determined to rock'n'roll all the way down to the pit. He
hadn't forgotten Claudette, who under a new alias, Angelina, 'rode a
donkey through the crowd', fulfilling another messianic prophecy.
This woman, though, was a friend of the Devil:

In the valley of judges, in the blackest of all holes
an Indian follows you, trying to acquire a soul
the one that you sold him was the one that you stole . . .
Now her vengeance is complete and her strength cards are showing gold
Now he's got stumps for arms and she's wearing a blindfold
And so are you, Angelina.

He had finally completed the trilogy-of-song about former lovers on
opposite sides in the final battle. Now he just needed to tinker with
'Caribbean Wind' and 'The Groom's Still Waiting'. And tinker with
them he did, only to discover he'd been right all along in telling *TV
Guide* back in '76, 'The hardest part is when the inspiration dies along
the way. Then you spend all your time trying to recapture it.' He was
also surely thinking of this imperfect pair when he later told Bill Flanagan, 'You go back and look at the stuff and say, "Wow, this is great," but
you can't get connected to it again.' 'Caribbean Wind' became particularly susceptible to such a disconnect as Dylan played Russian Roulette
with the rhyming dictionary inside his head:

Was she a queen or an angel, a saint or a mirage
Was it an accident or was it sabotage

That we happened to meet behind the back of the man of the hour . . .
Told her 'bout Jesus & the shadow & the mirrors
I could hear a man pounding iron and I could see the tears.

None of these lines are an improvement. 'The Groom's Still Waiting' fared better, but still lost that great chorus, 'Set my affections on
things above/ Let nothing get in the way of that love/ Not even the
rock of Gibraltar,' as well as the strongest image he had found to
describe the imminent Apocalypse, 'I can tell [it's] about midnight by
the way the trees begin to bend.'

For now, he still felt these three songs should form the spine of the
next LP, along with 'Every Grain Of Sand', the perfect album-closer,
even as he continued to write the songs which would ultimately dis-
place them. On the back of one such wonderfully evocative song about
lost love, 'In The Summertime', is what looks like a provisional sequence
for a side two: Angelina/ Need A Woman/ Dead Man/ Every Grain Of
Sand; three new songs and one he knew he could not supersede.

At the same time, to use David Mansfield's evocative phrase, he
began 'auditioning producers the way he used to audition drummers
back in '78'. The experience nearly killed one veteran auditionee.
'Bumps' Blackwell was the man who had produced the great early
Specialty singles of Little Richard,* but now cut something of a D.W.
Griffith-like figure, a legend rarely invited to lunch in this godforsaken
town. Dylan, though, was looking to get back to making records with
a live, immediate sound and thought Bumps might still know how.

On March 25th, the artist, musicians and old-school producer all
convened at Rundown. Chuck Plotkin, a modern producer who was
angling for the gig himself, was also there. As was Debbie Gold, dispatched from New York by Naomi Saltzman to find out what the fug
was going on. Plotkin walked in to see 'Bumps Blackwell was there.
They were rehearsing "Shot of Love" itself . . . Bumps was standing
there, conducting Bob and the band.' For someone used to working
with New Dylans who used tape like confetti, the distinction between

---

* During his 2007 *Theme Time Radio Hour* series, Dylan singled out the sound of Specialty, 'There used to be a lot of record labels, not like today, and each of those record
companies had their own sound. When you dropped the needle on a Specialty Record,
you knew it was a Specialty Record.'

a rehearsal and a recording seemed absolute. Not to Dylan, it wasn't. This was no rehearsal. They were rolling tape even as the song Dylan had already earmarked as the title-track for his next album took shape.

Dylan later lamented that Blackwell 'only produced [that] one song . . . I would have liked him to do the whole thing, but things got screwed up and he wasn't so-called "contemporary."' In fact, he produced two tracks, even if it would take until 2021 for a stately, seven-minute 'Angelina' to be officially mandated. Dylan evidently had a list of songs he wanted to cut first, and he'd been checking it twice.

At some point, perhaps the day after Blackwell's cardiologist handed him his cards, 'Every Grain Of Sand' was also cut at Rundown, possibly with Jimmy Iovine (the tape has been misplaced). Iovine was another of Gold's unwise suggestions for a 'contemporary' producer, and another one she knew from working for Bruce. If Iovine did oversee a session at Rundown, it was a runthrough for him, even if it was a recording for the artist. Having given Patti Smith her one hit single with 'Because The Night', he wanted to take Dylan into Studio 55 to do the same thing with another A-list song, 'Caribbean Wind':

> **Fred Tackett**: Studio 55 . . . used to be an old studio, but now . . . it had all the new equipment, all the newest technical stuff . . . All the musicians got there early, and [so did] Jimmy Iovine . . . and the first thing he did was separate us . . . Bob always liked to have everybody in a room together and just amps, no baffles, nothing separating, just all the music. Put a couple of mikes up and record it live, a real raw live sound . . . In Bob's style [of recording], you couldn't take anything in or out, it was just all in the room. It's the way they used to do it – old style. [But] Jimmy Iovine puts us all in little boxes. I was back in a closet somewhere, literally in a closet with my mandolin, playing 'Caribbean Wind' . . . Bob still hadn't arrived, and we cut a version of the tune . . . Then Bob comes in, and he's standing at the back . . . listening to the playback . . . The next thing, you know, the whole set-up is just taken apart, and he's got all of us . . . in the room together with our amps and stuff hastily set up . . . and then we just started doing what we normally did.

There was only one problem: the song the musicians thought they knew was no longer the one Dylan wanted to record. As Rosato relates,

'As soon as the musicians ran through it once, he goes, "Nah, nah, nah, that's all wrong." They could see it coming, because they had all worked with him before . . . Instead of that [original] version, he [had] turned it into this country and western thing, like boom-chika kinda stuff.' He even instructed the girlsingers to make whooshing noises, to emulate the wind. What he'd done to the lyrics was ten times worse, even as they persevered through eight takes, getting progressively further from that fire of unknown origin. Finally, Dylan turned to Rosato and said, 'Get me the music to "White Christmas," 'cause that's the only song we're gonna be able to cut in this studio. We're not gonna be able to record any of *my* music here.'*

Iovine took this as his cue to leave, along with engineer Shelly Yakus. As Rosato put it, Dylan had successfully 'managed to shatter him in one session'. He would go on to make a mint with *American Pop Idol*, but would not produce anything of note going forward. By now, as Tackett noted, 'The second engineer was the only guy left.' It didn't stop Dylan, who made the band switch to another instalment in the Claudette trilogy, 'The Groom's Still Waiting', and in a single six-minute take they nailed it, Dylan injecting couplets old and new – of which, 'Communists are falling, capitalists are crawling/ The hand of God is moving, Jesus is calling!' leapt out.

The next day he was back at the equivalent of a demo studio, called Cream, the next part of what Rosato described as 'a studio tour, to try and see if there was anything . . . different from our [own] studio. [So,] we went from some of L.A.'s great studios to converted garages in the Valley,' determined to roll tape and then review the results. Keltner was convinced, 'He was looking for a vibe . . . He didn't want to fall into that trap he [had] with *Saved*. He was looking to do something more *alive* than that.'

The Cream session had its moments – the raw outline of a fine new song, 'In The Summertime', which would come into its own a month later; good takes of 'You Changed My Life' and 'Need A Woman' – but nothing from any A-list. On April 2nd, he returned to a proper studio, United Western, where *Pet Sounds* and 'Good Vibrations' had been recorded. The best things he recorded there were both covers, the

---

* Dylan had just been informed Bing Crosby's version had been recorded at this very studio.

Everlys' 'Let It Be Me', sung with and to Clydie, and Leon Russell's 'A Song For You'.

He realized a rethink was needed if he was going to find takes that could stand alongside the five-minute 'Shot Of Love', the seven-minute 'Angelina' and the six-minute 'Groom's Still Waiting'. He also needed a producer with the hide of an elephant and the curiosity of Odysseus. As conversations continued with Gold, Plotkin emerged as front-runner.

But before he accepted the gig, Dylan had something to say, 'If you know my work, you'll know that I'm not a reliably effective record-maker. Record-making is not my fundamental thing.' Coming from a man who had already made half a dozen albums no-one in the rock field had (or would) come close to emulating, it seemed a strange thing to say. But within a month, an older, greyer, wiser Plotkin would know exactly what he had been trying to get across.

4.8

May to December 1981:
Stepping Back Into The Arena

One time . . . he didn't show up for a couple of days. And Arthur [Rosato] was getting sort of panicked . . . Finally, he [re]surfaced. And we were [asking,] 'Bob, where were ya?' . . . [But] I [already] got the impression that Bob walked around in a fog a lot of the time.

> Toby Scott, engineer on *Shot of Love*.

In order to get [*Shot of Love*] made at all, I had to relinquish a lot of control.

> Chuck Plotkin, producer of *Shot of Love*.

Pete Oppel: Do you think you'll ever paint that masterpiece?
Bob Dylan: No, I never think so . . . because I just finish things. I don't try to perfect them.

> October 1978.

I'm not interested in . . . laying down tracks and then coming back and perfecting those tracks and then perfecting lyrics which seem to wanna go with those tracks.

> Bob Dylan, to Dave Herman, 2nd July 1981.

My albums are just measuring points for wherever I was at a certain period of time.

> Bob Dylan, to Lynne Allen, 12th December 1978.

Helen Thomas: Do you have an idea of what you will be doing in the Eighties?

Bob Dylan: I'll be doing the same thing . . . I don't see any reason to stop.

12th March 1978.

*

Even at the time of its August 1981 release, there was a sense among fans that *Shot of Love* had not come close to capturing what was something of a creative renaissance. The Europeans had seen live performances of 'Dead Man, Dead Man', 'Watered-Down Love' and 'In The Summertime' that made the album versions sound undercooked; in the case of 'Dead Man, Dead Man', to the point of 'bloody rare'.

Dylan had also informed *NME* editor Neil Spencer just weeks before its release about 'a couple of really long songs . . . that we recorded . . . Do you remember "Visions of Johanna?" Well, there was one like that . . . We left that off the album. We left another thing off the album which is quite different to anything I [ever] wrote . . . [in] the way the story line changes from third person to first person and that person becomes you, then these people are there and they're not there. And then the time goes way back, and then it's brought up to the present . . . But that again is a long song, and when I came down to putting the songs on the album, we had to cut some, so we cut those.'

He was, of course, talking about 'Angelina' and 'Caribbean Wind', the latter of which was not released until 1985, the former not until 1991, though both circulated on bootleg from the early Eighties. As for 'The Groom's Still Waiting' – the other apex in this 'love triangle' in song – it appeared at the same time as *Shot of Love*, just not on it. It was the US b-side to the 'Heart Of Mine' 45, where it generated considerably more radioplay than the a-side, as his new sidekick, Debbie Gold, had told him it would.

To quote Paul Williams, what (the hell) happened? In a nutshell, the man had carried on doing what he did best – writing songs – only to promptly do what he did worst: a) selecting which songs to record, and then, b) which takes to release. In the three weeks between the United Western 'demo' session and the first *Shot of Love* session at Clover, Dylan began systematically dismantling the album previously conceived, the one he'd rehearsed and demoed the month before.

The song that first sent him off the rails he began on the back of a checklist of those he planned to (re-)record, comprising four covers ('Mystery Train', 'Leaving It All', 'Dearest' and 'Morning Has Broken') and six originals: 'Property Of Jesus' (no longer called 'Heart Of Stone'), 'Dead Man', 'Need A Woman', 'Shot Of Love', 'You Changed My Life' and 'Caribbean Wind'. The new lyric had just two lines at this stage, 'Love that's pure can be depended upon/ To go another mile when the feeling's gone.'

Like 'Caribbean Wind', it seemed to be an idea he'd been carrying for some time, having written, 'Love covereth a multitude of sin/ Love *never* has no breaking point,' on the back of an envelope back in January 1979. It was still barely an idea in early April 1981, when he included the working title in a provisional LP sequence:

dead man, dead man	every grain of sand
shot of love	angelina
you changed my life	the groom is still waiting
need a woman	love that's pure
property of jesus	caribbean wind

It's quite an album he sketched out here. If only he could have let it be. He couldn't. One song he'd been toying around with for the past fortnight was called 'Bolero', which was only an instrumental when the band assembled at Clover, the second week in March. Dylan convinced himself there was a set of words behind a burning bush somewhere.

Finally, mid-sessions, a rather mundane idea came to him, 'Heart of mine be still/ You can play with fire, but God will send you the bill.' Rather than dismiss it, he ran with it, at the expense of a far more promising fragment on the same page which told of a *Rolling Stone* reporter who finds himself 'holed up somewhere 'cross town/ long distance call interrupted me/ [It was] collect from Birmingham/ i accepted the call & it was coming from the conscience of the damned.'*

At least 'Heart Of Mine' had a tune – not as good a tune as the otherwise godawful 'Lenny Bruce', but a tune nonetheless. Which is

---

* This song fragment appears at the top of a draft of 'Lenny Bruce', so presumably dates from April '81.

more than can be said for the other song that occupied Dylan (and a lot of tape) through the first week in May. Called 'Trouble', it made 'Are You Ready?' sound like 'Like A Rolling Stone', and Billy Graham seem like a lyricist: 'Meditate on the mountain-top/ Stick a needle in your vein/ You can't depend on anything/ It'll become a ball and chain.'

Dylan would pull no less than *three* versions 'to master'. With more letters than notes, it made early April improvisations like 'Is It Worth It?' and 'Halleluiah' sound finished. Worse was to come. After he completed 'The Ballad Of Lenny Bruce' – its original title – he added it to the *Shot of Love* shortlist. After nine months of high water everywhere, that Caribbean wind of inspiration had blown itself out just as Dylan set about self-sabotaging what could have been his first bona-fide masterpiece in seven long years.

Of the nine songs on the original 1981 sequence, only the already-recorded title-track, 'Shot Of Love', and the Clover 'Property Of Jesus' and 'Every Grain Of Sand' warrant their berth. 'Trouble' and 'Lenny Bruce' weren't just beyond the pale, they were beyond redemption. 'Heart Of Mine', 'Dead Man, Dead Man' and 'In The Summertime' would all be released in patently inferior guises, despite turning up in their Sunday best at some point that week.*

Largely powerless to change any of this was Dylan's chosen producer, Chuck Plotkin, who had just spent the last fourteen months of studio-time turning a masterful single-album follow-up to Springsteen's *Darkness on the Edge of Town*, *The Ties That Bind*, into a double-album, *The River*, that should have been drowned at birth.

As with Springsteen's recent sessions, the main priority for Plotkin was to make sure that everything was taped, and nothing was lost. Before Dylan even arrived at Clover, his first task was to explain to his – and Springsteen's – engineer that they wouldn't be using headphones, something Plotkin himself – who had missed the era of recording live in the studio – had never encountered before:

Toby Scott: I [had] heard from Chuck one day, 'Hey, we're gonna be doing a Bob Dylan record but it's gonna be a lot of people and it's all

---

* Neither the first or last of these has been officially released, despite two Bootleg Series – in 2017 and 2021 – devoting a large chunk of multi-CD sets to the teeming *Shot of Love* detritus.

gonna be in one room. And Bob doesn't wanna use headphones. But everybody's got to be able to hear what everybody else is doing.' So, I got the rundown of players and I found a small speaker system that I could mount on short microphone stands and they would [put] the mix that would usually go into the headphones, into the speakers . . . The room was about thirty-foot wide and about twenty-five feet long. There was a little indent which sometimes we used as a little vocal booth. Nowadays, everything gets its own track. But back then, we're only talking twenty-four-track. [So, it was a case of,] 'Four background singers? Here's a mike. Adjust yourself. Be on it.'

This was just the start of a month-long re-education in recording, the Dylan way, for Plotkin and Scott. Almost immediately, Scott realized they'd need to run two sets of tapes – one 'multi', one two-track:

I think it was early in the first day that we realized [he was not gonna] say, 'Okay, everybody count [in,' and then] start playing. That was not gonna happen. Bob would just start playing and the band would sort of fall in. Sometimes Jim [Keltner], or someone who knew him better, would say, 'Okay Bob, are you ready to do it? One – two . . .' So, we started running two-track quarter-inch [tape 'cause] . . . one could never tell when some gem of inspiration would come out of Bob. So, we ran a . . . monitor [mix] whenever Bob was in the room and with an instrument . . . because if Bob had a guitar in his hands, at any instant he [might] start playing, the band would join in and he'd get to a microphone – maybe – and start singing the song . . . On one song Chuck ran from the control room and picked up the vocal mike, stand and all, and followed Bob around the studio pointing the mike at Bob's mouth while he (Bob) seemed unaware that he would have to sing into the microphone to be recorded properly.*

The result was a thorough audio record of the (de)construction of a pivotal album in his *oeuvre*, one that despite being plundered three times since 1981, still has some hidden jewels, two of them from the first couple of days at Clover: a one-time, off-the-cuff groove called

---

* Plotkin later claimed the song in question was 'Every Grain Of Sand'. His memory is playing tricks.

'Magic' that appeared on early sequences of the album, having both a better tune and superior ('dummy') lyrics to 'Heart Of Mine', and a six-minute 'In The Summertime' that entered 'What Can I Do For You' territory, thanks to its Coltranesque harmonica coda.

The approach Dylan adopted may have made Plotkin almost cut his hair, but for the musicians it was a delight, especially veterans like Tackett, who'd played on the previous debacle, 'It was a little looser . . . compared to the *Saved* sessions. We had not played the songs as much as we had on the *Saved* record. This was good, because there was even more spontaneous stuff going on . . . We did . . . a version of "Let It Be Me" when Bob and I were the only ones left in the room . . . We did it with just acoustic and electric guitars and Bob singing.' Actually, Clydie was present, too, and joined in. Cut in a single take, the penultimate song recorded, 'Let It Be Me', appeared as a b-side in Europe.

Keyboardist Benmont Tench, on sabbatical from Tom Petty's Heart-breakers, recalls, 'We cut everything live . . . with the backing girls really singing and playing percussion . . . We . . . just blazed through the songs . . . One of the songs . . . doesn't have a bass on it . . . because . . . almost everybody had packed up and gone home, including Tim Drummond . . . Two or three of us hung around . . . and then we went back into the studio, and cut the song without a bass. And that's the version they kept.' The song in question was 'Property Of Jesus', and as per, Dylan preferred serendipity to making the whole thing blend:

> **Toby Scott**: We recorded it two or three times and [took a break]. We came back, Bob starts to play, 'Okay, let's go.' . . . They did it once or twice, sounds good. [So,] everyone comes into the control-room and Bob comes in and we listen to it. [He] goes, 'Great, that was a good take.' Following studio protocol, I lean over to Chuck and go, 'Tim Drummond wasn't in the room.' 'What?!' 'There's no bass. Tim's still down at Ernie's having a burrito.' Then Tim walks in the room, 'Hi guys, what's going on?' Chuck goes, 'We can overdub it.' Bob goes, 'You wanna overdo it?' Chuck says, 'It's bass, it's on a direct. No problem. Won't be an issue.' Bob says . . . 'We said it sounds good. It seems okay.' Chuck goes, 'No, no, no. We gotta put the bass on it.' . . . Bob goes, 'Nope, I think it sounds fine without it. If it was meant to be there, he woulda been there. So, let's just move on.'

As one of just two songs from Clover where they used the best take on *Shot of Love*, Dylan's instincts were for once righteous.* The other pressing issue at the sessions, familiar to old hands but not Plotkin or Scott, was Dylan's complete inability to ever be on time. Scott recalls that by the end of 'the first day . . . I think [we realized] there was a thing that we began to call Dylan time. Which is whatever time you think he's going to be there, add three hours.' After two productive days, and a weekend break, Dylan went completely AWOL on Monday, April 27th. Returning late – even by his standards – on the 28th, his explanation caused Scott to wonder if this maverick genius was all there:

> He [said he] had gone down to Laguna Beach. I [had already] got the impression that Bob walked around in a fog a lot of the time [when] he said, 'Yeah, I was down in Laguna and I was in a phone-booth, and some kids saw me and said, Hey, what are you doing? And I just got talkin' to 'em and I ended up spending the day and the night and the next day with them, and finally I decided to come back.'

With a day and a half's work lost in the fog, Dylan decided to tackle 'Angelina' again, cutting three complete takes, uncertain whether to let the band cut loose. The second take – the one he pulled to master – was almost a solo performance, whereas the third take sounded like it came live from the Combat Zone, with the band sensing it was now or never, and emptying every cartridge. At least Dylan had remembered the A-list. The following day, he captured a near-perfect 'Every Grain Of Sand' after two other, equally great takes; the limit of Dylan's attention-span, as Rosato already knew:

> The most takes . . . for any session was usually . . . [on] the first day. After that, it was down to around three . . . Bob always put as much into performing any song the first time as the last, so 'record[ing] it in earnest' is what he does from the beginning.

At last, it seemed, the boss was starting to focus. On May 1st, the

---

* Were one to be ultra-finicky, the 'perfect' 'Every Grain Of Sand' would be the released take three with the harmonica coda from take two, a simple enough edit by 1981.

sixth (and supposedly) last Clover session, he didn't merely pull out all the stops, he plugged all the gaps in a marathon stint that went on long into the night. He finally tackled 'Caribbean Wind' and 'The Groom's Still Waiting' again, pulling two and three takes respectively 'to master' without even reviewing the Studio 55 tapes, along with 'master takes' of 'Trouble' and 'Heart Of Mine', trying in vain to salvage the unsalvageable. In the latter's case, he finally got a song that wouldn't have embarrassed *Nashville Skyline*.

'Caribbean Wind', naturally, occupied the most tape and engendered the greatest sense of frustration, as Dylan returned to a version of the original lyrics and cut out the wind noises, only to sabotage it anew with a maddening signature change at the end of every chorus, as if the band had stopped off to play hopscotch.

At least 'The Groom's Still Waiting' rediscovered the sound and the fury, before Dylan wound up proceedings with a glorious teenage prayer jam-session that took in a seven-minute version of Junior Parker's 'Mystery Train' that would have left Sam Phillips questioning whether Elvis really was the best white r&b singer he'd ever heard;* a 'Price Of Love' that went on so long, the tape op. had to change reels mid-song; the Dylan-King 'Let It Be Me', and 'Work With Me, Annie', a 1954 hit for Hank Ballard & The Midnighters. All in all, it was a glorious, life-affirming blast from the past and the perfect way to bring the curtain down on six days off the road, most of the time off-piste.

That Dylan enjoyed the experience is clear from one line in a 'to do' list he typed before flying to Europe in mid-June, which read, 'Arthur get let it be me – mystery train – price of love.' Both 'Let It Be Me' and 'Mystery Train' would be put on a reel of potential b-sides. Before that, it was the songs pulled to the album master reels that preoccupied Plotkin, Scott and Dylan. According to Scott, '[We] picked out ten or twelve songs, [and] Chuck [says to Dylan,] "Can you come in tomorrow? Why don't we take a list to everything we've got, to see how to proceed, and what we wanna follow up with" . . . Twelve songs from the rough mixes I had done off the monitor panel for playback at the

---

* The version on *Springtime In New York* (2021) is an edit of the May 15th version, *not* the superior May 1st version, which Dylan picked as a potential b-side and cut to acetate.

end of the day's recording . . . were assembled . . . Chuck [then] uses the ill-advised words, "We'll see if we've got a record or not." '

Scott has actually conflated two stages: one, to compile a master reel (or three); two, to sequence the album. Assembling the master reels on May 4th did indeed result in a twelve-song 'comp.', but what was actually put together comprised twenty-six *takes* of twelve songs. Never before had Dylan given himself so many permutations from which to cull a ten-track album; more options than even a double-LP could contain. After adding three more takes the following day – the Blackwell 'Shot Of Love' and two takes of 'Watered-Down Love' – plus the two 'b-side' covers, one of them seven minutes long, it was hard to see how he could trim it down to a single LP, especially given the length of some songs.

If he'd picked the best versions of 'Angelina', 'Caribbean Wind', 'Every Grain Of Sand', 'Need A Woman', 'In The Summertime' and 'Dead Man, Dead Man', they would have made for a forty-minute-plus album before they found room for the five-minute title-track or a similar-length 'Groom's Still Waiting'. And there was another issue which would not go away: how much time was Dylan prepared to allow Plotkin for remixing, given that all they had listened to in the last ten days were monitor mixes. Ever unwilling to surrender control, the answer was no time at all:

> **Chuck Plotkin**: The mixes that got released on the record . . . are all just the monitor mixes that we'd get at the end of each night. We'd do a tune, get a track we liked, and we'd just run off a rough monitor mix. Really rough. And those are the mixes you hear. Now, *I tried* to mix the record. Toby and I tried to squeeze some little level of aural finesse in there. But every time we had a finished mix and took it to Bob, he went, 'Naw, naw, no. The other mix . . . That's the record.' . . . And in part, I feel responsible . . . I had to relinquish a lot of control over things that I ordinarily would have . . . control over.

Welcome to a work-experience gig with an unswerving, unyielding artist of the first water, Chuck. At least Scott accepts that the monitor mixes had something the production mixes did not: 'At the end of [each] day we'd go, "Okay, this seems good. Let's put this mix down on tape." . . . We went through the week of recording [like this] . . . [And] we used to [wonder] why did the monitor mixes sound incredible, and the mixes off the console – where we're adding EQ [&c.] – not sound as good.'

Plotkin never imagined he wouldn't be allowed to do his own mix, a radio-friendly mix like the wafer-thin one digitally done to *The River*. Keltner, for one, knew from the outset how this would go down: 'Chuck [Plotkin] was wanting to get a nice mix at the end of each song, and Bob wouldn't have any of the nice mixes.' The drummer knew the whole ten days had been a series of misunderstandings from minds not destined to meet in the middle. As Scott informed me in 2017, 'I think Chuck thought we were rehearsing and selecting songs for the actual album-recording to take place after these sessions. Bob seemed to be of the opinion we were recording the record.' The outcome was never in doubt:

> **Toby Scott**: [Chuck] says, 'Well, I've put these into what feels like a sequence. We'll see if these'll work.' Then he plays the first [twenty-minute] reel and then he plays the second reel, and Bob goes, 'Sounds like a record.' And Chuck goes, 'Yeah, it sounds like a record . . . I should probably book out studio-time here at Clover, where we can record the record. And Bob goes, 'Whaddya mean?' Chuck says, 'Well, we gotta record it now in earnest.' Bob replies, 'You just said it sounds like a record. Sounds like a record to me! Master it and send me a copy.' . . . The [following] day he says, 'Look, do what you wanna do [to remix it]. You've got a week and then present it to me and I'll decide whether it's an improvement. Otherwise, this is the record.' . . . [At the end] of that week, Bob [just] said to Chuck, 'No, none of this stuff is working for me. Just gimme the tapes.' . . . Chuck, being somewhat maniacal, was like, 'No, I'm producing this.' . . . I remember living in Clover Studio [that weekend] with [the] back doors barred with two by fours; front doors barred. Bob [finally] sent men to retrieve all the tapes . . . When the album came out, it was all the monitor mixes.

At some point that week, while Plotkin fiddled and New Jerusalem burned, Dylan decided he wanted to redo a couple of tracks – to the sound of rending garments. Neither 'Heart Of Mine' nor 'Watered-Down Love' seemed to warrant such effort. In the former case Dylan admitted, while jamming with other musicians in 1984, it 'is not as good as some of the other versions, but I chose it because Ringo and

Ronnie Wood [sic] played on it, and we did it in like ten minutes.' Perversity, thy name is Dylan.

'Watered-Down Love' was subjected to fifteen takes, none of them up to scratch. Instead, Dylan cut a verse from the earlier Clover version, as he set about trimming the album. 'In The Summertime' and 'Shot Of Love' were both faded down when things were just getting interesting, and a tenth song, a 'Caribbean Wind' yet to be officially released, was scrapped altogether.* The album would now end with that sole survivor from summer 1980, the transcendent 'Every Grain Of Sand'.

He just wanted it out. Already, there was zero prospect of the LP appearing while he toured Europe in June and July. Just as he was leaving for the airport, Debbie Gold enquired, 'What about the album cover?' According to Gold, Dylan replied, 'Just make one up.' 'I can't just make one up. You're Bob Dylan!' 'I don't care . . . what you put on it. You're smart, Debbie. Just make one up.' The cover certainly looks like an afterthought, especially after someone inverted front and back, flipping the image of a Cadillac with the number of the beast heading into the clouds. By now, he knew he'd missed the boat, introducing 'Dead Man, Dead Man' at a warm-up show in Clarkston, Michigan, with, 'This is a new song we just recorded a couple of weeks ago. Should be out in a couple of years.'

But maybe he still had not given up on 'Caribbean Wind'. When Saltzman was asked if copyright-sheets should be sent his way for correction, she wrote back, 'Bob says he's going to re-record.' She should have known better. Although Dylan sounds almost wistful talking about the song to Spencer in July, he hadn't gone back to a song he'd previously recorded since January 1966. Leopard/spots. Meanwhile, Plotkin suggested marginally speeding up 'The Groom's Still Waiting', and having reinvented the wheel, he and Gold convinced Dylan to hide it away on a b-side. He would never play any of the 'Claudette' songs again. Like a man with a lame leg he moved on, having apparently decided 'elephant man dont get around much anymore'.†

---

* It would be released by the esteemed US bootleg label, Scorpio, on the first *Genuine Bootleg Series*.

† The line appears on a typed checklist that June, possibly prompted by Bowie's recent Broadway debut in *The Elephant Man*.

Above this line he typed a more poignant reminder he still had work to do: 'dylan thomas – do not go gently into the . . . night.' He had just turned forty, yet already felt he was raging against the dying of the light. At least the tour rehearsals were going well, as an escape to Europe loomed. But just as he thought he'd left L.A. to live and die without him, he was pulled back by a past partner-in-crime. Dylan heard via his accountant that Grossman was about to sue him.

He certainly should have known it was coming. Never shy of using legal threats, Grossman had been sitting on his hands too long. Indeed, according to papers filed in Kingston court, 'Beginning in 1974, [Grossman] disputed the accuracy of the Artist's accounts, and attempted to have the relevant records audited . . . Finally in 1978, [he] was permitted to conduct such audits . . . [But] after further negotiations with the Artist proved fruitless, the Lawsuit was commenced in May 1981 based on the claims identified by the Audit.'

So, if Dylan *was* surprised, he'd taken his eye off the prize, especially given it looked like a conscious strategy on his part, to hold back Albert's payments – as the judge in the ensuing case concluded – knowing that he held all the cards, whatever pack Grossman had. When he phoned Albert to ask why the suit, Grossman told him to read their contracts. He hardly needed to do that. Dylan had spent years poring over them, after he found out there was little that he could do to extract himself from under them.

The lawsuit, filed in New York state on May 18th, 1981, was Grossman's way of telling his ex-client he would not go down without a fight. According to the court papers, Dylan already owed at least $51,000 per annum since 1974 in back royalties and commissions from songs registered to companies in which Grossman retained an interest. Ever the optimist, he was also asking for $400,000 in punitive damages.

After firing the first shot, Dylan now brought in the big guns, including David Braun, now based in L.A., and a former employee of Grossman who knew where a number of bodies were buried. Things were bound to get dirty. Dylan had already decided this would be a fight to the death. It was not about the money. It was about what he supposedly said to Albert when they spoke, 'You've been paid enough.' And he had.

Having been obliged to return to L.A. for a conference with Braun,

Dylan flew direct to Toulouse to join his band, whom he found relaxing by the pool before the first show of a five-week European tour. Unlike America, there was still more than enough pent-up demand in Europe for Dylan to play arenas and stadia throughout, especially after a series of radio interviews assured punters he had put the last two albums behind him and was ready to reconnect with his largely agnostic audience. Unfortunately for his critical standing, he arrived in Europe just as Springsteen & The E Street Band were leaving, after a six-week victory procession that stretched from Stockholm to Edinburgh.

The last, dying flicker of Bruce's glory days as a performer was still enough for the critics this side of the pond, fed a steady diet of Hype for six long years, to go radio ga-ga. When one credulous culprit – Paul Gambaccini – asked Dylan if he knew 'that Bruce has included "This Land Is Your Land" in his concerts,' he didn't even realize Dylan was sending him – and his kind – up when he replied 'Oh he has? That's amazing! . . . Maybe he'll do an album with Bob Dylan songs!'

The singer revealed his true thoughts to a thoughtful Neil Spencer the following month, 'I feel very strongly about this show. I feel it has something to offer. No-one else does this show – not Bruce Springsteen, or anyone.' As for the notion of Springsteen positioning himself as Guthrie's natural heir, that position was already taken, even as Dylan stewed on the young colt's impudence a while longer. Indeed, it would be 2015 before he truly let rip, 'If you want to do a Woody Guthrie song, you have to go past Bruce Springsteen . . . Eventually, you'll get to Woody, but it might be a long process.' Bob was still holding Woody's baton and wasn't about to relinquish it. As he'd said in 1975, when Bruce was a genuine threat, 'I'm always changing, always moving around, forging new paths. I'm blazing a trail . . . They're all looking for a new Paul Simon. Or a new Bruce Springfield.'

As it happens, Dylan's European shows, or certainly the majority of them, saw him back to his energetic best, whereas Springsteen was raking over cooling coals. And though the elder statesman had a few things to say to critics like the *Sunday Times*'s Philip Norman – with whom he would cross swords again in 1986 – he said them from the Earl's Court stage, not in his hotel room, as he returned to the site of that triumphant 1978 residency for another six-nighter, during which he had several digs at critics who questioned his song selection, starting with, 'I know I've written a lot of songs, so I know I must have left something out. I hope I put something in,' before moving on to, 'We're gonna be here tomorrow night, and the next night and the night after that. You're bound to hear something that you know one of the nights.' On the final night we got, 'I wish we were going to be here tomorrow. We could do all the stuff we left out . . . [But] I get tired of reading things I don't like. I sometimes like to ask you what *you* think.'

The London crowd lapped up such remarks, and seemed to love the new songs – five of which were played, all of them improvements on their studio prototypes – even if Sunday night saw Dylan hint that the lucky many might be seeing the last of an artist who for two decades had previewed his new work in concert, 'I don't know how much longer I'll be playing new songs. People wanna hear the old songs. I was thinking of cutting out all the new songs.'

Those there on June 28th assumed this was nothing but a slightly sour Dylan bemoaning the commercial straitjacket that came with playing large arenas. But he was deadly serious. July 1st saw him play his last-ever live preview of an unreleased Dylan original. For the next forty-odd years, only after he released an album would he play anything from it. The loss to his artistry would be immeasurable.

For now, though, he delivered on his radio promise that fans would still hear 'the result of [those gospel] shows . . . [as well as] a few new things', and though the highlights were probably the really old songs (like a 'Barbara Allen' on opening night) and brand-new songs, he seemed to have reconnected with the gospel material, delivering a devastating 'Solid Rock' in Toulouse, along with a generally magnificent 'In The Garden' and an 'I Believe In You' that drilled the message home while some Keltner artillery provided cover. And the day after his London residency ended, he confirmed his commitment to Christ in a long, rambling interview with US DJ Dave Herman – not that the powers-that-be were about to broadcast the evidence:

Paul Rappaport: I was in . . . charge of promotion. So, I called Bob . . . 'You haven't done an [on-air] interview in years. Would you just do one interview?' 'Yeah, okay.' 'So, who do you want to interview you?' 'Ah, maybe Dave Herman, the morning guy.' . . . I tell David [beforehand], 'Do not ask him about The Bible. Do not ask him about being Christian.' . . . Damn if the guy doesn't [immediately] ask him [about his faith] . . . So, Bob does his Bob thing . . . [He] starts talking to him about The Bible and the 'beasts'. There's twenty minutes on the . . . weirdest shit in the world . . . So, I go in with Debbie [Gold] into CBS Studios . . . trying to get something that matters in between all the talk of the beasts . . . Debbie and I sat in that studio for two fuckin' days . . . trying to take the things that matter to make an interview . . . But at least we had an interview.

Another interviewer that month, *NME*'s Neil Spencer, was caught completely off-guard when Dylan started talking about Satan, 'What I absolutely didn't realize was that, far from Christianity being another station in Bob's quest, he had been "converted" by . . . some kind of dumb Sunday school for addled cokeheads.' At least Dylan didn't candy coat it to keep Spencer sweet, 'People don't know who the enemy is. They think the enemy is something they can see, and the reality of the enemy is a spiritual being they can't see . . . [Just like] people expected the Messiah to be someone to set things straight, and here comes a Messiah who doesn't measure up to those characteristics.' He was wholly unapologetic, which upset critics of the liberal consensus the most.

Spencer had unwittingly secured the last interview of consequence on a tour where those with ears heard him sing, 'Why must you criticise?' It would be two years before Dylan again spoke to the press at length, after a chastening reception for the album he named after what he called, in his next major interview in July 1983, 'my most perfect song. It defines where I am at spiritually, musically, romantically and whatever else . . . I'm not hiding anything. It's all there in that one song.'

The man who had once been his greatest critical champion, the man he once dubbed 'good critic paul', disagreed: 'The singer [on *Shot of Love*] often seems to think that he and Jesus are interchangeable on that mythic cross. Ultimate victims . . . You do wonder . . . if Bob Dylan is so full of God's love, why is he so pissed off at the rest of the world?'

Such was Paul Nelson's assessment of the new album in *Rolling Stone*, and even before the issue had appeared, Debbie Gold had rung Dylan from the magazine's office to warn him he was once again in the line of critical fire, prompting him to pen a new song that was a cross between 'When The Ship Comes In' and 'Ballad Of A Thin Man', addressed to some unnamed 'jerk that writes for *Rolling Stone*'. Who-ever could he mean?

Nelson's review stung, and though he no longer railed at students that fall before singing an increasingly tepid 'When You Gonna Wake Up', in Meadowlands at the end of October, he did 'say hello to all the editors of *Rolling Stone* magazine . . . [who] are here tonight, checking me out. They're gonna come backstage later, [and] I'm gonna check *them* out.'

By then, he was two weeks into his most disappointing tour to date, a Stateside stint that seemed more an afterthought than an ongoing crusade to convert fans to his new music. And it was the songs from the so-called gospel trilogy which were really suffering under the law at these shows. So disconnected had he become from his religious material that he sometimes barely got the words right. Encores of 'Are You Ready?' in Kitchener and 'Jesus Is The One' in Ottawa were bereft of passion or purpose. Even worse was a version of 'When He Returns' he played one night in Cincinnati on the guitar, without recourse to lyrics he could no longer righteously recall. He did not make that mistake again, even if he did insist on treating 'Solid Rock' and 'When You Gonna Wake Up' like he was Vincent Price draining the blood out of the last critic to give him a bad review.

Something had happened. He no longer knew who he was, even as the band who had done such solid service since November 1979 lost its compass and part of their charm, along with a departing Carolyn Dennis and Willie Smith. In the former's case, she had simply had enough of what she saw as Dylan's constant attempts in Europe to do 'everything he could to irritate' her, after she chose not 'to rekindle her relationship with him'. After Avignon, she decided to sever the ties that once bound her completely, while Willie Smith quit because, according to Tackett, Dylan wanted the shirt off his back:

> [In Europe] Bob would go over to [Willie's] wardrobe case . . . and take one of his Hawaiian shirts and put it on, and wear it on the show. He would get it all sweaty, and [then] put this thing back. So, when we started to do the next tour, Smitty went to Bob and said, 'Hey, Bob, I've got all these expensive silk Hawaiian shirts and they all got ruined on this last tour, because you were wearing them and . . . they didn't get cleaned. So I need you to replace those shirts for me. Otherwise, I can't

do the tour.' Bob kinda laugh[ed] and said, 'Oh yeah.' . . . It got to be the day before we were going to leave . . . and Smitty says, 'Bob, I'm not going to do the tour unless you give me . . . a thousand dollars for the shirts.' . . . So, he calls Al Kooper up . . . and said, 'Al, come and play organ with us.'

Kooper did not come cheap. Nor did he know the material or have the chops Smith did in spades. His 'fumbling for the light switch' approach worked best in the studio, and Smith's absence was keenly felt. Just as he needed his rhythm-section to fill the occasional melodic void, Dylan decided to experiment with two drummers – one professional, one not – simply to keep his right-hand man happy:

> **Arthur Rosato**: I was talking to Bob before the start of the tour, telling him that I was burnt out . . . I told him that I would fly out to the first gig to make sure things were okay, and then go home . . . [But then,] at the first gig, Bob was talking to me and Keltner about how great it would be to have an additional drummer. Keltner told him [it] could be a good idea and . . . Bob, knowing that I played drums, turned to me and said, 'Do you want to do it?' That was it . . . With no rehearsal, I was the additional drummer . . . I was doing all the regular pre-show production, the lights would go down, I would play the show.

It was an experiment Dylan should have abandoned after the opening gigs in Milwaukee – actually, the two best shows of the tour – or simply let Rosato play on selected songs. Instead, he tied the hands of the most dexterous drummer in rock. Only at a trio of shows in New Orleans and Houston was the experiment put on hold, as Dylan let Bruce Gary, recently departed from The Knack and hurting, to take Rosato's place and show what two real pros could do in tandem. At the end of it, Gary 'was invited to come down to Clearwater, but I decided to come home. I could see that everyone was crusty around the edges.'

At least he got to play on the one new song Dylan elected to try out live, 'Thief On The Cross', the first night in New Orleans, sung from the vantage point of an onlooker anxious to talk to the thief on the cross, presumably hoping for answers. The answer, if said onlooker was one of those who liked 'sinning by the rules', could perhaps be found in Dylan's June, 'to do' list: 'there's a price for going to the bottom/ + there's a chance you may not make it back (up).' In a couple of years' time he would phrase it differently, on another breakthrough song ('Foot Of Pride'): 'Be nice to people on the way up/ 'Cause sooner or later you're gonna meet them coming down.'

For now, the well was dry, unless an undated Eighties song in the Tulsa archives dates from the fall of 1981, just as Dylan was running out of steam, along with his steel-driving crew. It could have been prompted by a remark he jotted down on hotel notepaper, 'What I am attempting to do this year is let people know where I'm at – to break the ice.' If so, he was failing to win the many over, just as his predecessor and Messianic figure had, two millennia earlier. As he wrote in another early Eighties song fragment, 'No cure for my wicked imagination/ No cure for me in sight/ I'm running [a] race, had the realization/ I can't use no one tonight.'

He pulled up short of completing such a worrying thought. Instead, he wrote 'I Play To The Crowd That Jesus Played To'. As others got to perform for 'the righteous and the holy', Dylan felt he was singing for 'the cut off, the innocent, the ill-perceived, the disinherited', and even, 'twins, identical in every way except one is white and one is black,' perhaps proof he really was a fan of Star Trek.* This, though, is no 'Chimes Of Freedom'. He would prefer to 'play for the merciful and the humble . . . even if I wasn't paid', not 'the crowd that Jesus played to'.

Here is a fascinating, fully realized lost lyric, but if there was ever a soundcheck version, Rosato had stopped taping them. He was too busy setting up the drums. And when he wasn't doing that, he was chasing Dylan around with a camera while Howard Alk jotted down ideas, hoping he might yet get to make the sequel to Renaldo & Clara Dylan talked about back in 1978. Rosato took the view, 'It was just a home movie. We were always out shooting things, but it wasn't anything that involved. I think he was trying to let Howard go.'

Just as in 1976, when he had let go of the best band he had then played with, Dylan sensed he would have to do it again, near to the same Gulf Coast Highway. Though the 1981 US tour was to Dylan's mind ever only 'a regional tour', the fifth leg of a two-year zigzag

* The line directly references a famous Star Trek episode from Series Three, Let That Be Your Last Battlefield.

through the motherland, he never expected it to end where that Rolling Thunder leg began, in Lakeland. But the last scheduled show of the tour, in Tallahassee, had gone down the drain.

Originally, he had been scheduled to play the ten-thousand-plus Civic Center but it had been switched to the Florida State University, with a capacity of just 3,900, when sales proved disappointing. Evidently, the crowd Jesus used to play to was dwindling in size, even before this modern apostle was again attacked by the brethren of Tempe. A student paper in the town had apparently printed a letter highly critical of Dylan's religious stance and, with promoters like Bill Graham in short supply down south, the Floridian promoter simply cancelled the Tallahassee show.

It meant that the final show would be at the eight-and-a-half-thousand capacity Lakeland Civic Center on November 21st. Having been here before, he was determined to sign off with something special, and sign off he did, with the live debut of 'Every Grain Of Sand'. Dylan, though, was running on empty. He still knew all the words to the song, but had lost its meaning, along with his harmonica. It's a wretched runt of a rendition, bafflingly put out in 2017, capturing the sound of a singer clutching at straws.

He had reached the end of the road. It would be five long years before he would tour America again. Just days before that return, he did a phone-in on WBAI, where he was asked why he'd seemingly stopped touring. He set the listener straight, 'You can only play where people want you to play, and I was only doing regional tours. But I've never stopped working, you know . . . Nothing's changed around here. You all missed my gospel tours!'

The wounds cut deep, and would take half a decade – and more – to heal. A number of songs he played that night in Lakeland, and at the other shows that year, when he sang to crowds of 'the ill-perceived', would never surface again. One song that survived the cull came third in a six-song-encore. It was one he had played as a demented heavy-metal workout the last time he had played here. It still spoke for him:

I got nothing, Ma, to live up to.

Winterlude #4

1982:
Disappearing Off The Grid

I didn't have counterarguments for a lot of his [religious] arguments. [But] as a Jew, I just knew what I felt . . . After one of these discussions . . . I called Rabbi Friedman in Minnesota . . . I brought him out [to L.A.] . . . [Bob] started to study Torah and Talmud . . . And that's how I got him out [of Christianity].

Louie Kemp, 2020.

*

One of the oddities Dylan's unique place in popular culture throws up is an influence he is perceived to exert, often on those who stopped buying his albums pre-*Slow Train Coming,* which is out of all proportion to his record sales. Many still wanted to know whether or not he was 'still' a Christian. Those who seemed most upset were often orthodox Jews, even though there is no evidence Dylan had ever been a practicing Jew, merely someone born into the faith, like numberless outlaws and artists.

It wasn't just Dylan who got it in the neck when he 'converted'. His poor mother, now happily remarried, found herself on the receiving end of calls from well-known rabbis, forcing her to impart advice borne of four decades of motherhood, 'If you're upset, you try to change him.'

According to Dave Kelly, Dylan still ended up getting grief from Mum, 'The pressures that his mother was putting on him to submit to these very high Rabbis from the orthodox Judaic – it was like a war going on.' On one occasion – Kelly places it sometime early in

1980 – 'three or four rabbis, including Rebbe Menachem Schneerson . . .
turned up . . . They felt he had taken the time to study Christianity . . .
So, their position . . . was that they felt like he should give them a
chance . . . I remember them visiting a couple of times: once in the
Santa Monica studio and once while we were out on tour.'

Dylan's publicist, Paul Wasserman, also remembers 'these very religious Jews in the background, who had come in and were hanging out
[with him] . . . Dylan would also study the Torah with them.' This was
surely a reference to Louie Kemp. After a wild and wicked youth,
Kemp had gone in the opposite direction to his childhood friend,
becoming ever more Orthodox and increasingly convinced – after
attending a couple of the 1979 Santa Monica shows – that he needed to
save Dylan from himself:

> I knew he was studying the New Testament. I don't [know if] he con-
> sidered himself a Christian . . . [or just] a Jew who appreciated Jesus . . .
> [But] he studies a lot when he gets into something. And he has always
> been very spiritual. I went to a few of the shows during that period of
> time. I heard some of that [preaching] . . . People were shocked. It
> wasn't my cup of tea, and that was the beginning of me thinking, 'I
> gotta do something about this.' . . . I used to stay at the Beverly Wilshire
> for four to six weeks at a time in the Seventies, to hang out with Bob.
> Then . . . at some point he said, I got a house in Brentwood, I got plenty
> of room, why don't you move in with me?

Kemp says he moved into Dylan's Brentwood property some time
in 1980, 'And for about three years [sic] we lived there together, until I
got married in [January] 1983 . . . He'd be in one room studying the
New Testament, and I'd be in the other room studying the Torah. And
then we'd meet in the kitchen and we would try to teach or persuade
the other one about what we were reading . . . He thought Jesus
came to die for the sins of man, he was the Son of God, and he was
part of the Trinity, the Father, Son and the Holy Ghost . . . I saw Jesus
as a rabbi, teacher and another Jewish boy who'd made good . . .
Obviously we weren't on the same page.'

No great philosopher or thinker, Kemp was just another mid-west
boy done good. So, he had his work cut out facing off against an autodidact, but one who, when he dove into a subject, tended to go down

the full five fathoms. Even Kemp realized, 'after a few of these conversations . . . that he had been studying longer than me. He was more knowledgeable. I didn't have counterarguments for a lot of his arguments.' It was at this stage he made that call to Rabbi Friedman:

I said, 'Rabbi, I've got a friend who's studying the New Testament and we have these deep discussions, and I'm not equipped to counter the points that he brings up . . . If I bring you to L.A., will you meet with him?' . . . Bob liked him . . . It took a while, but I got him out . . . I probably brought Rabbi Friedman out in February or March of 1981. It was a gradual process, but within two years it was done . . . I still think he has some kind of historical appreciation for [Jesus], but he got deeply involved in studying Torah and Gemara and keeping Jewish customs and holidays . . . He went much farther in Judaism through the process of studying.

According to his childhood chum, this is what Dylan was doing in 1982 – being debriefed after going under the spell of the Vineyard Fellowship. In reality his appreciation for Jesus remained the fiery faith of an apostle, and the songs he started writing in the second half of 1982 showed only a marginal shift in his eschatological position, save to someone who'd attended those Santa Monica shows and came away *unsure* as to whether the singer was a Christian. Kemp had presumably gone for popcorn during those five-minute raps about the Devil, the true meaning of Passover and Christ's explanation to Nicodemus of what it meant to be born again.

When a cover-story ran in *Contemporary Christian* at the end of 1983, it was evidently Kemp who made himself the 'source close to' Dylan who was suggesting he'd reverted to the religion of his forefathers: 'In a sense, he never left his Judaism. My interpretation is that the New Testament and Jesus were a message he thought he got, but that he was still testing.'

Clearly, living in the same house with the man hadn't brought Kemp any closer to reading his old friend, even as he planted stories in the press that Dylan was 'again' a practicing Jew, something he had *never* demonstrably been. 'As far as we're concerned, he was a confused Jew. We feel he's coming back,' said Rabbi Kasriel Kastel. Meanwhile Dylan kept his counsel, as did his girlfriend, a devout Christian called Clydie, as they sailed the seven seas in 'his' schooner, whenever they weren't down on the farm, or in Brentwood.

But even as he kept his counsel, Dylan continued jotting down notes in another of his ubiquitous notebooks. One of those notes might have shocked Kemp, because in it he addressed the subject of evil, feeling there was too much of it in the world for it 'to be an accident'. He suggested that anyone who sought to 'expose an obvious truth' was done for, citing John F. Kennedy as one example. Only when one is 'standing on that foundation' – meaning the solid rock that is Christ – could one see things clearly, and realize that 'the purpose of this earth is to prepare you for the life to come, [because] your mind is shut off from the day you're born . . . and all you can go on is faith.' He would say something similar to the journalist Martin Keller the following July, 'I was born knowing the truth. Everybody is. Trouble is they get it knocked out of them before they can walk.'

In the same interview he also stated that he wasn't looking for his 'roots in synagogues with six pointed Egyptian stars shining down from every window'. This still proved too oblique for those comfortable with Dylan being a Jew, but not a believer in the same Messiah as those who arrived on the Mayflower. Dylan had little time for those who seemed obsessed about his private beliefs, 'People want to know where I'm at, because they don't know where they're at.'

Kemp was not the only old Jewish friend convinced Dylan was backsliding by the early Eighties. Even after Dylan released two albums in 1983 and 1985 that reaffirmed his Christian faith – *Infidels* and *Empire Burlesque* – that other unorthodox Jewish poet, Allen Ginsberg, a practicing Buddhist, was quoted as saying, 'It might have been expected that he'd evolve out of [Born Again Christianity] as something closer to his natural Judaism. Which he has . . . He hasn't been a born-again Christian for a long time now. People still think he is, and five years ago he changed.'

At much the same time Ginsberg was speaking his mind, Dylan was editing a TV special, a project he'd been trying to get to air since 1980. He was determined to ensure it opened with 'In The Garden', a song he prefaced on both nights filmed in Sydney that February with the following rap: 'We always sing this last song here. It's about my hero. Everybody's got a hero. [For] some people . . . money is a hero, success is a hero. To lots of people, Michael Jackson's a hero. [Or] Bruce

Springsteen . . . Well, I wanna sing about my hero, I don't care about those heroes. I have my own hero . . .'

The female director of the TV special, Gillian Armstrong, whose favourite film was presumably *Vertigo*, hated the song and didn't want it included. Dylan told her 'In The Garden' went first, or there would be no TV special. Guess who won that argument. And still, his spellbound friends continued to doubt his faith.*

---

* When the BBC decided to take it upon themselves to re-edit the *Hard To Handle* TV special prior to broadcast, they were royally ticked off by a furious Dylan. It was never shown again by the Beeb.

Part 5

Thief On The Cross

I would not put a thief in my mouth to steal my brains.
William Shakespeare.

Whoever is not a misanthrope at forty can never have loved mankind.
Nicolas Chamfort.

The Christianity of the majority consists roughly of two notions: first of all the saying . . . that one must become . . . as a little child [in order to enter] the Kingdom of Heaven; the second is the thief on the cross. People live by virtue of the former – in death they reckon upon consoling themselves with the example of the thief.
Søren Kierkegaard.

If God lived on earth, people would break his windows.
Yiddish proverb.

I have drawn from the well of language many a thought which I do not have and which I could not put into words.
G. C. Lichtenberg.

Success and failure are equally disastrous.
Tennessee Williams.

Success and failure are both difficult to endure. Along with success come drugs, divorce, fornication . . . medication, depression, neurosis and suicide. With failure comes failure.

Joseph Heller.

Success is feminine, and like a woman, if you cringe before her, she will override you.

William Faulkner.

Talking about Dylan is too complicated for just a few words. You can see why everybody writes books about him. It seems that anyone who likes him at all has a relationship with him, whether they admit it or not, that's just about as personal as any they have with people they actually know . . . No wonder he resents his fans.

Richard Hell, 2005.

Dylan is about the Individual against the whole of creation.

'Is About', Allen Ginsberg, 1996.

January 1983 to April 1984:
King Snake Will Crawl

Infidel: In New York, one who does not believe in the Christian religion; in Constantinople, one who does.

Ambrose Bierce, *The Devil's Dictionary*.

The Christian period . . . was a whole other 'moment' . . . [But] Bob's a guy who gets very passionate about living in the moment, and whatever his pursuit is in that moment. And then things just fade, and change.

Larry Sloman, *Isis* #104.

The artists that are really successful, that make platinum records . . . are compromising a whole lot . . . just calculating what the audience will want . . . I don't look at those people as true artists.

Bob Dylan, to Randy Anderson, February 1978.

Austin Scaggs: Am I crazy to love *Street Legal*, *Slow Train Coming* and *Infidels*?
Bob Dylan: . . . I . . . can't listen to those records. I'll hear too many faults. I was just being swept along . . . when I was making those records.

26th October 2004.

He's always talking about these people trying to force him into a mould, and they're not. It's just his story.

Barry Kornfeld.

Bill Flanagan: Do you think it's appropriate to write in the voice of a killer, as Bruce Springsteen did in [the song] 'Nebraska'?
Bob Dylan: I'm not too familiar with that particular song of Bruce's . . .

BF: Mark Knopfler told me that you wrote a song called 'Prison Guard' and Mark took that song to be a sort of reaction to *Nebraska*.

BD: Oh, yeah . . . I did write a song like that, but I never recorded it. I didn't think I needed to record it. It was a talking [blues] thing about this prison guard who's just sort of a rough character. He doesn't mind throwing people off the fourth tier and busting anybody's head in. And then it goes on to describe his family and his town. Then when I got done, I just thought it was pretty pathetic . . .

BF: But it wasn't inspired by or a take-off on *Nebraska*?

BD: Uh, I don't know what inspired it.

Bill Flanagan, March 1985.

using the pulpit for social change – . . . everything i do is amplified.

Bob Dylan, typed page of 'random' notes to himself c. July 1982.

★

So, what was Dylan *really* doing in 1982, a year when he jumped off pop culture's cliff? For the first few months, he was grieving, after a third confidant he had first known in the early Sixties had taken his own life, as Clayton and Ochs had done; doing so just hours before they were due to meet at Rundown Studios to discuss their latest film project. The meeting had been scheduled for New Year's Day, but when Arthur Rosato phoned Howard Alk on New Year's Eve to confirm the arrangement, Alk, who had a history of substance abuse, said he couldn't make it. When asked why, he said he was committing suicide. It turned out, he wasn't joking.

It was another blow from the hand of fate, to which Dylan had thought he was inured. As he told a girlfriend, after the late great Stevie Ray Vaughan died unexpectedly, 'It still seems so unreal, like it couldn't be so. But every once in a while, it'll sink in that I'll really never see him again. That he's in tiny pieces. The feelings just become overwhelming. But most of the time I just don't think of it as real. In my life there've been so many people that come and go, that I don't see for months or years at a time . . . Then I'll run into them again. So, I think of [him] that way. That he's just out there working somewhere.'

Alk's death would be the end of Dylan's cinematic ambitions for a while. It also signalled the end of the Rundown era. He duly disappeared between the cracks, not re-emerging until June 6th, when he joined Joan Baez to perform three songs at an outdoor anti-nuclear benefit show in Pasadena, 'Peace Sunday', having – according to Sounes – 'fled to Baez's home around this time after running into trouble with one of his girl-friends'. Note the emotive language – not just visited Baez, but 'fled' to her. Given that he was seen with constant companion Clydie King weeks later, between attending shows in the Twin Cities with his son Jesse, if there really was trouble, it was transitory. As was life. Hence, presum-ably, the self-conscious inclusion of Jimmy Buffet's 'Pirate Looks At Forty' at Peace Sunday a fortnight after 'the voice of a generation' turned forty-one.

If Dylan was fleetingly interested in some 'Genius . . . inflicted with poison & questionable virtue' – another cryptic line from that typed July 1982 list – it was presumably another flawed genius he had in mind. His own retirement he intended to be brief, signing a new con-tract with CBS on July 1st that committed him to five more albums in five years, though again with no album 'delivered earlier than six months . . . after the delivery of the preceding Album.' Those days were long gone.

It would be ten long months before he even began recording the first album of his new contract. On the day he signed on the dotted line, he furnished no evidence he had *any* songs in the works. The first song he felt compelled to write was, as per usual, in response to external events, in this case the release of Bruce Springsteen's sixth CBS album and first solo album, *Nebraska*, on September 30th, 1982.

Springsteen had made an album which reflected a remark from Len-non when accused of trying to emulate Dylan (on 1970's 'Working Class Hero'), 'Anybody that sings with a guitar . . . about something heavy will tend to sound like Dylan.' Dylan's skin was now easier to pierce, and he was evidently not amused by the comparison some crit-ics chose to make between his early acoustic work and Springsteen's album of home demos,* complaining to Mikal Gilmore, 'People say to me, "When you gonna make a *Nebraska* album?" Well, I love that record, but I think I've made five or six *Nebraska* albums.'

---

* *Nebraska* was originally intended as demos for the E Street Band to learn the songs prior to recording a full band version of these songs. That album *was* recorded, but remains unreleased.

It was a right-on rebuttal, but it was not enough. Having parodied Lennon's attempt to emulate an earlier style of his with 'Fourth Time Around', he now set about doing the same to Springsteen. He may have told *Musician*'s editor he didn't 'know what inspired' 'Prison Guard', but that was smoke'n'mirr'rs. When the first-person guard said he had 'a brother who works in a factory, making shoelaces to feed his family', we know his address is 'on the edge of town', and when he says he's 'a guard in a federal pen' who 'just for fun' loves 'to kill men', we know he's a friend of Charlie Starkweather. The final pay-off suggests Dylan didn't buy Springsteen's explanation for the deeds of men, even those from the badlands: 'Don't know what it is that makes me like to torture folks/ Guess I had a bad childhood – guess I couldn't take a joke.'*

Later, Dylan concluded his riposte to the great pretender 'was pretty pathetic', and even though he thought the dire 'Julius And Ethel' worthy of copyrighting, he never even demoed 'Prison Guard'.† Parodying Springsteen, though, remained on the agenda, flowering five years later with perhaps his wittiest pastiche-song, 'Tweeter And The Monkey Man', the highlight of his most successful album of the Eighties.

His real message for mankind, though, was that the Caribbean wind still howled, even if the distant ship of liberty had been hijacked by a jokerman wearing a disguise. The idea came as he sailed the *Water Pearl*. As he explained to Kurt Loder, ' "Jokerman" kinda came to me in the islands. It's very mystical. The shapes there, and shadows, seem to be so ancient.' A song that would go through more transformations than Lucius's *The Golden Ass*, taking in at least a dozen typed or handwritten drafts, the 'distant ships sailing into the mist' would not manifest themselves for a while. Indeed, on the first typed draft, we are near dry land, namechecking a Sinatra movie: 'Standing in the river catching fish with your hand/ while the eyes of the man with the golden arm are glowing . . .'

Throughout the process, the identity of the Jokerman would remain

---

* Almost certainly, a send-up of 'Nebraska's last line, "I guess there's just a meanness in this world." '

† Something called 'Prison Station Blues' was logged at the *Infidels* sessions, but if it was ever recorded, it was erased, replaced by a minute-long snatch of The Carter Family's 'Wildwood Flower'.

oblique: was he the false messiah, Dylan himself or some celluloid alter-ego? The image of him 'shedding off one more layer of skin/ playing hide & seek with the child within,' reminds one of Ginsberg's depiction of Renaldo, 'shedding . . . skin, just like a snake. If a snake doesn't shed his skin, he's through – he decays.' But a false Messiah also bestrides the song, as he shall throughout *Infidels* – hence, presumably, a note in pencil at the top of one 'Jokerman' draft, 'REVELATION TELLS YOU THAT THE RIGHTEOUS . . .', surely a reference to Revelation 22:11: 'He that is unjust, let him be unjust still; and he which is filthy, let him be filthy still; and he that is righteous, let him be righteous still.'

The narrator seems to have such a person in mind when a Dylan-esque character enters in verse four, 'Living like a madman suffering from love, polluted by nothing, reciting Keats and Shelley/ Your life has been a series of breaths – you played Hamlet . . . Macbeth and Machiavelli.'* Only at the end of the song is it clear that it is about two sundered souls, and this Jokerman was always destined to cross paths with the false Thief:

5. You're a milkcow blues preacher, from a country so torn
Great princes died the day you were born & it was predetermined . . .

[6.] It's a shadowy world – skies are slippery grey/ A woman just gave birth
   to a wolf today . . .
He'll run with the pack & be the man of the hour – he'll divide the house
   and have bargaining power -
Oh, Jokerman, you know what he wants . . .

Here was living proof that the Caribbean wind had not died, or loved, in vain. The messianic nature of the prince of plunder will become only more apparent, as the song is meticulously reworked and refined, passing through an interim stage where, 'He'll sit on the throne & step into power – divide the house & root out every flower in the garden,' until by the time of the recording, he'll have the power to 'take a woman who could have been Joan of Arc and turn her into a harlot'.

'Jokerman' definitively debunks the notion that Kemp and/or rabbis

---

* The only vestige of this couplet in the final song is the Keatsian reference to 'the nightingale tune'.

in his Rollodex had cured Dylan of his fascination with Revelation. As Dylan told Loder in March 1984, 'I've always thought there's a superior power, that . . . no soul has died, every soul is alive, either in holiness or in flames . . . I believe in the Book of Revelation'; and, to an English journalist, three months later, 'Ever since Adam and Eve got thrown out of the garden . . . the whole . . . planet has been heading in one direction – towards Apocalypse. It's all there in the Book of Revelations.' No ambiguity – no prisoners – no man righteous.

Dylan may have cut away the vine, but in 1982-3 Lindsey's redaction of St John the Divine continued to hold sway in this lapsed Jew's cosmology. And Satan, too, remained as real as ever, still hatching his masterplan, as evidenced by another new song which coloured in more of the Antichrist's picture profile, stripping away a few more of his disguises. As he later warned Scott Cohen, and *Spin*'s readers, the Devil's envoy won't be 'some crackpot lawyer or politician with the mark of the beast, but somebody who makes them feel holy'; someone who would present himself as a man of peace:

> 6. He'll take you to a mansion called the house of mirrors
> He'll be the answer to your prayers (he'll scratch your itching ears)
> Don't you worry sister, take it from me, there'll be a tax increase
> Sometimes Satan come as a man of peace . . .
>
> 8. He will spread the cards for you and he will pull the shade
> Jack of diamonds, six of clubs, ten of hearts, ace of spades
> But your heart is on the table and your soul is in the shadow of the beast
> Sometimes Satan comes as a man of peace.*

It takes until the ninth verse of the 'Man Of Peace' ms. for Dylan to remove the mask from this charismatic man, 'He will make you think his messengers are three kings riding from the east.' The released take, which only runs to eight verses, successfully lyricised the notion he'd imparted to Neil Spencer back in July 1981, 'The Devil, that's the real enemy, but he tends to shade himself and hide himself and put it into

---

* This verse, which Dylan marked as 'questionable', will be deleted from the final song.

people's minds that he's really not there, and . . . he's feeding you envy and jealousy, he's feeding you oppression, hatred.'

The third song from the first batch of *Infidels* songs tapped directly into the black hole at the centre of the Lindsey liturgy and was even more incendiary than 'Man Of Peace'. 'Neighborhood Bully' seemed, on the surface, to be a song about Israel's precarious existence, surrounded by Semitic states of hate, its very future perennially in doubt, articulated most clearly in a scrapped seventh verse:

> Wars are being fought every day, every hour
> Over vain ways of life, over economic power
> Some fight to conquer – others fighting to resist
> He's fighting for nothing but the right to exist.

Only later did Dylan admit to a more apocalyptic dimension, chastising Kurt Loder for trying to make it pertinent to 'what's going on today. But what's going on today isn't gonna last. The battle of Armageddon is specifically spelled out: where it will be fought and . . . when it will be fought. And the battle of Armageddon definitely will be fought in the Middle East.' In Israel, to be precise.

With these three songs, Dylan had the core songs for a natural successor to *Shot of Love*. He just needed to sweeten the pot. After all, CBS were expecting a more nuanced work after they vouchsafed their own act of faith with dollars. When the ever-contrary Dylan came up with the album title, SURVIVING IN A RUTHLESS WORLD, some of 'the whores on Seventh Avenue' began to get a bad feeling. He also wanted another line from Scripture on the sleeve somewhere, one that made a mockery of their worldly wisdom, 1 Corinthians 3:19: 'For the wisdom of the world is foolishness unto God.'

Even when he played his long-standing A&R man, Don DeVito, a song ostensibly about America's economic plight, 'Union Sundown', he never explained its underlying message, one he did reveal after the album's release to the redoubtable Robert Hilburn, 'The Enemy is . . . just going to buy America or steal America, and sell it back to them.' By then, he had deleted the most telling verse from the song, one which made the president complicit in the sale of his country to the Enemy's emissary:

> There's a man in a mask in the White House,
> Who's got no name or important ties.
> Just as long as he understands the shape of things to come,
> He can stay there till he dies.

Despite having hardly any new songs to his name when *Nebraska* appeared, Dylan had enough songs by the New Year to start looking for a new producer to help him make an album that pitched itself to 'pauper or pilgrim or permanent stranger', all namechecked in an early 'License To Kill'. Dylan had got his ambition back. Now he just needed someone to explain how to reach this audience with music that relied not on technology, but on a pair of ears and a beating heart. It was a growing concern, expressed as far back as 1978: 'Once you get into [all this] production, you aren't going to tell too much of the story at all. Records nowadays are all production . . . The old ballad singers . . . used to lay it out and . . . [you] could decide for your[self] which side was right and which was wrong.'

This troubled troubadour was worried his audience might not meet him halfway any more. Hence why, some time in January, he called on a recent collaborator more *au fait* with Eighties sounds at his New York home. Having failed to call ahead, he came away empty-handed. Only when Mark Knopfler returned home from an errand did his wife Lourdes inform him the maverick musician had shown up, looking for him.

Knopfler's own career had gone from strength to strength. Dire Strait's most recent pop confection, *Love Over Gold*, had been their most successful to date. Meanwhile, a despondent Dylan called at the apartment of Larry Sloman, beleaguered by doubt, 'He was unsure what kind of sound he wanted for *Infidels*. We spent at least six hours that night just listening to different albums from my collection. I made some suggestions . . . [including] Sly Dunbar and Robbie Shakespeare.'

If Sloman was indeed responsible for suggesting that Dylan use Jamaica's finest as his new rhythm-section, he did the music world a huge favour. In the slim notebook Dylan was carrying with him at the time he wrote down a provisional studio combo comprising 'Smitty' [Willie Smith], Steve Cropper, Jerry Scheff or Donald 'Duck' Dunn – all worthy of his trust – and Ian Wallace, the man with 'a beat like a cop'.

If Knopfler was to be the bridge between Luddite singer-songwriter and modern technology, that list of musicians was a non-starter. Dylan's goal – articulated to Hilburn the following June – was to provide a real alternative for people 'constantly being bombarded by insulting and humiliating music, which people are making . . . the way they make . . . Wonder Bread . . . I'm afraid roots music is going to be obsolete, the way we're going.'

To remind himself what the music he still loved sounded like, he took himself down to the Lone Star Cafe one evening in February, to sit in with old friends Rick Danko and Levon Helm and entertain the natives, only to find another old friend from the Sixties backstage, one he was not quite so happy to see:*

> **Al Aronowitz**: Danko and Levon Helm [are] in their dressing room at the old Lone Star . . . In walks Bob, with a sour look on his face . . . 'Get the fuck out of here!' . . . What's he angry with me about? . . . I look to Levon and Rick. After all, it's their dressing room. They keep talking to each other, pretending not to notice what's going on . . . I head for the door. The gorgeous creature [I'm with] follows me down the stairs to the street. She'd told me she was a professional dominatrix . . . She'd met Bob when she was a child . . . Her father was Dr Ed [Thaler], in whose house Bob lived for a while after his motorcycle accident . . . When my statuesque beauty and I get to the sidewalk, she tells me, 'Just before we walked out, Bob ran his hand down my side.' 'Did that bother you?' 'No, I liked it.'

This she-creature from the Catskills may have unwittingly inspired a new song which articulated what Dylan had failed to say to her in person, even after he got physical: 'What's a sweetheart like you doing in a dump like this?' The Lone Star was certainly a dump. As for 'the boss' who 'ain't here', there was only ever one 'boss' in Dylan's mind: mutual acquaintance, 'Uncle' Albert. He was certainly on Dylan's mind. The court battle between the two was heating up, just as he was depicting 'the boss' of this song as someone who 'caught the Red Eye, it left on time/ He's starting a graveyard down there.'

---

* Aronowitz admitted to me that it was his own crack-cocaine habit which had alienated him from Dylan.

'Sweetheart Like You' was one of eleven songs Dylan now listed at the end of another slim notebook, though the notebook itself contains just two lines from the song: 'Got to have done some worthless deed,' and, 'It's here all right, it's called the land of permanent bliss.' As for the ongoing court case, Dylan had already ramped up the pressure by stopping all payments to Grossman, as papers filed at Kingston court confirm:

> There were essentially two aspects to the Affirmative Claim: first, that the Artist's accountings over the years were simply incorrect and had not credited to plaintiffs their rightful share of income; and second . . . Decedent [was] entitled to share in an increase in the royalties . . . negotiated by the Artist after the Management Agreement had terminated in 1969 . . . The Artist thereupon asserted 18 counterclaims and 16 affirmative defences alleging . . . that he had been fraudulently induced into the various agreements by Decedent at a young age . . . The Artist, starting in January 1982, withheld all further management fees and income payments under the [various] Agreements.

Simply put, Dylan wanted to show Grossman he could not be bullied. If there was a neighbourhood bully in the new Woodstock, he was not called Al. If he was troubled by his own double standards, there's no evidence in either of the two 1983 notebooks housed in Tulsa, aside from a very rough draft of another new song, 'I And I', which suggested he was having trouble sleeping.

After this are three blank pages and those eleven shorthand songtitles, all readily identifiable: Sweetheart [Like You]/ I and I/ Death [Is Not The End]/ License [To Kill]/ Don't Fall [Apart On Me Tonight]/ Joker [Man]/ Neighbor[hood Bully]/ Julius [And Ethel]/ Tell Me/ Man Of Peace/ Union [Sundown]. Presumably, these are the eleven songs he had in some form at the end of February/ early March, but not all of them are oven-ready.

The first two songs are very much at the raw idea stage, with 'Sweetheart Like You' requiring a whole day of recording to knock into shape as Dylan speed-dialled some shape-shifting lyrics till he had her nailed. The other two songs where lovers converse – 'Tell Me' and 'Don't Fall Apart On Me Tonight' – would both go through a similar, surprisingly laborious process in the studio, but from a more formalised starting point, the latter appearing in fragmentary form on page one of the 'January 1983' notebook, before occupying nine drafts without ever becoming 'Just Like A Woman' revisited.

'I And I', an important song, had evidently come to him when all he had to hand was the notebook, occupying pages 26-28, 30 and 33 of the same notebook. The parts fell into place with surprising ease, though nothing like the ease he suggested to Leonard Cohen sharing a cappuccino in gay Paris the following year. Discussing songwriting, a favourite topic, Dylan asked Cohen how long it took him to write 'Hallelujah'. Cohen replied – honestly – two years, before asking how long 'I And I' took. Dylan said fifteen minutes. I think not, but its inclusion in one of his 'ideas' notebooks in a recognisable shape – the only song where this is the case – suggests it hit him like a tree. He'd probably been carrying the idea around after hearing the Rastafarian crew of the *Water Pearl* using the expression while blaring Bob Marley and Peter Tosh through the ship's speakers.*

Oddly enough, this sketchy attempt at 'I And I's lyrics appears below another cryptic title, 'While Men Die of Hunger'. Little more than a series of stray lines at this stage – 'It's been years since a strange woman slept in my bed . . . Don't feel like sleeping and I got much on my mind/ Besides if she wakes up, I'll just have to talk . . . Outside [are] two men on a train platform, they're waiting for a ghost' – it rather suggests the idea came to him whole. It was like back in '65, when he told Maureen Cleave, 'I write down the idea [in] say an hour, and then I just fill the [verses] in as time goes by.'

The lines he ends up discarding this time hardly comprise 'pages of vomit'. They just take the song somewhere he doesn't want to go: 'Don't want to make too much noise/ She'll think I'm leaving her behind . . . I never thought I'd see the day when I could whisper I love you to a deaf mute . . . No-one up ahead ['cept] the woman at the well . . . Up [ahead] the holy mountain of Zion, behind me ashes . . .' All mouth-watering images, none taking us anywhere. On the other hand, the evocative 'walking through the meadowland during the rain', will survive to the album take, only to be edited out at the death.†

---

* The expression means God is within all men, a Gnostic concept Dylan mirrors in the line, 'Never could look at your face and call it mine.'
† The complete take clocks in at 7.22; the released take is 5.13.

All he needs now is a bridge – which appears five pages later ('Took an untrodden path . . .') – and a less confessional line than, 'If she wakes up, she'll ask me my name.'

Though he never completes the song in the notebook, he knows what he has and where it must go. He needed this one, big-time. The song-list indicated he had an album's worth of songs, but what he did not have was an *album*. For the first time since *New Morning*, he was entering the studio light on songs of quality, and too many of a type.

Four of the songs – 'License To Kill', 'Union Sundown', 'Julius And Ethel' and 'Death Is Not The End' – had outtake written all over them, and needed replacing, preferably using some stray ideas scattered across the notebooks: 'Stared at the face of an angel and I learned her features well'; 'I was telling myself, ain't nothing worth stealing in here'; or howabout, 'Never could drink [Your] blood and call it wine.'

At forty-something, he still had a burning need to tell people the end is nigh. As he said in July 1983, 'Most people's sensibilities are determined by the newspaper they read . . . It's doing nothing to get you into the world to come.' The pulpiteer was wearing a disguise, but he was still selling pulpit fiction, even as he began playing some of the songs to interested parties, notably Mark Knopfler, with whom he'd finally reconnected and who had agreed to sign on for the duration as (co-)producer – just as soon as he stopped promoting his own new album. Now there's an idea! Thankfully, Dire Straits selling out shows and shifting product in equal measures gave Dylan time to develop an idea he'd jotted down at the bottom of an early version of 'Jokerman', 'I hear the tribes a-moaning . . . Nobody sings the blues like BWM.'

Who, pray tell, was 'BWM'? It turned out he was 'the Van Gogh of the country Blues', as Dylan described him in 1991. Blind Willie McTell (pronounced McTier) was a largely forgotten blues singer, save for his Allmanized 'Statesboro Blues'. Unlike Van Gogh, though, he had a long and varied career and one of the most scattershot discographies of any blues artist. What he didn't specialise in was songs about the end of the world, death and redemption. That would be Blind Willie Johnson, a far harder name to rhyme.

Again, Dylan locked into a song that really did come roaring in like Ezekiel's chariot. Just one draft exists, five typewritten verses and a handwritten final verse, with Dylan only ever changing a single line. What he had to say he'd been storing up since that early 'Jokerman' – a valedictory for the world, written the night he went for a walk, humming an old blues song in his head, knowing 'the world could end tonight'. The tune was 'St James Infirmary', which in its original form was closely modelled on 'The Unfortunate Rake', and as ripe for adaptation as 'Ye Tramps And Hawkers'.

Dylan had found the album's anthem, and starting point. Sure enough, when he joined Mark Knopfler, Dire Straits keyboardist Alan Clark, their de facto engineer Neil Dorfsman, the ex-Bluesbreaker who once saved the Stones from their more destructive demons, Mick Taylor, and Jamaican rhythm duo Sly'n'Robbie at New York's Power Station on April 11th, this was the song he wanted to nail to the studio wall on day one.

Working up this oh-so-familiar melody would also tell Dylan if this combination had what it took, and/or whether the technology Knopfler and Dorfsman had sold him on was laced with snake oil. Because Dylan had gone digital, ahead of most of his contemporaries, albeit a whole three years after Bruce. The idea that a digital dub was sonically identical to the master had proven so appealing to Dorfsman and Knopfler, after making *Love Over Gold* this way, that they had sworn never to use analogue again. The 1" digital tape they were using was called the 3M system, it cost $90 per 32-minute reel, and it would prove to be so future-proofed that forty years later exactly one studio in the world can play this format.

Not that it was the sound quality of the songs taped that really concerned Dylan, it was those Godawful headphones. As he said in 2015, still an audiophile agnostic, 'There's a complete disconnect. You can overwhelm yourself in your own head. I've never heard anybody sing with those things in their ears effectively. They just give you a false sense of security.' They also allowed the engineer, Josh Abbey, to feed a false signal into the phones that convinced the singer his electric guitar – an instrument Dylan still hadn't mastered – was in the mix, when it was barely there. If Dylan could hear the room, that little ruse was a non-starter.

The duo needed to convince Dylan to use 'phones. Placing Dunbar's drums in the so-called piano room, Knopfler and Shakespeare in a separate annex, and Mick Taylor, Dylan and keyboardist Clark in the main room, near the amps, still meant everyone could see Bob. It just necessitated everyone, Dylan included, use headphones. One participant watched on with amused detachment as the maverick refused to play ball, just as he had when Tom Wilson had tried a similar subterfuge way back when:

> **Alan Clark**: Bob would wander in, sit down, put his headphones on and struggle with his guitar strap for a couple of minutes, light a cigarette and then stub the cigarette out, take his guitar off, take his headphones off and walk across to the organ where I was sitting and write down about . . . half a dozen lines of the next tune in tiny, meticulous hand-writing . . . wander back over, maybe forget to put the headphones on, and start playing the track.

When not playing the piano, Dylan would insist on playing electric guitar, often vying with the two fine guitarists chosen to put their imprint on the album, cranking up his amp like it was a rehearsal. So, whenever a take seemed imminent, Dorfsman would dim the studio lights and instruct assistant engineer Josh Abbey to sneak into the studio and put Dylan's amp on standby, muting the sound to the room, while Dorfsman fed the signal for the guitar to Bob's head-phones. Dylan finally sussed out something wasn't right, and complained to Dorfsman, 'Neil, my guitar sounds like a banjo in my headphones.' Dorfsman assured him he would look into it. But he never did.

Some of the musicians were delighted by the easy informality Dylan brought to the process. Dunbar, in particular, who liked to read heavy metal magazines at his drum stool while the others listened to play-backs, always enjoyed playing by the seat of his pants. He remembers Dylan 'would just come into the studio with his 'armonica and his gui-tar, and he start to play the song, and we just fall into the groove. He would take different takes of a song in different keys and he would change words on the fly . . . I remember us running down "Jokerman" without realizing it was being recorded. Then at the end Bob said, "That's it!" ' Welcome to the world according to Dylan.

Heading off another quirk at the pass – Dylan's tendency to just start playing, never thinking to cue up the musicians – Dorfsman adopted the practice from *Shot of Love* of running quarter-inch, two-track reference reels throughout. According to Abbey, 'Running tapes like those was not standard procedure. I cannot remember ever doing it before . . . *Infidels.*' And still, as Abbey soon discovered, nobody can fuck with musicians like Blind Boy Grunt.

On day one, though, the signs were propitious, Dylan getting straight down to business. Even before he eulogized McTell, he did a vocal tryout on the other ready-to-record masterpiece, 'Jokerman', using a rather lovely melody line he will never revisit. Yet a warm-up is all it is – unlike take one of 'Blind Willie McTell' (released on 45 in 2021), which for most artists would have been a keeper. Take two is even better, Dylan leading the troupe with his driving piano, whooping it up with the harp, but fluffing the ending.

He knows he is near, but rather than nail it to the cross, Dylan switches to a seven-minute improvised blues called 'Oh Babe', where the vocals unfurl like a sailing ship in cross winds. Gloriously throw-away, it still said more than a whole box of 3M takes of 'Union Sundown' and 'Julius And Ethel'. It also put the band through its paces, testing their mettle preparatory to a 'McTell' for the ages; Dylan's best studio vocal since 'When He Returns', playing off musicians helplessly swept along by the moment.

Sensing a tide which, taken at the flood, should lead to fortune, he immediately switched to 'Don't Fall Apart On Me Tonight', recording a meticulously executed slow waltz (released on 2021's *Springtime In New York*), complete with meandering five-minute instrumental coda, a sure sign he was in the groove, asking for one more take before he called it a day; this one prefaced with the instruction, 'Let's do it all the way through, then listen to it, see what sounds right, what sounds wrong and then do it again. I want to play it so they can dance to it in an old folks' home.' One imagines he slept well at the Ritz-Carlton Hotel that night.

Taking up where they had left off the day before, the reassembled ensemble jumped right in on the 12th with two complete takes, the second of which said all this song was ever gonna say. But Dylan had forgotten the Rosato Rule – 'The most takes . . . for any [song] was usually . . . three . . . [because] Bob always put as much into perform-ing any song the first time as the last.'

Knopfler thought he still adhered to it, 'You try and get things run down before the thing is attempted, because after two or three times Bob would have moved on to something else.' Not with 'Don't Fall Apart . . .', he didn't. He would spend the whole of the inglorious 12th battering the song into submission, cutting five more complete takes, none better than this one, establishing a worrying pattern for the next three weeks of work.

Was it just an aberration running away with him? Certainly, for the next two days Dylan remembered Arthur's Dictum, cutting 'Jokerman' – already earmarked as the central song, probably the opener – in three takes and the admittedly superfluous 'License To Kill' in one on the 13th; a seven-minute 'Clean Cut Kid' good enough to be copyrighted; an earnest stab at Sinatra's 'This Was My Love' – Dylan picking out the tune at the piano, while a baffled band wondered when to come in – and that kick-in-the-balls to all unbelievers, 'Man Of Peace', captured the very first time on the 14th. Dylan wrapped up the session by doing a first rough mix on 'Jokerman'.

Four days in, he already had six usable originals – even if one of them was 'License To Kill', one of his sloppiest, stupidest lyrics. Though it could have been worse, Dylan later writing about the space programme – apparently the point at which 'man . . . invented his doom' – 'Can't build a tower of Babel. God says you don't come here.' Adding insult to injury, he mixed out Taylor's tasteful slide from the song, as great a mistake as removing Al Kooper's organ from 'Ballad Of A Thin Man'.*

But a week later – after six more days of sessions – he had not yet moved from this spot. Instead, the sessions became a series of song-rehearsals at best, melodious doodling and halting covers at worst. Four of these days were spent trying to get increasingly belaboured renditions of songs he would have previously tried thrice and then re-rolled the dice.

'Sweetheart Like You' and 'Tell Me' both needed work because Dylan simply hadn't finished them, or decided what to do with them. Part of the problem with 'Sweetheart' was that as soon as the band got a handle on the arrangement, Dylan changed it, prompting Knopfler to remark, 'It's different than when you played it at my place the other night.' Dylan, too, was growing frustrated, complaining, 'This song is giving me trouble. I don't know why. Feels so ordinary.' And there we

---

* Perhaps predictaby, Dylan delivered two of his finest-ever live performances with this misfiring rant, on *Late Night With David Letterman* in March 1984 and the third night in Prague, March 1995.

have it. A torch-ballad that *had* stood the test of time, 'This Was My Love', took up most of the 20th, yet even after six full takes was surely never a candidate for the album.

Only 'Neighborhood Bully' managed to keep the fire in its belly long enough to generate three full takes and a vocal that made 'Property Of Jesus' sound like a prayer. Unconcerned that he might be misunderstood, Dylan later added horns to the song – rather effectively – and just as promptly took them off. At least he had the song to mirror 'Man Of Peace's bleak worldview. What he didn't have was another couple of songs as good as 'Jokerman' or 'Blind Willie McTell'.

So, he was just gonna have to write them mid-session, something he hadn't done since *Blood on the Tracks*. He had a fine lil' tune for one called 'Someone's Got A Hold Of My Heart', which he taught the band at an otherwise wasted session on the 16th. Now he just needed some words. What he came up with by the 25th, when he first recorded the song with lyrics, proved that this man still had the sweet gift of gab and then some. Here was another testimony, à la Blind Willie McTell, to a Son of Man who really had grabbed a hold of his heart, and wouldn't let go, no matter how hard Louie and his rabbinical horde tried to dislodge Him. Its original lyrical form, never recorded, was as much of a confessional as 'Every Grain Of Sand', and just as heartfelt:

> What I used to find easy now I can't locate
> There is love now where there used to be hate . . .
> I know why I'm reeling, but [I] am focused and so still
> Because my mind is fixed upon what's keeping me fulfilled . . .
> I know why the sons of Adam killed each other and went broke
> In the golden age of voodoo, what was righteous was a joke . . .

And still he held off from explicating His identity, until revelation came like a freight train:

> It's getting harder and harder for me to sleep at night
> I keep seeing visions of you wearing a robe of white . . .
> The sound of a freight train blasts into my ears
> In the coolness of the evening, a vision appears
> It's just like you told me, it's just like you said it would be.

You plant yourself in front of me like a lightning bolt that burns
What I've taught so well to others, I see now myself I've got to learn.

If he really pulled all this together in a few nights, it was quite a
statement. But was it a statement he wanted to make public, or did he
prefer to continue muddying the waters? The very first draft was him
at his most personal, hinting at how he'd been called before, but failed
to hear the summons: 'Something has changed. I've changed/ I'm a
little different can't ya see . . . There's a melody I heard before some
place in the (my) past/ That long time melody, it just might've come
back to me at last.' But rather than letting a vision resonate which left
him unable to 'concentrate on what I used to be able to do so effortlessly', he began to make the lyric about two Yous: the ancient one
who taught him to drink His blood and call it wine, and the one who
told him how it would be, the precious angel of yore.

It was like the song had been infected by the same virus that now
infected 'Tell Me' – a song on that March checklist which in its notebook guise asked questions like, 'Who'd you like me to be? . . . Do you
see anything [of] me? . . . Is it too early or too late? . . . Is that the real
face that you wear?' Dylan now spent the whole of the April 21st session deflecting a woman's probing questions away from his real self.

Barely had he begun to work on 'Someone's Got a Hold . . .', than
he wrote a note to himself: 'do not be misled – don't hide in the
shadows – don't look this way or that.' It was the springboard for a
radically different narrative, another epic depiction of a man brought
down by pride, 'Too Late'. Having seemingly seen off 'Tell Me', he
produced 'Too Late' the following day, though not before discarding a
fine third verse that seemed to inhabit the same apocalyptic landscape
as 'Makin' A Liar' and 'Angelina':

Now the man upstairs with nine green eyes who walks on stilts gonna kiss
    yr mouth and write his laws upon yr heart
And Miss Brazil with her lights punched out is gonna contact you and
    when she does, you're gonna hope the seas will part
Some high cheek-boned queen who smells like peaches and chlorine is
    gonna call yr name and you'll wanna investigate
She'll feed ya after midnight . . . that is, if you don't mind sleeping with
    yr head face down in the plate.

Capturing 'Too Late' on the very first complete take – *if* the Rosato Rule still applied, and he had been prepared to do some minor vocal punch-ins – it was everything he'd been trying to say about this world of sin since his private note, the previous year, about the prevalence of evil. It all came together in a single song, about a man who had died in suspicious circumstances, set at his funeral, attended by characters straight out of a painting by Bosch.

And it seemed like the narrator might be next: 'Tomorrow they'll be nailing up posters on public walls with yr face on it staring into fairyland'; the sense of danger palpable, 'They don't come to party, man. They kill babies in the crib, then say, only the good die young.' And yet, 'Too Late' in draft-form ends on a surprisingly upbeat note: 'Ain't nothing here partner – just the dust of fools that've left their mark in spades / It must be time to choose to live, let the dead bury the dead & learn to forgive, the sun will surely rise as the darkness fades.'

Not much of this would make it beyond that first try-out,* let alone to the version he recorded last at a session a week later, having spent six sessions trying to extract the essence of a song that shifted like quicksilver in his hands. Never before had recording a song been this hard, not even 'Caribbean Wind', though just like that song, the number of discarded lines – many of them splendid in isolation – could fill a notebook: 'Look out Joe, there's a fire below . . . He got a brother from the Tombs / a man of many unlit rooms . . . [They] can turn you into the devil's daughter / Lead you into the valley of slaughter.'

What was truly unprecedented was for Dylan to *persevere* like this. It was as if he *knew* the album he was making needed this; that he, too, must climb that hill and make it to the top, like the Malloryesque character whose funeral he attends. Across five sessions (22nd-26th), Dylan worked industriously on this one song – taking a break just twice, on the 25th and 26th, to cut one, then two versions of 'Someone's Got A Hold . . .' And yet, as early as the 23rd he is telling the entire studio, 'Maybe we should just cut another song. I'll have to come back late at night, with nobody here, when all the lights are low . . . It's too complicated [as it is]. It's hard to throw all the words out there.'

Instead, Dylan went away for a whole day and came back with a new

---

* Frustratingly, none of the embryonic versions of 'Too Late' from that 1st session (April 22nd) feature on *Springtime In New York*.

narrative, 60% new lyrics, a new title, 'Foot Of Pride', and a new burden – 'Ain't no going back, when the foot of pride comes down' – but still very much marooned in the same hinterland of dishonourable deeds. If he thought he'd found the key, he was wrong. 'Foot Of Pride' would take up even more tape and time than 'Too Late'. On the 29th, at the end of his tether, he admitted to one and all, 'This is the toughest song I've tried to do in my entire recording career. I've never struggled with any song like this one.' By the final take that day, he was too burnt out to care if he got it. It was time to pull that final 6.22 take to master after admitting at take's end, 'There was one wrong change, but who cares at this point?'

By now, he was so weary of the process that he was almost rushing through the songs just to get the last few onto tape. The one master-piece he had kept in reserve all this time, 'I And I', was finally tackled on April 27th, on a day when he captured two complete takes of 'Foot Of Pride' (neither of them pulled to master); a version of 'Union Sun-down' with dummy lyrics which *was* pulled to master;* a single take of 'Julius And Ethel' that was more than it deserved; and two takes of 'I And I', both exquisite, after which Dylan exclaims, 'I've had it with that, I think. Maybe we can do it better and maybe we can't, but that's always the story.' In fact, he'd captured it on take one, a seven-minute paean to passing passion and permanent faith.

Sadly, such was his fading focus that when, on the 29th, he took a break from the foot of pride coming down, and began plunking away on a lovely song he had yet to formalize, called 'How Many Days?', he did it twice and left it at that. It was another 'Rock Me Mama' moment – one he at least recognized enough to tell Abbey, 'Can you mark that?' Even with dummy lyrics, it tugs the heart strings at every turn as Dylan blows his lungs out on a melody worth the effort. But he can't shake the thought, must finish 'Foot Of Pride'. Which he duly did. Along with an enflamed 'Someone's Got A Hold . . .' and that nocturnal emission from the brink, 'I And I', it gave him an album as good as any since 1974's fabled return to form.

---

* It would remain the chosen take until May 18th, when Dylan reviewed the reels and found a more promising take from two days later, which he promptly overdubbed, edited into extinction, and released.

He had just three more originals to capture at the final band session on May 2nd, none of them about to provide the icing on the cake: 'Union Sundown', which he'd admitted on the 27th, 'I don't have the lyrics for'; a promissory note for the afterlife, 'Death Is Not The End'; and an apocalyptic variant on 'Forever Young' for an unnamed son – perhaps the one he bar-mitzvahed in Jerusalem, the previous September. He was determined to get all three, even 'Lord Protect My Child', on which he prays his child will not lose his way 'till men lose their chains/ And Righteousness reigns', and which after seven takes still wouldn't make the master reels.

However, the song they worked on most that day – with the least obvious *raison d'être* – was Willie Nelson's 'Angel Flying Too Close To The Ground', a b-side candidate from a set of sessions remarkably free of covers. Neither of the two other covers on the 2021 Bootleg Series from this penultimate *Infidels* session – a savagely-edited 'Baby, What You Want Me To Do' that never catches fire, let alone burns, and an impromptu 'Green Green Grass Of Home' – scream, release me. After the latter, Knopfler opines, 'Not as good as Tom Jones,' prompting Dylan, never the best critic of his own work, to retort, 'It's a hundred times better than Tom Jones.' Sorry, Bob, it ain't.

Actually, the two best covers he'd already recorded in the first five days: a rather spirited 'Jesus Met The Woman At The Well' on the 15th, and a 'Do Re Mi' on the 13th that if it wasn't for a non-plussed Sly'n'Robbie might just have amounted to something. But for all their famous *feel*, neither knew the songs Dylan knew, nor related to them. There was a reason Sly read heavy metal mags.

Which is perhaps why Dylan pulls up short on the 26th after another wearying 'Foot Of Pride' work-out. Despite the presence of a return-ing Clydie, he can't quite revive the spirit of 'the two Hanks', Williams and Snow, on 'Cold, Cold Heart' and 'I'm Movin' On'. And yet, Dylan told the one reporter allowed to sit in on the mixing sessions that he had fourteen covers, 'one of [which], Willie Nelson's "Angels Flying Too Close to The Ground," may or may not end up on the finished product.' There simply wasn't room, though, for Nelson's song – or Nelson Riddle's 'This Was My Love', the only other Power Station cover in a releasable state.

Dylan had enough of a task ahead of him editing the quality originals he had down to a single album, without looking for a cover, or going back to a track he'd already perfected. But that is precisely what he proceeded to do, setting up a session on the 5th for him and Knopfler to rework 'Blind Willie McTell' as a piano/ guitar duet. Even Dylan seemed unconvinced as to the wisdom of this move, prefacing the first take by saying, 'We'll give it one pass,' to which Knopfler responds, 'It doesn't matter, we don't have to use this.' As it happens, they ran through it twice – both times beautifully – before calling time on what was potentially Dylan's strongest album since *Blood on the Tracks*.

But if Knopfler thought he was going to be there to ensure Dylan stayed on the straight and narrow, he was about to be sorely disabused. When Debbie Gold called in to see how things were progressing, she was astonished to hear Knopfler suggesting Dylan could 'go to the movies, and I'll mix the record'. Whether or not he meant it in jest, it was the end of Knopfler's involvement. He was summarily fired, and it would be some years before the pair were reconciled. The guitarist was still absolutely fuming when Josh Abbey gave him a lift to JFK, so he could resume making movie soundtracks with his brothers in arms. Despite the guitarist later denying there had been a falling out, his one contemporary on-the-record remark rather gives the game away:

> If anybody ever has the dubious fortune to end up in [Dylan's] producer's seat they'll find out for themselves that sometimes the best way to go forward is to respect others' feelings about things when they're directly opposed to your own.

'Twas a warning to which none of his successors would pay heed. When this marked man finally heard the released album, he couldn't believe his ears: 'Some of [*Infidels*] is like listening to roughs. Maybe Bob thought I'd rushed things because I was in a hurry to leave, but I offered to finish it after our tour. Instead, he got the engineer to do the final mix.' The album Knopfler left behind soon went AWOL.* He still hadn't realized no-one *produces* Dylan:

---

* A nine-track version that circulated before the official album came out featured 'Blind Willie McTell', 'Foot Of Pride' and the superior master take of 'Jokerman'. It probably accords with Knopfler's version.

Bob Dylan: I produce my own records, really. I don't even know what a producer does. Producers usually get in the way. They're fine for picking you up at the airport, and making sure all the bills are paid at your hotel . . . I haven't run into any that know any more about what I'm doing than I do. [1985]

As it happens, the mix – done in tandem with Australian producer Ian Taylor, brought in on June 4th – was the least of *Infidels'* problems. What he'd been brought in to finish up needed very little work. Also, it would be hard to argue with the chosen takes pulled to the four master reels on May 15th-16th: fourteen originals, just two of which came with alternate takes: 'Tell Me' and 'Blind Willie McTell'. But such was the length of most of these, six minutes-plus being the norm, a ten-song sequence was out of the question.

Perhaps unsurprisingly, the songs worked on the most in the next fortnight would be 'Tell Me', 'Union Sundown', 'Death Is Not The End' and 'Neighborhood Bully', only the last of which really warranted a berth, and only then because of its vituperative vocal. Not even under consideration was 'Someone's Got A Hold . . .', Dylan perhaps feeling it was the kinda song he once described to Cott: 'Very seldom do you abandon something with the attitude that you've gotten what you started out to get. Usually you think, well, it's too big; you get wasted along the way some place, and then it just trails off.'*

Despite this, sequencing did not come easy. Interviewed by Martin Keller in mid-June, he informed the reporter, 'All that's left to do is the song sequencing.' Yet almost everything he had overdubbed in May – the horns on 'Neighborhood Bully', a Dylan guitar overdub and backing vocals on 'Tell Me', Full Force on 'Death Is Not The End' – had gone unused. Instead, Dylan spent his time overdubbing his vocals using digital technology, something he had eschewed at every turn for two decades. Engineer Josh Abbey had shown Dylan how easy the new

---

* The sixteen takes of fourteen tracks on the compiled master reels are as follows: Union Sundown. Jokerman. Don't Fall Apart On Me Tonight. Neighborhood Bully. License To Kill. Man Of Peace. Tell Me (in D). Tell Me (in E). Julius And Ethel. I And I. Sweetheart Like You. Death Is Not The End. Blind Willie McTell #1. Blind Willie McTell #2. Foot Of Pride. Someone's Got A Hold Of My Heart.

technology made it, thus throwing a spanner into Dylan's work that would still be clogging up the machinery in 2020. Terry Gans identifies Abbey's input in his book-length history of these sessions, *Surviving In A Ruthless World*:

> Dylan . . . discovered he did not have to re-record an entire song to change a word or a line. [He] was working on 'I and I', where there was a lyric change in the fourth verse, substituting four words for five . . . 'You mean I don't have to sing the whole song? How would we do that? If I . . . sing it again, don't we erase what's already there?' Abbey showed him how the computerized switch worked . . . Dylan nodded and said, 'Pretty sneaky'.

Abbey thus set off a chain reaction that resulted in Dylan becoming the editor-*auteur* of his own audio canon, casting aside an aesthetic that had served him well for twenty-two years. The explanation he offered the following year for what he now perpetrated was as questionable as most of the calls he now made: 'We put the tracks down and sang most of the stuff live. Only later when we had so much stuff, we recorded it over [again] . . . I wanted to fill it up more, I've never wanted to do that with any other record . . . [So,] we decided to redo some of the vocals.'

The song that suffered the most was 'Jokerman', which he not only re-sang but rewrote. It would take him until 1991 to admit it was 'a song that got away from me. Lots of songs on [*Infidels*] got away from me . . . They hung around too long. They were better before they were tampered with . . . In my mind, it had been written and rewritten and written again.' Even when the rewrites were an improvement, as they mostly were, they came at the expense of a committed vocal, captured live in the studio, not an underheated overdub recorded in cold isolation.

He wasn't done deconstructing the album, either, not by a long chalk. This required him to remove the two central pillars which were keeping the whole edifice upright: 'Blind Willie McTell' and 'Foot Of Pride'. Even when he played the finished sequence to the man who'd recommended the rhythm-section, and saw his reaction, he merely laughed it off:

Larry Sloman: I was in the studio when Bob was doing *Infidels*, and heard most of the songs, and it's the final night in the studio and they're doing the sequence, and we're playing back each song, and Bob's getting back my reactions. I listen to the whole sequence . . . and I said to Bob, 'Wait a minute, wait a minute, where's Blind Willie McTell?' And he said, softly, 'That one didn't make the album.' I said to him, 'Are you out of your fuckin' mind?' . . . Bob looks at me . . . and says, 'Oh Ratso, just relax. It's just an album. I've got twenty-five of them.'

Dylan had told Keller his '25th album' – which he didn't send to Sony until Independence Day – would be out by September. Wishful thinking. By the time it did appear – on October 27th – he was not straying far from the green, overgrown grass of home. And nor was Clydie. A single interview with Robert Hilburn and his first promo video in eighteen years ('Sweetheart Like You') was his idea of pushing the publicity boat out. Having been introduced to Punk and Post-Punk by his son, Jesse, the previous summer, he instead bought himself a sharp suit and a skinny tie, and plugged in a band brought up on L.A. punk, for some music-making that did not require him to punch the clock:

Tony Marsico: He wanted some younger guys to jam with [at his] house at Point Dume. [This was] from the fall of '83 to around March '84 . . . Bob wasn't the best at stuff like plugging in a guitar and turning his amp off standby, [but] he was totally cool with us, offering us coffee . . . making sure we were comfortable . . . The rehearsals were quite long, but . . . we never worked on a section of a song or went over any one thing, we just jammed . . . I would record rehearsals . . . for my own reference . . . on a cheap old ghetto blaster over used tapes. Bob was curious how they sounded . . . Clydie King would join us occasionally. That was a real treat, to hear her and Bob sing together on songs like 'We Three' and 'Johnny Too Bad' . . . We would jam the whole day then head back home to Hollywood and up to a club to hear a band.

Also there on a regular basis, with the motor idling, was drummer Charlie Quintana, whose 'impression of what was going down [was] that he was trying to get back into playing, that he just wanted some guys, low-key, to jam. And that's what we did. We didn't sit around and talk a lot. He came in, we played, we had some coffee, we played again. He'd say, Alright, that's it, and he'd split.' Another occasional attendee, guitarist Charlie Sexton, was bemused to find he was expected to just play 'without any introduction or explanation – no keys, no chords, nothing! . . . I'd keep asking him, "Is this one yours?" and he'd just mumble in that gravelly voice, "Nah, it's from the Civil War."'

In fact, most of the time they stuck to instrumental jams, with an occasional foray into r&b from the likes of Roy Head ('Treat Her Right') or Sonny Boy Williamson ('Don't Start Me To Talking'). If Dylan was writing songs in these months – as a rehearsed 'Who Loves You More' and a 1983 notebook version of the whimsical 'Straight A's In Love' suggest – he kept them largely under wraps, along with any wider intentions. Only in March 1984 did he suggest they relocate to New York to do his first national TV since the 1980 Grammys, an appearance on *Late Night with David Letterman,* which he seemed determined to treat like another garage jam session:

> **Charlie Quintana**: The Letterman show came out of nowhere, really. I think it was about a week's notice . . . It didn't really matter whether it was a week or a month, because we didn't know what we were going to play until about a minute before we went on the air! . . . It was five minutes before we were supposed to go on and I'm asking Bill Graham, 'We're shitting bricks over here! Can you please go in and ask Bob what songs we're gonna do?' And he'd come back and say, 'He's not sure yet.'

Unbeknownst to Bob's band of rookies, this was the start of a second wave of publicity for the becalmed album CBS had released five months earlier to generally good reviews, but in the brave new world of MTV and Westwood One was struggling to garner the necessary airplay. A second promo video – for 'Jokerman' – set the song to an inspired montage of historical and archaeological images, with occasional cuts to a close-up of Dylan singing the chorus, the brainchild of Larry Sloman and George Lois.

Meanwhile, Dylan exchanged his first *Rolling Stone* interview in six years for a colour cover. Letterman's show, though, reached more than MTV, *Rolling Stone* and Westwood One combined. So, when Dylan delivered a blistering three-song set, including 'License To Kill' and 'Jokerman', fans hoped he had finally discovered the right sound for these songs – a stripped-down one. Now was surely the time to take to the road again and revisit the *Highway 61* sound, with a dose of the spirit of punk thrown in for good measure. Or was it too late; too, too late?

March 1984 to June 1985:
I'll Go Along With This Charade

These ballads . . . get harder and harder every year.

Bob Dylan, between takes of 'Sweetheart Like You', Power Station,
New York, April 1983.

It was April 24th, 1984. He kept circling [the house]. [Then] he talked for two hours. He [said he] came back to see his Dad's grave and visit some people. He didn't look like he was famous. He graduated with my Dad.

Patrick, son of the then-owner of Dylan's childhood home in
Hibbing.

I don't know how you'd spend a year on an album. How's it done?

Bob Dylan, to Christopher Sykes, 17th October 1986.

Empire Burlesque . . . seems to be chasing some kind of 'current sound'. And, to my tastes, the current sound of the Eighties was a horror show. So that colours [it] for me as an album.

Benmont Tench.

[The night before the first show in Verona,] I asked him if he ever considered doing 'Positively 4th Street', one of my favourites. We had another drink and he said, 'Let's make a list of the songs that you want me to do.' . . . Bob had no intention of doing *any* of the songs on that list . . . He was just having fun. And since he now knew exactly what we wanted to play, they wouldn't be mentioned [again]. Talk about contrary.

Ian McLagan, *All The Rage* (1998).

He tends only to trust his instincts. He doesn't like to think too much about anything, because he thinks it'll break the spell. Sometimes . . . he is the worst judge of his own work. But I don't know if he doesn't do a lot of that on purpose . . . He just has a completely different viewpoint [to most people] on things.

Dave Stewart.

When people sense that you've come through a certain heat and are still functioning in a semi-coherent type of way . . . they treat you as a legendary figure.

Bob Dylan, to Martha Quinn, 7th July 1984.

Q: How long have you been rehearsing?
BD: About two or three days.
Q: . . . Just three days?!
BD: Oh, that's a lot, three days!

Verona press conference, 29th May 1984.

*

On April 28th, 1984, Dylan officially signed with promoter Bill Graham for a five-week tour of Europe with another of Graham's clients, Santana, the band of *Abraxas* in name only at this point. With almost no crossover in fan bases, it was a tour only Dylan could headline, and it would still need regular bolstering with 'special guests' to keep the customers satisfied.

Graham – whose relevance to rock ended the night of January 14th, 1978, at the Winterland Ballroom – had been making his presence felt from the wings for a while now, phoning up Ed Bicknell, Knopfler's manager, during the *Infidels* sessions, to ask him if he 'could prevail on Mark to speed things up', like it was him who was making them a marathon, not a sprint.

No-one was about to tell ol' Bill that what he knew about all the exciting new music – and musicians – coming out of the west coast, post-Winterland, could be written on a head of a pin. It was him who began to push Dylan to start rehearsing with fossils brought up on pre-historic sounds, not young guns like those who had for the past six months been breathing life into the forty-something music-man fronting his first garageband/s since Hibbing High School.

Over the next three weeks, one by one, the colts were replaced by friends of the lead guitarist, Mick Taylor, a wonderful blues player but no bandleader. His one inspired selection, pianist Nicky Hopkins, turned up with a manager to discuss terms, which ensured that was the last anyone saw of him. The easy-going ex-Face Ian McLagan took his place. But the real stickler gumming up the works was drummer Colin Allen, the second time he'd used a British drummer, and the second time he'd been sold a dud. The one survivor from the garage jam-sessions was bassist Greg Sutton, who looked like a refugee from Robert Gordon's band, though all similarities ended there.

After the first rehearsal for the new combo, on May 22nd, a full six days before they opened in Verona, McLagan walked up to Dylan to say, 'Thanks Bob, it's an honour and a privilege to work with you.' Dylan, who already had a bad feeling about this, replied, 'I hope you feel the same when the tour's over.'

Rehearsals were so truncated, and the material they worked on so ad hoc, that they never even found time to work on song-endings. They would be halfway through the tour before Allen summoned up the nerve to ask, what gives: 'One day we were sitting in this hotel in Rome . . . We were sitting outside, and Bob was there, and I said, "Hey Bob, you know when you look at me at the end of a song, what's the story? Do you want me to end the song[s] immediately, as soon as possible, or wait till the sequence goes?" He said, "Well, I just figure we've done enough with the songs."'

In classic Dylan fashion, the day before starting a stadia/arena tour at the atmospheric open-air Arena di Verona, he spent most of the afternoon's rehearsal working on what McLagan called, in his 1998 memoir, this 'one beautiful song he played occasionally that he'd never recorded and never [properly] rehearsed with us, either. It was a tricky little number, we never knew the title, but he'd launch into it from time to time, leaving us totally in the dark.' Seemingly called 'Almost Done', or that's what he sings, it could actually be the fabled 'Angel Of Rain'.*

---

* 'Angel Of Rain' was one of three 'new songs' on a list handed out at the May 29th Verona press conference, along with 'Dirty Lie', also rehearsed, and 'Enough Is Enough' – the only one which was ever performed.

He'd done something similar nineteen years earlier, with another pick-up band, The Hawks, but they had been playing together for six years, not six days, and they only had to learn eight songs, not twenty-eight. Not surprisingly, the opening show was a train-crash of Casey Jones-like proportions, leaving all four songs from *Infidels* – 'Jokerman', 'I And I', 'License To Kill' and 'Man Of Peace' – barely crawling from the wreckage.

Fortunately, it was the first time Dylan had played Italy, and no barometer was available for most attendees, at least until the following night, when first-night nerves were less in evidence. But one thing was for sure, more rehearsals were needed, starting at the very next show, in Hamburg, where a first 'special guest' was lying in wait for him at the afternoon press conference. Joan Baez was aiming to 'catch him and practice the songs', only for Dylan to make a hasty departure just as she was arriving. As she wrote in her 1987 memoir, *And A Voice To Sing With*, she had flown 'into Hamburg to meet him and "go over some stuff," only to discover that he was not at the same hotel, and would not be in town until the next day'. After a second German show in Munich, Baez had had enough, having been promised much, just 'nothing in writing', by Graham, who'd first made money as a promoter booking a band of charlatans.

They would have to find some other special guests and/or Dylan would have to buck up his ideas. Unexpectedly, it proved to be the latter. Starting in Rotterdam, not Rome, Dylan began to shake things up, starting with new versions of 'Tangled Up In Blue' and 'Simple Twist Of Fate' that were a delight. Each written out on hotel notepaper during his Dutch stay, this was as impromptu as it got. The new lyrics of the former had him 'still walking towards the Sun/ Trying to stay out of the joint,' while the latter was a belated sequel to the cinematic post-*Desire* rewrite: 'Stopped into the Grand Hotel, where the desk clerk was dressed in white, with a face as black as night/ He said, Checkout time's at eight . . .' While both reinterpretations would stay in the set, only 'Tangled Up In Blue' would be included on *Real Live*, in its least effective, stadium incarnation.

By the time Dylan returned to Italy for three shows at PalaEUR in Rome, three weeks on from Verona, he felt confident enough to tackle 'Desolation Row' for the first time in ten years, as well as unveiling the first new song of the tour, 'Enough Is Enough', a raucous rockabilly romp that suited a band of ex-Bluesbreakers.

At last, the shows were attracting rave reviews and rabid fans in equal measure. After playing his first Italian football stadium, the legendary San Siro, he played two more soccer stadia in Spain, Madrid and Barcelona, the second of which featured an impromptu 'Lay Lady Lay' – with Dylan pointing to someone in the crowd, saying, 'That was for *you*!' – and a 'Blowin' In The Wind' where the crowd needed no cajoling to sing along, even after Dylan showed them just how it was done, resurrecting the meaning of a song he had long sung like an amnesiac.

Broadcast on Spanish TV, it proved they should have been taping all the shows since Rotterdam if they wanted an album to emulate *Get Yer Ya-Ya's Out*. Instead, they began taping *after* Barcelona, and then turned the tapes over to Glyn Johns, who danced all over them with muddy boots. The resultant album – *Real Live* – was a case of too little (a single album from two-hour-plus shows), too late (mostly the penultimate show at Wembley Stadium, on a baking hot day, not any of its July predecessors).

At least Dylan got out of Europe in one piece, having given the promoter of nostalgia a run for his money – telling MTV's Martha Quinn backstage at Wembley, 'This term "nostalgic" is just another way people have of . . . putting you some place they think they understand.' He even felt inspired enough to start work on the second album in his contract, already two years old, the minute he landed in New York.

Unsurprisingly, he did not bring the band with him, not even Greg Sutton, who had acquitted himself well enough. Instead, Dylan decided to check out the band Sutton would join at year's end, Maria McKee's Lone Justice, the great white hope of L.A. cowpunk and a signing made by Geffen Records' A&R newbie, Carole Childs, who was determined to make the precocious Maria a star, if only to solidify her own position.

The half-sister of Love's Bryan MacLean, the 19-year-old McKee had been fronting bands since she was fifteen, and had songs a-plenty of her own, but Childs wanted a debut album full of *names*. She had also already inserted herself into Dylan's life, offering a complete contrast to the home-lovin' Clydie. As a brief rival for Bob's affection described her, Childs was an 'energetic short Jewish woman . . . her hair . . . bleached a splintering platinum, her nails manicured in gaudy red . . . pretty, but too artificial . . . kinda tough, and her accent . . . strictly New York.'

Was Childs really his new Sweetheart? Had Dylan's tastes in women really changed that much? No-one seemed to really know. But he did do what Childs asked, just without throwing body and soul into it. As McKee put it at a Dylan tribute show in 2007, 'Carole Childs cornered Bob into writing a song for Lone Justice. I guess he woke up one day, had a cup of coffee and scribbled something out.'

On July 25th, Dylan turned up at the Power Station in the company of Ron Wood, both of them a little bleary, worse for wear and tear. McKee recalls, 'They were drinking Rebel Yell or Southern Comfort, their guitars were all out of tune and they sat around [making guitar noises] for six and a half hours. I was a little punk-rock kid, y'know, [with] a punk attitude and I was like, "Who is this old fart? This is my record, this is my moment! He's had his chance."' A battle-scarred Jimmy Iovine, who was at the console, told her in no uncertain terms to behave herself.

The song he'd penned after his first breakfast in America in a while was 'Go 'Way Little Boy', a transgender twist on a familiar Dylan scenario. But an eager Maria had been expecting a *song* from the old fart, not to audition for the role of a female Dylan. Much to her dismay, 'We ended up working on it a very long time . . . He didn't like the way I sang it . . . He kept saying, "No, no, no, you're singing it all wrong," . . . until I sang it like him! It got to the point where finally I just did my best Bob Dylan imitation – and he said, "Ah, now you're doin' SOME REAL SINGING! I knew you could do it."'

Apparently, it did not occur to Dylan that she could simply redo the vocal when he left, as he'd done to Knopfler on *Infidels*. According to Lone Justice drummer, Don Heffington, who was about to make an immense contribution to Dylan's next set of songs, that's just what she did, 'We did a version with Bob singing, so Maria could learn it, and then we recorded one with Maria singing a scratch vocal, which she later replaced.' What didn't need replacing was Dylan's harp-work, but 'when it was mixed, somehow the executive decision was made to wipe Bob . . . off the thing.' Adding insult to injury, the song was only released on a b-side, as Iovine inflicted his AOR vision on another immense talent he was determined to trivialize.

If Dylan had his doubts about the vocalist, he seemed impressed by her rhythm-section, so much so that Heffington was requisitioned on returning from a break, after he found Dylan 'in the back with

Benmont [Tench, McKee's then-boyfriend,] figuring out the chords [to a new song]. Bob had called Ronnie Wood down and we started workin' on . . . tryin' to arrange this tune . . . [It] was a blues, a slow 12/8 blues, just fooling around really . . . Benmont and Marvin [Etzioni] figured out the key and we played through this tune. "Baby, oh baby," he was singing. I never heard it back again after that night.' The song was logged – as 'I Love You' – before going the way of previous Iovine/Dylan co-productions.

According to Maria herself, in her 2021 *Variety* obituary of Heffington, 'They played all night through the morning because of Don . . . He was that good.' What would have made more sense would have been for Dylan to cut – or allow Maria to cut – 'Enough Is Enough', a song he'd now played live to over half a million people, but seemed not to want to record. Indeed, not one of the songs they'd semi-rehearsed on tour was ever excavated again. He had a new *modus operandi* he was looking to test-run:

> **Bob Dylan**: [Previously,] when making a record I'[d] need some songs, and I'[d] start digging through my pockets and drawers . . . In the past, what's come out is what I've usually stuck with, whether it really knocked me out or not . . . just from [a] lack of commitment to taking the trouble to really get it right. I didn't want to record that way anymore . . . [So,] I decided to get serious about it, and just record. [1985]

Two of the songs he brought to the studio the following day, for a session at Delta, with Ron Wood and another loose cannon from Lone Justice, guitarist Ryan Hedgecock, were older than Verona. 'Who Loves You More' was a rare original he'd worked on in garageland, while *Infidels* outtake 'Clean Cut Kid' broke a rule which had held for nigh on two decades, one he had just articulated to Loder, 'If I wrote a song three years ago, I seldom go back and get that. I just leave 'em alone.' Cut in two takes, it was the only song he seemed to consider worthy of some post-production. The other songs – including 'Driftin' Too Far From Shore' – were left to the whims of an engineer who seemed to consider Dylan a disinterested observer:

> **Ron Wood**: When we'd go in at . . . Delta for a playback, every time he'd have the same attitude. The weak side of him would come out.

They'd say, 'Hey Bob, we don't need this,' and he'd say, 'Oh, okay.' . . .
And I'd be saying, 'Hey! Look!! They've left off the background vocals!'
or 'What about the drums?!' But there would be something going on in
the back of his head which didn't allow him to interfere.

Possibly, Ron's new best friend already knew he would take the tapes
with him, and give them a thorough working over. He certainly
seemed to be finding it hard to immerse himself in the experience, telling Bert Kleinman four days later, 'Recording a song bores me. It's like
working in a coal mine . . . To do what I used to do . . . you have to stay
in the studio a longer time to even get that right, because technology
has messed everything up so much.' So much for getting 'serious
about' recording, or embracing the Eighties *zeitgeist*. Instead, he convinced CBS to accept his first European live album as the second album
of his 1982 contract, giving him some breathing space before *Infidels'*
true successor fell due. For now, he seemed more interested in getting
back to the farm, where he could work on further songs. Or at least
find some tunes to which others could put words.

The afternoon after the Delta session, Dylan turned up at the New
York apartment of 'Doc' Pomus, the songwriter responsible for 'Save
The Last Dance For Me', 'A Teenager In Love' and a raft of Elvis Sixties
hits, in the company of his son, Sam. He stayed for three hours, telling
the 'Doc' he wanted to give him a cassette of musical riffs which he
hoped he would like enough to add some lyrics. Sure enough, a tape
with 'Firebird' and 'Wolf', two backing tracks recorded at Delta,
arrived three days later. He also told him he had recently spent 'a few
hours' in Ellie Greenwich's apartment, where she had shown him the
crude home recording set-up she used to demo her material. Dylan
was impressed. Finally, as Pomus later wrote:

> He spoke about the days when he had started writing; [how] he had
> come to New York when he was very young with about 500 folk melo-
> dies in his head and he just kept putting lyrics to them on bits of paper
> everywhere . . . He said at times he had felt like a transmitter, but it was
> all so long ago that he couldn't really remember the way – and then at
> other times, it was hard work and it was like bits and pieces – but mostly
> he couldn't remember the process. And it sounded to me as though for-
> getting [how] was really rather frightening to him. He said he couldn't

concentrate any more in the particular way that was necessary to create
and that he had become self-conscious during the very act of creating,
and his thoughts and feelings kept wandering; it would all work for a
few minutes and then it would disappear.

The fog, it seemed, had closed in again. He even told Pomus he had
recently returned to Woodstock, looking for something – he didn't
know what – and that he had stumbled on the cabin where he had written so many great songs. There was almost nothing left, just charred
remains, save for the piano he used to play ideas on, which was somehow miraculously intact. Pomus was impressed by how serious Dylan
was about the art-form they shared, discussing Leiber and Stoller,
Spector and Elvis with a clear knowledge of what each of them had
brought to the party. But underlying it all was a nagging sense that
maybe he had shot his bolt; that he was *done*.

His decision to 'just record' seemed to be his one solution to this
new amnesia, even though he hadn't finished anything of note in fifteen months, and even when he had nothing he particularly wanted to
record. Such would prove to be the case when he summoned local
favourites, Willie & The Bees, to Minneapolis' Creation Studio on
August 28th. It had been two summers since he'd last checked them
out live, and the r&b outfit was on its last legs, but he remembered
them. They weren't about to turn down a summons from Minnesota's
most fortunate son:

Maurice Jacox: That's when the band was breaking up, [but] we were
being groomed as the next backing band for Bob. The recording we did,
we were not even allowed to tell our significant others where we were
going that evening. In those days, Creation Studios was in a farm twenty
miles from town. Bob and I knew each other in the Sixties, [but] I hadn't
seen him since '68, '69, when he came up the driveway, driving a white
Firebird. I was impressed by who gets out of the passenger seat, Clydie
King . . . one of the *great* backing singers. First thing Bob had us do was
overdub on something he'd done live in London.* He had us put a
drum-track on, and add a couple of horn parts. And then he just wanted

---

* It was 'Tombstone Blues', which Dylan seemed to think warranted a horn section,
then changed his mind.

us to try a few things, [and starts] go[ing], 'It kinda goes like this: danga-danga-dang.' What the hell is that, Bob? [He does it again.] Could you be a little more specific? How do you want the arrangement to move? Do you hear horns? We actually fleshed it out into a song – I think there were [actually] two of them. At one point, I went into the control room and was talking to Clydie: 'I can't tell if he likes this or not.' 'Oh no, he just *loves* you guys.' 'How the hell can you tell?' 'If he didn't love what you were doing, he'd have left here an hour ago.' That was the only approbation we got.

Aside from four instrumental jams, the only shape-shifting songs recorded that day were logged as 'Unfinished' and 'Footprints In The Sand'.* Neither was finished, nor would they ever be. The day's one significance was that it represented a last sighting of Bob'n'Clydie. By the time he returned to L.A., a relationship that had lasted longer than any since the end of his first marriage was in tatters, and nobody save the relevant parties seems to know why, though Dylan's growing reliance on two Jewish ladies in the Biz, Debbie Gold and Carole Childs, can't have helped.†

If Childs was now getting her tentacles around the rock star, it was Gold who continued pushing him to record with accredited musicians. But it was Dylan's personal assistant, Gary Shafner, who asked guitarist Ira Ingber to assemble another band of young guns, 'I was asked to bring a bass player, and a keyboard player. The drummer at the time was Charlie Quintana. The bass player I brought in was Carl Sealove. The keyboard player was another good friend, Vince Melamed. When Charlie bowed out, Don Heffington came in,' at Bob's behest:

Don Heffington: I came home [one day] and there's this piece of paper, this note, kinda kicked halfway under the bed and it said, 'Ira [Ingber] called and wants to know if you want to play with Bob Dylan.' So, we started going over to Bob's place and playing. He had a place at the

---

* I foolishly suggested these two songs – 'Money Blues'[!] and 'Footprints . . .' – came from 1975 in *Still On The Road*. Close. The former includes a potential proposal: 'Money, whole lotta money/ So I can get you a wedding ring.'
† On the 2021 *Springtime In New York* set, Clydie King is credited on the L.A. recordings from December 1984 through February 1985. I know not why. None of the musicians remember her there, nor is she audible.

beach. That went on for a while. He'd show up and we'd play for three, four hours straight. Very spontaneous. He just wanted to jam, I guess. I remember he worked out a Jim Capaldi tune once – actually worked on it! He doesn't teach a band a song, he'll just play it. He knows a lot of chords and he's got an amazing ear. Very musical. I think he's a lot better musician than people give him credit for. We went up there five or six times and then he wanted to go in the studio.

Ira Ingber: I wouldn't describe what we did at Bob's house prior to the recording sessions as being 'jams'. Rather, they conformed to Bob's concept of the rehearsal process. I recall that we were at Bob's house for a few weeks prior to the recording sessions. When Bob would start playing a song for us at Cherokee, the band looked at each other in recognition that [it] was one we had been rehearsing . . . Each rehearsal, and probably most sessions, ended with Bob's oft-used question, 'Can you come back tomorrow?'

On December 6th, 1984 – the true starting point of *Empire Burlesque* – the 'jam' band relocated to Hollywood's Cherokee Studios. Dylan was finally ready to record seriously, starting with a ballad version of the Western screenplay he'd never finished. Blurring fiction and fact, quoting and misquoting lines from movies – an idea he felt he could really run with – he produced something more than a half-decent album-filler. Rather, a work of epic proportions. So epic, in fact, that it was originally logged as simply, 'Opera', before Dylan gave it a name, 'Danville Girl', and then remembered there was a Guthrie song of the same name. So, 'New Danville Girl' it became.

Just as he had done the last time he'd attempted a similar cinematic sweep, and needed some help, Dylan turned to a playwright and fellow survivor of the Rolling Thunder Revue to lend a hand. Dylan's co-lyricist, Sam Shepard, explained the premise, '[It had] to do with a guy standing on line and waiting to see an old Gregory Peck movie that he can't quite remember – only pieces of it – and then this whole memory thing happens . . . He starts speaking internally to a woman . . . reliving the whole journey they'd gone on.' If the original idea had been to write an answer song to Lou Reed's 'Doin' The Things That We Want To', the result would make even 'Sister Ray' stop sucking on her ding-dong.

Presumably, 'Doin' The Things . . .' had been one of the songs from Reed's latest album, *New Sensations*, he played at the Hollywood Palace on October 28th, 1984, for a live TV broadcast. Also on the bill were Lone Justice and another new band fronted by another not-so-bashful blonde, Carla Olson's The Textones, to whom Dylan had 'donated' 'Clean Cut Kid' for their debut album, *Midnight Mission*. Dylan was there with one childlike woman, while perhaps 'speaking internally' to another. Days later Shepard got the call. Delighted by the idea of responding to Reed's song about going to see one of *his* plays, Shepard recalled, 'We spent two days writing the lyrics – Bob had previously composed the melody line, which was already down on tape.'

It seems Dylan had meant it when he told Karen Hughes six years earlier, 'I can imagine every situation in life as if I've done it . . . whether it be self-punishment or marrying my half-sister.' At the top of the page of an early 'Danville Girl', handwritten in pen, is the following hook, 'I'm trying to think of that movie but I can't remember it that well.' Handwritten above a second draft is the altogether more cryptic *Dark Rhythm of the Pale Rider Priest*, which sounds like a western film, just not the movie Dylan was trying to remember. That was Gregory Peck's best western, *The Gunfighter* (1950). Or was it:

> I'm standing on line in the rain to see a movie starring Gregory Peck
> But it's not the one I had in mind
> They put that one out to pasture so many years ago
> Like our love that was true, it's so hard to find . . .
> I don't remember that movie too well (too good)
> Or who I was supposed to be, or what part I played
> All I remember was Gregory Peck
> But that was a long time ago – maybe it was never made.

Below this draft Dylan has written, in blue pen, 'Danville Girl 'neath the moon above,' at which point he presumably junked the idea of calling the heroine Ruby, thus losing a neat little pun: 'Ruby, got a message for you/ Ruby, you're all I need to get by/ The best thing that happened to me . . .' She becomes an ancillary character, instead; an ex-stripper ('She used to show herself off in a niteclub for so much a nite'), married to a sorta 'Love Henry'.* The narrator and his new lover pull up at her homestead as she's 'baking a pie for no one', and when they tell her they're 'going all the way, till the wheels fall off and burn', she just smiles and says, 'I hope you don't have to return.'

All of this he will reshape and retain, but lost in transition is a 'state of the union' outburst from Ruby that probably came from the heart, 'She said it's as if the whole country needs a floggin', and the Son of Man has no plan to lay his head.' Such an overt reference to Christ the Redeemer didn't even make it to the first take.

How much time the poet and the playwright spent watching a VHS of *The Gunfighter* we'll never know, but they certainly took some liberties with William Bowers's dialogue (for which he rightly won an Oscar). They even improved on it in places, first tweaking the gunfighter's dying words to, 'Don't do him any favors, hangin[g]'s too good for him,' before they find the inspired, 'I want him to feel what it's like to every moment face his death.'† The movie flashback, though, like 'Tangled Up In Blue's opening, is little more than a device. The song is really about the lost love he can't shake or forget, even when he's in the car with a new lover, who knows she's with a haunted man:

> Well, we're driving this car & the sun is coming up over the Rockies
> She ain't you but she reminds me of ya when she leans towards the ledge
> I ain't in the mood anymore to remember the times when I was your man
> And she don't want to remind me, she knows this car might go over the
> edge.

What Bob'n'Sam produced by the end of their communal composition was his greatest narrative ballad, a song which could stand alongside anything in Child. Though the lines above were later tweaked, once work started on its transition into Song, the narrative arc never changed. The pressing question now was how to retain a sense of dynamics when it was verse-verse-chorus-verse-chorus for twelve minutes, a conundrum the singer had been wrestling with since

---

* 'What is it about the name Ruby? It's not even a real name. A rube is someone that's an easy mark. Easy to take for a ride.' – *The Philosophy of Modern Song*, p143. (2022)
† In *The Gunfighter*, what Peck says is, 'If I was doing you a favor, I'd let them hang you right now.'

February 16th, 1966. Thankfully, all the prep work with Ira's band of brothers came to fruition as Quintana's replacement took the song to the brink, but never over the edge.

Not surprisingly, it took almost a whole session to capture 'Danville Girl'. However, the version bootlegged by 1986, but not released until 2021, was just the third take. Dylan even seemed to think they might get it in one, telling the musicians before the first take, 'All right, we wanna get this one time,' before asking the engineer, 'How much tape you got?' Even that nine-minute run-through, which omits the towns-people and sheriff and doesn't get to the chorus till 5.44, has a touch of De Mille about it.

Rather than go again, though, Dylan takes a detour with an unfin-ished song called 'Look Yonder', which asks, 'How far to the horizon/ It don't look that far, not more than thirty miles/ But I been walkin' for thirty years, and I'm still walkin' all the while/ Look yonder, look yon-der/ love don't give up on me.' Dylan never develops the promising idea. In fact, the number of song-ideas he would leave unfinished, some-times barely start, at ten L.A. sessions between December 6th and February 14th, would break all records. This one was worthy of rein-spection, unlike the other December 6th discard, 'The Gravity Song'.

Soon, it's time to get back to the matter at hand. This time Heffing-ton drives the Danville Girl to the More-Than-OK Corral; Dylan puts the chorus in the right place, and the whole thing *burns*. He even hints at a possible melodic source by prefacing take two with a snatch of 'The Banks Of The Royal Canal'. Take three finally traps the beast. Indeed, at twelve and a half minutes, he has two-thirds of an LP side under his belt.

He only needed to put together an album worthy of this painted-desert masterpiece. Sure enough, some real songs, some unrealized tunes began to fill tape-boxes, the break-up with Clydie perhaps acting as a creative spur, much like previous romantic traumas. Eight days later, work resumed with a song called 'In Front Of You', Dylan laying down three complete backing tracks, then renaming it 'What's Come Over You?' and finally 'Something's Burning, Baby'. Again, he cut it at Cherokee with the garageband kids, Heffington recalling how he just 'kept working on it . . . He had scraps of paper and he was writing things on paper bags . . . whatever was around. It was amazing how he'd change things up.' It wasn't just the band who didn't know the

words. Neither did the poor backing singer Dylan entrusted with shadowing him vocally, Madelyn Quebec:

> **Ira Ingber**: ['Something's Burning'] is a very weird song. And Maddy
> did not know the words when they did the vocal, 'cause I watched her
> trying to follow him. She was trying to sing harmonies with him live,
> which is tough, because Bob doesn't necessarily know where he's going.

This one seemed real personal, with its narrator more concerned
with saving 'her' soul than their relationship, 'Are you still my friend,
baby, show me a sign / Is the love in your heart for me turning blind? . . .
Got to start someplace baby, can you explain? / Please don't fade away
on me baby, like the midnight train / Answer me baby, a casual look
will do / Just what in the world has come over you?'

Once again, he'd written something set against a now-familiar backdrop of Apocalypse, the fumes of hell rising like the final scene in
Charles Williams's *Descent into Hell* (1937), seeking to claim the sinner
at the moment he least expects: 'Somebody bigger than me is gonna
know what you're about / Somebody parked in a truck in the shade is
gonna figure you out.' Just in case His identity wasn't clear, Dylan duly
rewrote the last verse to remind her Judgement Day was just around
the corner: 'Something is burning, baby, something's in flames /
There's a man going 'round calling names.'*

It was the first time in Dylan's career a backing track had become a
song. Others weren't quite so lucky. The same day, he cut five takes of
a song logged as 'The Girl I Left Behind' – not the traditional song he'd
recorded in October 1961 – but with just a single line of lyrics, 'Miss
Arizona, Lola and Mona, all down the line . . .'† Entire songs were
being logged while the lyrics were lost in the mail.‡ In the case of

---

* He is referencing the Leadbelly song, 'There's A Man Going Around Taking Names',
first, and Revelation second.
† What seem to be cover versions at these sessions are usually not. Two songs logged
I have yet to hear. 'High On The Mountain' from January 28th, sounds like it should
be 'Mountain Of Love'. Two days later, 'Steady Rollin' (Highway Of The Blues)', suggests Robert Johnson's 'Steady Rollin' Man', but is probably not.
‡ Another song, recorded at the February 19th session, is called 'When The Line
Forms' ('So deep in the hole, so deep in the first war, when the line forms . . .'). It lasts
a full five minutes.

another, 'Fire In Your Eyes' – also pulled to a comp. master the following February – the only line sung over the six-minute instrumental track was, 'Baby, I see fire in your eyes.'

Fortunately, two of the better songs recorded that winter came with lyrics. 'I'll Remember You' took up where 'Let's Keep It Between Us' had left off, as he remembered how 'they tr[ied] to educate us/ In all the things we coulda done without . . . To divide our minds and plant the seeds of doubt.' 'Trust Yourself' took its cue from Shel Silverstein's 'A Couple More Years' (a song he'd previously sung with Clydie), before losing lines like: 'There are those who'd like to hinder you, your spirit to devour/ So you must recognize those who would help you, even though they do not have the power.'

Here would be the first two songs from his 1985 album to receive live debuts, to a national TV audience of millions, in refreshingly blistering guises, belated proof he meant what he said.

But a lot of the ostensible love songs he was now penning seemed to have been left out in the rain. Like the 'divorce songs' he wrote in early 1977, he had lyrics he wanted out of his system, but seemed to have no intention of releasing, or completing. One promising fragment seemingly raked over the coals of an old affair with a cousin of Claudette, 'I took a walk one day with Vanity, it was in the early fall/ She showed me the empires of materialism, she said I could have it all.' Written above a set of lyrics to 'The Very Thought Of You' was another orphan couplet: 'Nothing separates you from me, not even the long canal/ That winds its sickly way downhill to the bottom of the well.'

Other songs he began seemed more like song-writing exercises, some with titles nicked from the golden age of rock'n'roll, like 'The Very Thought Of You', 'The Queen Of Rock'n'Roll' ('Of all the lovers I never did love, she['s] the one I love the most/ It's all there it's all written down in the letters I so painfully composed') and 'Straight A's In Love'. Three Fifties-style song-titles – 'My Heart Is Full For You', 'Pied Piper' and 'When Hearts Turn To Spades' – appear at the top of the lyrics to 'New Danville Girl', but went unused.

The most cryptic title he assigned a discarded song, 'Prince Of Plunder', might just as well have been called 'Spuriously Seventeen Windows'. When he finally released the track in May 1986, he used instead the two words that opened every verse, as in: 'Maybe someday, you'll believe me when I say/ That I wanted you, baby, in every kind of way . . . Maybe someday there'll be nothing [left] to tell . . . There was no greater love than what I had for you.'

Don Heffington admitted to me, 'A lot of times we would just play off the chord changes of a song without him singing, so no-one would necessarily know what a song was called . . . He put the lyrics on later.' It was a methodology that left a lot of promising tunes behind. Those that did get words often got ones that lacked the tight connection of his pre-conversion ballads, like the unsalvageable 'Emotionally Yours' and 'Never Gonna Be The Same Again', both recorded in February when he already had enough torch ballads to fill the welcome table.

Altogether more promising was a song which used other writers' made-up words to say something true about a woman who had been false to him, 'Seeing The Real You At Last'. Shortly after he compiled this composite, Dylan claimed, 'I write lines down. I have notes scribbled all over the place. Sometimes I'll go out and say, "I'm going to write down all the lines that seem interesting to me, either that I think of or that I overhear."' He would say something similar in 1991, this time rather implying it was a last resort when inspiration failed, 'If you're ever hung up for things to say you can always use . . . lines overheard here and there. It works better sometimes than sitting in a room, staring at the wall.'

This song, though, was not composed from wonderful remarks overheard in a dark café, but rather lines of dialogue from movies and TV shows he'd caught 'sitting in a room, staring at the' screen; in this instance old Humphrey Bogart movies (*Key Largo, The Maltese Falcon*) and even the odd Clint Eastwood movie (*Bronco Billy*), a technique he would transfer less successfully to the contemporaneous 'Tight Connection To My Heart'.

By the new year, he was starting a lot of songs, finishing only a few. Before 'Queen Of Rock'n'Roll' on February 5th, he told the band, 'We're just rehearsing this thing. Okay, let's see if it happens.' It didn't. Seven days later, he worked on six distinctly different melodic ideas at the piano before breaking into 'Emotionally Yours', a song he had at least sketched out. Eight takes later – after breaking off at various points to work on other instrumentals – he still hadn't got it, save for one great little couplet – 'Just one kiss and I think I can make it/ Make it to the top and never get caught' – which he discarded before returning two days later to finish the song.

It seems melodic ideas were flowing again, but the lyrics were not. And yet, one song which went wholly unused seemed full of promise. Bearing the enticing title, 'Where Is This God?', it was a third-person exchange between someone still the property of Jesus and Satan's spokesperson; a case of Dylan re-engaging with the students of Tempe, five years on:

> CHORUS: They said where is this God?
> Where can he be, what [is] he made of, we'd like to see . . .
>
> 5. They said, 'Our gods are armies that can frighten the heart.'
> He said, 'My god drowns armies in seas that part.' . . .
>
> 6. They said, 'Our gods are nature and the moon and the sun,'
> He said, 'That's too many gods. My God is one.'

Rather than develop this powerful idea, he continued recording songs about a man and a woman estranged in the End times with sections of Tom Petty's Heartbreakers, a suggestion of Gold.

Of the fourteen songs* pulled to a comp. master reel on February 17th, 1985, six still needed lyrics. The remaining eight were still an album in disguise, especially with 'New Danville Girl'. Only five would make the album he sequenced six weeks later: 'Seeing The Real You At Last', 'Something's Burning, Baby', 'Trust Yourself', 'I'll Remember You' and 'Emotionally Yours'. Noticeably absent from that artifact? 'New Danville Girl'.

It was all the fault of Debbie Gold, who had been going around town playing the proof her bosom buddy remained first among equals. But as she told me after producing the man in the Nineties, 'If somebody likes something too much, he's bound to pull it. I'd sit there in the studio with him and, if I'd like something, I'd keep my mouth shut, because he'd *literally* take it away from me.' According to Ingber, Dylan

---

* They are as follows: Seeing The Real You At Last [25/1/85]/ Something's Burning [14/12/84]/ Trust Yourself [5/2/85]/ Prince Of Plunder [28/1/85]/ Danville Girl Opera [6/12/84]/ The Girl I Left Behind [14/12/84]/ I'll Remember You [5/2/85]/ Queen Of Rock'n'Roll [5/2/85]/Look Yonder [6/12/84]/ Gravity Song [6/12/84]/ Emotionally Yours [14/2/85]/ The Very Thought Of You [14/2/85]/ Straight A's In Love [14/2/85]/ I See Fire In Your Eyes [14/2/85]. The December 7th and 9th sessions in Krogsgaard's sessionography appear to be apocryphal, or produced nothing.

also made his own cassette of the epic and 'took it out and started playing it [to people]. He came back the next day we were working and
said, "Yeah, a lot of people like this thing." And then he didn't do anything with it . . . [It was] like he was doing it to spite [these] people.' As
an act of self-sabotage, it put even the substitution of 'Blind Willie
McTell' and 'Foot Of Pride' with 'Union Sundown' in the shade.

Though he already had an album, albeit one that needed a little
post-production, Dylan wanted to keep recording, three thousand
miles away, having written a major work that had the potential to be
the definitive account of a man and a woman torn apart by circumstance in the End times. It certainly had a great title, 'When The Night
Comes Falling From The Sky', and an opening verse that tipped its hat
to 'All Along The Watchtower' and – in its original guise – 'When The
Ship Comes In':

> You can look out across the fields, see me returning
> Smoke is in your eye, you draw a smile
> From the fireplace where my letters to you are burning
> You've had time to think about it for a while.
> I have walked 200 miles – now look me over
> If you're needing somebody baby, here I am
> I'll stand by you like a shield, and you'll know that I'm for real,
> When the night comes falling from the sky.

Fiery stuff, indeed. Having decided to relocate operations to New
York and resume his association with Power Station engineer Josh
Abbey, Dylan was in a hurry to record it, again taking advice from
Gold as to who should join him. Which was how E Street guitarist
Steve Van Zandt 'got a call from Debbie. Everyone knew Debbie. She
was like everybody's confidant/ intermediary, full of positive vibes.
"Stevie, Bob Dylan wants you to produce him." "Really? When?"
"Now. Get down to the Power Station." Bob was playing with Sly and
Robbie, the famous reggae rhythm section, and Roy Bittan . . . on
piano. Bob pointed to a guitar and I joined in . . . After a second take,
Bobby turned to me, "What do you think?" . . . "To tell you the
truth, I'm hearing this faster."' Once again, as at Delta the previous
July, Dylan went along with external input, having told Bert Kleinman
the previous July, 'If you don't want to do something, just ask

somebody's opinion and they'll just verify it for you.' And Van Zandt was never shy of offering an opinion:

Josh Abbey: [Bob] never threw anybody out. Al Kooper would come around; Paul Schrader would come around, Jimmy Webb . . . [And] Steve was very hot . . . [He] really wanted to show [he] could produce Bob's album. So, it was one of those moments. I was just sat getting the drum sound and Steve said, 'Solo the bottom snare mike.' . . . I do that engineer thing, pretending to turn the knob, and Steve says how much better it is now. I haven't changed anything. And Bob's eyes are really wide open . . . That night was it. Bob was having a great time. [Steve and Roy] took over the evening, and Bob never said, No. Bob's way of dealing with things [like that] was [to] let them do what they're gonna do . . . They're not gonna be here tomorrow.

Actually, Van Zandt called it right. The second take *was* too slow, while takes one and three would have been perfect for a Patrick Swayze soundtrack. But take four, the one on 1991's *Bootleg Series 1-3*, was the keeper, Dylan hurling himself into lines like, 'I gave to you my heart like buried treasure,' and delivering its *denouement* like the fifth horseman, 'You'll know everything down below and up above / When the night comes falling from the sky.'

But when Dylan went back the following day – actually four days later – he was wearing a pair of Casio's finest hobnail boots.* Engineer Abbey believes he understands Dylan's rationale for rejecting that consummate take four, 'There's nothing wrong with it, except it's a Springsteen record with a Bob Dylan vocal . . . [So] he put it in the box and never took it out again.' Perish the thought he might want to make a record that sold eighteen *million* copies, like the last album Van Zandt co-produced.

Six days later, he took another former masterpiece apart, the second *Infidels* discard to be resurrected. He had decided to take the as-yet-unbootlegged 'Someone's Got A Hold Of My Heart' and make it walk to Calvary, while its original self was scourged and denied.

---

* He began re-recording the song on the 23rd with a gratuitous reggae arrangement before giving it a rinse-spin in that Eighties synth wash, leaving it more than a little bedraggled.

Exactly one line retained that Someone's original identity, and even that put the non in sequitur: 'Never could learn to drink that blood and call it wine/ Never could learn to hold you, love, and call you mine.' A song once about the profoundest experience in this wretched sinner's life was reduced to one more lamentation on the charade of physical love.

He couldn't even pull the right take. The version which Jeff Rosen called up on January 15th, Dylan was convinced had the edge on the coruscating confession of a penitent recorded a day later, the one originally pulled to master. This was little more than a demo, ripe for a new vocal that made 'The Boxer' sound heartfelt, and lyrics that stripped the spirit of Christ from it. After this, he turned the tapes over to the new Tsar of post-production, Arthur Baker, who had already reduced several Springsteen tracks to a Dantesque dub version of diamond hell, thus ensuring he turned wine into vinegar:

> **Josh Abbey**: Arthur . . . was really a record company plant. He was kinda forced upon Bob. But Bob brought it on himself . . . People [had] started asking Bob, who was producing this album. And Bob was. He really was. He was picking the songs, he was saying, Let's do this, let's do that. He was producing. But Bob refused to say, I am. Bob would say, Nobody. So, everybody with an agenda all around town decided this was their opportunity to try to produce Bob Dylan . . . like we were a bunch of fucking retards . . . Bob went along with the Arthur Baker thing because the record company was just pushing him towards this kinda crap. One night, this other guy came along, some 12" . . . remixer . . . François Kevorkian . . . He never said a word to Bob, Bob never said a word to him, and [when he left,] Bob said to me, 'You know these 12-inch guys? What do they *do*??' . . . One night Arthur showed up, and within a week it's on the cover of *Rolling Stone*, Arthur Baker is working with Bob Dylan. Bob [just] took the opportunity to satisfy the record company.

Dylan himself was no idle bystander in the post-production process, which took until March 31st to complete the evisceration of something that had once pulsed with the lifeblood of salvation. By then, Dylan had been briefed on the 'virtues' of Eighties mixing:

Arthur Baker: When we got around to mixing [*Empire Burlesque*], he said, '*Blonde on Blonde* was a double album and we mixed it in two days.' I told him that was eight-track [sic], and we were now using 48-track, so it was going to take at least six times longer . . . [When] we'd already finished the record, he'd said to me, 'I'd like to make a record like Prince or Madonna.' [2021]

They'd spent twenty-five days putting horns on and taking them off tracks, and adding more girls no-one needed, while letting an infinite number of monkeys play with the in-house synthesizers. Finally, Baker Bob had an album with just two songs worthy of Rhino's 4-CD Eighties anthology, *Left of The Dial*, wittily advertised as 'All The Music That Matters From The Decade That Doesn't'. The one New York track that could have qualified for inclusion there, even Baker couldn't burn to a crisp. Cut at a session on March 3rd, it was Dylan's last attempt to salvage the album from its Eighties sheen. According to the *Chronicler*, doing it solo was Baker's idea. He wasn't even there:*

The night the album was being completed . . . I was staying at the Plaza Hotel on 59th Street . . . As I stepped out of the elevator, a call girl was coming towards me in the hallway – pale yellow hair wearing a fox coat – high heeled shoes that could pierce your heart. She had blue circles around her eyes, black eyeliner, dark eyes . . . She had a beautifulness,† but not for this kind of world. Poor wretch, doomed to walk this hallway for a thousand years. Later that night I . . . wrote the song 'Dark Eyes.' I recorded it the next night with only an acoustic guitar.

It took eight takes to get lyrics and lilting melody to sync. At one point he asked an attendant muse – perhaps Debbie Gold – 'What did that sound like?' She gushes, 'Yeah – fantastic. It was soft, but real dynamic.' An unconvinced Dylan thinks it might be 'a little too fast', and slows it down, before finally saying a restless farewell to an album that had started three months earlier with such promise. Sony had

---

* In *Chronicles*, Dylan writes: 'Baker kept suggesting that we should have an acoustic song at the end of the record . . . I thought about it and I knew he was right.' Actually, Baker had yet to be formally involved.
† The word you want is 'beauty', Bob.

their album, one that Dylan later told Aussie journo, Toby Cresswell, Baker had made 'sound like a record'.

The real question was, whose record? Certainly not a Dylan record. Even the 'big ballads' – 'Tight Connection', 'Emotionally Yours', 'Never Gonna Be The Same Again' – sounded like cartoon versions of songs they used to play on the radio. He had evidently convinced himself he could emulate the craftsmen who compiled the Great American Songbook, after professing himself unworthy of such company on being inducted into the Songwriters Hall of Fame in March 1982. Talking to Cameron Crowe, a mere three months after *Empire Burlesque*, he admitted he wanted 'to do a concept album . . . but I don't know if the people would let me get away with [things like] . . . "A Million Miles From Nowhere," "I Who Have Nothing," "All My Tomorrows," "I'm In The Mood For Love," "More Than You Know," "It's A Sin To Tell A Lie" . . . an album of standards.' At least he still had the voice for singing such songs, as live versions of 'All My Tomorrows' and 'I'm In the Mood For Love' from 1986 and 1988 demonstrate. Even that, time could take away from him.

His gift for album titles had already deserted him, 'round about *Slow Train Coming*. In 1985, he came up with a shortlist of three, the first of which gave the nod to Gurdjieff's *All and Everything (1950)*; the second, a 1951 John Huston 'lost' classic butchered by 'the system', *The Red Badge of Courage*. But he went with the third, after first asking engineer Abbey what he thought, 'Which one of these do you like better? He reads three titles . . . I said, *"Empire Burlesque."* And he says, "Yeah, me too. But the record company guys are telling me it doesn't mean anything." "Why does it have to mean anything?" "Yeah, that's what I said. I mean, *No Jacket Required*, what does that mean?" '

Did he really think Phil Collins fans treated the drummer's every utterance with the same reverence as his own fans? If the title was not great, the cover was worse. As for the contents, was this the shape of things to come – synths, click tracks and slick sound effects? For a while, it was.

Such was Dylan's determination to destroy all he might have wrought, he chose 'Tight Connection' as the first single, and then wheedled the budget out of Sony to make a 'real' video, with a proper filmmaker. Dylan had known Paul Schrader since the Seventies, even once pitching an idea for a movie 'about two Spanish aristocrats in love with the same woman,' to him. But when the video – made in Japan – went into rotation on MTV, Schrader dismissed it as 'a little piece of eye-candy I shot in Tokyo . . . [that] means as little as it looks like it means,' an injudicious comment that came back to bite him when he asked Dylan to provide the music for his 1992 movie, *Light Sleeper*. The songwriter didn't like what he saw, and when asked what could be done to make it acceptable, complained to a girlfriend, 'What can I tell them? Start over again?'

Dylan still felt like he hadn't found 'anybody that really thinks a certain way . . . like the German film-makers, the English film-makers.' In 1986, he apparently found one – the maverick director Alan Rudolph, with whom – or so he informed BBC journalist Christopher Sykes – he was planning to make a movie the following fall:

> It's a complicated story, about a piano player who gets into trouble because of a good buddy of his, and then he winds up doing some book work for a woman whose husband has disappeared, marries her, then falls in love with her daughter. And the other guy finally shows up again, and the movie comes to a screeching halt.

By then, he'd probably realized 'New Danville Girl' had all this and more, and was actually the kinda movie he should be making, having finally released it as the centrepiece of the fourth album in his 1982 record deal, and his 23rd studio album in all. The resultant artifact broke all records for a new Dylan album, selling *less* than any album he'd released since his March 1962 debut. Even as he fulfilled another contractual obligation, he knew deep down that he needed to bring the Hollywood soap-opera that his romantic life had become to a 'screeching halt' and get back to playing live. The impetus for this life-changing turn of events would be provided by Tom Petty's band; the suggestion of a good woman – just not one interested in marrying him: the sassy Debbie Gold.

1983–87:
There Ain't No Limit To The
Trouble Women Bring*

TIPS FOR GIRLS WHO'D LIKE ME TO LIKE THEM? Tell me everything.

Interview questionnaire answered by Dylan, February 1986.

I think he has this pattern of not being able to forge permanent relationships. I don't even know if it's serial monogamy. He's had a lot of relationships with a lot of women, but there seem to have been some that have [stuck] around through other [relationships] . . . There's always been a struggle to reconcile who he is personally with who he is creatively.

Ellen Bernstein, to author.

Bob's over twenty-one. He knows what he's doing. Besides, he has had a lot of women telling him a lot of things.

Paul Wasserman, Dylan's publicist, 1980.

He [dated] some of these black girls because they didn't idolize him. They were real down to earth and they didn't worship him.

Maria Muldaur.

'Do you change your conversation because you're trying to seduce someone?'

---

* A Warning to Sensitive Readers: those who have a rose-tinted view of the man behind the songs, and don't wish to see it shattered, may wish to skip this chapter.

'When I don't want them to see the real me.'

Exchange w/ Susan Ross, girlfriend.

I have a good understanding with all the women who have been in my life, whether I see them occasionally or not. We're still always best of friends.

Bob Dylan, to Scott Cohen, September 1985.

You shouldn't believe all those stories you hear about me. I'm only half the prick they make me out to be.

Bob Dylan, to girlfriend, 1989.

He has never been able to get the big picture from one woman.

Susan Ross, *Daily Mail* 16th May 1998.

He was brilliant, of course, but a lousy date. You'd be talking and he would get up suddenly and reach for his guitar and say, 'Oh, that reminds me. . .,' and he'd be lost for the night.

An ex-girlfriend, 2021.

Bob Dylan: I don't single out women as anything to get hung up about.
Ron Rosenbaum: But in the past?
BD: In the past, I was guilty of that shameless crime.

November 1977.

I still have desires that lead me around once in a while.

Bob Dylan, to Mick Brown, 27th June 1984.

★

If the break-up with Clydie King hit Dylan hard, he'd been pushing his luck for a while before it happened. In fact, he'd been pushing his luck ever since he first decided to tour with female backing singers, back in 1978. It meant there were times between 1978 and 1981 when it was akin to a travelling cathouse. That Clydie emerged as the victor from the battle of the backing singers was partly down to her two main rivals – Helena Springs and Carolyn Dennis – jumping ship. For Carolyn, Dylan's burgeoning relationship with Clydie was painful to behold, and ultimately too much to bear. She disappeared at the end of the European tour in 1981 to rebuild her life – starting with divorcing Raymond Lee Pounds.

So, when the call came from Dylan summoning her to New York's Power Station in February 1985, to add vocals to an album he was in the throes of completing – or completely wrecking, depending on your point of view – she probably couldn't quite believe her ears. She was even more non-plussed when the opening verse to one of these 'new' songs contained the couplet, 'Well, I had to move fast and I couldn't with you around my neck/ I said I'd send for you and I did.'

Was he talking to *her*? And was he speaking from the heart when he sang, 'You're the one I've been looking for/ You're the one that's got the key'? Or was he just looking for a rhyme to go with the part of a *Star Trek* episode that now replaced the poetry of 'Someone's Got A Hold Of My Heart'?* The Dylan with whom she reconnected seemed to be genuinely hurting, and at least Clydie seemed to have cut the cord completely.

That was not the way it was supposed to have gone down. The experience even seems to have led to some unguarded moments in the flood of interviews he gave at the end of 1985. When Dylan suggested to Scott Cohen, 'I have a good understanding with all the women who have been in my life,' he already knew of at least one major exception, who may even have been his second wife. Could it be that Clydie had thought he would take any marriage vows he might have made seriously? He certainly seemed to suggest he'd taken the plunge again in conversation with Charles Kaiser that fall:

> When I asked him if he had been married again after his brutal divorce from his first wife, Sarah, he said, 'Yes, in a manner of speaking.' A few minutes later he reconsidered and made that, 'Yes, as a matter of fact.' Asked if he was still married to the woman who became his second wife in 'about [19]80,' he said, 'I'm not sure.'†

---

*Sulu: 'How far do we go along with this charade?' Captain Kirk: 'Till we can think our way out.' – *The Squire of Gothos, Star Trek* Episode #17.

† According to Mr Kaiser, the interview was done on November 13th, 1985 and the relevant part of the exchange went thus: BD: What did I say when you asked if I was married again? CK: You said, "In a manner of speaking." BD: Oh, I meant to say, as a matter of fact I did.

However, amateur sleuth Howard Sounes seems convinced that if *he* couldn't find a marriage certificate, they *can't* have been married. But there are a lot of Caribbean islands the *Water Pearl* sailed by, and one later girlfriend, Susan Ross, who asserted unequivocally, 'Clydie King was Bob's second wife. I met them twelve years ago. She had two of his kids,' before going on to denigrate all previous biographers for not knowing 'why or how he married his wives, whether they were pregnant at the time, what his feelings on abortion are, and whether he married for love or because his accountant said alimony is tax deductible'.* Ross, who would enter Dylan's life in November 1985, would also make much of the fact that Dylan dedicated the 1985 edition of *Lyrics* to 'Narette', endlessly nagging him to reveal the unbelievable truth:

> I began to push [him] harder for answers. 'When is Narette coming?' I asked, fairly certain that was his youngest daughter's name. 'Who is Narette?' he asked, looking at me as if I had just asked about alien life forms. 'Well, it seems a little odd that you don't know anyone named Narette, but you dedicated a lifetime's worth of your work to her in your *Lyrics* book, which came out (interestingly enough) at the same time your youngest daughter was born. Plus, if you really want to get technical, Narette is not a name a white woman would choose for a child and your third wife is an African-American woman who is part of a culture of women known for inventing unusual names for their children.' He repeated, 'Who's Narette?'

Not that *Lyrics* was his only retrospective release that fall. Office manager Jeff Rosen had re-evaluated his boss's past for unknowing ears with a five-LP retrospective, *Biograph*, incorporating an extensive essay by Cameron Crowe, ex-*Rolling Stone* journalist turned *auteur*, which drew on several days of conversation with the creator of this impressive body of work. During this, Dylan talked about a record he once made 'of just me and Clydie King singing together and it's great, but it doesn't fall into any category that the record company knows how to

---

* Ms. Ross can't have read *Behind The Shades* very closely if she missed Sara was pregnant when she married Dylan.

deal with'. It sounded a mouth-watering prospect for anyone lucky enough to have seen them duetting together onstage in 1980-81.*

Also accompanying the essay was a full-page shot of Bob and Clydie far from the madding crowd, in happier times, busking on a porch. Dylan even remembered to send Clydie her own copy of the set when it appeared that November, signing it, 'For Clydie, My Greatest Love (that surpasses even my understanding), Forever & Always, Bob.' (qv. photo section). Perhaps inevitably, the gesture came back to bite him on the ass. She sold the item privately, and when a drunken art-director left it behind in a New York cab one night, it came up for public auction. Evidently, the tender words he wrote, no matter how heartfelt, failed to send her on a sentimental journey.

Nor would she feature again in Dylan's later career, or rise to rebut allegations in 1998 that they had been man and wife. There was little warm affection in his brief eulogy when she died unexpectedly of blood poisoning in January 2019, aged 75; Dylan merely described her in Rolling Stone as, 'my ultimate singing partner. No one ever came close. We were two soulmates.' It was all surprisingly uneffusive. So much for his assertion in 1985 that 'the women . . . in my life, whether I see them occasionally or not, we're still always best of friends.' Perhaps Clydie had finally come to realize that when Dylan sang, 'I could say that I'd be faithful . . . but . . . to me it surely would be death,' he wasn't joking.

For a while, King had seemed to keep his roving libido in check by playing the loving matriarch and sticking close. But they were always chalk and cheese. As Ron Wood said, 'Two [more] different people you couldn't hope to meet – a black, outrageous, hamburger-eating soul-singer, and Bob all quiet and white, nibbling off the side of her hamburger . . . She was bossing him around and stuff. He needed it at the time.' And although, according to Maria Muldaur, 'Each one of his back-up singers told me that when they got a call from him, they hadn't

---

* There's no evidence that such an album exists, except on Rundown rehearsal tapes, the ones from June 1981 seemingly being lost. The songs the pair rehearsed that month included 'Dearest', 'Leaving It All Up To You', 'Your Cheatin' Heart', 'Big River', 'Let It Be Me', 'Guess Things Happen That Way' and 'Smoke Gets In Your Eyes'.

a clue who he was,' Clydie was the exception. She'd recorded four Dylan songs with The Brothers & Sisters of Los Angeles back in 1969.

By the time of *Infidels*, he was back making records without her – save for a cover of 'Angel Flying Too Close' at the May 2nd session – and taking his friendship with Debbie Gold to another level. He knew he could trust Gold to be discreet, so much so that for years her close friend Paul Rappaport believed there had never been anything between them, until one day 'she confided that Bob and her had been an item at one time and that, indeed, one of Bob's songs had been written about their relationship'.*

Unlike some others, Gold never had any illusions about the man she was loving – indeed, the men she was loving (she also had an ill-fated affair with the distinctly-married Warren Zevon) – and his indeterminate idea of constancy. Which is perhaps why she never took his proposal of marriage seriously. It was also why she expressed incredulity when she ran into a recently excommunicated girlfriend in 1987, who told her he'd said he loved her. That was not like him at all. When the jilted gal proceeded to tell Gold, Carole Childs had found out about their 'affair', 'and the next day I was on a plane bound for Los Angeles', Debbie wondered aloud, 'What's she got on him, anyway?' It was a question to which she never really got the answer.

At least she had the sense to never admit which song he wrote about their relationship, unlike Margie Rogerson, who in 2017 tried to sell some poetry they had apparently co-composed, having been – in her own words, from an online auction catalogue – 'a successful San Francisco-based designer who . . . was contacted in 1977 by filmmaker and long-time Dylan friend Howard Alk and his wife Joan to purchase a cape for Dylan. The transaction eventually led to Dylan's first song with Rogerson in mind, "Is Your Love In Vain?" – written in response to a humorous note she'd added to one of his orders. Despite this evident chemistry, it was only in 1983 that Dylan and Rogerson became romantically involved. Their relationship was first immortalized . . . in the songs "Sweetheart Like You" and "Don't Fall Apart On Me Tonight."'

Not for the first time, a so-called girlfriend wanted to lay claim to

---

* Rap wasn't alone. Debbie repeatedly told me they were never 'an item', right up to her death in 2012. I knew better.

songs whose portrait of the female protagonist was hardly flattering. Certainly, Rogerson's claim to have inspired 'Is Your Love In Vain?' held very little water. But even if it had been air-tight, there was a far greater threat to Clydie on the horizon – ex-wife, Sara. According to stories in the press, Sara was seen spending time with her ex-husband, and not just at their son's bar-mitzvah or their daughter's graduation. She even snapped Dylan on the hill above Jerusalem for the back-sleeve of *Infidels*.

How much did Sara know of Clydie at this time – and any children she may have had by Dylan? On the evidence of a phone call to Dylan's suite in October 1987 – when Britta Lee Shain was sharing his bed – having only *just* found out about his latest daughter, Desiree, not a lot. Of any other children, she seemed completely in the dark, and yet still convinced it was somehow her business, a decade after their divorce:*

> In the morning, the phone in Bob's suite awakens the two of us. It's Sara. Somehow word has gotten back to her about this baby Bob's been buying clothes for. It's the baby he's had with one of his black backup singers, another Carol. Sara's worried that the news of a little illegitim-ate Dylan running around New York will upset the five children who rightfully carry his name. She's angry that Bob didn't tell her and the kids himself, instead leaving the gossip to be dropped on them like a bomb. All I hear on my end is Bob telling her over and over to calm down . . . 'A whole lotta women in this world have had my babies,' Dylan huffs [to me].

The 'Carol' in question was none other than Carolyn Dennis, her daughter Desiree having been conceived shortly after she and Dylan had started working together again at New York's Power Station in March 1985. If Clydie's own reaction to the news of Carolyn's preg-nancy might have made Sara's seem tepid, Dylan's views on children, abortion and marriage were an open secret long before Susan Ross entered the picture to 'set the record straight'. In fact, Ross simply hadn't been paying attention, given that CBS released a promo LP in 1981 of a conversation in which he states, 'I personally don't believe

---

* She wasn't alone. As of 2005, son Jakob told a reporter, 'My dad belongs to me and four [sic] other people.'

in [abortion], unless of course somebody needs to have their life saved.'

And so, when Ross herself became pregnant *by him* after their 'first night together' in July 1986, she had an abortion without consulting him. His response? 'Bob was horrified. He loves children. But . . . I didn't want him to think I was trying to trap him.' Again, she didn't know he had told a Canadian reporter, long before he ever met Clydie or Carolyn, 'If you're having children, you should be married . . . I'm just old-fashioned that way . . . [You] have to have something . . . in [your] relationship, other than just looking [into] each other's eyes.'

As for having children out of wedlock, his views seem to have been known to Victor Maymudes, who told Britta Lee Shain in October 1987, when she was fleetingly warming his cockles, 'Why don't you have Bob's baby? Then he'll be in your life forever. Bob always takes care of his kids.' Ten months later, Dylan implied there were a few, telling Kathryn Baker, 'I [was] always taught that if you were blessed to have [children], you just had more of them.'*

Initially, Dylan seemed unfazed by the bombshell Carolyn delivered after he put *Empire Burlesque* to bed. She had stayed in New York, where she was appearing in the *Big River* musical on Broadway, the ostensible reason she was there in the first place, recording with her lover at night and rehearsing during the day. Only after it opened, did she discover she was pregnant with Dylan's child. Mortified at the prospect of raising her daughter as a single mother she phoned the father, who assured her it would all turn out fine. Unfortunately, Dennis had just discovered that Dylan 'had more than just a business relationship with a woman she had met a year prior, Carole Childs'. And this rival had claws,

---

* Certainly, Dylan seems to have been taking very few precautions against pregnancy in this period, if a short story published in 2021 has a grain of truth. Entitled 'The Silent Type', by Sam Sussman, it purports to be an account of a relationship between Dylan and a fellow student in Norman Raeben's art classes in 1974, later briefly rekindled: 'In the spring of 1990, [my mother's] sister received a phone call from a man asking for my mother. The caller said Bob Dylan wanted to talk to her . . . My mother made plans to meet him at the old apartment. Dylan arrived in red cowboy boots, whether out of habit or nostalgia she never knew. As I registered the date – roughly nine months before my birth – my mother went silent.'

calling her up and screaming when 'her' boyfriend went AWOL one time, 'Is Bob there?!'

At least Dylan had agreed to support Carolyn and her child 'until she got back on her feet', after initially telling her he was not a bank. He also bought her a home in the Fairfax area of L.A. On January 31st, 1986, Desiree Gabrielle Dennis was born at Humana West Hills Hospital in Canoga Park. Her birth certificate did not show her father's name, in the hope she could have as normal a childhood as possible. In the box where the father's name usually appeared was written 'Mother declined to state'. Meanwhile, both parents drew up an agreement allowing Desiree to make the decision to take her father's last name herself when she felt ready, which she duly did when she was twelve.

Dylan, though, was not sticking around. He had a Far East tour to do, beginning in New Zealand's Wellington on February 5th. Carolyn was in no fit state to join him, having a baby to breast-feed. One somehow doubts he promised to be a good boy. And if he did, his resolve lasted less than a fortnight, until the night he met the provocatively-named Gypsy Fire, who fit perfectly the profile a confidant gave to Nick Kent in 1990 of Dylan's 'type', 'There are a lot of different women he sees, from all different walks of life. But they all tend to have one thing in common. They're invariably all very weird [and/]or very intense.'* Gypsy Fire shared another common conviction, a sense their meeting was preordained:

> I loved Bob Dylan's songs, and I knew that I was going to meet him, for eight years I felt this in my heart and sent my love to him in my meditation . . . In 1986, I am given backstage passes by a friend of my sister, the manager of Dire Straits . . . My seat is with members of Mark Knopfler's band. I don't sit there, I stand on the side and when Bob comes out, I know my psychic feelings have all come true, and I will be with Bob . . . As soon as Bob starts singing, 'Everybody Must Get Stoned' [sic], I walk in front of [the] stage, and dance and dance and dance . . . Bob gets to the edge of stage and starts talking to me . . . The people next to me told me, he wants me to get up on stage with him, so

---

* In a 1987 proposal by Faridi McFree for a never-written book about their affair, she wrote, 'I can't seem to get you out of my heart. You've bitten into it too deeply and for too many centuries. How many years do we go back? Osiris and Isis?'

I did . . . [Afterwards,] too many people were trying to get to Bob's dressing room. Even though Bob invited me to meet him backstage, I left, and went to the hotel and waited for him. When he arrived, I went up to him, and he said, 'There you are.' . . . He told me to wait for him at the bar, I was chatting to someone and after a while . . . I jumped off the stool and went into the lounge area, and there he was talking to a woman . . . They were discussing The Bible. Bob told me he loved my boots and stockings and to pass him the ashtray. We talked and I told him I was leaving – I thought this woman might have been his lover. As I got up and started to walk away, he came after me and told me he wants to talk to me. So, he took me to the phone area and asked me to phone him the next day after midday and ask for a fake name he gave me . . . [The next day] he [said he] wanted me to stay . . . [When] we were alone, he told me he wanted me to be in a video an Australian director was about to shoot . . . I could dance in it . . . He told me to take my clothes off . . . we talked some more and then we made love.

Here was a replay of another ships-passing liaison on the previous tour. An infatuated painter, Claude-Angèle Boni, had spent the night with him in Paris, after he told her, 'I want to play until I'm 90.' He then 'grabbed his little Martin and started to strum it walking around in circles in the room. He said it was time for him to go to bed. I don't remember all the details, but I know I followed him.' The following morning, she found out that if she wanted to continue to hang around, it would have to be on Dylan's terms:

[Back at my hotel,] I was trying to sleep when the telephone rang. It was . . . one of the road managers. He was calling to tell me that Dylan wanted me to go with him to Grenoble, where he was giving his last concert before [he left for] England . . . After that I received another call from Stan, Bob's bodyguard . . . I said that I was okay for Grenoble but that I wanted to travel . . . with Dylan in the same plane. He said that was impossible, that I could not travel with them and I had to take a train . . . Then he phoned somebody to say, 'She agrees to go to Grenoble incognito.' I asked him who was on the phone, if it was Bob, but he didn't want to tell me.

Gypsy Fire also found herself treated like a puppet on a string as

Dylan continued touring Australia. If their grand affair lasted barely a fortnight, during and after which she was neither discreet nor taciturn about their brief fling, by August 1986 a Sydney newspaper suggested she claimed, 'I Was Bob Dylan's Sex Slave', printing their salacious piece of tittle-tattle alongside a racy photo of the lady in stockings and suspenders. (How did that happen?) She sued for damages – and eventually won – but the damage was done. Whatever impression Gypsy Fire tried to convey regarding their souls-entwined liaison, it was no great meeting of minds.

Something like this did happen in Melbourne. But it was with an older woman whom Dylan had long admired, and to whom he willingly admitted, when she directly asked him about his relationships with members of the opposite sex in a tiny seafood restaurant at the Melbourne Marina, one Sunday afternoon, 'I am not good at that. I am a disaster when it comes to women.'

The lady in question was legendary Hollywood actress Lauren Bacall, who at 61 was 'in town' appearing in Tennessee Williams's *Sweet Bird of Youth*, directed by her good friend, Wilton Morley. It was Morley's idea to invite Dylan to a performance: 'The next afternoon Bob brings his three black backup singers to the matinee of *Sweet Bird of Youth* . . . He sits through the whole performance in sunglasses.' When it came to Bacall, Dylan was the eager fan hanging on the words of his teenage prayer, the love interest in movies like *Key Largo* and *To Have And Have Not*, which he could quote almost verbatim. Bacall, though, was not about to play the coy mistress.

Wilton Morley: The thing you have to remember about film stars is that most people never quiz them about Hollywood. They assume, for example in Bacall's case, that questions about Bogart or Sinatra are off limits. But movie stars are just like the rest of us, they want to reminisce and if you give them enough space and they trust you, that's often all they talk about . . . [and] Bob Dylan is a sponge . . . When he does meet someone who is not intimidated in his presence, which must be rare, he soaks it up. 'Media,' says Betty, at one point, 'I always say [is short for] mediocrity.' Bob will use that [line] on stage the next night.

Bacall wasn't the only Fifties screen goddess for whom Dylan had carried a torch. Indeed, he unintentionally wound her up by talking about his friend, Elizabeth Taylor, boasting of recently getting to know her, and telling Bacall how much he had in common with her. This did not go down well with 'Betty', who confided to Morley, 'I don't know why he had to keep going on about Liz Taylor . . . like a little boy, for Christ's sake!'

Such was Dylan's yen for Taylor that he admitted to the English video directors who shot two more *Empire Burlesque* promo videos in August 1985, that 'Emotionally Yours' was a song he'd written 'with Liz Taylor in mind'. Indeed, as director Markus Innocenti recalls, '[When] we went back into the [church] hall to shoot "Emotionally Yours" . . . he'd noticed that Monica Getchell, who was playing the discarded girlfriend, had a similar bone structure to the young Elizabeth Taylor. He asked if a wig could be found, so that Monica could become the image of Taylor in the 1950s.' He also told the girlfriend of his right-hand man, Gary Shafner, he thought Taylor was 'the very definition of celebrity . . . so elegant and poised.'

Just nine years older than Bob, and a fantasy figure for him since at least 1962's 'I Shall Be Free', Taylor had been his personal guest at an evening at New York's Whitney Museum in November 1985 (during which he met and obtained Susan Ross's contact details), and was at her 55th birthday party in February 1987, in the company of Carole Childs, who offered the perfect contrast to Taylor's elegance and poise.

Whilst in Melbourne, Dylan took the opportunity to return the favour with Bacall, giving her and Morley tickets to his show, which she loved (writing a caustic letter to the local paper after a less than favourable review). Afterwards, the two icons continued swopping stories back at the hotel, until, in Morley's words, 'three late night revellers happen in on this scene and see an opportunity. The two men, wearing dinner jackets and evidently fairly drunk, egg the woman onto the piano stool, and she breaks out singing . . . a dreadful rendition of "Sometimes When We Touch." Bob takes control of the situation. He beckons Stevie [Nicks] over. "Stevie, anything you can do about this?" Stevie edges onto the piano stool, next to the singer and gently takes over . . . Bob is able to continue his conversation with Betty Bacall.' The Fleetwood Mac singer, ostensibly there with Petty but leaning to the Jack of Hearts, had been hoping to join Dylan onstage, but without a work permit had to confine her singing to hotel bars.

Nothing in Dylan's behaviour as he weaved his way across the

Antipodes and on to Japan, suggested he was looking to settle down. Or that he was running out of opportunities for encounters with women who'd convinced themselves they had known each other in another lifetime. As Heartbreaker Stan Lynch told Mikal Gilmore that summer, 'I pretty much saw it all. I saw the girl who slept in the elevator claiming to be his sister from Minnesota; I saw the one who claimed to be his masseuse, who flew in from Perth and was riding up and down the elevator trying to figure out what floor he was on . . . They forget one important thing: Bob doesn't know them; they just know him.'

Which makes it all the more surprising that the mother of his new baby girl was confronted, on the father's return Stateside, by a man seemingly determined to marry her, as he had married a pregnant Sara (and possibly Clydie) before, ensuring slightly belatedly that their daughter was a 'legitimate' Dylan, as it were.

According to Dennis, his proposal went something like this, 'You know, Carol, out of all the things I know about you, you are strong and aggressive. But I [also] know that you love the Lord and I need a woman like you on my side praying for me . . . I don't want to be on my death-bed and have to ask a minister or rabbi to come and marry us before I go across.' When she failed to see the romance in this plea, he raised the ante, 'If you cannot marry me just because you love me, then do it for the sake of our daughter . . . I want to make sure that you and the baby are all right. They write about my life, and I want them to know that you were not just one of my girlfriends. You were my wife.'

Oddly enough, this did the trick. He promptly asked her if she could make all the arrangements for the ceremony as he had another album to record, and even less idea what to put on it than when they'd reconnected in New York. The mother of Desiree was keen to ensure the whole thing was done discreetly so that 'it wouldn't belong to the world'. She later said, she didn't want him penalized for being 'in love with this woman from another culture', having seemingly forgotten he was Bob Dylan, oh, and for the past eight years had been constantly carrying on with one black woman or another.

Dennis duly discovered California had such a thing as a confidential law of marriage. Using this, she arranged for her and her fiancé to meet at the downtown office of the State Commissioner of Marriage, Iris Spencer, on June 4th, 1986 – just five days before they were both scheduled to start a two-month tour in San Diego – to conduct a private ceremony before regular office hours.

After the ceremony, the newlyweds left the building separately, hoping to avoid drawing any attention to the odd couple, meeting up at her car. According to Dennis, she drove him back to his house in Malibu, kissed him on the lips and told him she would see him at rehearsals. The rest of the band were none the wiser. According to Dennis, it was her decision to hide their marriage from the world, 'grateful that the Lord had somehow sheltered me throughout my life from knowing anything about him'.

If she really didn't know whom she had married, and what kind of man he was, she was in for a rude awakening. She had not yet joined his touring band when he confided to a female Aussie journo that 'anyone who is in my life at all respects [the fact] that . . . I don't come home every night.' Still nursing Desiree, and backing her child's father onstage every night that summer, less than six months after their daughter entered the world, she found herself being asked to ride in the back bus with the other singers whenever Carole Childs joined the tour.

He seemed determined to convince the green-eyed Childs she was the only woman in his life, prompting her to later tell Sounes, 'He has been a stand-up guy with me. [So] it wouldn't matter to me what he did. That . . . might seem foolish.' Actually, she had a temper, their relationship was always tempestuous and at times it hung by a thread. As for his predilection for the stereotypical tart-with-a-heart lauded in his Eighties' lyrics, it seems it only went skin deep. When Childs's outfit attracted wolf whistles from passing taxi drivers one time in New York in 1986, Dylan turned on her and said, 'That's it! You're dressed like a whore. You're going home!' And he meant it. Just as he did when, during a night of heavy drinking in Tel Aviv with Kurt Loder in September 1987, he forgot there was a tape-recorder nearby, and let slip his view on those who took the Madonna's name in vain, 'I hate to see chicks perform. Hate it. Because they whore themselves. Especially the ones that don't wear anything. They fuckin' whore themselves.' (Loder, to his credit, never quoted these lines in his Rolling Stone article.)

Not that Dylan was under any illusion about how his relationship with Childs would end. As he confided to Sam Shepard one afternoon in August 1986, at the end of his most successful US tour in *years*, 'You gravitate toward people who've got somethin' to give you . . . And then maybe one day you wake up and see that they're not givin' it to you anymore.'

Not surprisingly, the tour in question offered plentiful opportunities for the Mr Hyde in Dylan to smooth talk women into bed and disappear down the highway. He even spent a night with the lovely Chris O'Dell, whom he had put on notice as far back as 1975, when Sara was sharing his bed, 'I know that you know I'm making a pass at you, and you know that I know that you're interested.' Eleven years later, he seized the day, even if he didn't look like that lean, mean coke-machine any more, holding up an earlier photo and asking her, 'Did I ever really look like that? Was I ever really that person?' At least he confirmed a decade-old suspicion that she was interested, willing and able.

Nor was Dennis the only duskier dame to share his bed. On one occasion in 1987, he told Shafner's girlfriend to 'pick up a woman named Darlene at the airport. He says she's black. "You'll know her when you see her." . . . She tells me she met Bob the year before in Texas when he was on the True Confessions tour . . . She says Bob begged her to accompany him on his bus to the next destination. After a lot of soul-searching – she tells me she's a devout Christian – . . . she'd agreed to go. Later, she was horrified to learn that there was a woman on the backup singers' bus right behind them who was carrying Bob's baby, but she spent the night with Dylan anyway.' So, not really *that* conflicted.

The True Confessions tour also finally provided Dylan with the opportunity to have a first sexual encounter with the woman he met at the Whitney, the previous November. According to Susan Ross, this was the beginning of some great decade-long love affair, which curiously seemed to comprise a series of one-night stands anywhere up to a year apart. Heloise and Abelard, it was not. When she tried to sell her story in 1997 – and found no takers – she insisted she had replaced Childs in Bob's bed, thus passing the gullibility test with flying colours:

With him [at the Whitney] was a small blond[e]. I later found out [it] was Carole Childs, who apparently was telling everyone they were going to be married. That was typical of him, allowing his women to say anything they wanted, then taking no action. He swore to me whenever her name came up in articles or books as his girlfriend, that they stopped being lovers shortly after the Whitney party, but remained friends.

That was in November 1985. The Washington shows were the first week in July 1986. When he made his move, she later told a tabloid reporter, he had. 'all the finesse of a tenth grader, struggling with his zipper in the back of a car'. And yet, the flame still burned. Unfortunately for her, opportunities to rekindle their burning love would remain few and far between. Her next trip to see him was not until the following October, when she joined him in Montreal as he was wrapping up his first film-role in eight years, *Hearts of Fire*. With Childs due to arrive any minute, he dispatched her to Tucson, apparently 'to research Josephine Earp, Wyatt Earp's third wife, in order to write a screenplay for Dylan to produce'.

Again, she conformed to a type Dylan liked – attractive, wacky women who deluded themselves into believing they were undiscovered writers, when they barely knew how to use an apostrophe. Not that Ross was wholly blind, or entirely naive. She soon realized 'his life . . . was rigidly compartmentalised, and he was a control freak, who kept each compartment hermetically sealed.' As she kept on at him, 'Why don't we live together?', Dylan used a stock answer that contained a kernel of truth, 'Because I can barely live with myself.'

It was a line that failed to work on another demanding female, which is why in 1994 he found himself on the end of a lawsuit from a woman he had known since 1975, the actress Ruth Tyrangiel. Where she fits into this picture of a forty-something man adrift, bouncing from bed to bed while his career sank ever more down the pan, is not entirely clear. In the years between their first interaction, when she played 'The Girlfriend' – typecasting or what? – in *Renaldo & Clara* (acting alongside someone pretending to be Bob Dylan, Ronnie Hawkins), and 1994, when she claimed to be the L.A. equivalent of Dylan's common-law wife, their relationship was about as public as Marilyn Monroe and John F. Kennedy.

Just like in that relationship, one of them – it turned out to be Ruth – was married for much of the time to someone else. Her suit thus rather foundered when her actual husband testified to this effect. The lawsuit was thrown out, and she was a million bucks poorer. (Dylan told another girlfriend at the time of the suit he would have paid her off, if only she'd come to him first, and not brought suit.)

Such was the weird and wacky life of Bob Dylan when a familiar face re-entered his orbit in September 1987, someone whom Ross described in her 1997 proposal, with some asperity, as 'the gargoyled bodyguard who used his association with the Dylan entourage to seduce young girls'. It was a name familiar to anyone who had known Dylan when he *really* did misbehave, sometimes dangerously so: Victor Maymudes. He was (re)hired, in part, to ensure that the crazier wannabe groupies were kept firmly at arm's length. Ross herself had not yet become one of those on whom the Dylan office kept files – called, euphemistically, 'profiles'.

The previous October, Dylan had become quite animated when one of these 'profiles', the infamous 'Sara Dylan', actually a French woman who had changed her name by deed-poll and been following Dylan around claiming to be his lost half-sister, came up in conversation with Christopher Sykes: '[These kind of people] think they know me because I've written some song that happens to bother them in a certain way . . . That's got nothing to do with me! . . . I think I could prove that in any court!'

Two years after the Whitney, Ross suddenly received a visitation from the terrible two, when 'a long black limo pulled up in front of my building. [Dylan] had told me to meet him downstairs, so I was standing in the darkened alcove, waiting until he arrived. Victor got out, looked up and down the street, then at the building, and after making his assessment for Bob's safety, opened the door.'*

By then, Maymudes had already met, assessed, humoured and dispatched the latest threat to Dylan's emotional well-being, Britta Lee Shain. For once, the singer's radar doesn't seem to have been working where Lee Shain was concerned, perhaps because he thought she was sidekick Gary Schafner's girlfriend.

It had certainly taken her a while to get under his skin. She had been just his employee's girlfriend when she attended a party the previous year when someone raised the subject of the film, *Fatal Attraction*. The

---

* Ross claims this was three days after the Whitney Museum, but Maymudes was not rehired by Dylan until September 1987, some 22 *months* after the Whitney.

ever-wary Dylan had said he couldn't believe it had taken this long for Hollywood to tackle the subject: 'I've had that idea a million times.'*

Shain had found it hard to pierce the man's outer armour, and had initially complained to her ostensible boyfriend, 'He shuts down so quickly,' only for Shafner to patiently explain, 'He has to do that. He can't just let anyone in . . . He'll do that the first four or five times he meets you. Then one day, he'll just sit down and have a conversation with you.' Duly noted.

By the time Dylan initiated such a conversation with her, Britta's relationship with Shafner was on the skids and she was inveigling herself into Dylan's inner circle, gaining his trust long enough to accompany him on the 1987 Temples In Flames tour, evidently believing – foolishly – that what happened on tour, stayed on tour. She didn't survive long, not even long enough to inspire a song from her beloved songwriter, despite being the niece of the co-author of one of Dylan's favourite songs of misplaced love, Bobby Sharp's 'Unchain My Heart'.

Perhaps this was a blessing. For the past half a decade, the greatest writer of love songs in modern times had been writing some of the most one-dimensional torch ballads a major label ever foisted on the record-buying public. These included such unregenerate dreck as 'Driftin' Too Far From Shore', 'Tight Connection To My Heart', 'Never Gonna Be The Same Again', 'Had A Dream About You, Baby' and 'Night After Night'. The last two were his musical contribution on his return to movieland, *Hearts of Fire*, and were so bad he had to record an impromptu version of Shel Silverstein's 'A Couple More Years' to inject some honesty and perspicacity into the film's soap-operatic narrative.

As Robert Graves could have told him, not every woman one sleeps with is a muse. If ever there was a correlation between inspiration and libido, it was no longer working for Dylan. As for the claim, made to Bill Flanagan in March 1985 – the mid-point of his four-year-long lost weekend – that he 'never really . . . thought I was giving away too much [in my songs]. I mean, I give it *all* away, but I'm not really giving away any *secrets*,' he had been living that lie too damn long.

---

* Clint Eastwood made a far better film on the subject in 1971, his directorial debut, *Play Misty For Me*.

In September 1987, he would embark on what would prove to be his last tour where girlsingers were part of the travelling troupe, leaving him prey to temptation, having failed to rehearse the one song from the Eighties that went, 'Trouble – nothing but trouble.' For too long, he had been down in the bottom, playing the back door man. Time to atone, and maybe even start treating women with dignity again.

5.4

July 1985 to June 1987:
Meet Me In The Bottom

He's had his patchy periods, but we all hang with him because we know any day he might write the best thing he's ever done.

Tom Petty, 2006.

It's not important what other people call you. If you yourself know you're a fake, that's tougher to live with.

Bob Dylan, to Bob Brown, 19th September 1985.

One thing that people have to understand about Bob is that he's not trying to prove anything.

Dave Stewart.

He [told me] that the words stopped coming. Suddenly, it just wasn't there anymore, like the well ran dry.

Ted Perlman, guitarist on *Empire Burlesque*.

My enthusiasm for making records might not be what it was twenty years ago.

Bob Dylan, to Denise Worrell, November 1985.

After you make so many records . . . sometimes you just don't know any more whether . . . [you] do it because you think it's [what's] expected of you . . . And you'll try to do something [different], but it just won't come out right. At those times, it's best just to go sing somebody else's song.

Bob Dylan, to Bert Kleinman, 30th July 1984.

I went [to Australia] for thirty-two days [in 1986] and became good
friends with Bob – as good a friend as you can be with Bob . . . He's very
much by himself. You don't run up to Bob and say, 'Hi, Bob.' You kinda
wait for him to even notice that you're in the room.

Stevie Nicks, 1994.

Most of my dealings with Dylan were either on the phone or through
his woman-Friday, Naomi Saltzman, a nice Jewish mother-hen who
made his everyday activities possible and was great to work with,
because she was utterly devoted to his interests, yet also practical and
realistic. One night she had me and my woman-Friday . . . to her apartment for dinner with just her husband [Ben], and Bob. It was a revelation.
This genius rebel . . . was almost child-like – you felt he barely knew
how to tie his shoes, let alone write a check.

Robert Gottlieb, editor of the 1985 edition of *Lyrics*.

Bob lived in a parallel universe. He was with us, but not with us . . . He
would come into the trailer and collapse into the make-up chair, like a
wild animal that had been shot with a tranquilizer . . . He often wore a
huge fur-trimmed parka, his head peeking out from the shadowy inter-
ior of the hood.

Rupert Everett, co-star on *Hearts of Fire, Red Carpets &*
Other Banana Skins (2006).

★

At what point did Dylan start to hate the sound of *Empire Burlesque*, or
doubt himself and / or his new methodology? Not right away, for sure,
as he persevered with that godawful Eighties drum sound for at least
one more album, even resurrecting three of its discards. Thankfully,
these included the monumental 'New Danville Girl', which was subject to yet more post-production and rewrites. The decision to open
himself up to the idea of overdubbing vocals and layering tracks ad
infinitum was destined to have consequences that would challenge the
Artist Known As Dylan like never before.

To no longer record 'in the moment', once unthinkable, still seemed
to go against the grain. But he had been harbouring doubts about his
previous methodology for a while. Sat around a table with Paul 'Rap'

Rappaport around this time, he enquired, 'How come Fleetwood Mac sell six million albums, and no matter what I do, I can only sell a million?' Rap's light-hearted response was to have more consequence than he realized at the time, 'Bob, Fleetwood Mac goes into a studio for six months, writes catchy tunes designed to be radio hits, takes the time to do many overdubs, and then works on polishing up the sound of the whole thing for another couple weeks. You go into a dentist's office, pull up a sound truck, and in two weeks . . . you've completed your album. But . . . no matter how many records they sell, they'll never be Bob Dylan!'

The very idea Dylan cared about commerce cut to the core of a carefully constructed public persona. It was like he was letting the cat out of the bag, just as his commercial clout was at an all-time low. It turns out, he really *did* care. When an English journalist in 1989 joked about how he 'cleverly avoided' having hit singles, Dylan rose to the bait, 'Cleverly avoided! That's a nonsense, isn't it? Who wants to cleverly avoid hit singles? Everybody'd like 'em. But it's just not been my lot to have them.' Well, not many of 'em.

That he still harboured doubts about the wisdom of the course he'd taken with *Empire Burlesque* – meeting some illusory mass audience halfway with a sound as artificial as the era's shoulder-pads – is clear from who he chose to play the album to. The first fresh pair of ears belonged to Mick Jagger, who heard it at Right Track right after Dylan sequenced it; 'before anyone other than us heard it', engineer Abbey recalls. Jagger had just released the slick-as-shit *She's The Boss*, proof that he a) thought he could do Funk, and b) could do without the Stones. He proved the exact opposite, even if the album initially sold well, convincing Dylan he might know his audience.

His second choice of sounding board was even more left-field. Turning up unexpectedly at Allen Ginsberg's Lower East Side apartment with a cassette, he played him – and his friend, Raymond Foye – the entire album, as Richard Hell (an altogether more trenchant sounding board) slept fitfully upstairs. At one point, Allen asked Dylan to be quiet so he could hear the words, not realizing the album had been Bakerized, and there was precious little chance of hearing anything over the sound of airlifted kitchen sinks.*

---

* Hell, the original punk, was also a fan, having recently released his original version of 'Going Going Gone' on *Destiny Street*.

Within six months, Dylan was telling Robert Hilburn, 'I haven't even listened to [*Empire Burlesque*] since it came out. I'd rather spend my time working on new songs, or listen to other people's records.' And 'working on new songs' was precisely what he had been doing. He just hadn't bothered to finish any of them. Despite being contracted to deliver two more albums by July 1st, 1987, he spent a whole day at Cherokee in June 1985 working on Allen Toussaint's 'Freedom For The Stallion', a song given over to funk by The Hues Corporation back in 1973, before returning to Oceanway five days later to continue crafting the song, along with versions of (an uncirculated) 'I'm In The Mood For Love' and 'In The Summertime' – Ray Dorset's, not his.* None of these seemed like obvious album material, and nor were the multiple instrumentals also cut, helpfully logged as 'Ideas', 'Track X', and 'Blues Jam' (which apparently had a 'good last ½ min').

It only became apparent he was really looking for musicians to jam with after his next 'session' in August. This time there was an ostensible purpose – to shoot a couple of promo videos for the album he was already looking to disown. Asked the following month why he was prepared to pander to the label this way, he replied, 'Because my records aren't exactly selling like Cyndi Lauper's or Bruce's, I didn't feel I had the credibility to demand that control.' Even his choice of video producer – the Eurythmics' Dave Stewart – suggested he thought he needed to make a pact with contemporary pop. Stewart promptly explained he was not a video director, but he knew a man (or two) who fit the bill:

Markus Innocenti: Dave recommended Eddie [Arno] and I, and Dylan agreed. We then hung around in L.A. for three weeks whilst Dylan was incommunicado in Russia . . . Dylan arrived back, approved Dave's concepts and added a few of his own ideas . . . Dylan had requested that all the musical equipment was 'playable' . . . and he jammed extensively with the band . . . Dylan himself didn't sing, being more interested in riffing or taking solos on guitar. Dylan had brought two girls with him to audition the female voice in 'When The Night . . .' . . . [and] also a teenage girl called Angel, and asked if she could play guitar in the band.

---

* What a shame it wasn't Mungo Jerry's follow-up to that #1 hit, the peerless 'Baby Jump'.

Angel had never held a guitar . . . Everybody was under orders from the producer not to speak directly to Dylan . . . and that included us . . . Dylan asked Eddie why nobody was speaking to him, and was annoyed when he learnt the reason. He said that this happened all the time.

What Stewart had failed to explain to the two directors was the reason Dylan wanted to shoot in black and white, 'We were simply told by Dave that black and white was required. We weren't told why . . . We wished that Dylan had talked directly to us earlier, because we learned [later] that Dylan wanted it to look like an old Japanese movie,' something by Kurosawa, say, or even Paul Schrader's recent arthouse movie, *Mishima*. The other thing Dylan hadn't told the directors was that he wasn't really an actor, Innocenti recalling one 'moment during filming when Dylan was required to act like he was dismayed. He seemed worried about it. I quietly told the cameraman to start filming, [before I] asked Dylan what was wrong. He let out a sigh and said, "I'm not sure I can do this," and gave an uncertain shrug and shake of his head, "Cut." '

At least the itch to perform and play was real. Even when they were having lunch on the first day, Innocenti noticed, 'Dylan quietly played acoustic guitar at the table . . . He couldn't pass a piano or guitar without stopping to play a while.' The band Stewart had assembled for the shoot, which included Blondie's Clem Burke on drums and Feargal Sharkey on tambourine-bashing, seemed to delight Dylan:

[Dave] put together a great band for this lip-sync video . . . somewhere in West L.A. So between all the time they took setting up camera shots and lights and all that stuff, we could just play live for this little crowd that had gathered there. I can't even express how good that felt – in fact, I was trying to remember the last time I'd felt that kind of direct connection. [1985]

It was just the kinda set-up he loved: an invited audience of extras, no set-list. It was a much-needed antidote to his last US performance, at a stadium in Philadelphia to a TV audience of close to two billion, somebody having come up with the hare-brained idea of having Dylan headline Live Aid, the biggest charity concert of all time. But then, according to Bill Graham, 'Lionel Ritchie came in at the last minute to join the show. Before that, I had Dylan as the closer. I didn't want "We Are the World" . . . I wanted "Blowin' in The Wind"!'

Dylan wasn't even sure he wanted to do the show, remaining sceptical of the whole pat-oneself-for-caring aspect, telling Mikal Gilmore six weeks later, 'Some guy halfway round the world is starving, so put ten bucks in the barrel. Then you can feel you don't have to have a guilty conscience about it . . . [But] as [for] any sweeping movement to destroy hunger and poverty, I don't see that happening.'

So, when Elliott Roberts phoned to tell him he would be closing the show, Roberts was stunned to hear the singer not asking him when and where, but rather, 'How does it work?' Roberts tried to bite his tongue before riding roughshod over Dylan's interjections, 'You mean how does the money get to the people in Africa? Well, I'm not sure . . . No, Bob, I don't think it's a scam . . . No, I can't guarantee you that all the money will get to the people [starving] . . .,' until he finally blew his stack, 'Why should you do it?! How about, 'cause it's fucking great for your fucking career!!'

Actually, Dylan – who would be proven right to voice concerns about where the money was going – was not now closing the show, Patti LaBelle was (and woe betide anyone who tried wrestling *her* microphone away). As for it being great for his career, if doing his worst-ever set to his largest audience qualified, then yes, it was great for his career. Fortunately, the worldwide audience – Willie Nelson included – stayed tuned long enough to hear Dylan ask folk to spare a thought for all the farmers who were also struggling (leading to another foul-mouthed rant from Bob Geldof, thankfully off-mike).

That single comment would spark no less than thirty-three Farm Aid benefits between 1985 and 2021, raising tens of millions of dollars for US farmers, doing more actual good than anything anyone looking to further their own careers did that day in July 1985. But it sure would have helped if Dylan had told backing musicians Ron Wood and Keith Richards which three songs they were doing some time before, in Wood's words, 'we were walking up the steps to the stage'. It would also have helped if the organizers had given the trio some stage monitors. Dylan later complained, 'We couldn't even hear our own voices, and when you can't hear, you can't play; you don't have any timing.' It was like he was back at L'Olympia. This time, though, the whole world was watching.

If Dylan's Live Aid performance did not have the positive knock-on effect on album sales the likes of Queen and David Bowie experienced, it did galvanize him into getting a proper band to back him next time he did a benefit gig, which would be on September 22nd, in Champaign, Illinois, at the first Farm Aid concert. Having spawned the entire event with his Live Aid speech, he could hardly refuse. This time he decided he might even rehearse some of the songs he intended to perform, do an actual soundcheck,* and listen to Debbie Gold, which meant finally utilising the ultra-professional Tom Petty & The Heartbreakers as his backing band. When he did, he once again felt 'that kind of direct connection'. When a film-crew turned up three days before Farm Aid to film rehearsals for a news story, they captured one of the great Dylan performances, a rendition of the Ray Charles standard, 'That Lucky Old Sun' that was close to heaven.

He reprised it, too, at Farm Aid itself, just as the Nashville Network decided now would be a good time to take an ad-break. But even the half of the six-song set they deigned to broadcast proved he was back to his brimming best, oozing confidence, revelling in the restoration of full power. He was visibly enjoying himself, as he had been all day, chatting animatedly backstage with the likes of Randy Newman, Lou Reed and Emmylou Harris, who was probably thankful it was poor Madelyn Quebec who was up there having to fly by radar, sharing a mike with the man.

The alliance Gold had been angling for all along clearly clicked – no argument brooked. The ensuing jam sessions – euphemistically dubbed rehearsals – confirmed guitarist Mike Campbell, organist Benmont Tench and the Lynch-Epstein rhythm-section could confidently rise above anything Dylan might throw at them.

And yet, when Dylan returned to Cherokee to record some 'songs' at the end of October, the Queens of Rhythm, his latest gaggle of backing singers, were along for the ride, but not The Heartbreakers.[†] At times it sounds as if he jotted down a bunch of song titles, and then

---

* Which I presciently taped on my Sony D-6, thus capturing a one-off performance of 'I Like It Like That'.

[†] It could be Tench on organ. A pristine 15-track bootleg CD was released in 2016, called *After The Empire*. Björner assigns its contents to this October 31st, 1985 Cherokee session, an educated guess, probably correct.

tried to jam random pop/r&b lyrics into them. In one instance, after singing, 'Baby, Coming Back From The Dead' for eight minutes, he asked, 'What was that called?'

Though he attempts 'Nothing Here Worth Dying For' three times, he is not really knocking anything into shape. Perhaps he simply wanted to prove he meant what he said when he told a reporter, 'I don't write songs if they're not easy to write . . . I don't usually struggle with it. I have done that, but I don't usually like the results.' None of the song-ideas would re-emerge at the *Knocked Out Loaded* sessions, six months later, but a matter of days after the Cherokee session he told *Time*'s Denise Worrell:

> [I] go through long spells where I don't really write anything. I just jot down little phrases and things I overhear, people talking to me . . . Sometimes I'll play on the guitar or piano, and some kind of thing will come. Other times I'll just go into the studio and play riffs with other people, and then later on listen to the tapes and see what that wants to be.

These particular tapes he seemingly left at the reservation, even the promising 'Twenty-Six Storeys High'. Instead, after doing another spate of promo interviews for the surprisingly popular five-LP *Biograph* boxed-set, Dylan flew to London and recorded four days' worth of instrumentals at Dave Stewart's Crouch End studio, The Church, with another smorgasbord of session-men. Again, he just seemed to be fooling around, or so one attendee, Waterboy Mike Scott, concluded:

> It was basically a free for all. Dylan turns around and says, 'Just keep playing. It doesn't matter if you overplay, it doesn't matter what you do, just keep playing and we'll keep the best bits' . . . He had a verse, a chorus, a middle eight and that was the structure . . . but he didn't actually stand at the mike and sing.

'Producer' Dave Stewart, perhaps had his tongue firmly in cheek, when he told *The Whistle Test*'s Andy Kershaw, who gate-crashed a session with a BBC film-crew, 'They're all Bob's tunes. He makes them up on the spot, and then we just record them as soon as he makes them up.' Again, Dylan continued stockpiling tunes, as opposed to songs – pulling twelve of them to a comp. reel and shipping ten boxes of multitrack tapes back from Blighty,* but not before an alcohol-fuelled evening spent listening to the tapes with Dave Stewart and Eurythmics' singer Annie Lennox.

According to Stewart, 'We were all drunk on tequila. Dylan was reciting the lyrics to these songs as the backing tracks were playing, but he was just making them up on the spot . . . He did it for about nine songs.' The experience inspired Lennox to write her own song using half-remembered lines Dylan sang, calling it 'Missionary Man', a Dylanesque figure who's 'got God on his side/ He's got the saints and apostles backin' up from behind.'

Meanwhile, Dylan's own hunt for lyrical subject-matter went on. Perhaps he didn't think the world was quite ready for the truth, having told Scott Cohen in September, 'The things I have to say about such things as ghetto bosses, salvation and sin, lust, murderers going free, and children without hope – messianic kingdom-type stuff . . . people don't like to [read in] print.' Or want him to record.

And yet, this was the very subject-matter of his next record, a single called 'Band Of The Hand (It's Hell Time, Man!)', recorded the following February in a hurry (a.k.a. Sydney), mid-Antipodean tour, as the theme tune for a film that went straight to Blockbusters. For the first time, The Heartbreakers sat in.

Again, the session-tapes suggest he only brought a set of dummy lyrics to the first session on February 10th. Early versions lack even the hook-line, 'It's hell time, man.' But a set of lyrics on Park Royal, Wellington hotel notepaper confirm he'd been sketching away since the week before, in the process losing the image, 'Got to find the fountain of courage and drink from its breast,' as well as a couplet with some relation to the plot – in which the kids threaten to take back the streets – 'Close the book, write the final report/ This is a direct order, this is your day in court.' (A 'lost' song of the period, 'Anything For A Friend', contains a similarly gung-ho couplet, 'Gonna bring down the

---

*In this case, he did 'listen to the tapes', applying lyrics to two of them, eight years apart. 'Time To End This Masquerade', called simply 'Pipe Organ Ska' on the Church reels, would not be released until 1996 by Gerry Goffin, with whom Dylan wrote a darkly humorous set of lyrics.

corporations that rule the land/ Gonna have 'em all eatin' out of the palm of my hand.')

Despite telling *Omnibus* later the same year, 'A lot of times I . . . think of something, but if I'm not in the right place to carry it through, it just won't get done,' here was one instance where he did get it done, perhaps because the Heartbreakers were on hand and Campbell, as always, had fire in his fingertips. The record, rush released by MCA, confirmed he was still not due a hit single, though it deserved better, being angry in all the right places about all the right things.

It also reminded Dylan that the Heartbreakers could cut it in the studio, after spending a couple of months rehearsing a live set he was never going to be allowed to play, full as it was of songs from his last three albums and covers he would have to put aside for that album of standards. Surprisingly, Dylan admitted he made certain compromises in a Melbourne radio chat, 'There's material that I WANT to play, there's material that I feel I HAVE to play, and I try to get . . . into the frame of mind where I want to play the material that I have to play.'

As so often in the Eighties, if he'd have taken the rehearsals into the studio, even if it was just to record standards, he'd have had an album that would have put his next two albums in the shade. The extra vocal commitment he brought to songs like 'This Was My Love', 'That Lucky Old Sun', 'Across The Borderline', 'Red Cadillac And A Black Moustache', 'Lonesome Town' and 'Sing Me Back Home', he simply wasn't bringing to his own crown jewels – the ones his Antipodean promoter expected him to perform in order to fill the arenas he had agreed to play.

By the second fortnight of the True Confessions tour, he had already shed a couple of *Shot of Love* songs; while only one of the four *Infidels* songs rehearsed ('I And I') had become a regular inclusion.* At least *Empire Burlesque* held its own, with four or five nightly selections, including a 'When The Night Comes Falling' that almost revealed itself at last.

What didn't survive to the shows was a version of 'I Shall Be

---

* Possibly a blessing. The one night he did 'License To Kill', in Sydney, he referred to the recent NASA disaster in less than tactful tones, 'These people had no business going up there. Like there's not enough problems on Earth to solve? So, I wanna dedicate this song to all those poor people who were fooled into going up there.'

Released' they'd not only rehearsed, but Dylan had performed on a 'Martin Luther King' national telecast in January. A rare song from the Woodstock era to contain a Biblical allusion, it now took on elements of 'The Wicked Messenger' in the new lyrics: 'You're laughing now, you should be praying/ You're in the midnight hour of your life.' He could have been singing to his ex-manager – and co-owner of the song – with whom he was still embroiled in a legal dispute, a New York County Supreme Court judge having concluded in April 1985 that 'extensive issues of fact and law remain to be determined by trial'.

Grossman's suit now stood at just over three million dollars and counting. But he was fast running out of the money needed to take it all the way, and as his advisers explained at the beginning of 1986, 'The Songwriter's strategy [i]s very clear . . . to delay and to prevent the case from coming to trial as long as possible . . . After years of [legal] discussions it [i]s painfully clear that Songwriter [i]s not bargaining in good faith.' As it happens, time was also running out – fast. Less than ten days after Dylan had a dream, he was free at last. On January 25th, Grossman the gourmand died of a heart attack on a flight to London, aged 59.

The way was finally clear to reach a settlement with Sally, the grieving widow. Not that Dylan was about to make it easy on her. As the papers filed by Grossman's lawyers at Kingston court confirmed, Dylan was being obdurate: 'From the outset, the Artist insisted that any settlement must involve a total buyout of all plaintiffs' rights to future income under the 1970 Agreement and all prior agreements, including Witmark . . . Finally, in May 1987, the Artist made an offer which permitted the Estate to retain its rights in Witmark, and agreed to pay $2 million to settle all plaintiffs' other claims.'

In the interim, out of the blue, Sally received a personal letter from her former neighbour (and lover?), telling her just how important her late husband had been to him, and how much he had done for the singer early in his career. It was a side of Dylan he rarely shared – the one who could step back from a current conflict and remember when he felt he could trust someone other than himself.

He continued being powerfully affected by the death of those whom he had been close to in simpler times, even if he hadn't raised a glass to them in years. Richard Manuel was someone who had been trying to get in touch with him in Japan, without success. Sadly, Dylan would never find out what Manuel wanted. Instead, a day or two later news reached him that the man had taken his own life on March 4th in a hotel in Winter Park, Florida, hanging himself as Phil Ochs had done, having struggled for years with chronic alcoholism. Another man in the 'midnight hour of his life' had been released from his earthly woes. That superb tenor voice would not rise again.

Though Dylan made no reference to Manuel's passing at the March shows, he was prefacing a song every night with a Tennessee Williams quote from the play Bacall had been touring, *Sweet Bird of Youth*, about 'time, the enemy in us all', fully aware that Williams had 'died all by himself in a New York City hotel room, without a friend in the world. Another man died like that . . .' He meant Lenny Bruce, another talent crippled by his addiction/s, but the spectres of Manuel, Ochs and Clayton were whispering in the wings.

By Japan, the shows had settled into a routine, and any sense they were taking the spirit of the rehearsals onto the stage had largely passed. But Dylan had not entirely abandoned one recent habit, playing at least one song nightly that resembled the r&b with which he grew up, given a Dylanesque twist, much as he had done at Big Pink with 'All-American Boy'. In the Antipodes, he had been playing a thing called 'Shake', debuted at Farm Aid. Tipping its hat to Roy Head's 'Treat Her Right', it was both a homage and a straight lift – half-cover, half-pastiche – as was the song that replaced it, '(Cross On Over And) Rock 'Em Dead', which sounded a lot like Warren Smith's 'Uranium Rock', but wasn't.

If audiences and tape-collectors were slightly baffled, Dylan was allowing them a glimpse of the methodology he was considering carrying into the studio, continuing his October Cherokee experiment. Consciously blurring the line between original and cover, he really might be hung as a thief this time, while giving poor Naomi Saltzman a heart attack. It seemed symptomatic of a new kind of writer's block from a man who once was his words. As he would write about this time in *Chronicles*, 'When and if an idea would come, I would no longer try to get in touch with the base of its power. I could easily deny it.' The scraps of paper with song-ideas would remain just that, even when as promising as the following:

I'd climb the high ladder, but it's broken and bent
I'd give you my mansion, but all it is, [is] a tent
I'd give you the stars, but they're burnt out on coke
I'd take it all seriously if it wasn't a joke.

He needed help, and he knew it, even if he wasn't sure he could be
bothered to seek it out. As he confessed to Mikal Gilmore, the previous
September, 'If the records I make are only going to sell a certain
amount, then why do I have to spend a lot of time putting them
together?' Luckily for him, the folk at Sony didn't read the *L.A. Herald
Examiner*. The last time he'd felt this way, after *Nashville Skyline*, it led
him to lurch into a genre of popular music he never quite made his
own. What came next was *Self Portrait*, which featured Dylan's recreation of Elmore James's 'It Hurts Me Too', impertinently copyrighted
to himself. Seventeen years of mainly good luck later, Dylan was back
making a covers album, telling the guitarist he'd recruited to play at
the first session on April 28th, 1986, The Blasters' Dave Alvin, it was
going to be *Self Portrait Vol. 2*.

He had been recommended a studio in the bucolic setting of
Topanga Canyon that tipped its hat to his 1969 album, having mentioned to Ira Ingber, 'how much he didn't like the long drive from his
house in Malibu to Cherokee, which was in Hollywood. I told him
about Skyline [Studios], which was under a half hour from his house.
I . . . show[ed] him around, and he loved the place.' And so, Dylan and
a motley crew of musicians convened at Skyline, Dylan hoping he
could wrap the whole thing up with a minimum of fuss:*

Ira Ingber: He said, 'Can we do it in a week?' I said, 'I don't think we can
do it in a week.' He just wanted a band to play and to sing, but then we
got into the recording world, which is a different mentality. He realized
he was into this thing a little deeper than he initially thought.

After the first day, though, he perhaps believed he might buck the
trend. They certainly racked up quite a list of recorded tracks – some

---

* The Heartbreakers, save for one spare night, were unavailable. They had their own
LP, *Let Me Up*, to record.

on two-track, most on 24-track. It really did seem Dylan was up for this, at least to Mikal Gilmore, who had been offered the rare privilege of watching him record, because he was writing a much-needed *Rolling Stone* cover-story on the back of the announcement, at a Westwood One press conference a fortnight earlier, that Dylan in tandem with Tom Petty & The Heartbreakers was embarking on a two-month-long US tour, starting June 9th in San Diego:

Mikal Gilmore: They were playing some really good stuff, and he was sort of tossing out vocals as he was going along. It wasn't always easy to hear what was being said, but the stuff that they were doing sounded really great . . . They recorded a lot. I was there for at least twelve hours, over a two, three-day period, and they were recording pretty much the whole time, and some of it was pretty wondrous. He had a nice big rock & roll band . . . James Jamerson Jnr, T-Bone Burnett, and Al Kooper – and they were really wailing . . . Sitting there in a studio, it didn't sound to me like he was somebody with a studio problem – he was working very fast, moving from track to track, and really directing the sound.

Nor was Gilmore deceived or deluded. The multitracks of these sessions – only recently excavated, cleaned and transferred in a joint operation between the Dylan Archive and Sony Music – finally prove it. Over four days of sessions [April 28th-30th, May 2nd], Dylan cut at least twenty-two songs, only three of which would make it onto *Knocked Out Loaded*, much to the chagrin of at least one familiar participant – the only one who also played on the original *Self Portrait*. As Al Kooper told me back in 1990, 'There was enough stuff cut on *Knocked Out Loaded* to have put out a great album . . . but I don't think we'll ever hear 'em . . . I made suggestions [that were ignored], and then I just sort of fucked off.' Another musician did not hang around, either, claiming he had other commitments:

Dave Alvin: [Dylan] was a big fan of The Blasters . . . We met at the first Farm Aid [in 1985] and . . . he sang me my guitar solo from 'Marie Marie' . . . note for note . . . Six months . . . after meeting him, I get a call . . . They wanted me in there for like four days, but I only had one day free. It was thirteen hours . . . We did 'Look On Yonder's Wall', 'Got Love If You Want It', 'Rollin' and Tumblin'' and a couple other things

like that. We did a Warren Smith song, 'Red Cadillac and a Black Moustache' . . . [] . . . Then we cut Johnny Carroll's 'Rock with Me Baby' – we
cut it once with the core band, and then this girl choir came in with a
horn section, and they tracked it again . . . [] . . . Eventually, we did a
version of an old spiritual that we cut previously with The Blasters
called 'Samson & Delilah'. Then out of the blue Bob wanted to record,
'You'll Never Walk Alone', (sings the verse) and I was like, 'I can't fuckin'
play that.' . . . Al [Kooper] managed to get him out of the studio for five
minutes, and he ran back in and wrote charts for everybody . . . When
Bob came back to the studio, he got kind of upset that there were
charts . . . [Anyway,] we wound up recording what's probably a pretty
good version of 'You'll Never Walk Alone' with the horn section and
the gospel choir and the whole bit . . . We did two or three takes of it,
and the second or third take I remember looking up and watching him
do it, and he was so sincere that it blew me away. He was putting his all
into that song . . . . . . He [ended up] releas[ing] an album called *Knocked
Out Loaded*, that was mainly stuff recorded the following week.

Alvin's memory wasn't playing tricks either.* The performance of
'Samson And Delilah' – as untamed as an unshorn Samson – showed
just where Dylan had got 'Trust Yourself's riff. There were actually
nine takes of 'You'll Never Walk Alone', at the outset skirting very
close to parodying the 1945 *Carousel* original. But by the end, Dylan is
throwing himself into the song like a man possessed, and though some
notes remain out of reach, he is undaunted. In fact, this becomes the
motif for these sessions – going for it vocally, without a safety net.
According to Ingber, he even 'wanted me to do an arrangement . . . of
"Come Rain or Come Shine." . . . I showed him, but there's some really
weird chords because it's an orchestra arrangement, not piano or
guitar – the chords more or less reflect the complexity, and Bob couldn't
[really] play those chords.'

If the song was left unrecorded, 'You'll Never Walk Alone' was not
the only song where Dylan pushed his voice close to the edge. He
attempted a full girls'n'horns version of 'Without Love', from Elvis's

---

* Though the now-transferred reels do not include 'Got Love If You Want It', 'Rollin'
And Tumblin'' and 'Red Cadillac And A Black Moustache', some two-track reels are
missing, specifically Reel #1.

1969 Memphis sessions, a hugely ambitious undertaking and one where he did stumble and fall. On the other hand, a song logged as 'No Setting Sun' – actually a 1907 parlour ballad called 'A Different Life' – covered by everyone from Johnny Cash to The Statler Brothers, was cut in three takes. Requiring an equally challenging vocal, it was another 'Lucky Old Sun' moment for a song with a similar sense of mortality: 'Life's *evening* sun is *sinking* low/ A few more days and I must go/ To meet the *deeds* that I have done/ Where *there* will be no *setting* sun.'

The first take, which in six high-octane minutes included a short segue into 'Dearest', is probably the highlight of these sessions. After trying it twice more, he admitted, 'I sorta liked that other take. We could just go back and repair it all.' Or not. For here was the crux of the problem – what exactly did he intend to *do* with these songs? Send them to Nashville to drown them in strings? Have Arthur Baker synthesize them to death? Or how about finishing them in the here and now?

Whatever the plan, some repair work was going to be required, because he wasn't finishing anything. After a decent complete take of 'You'll Never Walk Alone', he suggests they 'take a break. We're just practising this thing.' If that was the case, why was he eating up all this 24-track tape? What was he rehearsing for, exactly? Why was he stock-piling songs at a rate of knots? Because, as Gilmore wrote in his *Rolling Stone* feature, he was 'piling up instrumental tracks so fast that the dazed, bleary-eyed engineers who are monitoring the sessions [we]re having trouble cataloguing all the various takes – so far, well over twenty songs, including gritty r&b, Chicago-steeped blues, rambunctious gospel and raw-toned hillbilly forms.'

Not that Sony knew whether they were getting an album of covers or not, as Dylan blurred the line between original and cover at every turn. Vocals were being left unfinished, songs unresolved, Dylan having seemingly convinced himself all could be corrected in post-production. After a spirited 'Angels Rock Me To Sleep', sung without access to a copy of Bill Monroe's lyrics, he said, 'We'll punch in at the end.' What it needed was a completely new vocal. And after an original fragment called 'Ride That Man Down', Dylan instructs Britt Bacon, engineer and owner of Skyline, 'Just keep that little bit there. How many tapes today? We don't really have any[thing]. We don't really want to start piling up tapes.'

Still the tapes rolled and the songs kept coming, some half-familiar, some not. What started out as Junior Parker's 'You Wanna Ramble' ended up as nothing of the sort. Something that sounded at first like Muddy Waters' 'Come Back Baby (Let's Talk It Over)' became another blues template for him to rework. A glorious uptempo blast of r&b called 'I Need Your Loving' – to which he would return – had countless precedents but no nailed-on cop. He really was covering the waterfront of 'gritty r&b, Chicago-steeped blues, rambunctious gospel and raw-toned hillbilly forms', without ever dealing in specifics. When he did shadow someone else's original, it was usually some r&b classic like 'Lonely Avenue' or 'Unchain My Heart'.

At such junctures it seemed less a recording session, and more like a rehearsal. Which is why, for all the energy expended, he did not have an album at the end of five whole days. He had a set of songs he would still have to slap into shape. Which meant more time, more application, and he wasn't sure he had the requisite strength or sense of purpose to address head-on the rhetorical question he'd raised to Gilmore eight months earlier – 'If the records I make are only going to sell a certain amount, then why . . . spend a lot of time putting them together?'

He already sensed his label was none too happy at the news that the album which would accompany Dylan's first national tour in eight years was a successor to the shitty *Self Portrait*. He knew not where to turn for advice. Oddly enough, it was to 'good critic' Paul Nelson, whom he had forgiven for his *Shot of Love* review in *Rolling Stone*. He put in the call, complaining to the mystified scribe that the label didn't want him to do an album of covers, even though that is what he had. Nelson, predictably, told him he should tell the label to shove it, as he'd told Mercury himself in 1974. It was the last time they spoke. Still unsatisfied, Dylan called up one of his few allies at the label, Paul Rappaport, and told him, 'I don't think people want to hear my shit anymore. I think I'm gonna quit.'

It wasn't what Rap expected or wanted to hear. They talked for a solid hour as he tried to talk the maverick down. Dylan had once again allowed himself to become belittled by doubt, even confiding to Gilmore, 'These lyrical things that come off in a unique or a desolate sort of way, I don't feel I have to put that out any more,' which was Dylan-speak for, those kinda songs just won't come.

He feared he was fast becoming an anachronism, telling David

Fricke the previous fall, 'I've made all the difference I'm going to . . .
I'm not worried about having to do the next thing or keeping in step
with the times.' Actually, he *was* worried, even as he jotted a note to
himself, 'I'm not making . . . any kind of comeback – I'm just doing the
same thing I [have] always been doing, . . . Did the same thing last year
and the year before. Not trying to appeal to any new crowd – I'll leave
that to the teenagers – chocolate syrup.'

Perhaps he should construct an album from all the odds'n'ends left
lying around from three years of recording. Hell, he had stockpiled
more than enough songs fit for purpose. The first track he called up
was from the *Infidels* sessions, which was brimful of great lost songs.
'Death Is Not The End' just wasn't one of them. It was a troubling
choice,* as was the next one, a backing track from the November
Church sessions. He just needed some lyrics, and preferably someone
to lend a hand. Carole Childs was only too eager to suggest a candidate, her old friend, Carole Bayer-Sager, another lyricist steeped in a
Pop sensibility, who was summoned to Point Dume to help him produce an album-closer:

> [I] drive out to his Malibu ranch . . . He really was a man of few words.
> 'Let's go out to the barn,' he said . . . The ground on the walk from his
> main house to his barn was more uneven than his beard . . . He [was]
> completely dishevelled from head to toe and [there was] I in full makeup,
> tight jeans, tee shirt and studded leather jacket . . . He could have told
> me he had come in from just rolling around with some farm animals,
> and I would not have disbelieved him . . . I appreciated Bob's thorny
> poetry as a lyricist, but I was always in search of a great melody . . .
> There was no melody to speak of . . . He started strumming his
> guitar . . . And then he began humming a melody. It was a simple one.
> He didn't ask me if I liked it, but [instead] sang, 'Something about you
> that I can't shake.' And he played the melody to the next line and I ner-
> vously said, 'Feels like it's more than my heart can take?' . . . And he
> sang, 'Don't know how much more of this I can take / Baby, I'm under
> your spell.' . . . 'That's good,' I said, feeling more like a stenographer
> than a lyricist. I kept offering him lines. Sometimes he'd say, 'I like that'

---

* The tape-logs confirm it was originally considered for *Knocked Out Loaded*, before
appearing on the even more cobbled together *Down In The Groove*.

and I would be so happy as I wrote something down . . . Most of the lyrics of mine that I thought he'd liked weren't even written down – just
one or two lines. Finally, I said, 'I feel like you don't really need me here
writing this with you, because you seem to have your own idea of what
the lyric should be.' . . . 'No, I need you here,' he said. 'I wouldn't be
writing this if you weren't here.'

Here was Dylan admitting Sager was there primarily to motivate
him to write, when he'd rather be doing something else. A few days
later he sent Sager 'a rough version . . . on a cassette . . . Of the twelve
lines I thought I had written, maybe there were three or four left in the
song.' Not that she need take this personally. Dylan also took out some
of the better lines he came up with himself, including, 'I'll call you
tomorrow if there are phones where I am/ And Baby, I hope it ain't
hell,' and, 'I will stand up and I will survive/ I'll climb back out of here
till I know I'm alive/ And maybe I'll ring your bell.'

Suddenly, he was shuffling through old tape-boxes, looking for
songs he never quite finished from the last couple of years. One of
them, 'Maybe Someday' (formerly 'Prince Of Plunder'), needed very
little work, whereas the July 1984 Delta 'Driftin' Too Far From Shore'
was little more than a demo, requiring new words and a bouncier
rhythm-track. What he came up with still left him dissatisfied, initially
rhyming the title-line with 'I hear another man call you his whore' in
verse two. A deleted verse three suggested an ongoing preoccupation
with the prince of darkness, 'These times these figures are haunted,
we['re] living in the shadow of a beast/ I've waited years sometimes for
what I've wanted, it always came when I expected it least.'

When he returned to work on May 12th, a mere ten days after 'finishing' the tracking sessions for his latest album, he was a changed
man. As Gilmore noted, 'His mood was entirely different, the music
wasn't as inspired. He still could hit it vocally at moments, but he was
not in a good mood and he told me he'd thrown out all that other stuff,
and now it was just gonna be an album of bits'n'pieces.'

His attention span wasn't what it needed to be, either. According to
Gary Shafner's new girlfriend, some wag came up with 'the notion of
making a short film called *Waiting for Bob* [because of] those not so
infrequent times when Dylan called for a midnight recording session
and didn't show up till 4 a.m. . . . [Then,] when Bob finally shows up at

these sessions, it's with a distracting girl on either side, or both, of his arms.'

He still had his good days, though, and on the 16th, he turned up early and stayed late, blasting through a series of semi-improvised, quasi-originals, two of which warranted inclusion on the finished platter, the six-minute 'I Need Your Loving', and a vocal tour-de-force called 'So Good', light on lyrical content but with a vocal set to eleven. Yet even these tracks would have needed work. It was the last day of recording, and Dylan was still saying, 'Let's try and do a *rough* track on this,' and before 'Baby, What Am I To Do?', 'We'll go back and repair it.' When exactly? At the end of one song, he asks how many songs they'd recorded. A musician responds, 'Four albums, five singles.'

If the women on his arm were sometimes distracting, so were the women hovering around the microphones, as he gave the girlsingers far too much latitude on the overdubbed 1984 tracks, notably a recast 'New Danville Girl', now from Brownsville, the one track that might give the album 'a theme or a purpose'. Where the girlsingers came into their own was during those inspired offhand moments, like the one Gilmore witnessed when Dylan led them 'through a lovely a cappella version of "White Christmas," then moves into a haunting reading of an old gospel standard, "Evening Sun."'* An attendant Tom Petty exclaimed, 'Man, we've got to get this on tape.'

This was hardly an uncommon occurrence. As Benmont Tench told Gilmore, 'That was the stuff that would really blow his mind . . . And yet, [we] couldn't convince him to take that stuff to the stage . . . I saw great performances in rehearsals that were just of a very different tone and temperament [from] the live performances.'

None of those stolen moments from the Skyline sessions made it to the album Dylan sent to the label at the end of May, after informing Gilmore, 'I've got a lot of different records inside me, and it's time just to start getting them out.' The label didn't really want to hear all these different records – they just wanted an album they could market to a mid-Eighties audience. *Knocked Out Loaded* was not it. Dylan didn't even pretend to push it, playing exactly one song from the wretched record, 'Got My Mind Made Up', on opening night in San Diego, and not performing anything else for the next two months.

---

* He surely means 'No Setting Sun'.

For the first time, he couldn't even pretend he wasn't doing an Oldies show, which makes his comment to David Hepworth backstage at Madison Square Garden in July – talking about a movie he was due to start shooting in the fall – doubly ironic, 'It seemed like I knew that character . . . It's a guy who plays oldie shows.'

Only rarely on the US leg – usually on the covers – did he break out of this trap of his own making: a 'House Of The Rising Sun' in New York; a rather lovely 'We Had It All', most nights; 'Shake A Hand' at a well-oiled benefit gig on June 6th; the hit single he thought he should have had, 'Band Of The Hand', played nightly to the gallery; and a hilarious Meadowlands show where Dylan the Chatterbox went kite flying.* Arthur Rosato, recently returned from videoing the biggest rock tour of the era, one born in the USA, recognized the symptoms, 'He doesn't know who he is. He's wearing the black leather, he's got the earring . . . He [really] doesn't know who he is in the rock pantheon.'

Maybe he was just getting into character for his next cinematic role, Billy Parker, an ex-rock star who robs toll booths for kicks (or does, in the script). Director Richard Marquand had somehow sold him on the idea, knowing, 'he's always been interested in film – I mean . . . his own film; it's always something that has intrigued him.' But if *he* seemed like perfect casting, the female lead, Fiona Flanagan – who had the *chutzpah* to call herself just Fiona (as in, just Madonna) – was a chorus girl in disguise.

Rupert Everett, who played the current rock star in this improbable *ménage à trois*, later wrote, 'I should have known better . . . *Hearts of Fire* was the full-on, no-survivors crash of my career . . . Fiona was sweet, if irritating . . . Yet even when the poor, terrified girl jumped out of the bed during our sex scene, and ran screaming to her dressing-room, I was strangely unperturbed.' Dylan had shown the script to his friend, Debra Winger, a real actress, who snapped, 'Why would I want to do that?' An unperturbed Dylan replied, 'Why? For the money!'

She wasn't the only one who wondered what he was doing in a turkey like this. Everett realized immediately – '[Dylan] knew he was

---

* He was definitely on *something* that night in New Jersey. According to someone backstage, he was doing industrial quantities of cocaine, a sign of the times.

taking part in a piece of unmitigated rubbish. His hangdog eyes said it all' – as did the entire corpus of English pressmen who assembled for his first London press conference in twenty years on August 17th, eleven days after the end of the True Confessions tour. The obnoxious Philip Norman was particularly persistent, 'Why aren't you writing poetry? Why aren't you doing the things you're really great at?' This, from the man who slammed one of the decade's finest concerts, opening night at Earl's Court 1981.

Norman also persisted in wanting to know about these six songs he'd apparently written for the film. It quickly became apparent there were no six songs, even though Dylan was booked to record at the Townhouse in ten days' time. It was *Knocked Out Loaded* Take Two. One lyric he half-wrote, 'To Fall In Love With You', in one draft had the promising line, 'Being able to watch people suffer has never been one of my stronger qualities.' But it was never finished. This was particularly frustrating because when he broke into the song at the sessions, it was the most tender moment of the whole damned project as Dylan reached for words that would not come, yet still expressing the raw emotion he was feeling, as another 'Rock Me Mama' fell by the way.

The rest of the session was a bust. The two originals he did finish – 'Had A Dream About You, Baby' and 'Night After Night' – should have had Reject stamped on their tape-boxes before he mixed a note. Even cajoling old friends Eric Clapton and Ron Wood into lending a hand couldn't save the sessions, or the soundtrack. He padded it out – just as he had in May – with a Billy Joe Shaver song ('Old Five And Dimer') and a John Hiatt song ('The Usual'), only the latter of which would be used. He might have to come back to this. And maybe he did. By September 9th, he'd 'adapted' a Neville Brothers song called 'Fear, Hate, Envy & Jealousy', which was more like it:

> You know the wicked have sold their souls for gold
> And everybody knows their wealth is in the sky
> And the very, very, very sad part about it all
> There ain't nothing that nobody gonna survive.

He was still grasping for ideas in Toronto, where production moved in October. He had heard that Scottish siren Linda Thompson was loitering on the set, with her new husband, the agent Steve Kenis. Aware of her work with her ex-husband Richard, but also possibly a song she'd released the previous year, 'Telling Me Lies' – which would later win her a Grammy nomination – 'He expressed an interest in meeting me . . . This is like half-past ten in the morning and he's got a glass of brandy . . . His guitar was lying in the trailer and he handed it to me, "D'ya wanna write a song?" He gave me these two lines. They were absolute crap: . . . "I knew him when I was a little girl / His Daddy knew my Ma."' A fine actress in her own right, the luscious Linda should have been playing Fiona's role, not helping him write songs. She might have taught him how to act, something he still patently couldn't do:

> **Rupert Everett**: Dylan was the real thing. I think he lived to create. At the same time, he was also desperately retiring. On the film set he could interact and somehow keep himself from calcifying. He never said a bad word about anyone. Actually, he never said a word. But he listened and watched and nothing escaped him . . . But he had a hard time remembering his lines . . . I don't know whether Bob learnt the lines beforehand. Possibly, it never occurred to him . . . Probably he thought he could wing it once he got onto the set. But, actually, he just drowned in front of the camera.

Nothing escaped Everett, not even Dylan's secret drinking, '[Make-up artist] Meinir . . . adored him and always gave him a drink from her portable bar: Jim Beam was his favourite tipple.' Everett was not averse to taking part in revelries himself, which led to a face-off with the director that was only ever going to have one outcome:

> The production moved to Toronto in November to film all the big concert scenes. Winter had set in and it began to snow. We worked in the Maple Leaf Stadium, and played to the sixty thousand fans of some other band . . . Suddenly Bob was in his element, unruffled like a duck in a thunderstorm: 'You gotta stand up to them when you get on stage,' he advised, 'otherwise they just wash over you.' We all piled into his trailer before the show and got incredibly drunk . . . By the time we got to the wings we were in extremely high spirits, but Bob was too wobbly to make it up the very steep steps onto the stage [and needed

help from the two girls] . . . By now Richard [Marquand] was on a short fuse . . . He stormed over to Bob . . . All his habitual tact and diplomacy evaporated and months of frustration poured out into the deaf ears of our star . . . But no-one raised their voices to Bob Dylan. 'I always have girls take me on to the stage.' . . . [After] the [film] studio . . . heard that his girlfriends were none other than the make-up lady and the hair-dresser, they had a meltdown.

By then, frankly, Dylan didn't give a damn. He just wanted to get out of this artificial world alive. On the final night they shot a scene in a limo, Everett recalling: 'Bob was his usual self in the car . . . We chat-ted between takes. We had drinks in the scene and they were constantly refilled – the real thing, needless to say . . . When we finished, the first assistant opened the car door. Bob climbed out. He looked around squinting, 'Where's the hotel?' . . . He didn't attend the bloodbath of a premiere in London.' He didn't need to. The film sank faster than the *Titanic*. When Mikal Gilmore bumped into him in June 1987, rehears-ing with the Grateful Dead – the musical equivalent of *Hearts of Fire* – he asked if he'd finished his movie. He replied, 'Oh yeah, that. That came out. It was called *Citizen Kane*.'

It hadn't come out, and it never really would. A week in London's West End, and then straight into the racks of Blockbusters, next to *Band of The Hand*. He was still looking for someone who could harness that certain indefinable visual quality he had. As the film's producer Iain Smith noted, 'He's funny and quirky and strange and you watch him on the screen and you think, "Well he's not acting . . . but he's very, very watchable."'

Funny, quirky and strange perfectly describes Dylan's next perform-ance for the cameras – a Gershwin Gala evening at the Brooklyn Academy of Music on March 11th, 1987. He got up on stage and per-formed 'Soon', from *Strike Up the Band*, solo, acoustic, a daring adventure in sound without a safety net, which he had removed of his own free will, trying to find that 'country, backwood, alley cat element to [Gershwin's music] that . . . he was [somehow] able to capture.' A month earlier, he'd recorded the song with a full band, intending to use this arrangement at the show. Yet here he was, alone, crooning a tune in March, on national TV. What next? An album of standards?

Sure enough, a fortnight later there was an album in the works – the

one Paul Nelson had told him to make the year before, an album of
covers called *Fuck What The Label Wants*. It wasn't like Dylan hadn't
threatened to do such a project for a while. Back in 1985, he had told
Denise Worrell that his 'favorite songs of all time aren't anything I've
written . . . My favorites are old forties songs . . . I will do an album of
standards . . . I [just] don't know what's going to be on it.'

He would later pass off the 1987 project as 'just [a way] to keep yourself straight . . . Every so often you've gotta sing songs that're out
there.' In fact, it was simply that old writer's block that had him in its
spell. In a 2015 interview, he insisted he had envisaged such a project
even earlier, 'I heard Willie [Nelson]'s *Stardust* record in the late
Seventies . . . I went to see Walter Yetnikoff . . . president of Columbia
Records. I told him I wanted to make a record of standards . . . He said,
"You can go ahead and make that record, but we won't pay for it, and
we won't release it." '

Actually, Yetnikoff, a belligerent, coke-snorting bully, had absolutely
no say in the matter. Dylan's contract didn't allow the label to reject
anything that vaguely resembled a record from The Artist Formerly
Known As The Voice of a Generation. And if ever proof was required,
it was the runt of an album Dylan delivered just as his July 1982 contract was expiring. It was called *Down In The Groove*, but *Down In The
Bottom* was more like it.

Once again, he eschewed the work of his contemporaries – though
he later told Nanci Griffith, he had wanted to record 'her' 'From A Distance', 'but then a whole bunch of people started doing it'. So, he set
about recording songs by Merle Haggard, Otis Redding, Elizabeth Cotton, Wilson Pickett and Ralph Stanley. The common denominator?
There wasn't one, as across seven sessions in five weeks he recorded a
couple of dozen cover songs in ad hoc arrangements that sometimes
flattered, sometimes deceived.*

---

* The 26 documented songs recorded that spring, some of which have only working
titles on the tape-boxes, are as follows: Branded Man/ Chain Gang/ 'Bhidie'/ Dark-
ness By Dawn/ Just When I Needed U Most/ [?Piece of] Wood N Steel/ Sally Sue
Brown/ Sidewalks/ Involved With You/ [Shake] Sugaree/ My Prayer/ Street People/
When Did You Leave Heaven?/ 'Axe'/ Sing Me Back Home/ Almost Endless Sleep/
Barefootin'/ Got Love If You Want It/ If You Need Me/ Silvio/ Ugliest Girl In The
World/ Ninety Miles An Hour/ Let's Stick Together/ Shenandoah/ Rank Strangers/
Willie Boy.

The album of standards appeared to be on hold, save for a series of futile attempts to capture 'Just When I Needed You Most' and the mawkish 'When Did You Leave Heaven?' Not even 'We Three' or 'All My Tomorrows' – both songs performed (albeit infrequently) on the True Confessions tour – got the treatment. The more intriguing the choice of song – Haggard's 'Branded Man' and 'Sing Me Back Home', Otis Redding's 'Chain Gang', Elizabeth Cotton's 'Shake Sugaree' – the less likely it was to make the cut.

At least this time he was sticking to covers – or he was through May 1st. Four weeks later, on May 28th, after knocking all the songs he wanted on the album into some kinda shape, he decided to add a song given to him by Grateful Dead lyricist, Robert Hunter. 'Silvio' turned out to be another bridge to Babel; an amusing little diversion that set Dylan scuttling off down another blind alley.

By the beginning of July, the album of covers had turned into *Knocked Out Loaded* Mk. 2 – the *Dylan* to its *Self Portrait* – save that this was Dylan's revenge-album on the label, not the other way round. Shuffling songs from other projects – two from the *Hearts of Fire* soundtrack; the dreadful 'Death Is Not The End' from *Infidels*, via *Knocked Out Loaded* – and adding another of Hunter's hack effort, 'Ugliest Girl In The World', an inferior, kissin' cousin of *Burlesque* reject 'Straight A's In Love', he turned *Down In The Groove* into an album without identity, and himself into an artist who released albums to fulfil contracts, not change the world, as he once used to do.

Perhaps the problem was that he no longer wanted to be that person. Hanging out with U2's Bono in April between L.A. sessions – just as U2 hit their commercial peak with *The Joshua Tree* – he suggested they try writing a song together. Unfortunately, as Bono discovered:

He's very hung up on actually being Bob Dylan . . . Like, we were trading lines and verses off the top of our heads and Dylan comes out with this absolute classic: 'I was listenin' to the Neville Brothers, it was a quarter of eight/ I had an appointment with destiny, but I knew she'd come late/She tricked me, she addicted me, she turned me on the head/Now I can't sleep with these secrets, that leave me cold and alone in my bed.' Then he goes, 'Nah, cancel that.' . . . He thought it was too close to what people expect of [him].

Perish the thought he might give people what they wanted. In truth, he no longer *knew* what people wanted. The one thing he seemed sure of was that he was done. As he informed Shafner's girlfriend, Britta Lee Shain, that September, as Sony tried to persuade him to stick to a sequence on his latest album, 'I already wrote all my songs.' A month later, he was stood outside a rehearsal studio in New York with Lee Shain's replacement, in whom he confided, 'You know, no matter what anyone says, I have written my share. If I never write another song, no one will ever fault me.'

Retirement – at the grand old age of 46 – loomed, or so he would suggest in one of the few passages in *Chronicles* to ring true, 'The previous [few] years had left me pretty whitewashed and wasted out professionally . . . I'd been on an eighteen month tour [sic] with Tom Petty and The Heartbreakers. It would be my last. I had no connection to any kind of inspiration. Whatever was there to begin with had all vanished.' What was he doing then, standing outside a rehearsal studio in Hell's Kitchen, having a sneaky smoke, leafing through the 1985 edition of *Lyrics*, looking for songs to play with his new band?

June 1987 to December 1988:
Struck By Lightning

He doesn't hang out with everybody as much as others might like him to . . . but how else is he going to preserve what he's doing? He's a worker and he works hard and he's worked a long time. He's given us his life, his life energy, his life force, and we should be grateful.

Ronee Blakley, 'Dylan at 70', *Mojo* May 2011.

When I told Bob about [*The Last Waltz*], he said, 'Is this going to be one of those Frank Sinatra[-style] retirements where you come back a year later?'

Robbie Robertson.

He'd rather play music probably than do anything else. He doesn't relate well to people.

Joni Mitchell, *Rolling Stone* 30th May 1991.

Elvis did thirty movies . . . but they never were enough for him. He eventually had to go back on stage. Once you pick up the guitar, you can't put it down.

Bob Dylan, to Robert Hilburn, *L.A. Times* 28th May 1978.

I have to play songs which're gonna relate to the faces that I'm singing to. And I can't do that if I was spending a year in the studio.

Bob Dylan, to Dave Herman, 2nd July 81.

Wasn't it dramatic back [in 1988]? I think they handed me a guy who was wild . . . He was definitely like a wild horse when I got him . . . You couldn't ride him, that's for sure. You could hardly communicate.

César Díaz, guitar-tech, to author.

He would talk a lot about Ernest Tubb, and he'd say how . . . the object of the game is to die on the bandstand. Seriously!

G.E. Smith, Mojo 2017.

I'm not looking for anything special in a band. I'm looking for guys who are enthusiastic and know the kind of music I know, who can play strongly on the structure of the song.

Bob Dylan, to David Fricke, October 1985.

On record, it's deceiving . . . but when you see that person doing it live, you can tell if it's real.

Bob Dylan, to Edna Gundersen, 21st September 1989.

I've been to the mountain top and I've seen how the eagle flies / I drank the cup of deliverance before the bloody sun could rise.

'I Have Prayed For Liberty', c. 1987.

★

The impending completion of *Down In The Groove* would be interrupted in July 1987 by a sold-out, six-date, stadia-only US tour. In the very depths of Dylan's deepest commercial trough, a mere year after a two-month-long arena tour of North America, his name was somehow packing them in. And still he insisted he wanted to be out and about, telling one journalist, 'Music is a live thing. For me, it's always of the moment . . . That's why I can't get away from it,' and another, 'I've tried to get away from [touring] but . . . it's all I've ever done, really . . . I wouldn't know what else to do. I would be lost.' This time around, the evidence was against him. He didn't admit the real reason people were still coming to see him, even to himself, until 1991:

A lot of the shows over the years was people coming out of curiosity and their curiosity wasn't fulfilled. They weren't transported back to the '60s. Lightning didn't strike. The shows didn't make sense for them, and they didn't make sense for me. That had to stop . . . A lot of people were coming out to see The Legend, and I was trying to just get on stage and play music . . . You're either a player or you're not a player. [This] didn't really occur to me until [I] did those shows with the Grateful Dead [in 1987].

Night one, Independence Day, Foxborough, Mass., the amnesiac in him is visibly in the ascendant. As he admitted to Christopher Farley in 2001, referencing this very tour, 'I'd become a different person and, frankly, [my old songs] mystified me.' The second amnesia had him in its iron grip, as it had since before rehearsals began in June. To the exasperation of the member of the Dead with the least grasp of Dylan's vast contribution to music, Bob Weir, 'He wouldn't want to rehearse a song more than two times, three at the most. And so we rehearsed maybe a hundred songs two or three times.'

As this lesser Bob should have known, this was standard procedure with Dylan, and had been as far back as 1980, when, as Fred Tackett once observed, 'We'd rehearse all kinds of songs, but we wouldn't rehearse the songs we were going to do . . . He didn't want you to learn the songs real well. He wanted to have the spontaneity . . . All kinds of interesting things would happen that way.' Back then Dylan was fronting the most musical band in America. Now, he was in the least. Whatever the musical merits of the Dead – and I fully admit they're lost on me – they simply couldn't play songs on the hoof. Sure, they could extend tunes to the crack of doom, but that didn't require any actual 'chops', just an audience for whom a twelve-minute version of a song was de facto twice as good as a six-minute version.*

Dylan arrived in San Rafael on June 1st hoping, in the words of Jerry Garcia, 'for a new direction in which to take his songs . . . We talked about people like Elizabeth Cotten, Mississippi Sheiks, Earl Scruggs, Bill Monroe, Gus Cannon, Hank Williams. We tried a few of those things out at rehearsal. I showed Bob some of those songs: "Two Soldiers," "Jack-A-Roe"† . . . Bob seemed to prefer to do these, rather than . . . his own songs.' This was because these songs never mystified

---

* On Cream's first US tour in 1967, Eric Clapton says he realized the more they extended the songs, the greater the reaction. By the end of the tour a four-minute 'Crossroads' was now eight minutes, and half as good.
† Both are traditional songs he surely already knew. 'Jack A-Roe', a track on Tom Paley's 1953 Elektra LP, *Folk Songs from The Southern Appalachian Mountains*, was a staple item in most folk revival repertoires.

him. Twenty years on, they remained 'the only true valid death you can feel today'. The few such venerable relics they did run down in rehearsal – 'Roll In My Sweet Baby's Arms', 'John Hardy', 'Stealin' – were but the tip of an iceberg he hoped might melt minds among the baking summer stadium audiences, all of whom already knew the likes of 'Pretty Peggy-O', 'In The Pines' and 'Walkin' Blues', songs Dylan wrote down as potential candidates to perform that July, but never did.*

Instead, the Dead tried to push him into performing the Dylan songs *they* knew, even if he didn't. One of these was 'Joey', which Dylan later admitted, 'Garcia . . . got me singing . . . He said that's one of the best songs ever written.' What a shame he often killed Joey off a verse or two early, once in the second verse. (When a later girlfriend teased him about this, 'he wrinkled his brow thinking and debating over when that was.')

In isolation, the list of songs performed at the six shows seemed like every Dylan fan's teenage prayer. 'Queen Jane Approximately', 'Joey', 'The Wicked Messenger', 'The Ballad Of Frankie Lee And Judas Priest' all received live debuts. Other songs they semi-rehearsed – 'In The Summertime', 'If Not For You', 'Walkin' Down The Line', 'Under Your Spell', 'Pledging My Time' – would have been equally enticing, had the audience he was playing to been his own.

As it is, the format was a 75-minute Dylan/Dead set at the mid-point of a gruelling four-hour Grateful Dead show. Already jettisoned by July 4th was a plan to do a short acoustic set, which had an enticing provisional set-list including 'Frankie & Johnny', 'Dark As A Dungeon' and 'Blues Stay Away From Me'. According to a story Dylan told Dana Gillespie in 1997 – later reworked for *Chronicles* – there had come a moment during rehearsals when he decided to go out and go for a walk:

> He had thought it would be a piece of cake to get up and sing his songs with the Dead, as he had been doing most recently with Tom Petty and his band, but the Dead were a totally different animal. They wanted to do songs that he'd long forgotten, and he surprised me by saying how he felt his confidence slipping away – knowing he would never be able

---

* On the list was Johnny Horton's 'North To Alaska', 'Junco Partner' – from which he got *Knocked Out Loaded*'s title – 'This Train', 'Go Down Moses', 'Streets Of Laredo', 'Johnny I Hardly Knew You' and 'Down In The Valley'.

to remember all the lyrics . . . It got to the point where he felt so uncomfortable about this that he told the band he'd left something at his
hotel, then walked out of the rehearsal room with no intention of
returning . . . Fate, however, led him into a little nearby bar where a jazz
band was playing in the back . . . As he stopped to listen to the musicians . . . [a] revelation came over him; he said it was almost like he was
being propelled into another dimension. Somehow, he suddenly knew
that he had the power to go back . . . and sing those old songs that had
previously scared him so much.

In reality, by the time of the tour Dylan was more than ever convinced he'd made a foolish move. After being booked into a hotel 'too
far for comfort from the [Foxborough] gig', and leaving to move somewhere else at three in the morning, Dylan made his feelings known to
management. As Shafner's girlfriend observed, 'It's clear from the outset that he wants very little to do with their band.' When he discovered
those huge video screens served a purpose, beaming close-ups of a
shuffling singer around the stadia, his discomfiture grew. After Foxborough, those screens pulled back to full stage for the entire Dylan set,
but no amount of panning could disguise the sheer incompatibility in
this misalliance.

Later statements, including one at a 1997 London press conference,
that 'playing with the Dead . . . taught me to look inside these songs',
have convinced Dead apologists he meant they showed him the way.
He did not. The full quote is nothing short of a true confession, 'At the
time of that tour, I couldn't even sing . . . The spirit of the songs . . .
had been getting further and further away from me.' To Mikal
Gilmore – once commissioned to write a book on the Dead before fate
ensured he left all his notes in a taxi, prompting him to write the magnificent *Shot In The Heart* instead – he was more explicit still:

I had already been on a long string of dates with Tom Petty and the
Heartbreakers . . . playing fifteen to twenty of the songs I had written,
and I couldn't really grasp the older ones. But when . . . I went back and
played with Petty['s band] again . . . I found I could play *anything*.

Babe, this ain't no lie. All of the ostensible highlights of the Dylan/
Dead shows – 'Tomorrow Is A Long Time', 'Joey', 'Dead Man, Dead

Man', 'John Brown', 'The Wicked Messenger', 'Frankie Lee And Judas
Priest' – were born again when Dylan resumed an altogether more
musical association in September, a six-week European tour with Petty
and co. Like Pygmalion breathing life into his statue, all these songs
came alive; indeed burst into flames, though only after bubbling under
for the first three shows.

The reason? The Heartbreakers *responded* to their leader, embracing
the experience, Petty admitting at the end of it, 'I always felt he taxed
us to the limit every night because he did throw you some curve[ball]s
up there.' Drummer Stan Lynch read the runes too, describing some
'gigs where the songs have ended in all the wrong places, where it's
fallen apart, and it's almost as if, in some perverse way, he gets energy
from that chaos'.

The Temples In Flames tour, the third instalment of their alliance,
was conducted with Eris hovering nightly. Early on, the auspices were
not good. As with Foxborough, so with Tel Aviv, six weeks on from the
last Dylan/Dead requiem in Anaheim. His newly appointed assistant
later recalled, 'When we arrived in Israel, Bob came to me and asked
me not to associate with the Tom Petty group . . . For the next few
concerts, we kept our tours separate from Tom's, despite playing the
same shows. We didn't move at the same time, we didn't use the same
equipment; we didn't use the same boats or planes to travel.' That
'new' assistant was none other than Victor Maymudes, who discovered
that twenty-one years on, his boss hadn't changed; he was the same
man:

In 1987, I found myself in dire straits financially . . . I gave Bob a call in
my desperation. He answered and I simply said, 'Bob, I need a job.' . . .
He told me, 'I'm going on tour . . . I don't really have a place for you.
But I'll pay you and . . . we'll see what happens.' . . . The day before we
were supposed to be flying to Athens [sic], Bob called me up and told
me to drive out to the house and we would ride to the airport
together . . . Bob sat sideways in the front passenger seat. He didn't look
up once, just kept flipping through a big handful of photographs, snapshots that he had taken with his camera from some other place in
time . . . He was looking at each one closely and then throwing it out of
the window, one by one, the whole distance I drove . . . If someone was
lucky enough to have been in the exact right place and time they would

have had a personalized, stop-motion film displaying the depths of a moment in Dylan's life that he so [desperately] wanted to leave behind.

Also along for the ride as the wheels again caught fire was Shafner's girlfriend, the adhesive Britta Lee Shain, and Dylan's middle son, Sam. Arriving in Egypt on September 2nd, three days before his first-ever show in Israel, the Heartbreakers – more in hope than expectation – were looking to rehearse. It had been thirteen months, after all. But as Lee Shain found, 'Bob is so enamored with Egypt, we stay an extra day . . . Time is now of the essence in terms of making rehearsals for the Tel Aviv show . . . [but] he wants to take a bus across the Gaza to Israel . . . For ten hours, the view through the grimy windows will be of dust, dirt and desert.' Dylan told Robert Hilburn, 'I wanted to see the prison where Joseph was in and the place Abraham took Sarah.'

His mind was not as yet on the job in hand, and wouldn't be until he left Israel. The Tel Aviv show did not live up to the 'homeland' hype – how could it? – despite Dylan encoring with a heartfelt 'Go Down Moses (Let My People Go)'. When Hilburn mentioned the lukewarm local reviews the following night, Dylan shrugged it off, 'Some nights . . . you just feel like you are on a sinking boat. There's nothing you can do about it. But . . . you can't just stand there and guess what the audience wants to hear.'

He certainly couldn't be accused of trying to pander to the masses, performing the likes of 'In The Garden' and 'Dead Man, Dead Man' to the largely Jewish crowd. The Jerusalem show on the 7th was more of the same, yet entirely different. Not a single song in the thirteen-song set replicated Tel Aviv, as he found room for 'Man Of Peace', 'Shot Of Love', 'Gotta Serve Somebody' and 'Slow Train'. The message remained the same, even if the songs didn't. According to *Chronicles*, it was all part of some master plan, 'In these first four [Temples In Flames] shows I sang eighty different songs, never repeating one, just to see if I could do it. Night after night it was like I was on cruise control. Regardless of all this, I was still planning to quit.'

Actually, it was the first three shows and 42 songs but, hey, who's counting? Certainly not Dylan, who was probably still nursing a hangover when he boarded the plane to Basel, Switzerland. He'd spent the wee small hours after the Jerusalem gig being interviewed by Kurt

Loder for a twentieth anniversary issue of *Rolling Stone*, and 'drinking Kamikazes like they were Kool-Aid'.

Fortunately, there was only room for a much-edited version of their conversation in *Stone*, thus losing his remarks about Mick Jagger 'jumping around like he does . . . It's got nothin' to do with jumping around,' and how he, 'hate[s] to see chicks perform . . . because they whore themselves,' as he and Loder sat 'out on the patio for four hours, talking and toking', after which Dylan told Lee Shain 'to go wake everybody up. He wants to go to the Wailing Wall.'

The praying seems to have done the trick because, according to the Chronicler, 'Suddenly, one night, in Locarno, Switzerland . . . everything came back.' Save that it wasn't Locarno, it was Basel – the show after Jerusalem – when he realized with a start, 'Nobody was looking at the girls anymore. They were looking at the main mike.'* Even before he published his own authorized version of events, he was telling Mikal Gilmore, 'That night in Switzerland, it all just came to me . . . Before, I wasn't controlling it. I was just being swept by the wind,' and *Newsweek*'s David Gates, 'After that . . . I sort of knew: I've got to go out and play these songs. That's just what I must do.'

If all of this happened near the Swiss border, it was in Turin, the following night, that full transmission was restored. 'Wicked Messenger', 'I Shall Be Released', 'Heart Of Mine', even 'License To Kill', came from the other side of some deep, dark, truthful mirr'r, as the magical moments just kept coming. At the next show in Dortmund, 'Tangled Up In Blue' and 'Shelter From The Storm' were as good as any of their precursors – A&R included – while the 'Simple Twist Of Fate' in Helsinki (23rd) sat at the same welcome table. In Copenhagen, two nights earlier, he had decided to do an electric arrangement of 'Desolation Row', giving the band a full minute's notice. It felt like something he'd been mulling over for the past twelve years.

Every song which had lurched from pillar to post in July, while Bob

---

* In fairness to Dylan, he has been quite consistent about claiming it was Locarno. But the audio evidence is against him. Basel was on September 10th, Locarno October 5th. The shows inbetween have moments better than anything from 1984 and 1986, and as good as 1979-81, so I wouldn't cling too much to the Chronicler's selective memory. After all, he has the tour ending in December, not October 17th.

the backseat driver tried steering the Deadmen at the wheel right, had become a revelation. In Gothenburg, Benmont Tench recalled, 'We were just about to go on stage and I asked Bob what slow song he wanted to play in the middle of the set . . . He said, "Do you know 'Tomorrow Is a Long Time'? Let's do it, just me and you." . . . It was genuinely transcendent.' It was the first time they'd done a piano/guitar duet, but from hereon it was a nightly highlight.

However, anyone who fondly imagines plaudits raining down must be a glass half-full person. The reviews of the shows were among the worst he'd ever had in Europe. In Basel, after reading the reviews, he was heard to complain, 'I don't think everything I've done since 1965 is irrelevant!' And in Helsinki – a truly great show – he asked a female fan he met while searching for a synagogue to translate the local paper:

> **Bob Dylan**: What's it say, there in the paper?
> [She shakes her head]
> **BD**: Just the headline. Maybe you could translate.
> **Girl**: No.
> **BD**: Why?
> **Girl**: It's not good.
> **BD**: It's okay. Go on, just the headline.
> **Girl**: 'The God arrived. The man performed.'
> **BD**: [laughs] What else?
> **Girl**: It says you would have been better off if you'd have died young like other legends – like Elvis and Marilyn or James Dean.

It was Faridi reading him the *Renaldo & Clara* reviews all over again. He professed not to care, but after the Basel show, Lee Shain noticed he was getting 'more and more sloshed. At one point he gets involved in a singalong with a couple of his backing singers . . . Not long after this, the almost totally incoherent Bob Dylan falls out of his chair.'

He was certainly putting it away, leading to some nights where he needed two or three songs to establish that tight connection to his muse. Before the show in Verona, he asked Lee Shain to 'make him four Kahlúa, cream and VSOPs – his drink of the week'. And yet, the set itself was one of the best to date. He had once again plugged in onstage. But not in bed. According to Lee Shain, 'only once on the tour . . . did he apparently sleep on the same bus' as his wife – the long-suffering Carolyn Dennis – 'and even then, [he] was the worse for wear – as he was for much of that tour.'

If he couldn't always manage to perform in both arenas, this didn't stop him 'consoling' Michael Bloomfield's widow one night, or flying in a concubine for the week in London at tour's end. She arrived to find he was now sharing his bed with Lee Shain, from whom she wanted to know, 'What did he fly me in for, then?' Maybe to keep him from making a fool of himself, and losing a trusted lieutenant in Shafner? Ironically, Lee Shain describes this woman in her memoir as 'a bimbo . . . coarse, overly made-up, but not stupid.' So much for any solidarity among the sisterhood who sleep with superstars!

Shain did not see the inevitable coming. Just before the axe fell, Maymudes and her were looking at some pictures she'd taken of Dylan, and she said, 'I think we should use it as an album cover.' The sharp-as-a-tack Victor snapped, 'We?! I'm starting to get a bad feeling about this.' It did not need Victor voicing his concerns for word to make it back to L.A. Lee Shain now told Shafner (that she loved Dylan, not him) who told Childs, who informed Dylan she would be on the next plane to London, the following morning. Britta had blown it, losing her fiancé into the bargain,* and Dylan had burnt his bridges with Shafner, who never forgave him, going on to become a multi-millionaire anyway, while Childs took the flight to London to bring 'her man' to heel.

The Teflon man was unfazed. No sooner had he returned to New York – after a triumphant four-night residency at Wembley Arena, the import of which the UK dailies predictably blinked and missed – than he was calling up Susan Ross, with the newly-promoted Victor in tow, after a year in which nary a word had passed between them.

He knew he wanted to keep going and that retaining the Heartbreakers beyond Temples In Flames was never an option. They had served him well, but as he later told Stuart Coupe, 'If you're only going out once in a while then, you know, you have a problem trying to find . . . people who aren't playing with somebody else at that time.' It was time to get a(nother) standing band, and he already had a few

---

* According to Lee Shain, Shafner flew to New York shortly after their break-up to confront Dylan, but was apprehended by security. He must have known physical confrontation was never Dylan's dish.

ideas. Which is how Danny Kortchmar, Steve Jordan and Randy Jackson all found themselves summoned to Montana Studios to 'rehearse', closely followed by G.E. Smith, a guitarist with a growing reputation, thanks to his weekly stint as bandleader on TV:

> I was playing on *Saturday Night Live*, and Elliot [Roberts] called me at work one day and said, 'Hey, can you get a bass player and a drummer tomorrow night and be at this rehearsal studio called Montana? Bob's coming to New York and he wants to play.' So, I called T-Bone Wolk and Chris Parker and we're meant to be there at ten in the evening . . . We got there, there was no-one there . . . The lights were very low. But we saw . . . the gear laid out. We plugged in . . . Still nobody [was] there. Then, about half an hour later, maybe more, out of the darkness . . . steps Bob. I don't know how long he's been there. So, he . . . picks up an electric guitar and starts to play. And we start to play along. There's no conversation or instructions or anything . . . Then at some point he turns . . . and says, 'Do you guys know Pretty Peggy-O?' Me and T-Bone say, 'Sure.' 'You do?' And he starts playing it . . . We continued on for maybe a couple of hours pretty much non-stop, and again with no talking at all. He'd just go straight into another song. Almost all old stuff – traditional songs, country stuff, some rock'n'roll, no Bob Dylan songs I can recall . . . [Then] he put down his guitar, said thanks, and he was gone.*

And that was that. Or so it seemed. Something now made Dylan take stock, instead; possibly a hand injury he says in *Chronicles* he sustained. Equally possibly, his management team informed him *Down In The Groove* – which was already circulating in two incarnations, neither of which would end up released[†] – wouldn't be out till May,[‡] which was also the earliest date he could realistically embark on a national tour, however much he wanted to start blazing a trail again.

He would just have to stay home and write a song or two. It wasn't

---

* A two-CD bootleg of a G.E. Smith rehearsal from November 1987 was called *Dancing In The Dark*.
† Both 'Important Words' and 'Got Love If You Want It' were replaced, though not in time to stop the latter appearing on the Argentinian version.
‡ Not that he exactly promoted it, save for 'Silvio', which soon became a stage favourite.

like he didn't have subject matter. How about his recent treatment of women, for starters? The song he came up with was another major breakthrough, opening up a potentially rich vein to mine. It was called 'Dignity', and in *Chronicles* Dylan describes how he 'heard the whole piece in my head – rhythm, tempo, melody line, the whole bit . . . a song like this, there [was] no end to things,' which all rings true. Less credibly, he also claimed 'he started and completed the song . . . the same day,' and that 'there were more verses with other individuals in different interplays: The Green Beret, The Sorceress, Virgin Mary, The Wrong Man, Big Ben, and The Cripple and The Honkey'.

He certainly had more verses, countless more verses, but not one of these characters appears in any of the nine drafts that reside in the Bob Dylan Archive. I think we can safely assume he didn't write nine drafts in a single day, especially as the essence of the idea had yet to be extracted in the first few drafts. What he did have, though, was a juxta-position between men forever searching – à la Joseph Campbell's *The Hero with a Thousand Faces* – and Dignity itself, portrayed as endlessly suffering at the hands of men across all nine drafts:

> Dignity is a woman that bleeds in the hot Egyptian sun . . .
> Dignity is a woman who cries, in love with a man with death in his eyes . . .
> Dignity is a woman enslaved to the pavement of the night . . .
> Dignity is a woman that wails in the broken down lonely night . . .
> Dignity is a woman in need who'll go to the ends of the earth for you . . .
> Dignity is a woman in chains, in Love with a man in the passing lanes . . .
> Dignity is a woman entrapped, in love with a man whose mind has snapped . . .
> Dignity is a woman on the rails, in the shadows, at the end of the world . . .
> Dignity is a woman in shock, caught in a crossfire of the auction block.

His futile quest leads the narrator to look east and west, 'see[ing] people [who] are cursed and people who are blessed . . . asking every-body, like a man possessed,' but he continues looking in the wrong places. He is Everyman: 'Black man looking through a crown of thorns/ Yellow man looking through a veil that's torn'; white man, angry man, shadow man, poor man, empty man (sitting 'in the church of the abused and confused'), gamblin' man. At the end of draft nine, the narrator is 'looking at a glass that['s] half-filled . . . looking at a dream that [has] just been killed . . . asking everybody that's strong willed . . .' But still, he can't find dignity, though she stands in plain view, a face in the crowd. A majestic work, it has come too soon. He hasn't an album he's ready to wrap around it. By the time he has, the Caribbean wind will have not so much whipped 'Dignity' into shape as spirited the women that are Men's crutches away. All that's left is a heartsick man on an endless seeking trail, westron wind blowing.

At least the doors of inspiration had swung firmly open again. Almost immediately, a second potentially great song took his imagination hostage, 'I Have Prayed For Liberty' (see chapter heading). This time he filed it away in the cupboard, marked Beware the Leopard. The loss is considerable as Dylan describes standing on the mountaintop, where he has 'seen the devil's eyes', having revisited all Ten Commandments 'while stationed on a hill'.

Having finally relearnt to drink the blood of Christ, he knows for sure that 'the eternal prince of darkness digs a deep and dirty grave'. He will not be tempted. The liberty he seeks can only be found in the freedom of faith; he will not succumb to the vision of a world he could own, which the Devil has shown him. At the end of the sixth draft, Dylan asks of his listener: 'Judge me by appearance, judge me by the storm, that rolls in with me, like Mystery . . .'

He had rediscovered his higher purpose – to write songs which do not so much save souls as lead people not into Temptation. Hence, a song called 'Silence Is Golden' that insisted, 'Faith is a river that never runs dry.' He has reacquainted himself not just with his Muse but also his Messiah. His race memory restored, he remembers a time when he sailed 'the seas of good fortune', when the flame of his youth 'blew like a torch and delivered the message of truth', pouring this notion into another vat of verses, 'When You Pass Me By', before it could be drained.

He knew these songs were in direct opposition to the things he now heard on the radio. As he told Denise Worrell, when amnesia reigned, 'The stuff you hear on the radio would make it seem like everything's all right everywhere. You really have to seek your salvation in some other place than the popular radio.' He would be blunter still to Edna Gundersen after delivering a second album of original songs in twelve months in 1990, 'It's not difficult to get people throbbing in their guts. [But] that can lead them down an evil path, if that's all they're getting.'

In *Chronicles*, he would suggest that 'Political World' was 'the first of twenty songs I would write in the next month or so', among which – he claimed – were 'What Good Am I?', 'Disease Of Conceit', 'What Was It You Wanted?' and 'Everything Is Broken'. It's possible but unlikely, and if so, the working title of the last of these was 'Broken Days', and it was little more than a series of broken images: 'nothing she wrote/ laws jaws/ eyes feet/ hands street/ ... everything is broken/ food in broken cans.'

What certainly never featured in any draft was the line, 'I'm crossin' the river goin' to Hoboken,' quoted in a series of patently fabricated alternate verses for these five songs in *Chronicles*. Twelve years before the Tulsa archive gave a glimpse into the real *Oh Mercy* writing process, anyone with an inkling of the real songwriter in him knew lines like, 'What good am I if I'm walking on eggs/ If I'm wild with excitement and wet between the legs?' ('What Good Am I?'), or, 'I'll hump ya and I'll dump ya and I'll blow your house down/ I'll slice into your cake before I leave town,' purportedly from 'Disease Of Conceit', were the work of a post-modern poetaster, perhaps the same one who 'discovered' handwritten manuscripts of his most famous Sixties songs in the 2010s.

Unfortunately for him, it was still those songs that continued to cement his position in popular consciousness, as was confirmed in January 1988, when he was inducted into the newly-formed Rock'n'Roll Hall of Fame by his dear friend, George Harrison. That Dylan had doubts about this whole rock'n'roll circus was clear from his acceptance speech, which noted how much 'more important was the recognition of Leadbelly and Woody'.

He would continue sniping at the very idea of such an institution, both from the stage in 1991 – when he said that if Johnny Cash wasn't in it, 'there shouldn't be a Rock'n'Roll Hall of Fame' – and during his infamous 2015 MusiCares speech, when after talking about the late great Billy Lee Riley, he gave vent to his true feelings about the name of this hall of fame: 'You won't find [Billy] in the Rock'n'Roll Hall of Fame. He's not there. Metallica is. Abba is. Mamas and the Papas ... Steely Dan – I've got nothing against them. Soft rock, hard rock, psychedelic pop. I got nothing against any of that stuff, but after all, it is called the Rock'n'Roll Hall of Fame. [And] Billy Lee Riley is not there.'

Of course, the Rock'n'Roll Hall of Fame was never about 'that rock'n'roll music', being really the *Rolling Stone* Hall of Fame. Located in Cleveland, Ohio, four thousand miles from the home of Rock music,* it grossly exaggerated the importance and quality of the middling brand of 'west is best' reactionary rock Jann Wenner, Jon Landau &c. preferred.† The perfect paradigm for these wine-drinking businessmen was the frat-rock of Bruce Springsteen, who in his own speech at Dylan's induction very much placed himself on the shoulder of this giant: 'To this day, where great rock music is being made, there is the shadow of Bob Dylan . . . Bob's own modern work has gone unjustly under-appreciated for having to stand in that shadow.'

Eloquent, indeed. And to show how much Dylan appreciated it, three months later he deconstructed Springsteen's entire songwriting *schtick* in a single satirical song that was superior to anything Bruce had written this side of 'The Promise'. That song was 'Tweeter And The Monkey Man', and it formed the centrepiece of a triple-platinum album released that very year under the *nom de plume*, The Traveling Wilburys.

Dylan had been gunning for Bruce throughout the Eighties, as all close to him already knew. These included Paul Rappaport, who remembered Dylan visiting him just after Bruce released *Born in The USA*, thus becoming King Midas minus the curse: 'He walks into my office and spies a large, [signed,] Bruce Springsteen poster . . . He was always after me, asking, "What's that guy doing now?" . . . He looks at the poster, turns around, looks at me sitting behind my desk, cocks his head, and in that very recognizable Dylan timbre, asks, "Is this guy still driving that stolen car?" '

Sure, that was a private joke, but the public digs weren't too far away. When he told *Rolling Stone*'s David Fricke in 1985, 'I'm too old to start over and too young to blow my horn about all the people that ripped me off,' he was responding to a question about *Nebraska*. And to Mikal Gilmore, the following summer, as his own calliope crashed to the ground, he confessed, 'I'm not particularly into this American[a]

---

* Not a hard one to prove. Five of the six most influential bands in Rock music – The Beatles, The Rolling Stones, The Who, Led Zeppelin and the Sex Pistols – are English. The only US band of commensurate importance – The Velvet Underground – would not be inducted until 1996. 'Nuff said.

† Cleveland's most innovative rock band, the hugely influential Pere Ubu, have yet to be inducted.

thing, this Bruce Springsteen/ John Cougar/ "America first" thing . . . I personally feel that what's important is more eternal things.'

So, when his friend and fellow inductee, George Harrison, cobbled together the Eighties' finest supergroup from his little black book, the ex-Beatle was delighted to find 'Tom Petty and Bob sitting in the kitchen . . . talking about all this stuff which didn't make sense to me – Americana kind of stuff. [But] we got a tape cassette and put it on, and transcribed everything they were saying.'

The pair had already collaborated on two songs at the time of *Knocked Out Loaded*, the second of which, 'Jammin' Me', came about because 'Bob . . . said, "I got this idea for a song . . . [about] too much information." So, we put a pad down and picked up a newspaper and just started coming up with lines. We had a lot of fun doing it.' Ditto, 'Tweeter And The Monkey Man', Dylan's (and Petty's) wittiest song in years. In fact, the whole Traveling Wilburys album, recorded over ten days in May, was full of a rare wit and abiding affection for traditional pop forms. Yet it had only come about because of something as mundane as Warner's needing a song to put on a George Harrison 12" 45:

George Harrison: I didn't have another song, I didn't have an extended version, so I just said to Jeff [Lynne] – I was in Los Angeles and he was producing Roy Orbison – 'I'm just going to have to write a song tomorrow and just do it.' I was kind of thinking of 'Instant Karma' – that way. And I said, 'Where can we get a studio?' And he said, 'Well, [what about] Bob? 'Cause he's got this little studio in his garage.' . . . We just went back to his house, phoned up Bob; he said, 'Sure, come on over.' Tom Petty had my guitar, and I went to pick it up; he said, 'Oh, I was wondering what I was going to do tomorrow!' And Roy Orbison said, 'Give us a call tomorrow if you're going to do anything – I'd love to come along.'

Even Warner's realized the resultant track, 'Handle With Care', was far too good to hide away on a b-side. What, then? The legendary Roy Orbison takes up the story, 'Then we had the idea of putting together [an] album. We had all enjoyed it so much; it was so relaxed, there was no ego[s] involved, and there was some sort of chemistry. So, we'd go to Bob's house [sic] and we'd just sit outside, and there'd be a barbecue, and we'd all just bring guitars, and everyone would be throwing something in here and there, and then we'd just go to the garage studio, and put it down.'

The two other songs where Dylan took the lead – 'Congratulations' and 'Dirty World' – were pastiche pop at its basement best. But he was not making music at Big Pink. He had a major time restriction, Harrison confirming, 'We had nine or ten days that we knew we could get Bob for, and everybody else was relatively free, so . . . [we decided] we'll write a tune a day and do it that way.'

For Dylan, who had tried a few collaborations in the last two wasted years – even writing a song with Britta Lee Shain – the album came surprisingly easily. So easy, he barely remembered doing it when Harrison wrote to him later in the year and thanked him for doing the record, 'It was great being in the band with you . . . I hope it was not too embarrassing for you.' In fact, the album charted at three in the US charts, and was a huge worldwide success, reminding Dylan that songwriting could sometimes be fun.

Its release came as he was wrapping up six months of almost solid touring with four sold-out shows at New York's Radio City Music Hall, where he predictably failed to acknowledge this commercial comeback in deed or word. He was too busy finding 'a new audience, because my audience at that time had more or less grown up on my records and was past the point of accepting me as a new artist . . . They came to stare and not participate.' That process had begun in earnest in May with another band G.E. Smith had assembled with drummer Chris Parker on the off-chance it fit Dylan's remit. For a few days it included Marshall Crenshaw, a singer-songwriter in his own right:

I was sittin' in my kitchen in Nashville. My phone rang and it was G.E. Smith. . . . He said, 'Are you doing anything this summer? How'd you like to go on the road with Bob Dylan as a bass player? . . . Here's the deal . . . The band's . . . gonna rehearse for a week and then on the seventh day, Bob will play with us.' . . . But then what happened was Bob turned up on the second day, unannounced, and freaked everybody [out] . . . I knew like twenty-five Bob Dylan songs. I mean, everybody knows at least 25 Bob Dylan songs! . . . I really started to cram the stuff as much as I could . . . But I [had] walked into it dabbling . . . So we played for about three days and it wasn't really clicking at all . . . It just kinda fell apart after three days.

Crenshaw's replacement was Kenny Aaronson, who was left as much in the dark as his predecessor, 'They didn't even tell me if I had the gig. They just had me playing for days, and I was learning fifteen to twenty tunes a day.' Finally, it got to the first week in June, and he was informed, 'Oh yeah, you got the gig.' Oh, and could he be in Concord, California, on the 7th for the start of a two-month, forty-date tour of North America.

The spirit of adventure was once again abroad, as Dylan again ripped up the set-list, abandoned cherished favourites and played some gut bucket rock'n'roll that would itself have qualified for the Rock'n'Roll Hall of Fame. Smith was delighted, 'I love that kind of seat of your pants playing . . . He kept the music alive. He kept me guessing. But I think it was really for himself . . . He would play anything. He [once] asked me, "Do you know that Springsteen song, 'Dancing in The Dark'?" And I was, "Kinda." . . . He would do stuff like that from time to time.' Actually, Springsteen's attempt at disco-synth was the first song they ever rehearsed, in November 1987. They just never played it onstage until one memorable night in January 1990, by which time Dylan only 'kinda' remembered the lyrics. His purpose in murdering Bruce's biggest hit? God knows.

The summer '88 tour – just like the Wilburys LP – gave him a much-needed commercial and critical shot in the arm. Supported by The Alarm, Wales' answer to U2, with just a three-piece band, Dylan was delivering his most stripped-down sound ever. The set was a locked-in-tight seventy-five minutes, with a three-song acoustic interlude at mid-point, where Dylan and Smith got to busk.

Every show Dylan was opening with 'Subterranean Homesick Blues', of all things. Though it was a nightly roll of the dice how many lines were intelligible, it was a gloriously ballsy opener that set the tempo and tenor for the show to come. Some of the electric arrangements were astounding – a *götterdämmerung* 'Gates Of Eden'; a 'My Back Pages' that reclaimed it from the twee Byrds bastardization; an 'Absolutely Sweet Marie' that scorched earth. He was also back to doing covers galore, always a good sign. Traditional ones like 'Lakes Of Pontchartrain', 'Eileen Aroon', 'Wild Mountain Thyme' &c. were usually reserved for the acoustic set. Yet an electric 'Pretty Peggy-O' showed the Dead it actually went like *this*. The other electric covers could be anything that took his fancy, from Chuck Berry's 'Nadine' to Leonard Cohen's as-yet-unlauded 'Hallelujah'.

Returning to California in early August, for three shows at Holly-wood's open-air Greek Theater, Dylan sensed he was on a roll. After forty shows with The Alarm, he was wrapping it up with another open-air show at Santa Barbara's County Bowl, and a Sunny 'Big River' followed by a communal 'Knockin' On Heaven's Door'. The Alarm may have been switched off, but Dylan was determined to keep going, resuming touring after just twelve days off the road in Portland, Ore-gon, concluding another 25-date leg of what – unbeknownst to the world – he intended to be the Never Ending Tour, in New Orleans on September 25th.

Finally, his mind began turning to all those songs he had in his locker, and what to do with them. Firstly, he needed a producer. He knew what he didn't want. As he'd told Loder while getting loaded in the homeland, 'Personally, I don't believe in separation of sound. I like to hear it all blended together. The world could use a new Phil Spector record.' How about trying to make a record that – as his 21st century engineer would put it – sounded like one he'd made 'on some of the old four-track [machines] . . . [with] drums and organ on one track and Bob and his electric guitar bleeding into everything else, all mushed together . . . ['cause] Bob is constantly trying to get back to that sound'?

It was certainly a subject he had firm views on, ones he shared with U2's Bono at Slane Castle in 1984, 'The studios now are so modern, and overly developed, that you can take anything good and you can press it and squeeze it and squash it, and constipate it and suffocate it.' Bono assured him it didn't have to be that way, and in 1988, having been privy to some of Dylan's new songs, 'suggested that Daniel [Lanois] could really record them right. [So,] Daniel came to see me when we were playing in New Orleans.'

Lanois seemed, on the face of it, an odd choice. As Dylan told Adrian Deevoy, shortly after recording 1989's *Oh Mercy*, he had spent years 'working with people who for one reason or another happen to be there, but don't have a great understanding of what it is that [I'm] try-ing to do . . . They'd rather say, . . . "Let me think what else I can put on it."' In what way was Lanois – a determined meddler who mar-keted himself as a producer/ musician – not a member of this club?

Dylan had already encountered two more suitable candidates, Don and David Was, after an August show in Toronto, when, Don recalls, 'David and I were ushered into a room to meet our hero . . . We had a

good laugh together and the vibe was nice.' But Lanois was in pole
position once Dylan heard the record he'd been doing with the Neville
Brothers, whose *Yellow Moon* he was producing when Dylan rolled into
the Nevilles' hometown. It was Lanois who had his doubts, after seeing
the show at the local zoo:

> Bob was travelling with an aggressive, powerful trio, and I went to hear
> him in New Orleans, and I had no connection with what was going on
> onstage. I had no criticisms toward those players, [but] I didn't know
> what to do. I thought, 'Is this where Bob is at? Is this the kind of record
> he wants to make?' We huddled [together] after that performance and I
> said to him I didn't think . . . that particular band would work out.

Only when he persuaded Dylan to come down to the studio and
heard what he was doing with the Nevilles, did they find common
ground. The way Lanois describes it in his 2010 memoir, 'Dylan walked
into my studio and I knew [right away] he had an appetite for dedication. He had a vibe on him like a boxer who had fallen out of the
limelight, looking to come back in to regain his throne . . . [He] listened to a few songs of the Nevilles' record, including a version of his
own "[With] God on Our Side," sung by Aaron Neville . . . And at the
end of the playback, Bob looked at me and said, "That sounds like a
record."' As always, it was meant as a compliment. In this watershed
moment, they agreed to reconvene the following spring and make
something that 'sounds like a record'. It was tough on G.E., who had
certainly harboured hopes that after a summer making marvellous
music, he might help define the studio sound himself.

Another homecoming of sorts at Radio City Music Hall signed off
on NET shows for the year, after which Dylan opened the locker and
looked at what he had to record. It was not enough, and he knew it.
Time to get down and get with it. Which required some time spent
home alone. As he'd informed Kathryn Baker that August, 'You need
to be able to . . . shut yourself off for long periods of time . . . in order
to come up with [songs]. You're always capable of it in your youth . . .
But once that all ends, then you have to create not only what you want
to do, but you have to create the environment to do it in.'

Some of the songs in his head he had been carrying around for a
while, possibly as far back as January 1986, when he alluded to 'a bunch

of songs I want to write that I haven't been able to get close to at the moment. They're songs I almost have to go out and . . . get . . . [They're about] real things that have happened . . . I hope to have some of that . . . on the next album I do.'

There were no such songs on *Knocked Out Loaded* – unless 'Got My Mind Made Up' counts – or the irredeemable *Down In The Groove*. But he was determined to knock some of them into shape now. One even had the marvellous title, 'Blackbeard Was A Woman'. It was another 'state of the union' address: 'So much disease, so much alarm/ So much disharmony, so much harm/ So much black masquerading as white/ Under the moonlight.' This Jew for Jesus was once again Jeremiah incarnate, as he penned another scathing portrait of a 'Mr Moneybags' who was rock'n'rolling all the way down to the pit. He may even have had a lapsed Jew who worked at the label in mind; a man who liked to be whipped like a baby while chained to the bed; who had 'gained the whole world . . . and watched it crash'. In the final verse of a cogent lyric, he described meeting Mr Moneybags in the elevator, 'I was going up, he was coming down/ He was tryin' [to] figure out the chords to a Top Forty hit/ A most intriguing song called "[The] Bottomless Pit."'

Splendid stuff, righteously spiteful and sarcastic, it was not even attempted at the March 1989 sessions. Nor was another of his 'Jesus Is Another' songs. Called simply, 'If Jesus Walked The Streets Today', it raised questions like, 'Would they lock him up and throw the key away? . . . Would they kill him again, 'cause it's written that way? . . . Would he go to the Vatican, where would he stay?'* Again, Dylan would shy away from recording, let alone releasing, a song with the J-word in the title. Also cast on stony ground were 'By The Look In Your Eye', 'Love Ya Easy' ('Love ya in a ring of fire/ Like a bird upon the wire'), and 'You Are My Destiny', which duly donated the following bridge – 'I sent you roses from a heart that was truly grieved/ I sent you roses that someone else must've received' – to 'Broken Days', where it was claimed by an old actress-girlfriend, Sally Kirkland.

He had done it again – reinventing himself and erasing recent foolish moves. All of which made his next one particularly baffling. Yes,

---

* The last of these lines is surely a reference to the famous Lenny Bruce skit where Christ returns and turns up in a church in Chicago. Cardinal Spellman calls the Pope and asks what he is paying protection money for.

he'd agreed to do a live album with the Dead at the time of the 1987 shows. But now was not the time, nor the place. And yet, on February 6th, 1989, Sony released a seven-track live album called simply *Dylan & The Dead*, that raked over the coals of a catastrophic series of concerts. At least the Dead tried their darnedest to present the slightly tarnished legend in the best possible light, compiling a nine-track LP that featured the best of a bad lot – 'The Wicked Messenger' in East Rutherford, the 'John Brown' at Foxborough, the 'Chimes Of Freedom' in Anaheim – only to be summoned to Point Dume, and told to bring along their suggested sequence.

Garcia was stunned to find, sitting there 'on the table . . . a $39 ghetto blaster, and he's got the cassette [we'd made,] and he sticks it in there and he says, "Don't you think the voice is mixed a little loud in that one?" So, we just sat and listened to it on this funky little thing, [while] he'd say [things like], "I think there ought to be a little more bass." '

A little more bass and a little less inspiration. Just three songs from the Dead's preferred sequence – 'Joey', 'Slow Train' and 'Queen Jane Approximately' – would make the final cut. Dylan was determined to tell it like it was. Maybe people would then realize just how far he'd fallen, so that he could rise again with a new album which showed he was back to his Blakean best, minus the songs of innocence.

5.6

January 1988 to December 1989: The Quality Of Mercy

I like to sing to the people. I just don't like to sing into microphones in a studio.

> Bob Dylan, to Karen Hughes, 1st April 1978.

Q: How much of the music comes from the sub-conscious?
Bob Dylan: . . . I used to pull a lot of it up. I pull some of it up once in a while now, but not too often.

> Sydney press conference, 10th February 1986.

An easy way out would be to say, 'Yeah, it's all behind me, that's it and there's no more.' But you want to say there might be a small chance that something up there will surpass whatever you did.

> Bob Dylan, to Edna Gundersen, 21st September 1989.

I asked him how he gets his ideas for songs and he said, 'I walk around in crowds and I listen to what people are saying.'

> Mark Howard, engineer on *Oh Mercy*.

A lot of these guys who are in their fifties just don't bother with it anymore. It's not that they've lost their muse, it's [more] like, 'I don't wanna cut my grass anymore. I'm gonna hire some kid to come do it for me.' That explains a lot of what you hear on records today from people who've been doing it for a long time.

> Don Was, to Peter Doggett.

It's not for me to understand my songs. I don't need to understand
them . . . They make sense to me, but it's not like I can explain them.

Bob Dylan, to Denise Worrell, November 1985.

*

It was *Infidels* all over again. He had renewed his contract with Sony on
January 18th, 1988, even though he didn't have a great deal ready, and
then did nothing to fulfill it for a full fifteen months. At least he reined
back the label's expectations, committing to four albums in the next
five years, with the still-unreleased *Down In The Groove* 'deemed to have
been Delivered under the 1982 Agreement'.

Remarkably, the experience of sitting down 'twice a year . . . with
this smokey old gypsy who isn't remotely interested in releasing singles, shrivels up at the thought of going on the radio or TV, and only
ever approves pictures of himself in which his eyes are closed,'* had
not dissuaded Mr Moneybags himself, Walter Yetnikoff, from agreeing
terms; not that he was taking a huge risk given that Dylan's current
releases were cross-collateralized with his catalogue sales, which
remained – and would continue to be – buoyant.

The man mattered. But he was edging ever further from the mainstream, and he professed to care not a jot. As he subsequently told Alan
Jackson, 'The people I . . . still listen to were never fashionable . . .
Robert Johnson – how many records did he sell in his lifetime?' It was
certainly hard to imagine his latest song – the hypnotic 'Series Of
Dreams' – ever getting onto AM radio, or indeed AOR radio, as it self-
referenced the symphonies he was seeking to emulate in spirit:

> i was thinkin' of a series of dreams
> where the chambers vary the tones
> where boxcars rumble in statements
> and ladders are built out of bones
> wasn't makin' any connection
> between the ingoing and outgoing themes . . .

---

* The description comes from David Hepworth, obliged to pad out a non-interview
with Dylan from 1986 with his own mordant observations.

The ever-present rumbling in his head was once again coalescing into songs of stature. He was also writing in the first-person again. 'Most Of The Time' was as disarmingly confessional – three years after he insisted to Cameron Crowe, 'I don't write confessional songs' – as it was disaffected with love, or perhaps more specifically, a single love, 'Most of the time I can't (even) remember who she was/ If she was real or unreal, it doesn't matter, it never does.'

Which Another all this self-analysis re-examined he wasn't saying, but when he claimed, 'I can disarm the confused, I can tolerate pain/ I can help the abused & I hardly ever complain/ I can smile in the face of mankind,' at least no-one was about to shout, 'I don't believe you – you're a liar.' Always at his best when he appeared to be laying it on the line, this was an older, wiser populist poet, the same person who told Scott Cohen in 1985, 'If I'm talking to me in a song . . . [I] say, Alright, now I'm talking to you. It's up to [the listener] to figure out who's who.'

Another major song which he seems to have penned that winter, after a year renewing his pact with his audience, was 'Ring Them Bells', which reined in the admonishments but was still a clarion call to repent and confess while there was time: 'Ring those bells ye heathen, where the lone wolf calls/ Ring them from the sanctuaries with the trembling walls . . .' Probably also composed at this time was 'What Was It You Wanted?', which, he informed *SongTalk*'s Paul Zollo, was just 'another way of writing a song – just talking to somebody that ain't there . . . Then it just becomes a question of how heroic your speech is.' The poor recipient on the receiving end of this particular 'truth attack' might not have shared his point of view, but it was another fine song.

One song he worked on extensively would not appear until September 1990, in another quite distinct incarnation. It may have been one of those he meant when talking about 'want[ing] to write . . . songs [that are about] real things that have happened.' In the same January 1986 interview, he had also vented some real venom towards the medium which had saved his life as a teenager in Hibbing. Indeed, his comments to Toby Cresswell could almost be a precis of 'TV Talkin' Song', the song he started three years later:

There's a time to turn off the tube . . . With the way it's projected into society now, there's not much of a chance that you could get to do

that . . . In America, it's everywhere, it's invaded your home, it's in your
bed, it's in your closet . . . It's hard to stand outside of all that and remain
sane . . . If . . . it['s] destroying the fabric of our minds, then we just have
to [learn to] shut it off. . . . You can't meet it head-on, because it's [always]
there.

Nor was this an isolated example of him voicing an abiding mistrust
of the medium. In September 1987, he privately told Britta Lee Shain,
'The media is the devil, and it won't be long before all it'll take is one
charismatic leader to bring the whole world to its knees.' In public, on
camera the previous October, he warned all unmarried men *and*
women, 'Even if you do see [an incident] . . . on the news . . . [it] is
[just] a replica of anything that really has happened.' 'TV Talkin' Song'
sure feels like a man who once passed through Tempe, especially in its
original manifestation:

The man who invented it can't be blamed, he died and left it behind
How was he to know that it would go into the hands of those who want to
    control yr mind? . . .
Get in touch with your own life while you still have a chance
Don't let that thing penetrate your head under any circumstance . . .
Grown men & women with their hands between their legs
Just keep wanting more – just like a dog that begs.

The original ending makes the narrator as culpable as the mob who
hang the truth-teller, crossing 'Talkin' World War III Blues' with 'Black
Diamond Bay' as the song switches to first-person: 'About this [time] I
woke up, glad the dream was gone / I wiped the sleep out of my eyes
& turned my TV on.' It's all fish-in-barrel stuff, but Dylan's aim is
unerring. 'Tis hard to argue with the observation, 'If your face ain't up
on that screen, it's like you don't even count at all.' But anyone convinced they were seeing the real him at last should first pay heed to a
comment Larry Charles made after Dylan repeatedly ranted and riffed
about the real world during their collaboration on *Masked and Anonymous*: 'He will never say, "This is what I think." He will have something
and he will say it, and I will say "Wow, you really feel strongly about
that!" and he'll say, "Well, somebody does." '
What we don't know is if this was one of the songs Lanois heard

that winter 'on the piano, back at his place'. The fact that Daniel was summoned to the lion's den confirms a Dylan getting serious again. The last time he'd given a producer a sneak preview of impending work was *Infidels*. For now, Dylan seemed to feel he'd made the right choice – a fellow musician-producer. As he told Edna Gundersen later that year, 'It's very hard to find a producer that can play. A lot of them can't even engineer. They've just got a big title and know how to spend a lot of money . . . [But Lanois is] someone who knows my music inside out.'

He was less inclined to mention that, in an era when producers expected 'points' on any product they manhandled – an innovation for which his friend Debbie Gold was partly responsible – Lanois was offering, 'record companies [back then] a package deal . . . Pay me $150,000 and I'll deliver you a great record, no questions asked.' Apparently, he included U2. Fortunately for him, Dylan was a true artist and for now, he had no intention of looking back, or stopping accumulating songs.

The latest was a gem called 'Born In Time', and if this wasn't confessional, St Augustine was a hippo. It was one of three songs that winter written with someone in mind. He presumably meant in their 'style', not as a recipient,* since Marvin Gaye – the designated driver for 'What Was It [You Wanted]?' – was dead. Nor did he pass '[Series Of] Dreams' to Leonard Cohen, even after it turned out that he had no immediate use for it himself. But why, pray tell, was the name 'Clydie King' written next to 'Born In Time'? Was she the song's succubus, ghostly presence or voiceover? Or even its original subject-matter?:

> a pretty face . . . a pretty cloud
> like the prince of peace, like a face in the crowd
> like a kansas wind, like a palace of sin, like a texas twister
> behind what flame . . . behind what fire . . .

If so, the song would become about two loves, a lost love and a new love, to whom Dylan sings, 'Open up your eyes and see/ That the only

---

* He later named certain *Time Out of Mind* variants after favourite singers: 'Little Walter' for 'Million Miles'; 'Charley Patton' for 'Till I Fell In Love With You'; 'Howlin' Wolf' for 'Mississippi'.

one for you is me', as he reworked it in the fortnight between a surprise guest appearance at an L.A. Forum Grateful Dead show on February 12th – six days after the atrocity exhibition that is *Dylan & The Dead* was released – and arriving in N'Orleans to begin work on his own confessional jazzfest.

A new muse entered his life that night at the Forum, after a mysterious package arrived backstage with a business card, a covering letter explaining how this lady came to meet a mutual friend who passed along the package, and a copy of a Dylan fanzine, of all things, *Look Back* #14. The US-based zine contained a review of the recent stage musical, *Dylan: Words & Music* by the lady in question, Sylvia Tribelhorn – known to one and all as 'Cooky'. More importantly, it contained a photo of a radiant Cooky, standing with the show's 'Dylan', Bob Miles. The following day, a messenger arrived at Cooky's L.A. hotel room, inviting her to a party at Point Dume the next afternoon.

She was nervous as heck, and when the guests started to depart, and he hadn't even said a word to her, her resolve to remain wavered further as she told her cheerleader, 'I don't think he even knows I'm here.' 'Oh, *he* knows you're here all right.' Finally, he approached, 'I see you made it. How ya doin'? Well?' Nerves got the better of Cooky, 'Well, what? Is this where I'm supposed to say how you're different up close in person?' 'Yeah.' 'Well, your ears are bigger than I thought.' 'So, we're going to be honest, are we?' Dylan was enjoying the drift of their conversation and as the other guests began to drift away, he invited her upstairs.

The following morning, she woke up, the room was bare. She hurried down the stairs to find Dylan sat at the table reading the newspaper, with a cup of coffee and one more cigarette for the road. He hoped it was okay with her, but they were all going down Highway One to Malibu for breakfast in the colony of the beautiful people. He signed for the check, and that was that, until about a week later, when Cooky's home and office in Phoenix, Arizona began to be plagued with silent, hang-up calls.

On one of these late-night occasions, she caught the phone in time to berate the silent suitor, 'Okay, don't talk. I'll just sit here and hang on as long as you do. I'm in no hurry. I can wait all night.' Finally, he spoke, pumping her for information about herself, her work, her family, her *marriage* and finally, if she ever got to L.A. It was the start of multiple visits to the coast on her part, and occasional visits to Arizona on his.

Perhaps this time he had bitten off more than he could chew. Sure, Cooky was a sexy, leather-jacketed rock'n'roll chick, with a ready wit and a rapier-like turn of phrase, who could more than hold her own in conversation. But she was also – as he well knew – a bona fide Bobcat, with a foot in both camps of the Dylan fan base; a married woman (as in 'Don't Want No . . .'), and a practicing Catholic. Three strikes, surely. Not this time.

Dylan was smitten. Even as he was packing his bags to leave for New Orleans, he was making plans for another rendezvous. And soon. But now was the time to get down to business, and when he got to the Crescent City, he was delighted to discover Lanois had everything syncopated for the sessions ahead. Hell, maybe they'd even be finished by the time of Cooky's birthday, in two weeks' time:

> **Daniel Lanois**: We found an empty turn of the century apartment building – a five-storey building, a fantastic place . . . it had a bordello-ish overtone. We essentially turned the control room into a swamp . . . we had moss all over the place and stuffed animals and alligator heads . . . [] . . . The *Oh Mercy* studio was essentially a kitchen. Bob and I sat like two guys on a porch. He played on my 1952 butterscotch Telecaster that I plugged into an early Sixties Fender Concert amp tucked around the corner, five feet from Bob, with moving blankets around the mike to avoid vocal spill . . . That was the rig: we never changed it. My red Peavey bass from Mississippi was plugged in D.I. [direct input], and at the end of the night if we had a take, I would overdub the bass part . . . If we needed a drummer, I'd call in Willie Green, drummer for the Nevilles.

Alienated by his experiences on *Infidels* and *Empire Burlesque*, Dylan wouldn't wear headphones. Instead, as assistant engineer Mark Howard recalls, 'I had to have a set of stereo speakers in front of him.' Neither Howard, nor the other engineer, Malcolm Burn, were quite sure what to expect, especially as, the latter remembers, 'A week before we were due to start recording, we received a cassette from Bob . . . It had this little note from Bob: "Listen to this, this'll give you a good idea of what's going on." . . . We put it in the machine – and this Al Jolson music started playing.'

Welcome to the world of Dylan. He followed it up on his arrival by almost immediately telling Burn, 'Y'know, I really love the way my vocals sound when you record them on a boom-box, that little microphone.' He meant, of course, the condenser mike which overloaded at the slightest provocation and distorted like the Devil. Determined to be obliging, Burn insists, 'We actually tried recording with a boombox . . . He really pushed us so hard to get this really great vocal sound.' Already, he sensed humouring Bob would be a large part of his job. What he hadn't expected was the lack of interaction between Dylan and the other musicians, save when tape was rolling:

> While we're working, he never really spoke to the other musicians we had assembled. He'd speak to the people he knew . . . but he wasn't really interested in making buddies with anyone. And he always wore this hoodie . . . For the first two or three days while we were recording, we had the Neville Brothers' rhythm section there . . . And then the bass player, Tony, comes in and . . . he didn't know this was Bob sitting here. And he says, 'Man, that Bob Dylan is some weird motherfucker, man.' Bob just sorta looked up and raised his eyebrow, and then [just] went back to working on his lyrics . . . Every night he would come in with a rolled-up bundle of paper, wrapped up with a rubber band, [the] lyrics that he was in the process of working on.

One attendant muso, guitarist Mason Ruffner, whose highly respectable CV included everyone from Ringo Starr to John Lee Hooker, just thought he had a bad case of nerves: 'Before Dylan realized he had a record there, I think he was aggravated, maybe even a little nervous about the outcome of this project . . . Sometimes he'd argue with Lanois . . . just for the sake of arguing.' Perhaps he just wanted more give and take from the producer, who in that first fortnight seemed a tad intimidated. Thus, when Dylan asked him if he preferred 'Most Of The Time' on the piano or guitar, Daniel replied, 'I'm just a sucker for [piano]. I like [this] too, but I just don't know how to arrive at it' – about as useful as tits on a hog.

According to Burn, '[Even] when we were working on something like "Most of The Time", he'd be finishing the lyrics . . . One night, we were going to do "Most of The Time" and he sat down with his guitar . . . and he said, "Well, we could do it like this," – and he played the entire song, just . . . guitar and harmonica, the archetypal Bob Dylan thing, [and said,] '"That would be like a typical Bob Dylan way of doing it,"' before promptly reverting to piano.

Here was a song – one of many that year – where the lyrics never stood still. On the 'guitar' version he recorded on the 12th, he suddenly inserted the couplet, 'I can follow the path, I don't ask where it goes/ I can stay right with it, I don't even have to change my clothes,' absent from the fair copy he had made – and dated! – two days earlier, giving it the ironic title, 'May You Rest In Peace'. In this version, he had boasted of his prodigious memory, an admission he would not have made a decade later: 'I can rise to the occasion and not have a regret/ I can remember anything someone else might forget.'

At least there was never any doubt he was gonna include this song. At the bottom of a draft for 'Disease Of Conceit', dating from his time in N'Orleans, was the first of a googol of provisional sequences. It included no less than four songs which would not make the final cut:

What Good [Am I?]	?????
God Knows	Shooting Star
Dignity	TV Song
Political [World]	Most of [The] Time
Born [In Time]	Ring [Them] Bells

Said sequence also gives the lie to another unreliable part of his *Chronicles* account of these sessions – the last-minute composition of 'Shooting Star'. He'd apparently 'gotten back to New Orleans with a clear head. I'd finish up what I started with Lanois, [I'd] even write him a couple of songs I never would have written otherwise. One was . . . "Shooting Star." . . . I could vaguely hear it in my mind . . . I thought it might be something Lanois was looking for.' In fact, he recorded the song on the 14th, *before* he left town for a five-day break, and six days after the aforementioned 'Disease Of Conceit', having commenced recording on February 28th with a demo version of 'Born In Time' and a long instrumental called 'Rumble'. *

They were just testing, testing, testing, not starting in earnest until

---

* This version of 'Rumble' was one of three instrumentals preserved on the *Oh Mercy* multis.

'The farm was really where he got back up on his feet again.'
With the children, summer 1977.

Faridi, snapped by the man in him.

Miming to 'When The Night Comes Falling' like he means it, August 1985.

Trying to remember how it goes, with Dave Stewart & Mike Campbell, August 1985.

Dylan at Farm Aid, September 1985, all guns blazing.

I stare in
Wonder at
Mona Lisa
And I ask
My self
"Is she
Smiling
At
Yardbird?"

Dylan

The LINE it is drawn the curse it is cast
The slowest now will later be fast
As the present now will later be past
The order is rapidly fadin
An the first now will later be last
For the times they are a changin

me
Bob
Dylan

Dear Mr.Dylan,

    I've been trying to contact you personally but have
failed miserably.Roy Guest suggested I write to,you straight.The reason
I'm writing is that the students here at Cambridge want to know something
about your songs,rather than just about your private life-that's all we've
got out of the national papers.Could you just take a moment off to answer
these questions?

    Does it usually take you a long time to write your songs?Are you sudd-
enly seized with inspiration or do you have to sit down for hours and work
at them? songs come in ideas/ people good bad indifferent, situations
anything / takes me short time to write it out)
usually changes somewhat constantly

    You're quoted as saying,"I can't listen to my old songs any more?Why
not? old songs tend to be motivated by private desires

Very truly yours,

CBS RECORDS, A Division of Columbia
Broadcasting System, Inc.

By Clive Davis
Sr Vice President and General Manager

CBS RECORDS, A Division of
CBS Inc.

By Walter Yetnikoff
Bob Dylan
Bob Dylan

ACCEPTED & AGREED TO:

Bob Dylan
BOB DYLAN

leaving town for
Francisco, will call you
from up there — love
Bob

BD sequence MAY 2 1989

A DATE
N.R.   ☐ YES ☐ NO

B DATE
N.R.   ☐ YES ☐ NO

POLITICAL WORLD
WHAT WAS IT YOU WANTED
RING THEM BELLS
MOST OF THE TIME
EVERY THING BROKEN
- LONG PAUSE -
MAN WOMAN in the long BLACK COAT
DISEASE OF CONCEIT
BORN IN TIME
WHAT GOOD AM I
SHOOTING STAR

The shape-shifting penman with a series of messages, 1960–89.

A contingency of assholes: Cooky, Shasta, Bev, Glen and CH, June 1990.

Cooky and I, October 1992.

With Debbie Gold, good as she's been to him, 1992.

Tweeter and the Monkey Man, sharing a joke, 1996.

A rough and rowdy gunfighter in San Antonio, 2022.

four days later. Between the 4th and the 14th March, Dylan realized
eleven songs,* the bulk of the album and the majority of A-list material
he had written in the last eighteen months, suggesting the sessions
were going well. All of which rather contradicts assistant engineer
Mark Howard's recent claim, 'It was slightly uncomfortable for the
first two weeks. Dylan was being a bit snotty . . . There came this one
point when Dan finally really lost it with him . . . it became – not a yell-
ing match, but it became uncomfortable in the studio . . . Dan was
trying to get something out of Bob and he wasn't responding. Dan . . .
kinda put him in his place.' Sounds haile unlikely. It just took Lanois a
while to stop treating him with kid gloves, and start to box clever.

Malcolm Burn, the main engineer, had his own explanation for
Dylan's 'unsociable' behaviour: 'He's really focused. Most people
spend a lot of time yapping and gabbing and bullshitting around,
but . . . those seven or eight hours [each day] were full-on . . . I remember thinking, yeah, this is why certain people achieve what they do . . .
They don't waste time.' Lanois concurred: 'Bob was . . . one of the
most focused people I've ever worked with. I had a little coffee machine
that he would wander up to, as he stood touching up his lyrics.'

A good way to gauge Dylan's mood, even in 1989, was to note how
often he broke into a cover version mid-session. If it was delivered in a
perfunctory way, he was just killing time, singing while he slaved. If he
went for it, he was in the mood. Well, in those first ten days, Dylan
broke into impassioned versions of 'You Don't Know Me', 'I Heard
That Lonesome Whistle', 'Confidential To Me' and a 'Some Enchanted
Evening' I'd trade for all three so-called 'Sinatra' albums. All revealed a
man focused on the prize, but still riveted to his roots. The best of the
lot was a 'We Three' (a.k.a. The Inkspots' 'My Echo, My Shadow And
Me') on the 14th that was cut complete twice and pulled to master,
where it was misleadingly logged as 'Three Of Us', creating another
'lost' track for the next Dylan rumourography.

Also recorded that day was 'I'm In the Mood For Love', and indeed

---

* The eleven tracks are as follows: Born In Time/ Ring Them Bells/ What Good Am
I?/ Series Of Dreams/ Political World/ Dignity/ Disease Of Conceit/ God Knows/
Most Of The Time/ Broken Days/ Shooting Star, in that order. Krogsgaard's *Oh
Mercy* sessionography has the wrong dates, the wrong take numbers and the wrong
songs, but is otherwise an exemplary piece of research. All the reference DATs and the
multis reside in Tulsa.

he was. At the end of the session, Dylan simply took off for a mini-break at a golf-resort in Carefree, Arizona, where he was ostensibly due to rendezvous with Jerry Garcia and Dead lyricist Robert Hunter 'for some kind of sound mixing and fermenting' at the Phantom Studios in Mesa. He would be back in a few days. How much of the Garcia/Hunter meet-up was a smokescreen is unclear (boom, boom), but Dylan spent most of his time with Cooky, trying to read her fortune. She later relayed the details of these intense discussion/s to her constant confidant, Bev, who duly noted:*

> They shared examples of their mutual ardent attachments to children, animals, motor vehicles and independence. She eyed his constant scribbling of notes to himself, fascinated by how they ranged from the mundane and practical, like invest in x, or call y, to snatches of reeling rhyme. She measured whether his alcohol intake seemed controlled, and how at least in front of her, he never shared the cocaine his friends proffered around . . . They mapped out certain parameters, like when and how he could or shouldn't call her, [and he told her,] 'The secrecy is for your sake not mine. I've got nothin' to lose. I'll never deliberately hurt you. I'm not enemies with any of the women I've known. Just don't put me on the spot or take me by surprise.'

Perhaps these conversations informed some rewrites on a song he finally got around to completing on his first day back, the 21st, 'What Was It You Wanted?' The arrangement took a little work, Dylan confiding to Lanois, 'I'm having trouble telling whatever it is.' All Lanois could offer was, 'It never gets specific.'

Maybe they needed to try something different. For the rest of the day's session and the next, Lanois drafted in a local band, Rocking

---

* Bev kept notebooks documenting all her conversations with Cooky, from which she eventually penned an 80,000-word memoir of Cooky et al., including verbatim exchanges with Dylan. This has kindly been made available to me. In a 2021 communiqué with the author, Bev gave more details about this trip after checking her notebooks, 'He'd called to tell her he'd be there and to come to the Boulders Resort Hotel. He had a "retinue" of about a dozen people with him. One of them was problematic and worried her because he recognised her. The guy owned a music store in Phoenix and also rented equipment. They were all working on something in Phantom Studios.'

Dopsie, whom he had seen playing at a local club, The Maple Leaf. According to Howard, the collective 'we thought . . . [they] would work great on a couple of tracks, so we got them in. They had this really amazing saxophone player, Johnny Hart, who was blind . . . They're playing – and Dylan, right in front of them . . . goes, "Where'd you *get* these guys from?" ' It took Lanois to belatedly realize 'Dopsie could play only in two keys, D or G. The button accordion is a great but limited instrument.' The collaboration yielded just two potential album cuts from a day and a half, 'Where Teardrops Fall' (recut a week later) and 'Dignity', which Dylan had already spent a session and a half working on.

'Dignity' was proving to be 'Foot Of Pride' revisited. As Dylan later wrote, 'It was a strange bull we were riding. [Dopsie] and his band never lost their composure, though. . . . I couldn't figure out why we weren't getting it. You work hours on something and you get dizzy. After a while you lose your judgment. At about three in the morning, we had played ourselves out and just started playing any old stuff: "Jambalaya," "Cheatin' Heart," "There Stands the Glass." ' No such 'country' jam session exists, even on the reference DATs that were running continuously. They did jam, though, doing a better job on 'Stealin'' than the Dead, and attempting to recut 'Congratulations', unsuccessfully.

Dylan was clearly frustrated by his failure to capture 'Dignity'. He knew he had another breakthrough song, but it refused to reveal itself. He was still searching high and low on the 23rd, even as the version cut ten days earlier, pre-break, was pulled to master. The 23rd also saw him tackle 'TV Talkin' Song' (at the end of which, he opined, 'Yeah, that might be interesting,' before promptly forgetting all about it) and 'Series Of Dreams', two other majestic musical works he didn't feel he could quite get a handle on.

Contrary to Howard's not-so-total recall, the second set of sessions were not proceeding as smoothly as the first. When Dylan attempted a new song, 'Don't Be Deceived' – 'That's not a lesson that you're learning/ That's just the wheel of fortune turning . . .' – on the 29th, he pulled up short, telling Lanois, 'I'll finish the lyrics on it if I can.' He never did. Instead, he returned to two songs already secured – 'Broken Days' and 'Ring Them Bells' – both of which would ultimately make the album in pre-Arizona incarnations.

In the case of 'Ring Them Bells', he now added musicians when he should have been subtracting them, the best version being recorded solo at the piano on the 6th. He was also now changing lyrics for the sake of it, a worrying presentiment: 'Ring them from the sanctuaries 'cross the pages of time/ For the book is wide and the world is on its side/ And time is running backwards for one more ride,' were lines best left well alone.*

He also convinced himself 'Broken Days' needed work, after one of the musicians suggested 'it needs to resolve itself at the end'. He'd already done a Hollywood-style rewrite, intending at this stage for the final line to go, 'Everything is broken/ And it can't be fixed.' He tells the session-man, 'It's hard to say whether it's gonna succeed.' The experience reminded him there was no success like failure. The one from the 13th got the vote even as he carried on regardless, trying songs already cut every which way:

> **Mason Ruffner**: Seems like we were cutting these songs all kinds of ways. Rock groove, slow groove, a funk or folk kind of groove, just try-ing different grooves and different tempos to this stuff. He didn't say much about what he was after . . . It just seemed like it was all a big experiment, try the song twenty different ways . . . I guess he'd probably just doodled with these songs on the guitar or piano, and now that he was trying them with a band, it was up for us to try and create then, try different ways, and latch into one that he'd like.

Howard had convinced himself that because Dylan 'writes on a typewriter . . . he has no idea where these songs lie, in what key they live in, what tempo . . . Musically, there's no chords written . . . he just finds where it sounds best.' Actually, doing a song multiple ways had nothing to do with the absence of a tune in his head. It was simply him trying to latch onto the unique key that gave a song life. Again, Burn read it right:

> It occurred to me that the treatment of the song was secondary . . . He wasn't really precious about that aspect of it. The only thing that made

---

* Three versions of 'Ring Them Bells' were pulled to master, reflecting his uncer-tainty. 'Man In The Long Black Coat' and 'Where Teardrops Fall' had two takes pulled to master. The other eleven songs were all single takes.

any real difference to him was whether what he was saying was in place . . . He . . . doesn't care if the bass player sounds great, he's only interested in the songs.

Inevitably, the process itself had now begun to wear on his nerves, and this time words *were* exchanged, Lanois recalling, 'There came a time . . . when I felt he fell into old habits – He'd say, "Get somebody else to play on it," or, "Just hire somebody," when really he should have been playing the parts. And I made it clear to him that we weren't going to fly anybody in.' Dylan later acknowledged the ticking off he received to Edna Gundersen, complimenting Daniel for constantly prodding him, 'You can do better than that, you can surpass *that*.'

Sometimes he needed such cajoling. But he also needed to know when to stop recording more material, something he didn't accept until March 31st. The tape of this session includes a song called 'You Must Be Someone Important', after which Dylan suggests, 'Just put out another one after [this album]. 'Cause we could just go on like this forever. In another month you could see another two extra songs, maybe four, and what we gonna do with all the stuff we do, y'know?'

He had finally realized he had too much for one album, and was slowly opening himself up to the idea of a sequel of sorts – the album that would become *under the red sky* – even if he promptly inserted one last song of the wet-ink variety. It was born on the bayou and he was resolutely determined to record it. Lanois claims it was captured immediately:

Bob likes to get something quickly, if possible, in the name of spontaneity. On [*Oh Mercy,*] . . . some things came quick and we grabbed them that way. [But] then we spent a lot of time on detail. Some of the vocals we worked on quite a bit, and the lyrics were changed and we chipped away at them . . . [But] 'Man in a Long Black Coat' was written in the studio, and recorded in one take.

If Dylan rather gives the impression that the song came to him fully formed, and Lanois has him writing it 'in the studio', the various manuscript versions suggest otherwise. 'People don't live or die, they just are/ If you get beyond that, you've gone a little too far,' was just one couplet he replaced with something inferior (float/coat). The preacher's sermon was also more fire'n'brimstone originally: 'The preacher is talking, he says man is enslaved/ The conscience is evil, life is depraved/ How can it guide you – the servant of sin . . .' As for the *daemon lover* aspect in the song – and it could be considered a version of Child Ballad 243 from the house carpenter's point of view – it is more pronounced in its original second verse: 'He came in the morning, 'bout a half-past five/ Someone said he looked more dead than alive.'

If the song was composed by a man left lonely, its recording was a collective effort, beginning on the 28th with various band versions, even as Dylan finished up the lyrics. Ruffner recalled, 'He was always making changes and additions and subtractions as he went.' Burn remembers that in those early versions, 'he was singing it maybe an octave higher. And it didn't sound very good . . . Someone recognized it wasn't really working, and suggested singing it an octave lower, and . . . and suddenly the phrasing came and I was like, "Fuck, this is really good."' By then, Burn had surrendered the console to Howard, who credits his fellow engineer with the idea of 'playing [a tape loop of] these crickets – it made it really haunting'. The result was probably the most powerful track on the album.*

The congenital tampering first manifest on *Infidels* would continue long after the other musicians got their AFM cheques. For starters, Dylan was determined to keep chipping away at lyrics *after* he'd recorded them; sometimes going for a spin on a 1966 Harley Davidson that Howard had found for him: 'He'd go for a ride and think about what was going on.' The tunnel he'd disappeared down in post-production on *Infidels* loomed into view again. He would keep going, redoing vocals and reworking lyrics until he found the man in him:

Malcolm Burn: If he was fixing a vocal part . . . it was never about whether it was in tune or out of tune or anything like that. . . . He'd sing it and you'd try to mix it into the original track, he'd listen to it and he'd say, 'Ah, nah, nah, nah. That's not the guy.' And I'd say, 'The guy?' And he'd say, 'Yeah. It's not the same guy.'

---

* Dylan still hedged his bets, pulling a band version to master, too.

For a fortnight in April he worked on the vocals,* and when he wasn't working on the vocals, he was working on the lyrics, impressing even Howard: 'I've never seen anybody work so hard on lyrics in my life. He'll . . . take the last line of the song and put it in the first part of the song . . . [so] you can't figure out what it is he's talking about right away . . . From the time he walks in till the time he leaves, he's totally focused . . . He'd have a piece of paper that had words every which way you can think of – upside down, sideways. If you looked at the paper . . . it didn't make any sense to you, 'cause it [was] just words on paper.' At a certain point, though, the process itself had taken him over, as if afraid to let go of the album.

A fear of completion in middle-age had begun to consume him. As Burn notes, 'Even when we were mixing the record, I'd be in the middle of the mix and he'd suddenly say, "Y'know what, I've just rewritten that line, can I re-sing it?" ' Mr Single Take was no more. He was now using the multitrack technology he had long berated on almost everything. In the end, very little remained from a month's worth of live singing, his true forte. Of the thirteen originals pulled to master – the ten album tracks, plus 'God Knows', 'Born In Time' and 'Dignity' – just two retained their live vocals: 'Ring Them Bells', which needed no post-production, and 'Disease Of Conceit', which just needed scrapping. Perversely, one original that didn't make those 'master' reels, though it got a test edit on the 17th, was 'Series Of Dreams'. By then, Dylan was working on a series of sequences, in which 'Series Of Dreams' would play no part.† Dylan even offered some sort of explanation to a baffled engineer – just not one that washed, or held water:

Malcolm Burn: The one song that didn't end up on that record, that Dan and I were really pushing for, was 'Series Of Dreams'. . . . We were standing in the courtyard of this house in New Orleans where we recorded, and Bob said, 'Y'know what, I only put ten songs on my

---

* Vocal overdubs dating from April 1st-3rd, 6th-8th, 10th-12th, 15th-16th are indicated on multis, along with instrumental overdubs.
† What appears to be Lanois's preferred sequence included both 'Series Of Dreams' and 'Born In Time', but at the expense of two equally great songs, 'Shooting Star' and 'Most Of The Time'.

records.' . . . Finally, he said, 'Look, I don't think the lyrics are finished, I'm not happy with them. The song's too long. But I don't wanna cut out any of the lyrics.'

Also destined for the chop was 'Dignity', though two vocal overdubs on April 11th confirm a continuing interest in the song. Having recorded a set of original songs which gave him even better options than *Infidels*, he had already jettisoned two. Also falling out of favour was the exquisite 'When We Were Born In Time' (to give it its full title). After he redid vocals on the 7th and 13th, he used 'Where Teardrops Fall' – and the Dopsie version at that – instead.* It was almost like he didn't want to release the song with the more personal relevance. Yet there it is on Dylan's own May 2nd sequence, written on the cassette inlay card in his own hand:

Political World/ What Was It You Wanted?/ Ring Them Bells/ Most Of The Time/ Everything's Broken/ Man In The Long Black Coat/ Disease Of Conceit/ Born In Time/ What Good Am I?/ Shooting Star.

He was still sequencing a month later. In the same year as two of his near-peers, Neil Young and Lou Reed, both put out really strong albums, *Freedom* and *New York*, that were over fifty-five minutes long – recognising that the majority of listeners now listened to such artifacts on CD as one sustained listening experience[†] – Dylan was firmly stuck in the vinyl era. He never even countenanced the idea of a thirteen-song album. He even trimmed the album opener, 'Political World', down from five minutes to 3.47, losing perhaps the most telling insight into his worldview:

> We live in a political world
> Everything's a little bit strange
> Prayers are prayed, orders are obeyed,
> Though everything is subject to change.

---

* Vocal overdubs occupied both the 3rd and the 8th, the latter being annotated, 'New words'.
[†] Lou Reed even provided instructions for the listener, 'It's meant to be listened to in one 58-minute sitting.'

One person he did not use as a sounding board when it came to sequencing the album, or even choosing the songs, was Cooky, even though she certainly knew the breadth and span of his work better than anyone who worked on *Oh Mercy*. Instead, they spent quality time together at various interludes, even as post-production again lasted longer than the recording. Perhaps it was enough that he dedicated the album to her and her kind – 'This is for you, you who still hasn't paid for it with your soul – for those who still have the courage to understand' – only to then change his mind.

When he finally said farewell to Lanois's New Orleans kitchen for good, engineer Burn imagined, 'He got on the tour bus, and he was gone, back on the endless tour.' In fact, he was heading west to see Cooky, briefly. Tour rehearsals could wait, though not for long.

He still wasn't quite sure he could read her, or trust her. On one occasion she teased him, after clipping off locks of his famous hair, 'I'm going to keep it for a voodoo doll in case I need to get back at you. Or maybe I'll send some in for DNA testing to find out what drugs you're taking.' He responded, a little uneasily, 'I'm never sure when you're serious or not.' And nor was he. He was certainly infatuated, placating her yen for souvenirs by letting her have the shirt off his back, as they did the rhumba in the back seat of one of his many cars: 'Let me have your shirt . . . No, don't take off your tank. I mean that blue silk one up in the back window.' 'Oh sure, take the new expensive one.'

The Never Ending Tour was heading for Europe, opening the year's proceedings in a park ostensibly near Malmo, on May 27th, where he played just one song from the recent sessions, which happened to be Eddy Arnold's 'You Don't Know Me'.

Once again, Fifties covers were in favour. Dylan also gave Johnny Cash's 'Give My Love To Rose' an outing on the outskirts of Malmo, but not 'Mystery Train', 'I Heard That Lonesome Whistle', 'Poison Ivy', 'High School Confidential', 'Mountain Of Love', 'Ring Of Fire', 'Love's Made A Fool Of You', 'Not Fade Away', 'Peace In The Valley' or 'Lonesome Town', all songs rehearsed at Montana days earlier.

Not everyone in the band enjoyed the experience. Bassist Aaronson told me, 'Second time around . . . he was pulling out tunes that I'd never heard, and I was having a hard time there . . . [And] he was a lot more distant . . . He hardly said a word, or even hardly looked at me at all for [the] two, three weeks I rehearsed with him in '89.' Ray Price's 'Hey La La', plus 'Confidential To Me', 'Lonesome Town' and 'Congratulations' were all thrown at him (and audiences) in the ten days before he went down to St James Infirmary.

Aaronson had discovered at the last minute he needed a minor operation in the middle of the European tour and though Dylan assured him, 'If you ever get better, you can come back and get your gig. This is your gig,' when he turned up at a US show in July, ready for duty, Dylan blew him off ('He actually said to me, "I don't give a shit who plays bass." ') His replacement, Tony Garnier, no Danko or Stoner, still plays with Dylan in 2023. It seemed a low blow, and the 'G.E.' band was never quite the same. That ballsy, gung-ho trio said farewell on June 8th, 1989 at Wembley Arena. A further wedge was driven between Bob and the band in early July at the start of a two-month US tour of the picnic circuit. Maymudes had convinced Dylan he should get his own tour bus:

> It didn't make much sense to me that Bob was still travelling in the band bus with no actual bed. No privacy. No place to write. I told Bob I'd look into it. I researched it and found out where . . . guys like Willie Nelson . . . were buying their personal buses . . . The very first time I showed the trailer to Bob, he was on the start of a West Coast tour . . . and [I] heard Bob yell at me from across the parking lot . . . 'This is not what I wanted! You're an asshole for wasting my money.' On and on, Bob just hammered [on at] me on the trailer . . . He felt bringing his own bus on tour was premature. He was worried about alienating the band, with whom he had shared a bus up until this point. But . . . he agreed to a ten-day trial period at my request . . . Carolyn Dennis, Bob's second wife, and their three-year old daughter, Desiree Dylan, arrived on Saturday, 8th July . . . Bob seemed very happy and comfortable with his family travelling together; it would have been a much different dynamic on the band bus.

Once again, after complaining, Dylan acquiesced. The days of pit stops at junkyards with a bemused band lagging behind were fast receding, even if it sure made it easier for all those female cousins to share a berth. Cooky, though, was not one of them. She was far too familiar to the crew, especially César Díaz, who was passing her board tapes, a firing offence if Dylan had ever found out. She it was, though, who was waiting for him after the September 10th Hollywood Greek Theatre show. Though a month respite from the road lay ahead, she found him 'in a swearing rant against media people planting stories in the press, while at the same time responding to their complaints about his deteriorating voice by [stopping] smoking'.

What was really annoying him was the failure of Sony to get behind his best album in a decade, whatever its largely self-inflicted shortcomings. As he bemoaned to Gundersen, 'It's discouraging when you ask the vice-president of your record company why he hasn't sold more of your records and he says, "Well, the title isn't all that great." ' For once, it was a piece of work he could believe in.

At least Cooky was blown away, listening to the album while driving around Phoenix until, overcome by its intermittent greatness, she pulled over to a phone booth and called its creator. She needed to see him. He told her getting away right then was impossible. But then, there he was, checked into the Crescent Motel. It was the first personal demand she had made on him, and the swiftness of his response took her by surprise. When she queried his prompt appearance, he responded, 'Did you ask me to come? Okay, I'm here.' It gave him a chance to press her into joining him in New York in October for what would be a momentous four-night residency at the Beacon Theater, the unveiling of *Oh Mercy* live.

When she agreed, he assiduously avoided looking at her throughout, later claiming it was because seeing her bothered his concentration. But he generously paid for her hotel room, and as such inadvertently paid for the late-night pizzas of the 'contingency of assholes', as he christened the retinue of fellow Bobcats that provided cover for the married Cooky's sorties. These included four young tykes who followed him and Victor into a bar near the Beacon pre-show in search of some Dutch courage, only for them to hear these fans loudly discuss their favourite Dylan shows of yore, after Maymudes had warned them not to approach the inconspicuous individual, sat in a dimly-lit

Upper West Side bar on a humid October night with a hood over his head.*

So, imagine his annoyance when all four were sat centerstage, row AA, as he opened the first Beacon show with a medley of Eighties' greatest hits: 'Seeing The Real You At Last', a live debut for 'What Good Am I?' and 'Dead Man, Dead Man', every one a winner, before unveiling a nine-minute 'Rank Strangers' with four harmonica breaks (one of them in the right key), as well as 'Everything Is Broken' and 'Most Of The Time' from his first album of original songs in four years, into the set of a man determined to get back to the future.

Meanwhile, Cooky and her friend Bev racked up an impressive bill at the Hilton. Finally, on the Saturday after the final New York show – made extra special when 'Man In The Long Black Coat' was unveiled, before he jumped into the audience during 'Leopard-Skin Pill-Box Hat' and exited the theatre – Dylan phoned her room, wanting to know where she'd been. She told him about bar-hopping with 'the guys'. A jealous guy, he took her to Macy's, where they strolled around unnoticed. After perusing the jewelry department, they retreated to his Village townhouse, where he asked her to 'gimme your arm', over which he dangled a dainty little gold bracelet. 'I thought you didn't give gifts.' 'You shouldn't believe all those stories you hear about me.' Especially those that came from the contingency.

Not even the c. of a. came up with anything like the next jape the tour crew and band played on their paymaster. Also not in on the gag was Maymudes – always an outsider – who was stunned when, at the second Sunrise show on November 13th, 'a girl from the audience got up on stage and started to strip. Bob let her do her thing to the cheers of the audience.' In fact, the band – closet fans of The Stranglers – had secretly hired a professional stripper to jump on stage as Dylan was performing his first acoustic 'Tangled Up In Blue' in five years, a most apposite choice.

If 'Tangled Up In Blue' had gone back to acoustic, 'Don't Think Twice' went electric in Ann Arbor, as did the traditional 'When First

---

* Even the road-crew thought Dylan's casual wear a tad odd. So much so that in Chicago on Halloween, they all wandered around the venue in identical navy sweatshirts, with hoods raised.

Unto This Country' in Norfolk, as Dylan put the set-list in the blender to accommodate three or more (permed from six) *Oh Mercy* songs. A live debut for 'To Be Alone With You' in Philadelphia proved the *Nashville Skyline* voice wasn't the result of him giving up smoking, as he had just done again. He was singing his heart out, and that was all that mattered, pushing the new album across all twenty-seven shows, as he largely stuck to the eastern seaboard. At the end of it all, *Oh Mercy* was stuck at thirty in the US charts, faring far better overseas without the benefit of shows, making him wonder why he bothered.

As year-end approached, and Bob and Cooky met up in Minneapolis, his mood swung to the dark side again as, 'angry, depressed, and drunk, he vented his spleen in language she'd never repeat over the ineptitude of the record company marketing department, their not correctly promoting *Oh Mercy* and its lack of sales'. The one time she was hoping for reassurance that he felt the journey was worth it, he set her straight, 'If I didn't think it was worth it, I wouldn't have come,' as he again warned her about his low tolerance for *her* issues, 'The day you say it isn't worth all the complications and risk will be the last you see me.'

Cooky also found herself obliged to defend her fellow fans from Dylan's wrath at the news that manuscripts of his from 1963-65 – the so-called Margolis & Moss ms. – were being privately sold. He insisted they must have been stolen from Grossman's house. He'd heard there were markings in the margins and penciled changes in different colored ink and insisted he never did that; that he never made extensive corrections or changes in the margins. He had convinced himself other people had altered his work.

Turning on Cooky, he wanted to know which of 'her crowd' was behind this and made various threats as to what he'd do to them when he found out their identity. When she said, 'I don't know who it could be,' he exploded, 'Well, why the *fuck* not?' It was the first time she had seen the man who wanted to know 'who threw the fucking glass'. Handy dandy was throwing a paddy. Thankfully, after she sent him copies of the largely innocuous (if historically important) material, his fury abated as instantly as it had arisen, and his mood improved, even as he continued pushing her to come with him to Rio and/or London in the new year, as if he'd forgot he was carrying on with a married woman, with a small business and a teenage daughter to consider.

He continued brooding about the sub-par sales of his best (and best-sounding) album in a decade, not knowing that at forty-nine he had just made his last album where the masterpieces would outnumber filler two to one. He would take one more shot in the dark before turning fifty. The good news? He had finally had enough of trying to make his peace with the synthetic sounds of the Eighties. He was going to make a rock album, taking the sound of the stage into the studio so we could again see the real him.

5.7

January 1990 to August 1994:
The Contingency Of Assholes

There were times when we offered suggestions that were based more on preconceptions about the legend than what was right for the moment. But that doesn't mean that Bob actually *listened* to those suggestions.

Don Was, to Rob Hughes.

I started to develop this unified field theory, that if something was too beautiful, if it looked like it was trying to please, then it was against his purposes.

David Was.

Bob considers himself a simple man who performs a trade. Like a plumber, carpenter or stone mason. As with those trades, one does not stop for a period of time only to pick it up again at a later date. So, Bob sees himself as a musician, that's his trade, and musicians play concerts. That's the simplicity behind the Never Ending Tour.

Victor Maymudes.

Every night I'm looking out to see who comes and [I] see those people react in an honest way. It's more important than all those people that write.

Bob Dylan, to Marc Rowland, 23rd September 1978.

The only fans I know I have are the people who I'm looking at when I play, night after night.

Bob Dylan, to Jonathan Lethem, August 2006.

Having gravitated towards bringing my work alive again night after night on stage, I find that [is] what's important to me now. I can't say that it's never been my turn commercially . . . but to have it again? I'm not really counting on it.

> Bob Dylan, to Alan Jackson, 4th October 1997.

I remember . . . Don [Was] was just sitting down on the floor and asking Bob: 'So, did you ever wonder, why me?' . . . Dylan didn't say anything.

> Robben Ford, musician.

Despite the overt richness of his work, life and even the rewards of his warm connectedness to his children and friends, he still appears to feel some hollowness as tentacles reach for him from the void. He seems to be in a constant fight with the enemy within.

> 'Cooky', March 1990.

★

By the time he got to Phoenix next, in March 1990, Dylan had rediscovered his mojo. It had started with a one-day studio session on January 6th that resulted in four usable tracks before the year was even out of the traps; a week later he followed it with a four-set, fifty-song warm-up show in New Haven which opened with Joe South's 'Walk A Mile In My Shoes' ('before you accuse, criticise or abuse . . .'); then, a huge open-air show in Sao Paolo, his first in Brazil; and best of all, two landmark theatrical residencies, six nights at Hammersmith Odeon and four nights at the Rex in Paris.

The London residency, in particular, generated enormous interest in a country that had always been a commercial stronghold, and where *Oh Mercy* charted at six. The final show saw him attempt 'You Angel You', minus a lyric sheet, a powerful 'Disease Of Conceit' at the piano and an encore of 'Hang Me, Oh Hang Me', a song he last sang in SW6 for *Madhouse on Castle Street*.

It was triumphal stuff, of which the most impressive component was the studio session, barely two months after he told Adrian Deevoy, 'The odd song will come to me every now and then and there'll be some kind of responsibility on my part to . . . take it down. But a lot of my ideas don't even get developed anymore.' Ostensibly set up to record an *Oh Mercy* leftover, Dylan suddenly produced three new lyrics, all of which he captured the same day. It is – not was – just like the old days:

Don Was: Bob called and asked if I'd be interested in producing a new version of a song called 'God Knows'. David and I . . . booked a day at the Record Plant recording studio for our first session with Bob Dylan . . . He made a real effort to put us at ease . . . He was humble and very funny . . . 'God Knows' was our audition . . . Bob played it on the piano for us once through, and then we cut it. The *modus operandi* for all subsequent sessions was immediately established: listen to Bob and respond sympathetically . . . The first take was a mess – too many musicians. For take two, we began with just Bob and Stevie Ray [Vaughan] and built up the arrangement very, very slowly. His singing was great. It was a keeper take. The rough mix from that moment is the mix that appears on the album.

Actually, it wasn't quite that spontaneous, Don later admitted to *Record Collector*'s Peter Doggett, 'The very first session I did with Dylan . . . happen[ed] to start with a section where Bob was at the piano, telling me what he wanted to do, and I was telling him why it wouldn't work . . . [It didn't occur to me] the Bob Dylan of 1989 [sic] may not have the same priorities that he did in 1966.'

The Was Brothers had assembled quite a band: Stevie Ray and Jimmie Vaughan on twin guitars, multi-instrumentalist David Lindley, the keyboard player from Was (Not Was), Jamie Muhoberac, drummer Kenny Aronoff, Don on bass and Dylan at the piano. Don also got to witness, 'Stevie walk up to him and said, "Hi, Stevie Ray Vaughan." But Stevie didn't have his hat on, [so] Bob [was] just like, "Yeah, sure," and kept going.' Once he knew it really was that fine guitarist, he befriended the Texan. Others who worked with him on later 1990 sessions weren't quite so lucky. Slash, from Guns N' Roses, felt like he was meeting the masked man, 'Even when he was talking to me, all I could see behind all those fuckin' hoods was his nose and his upper lip.'

If Stevie Ray was still feeling his way on the two takes it took to get 'God Knows', him and brother Jimmie were in their element on the next three songs Dylan showed to them, as a demo session turned into two-fifths of an album. And it was immediately apparent he had decided to let this froggy go a-courtin'. After recently recording his first nursery rhyme, 'This Old Man', for a children's charity album, he was the same man.

The new songs were shot through with all the darkness of early nursery rhymes like 'The Strange Wedding Of The Frog and Mouse' and 'The Carrion Crow'. He began with his first-ever apocalyptic nursery rhyme, 'Cat's In The Well',* in which the six white horses of 'She'll Be Coming 'Round The Mountain' were 'just about ready to explode', and 'Papa['s] reading the news/ He ain't got much to say, sister's dancing to the mushroom cloud blues.' Originally running to ten verses, the song quickly found the right groove, only coming up for air when Dylan gave his final benediction: 'May the Lord have mercy on us all.'

Just to prove every apocalypse has its man of peace, the next track was another ten-verse opus trimmed to fit, (re)introducing a dedicated follower of fashion. Controversy surrounds 'Handy Dandy',† who in the original typed draft was 'a tower of strength & stability/ he does it with mirrors but he don't need to lie . . . handy dandy, compulsive & healthy, plausible obsessive automatic/ blowing his horn for the girls & bringing them up to the attic.' However, the man has blood on his hands, as the original finale explicates: 'He calls life a prison & tells it to anybody who will listen/ He invites you to the bloodbath, he says you don't know what you're missing.'

The band once again excel themselves, the Vaughan brothers weaving a spell as a delighted Dylan picks up the slack. They are having fun, so much so that Dylan starts to play a song he hasn't even finished as the engineer hastily hit play.‡ In the process he may have lost a coupla verses from 'Ten Thousand Men', including the ominous, '10,000 men law books in their hands/ all studying medicine and law/ gonna create something of their own, the likes of [which] you never saw,' and an image Dylan ended up transferring to the album's title-track, 'My baby

---

* The title comes from a nursery rhyme dating back to at least 1609.
† A children's game Shakespeare knew went 'Handy dandy, riddledy ro/ Which hand will you have, high or low?'
‡ That sound at the beginning of side two is apparently the multitrack lurching into life.

and [I] were baked in a pie/ She leaned in right next to me, she put her finger in my eye.'*

The question became, what to do now? Any thought of making a 'sequel' that relied on the detritus from the *Oh Mercy* sessions had gone out of the window, along with 'Dignity' and 'Series Of Dreams', as Dylan returned to 'the only true valid death you can feel today'. He would instead write the songs needed to complete another ten-song collection across two months of travels.

When sessions resumed in mid-March, after another trip to Phoenix, just two songs from the previous spring had the welcome mat rolled out: 'Born In Time' and 'TV Talkin' Song', both barely recognisable. Each was recorded at the final *under the red sky* session in March, along with 'a very cool Grateful Dead-style extended instrumental that featured Bob on harp'. Co-producer Don Was didn't even know the former was an old song:

> At the time, I didn't even know that 'Born in Time' was left over from *Oh Mercy* . . . At the session, he just sat down at the piano and played it for everyone. Once the groove was established, Bob yielded the piano bench to [Bruce] Hornsby and picked up an acoustic guitar . . . There is a world-weariness in Bob's vocal that is integral to the song . . . It's a mood that foreshadows the sensibility of *Time Out of Mind*.

Its world weariness may have stemmed from a feeling he hadn't quite retained the raw emotion of the original, neither in his rewrites nor the vocal. What had been a song about a love affair in the past tense was now very much about an affair which was still smokin', especially in its new bridge, 'Not one more night, not one more kiss/ Not this time baby, no more of this/ Takes too much skill, takes too much will/ It's too revealing.' Did he mean someone who made him fearful of revealing too much of himself, who had 'married young, just like your Ma'? It was the one song he confided to Cooky was written 'for' her, though *rewrote* may be more accurate.

The fact he cut three versions in March, then picked the least convincing vocal merely confirmed that the song had gotten away from

---

* Dylan may have redone the vocal at a later date, amending the lyrics in the process, an increasingly common methodology. The *Red Sky* tapes are not in Tulsa.

him. As would 'TV Talkin' Song'. As brother David noted, 'I didn't think he was improving upon it after a certain point.' Initially, though, Dylan retained a grip on it, even linking it to the songs recorded in January with an appropriate new couplet, 'TV judges and TV clerks, TV repairmen to fix it so it works/ TV dads and TV mums, living in TV cities, under bombs.'

Even as he continued lambasting the medium – telling folks, 'If you wanna know what's happening, shut off that damn TV/ it steals your precious time away, it's your mortal enemy' – he abandoned the idea it was all a crazy dream. Instead, he returned to Hyde Park's Speaker's Corner fourteen years on, in the company of Dave Stewart. Now the song was set in the one place where such calumnies were countenanced. With a lurching bass and a vocal that wouldn't have been out of place in a spaghetti western, Dylan took the song where it needed to go. But he refused to let it remain there. In its eventual recorded guise he spared the life of the speaker of truth at the end of a song which sounded more and more like one of those 'moody old bugger' rants Van Morrison specialised in.

The stardust someone's saving grace had sprinkled over the January session had dissipated somewhat by the time sessions resumed in March, but he still seemed to be in something of a hurry. One session with NRBQ was aborted because, in the words of Don Was, 'he never finished writing those particular songs', not even one with the intriguing title, 'Night Of The Living Dead'. Another song he never finished, 'Heartland', was a kindred spirit to the title-track, recorded on the same day – what Was called, 'All Jews Day'. Again, he seemed to want to get the latter down posthaste, cutting 'Under The Red Sky' in two takes. In its original form, it read like an English Civil War broadside balladeer had crossed 'Nottamun Town' with 'Twa Sisters':

> Oh, the wind blow low and the wind blow high
> A black man on a white horse came passing by
> Two sisters are dressed in green, come wandering by
> Going into the woods to gather flowers.

In conversation with Don Was, he seemed to imply the song was about his hometown, but he never said which hometown. Whichever

Minnesota town he meant had become 'the way it looks/ when it's upside down.' Was wasn't entirely convinced he'd lived with these songs the way he had with those on *Oh Mercy*:

> *under the red sky* was done very quickly . . . so quickly, in fact, that when he did his initial vocals, he did them in two days . . . It's possible he wrote them all the night before! There are these lyrics that [sound like] he just threw [them] on . . . [But] if you're singing a line three seconds after you wrote it, your performance isn't going to have the nuance that living inside these things will allow you to have.

I don't buy that explanation. If the lyrics had a problem, it was the opposite one – he just kept tinkering. As brother David witnessed, 'The first song we were mixing, he breaks out his papers again and says he's gonna redo the vocal . . . Well, in fact, it happened on every song. He redid the vocal . . . At the moment before he sings it, he's still writing, and after he's recorded it, he's still writing, and then at the mixing session, he's still writing.'

Another problem was that he was pruning the songs even as he was recording them. As Robben Ford, who'd played on 'All Jews Day', described it, 'Bob ha[d] a table in front of him, with pages and pages and pages of lyrics, and he would just start some kind of a thing going on the guitar, and we'd all fall in behind him . . . And as soon as he kinda liked what was happening, he'd start . . . going through the pages, and just start trying to sing it over whatever we were doing.'

'Unbelievable', recorded the same day as the title-track, was a case in point, losing key verses that referred to 'the juggling of the dream' and 'the manipulation behind the plan', as well as one which delineated 'the madness of each chilling chance/ that takes its turn while vipers dance/ upon the winds when victory knows no play/ Unbelievable, that it would go down this way.'

David Lindley, who then returned to do overdubs, remembers how 'he was always working on stuff, organising verses and finishing things, changing words if he felt they worked better . . . within the structure of what was going on.' Yet Dylan seemed anxious to only get first impressions from those musicians he brought in to embellish the songs in post-production, including an old friend, a pre-fab guitarist:

Don Was: Bob sat down behind the board in the engineer's seat, hit the record button and said, 'Play!' . . . The guitar was way out of tune, and George [Harrison] didn't even know what key the song was in. Bob indicated that the solo was perfect . . . George rolled his eyes, turned to me and asked, 'What do you think, Don?' I said, 'It was really good, but let's see if you can do an even better one.' . . . Bob laughed, rewound the tape . . . George nailed the solo on the next pass.

The song in question was 'Under The Red Sky', and with it he had an album that for all its jaunty musicality was dark as night. Harrison's presence was no coincidence. Even as Dylan put the finishing touches to his second album of original songs in a year, he was working on a sequel of sorts, a second Wilburys album called, er, *Volume Three*. Once again, the plan was to do it all on the hoof. However, without the trembling Wilbury himself, Roy Orbison, who'd passed on, it was not the captivating concoction its predecessor had been. As Petty noted, 'Whereas the first one was just sort of a party, this was more serious work, and yet [still] done in a hurry . . . I just don't think it was a commercial record, and I don't think it was intended to be.'

I somehow doubt Warner's knew any of this in advance. Jim Keltner rather implies the residual trio were rather pushed into doing it, 'They knew they sorta had to do it, but it wasn't the same at all . . . [It was] recorded at this big old estate at the top of Coldwater Canyon, [in] this big old room . . . [but] Roy wasn't there . . . [and] the tremendous spirit from the first one wasn't there.' The commercial failure of the album put the kibosh on a summer Wilburys tour which had been 'a semiplan that came up several times' that spring.

Dylan twice gave the impression in the Noughties that he was browbeaten into doing *both* 1990 albums, telling author Jonathan Lethem, 'I wasn't bringing anything at all into the studio, I was completely disillusioned. I'd let someone else take control . . . Too many people in the room, too many musicians, too many egos,' and Mikal Gilmore, 'I didn't feel I was writing any of the songs that I really wanted to write. I wasn't getting the help I needed . . . I didn't like the sound . . . I reckoned I was done with it.' He also claimed he 'worked with George [Harrison] and Jeff [Lynne] during the day . . . and then I'd go down and see Don Was. And I felt like I was walking into a wall. He'd have a different band for me to play with every day.'

In fact, the sessions didn't overlap – only the post-production on *red sky* clashed with *Volume Three*. As for the post-production on *Volume Three*, Dylan simply left Lynne to it, with calamitous results. He yanked the best Dylan song, 'Like A Ship', from the album before proving he was an uber-exemplar of a producer with no 'great understanding of what it is that [I'm] trying to do . . . [but] would rather say, . . . "Let me think what else I can put on it." ' Owning the Surrey concession on kitchen-sinks, Lynne went to town.

On the other hand, *under the red sky* – had Dylan finished up 'Heartland', included the right 'TV Talkin' Song' and disabled the fader on some tracks – could have been all he hoped for. Instead, it was left to the label to market an album that was to *Oh Mercy* as night was to day, yet still something of a lost latter-day gem.

At least the road beckoned again, providing – he hoped – an opportunity to get away from any reminder of his spring studio activities. Not for long. When G.E. Smith found out his boss had made an album without him for a second time, his mind began to turn to taking his leave. If he wasn't appreciated now, when?

The shows through May and June saw Dylan lead Smith and the band a merry dance. But not once did Smith miss a beat, even when Dylan started taking requests, as he did second night in Toronto, when a Chicago drug-dealer shouted 'Tomorrow Is A Long Time' as Dylan prepared to play 'Baby Blue'. In a heartbeat, he replied, 'Sure is. Awfully long,' before switching song. Had he recognized the rogue's dulcet tones? After all, he had played five of his requests at Toad's in January, little knowing that in the next few months said dealer would be supplying half the band and crew.

Dylan himself was sticking to more traditional moonshine to get in the mood, so much so that in Toronto he surprised one of the hardiest party animals on the planet, Ronnie Hawkins, 'He was having a little bit too much fun at the O'Keefe Center. Too hard for him. He's too old to be drinking and doing all that shit now. That's strictly for under thirties.' Dylan did not agree. He was enjoying himself, and looking forward to seeing Cooky in three days' time in Alpine Valley, only to find he couldn't get close to her. So, he poured every ounce of feeling into a live debut of 'Shooting Star' sung directly at her, sitting in the front row, surrounded by the full quorum.

When he finally got to speak to her, he complained, 'I was just frustrated I couldn't get a message through. You were always with other people. How'd that crazy kid [the drug dealer] get in your group?' A defensive Cooky replied, 'I just met them on this tour. I didn't know those kids before.' Later on, she heard from others how pissed off he was over her hanging out all the time with 'that rowdy group of assholes'.

To make matters worse, she had confided 'that even when she had seen a chance to get to him, she held back because of their understanding, reminding him, "Don't you remember way back at the start when we set up the rules, we agreed to never put each other on the spot? And I had no way of knowing if you were alone."' Dylan's response took her by surprise, 'Yeah, we should have changed the rules.' And still, he couldn't quite grasp how the c. of a. provided her with both necessary cover and a social framework, even as she explained, 'I'm not the head of anything. I just keep in touch with people because it eases the boredom.' When she tried to point out all the complications, he didn't want to hear it: *'Why can't you get away?' "Cause I'll end up divorced and standing on your doorstep.'* 'Well, you know where the key is.'

Cooky was not the only one on the receiving end of complaints about his chosen lot that summer. In a letter to *Sister2Sister*, a feminist 'zine, he wrote, somewhat tongue in cheek, 'My soul is unaware of any time, only my mind, my Poor mind which is so bombarded with dates, calendars and numbers has been deceived into believing there is such a thing as time, woe is me.'

It was the shows – some of the best he'd given in years – which were keeping him sane, but not, as it happens, off the sauce. When he heard new friend Stevie Ray Vaughan had died in a helicopter crash on August 27th, it seemed to send him slightly off the rails. Even his guitar-tech César noticed, 'He was all teary-eyed. He was really highly affected by friends that die, it was like tearing [out] a chunk of his heart.' He wasn't just teary-eyed. He was trashed, his reaction to the news being to immediately pick up a bottle and get as drunk as possible as fast as possible, despite being due to perform the first of two shows in Merrillville, that night. Eyewitnesses were astonished to see him sat all alone on the hotel patio strumming on his guitar and singing while the opening act was on.

Members of the c. of a., who recognized both 'Friend Of The Devil' and 'Lonesome Whistle', came up and asked if his new album was any

THE CONTINGENCY OF ASSHOLES

good. He strummed down hard on the guitar and proclaimed, 'All my albums are good.' 'Friend Of The Devil' featured that night. It could almost have been tailored for the occasion, its narrator singing of how he's 'got a wife in Chino, and one in Cherokee / First one says she's got my child, but it don't look like me.' However, it was the one-off performance of 'Moon River', prefaced with, 'This one's for Stevie, wherever you are,' that reached the parts other songs and singers simply couldn't reach.

His drinking, though, was now becoming a cause for concern, just not to Dylan, who would insist to Mikal Gilmore in 2001, 'I can drink or not drink. I don't know why people would associate drinking or not drinking with anything that I do, really,' a clear dig at me for raising the matter of his early Nineties drinking in the 2000 edition of *Behind the Shades*. When Cooky addressed it, he retorted, 'You sound like a wife,' to which she retorted, 'I am a wife. Just not yours. Can't you take it as advice coming from a friend?'

He even used it as his get-out-of-jail-free card when Susan Ross accused him of being 'a vicious person when we met'. 'But I was drinking,' was his line of defence. Ross would later affirm that 'he combated his demons with such heavy drinking, many friends and employees thought he would not make it through another day'. He was not at such a point yet, but he was getting there.

Having arranged his next rendezvous with Cooky and the contingency, a five-night return residency at The Beacon in October, 'he called [her] after midnight on the second night to invite her over, [but] his condition fueled her prompt decline . . . He'd clearly started drinking before the show, so the performance was faster and his timing was off, waving his arms around and his movements around the stage jerky.' The following night he killed off Joey Gallo in the second verse, and introduced 'Man Of Constant Sorrow' by enquiring whether anybody else had 'woken up drunk today'.

The same day, Dylan switched hotels to the Mayflower, where Cooky was staying at his expense, which merely meant they spent half the afternoon flirting on the internal phone eleven floors apart. Finally, Dylan began to open up on the subject of marriage, admitting, 'Relationships are constrictive . . . Monogamy is not the accepted norm in most cultures. Relationships have to evolve. Every seven years you shed yourself.' When she enquired, 'What if I walk in and there's another woman?' he took it in his stride, 'Then you just walk up to the table and I'll introduce you?'

Their personal ding-dong continued through the end of the year and into the next, when he told her straight, 'I'm not ashamed of you. I don't care what anyone says or writes about me. The secrecy is for your sake, since you're the one with something to lose.' The moment had come for him to let Cooky know he was ready to take their relationship to another level, and it was her putting stones in the passway. Cooky suddenly saw that her marriage, rather than preventing him from being scared off, was a major stumbling-block. Something else kept him wary, too. He still knew he was sleeping with the enemy.

When he suggested that he never set out to hurt anybody, she pointed out that some people end up getting hurt anyway. He responded just as he had in 1966, insisting that they usually do it to themselves. When she tried to redirect the conversation, 'I understand you're going through changes lately,' he snapped back, 'I'm always going through changes. Don't you read what *your* people always write about me?' One evening around this time, he became particularly verbose, being 'two sheets to the wind', and she told him he should check himself into the Betty Ford Center. He warned her, 'If any of this gets out, I'll know where it came from.'

One of the more bizarre manifestations of his paranoia about Cooky's contacts was the pretense he maintained throughout 1991 that there was an album he was working on, and it was almost completed. In reality, the shutters had firmly come down again, Dylan confiding in another woman, 'I used to know what a song is, but I don't know anymore.' The lady, who came from the Canyon, thought she knew only too well how inspiration 'gets beaten out of you, because we make this music and we put it out and the critics have gotten into the scheme of reducing Wild Things Run Fast to I Love Larry songs'.

That wasn't it, at all. The transition from fragments to verses to songs simply wasn't happening. Thus, when in the middle of a conversation with Robert Hilburn in November 1991, 'he pulls out a notebook from his jacket and starts scribbling – [explaining,] "It's a song I'm workin' on"' – nothing comes of it. He fully admitted to this man he respected, critic or not, 'There was a time when the songs would come three or four at the same time, but those days are long gone.'

Although he knew isolation was a writer's best friend, he now hated being alone with his thoughts. As one of his close friends confided to Cooky, 'He pulls a curtain down around himself for periods of time.' But it had been a while. As Dylan admitted in conversation with Paul Zollo that April, 'It's [important] to be able to put yourself in an environment where you can . . . accept all the unconscious stuff that comes to you from the inner workings of your mind. And . . . control it all, take it down . . . You have to be able to get the thoughts out of your mind . . . The environment has to bring something out in me that wants to be brought out.'

Girlfriends never saw this process, which led one to conclude, 'Left to his own devices with free time on his hands, he does not generally write. He wanders from place to place . . . seeing people.' Meanwhile, the lyrical scraps he kept from 1991-92, when he was again becalmed creatively, were few and far between, showing no great shift in worldview. He was troubled, that was for sure, threatening at any moment to head for Speaker's Corner and tell it like it is: 'He was dressed like a woman, it ain't right/ He came on like a black man, but he could've been white,' said one fragment; 'Unmarried mothers having babies, some people say abortion's the thing to do/ Kill the baby before it's born and then kill the mothers and fathers too,' another.

At least his faith continued to survive, to endure, 'Can't kill the spirit, it can always be torn/ Can crucify Jesus but he's always reborn.' As did an unwavering belief in a land way up yonder, 'You think you're going to heaven but who's gonna pay your fare?/ It's a proven fact you can't get in unless you know somebody there.' He also hadn't entirely abandoned warning married women and men: 'Voodoo king laying in a ditch/ With his head cut off, his body beginning to twitch/ Car down the street out of gas/ Little girl saying, "This too shall pass." '

This one – possibly called 'Altar Of Pride' – had some potential, but as 1991 turned to 1992 (and then 1993, &c.), it became apparent such fragments were stoutly refusing to fuse together. Asked in April '94 if he was still writing new material, he dissembled, 'Well, I do have a bunch of papers and notes and things lying around, [but] only time is going to tell when those things come out.'

He was more upfront to a more trusted journo, Edna Gundersen, the following spring, 'Unless a song flows out naturally and doesn't have to be chaperoned, it just dissipates . . . I get thoughts during the day that I just can't get to. I'll write a verse down and never complete

it.' Even his complicated romantic life wasn't inspiring songs, no matter how hilarious or surreal a relationship became.

When an article appeared in the premier Dylanzine, *The Telegraph*,
describing a brief fling with poetess Anne Waldman in the late-
Seventies, Cooky took belated umbrage, confronting him with, 'Who's
Anne Waldman?' He claimed he didn't know. When she told him about
the article, he responded, not unreasonably, 'That was a long time ago.'
'How long? Your methods are still the same.' 'You mean you're getting
on me for something written in one of *your* magazines, by one of *your*
people?'

It prompted him to reiterate monogamy was not part of his plan,
even quoting St Augustine, of all people, 'Lord make me chaste, but
not yet.' What he didn't do was contextualize the quote, which was
from *Confessions*, a scathing self-examination of a life misspent. Cooky's
response was to leave messages answering his silent hang-ups like,
'This is girlfriend number 322 if you want to call back.'

At the end of 1990, though, when he was as close as he ever came to
making a real commitment to Cooky, it was she who pulled back. He
was even starting to miss the c. of a., complaining to her after a show
in Chicago, 'There's no familiar faces in the audience. I didn't see anybody I recognized.'

He was not enjoying himself. Having sabotaged his own band by
not considering the feelings of anyone else – in this case G.E. Smith,
who had quit after the second Beacon residency – he was back in diamond hell, auditioning guitarists onstage in front of paying punters.
And it was not going well, with Miles Joseph having to be fired for acting like a fan, Steve Bruton having an 'attitude' and John Staehely
needing a pint of Jack Daniels every night to get up and play. Bruton's
'attitude', according to Díaz, amounted to flying his wife in for the
Beacon shows. It was going to get worse, before it got any better.

Rather than ride it all out, Dylan fired Chris Parker, the last survivor
of the great G.E. trio, at year's end and brought back 'the man who got
a beat like a cop', Ian Wallace. As he continued auditioning different
drummers and guitarists, the clock was ticking. Finally, he gave G.E.'s
slot to a promising young Southern axeman Tom Petty had recommended, J.J. Jackson. He then agreed to let guitar-tech César Díaz share
the stage with the new man, just to muddy the waters, all the while
failing to recruit an actual bandleader. So, when he returned to

Hammersmith Odeon for eight more shows during a bitterly cold snap, he was strapped to the mast of a ship without a sail.

The winter 1991 shows have become the stuff of legends. This time, Dylan crawled inside a bottle to escape the cacophony in his head (and, nightly, onstage). The Hammersmith shows undid any good achieved the previous February. The spring shows and European return in June were worse. In Stuttgart, he 'sang' an eight-minute version of 'New Morning' that almost caused a fist-fight in the bar afterwards, when a German fan asked an English fan which song it was, and was told, 'New Morning'. 'Nein. I know "New Morning." That was not "New Morning!"' It was, but only in Dylan's head.

As he told Elliot Mintz the month after London, 'I'm usually in no frame of mind before a show . . . Usually it takes me one or two songs, sometimes it takes me . . . to the encore.' Never was a truer word spoken. Yet each time he called Cooky from his London hotel – and their regularity (at overseas rates) was most unusual – he put on a positive front, so much so that, 'she really couldn't tell what was fuelling his disquiet: personal relationships, the lingering unease over the Gulf War, an unnerving Grammy Lifetime Achievement Award hanging in the shadows like a noose, the head-shaking disarray of his current band, drugs . . . alcohol.'

The contingency and her friend César were, of course, keeping her fully updated as to how the shows were really going – disastrously – even as Dylan pressed her to come with him to the 'prestigious' Grammy Awards at Radio City Music Hall on February 20th, where he was due to receive a Lifetime Achievement Award, even as he hoped he still had half a lifetime to go. As he told a member of the contingency the night before the ceremony, 'It's like going to your own funeral.' The way he was going, that event might not be too far away.

He had turned up to Radio City on the 19th to rehearse a song they had been playing every night for the past three weeks. On his way back to the hotel, he was approached by one of the contingency, whom rather than rebuff, he engaged in conversation as he walked the ten blocks back to The Westbury. When she asked what he was planning to perform, he replied, 'Masters Of War'. 'Why are you doing that one?' Rather than say it was because the first Gulf War was still raging, he claimed, 'Well, the band doesn't know that many songs.' 'They'll

say you're being political again.' 'Fuck 'em.' What he didn't let on was
that he wasn't a well man:

> **César Díaz**: He was very sick right before we got [back] to the States . . .
> He came down with a cold, and he doesn't like to take regular medi-
> cines. He's really very holistic about it, herbs and teas, and crap like that.
> I blame Suzie [Pullen, his dresser]. She wouldn't let anybody else sug-
> gest anything, or get close to Bob.

Try as Pullen might, though, she had no say when it came to Cooky
accompanying Dylan to what was a very public event (so public that
reports soon made it back to the c. of a. that she'd been seen there).
Not surprisingly, she began to feel very uncomfortable, so much so
that Dylan kept encouraging her to sip some Scotch. She assured him
that if she did, she'd be throwing up. In fact, it was Dylan who ended
up puking up his guts, having fortified himself from a bottle Jack
Nicholson had given him. Every time he went to the loo, he returned
looking pale and shaky. Cooky grew increasingly convinced he wasn't
gonna make it across the stage without totally embarrassing himself.
She was right to be worried. The way Dylan described the occasion to
Mikal Gilmore a decade later, it was Night of the Locusts:

> The Grammy people . . . said that they wanted to give me this Lifetime
> Achievement honor. Well, we all know that they give those things out
> when you're old – when you're . . . a has-been . . . I wasn't in a good
> state of mind that night. I was frustrated. It's difficult to be paralyzed by
> the past in any kind of way . . . I was glad to have gotten out of there
> [alive].

The message he delivered that night, after a 'Masters Of War' so
incoherent one tabloid reporter wondered if he was singing in Hebrew, wasn't 'Fuck 'em', but it might as well have been. Instead, he
admitted it was 'possible to become so defiled in this world that your
own father and mother will abandon you, [but even] if that happens,
God will always believe in your own ability to mend your own ways.'
Presumably Beattie, along with most of America, was tuning in.

The evening, though, had only just begun. After he dropped Cooky
off at her hotel, 'she wasn't bothered that he was obviously going to

continue all night partying, because by then he was so plastered, he was in no shape to do anything but pass out'. What she didn't realize was that it was about to become the night of the returning girlfriends. Ross was hovering somewhere, claiming to be Dylan's date, as was Carolyn Dennis, who didn't have a ticket for the post-award party but got a friend at Sony to sneak her in.

She found Dylan sitting with Diana Ross and Cyndi Lauper, and profoundly embarrassed to see her there. According to Dennis, it was this experience which convinced her she couldn't 'handle any more of the chaos around the personal situation in his life', and she asked him for a divorce. Back in Malibu, he expressed exasperation at having to constantly keep one girlfriend from running into another, knowing the Grammy had been a close run thing. When Dennis said she was tired of his infidelity, Dylan responded, 'Why can't you just accept the other women, knowing that you will be my only wife?' Even when she filed divorce papers, he didn't respond, and wouldn't sign or receive them.

Only when she went on tour with Springsteen in 1992 – having been recommended for the gig by Debbie Gold – did he sign the papers, after she finally waived her rights to a share of any songs written during the course of the marriage, David Braun claiming – not unjustly – that these years had not been his 'best years as a writer' and that 'the songs were not very valuable'.

He still wanted control of them. It had taken him until 1990 to (re)gain complete control of his catalogue, as the Witmark songs began reverting to him under America's peculiar twenty-eight-year rule. Dennis agreed to not pursue the matter and their divorce became official in 1992, without any of the multi-million-dollar settlement or emotional trauma Sounes fondly imagined. The pair met and signed the agreement at a 76 gas station on Ventura Boulevard one sunny afternoon. Who said romance was dead?

Just as the marriage had passed the media by, so did the divorce, as Dylan revelled in his lack of newsworthiness, while plying his wares from town to town. He later told Gundersen, 'In the early '90s, the media lost track of me, and that was the best thing that could [have] happen[ed] . . . Five or six years later, I'd fully developed into the performer I needed to be.' In the meantime, almost the only people privy to his public thoughts were Gundersen and Hilburn, especially after sleaze-seeking reporter Joe Queenan claimed he was doing an interview for the *New York Times*, but was actually writing an 'exposé' for *Spy* magazine.*

Only Hilburn and Gundersen, it seemed, were trusted to respect the rules. As Hilburn let slip in a 1992 cover-story, 'Any talk about his former, 13-year marriage to Sara Lownds, or their four now-grown children is strictly off-limits. So is his longstanding relationship with Carole Childs,' leaving the way free and clear for any new biographer whose work – or so he now told Cooky – he found 'too personal, too probing'. Of course, he never kept up with what people wrote about him, which is why he ranted about a local review of the first Ottawa show in June 1990 the following night;† and why, when Cooky tried to unobtrusively pick up a copy of Queenan's *Spy* article at Busters, in his company, he called her out, 'You don't have to put on an act.'

When he did allow someone to interview him who knew *his* work, he would test them to see how well-read they were. Thus, when *Song-Talk*'s Paul Zollo interviewed him in 1991, he told him, 'A Byron line would be something as simple as, "What is it you buy so dear / with your pain and with your fear?" Now that's a Byron line.' He knew full well it was a Shelley line, from 'Men of England'. Twelve months later, he told Stuart Coupe, 'It's been necessary for me to find some time to go back and re-read . . . Blake, Shelley, Byron.'

Even here, he framed such reading as his way of avoiding Dylan biographies, telling Coupe, 'It doesn't knock me out to read a book about myself.' His most revealing bum-steer, though, came in a 1997 interview – just before search engines ruined his fun – to the *New York Times*'s Jon Pareles, a partisan of the man's work. Dylan quoted a line from The Bible, 'Work while the day lasts, because the night of death cometh when no man can work,' insisting 'a lot of that [idea] is instilled into [my new] record'. He promptly attributed it to Psalms, a book

---

* The hack in question even tried to get tittle-tattle from me, pretending to interview me about *Behind the Shades*. It was 1966 all over again. As Dylan said in '86: 'Record companies would send me over to do an interview with someone and you'd be honest with that person and . . . he'd take quotations and turn things around and make you seem like a different kind of person by using everything that you gave him.'

† A magical moment it was, as Dylan told the crowd, 'There was an article written in the paper about me saying that the girls should come back and the harmonica should go! . . . Anyway, the girls might be back next time, but it's OK if I play harmonica on this one, right?' Cue roar of approval.

from the Old Testament, knowing it was really from the gospel according to John [9:4]. The actual quote, 'I must work the works *of Him that sent me*, while it is day: [for] the night cometh . . .' were the words of Christ himself, and they refer to a Christian's evangelical duty to preach the gospel from place to place, something Dylan had not done in a while.

Such were the games he continued to play on the rare occasions he exposed himself to media scrutiny. Most of the time during the first half of the Nineties, he simply played shows, dozens of 'em, once again regaining his sense of purpose in 1991 as summer turned to fall. Stripping the sound down to a trio again, he called for band rehearsals in early September, even though the next shows were six weeks away. When he finally resumed gigging, something commensurate with Basel '87 occurred. It was a case of, hello, hello, I'm back again. An attendant Cooky was delighted, even if at Ames, Iowa, a week in, he looked so sick she wanted to jump onstage and hold him up. At one point he doubled up in pain and hung there for a minute, covering it up by pretending to check the monitor.

At other shows he continued projecting inviting looks in Cooky's direction, but when she told him she wasn't sure they were meant for her, he replied, 'I always mean everything I do.' If so, he also meant every word of his stunning reinterpretation of Eddy Arnold's 'You Don't Know Me' ('You think you know me well, but you don't know me'), and the crooner classic, 'Answer Me, My Love' ('If you're happier without me I'll try not to care / But if you still think about me, please listen to my prayer'). Passion was back in fashion, even as Dylan told a travelling Hilburn in Madison – a particularly magnificent show, topped off with a heavenly, acoustic 'That Lucky Old Sun' – 'What's important isn't the legend, but the art, the work. A person has to do whatever they are called on to do.'

The crowds lapped it up, prompting Dylan, ever the optimist, to believe he had found a new audience who 'are not enchanted by the past'; who 'react immediately to what I do, and . . . don't come with a lot of preconceived ideas.' If the fall tour was a return to form devoutly to be wish'd, his girlfriend from the contingency seemed less and less inclined to settle for what they had.

When they got together in New York, after Dylan performed at David Letterman's 10th anniversary show on January 18th, 1992, Cooky

confronted him about Susan Ross, who was back on the scene. She told
him it was time for her to pull back, and put her own house in order. It
prompted an educated rap from the man, 'You probably hate me
because I'm not what you expected. I run into that all the time.' He
made it clear that although he wanted to continue the relationship, if
she was really determined to end it, he would not undermine her
efforts by contacting her.

Ironically, a sidelined Ross was about to bail, and with some cause,
having long been relegated to stand-in status. As she later complained,
'He would call me every day for three weeks, then disappear for a
month . . . [And] he lies about little things such as where he's calling
from, or whether or not he's coming to town, as well as about big issues.'

When she naively tackled him on why they didn't live together, he
told her 'he could barely live with himself'. So, despite their souls having known 'each other intimately from another lifetime or two', she
wrote to him in September, asking him not to call her again. His reply
from Stamford, dated October 24th – a brief, typed, unsigned postcard –
was hardly Petrarch, 'Everybody has [feelings]. Mine sometime may be
a bit penurious, but they're there. Anyway, if there's a change lemme
know.'

By then, Cooky's own short-lived resolve had dissipated as quickly
as her season of discontent, as reports reached her of Dylan's dispirited mood on his latest Antipodean tour, which began in spectacular
fashion on March 18th, in Perth, with full-on electric covers of Hendrix's 'Dolly Dagger', Robert Hunter's 'West L.A. Fadeaway' and the
traditional 'Little Maggie'. The unexpected covers kept coming, two
of them from his 1961 set, 'Little Moses' and 'Golden Vanity', the first
Child ballad he had ever learnt. But the song that sent the contingency into a tailspin was resurrected first in Melbourne, on April 2nd.
'Idiot Wind' was back, and it was near word-perfect. Someone, it
seemed, needed reminding of all 'the hurt I suffer [and] the pain I rise
above'.

Cooky rose to the bait, insisting to friends she would come to west-
coast shows in May, but only because 'it would give her the opportunity
to test if she could enjoy friends and the shows as a spectator only'.
Who was fooling who? Dylan spotted Cooky the first night at San
Fran's Warfield Theater (May 4th) – the first time he'd played there in
twelve momentous years – as his roving eye checked out who had

joined the stage rush. As he took his bow at the end of a guns-blazing show, he reached out his arm to Cooky in the dark.

The following night, joined by Jerry Garcia on guitar for two songs, he delivered an 'Idiot Wind' as nuanced as any mid-Seventies rendition and at song's end very deliberately nodded in someone's direction, as if to say, 'So, worth coming?' The contingency howled their approval, and two days later, in Berkeley, he reciprocated in kind, playing most of the show to these familiar front-row faces, even pointing at all four witches of Westwick in turn during the encore. He was upping the ante. In San José, he played 'Most Of The Time' for the last time, the sweat dripping from his brow, as he wrenched every word from the depths of his soul, looking directly at Cooky, who was leaning to the Jack of Hearts, directly in his sight-line, buffeted by the entire contingency.

When Cooky found the will and the means to return to L.A. a few days later for a week of shows at the Pantages, she allowed herself to be picked up from the airport by the partner of the friend who had introduced them. He brought her the message that Bob wanted to talk to her: 'He really wants to know what your purpose and intentions are in coming to the shows. Is the break-up off?' At the Saturday night show, a well-juiced wunderkind spent an inordinate time playing right to Cooky. Come Monday, they agreed to meet on the corner across from the big white Hollywood church where he filmed 'When The Night Comes Falling', right after the show, to talk.

A conciliatory rock star even seemed to have come to accept her need for a group of friends to travel with, beyond just a cover story. When she explained how the group's make-up changed from tour to tour, he admitted, 'It sounds like some living, breathing animal.' (No shit, Sherlock.) Inevitably, the conversation soon turned to the usual subject – their relationship – as Cooky continued asking the relationship-equivalent of how long is a piece of string:

'How long can this all last?'

'I wish I could give you those kind of answers. But I don't have them myself. Do you live your whole life like that? Planning it out in segments and thinking of it in periods?'

'I guess I do. At least at what point will I know you're not going to call again? Like, if I don't hear from you? Three months? Six months?'

Later, while digging in her purse, her calculator fell out. Dylan picked it up and started punching the buttons: 'Answers to all Cooky's questions . . . Time lines . . . etc.' When the display was full of numbers, he held it up: 'Here.' Nothing was resolved, and though those silent hang-ups resumed as soon as she returned to Arizona, the sense that they were merely delaying the inevitable was becoming palpable.

When Dylan played a five-night high-summer residency at the recently-restored Orpheum Theatre in Minneapolis (in which he had a part share), to record a possible live album, the contingency was out in force. Cooky was not there to see the end of an era, the final night including two messages to Mum and brother, sat in row six: 'I Believe In You' and 'Every Grain Of Sand'. But the defining moment came on night three when Dylan turned to the drum rise during 'Simple Twist Of Fate' to ask Letterman '84 refugee Charlie Quintana, who'd replaced Wallace at the start of the year, not to quit. The high watermark for the post-G.E. band had been reached, and the only way was down, even as Quintana called up a replacement who could teach the band how to drive with a stick:

> **Winston Watson**: [Charlie] called me as I was burning dinner. I thought [he] needed a tech to come out, and then he said 'No, you're gonna play with Dylan.' I go, 'Ha ha ha, not the dead Welsh poet . . . When do rehearsals start?' He goes, 'No, no, no, you're flying out to Kansas City tomorrow to play with the guy.' And I said, 'An audition?' He said, 'No, you're gonna do a show with him.' . . . We land and nobody's there . . . The first person I saw was Victor [Maymudes] and he was no help whatsoever . . . After the show, there was some commotion and it was [Dylan] making his way through this crowd of people, and he came up to me, and he looked me up and down, and he shook my hand and gave me a hug, and he said, 'Hey, you play really great, I'll see you tomorrow.'

Watson arrived just as the boat was rockin'. The internal equilibrium of the band and crew wasn't helped by Dylan's mood swings, or by the fact that Maymudes was now carrying on with another member of the contingency, a gorgeous Jewish-American princess called Michelle, young enough to be his daughter.

When Cooky left her address-book in Michelle's car on a ride from

Kansas, she began to freak out as to whether Michelle saw all the 'interesting' numbers in there. Also now an issue was another contingency member, Roy, the young drug-dealer whom Dylan tried to ban from the shows, was still supplying Maymudes with his pot, as well as 'half the crew'. On one occasion, Victor told Cooky's own conduit to Dylan to 'warn Cooky that Roy knows a lot more about what's been going on than she probably thinks'.

It was all becoming a little too incestuous, and when Sony Music organized a special 'thirtieth anniversary' celebration of Dylan at Madison Square Garden on October 16th, Cooky stayed home.* By the end of it, Dylan might have wished he'd done so, too, even with the lucrative pay-per-view revenue that flowed directly into his coffers, something which amused Maymudes greatly: 'It ended up being a [huge] financial windfall for Bob, but it pissed off a lot of the performers that night. George Harrison was so angry about it being a for-profit show, he made T-shirts with dollar signs on them and sent them to Bob.' Though the rehearsals had been promising – Dylan joining Eric Clapton on the first song they ever played together, 'It Takes A Lot To Laugh' – the only part of the evening Dylan seemed to enjoy was an impromptu afterhours party at Tommy Makem's Pavilion.

It was just like old times. As Liam Clancy recalled, 'We were drinking pints of Guinness. As the night wore on, I said, "Let's get a guitar," and we started singing Irish drinking songs . . . I looked up as we were singing and this group of guys were singing . . . with their arms around each other . . . George Harrison, Tom Petty, Dylan and me.' This was also probably the evening where Liam turned to Dylan 'after about thirty pints of Guinness', and said, 'Remember, Bob, no fear, no envy, no meanness.' Though he still recalled the advice eight years later, Dylan would find it a real challenge to abide by it, given what the next two years held in store.

The marriage that had erected a semi-permanent barrier between Bob and Cooky had been shaken to the foundations by the revelation that her husband, Karl, had hidden a long-standing gambling addiction which now threatened to cost them their home, their daughter's home,

---

* The only thirtieth anniversary with which it coincided was Hammond's betrayal of the young Dylan, and the label reneging on promises to amend a contract he'd signed as a minor.

even his very freedom.* Even now, Cooky couldn't commit – or keep away. A third Hammersmith residency in February 1993 saw her travel to London, but when she called Dylan at the Royal Garden Hotel in Kensington, it was to lay into him about two young Italian girls she had seen hanging on the lip of the stage every night. It led to the usual unresolved, irreconcilable, oxymoronic circle game. One moment he'd express a desire to be married, the next he's expecting her to know he'd never be faithful. When he gave her his phone number, 'in case she needed to reach him' in London, she said:

> 'I'd be afraid to call. You might be busy.'
> 'I thought you'd be more immune to that kind of thing by this time.'
> 'It really hasn't happened before.'
> 'I thought we had discussions about this a really, really long time ago.'
> 'Discussions, yes. But that doesn't mean we came to any *agreement*.'

Which is where they left it. Yet it was clearly eating him up, her being there, as he again put the blame for the infrequency of their interactions on her being with her gang, which was especially large and avid here. When he suggested she should have known, she admitted she'd had some idea it might be like this. 'Just being in the same country is making me blue,' he later wrote, in a song he wouldn't release for another four years, and then not with this line.

He still wanted her to know he really cared, though, even if she found it hard to believe the message was for her when she opened her daily paper, the *Arizona Republic*, on Valentine's Day: 'Grandma Cookie, I love you forever, I like you for always. Forever and always my grandma you'll be. Happy Valentines. [signed] Dylan.' It couldn't be. When he finally admitted it really was him, he couldn't help adding, 'It took ya long enough to figure that one out.'

In May, he gave himself a birthday present of a weekend in Phoenix, staying at the Windham Garden Hotel. He even brought some crystal meth to make the party go with a zing. When he suggested taking a ride out in the desert, Cooky briefly objected, worried they might get stopped, to which Bob replied, 'Cooky, the cops don't pull you over and

---

* He would end up doing time for fraud, even as the marriage crumbled to dust, not because of Cooky's infidelity but because of Karl's criminality.

make you pee in a bottle.' A good time was had by all, despite arguing over the faults of particular members of her crowd and even though the Sword of Damocles hung over their relationship. At the end of the stay, a tearful Cooky cried, 'I don't know if or when I'll ever see you again.' He reassured her, 'You'll see me.' He did eventually come back for one more visit, but shadows were falling – or lengthening, even.

It would be almost a year before they spent any quality time together again away from Point Dume, and by then, the shit really had hit the fan back home. In Chicago, in mid-April 1994, Dylan booked her a room at the Omni on the same floor, so she was able to pop by his room 'for quick feel-up visits and hallway meetings', but again he ended up complaining about their lack of time together. Feeling penned in by his own retinue, he wasn't happy with her being chummy with them, or her own crowd. She couldn't win.

Five nights later, in Milwaukee, as she was preparing to head back to Phoenix for the inevitable showdown with her deceitful husband, she left a message on Bob's machine telling him this was one final opportunity to do 'Born In Time' for her, since she was going home after the show. It was the last chance saloon and Dylan came out swinging. The song that he wrote about a lost love, and rewrote when he fleetingly found love, had an air of finality that night in Wisconsin.

The minute she got home, though, she phoned him, waking him up. They still talked for two hours as Dylan turned counsellor to Cooky, informing her, 'You first have to figure out what you really want . . . But you have to realize you're not in control. You've got to get yourself together. When I look behind your eyes, I don't see Cooky there anymore . . . You have to stop and think about exactly what it is you want to do and go ahead and go after it, and don't let anything stop you. You're dealing too much from situation to situation . . . When you do get it all straight, if there's anything I can do to help, I will.' He meant it. Just as he had meant it when he told her previously that when the end came, 'It won't be me. It'll be you. We'll change and it'll evolve and end on friendly terms.'

She thought back to another of those 'why we have to break up' arguments. He had told her he knew what was happening, and that this was why he'd told her long ago that she'd be the one to end their relationship, not him, as she had feared at the start. He said he'd experienced it so many times before. He described how people are drawn to

him because of what they *think* he's like, but then when they find out
what he's really like, and the novelty of the fame etc. has worn off, they
get disillusioned and want out. The end of the line was in sight, and
Dylan sensed loneliness closing in again. All this may even have had a
direct bearing on what for him was a momentous decision, one which
took even Victor by surprise:

> Another important milestone in Bob's life happened in 1994: He stopped
> drinking. He just stopped on a dime. He didn't talk as much once he
> stopped, and he didn't laugh as loud either . . . He was capable of deal-
> ing with a broader range of personalities when he was drinking and
> after stopping, his tolerance for certain types of behaviour diminished.

If he was going to continue touring into his sixties, he couldn't keep
treating his body like the wrecking crew at a derelict temple.* That he
needed to commit himself to the road had been impressed upon him
by eighteen months of touring with a band that was all too often on
auto-pilot. The two highlights in that period had both been when he
departed from the Never Ending Tour format: first, to film four shows
in an intimate night-club setting in New York in November 1993, the
legendary Supper Club shows, one of which should have been released
officially, years ago.

Cooky found herself in Malibu when Dylan was discussing with
Tom Petty the possibility of releasing a live album from the Supper
Club, only to warn him, 'Well, if you're going to, you better hurry up
before the bootleggers beat you to it.' Needless to say, the bootleggers
won the race, releasing all four shows in less than two months, featuring heart-stopping semi-acoustic versions of 'Ring Them Bells', 'Queen
Jane Approximately', 'Delia' and 'Weeping Willow', and letting MTV
know he could do without them.†

Originally, he may even have intended to introduce some special
guests. He'd phoned Roseanne Cash to ask if she would 'like to sing

---

* In 1993, he had to cancel a show in Lyon after his chronic back pain flared up again.
Indeed, he was laid flat from the pain. This was the first time in thirty years of touring
he'd cancelled a show at the last minute.
† They had been pursuing him to do a show in their *Unplugged* series, prompting him
to opine, within Cooky's earshot, 'What the fuck did MTV ever do for me?' Aside
from the viaducts.

backup? He asked if we could get together. I said, how about Tuesday? He said, how about right now? He played a lot of really obscure songs . . . I couldn't really tell what to do . . . Occasionally I'd throw in a harmony . . . Nothing came of it.' Such intimate shows were a special moment for the band, even if for drummer Watson the really special time were the pre-Supper Club rehearsals, '[be]cause everyone had their street clothes on, there's people milling around doing stuff, and we were just playing for the sake of sheer playing'.

Even better was Dylan's three-song, final night set recorded and filmed as part of The Great Music Experience, in Nara City, Japan, the following May, two days before his 53rd birthday, backed by a full orchestra conducted by Michael Kamen. It included a transcendent 'Ring Them Bells' from the land of the rising sun. He also proved he still enjoyed the odd mind game on the obligatory 'I Shall Be Released' communal encore, the organizers having stuck Joni Mitchell at the mike with him, 'And if you look closely at it, you can see the little brat, he's up in my face – and . . . he's mouthing the words at me like a prompter, and he's pushing me off the mike.' Maybe he was reminding her, he wrote the song and it was his to do with as he wilt.

A further reminder of his time in Woodstock came three months later, when promoters of a 25th anniversary Woodstock concert did what Michael Lang could not, they persuaded Dylan to perform there as part of a live telecast. For him, it might have been just another NET show, sandwiched between Scranton and Lewiston, but he came, he sang, he conquered; opening with 'Jokerman', and refusing to be cajoled into dropping his acoustic set while the mosh pit yelled for rock'n'roll; performing versions of 'Masters Of War' and 'It's All Over Now, Baby Blue' which proved there were no songs in his catalogue that, when the night was right, were rank strangers to him. He had shaken the mud off his feet, and was again heading toward the Son. And still, MTV kept a-callin'. What was a poor boy to do, especially one who sang in a rock'n'roll band?

5.8

June 1992 to March 1997:
Meeting The Criteria

There is an enemy at the doors of folk-music, which is driving it out, namely the common popular songs of the day, and this enemy is one of the . . . most insidious.

Hubert Parry, composer of 'Jerusalem', 1899.

By 1950, when Leadbelly died, it was clear what a folk singer actually was . . . He was someone who was unemployable as a singer in any other context.

Stephen Calt, *I'd Rather Be The Devil*.

The[se] are such old verses as have been done *time out of mind*, and only wanted to be rescued from . . . blundering Transcribers.

Allan Ramsay, *Tea-Table Miscellany*, 1725.

I tend to base all my songs on the old songs, like the old folk songs, the old blues tunes; they are always good. They always make sense.

Bob Dylan, to Ron Rosenbaum, November 1977.

You know why th[is] record sounds so good? Because it was a performance. The whole band was playing together in the studio. It wasn't a thing assembled from parts, put together in little bits and pieces, until you had a complete take. Everyone started at the same time and finished pretty much at the same time, and all the time in between you just hung on for dear life.

Bob Dylan, *Theme Time Radio Hour*, 2007, referencing Hardrock Gunter's 'Gonna Dance All Night'.

I found myself spending more and more time in the studio, doing less
and less.

Bob Dylan, to Jon Pareles, September 1997.

[On] my records, solos don't mean that much . . . The vocals mean a lot
and the rhythm means a lot. And that's about it . . . . It's more [about]
getting the structure of it down right.

Bob Dylan, to Toby Creswell, January 1986.

Q: What do you expect from a record producer?
Bob Dylan: Somebody who can differentiate between what to play and
what not to play . . . Technology is not really my friend. It just . . .
trivialises my particular style of music.

Bob Dylan, London press conference, 4th October 1997.

Let me tell you: you don't force Bob to do anything.

Dave Bromberg, 2013.

He doesn't like too much democracy.

Daniel Lanois.

*

In the interregnum between *under the red sky* and its legitimate heir,
Time Out of Mind, seven years on, Dylan again resorted to making
albums of covers (two of them) and a live album to fulfil and renew his
recording contract with Sony. Throughout that period, he recommit-
ted himself to the road and seemingly abandoned committing himself
to relationships 'for good'. But the search for subject-matter and inspiration continued to preoccupy him, even as he wrote (to himself) that
he hated the idea he was spokesman for a generation – 'I'd like to think
I was speaking for myself.' Even the events in Tiananmen Square failed
to inspire more than a single thought, 'A crowd . . . can be photographed & massacred,' though Canadian singer-songwriter Sue
Medley's timely 'Dangerous Times' featured nightly in her support
slot at the spring 1990 shows.

He still felt there were people he'd hate to be on that dreadful day.
Surprisingly, these included the FBI agents in Waco, Texas, who laid

siege to the home of a religious cult in February 1993. In a lyric he left behind for Maymudes to scoop up, he called that siege, 'a diabolical piece of work/ To burn . . . women and children/ Even if you think the guy's a jerk/ What a blood curse on the government . . . Who now supplies the alibis?'*

Such fragments, though, refused to complete themselves. By the time he began making his 1993 covers album – two and a half years after *red sky* – he still only 'had bits and pieces of songs', or so he told a 1997 press conference. Some of these he tried to complete, as he had in 1968-9, by accepting help from fellow songsmiths, starting in early 1991 with a song called 'Steel Bars' and a certain Michael Bolton, who claimed at the time, 'He's kind of hungry to get back out there and wants to work with a few contemporary hit songwriters.' The key word here was 'hit'. The experience merely proved communication is only possible between equals:

> **Michael Bolton**: [When he suggested a] line like, 'It was your resistance/ It was my persistence' – if I didn't love it, I just kind of counted to ten and thought about how one would say to Bob Dylan, 'I'm not sure about that one.' I couldn't do it. But I didn't have to. He kept coming up with alternatives. During downtime, [he] talked about touring.

What Bolton omits from his own account is the one exchange that illustrated the great divide between the twain. Having almost finished their work, Bolton informed Bob, 'Now we have to do this, this and this.' When Dylan asked why, he replied, 'To ensure radioplay.' Dylan spluttered, 'I don't write my songs to get radioplay!' And nor did he. At least they finished the song, Bolton generously including it on his next smash-hit LP, *Time, Love & Tenderness*. Even less productive was the day Dylan spent with an altogether worthier companion of the Canyon, J.D. Souther, who recalled, 'We never did finish a song, but we had a great day playing with my dogs and talking, mostly about early English poets.'

Such was the dearth of inspiration, Dylan ended up re-examining a

---

* Dylan had taken to writing down song-ideas on index cards c. 1994–5, some of which Maymudes appropriated. His son later tried to auction them, unsuccessfully, at Sotheby's in London.

couple of songs he'd rejected from *under the red sky*, both at Don Was's prompting. Back in 1990, the Was Brothers had been asked 'to write a song for Paula Abdul's next album and we asked Bob if he'd [like] to join us in the enterprise. We turned the TV off, and wrote a little song called "Shirley Temple Doesn't Live Here Anymore" . . . conjuring up images of a dying town and a disappearing way of life . . . [Abdul] subsequently passed on the song. A couple years later, we thought we'd funk it up . . . Bob was cool with the idea, but wanted to change a few lyrics.' The result was 'Mr Alice Doesn't Live Here Anymore', which Was (Not Was) themselves cut in 1992, although it was not released until 2008.

Also finished by Dylan, with the help of Willie Nelson, was another abandoned song 'conjuring up images of a dying town and a disappearing way of life'. Nelson wanted a song for the Was-produced album he was working on in 1992, *Across The Borderline*. 'Heartland' had begun life in 1990 as another 'Rock Me Mama' moment, Don Was recalling, 'We'd cut some other song, and while the band came in to hear the playback, Bob stayed out there and the assistant engineer was smart enough to observe him playing, and turned the recorder on . . . when Bob started humming this song.' What he came up with lit a fire under Nelson:

> There's a home place under fire tonight in the Heartland,
> There's a well with water so bitter nobody can drink,
> Ain't no way to get high, and my mouth is so dry, that I can't speak,
> Don't they know that I'm dyin', why ain't nobody cryin' for me?*

Nelson completed the lyric, and after Don checked Dylan's schedule, he booked a session 'the day after the Columbia 30th anniversary show . . . That's why everyone was in New York . . . Bob came in and Willie was already seated in the vocal booth, and they just nodded hello to each other. I thought the mike was off . . . And then I realized they are two guys who are so deep, they don't need to engage in small talk.' The pair were similarly uncommunicative and equally inspired the following April at Nelson's 'Big Six-O' telecast, where they duetted

---

* See my 2010 study of Dylan's songs, *Still on The Road*, for a fuller explanation of its composition.

on a particularly fine version of Townes Van Zandt's 'Pancho And Lefty', the song Dylan had used as a template for 'Tweeter And The Monkey Man' and subsequently made his own in concert.

If the Dylan/Nelson friendship went back to at least 1976 – when Nelson rode to his rescue one night in Houston – the next potential collaborator went back even further, to his most successful album, *Desire*, after Dylan re-established contact with his old friend, Claudia, now Mrs Jacques Levy:

> We would talk painting because I was some[one] he could talk painting to . . . [Around '93], we were living up in Hamilton, [Ontario] . . . Bob wanted to work with Jacques again . . . He was trying to figure out a way to . . . work together again. He was very nervous that he would be in a college town, and people would see him and not leave him alone . . . Jacques thought he could find a place for Bob where he wouldn't be exposed. But it never worked out.

If Levy once unlocked an album of songs in him, Dylan's next collaborator, Gerry Goffin, was a member of the *pantheon*. His Sixties collaboration with his then-wife, Carole King, had redefined the craft of the pop lyric. Dylan first gave Goffin a song scrap, like Nelson. This one was from the November 1985 Church sessions, an instrumental called simply 'Polka'. The song they came up with – 'Masquerade' – was a withering putdown of the world of entertainment: 'I'm at a loss to entertain/ You see the cells are paralyzed inside my brain/ I bid adieu to all of you/ I think it's time to end this masquerade.' Their other co-composition on Goffin's 1996 album, *Back Room Blood*, not only gave the album its title but suggested a shared worldview and a sacred bond: 'The world's been run with back room blood/ Long before the time of the flood.' Vestiges of that vertiginous vision remained.

He continued calling on old collaborators, hoping they had kept a note of his muse's current address. A mid-Nineties week-long stay at the Mill Valley home of Robert Hunter, ostensibly to write songs together, merely confirmed to wife Maureen that their guest was a doubtful one. Another Bay Area resident, Neil Young, also spent time with Dylan in 1992 and 1994. Though the idea of writing together never came up, in 1994 Young ended up sidestage for the final night at Dylan's first New York residency since October 1990, at the Roseland Ballroom, with Bruce Springsteen as his date.

Both would-be peers had probably been on Dylan's mind back in 1988, when he told Kathryn Baker, 'People think that people who play the acoustic guitar and write their own songs are folk singers . . . [but] their own songs . . . are not really based on anything,' a sentiment he reiterated in 2001 to Gundersen, 'People who came after me . . . didn't play folk songs. They heard me and thought, . . . "I can do that." . . . [But] those songs don't have any *resonance*.' Confirmation he meant Springsteen came backstage at the Supper Club in November 1993, when arch-critic Dave Marsh asked Dylan if he thought Springsteen could speak for an audience other than the established one 'that could produce huge sales for a greatest-hits package'. Dylan told him, 'People like Springsteen . . . weren't there to see the end of the traditional people. But I was.'

It was also presumably Dylan's idea for him and Young to venture down to The Bitter End after one of Young's February 1992 Beacon shows to catch one of the last Sixties folk revivalists still ploughing that furrow, David Bromberg. For the first time in twenty years, Young was (briefly) outselling and outwriting Dylan by pandering to that audience 'that could produce huge sales for a greatest-hits package'. So, when he attempted to debut the songs written for the as-yet-unreleased *Harvest Moon* album at The Beacon, he was faced with a barrage of requests for his old hits.

Dylan, who had apparently been considering a similar solo residency, left dispirited and dissuaded. Hence, perhaps, his trip down to The Bitter End, like it was February 1969 again. There he found Bromberg still singing songs like 'Dehlia', from his 1972 debut album (on which Dylan contributed harmonica for 'Sammy's Song'), as well as other originals in a distinctly traditional style, like 'Sloppy Drunk' and 'Kaatskill Serenade', both from his 1976 album, *How Late'll Ya Play 'Til?* Knowing full well, 'People identify me with the songs I write, they don't identify me [with] what I can do with a song that's already been written,' Dylan almost envied Bromberg's ability to blur such boundaries.

Having reconnected, Dylan at some time that spring suggested they do an album together of electric folk/blues covers, having opened the year's touring in Perth with an electric 'Little Maggie', and a show in Sydney in April with 'Don't Let Your Deal Go Down', before performing 'Delia' in a similar guise at the Pantages in May. In fact, he spent much of 1992 referencing 'songs . . . already written', performing no less than twenty-six 'covers' live, twenty of them either traditional or in the traditional style. This being Dylan, exactly one of them featured on that year's album of covers.

A Tulsa-based list of such songs in Dylan's hand – perhaps a shortlist of songs he intended to record – includes, in the margin, eight songs of a traditional hue: 'Polly Vaughan', 'Streamline Cannonball', 'Casey Jones', 'Lonesome Valley', 'Four Strong Winds' and 'The French Girl' (both by his old friend, Ian Tyson), 'Blackjack Davey' and 'Goodnight Irene', as well as the Presley classic, 'Don't'.

In the *World Gone Wrong* notes, he would talk about 'learning to go forward by turning back the clock', a topic he warmed to in contemporary interviews, 'It was necessary for me to get back to the stuff that meant so much to me at one time.' Once he reconnected with his wayward muse, he gave credit where he felt it was due: 'If you understand those [old] songs . . . there's nowhere you can't go'; which is why he 'recorded two LPs of old songs . . . so I could personally get back to the music that's true for me.'*

The first of them he would have to do twice before it was alright, having initially tried to recreate the *Oh Mercy* vibe by renting a big old house in Chicago's Highland Park and recording there, even letting Maymudes use his Dylan-crazy girlfriend, Michelle, a native Chicagoan, to do some of the initial scouting.

The 'old songs' *schtick* was not hard and fast. These sessions included not just three of Bromberg's own songs – 'World Of Fools', 'Sloppy Drunk' and 'Kaatskill Serenade' – but also Tim Hardin's 'Lady Came From Baltimore', Ian Tyson's 'Summer Wages', Mose Allison's 'Everybody Cryin' Mercy'† and the 1977 gospel song, 'Rise Again'; while the subsequent Debbie Gold-produced sessions would include Fifties doo-wop classic, 'You Belong To Me', Lonnie Johnson's 'Tomorrow Night', Stephen Foster's 'Hard Times' and Mick Slocum's modern

---

* At MusiCares in 2015, he reaffirmed, 'Folk songs . . . gave me the code for everything that's fair game.'

† Also one of sixty-six songs in his *Philosophy of Modern Song* (2022), where Dylan suggests we 'leave justice and mercy to the gods of heaven . . . Mercy may be a trap for fools.'

arrangement of the traditional 'Jim Jones'. He got himself into legal trouble as a result. Although he insisted, 'Those songs . . . nobody knows who wrote them, if anybody did write them,' every self-respecting folkie knew Slocum, an Antipodean Van Ronk, came up with his own tune, and that was the one Dylan copped.

The idea of doing an all-electric album with Bromberg had come about – according to the ever-curious Susan Ross – because he wanted to go 'into the studio with a producer from the old days to make a perfunctory album for the label. In theory, he liked the idea of working with David again, but when he got there, he found the songs were wrong, the musicians were wrong and the mixes were terrible. He fought at first, thinking his will would prevail, but after three weeks, he saw [there was] nothing to do but walk away.'

Bromberg even vouchsafed Ross's cutting assessment halfway, admitting in 2007, 'There was some good stuff there, but Bob let me mix it and I did a terrible job. The roughs are way, way better. If you listen to Dylan records around the time of *Highway 61 Revisited* . . . there is a particular sound . . . the sound of the room. Those are rough mixes, [but] they have so much more immediacy.'

There was certainly no shortage of material stockpiled in that fortnight. According to engineer Dan White, twenty-six songs were cut, seven of them on the first night when 'there was electricity in the air . . . At times we would get what would sound like the recording of the year – it would be one of those magical musical moments – then Dylan would say, Erase it . . . I thought he was just teasing us.'

Fifteen of these tracks were mixed, possibly including a version of 'Hey Joe' cut 'as a warm up', but, as he confided to Cooky, 'He knew immediately, even before leaving the city, that they weren't what he'd hoped for. He called from . . . the Omni, while packing up for home. In a short, businesslike check in, he [said,] "I got three keepers."'

He surely had these sessions in mind when observing, the following year, 'I'm most disappointed when producers overlook the strength of my music. When producers try to equal[ize] everything out, it's to dismal effect on my records.'

The chameleon cover-artist, having abandoned the idea of an acoustic residency, decided to make an all-acoustic album instead, even if Debbie Gold later told me, 'It just turned into a record, really. [Initially,] we were dealing with a problem he had with that [Bromberg] record.' As with the first Wilburys' album, a happy accident finally made use of the home studio Dylan had owned all these years. When engineer Micajah Ryan arrived, at Debbie's behest, he was informed the plan was 'to record just a couple of songs for a day or two . . . [But] Dylan was on a roll, and I didn't get back to my family until . . . we finished what became *Good As I Been To You*,' more than a fortnight later. Gold herself had represented producers, befriended producers, but never, ever *been* a producer, making her a perfect sounding board for an unproduceable maverick:

> **Micajah Ryan**: He'd come in each day with at least a couple of songs to work on. He'd do several takes in every key and tempo imaginable; speeding up or slowing down, making it higher or lower in pitch until he felt he got it. He didn't talk with me at all about songs or what he wanted to do, but he consulted Debbie on every take. He trusted her and I got the feeling that was unusual for him. She was never afraid to tell him the truth, and, boy, was she persistent; often convincing him to stay with a song long after he seemed to lose interest in it.

Dylan exacted his usual retribution, refusing to include Debbie's favourite track, 'You Belong To Me', which ended up on the *Natural Born Killers* soundtrack instead. She hung in there, though, even when he insisted on making her sit with him as he set about 'sequencing it in the car. He'd . . . play me tapes . . . do[ing] various sequences on a really bad ghetto-blaster.' He even wanted to add some tape hiss where there was none, telling engineer Ryan about 'different techniques that he had heard of – like not letting the digital recording ever go completely to "black." This was in an effort to simulate the analog recording medium that always has some sound on it – even if it's hiss.'

The resultant album had one song dating back to 1549 ('Froggy Went A-Courtin'), one song he first recorded in 1962 ('Sitting On Top Of The World'), just one song he'd played in concert that year ('Little Maggie') and no obvious identity save that, in Cooky's words, it 'sounded like his usual around-the-house daily fare. He was always casually singing these kind of old song stories, switching to another [on a] whim before the previous one had time to be absorbed.'

Its acoustic nature and the familiarity of the material almost guaranteed him good reviews, though he was rightly castigated by *Folk Roots*'s

Ian Anderson for claiming arrangement credits – and therefore the publishing – on songs he had self-evidently appropriated from modern interpreters like Nic Jones ('Canadee-I-O'), Paul Brady ('Arthur McBride'), and Mick Slocum, all of whom could have done with the money. 'Leave that kinda thing to Paul Simon,' was Anderson's implied subtext.

Although Dylan gave the impression to Cooky that 'the material . . . would have special meaning for her,' and implied to Susan Ross that what 'had begun as a fluke . . . would put him back on the map as a serious artist,' when *Good As I Been To You* was released he immediately stopped touting it. The only two songs he played at the London shows Cooky saw in February 1993 were Mick Slocum's version of 'Jim Jones' and Lonnie Johnson's 'Tomorrow Night'. The latter was, as Dawson and Propes wrote in *What Was the First Rock'n'Roll Record?* (1992), 'an odd recording from the start. Subtly backed by piano and bass, the old bluesman sang in a high, mournful hillbilly voice, [a] song . . . written in 1939 for Horace Heidt's pop orchestra by a couple of Tin Pan Alley journeymen.'

By May, with 'Hard Times' now opening the shows, Dylan decided to repeat himself – something he'd never done before in a thirty-year recording career – taping another coupla dozen songs of a traditional hue from which he and Debbie could compile a sequel of sorts, *World Gone Wrong*, the final album of his 1988 Sony contract. This time he stuck to songs in the public domain, having stockpiled twice as many songs as the previous summer, only to issue a ten-track album with just one 'composed' song on it, the 19th century gospel hymn, 'Lone Pilgrim'. He had recorded lovely versions of The Platters' 'Twilight Time' and croon-tune, 'Goodnight, My Love (Pleasant Dreams)', but preferred to take liberties with the songs of the Mississippi Sheiks ('World Gone Wrong' and 'Blood In My Eyes') and Blind Willie McTell ('Broke Down Engine'), sure in the knowledge that they had taken liberties with tradition, too.

At least this time he wrote a set of sleeve notes which ostensibly addressed the sources of such songs. But only ostensibly. Originally one long off-shoot from a remark Tommy Lee Jones made when asked what it was like when he started acting, and quoted the 'revolution in the air' line from 'Tangled Up In Blue', it prompted Dylan to wonder if the actor knew the source. He concluded, 'One thing for sure, it was merely in his head, like these songs are in mine.' In the end, the notes were trimmed top and tail, either by Sony or its *auteur*, losing an uncited line from Friedrich Schiller's *The Maid of Orleans*, 'When is nature so in struggle with itself that heaven doth the righteous cause desert & that the devil it defends?' and a 'state of the nation' element which concluded, 'Something tells me that the Brainwashing is complete. That there's no more to achieve. Evil charlatans have tipped the balance.'

The draft version, housed in Tulsa, confirms Dylan worked long and hard on these notes – his first since *Desire** – even as a surplus of songs again induced him to make calls he alone would. In the process, he sleighted the British bedrock of his repertoire, using only 'Love Henry', a bowdlerized American variant of Child Ballad 68 ('Young Hunting'), and 'Jack A-Roe', the second cross-dressing sailor song he'd sung in a year.[†] He had also recorded the timeless 'Seeds Of Love', 'Roving Blade' – debuted in Reims on July 1st, 1992, and never bettered – and two songs he plundered from Paul Brady's repertoire, 'Mary And The Soldier' and a 'Bonny Light Horseman', which he dismissed for being 'too fast' when it was actually just right.

Once again, Miss Gold had to bite her lip, 'If I'd like something, I'd keep my mouth shut, because he'd literally take it away from me.' She was equally sad to see two Irish folksongs bite the dust, 'Twenty-One Years' and 'Till This Day Is Done'. At least he finally released his own 'Delia', but only after asking Gold, 'Was there good parts in there?'

Of the seven acoustic songs he'd played all around the world in 1992, only 'The Two Soldiers' – which he said he learnt from Hazel & Alice, not Garcia – made the cut. Not even 'Little Moses', which he sung almost every night, made the requisite pay grade, even though he had issued a fifty-five-minute album a year earlier, and he sure as hell wasn't doing this one for the publishing. It smacked of another contractual obligation, fulfilled in time to sign another contract with Sony on December 21st, 1993, this one for *ten* albums, 'each New Album [to]

---

* There were notes supposed to accompany *under the red sky*, but they were never used.

[†] The obscure 'Female Ramblin' Sailor' had featured regularly at the Australian shows.

consist entirely of Master Recordings made in the course of that New Album recording project'.*

That clause immediately excluded his next album, *Greatest Hits Vol. 3*, released on November 15th, 1994 as stocking-filler. Because Sony let Dylan pick the tracks, not many stockings were so blessed. His two big European hits from the past two decades – 'Baby Stop Crying' and 'Man Gave Names To All The Animals' – were both omitted. He preferred two non-album tracks, 'The Groom's Still Waiting At The Altar' and 'Series Of Dreams', and a ghastly remix of 1989's 'Dignity', even though he recorded three Elvis covers that September at Sony. None of them, not even a devastatingly intense 'Anyway You Want Me', would suffice, producer Don Was concluding, 'I don't think he felt the band was swinging enough. It was his live band and he was trying it out, seeing what it would be like to record with them . . . Carole Childs was the A&R coordinator on the project, and I think she sorta pushed him into it.'

He remained stuck in a rut, recording covers, the good and the great, including 'My Blue-Eyed Jane' for a Jimmie Rodgers tribute CD that was his idea but took three years to appear, and a sprightly 'Hollis Brown' for a Mike Seeger LP cut at the time of the *World Gone Wrong* sessions. As he later confessed to Hilburn, after the drought ended, 'I didn't feel like I wanted to put forth the effort to record anything. The acoustic albums were easy enough, [but] I was pretty content to let it be that.'

Equally easy, and a lot less enjoyable, was the first album to count against his new contract, the entirely redundant *Unplugged*, a pale shadow of the Supper Club quartet, compiled from two November 1994 shows at Sony Studios to a select audience of Bobcats, bimbos and businessmen. Dylan claimed, on its release, 'I would have liked to do old folk songs with acoustic instruments, but there was a lot of input from other sources as to what would be right for the MTV audience.' All it really required was some of that fabled willpower on his part to have made it something worthwhile.

Even his one sop to the faithful – a live version of 'Dignity' – only hinted at the song's latent greatness. Thankfully, by the time this demo-like 'Dignity' appeared, in May 1995, he had delivered a 'Dignity' worth

---

* This surprisingly long-term new contract would run through 2012.

dying for, a shotgun blast from the recent past fired off at the Brixton Academy on March 29th, at the midpoint of a 26-date European Tour that spring which was the high watermark of 'the J.J. Jackson era' (1991-97).

It started on March 11th with a show in Prague that bore comparison with any from Dylan's Seventies heyday. Crippled by back pain again, he had been obliged to reschedule the first show, but he repaid the travelling fans (and over a hundred from London alone came a-calling) in spades, performing without a guitar, whipping out his harmonica on song after song, introducing the Palace of Culture to performance-art of the highest order, including a 'Down In The Flood' opener to audible gasps from fans on the front-row. Once again, he had somehow been renewed inside.

The 1995 shows saw Dylan often performing at the peak of his powers, culminating in December with a series of joint shows on the north-east seaboard – dubbed The Paradise Lost Tour – organized at the last minute to allow grieving widow Patti Smith to return to touring for the first time in sixteen long years. Dylan even took Patti aside at a 4 p.m. soundcheck, first night in Boston, to tell her, 'Patti, I was worried about you. You gave your soul away to somebody else. Don't ever do that again.'

The following night, at the end of Dylan's acoustic set, Patti joined him for what became a nightly ritual. According to a 2021 online Patti post, 'After the death of my husband, the poet-activist Allen Ginsberg encouraged me to perform again. He had appealed to Bob, asking him to help me ease back onto the stage. After the first few jobs I was given the Bob Dylan *Lyric[s]* book and invited to choose a song that we could perform together. I spent a sleepless night going over the many songs I loved, and decided by daybreak on the song, "Dark Eyes."' Actually, Patti had already been performing this song for a couple of months, and the circumstances were more like those relayed to me by Patti's then-tour manager, Renaissance man Raymond Foye:

On the second night, at a gymnasium in Connecticut [sic], Dylan came out from his dressing room with Jeff Kramer, and watched a song from Patti's set, from the edge of the stage. Patti didn't know he was doing this. By chance, the song she was singing was 'The Wicked Messenger'. At the soundcheck to the first show in Boston, Bob came up to

Patti and asked her how things were going, if everything was all right for her on the tour, was there anything she needed, was she being treated well, and was she getting enough time to soundcheck with her band . . . Bob was wearing his sweatshirt with the hood pulled up, and Patti had adopted the same dress, so they were both standing face-to-face, hood to hood. Bob asked Patti if she wanted to do a song with him. 'Any song you want, I'll do any song at all.' 'What about Dark Eyes?' Patti replied. This clearly took Bob off guard. 'Uh, yeah, we could do that, sure,' he stammered. 'Jeff, where's that book? Go get [*Lyrics*].' Kramer ran off . . . and returned a minute later . . . J.J. Jackson came over with his guitar and they begin to work out the chords. Later, I asked J.J. if that was the first time he'd ever played it and he said no, they had rehearsed it a few times, but apparently Bob [had] decided not to play it publicly. The song was premiered that night. It was a rocky performance. Bob . . . messed up the lyrics several times. After the show he apologized to Patti, saying, 'I'm sorry Patti I messed that all up. I'm gonna go home and study the lyrics.' They continued to do it every night thereafter on the tour. And it got better and better . . . The last performance was the best one – the third night at the Electric Factory in Philadelphia. That night Patti walked out on stage in a Comme de Garçon dress that Michael Stipe had bought for her. She looked ravishing, and Bob did a double take and smiled broadly.

The last of three Philly shows was a fitting end to a tumultuous year, in which Dylan finally put the 'J.J./ Winston' band through its paces, Patti joining him a second time for a wholly unexpected 'Knockin' On Heaven's Door' encore. Dylan was delighted, even as he slid into the snow on Interstate 80, heading for Minnesota and the ubiquitous family Christmas.

A north country boy, he remained unfazed as the wind continued to hit heavy on the borderline, but when by mid-January, the winter winds showed no sign of abating, he apparently phoned his tour-manager Jeff Kramer and told him, 'Well, I'm snowed in, so I'm writing songs. But I'm not going to record them.' He later confided to Mikal Gilmore, 'I'd been writing down couplets and verses and things [for a while]. It was starting to pile up.' So was the snow.

These songs addressed two themes which had been weighing him down for the past few years: an unspecified heartbreak that for him

drew a line in the sand, and his own mortality. He later tried to suggest
the resultant album dealt not with *his* fear of death, but rather his critics': 'People say *Time Out of Mind* deals with . . . my mortality . . . Well,
it doesn't deal with my mortality. It maybe just deals with mortality in
general . . . But I didn't see any one critic say, "It deals with my mortality" – you know, his own . . . like whoever's writing about the record
has got eternal life, and the singer doesn't.'

Of course, in the good old days he would immediately have booked
a studio and taken his touring band in to record these songs, but this
time, or so he claimed, 'I was reluctant to record them, because I didn't
want to come out with a contemporary-sounding record.' Which fails
to explain why the first person he shared the songs with was Daniel
Lanois, who had just perpetrated an even greater sonic assault than *Oh
Mercy* on Emmylou Harris, the appositely-named *Wrecking Ball*, burying her in a swamp of sound that also sank one of Dylan's greatest-ever
songs, 'Every Grain Of Sand'.*

It was an album where the demos were better, perhaps convincing
Dylan to see what all the fuss was about, cutting his first-ever set of
album demos. Taking a break from the unending road while he looked
for a new drummer after Watson said a fond farewell at an early August
1996 two-night residency at the House of Blues – filmed for a possible
telecast – Dylan met with Lanois in New York, 'I called [Lanois] and
showed him a lot of the songs. I also familiarized him with the way I
wanted the songs to sound. I think I played him some Slim Harpo
recordings.'

It seems that he *literally* showed Danny Boy these songs, Lanois later
stating, 'We didn't even have any instruments . . . He just had a stack of
lyrics.' He also had a music player and began to play Lanois, 'all these
old blues recordings, Little Walter, guys like that. And he'd ask [me],
"Why do those records sound so great? Why can't anybody have a
record sound like that anymore?" ' Dylan told him he was looking for
'an identifiable sound . . . more traditional, like a record on a record
player.' Perhaps he also played him one new song, 'Can't Wait', which
he had just demoed in London with Ron Wood, after an open-air Hyde
Park jamboree in late June.

---

* A 2014 deluxe edition of *Wrecking Ball* does at least include a set of swamp-free
demos.

The meeting, according to Lanois, resulted in 'a lot of philosophical exchanges . . . It was clear to me that he loved records . . . made at the birth of a medium . . . There's a vibrant tone to [such] works . . . and Bob wanted that vitality in his work . . . I left with inspiration and a list of records that Bob recommended as good rock'n'roll references: Charley Patton[!], Little Walter, Arthur Alexander [etc.] . . . Bob wanted that sound and I felt I knew how to get it.' Such self-confidence would not survive the six-month process required to extract a new album from a reluctant recording artist.

The lyrics Dylan read to Lanois he later described as 'liv[ing] within that line between despondency and hope', combining with elements Jack Fate might have suggested had 'got a radical hostility towards sensuality'. Sometimes, despondency seemed to be winning, as in a lost couplet written on the back of a March 1996 *L.A. Times* article, 'Without a guide, without a chart/ Grief can cut you to the heart.'

He was still grieving at the loss of his friend, Jerry Garcia, who had died the previous August, the victim of his own unquenchable appetites. Dylan's brief obituary described the man-mountain as 'the very spirit personified of whatever is Muddy River Country . . . There's a lot of spaces and advances between the Carter Family and say, Ornette Coleman . . . but he filled them all . . . There's no way to convey the loss.' His fate also served as a timely reminder to the newly abstinent artist to rein in some residual vices.

If the new songs were anything to go by, he had come to realize his passion for women was the most dangerous vice of all, and not just because an ex-girlfriend – Ruth Tyrangiel – had brought suit in L.A. Superior Court in 1994, claiming that 'in or about February 1974, Plaintiff and Defendant . . . agreed that Plaintiff and Defendant would hold themselves out to the general public as husband and wife.' Unfortunately for Tyrangiel, her *actual* husband scuppered her assertion. But it was a warning shot across the bows.

When Lanois, engineer Mark Howard, hip-hop drummer Tony Mangurian and Dylan convened at a converted, disused cinema in Oxnard, California, in mid-August 1996, Dylan had a dozen original songs he was looking to demo. What he had yet to express was just how sick he was of love, even if the sentiment informed almost everything he now demoed. He began with perhaps the most love-sick song of all, 'The Water Is Wide', as if prepping for a third album of traditional covers. This time, it was a one-off – its purpose seemingly the same one which inspired the 16th century 'knitter i' the sun' who first gave the song form, as 'Waly, Waly'.

Five weeks later the quartet reconvened at Oxnard. Time to get down to brass tacks. The wrecking crew had done their homework, Lanois having 'listened to a lot of old records that Bob recommended I fish out . . . some Charley Patton records, dusty old rock'n'roll records really, blues records.' And that wasn't all he had done: 'Tony and I played along to those records, and then I built some loops [out] of what Tony and I did . . . And we built a [set] of demos around them . . . Some of the ultimate productions [on the LP] ended up having those loops in them.'

These are presumably the eleven untitled instrumentals, all running to between one and five minutes, found among the Teatro tapes. In Lanois's own, somewhat overactive imagination he fondly imagined, 'Tony and I . . . [had] closed our eyes and transported ourselves [in]to the Charley Patton Orchestra, fast and furious . . . [We] listened back to our jams, and selected the best . . . , eight-bar sections. We then deleted the source inspirations and just listened to our performances – they had a vibe.'

Initially, Lanois and Howard struggled to convince Dylan to sing any full versions of his new songs, even with a piano to hand, and a percussionist in situ itching to play along. After a ragged but righteous four-minute demo of 'Red River Shore' on September 26th, Dylan informed them, 'That's good enough for reference.' 'Mississippi' was similarly truncated. And on the same day, he cut a gripping 'Not Dark Yet', but only included the first couple of verses. When Lanois asked if there is more, Dylan replied, 'There's a *lot* more words,' but refused to do them until, finally, he summoned up the strength to return to 'Red River Shore' to deliver the full eight-minute epic, only to be audibly dissatisfied with the outcome, 'I dunno, man. I gave it my best bash. I bashed it as good as I could. I think we killed it.' It took until October 1st for him to finally cut loose on 'Dreamin' Of You' and 'Can't Wait'. But in both cases the results were superior to any later take and more than good enough to warrant inclusion on the result-ant album:

Mark Howard: When Dylan first came in . . . he'd say, 'Yeah, I've got this song,' and he'd go over to the piano, and he'd play just a little bit . . . And Dan goes, 'Well, it sounds really great, but I need to hear some lyrics.' But Bob wouldn't sing any lyrics. Next day, he'd show up, 'I got another song for you.' He'd play a little bit of piano. 'Whaddaya think of that one?' Dan would go, 'Well – I really need to hear a song.' . . . Finally . . . he . . . plays this song on the piano, called 'Can't Wait' . . . Tony just went over to the drumkit and started playing this groove . . . and Bob is hammering out this gospel kind of piano and really singing . . . It was stunning.

He had his starting point. Through October 7th, Dylan and the Charley Patton Orchestra demoed at least thirteen Dylan song-ideas, with titles hinting at his own mortality like 'Tryin' To Get To Heaven' and 'Not Dark Yet (But It's Getting There)' along with tales of heartbreak like 'All I Ever Loved Was You', 'Can't Wait (For You To Change Your Mind)', 'Make You Feel My Love', 'Dreamin' Of You' and 'Till I Fell In Love With You'.* Lanois was particularly enthused about Dylan's piano-playing: 'Bob is a roaring piano player with a great left hand, and he made my old Steinway sound like a barrelhouse full of birds, [and] the vocals he sang [in Oxnard] were full-bodied and deep . . . I felt that we were on the verge of something great.'

Even the musicians who worked on the later studio sessions were enthused by some of the demos they heard, Duke Robillard talking about 'a beautiful take of "Not Dark Yet" that was more basic . . . I don't mean basic as in demo, but basic as in the feel . . . more acoustic.' Inevitably, though, there came a day – about a week before Dylan went back on the road with new drummer, ex-Garcia Band member David Kemper – when he duly announced, 'Hey, it's too close to home, I can't work here, I gotta get away.' Lanois had not seen this coming, 'Things were going well with Bob, and I was the most excited I had been regarding production in a long time. Then came the crushing phone call, he wanted to leave the Teatro. He explained to me that . . . we needed to assemble a band, [because he wanted to] make the record in Miami.'

Lanois and Howard were left with a collection of tape loops, two of which would inform the finished album; a handful of finished demos – among which were releasable versions of 'Can't Wait' and 'Dreamin'

---

* Other songs include an eight-minute 'Song Sketch', 'Red River Shore', 'King Of Them All', 'Doing Alright', 'Dirt Road Blues' and 'Highlands'.

Of You' and a conviction that this was a big mistake. Howard, in particular, came to feel throughout his time in Florida that 'we tried to get back and capture what we had [at Oxnard], but it turned into a whole other thing'.

Dylan had stockpiled a number of songs which said much the same thing, hence the ease with which he could shuttle lyrics back and forth between different cuts. Time to separate the wheat from the naff. As he told Alan Jackson, 'We actually had twice as many songs as we needed . . . Those you hear on the album . . . are more concerned with the dread realities of life than the bright and rosy idealism popular today.'

As per usual, his solution to having too many songs was to write three more – 'Love Sick', 'Cold Irons Bound' and 'Standing In The Doorway' – all of which were destined for the album, and a set of lyrics, 'Make You Feel My Love', that just needed a tune. He was giving himself choices galore, à la *Shot of Love*, even as interstate trooper J.J. Jackson said a farewell to the Never Ending Tour after a February Japanese tour. Feeling he had 'twice as many songs as we needed' – only true if he intended something LP-length – Dylan did something he hadn't really done since 1983's 'Too Late': he began to 'frankenstein' lines, couplets and entire verses, moving them from one song to another, embracing a new conceit: 'I had to scramble around to find the right types of lyrics and basically moved lyrics around and put together the puzzle.'

The result was more puzzle than product. One song, 'Until I Saw You' – as in, 'Didn't think I could love anyone until I saw you . . .' – had already been traded in for parts, becoming 'All I Ever Loved Is You', after he discarded its first and last verses and with it a Pygmalion-like character who 'married a statue made out of solid stone', a premonition of 2020's 'My Own Version Of You'. Also taken out was someone who could 'get away with murder', shooting somebody twenty times and making it look like suicide. The original even contained the one and only known reference in Dylan's canon to 'a higher power', a term more common at AA meetings than Bible classes. Maybe the drinking had gotten even worse than friends feared.

Even 'All I Ever Loved Is You' wasn't safe from the scrapyard. After cutting eleven takes at Oxnard in the period he was just recording instrumentals, he decided to separate the tune and the words. The former he adapted to a new song called 'Million Miles'; the latter's five verses* became the core of a song whose central idea, and a number of lines, derived from tradition; in the case of 'I'm trying to get to heaven before they close the door', an old gospel song. The original denouement seemed to fit fine. And yet it was discarded: 'Judgement Day is coming, it must be overdue/ The silent sun is heavy, all I ever loved is you.'

Next for the chop was 'Dreamin' Of You', one of three songs whose title referenced some female heartbreaker in the accusative second-person. Thankfully, before it could be sliced and diced, it was captured on day one at Criteria, an overnight session on January 2nd, along with another composition that dripped with the blood of a poet, 'Not Dark Yet'. Running to nine minutes, the prototypical 'Not Dark Yet' saw the world as a dark place not because the 'night is coming when no man can work', but because he has lost 'a love that I know I never [felt] else-where'. At this juncture, 'Just being in the same country as her is making me blue,' so he heads for 'the land of the lost, where dreams come to die.'

The last two verses suggest a man utterly bereft, 'When I close my eyes, I can see her from a long way off/ Her lips so tender, her skin so soft,' and on the verge of losing faith, 'I've gone too far down life's beaten track/ I'm hoping the Master will guide me back/ The vines are fadin' and the trees are bare . . .' The fifth and final verse he sang on that first night sees him surrendering to despondency:

> Well, I'm thinking about the things that have slowed me down
> And I tried to convince myself I can turn it around.
> The truth sinks its teeth in and it's biting down hard
> Feel like a three-time loser who's played his last card
> Sometimes my burden is more than I can bear
> It's not dark yet, but it's getting there.†

---

* As follows: 1. The air is getting hotter . . .; 2. When I was in Missouri . . . ; 3. Gonna sleep down in the parlour . . . ; 4. There's people at the station . . . ; 5. Going down to New Orleans.

† Another early take has an even better first couplet, expressing how the love he has lost almost consumed him: 'Well, somewhere I can smell a wood-burning fire/ And I'm thinking about the things that fed this desire.'

For now, he continued cutting the songs live, as he had always done, even as he tinkered with and transplanted verses as the whim took him. Having assembled a band that was partly his, partly Lanois's, by fortnight's end it would be almost entirely his. The setting itself – Criteria Studios – even prompted him to remember an aborted March 1970 session which was supposed to feature guitarist Jim Dickinson's band, The Dixie Flyers. Having, in Dylan's words, 'started out playing the same time as me, in about '57 or '58, [and] listened to the same things,' Dickinson imagined he'd be meeting some remote rock star. He was soon set right:

> When they picked me up at the airport, on the way back to the studio, one of the bodyguards was telling me, 'Don't look at him, don't talk to him,' all that stuff. First night, I don't even know if we'd done a song, I was standing out in the parking lot smoking a joint, and here he comes, 'Hey, didn't you used to play with Sleepy John Estes?' . . . He talked to me the whole time. In fact, it pissed Lanois off: 'He doesn't talk to me. He thinks I'm a whippersnapper!'

Dylan also requisitioned an old friend from the Doug Sahm Band, accordionist Augie Meyers, who, like Dickinson, quickly realized there were two camps at Criteria, and never the twain: 'Daniel Lanois wanted to use his band on the session. And Bob wanted his friends. And so – Bob used his friends . . . Daniel wanted it one way, Bob wanted it another . . . It came out like Bob wanted it.' In fact, Dylan stuck to his guns most of the time. Much to Lanois's chagrin he insisted on all the following, 'Tony Garnier, [from] Bob's road band, was invited to play . . . Bob [also] suggested . . . Cindy Cashdollar; Bucky Baxter, Bob's pedal-steel player; Duke Robillard; Robert Britt and Augie Meyers.'

Another key component Dylan called up directly was timekeeper extraordinaire, Jim Keltner, who knew Bob's m.o. by heart, 'You can either let somebody else get the musicians for you, and then figure out how to try to tell them to do it, or you get the musicians yourself, who you think can pull off your ideas . . . On *Time Out of Mind*, Bob called me and a lot of other guys specifically,' putting Lanois's nose distinctly out of joint. Mark Howard saw it all first-hand, '[After] Dan had put together a band . . . Dylan brought in all these Nashville people, and I think that made Dan a little mental, having all these Nashville strummers strumming. It was a bit too much.'

The first thing Dylan did was play the assembled cast, Keltner included, 'some demos of the songs . . . that had been done prior to the sessions . . . [He] wanted to do [them] again and flesh [them] out another way.' The early results were not entirely promising. After a formative 'Standing In The Doorway', Dylan complained, 'I didn't really hear it that way. On the demo, it was this kinda rough [thing].' Rather than work on it further, he tackled a song which at Oxnard was just a title and a tune, 'Make You Feel My Love'.

When Dylan told Meyers he'd written it on the piano, Augie suggested, 'Play piano . . . I'll play organ, let's just have one bass, one drum and one guitar.' For the only time at these sessions it injected some spontaneity into proceedings, Dylan cutting the song live in a single eight-minute take that was actually two takes back-to-back, Dylan calling out to the band three minutes in, 'Do that verse again.' The vocal almost salvages one of his tritest lyrics and – Adele be praised – most valuable copyrights. It would be the only live vocal on the entire album, as Dylan continued to believe he could redo any vocal and improve it.

In those first four days at Criteria, he continued to live in the moment, cutting the likes of 'Marchin' To The City', 'Mississippi' and a twelve-minute version of 'Red River Shore' (called 'Tombstone Dancehall' on the multis) live. All were later deemed surplus to requirement – as was a stab at surpassing the Teatro 'Can't Wait', dubbed by Dylan 'psychedelic'.* Lanois still preferred the original. Two other songs also attempted at these sessions Dickinson remembered causing ructions:

> 'Mississippi' and 'Girl from The Red River Shore' . . . represented the most conflict in the studio between Dylan and Lanois. In the case of 'Mississippi,' there was a cut that we had that was very swampy . . . that Lanois really liked. And it just wasn't the direction that Dylan wanted to go . . . The two of them really got into it over that one.

But neither compared to the spat over 'Can't Wait', which prompted

---

* It appears on disc three of *Tell Tale Signs* (2008), along with an edit of the twelve-minute 'Red River Shore'.

the producer to utter the immortal line: 'The world doesn't need another two-note melody from Bob Dylan,'* a summation of sorts for Dylan's entire post-*Red Sky* recording career. As Lanois wrote in his 2010 memoir, 'I felt that its potential as a hit was disintegrating in front of my eyes. I begged Bob to reconsider [using] the feel of the demo . . . [The new version had] a conventional feel . . . It did not become a hit.' Lanois, a name producer now, kept pushing Bob. Finally, the latter snapped, 'I don't wanna hear about this song anymore. We got a version down':

> **Mark Howard**: We [ended up with] three other versions of 'Can't Wait' . . . But Dylan wouldn't go back to the piano, because we had Dickinson there, and Bob wanted his vibe on it . . . Dan would be saying, 'You know, those are good takes, but . . . I gotta get back to *that.*' Dylan wasn't interested. He thought it was . . . done – over . . . There was a tension between Dan and Bob that got quite uncomfortable. There was a situation where Bob wouldn't actually talk to Dan for a little while. Dylan would only talk to me . . . I was like their go-between.

After this blow-out, the sessions never quite returned to an even keel. Lanois confined himself to taking it out on those musicians handpicked by Dylan, like Duke Robillard, 'Lanois had a hair across his ass about me from the word go . . . I tried to give him what he wanted but he just kept complaining about me . . . I didn't realize . . . that I was replacing Daniel Lanois in his role as guitar player . . . Thus began a really strange battle . . . Lanois would . . . say, "I want you to sit this one out." . . . [Then,] fifteen minutes later, he and Bob would go into the corner and argue. Lanois would come back into the control room and tell me to go back into the studio and play.'

After a short break on the 7th, Dylan reconfigured the line-up again, insisting David Kemper, who'd been playing with him since October, be brought in. Arriving on the 9th, Kemper was just 'sat back at the drums . . . playing, and there was nobody there . . . [but] then Bob snuck up behind me and said, "What are you playing? . . . Keep doing

---

* Sources disagree as to whether the comment relates to 'Cold Irons Bound' or 'Can't Wait'. It applies to both.

it." And he went and got a yellow pad of paper and sat next to the drums . . . He just started writing . . . for maybe ten minutes, and then he said . . . "Alright, everybody come on in, I want to put this down." . . . He stepped up to the microphone, "I'm beginning to hear voices, and there's no one around . . ." . . . Daniel Lanois wasn't happy; he didn't like it.' He sure didn't, breaking a guitar in frustration. The song was called 'Cold Irons Bound', and its two-note melody would infest the shows well into the 21st century, by which time Lanois had expressed exactly how he felt about these kinda songs:

> If you want to respond to the singing, then you should have a signature or a melody and not ramblings . . . I didn't want ramblings . . . It becomes like a mosquito in the room . . . I want to hear the singer . . . I wanted Bob's vocal and lyrics, and then if we had something to say musically aside from that, then let's say it loud and proud, no meanderings.

After the reset, Dylan junked pretty much everything recorded to date.* In the case of 'Dreamin' Of You' and 'Marchin' To The City', the songs themselves were sacrificed for some abstract greater good, with 'Dreamin' Of You' surrendering most of its best lines – though not the revelatory couplet, 'Your love is my link to the outside world/ And always it will remain' – to a revamped 'Standing In The Doorway'. 'Marchin' To The City' was likewise subsumed by the slighter 'Till I Fell In Love With You'.

A new 'Not Dark Yet' – originally one of his most heartfelt love songs in a decade – was cut on the 18th, and was now almost entirely about the night closing in. It was still one of the best things he had. Likewise, 'Standing In The Doorway' stopped rubbing salt in its wounds, and turned state's evidence at 'her' expense, but still came out cogent, though at the expense of a song the album needed, 'Dreamin' Of You'. 'Tryin' To Get To Heaven' also dialled down the heartbreak, losing the couplet, 'I'm crazy for you and another girl, too/ But I'm trying to get to heaven before they close the door.'

---

* Just three performances from week one would be pulled to master: 'Red River Shore' on the 4th, and 'Can't Wait' and 'Make You Feel My Love' from the 5th. Only the last of these made *Time Out of Mind*.

Lanois even convinced himself, 'His constant amendments seemed to improve the songs at every turn.' Yet it was Howard whom Dylan would ask, 'what I thought about lyrics . . . I'd just try and be really honest with him. He appreciated that. But if it was *Dan* who said something [positive], Bob was like, "Let's change it, right away."' Keltner, with more experience of Dylan sessions than the other musicians put together, recognized an underlying purpose:

> Bob is a hands-on guy . . . If you're called to produce a record for him, it's more likely you're producing *with* him . . . It can be difficult for a producer to try to produce somebody like Bob who is very strong in his own ideas. I saw Dan struggle [quite] a bit . . . Bob probably knew there'd be some butting of heads [and he] was able to use that . . . What I saw was that Bob really was bouncing off Daniel. This may have appeared to some people to be Bob abusing Daniel, but I'd say it was more that he was using Daniel to bounce off.

Lanois would bitterly contrast his experience at the Teatro, which 'had [a] vibe dripping from the walls', with recording at Criteria, where 'it felt like everything that I had worked for . . . slipped through my fingers . . . The drums sounded crap and the room was dead.' Even when the studio manager agreed to move them 'into the orchestra room down the hall', it failed to mend bridges, even as Dylan was going into overdrive. The takes just kept piling up, as rather than resolve who was playing on what, producer and artist decided to record musicians playing the same instruments in opposition to each other – a way of extending their personal battle into the very grooves of the album they spilt blood, sweat and tears making.

When steel guitarist Cindy Cashdollar arrived, again at Dylan's insistence, her first thought was, 'This is Noah's Ark, there's two of everything . . . two steel players, two percussionists, two keyboards. You've got instruments in the same register, [meaning] you [have to] try and weave in and out of everybody's way . . . I realized this was not gonna be [a case of] people playing solos.'

Jim Dickinson, an experienced producer in his own right, who had worked with Big Star, Green On Red and The Replacements, explained at the time, 'The biggest problem . . . was the set-up; there were like twelve musicians live on the floor, three full drumkits . . . He was definitely into the spontaneity of the moment . . . He wants the first interpretation he can get . . . Sometimes, when it was all going on, it would be chaotic.' The one occasion Dylan hadn't embraced the chaos was when he took Meyers's advice, on 'Make You Feel My Love', asking, 'If you and Doug [Sahm] were in the studio, how would you do it?' Meyers had replied, 'Well, we wouldn't have two drummers, four guitar players.' Ouch.

At the end of one take of 'Standing In The Doorway', Dylan admitted, 'That had a pretty big train wreck in the middle.' Cindy Cashdollar concurred, 'Yeah. Amtrak.' Likewise, at the end of an unsalvageable 'Cold Irons Bound', its author had to own up, 'The song is there, but I don't know if we're hitting it.'

It was as if Dylan thought he was remaking *Bitches Brew*. If that sounds far-fetched, he had told Don Was during sessions for his last original album that 'he'd [once] been to a Miles Davis session, [and] the band improvised for an hour and then Teo Macero, the producer, took a razorblade to tape and cut it into a coherent five-minute piece'.* The raw *TOOM* takes of the songs suggest he really thought he could do a Macero, 'Million Miles' running to 9.02, 'Red River Shore' to 12.24 and 'Till I Fell In Love With You' to 7.28, with long, meandering instrumental sections weaving around the melody and in the third case, protracted, punchy harp bursts inserted.

Howard, now engineer-in-chief, thought the fact that 'each take [was] in a different key', was, 'because he hasn't figured out the song'. Keltner offered a more plausible explanation, 'Bob is often happy to kind of jam a song together . . . [He likes] to come in and see what the players have to offer.' Some of Dylan's other chosen few were impressed at the ease with which he switched tack:

Augie Meyers: He might change the key two or three times and do it different. I never really knew the titles to any of the songs . . . until after the album came out. Bob actually called them 'sketches.' . . . It amazed me the way he could instantly change keys, hit all the chord changes. No matter what key he went into, he didn't have to search for the chord, he could just go straight to it.

---

* Dylan did not attend the August 1969 *Bitches Brew* sessions, but Harvey Brooks – with whom Dylan spent some time in spring 1970 – played on all three sessions.

Dylan's way of keeping the musicians on their toes, though, was driving Lanois to distraction. At one point, Howard saw him have 'a bit of a freak-out', shouting, 'If you can't make the changes, don't play! These takes are sounding junky!' The multis – faders up – bear the producer's plaintive plea out. Dylan, ever accepting of chaos, was no help. As Dickinson recalled, he would say 'almost nothing . . . until after we'd got something, and then he'd discuss it. But it was very abstract . . . Either he liked it, or he didn't like it.'

That impulse to jam to a preordained groove till it found the song's core and Lanois's conviction that the loops made in Oxnard served a purpose – other than to convince Dylan to avoid such technology like the plague – did find common ground on three occasions, none of which *should* have made the final cut, certainly not 'Dirt Road Blues', built on the quicksand of a groove taped at a summer 1996 rehearsal. On the other two, 'Million Miles' and 'Highlands', Lanois confirms, 'the grooves that we built [in Oxnard] were . . . piped into the headphones of the drummers . . . as beacons of time and vibe.' Certainly, an Oxnard loop was the basis of 'Million Miles', but it's not there on the multis. In the case of 'Highlands', the loop *is* on the multi, but is a mere four minutes long, looping on repeat. The way Dylan described the latter's construction to Hilburn, 'I had the guitar run off an old Charley Patton record . . . and always wanted to do something with that . . . The riff was just going repeatedly . . . then the words eventually come along.'

The result was a seventeen-minute slog that never left the sidings, let alone reached those mythical highlands. It would never reward repeated listenings. According to Dickinson, the one Dylan chose was 'the rundown, literally'. At least the lyrics stayed largely put, save for Dylan losing the un-PC couplet, 'I look out the window, I know it's a lost cause / I'm watching Ivy League boys walking with them young white squaws.'

'Highlands' wasn't recorded until January 16th, two weeks in, as Dylan – true to form – began introducing last-minute lyrics like 'Love Sick' and 'Million Miles' as well as shape-shifting rewrites of 'Not Dark Yet', 'Till I Fell In Love With You' and the ill-fated 'Mississippi', a key song that try as he might, he couldn't get a handle on.

By now Daniel and Dylan had partly made it up, albeit at the expense of Daniel's brother Bob, who at Lanois's suggestion, had been brought in 'to film the recording process'. Even Lanois admits this was 'not a great idea, as Dylan was not really in a filming frame of mind. My brother was asked to go home.'* Dylan, as ever, needed to be alone when communing with the inner darkness. Lanois even arranged for 'a little private area [that was] curtained off from the rest of the studio where Bob liked to have his meal[s]. He had a friend with him and they'd have some time to talk in privacy during the eating hour.' Actually, all it took was one look. As Duke Robillard remarked, 'You could tell times that you could talk to him and . . . [the] times that you don't go near him.'

Finally, on January 20th, they wrapped up live recording and the musicians scattered to the four winds. But one of them saw trouble ahead. Jim Dickinson, interviewed a week later for the *Perfect Sound Forever* website, remarked, 'When Dylan comes to mix it, I think he's gonna be in a lot of trouble.' Got it in one. To start with, Dylan was determined to redo just about every vocal – while still refusing to wear headphones. Lanois had a solution, 'Whenever we had to replace a vocal line . . . we set up speakers around the room . . . and the music was piped through those speakers, simulating the presence and volume of the band in the room.' But it meant the band sound bled into the vocal track, muddying some already murky waters.

The eleven songs that make up *Time Out of Mind*, plus 'Red River Shore', 'Mississippi' and two further takes of 'Can't Wait' – dubbed 'Psychedelic' and 'Rag Doll' – were now pulled to master. The reconfiguring of an album that had already gone from pillar to post began the minute the musicians left, Dylan rewriting and re-recording vocals on 'Cold Irons Bound', 'Dirt Road Blues', 'Highlands', 'Love Sick', 'Not Dark Yet', 'Standing In The Doorway', 'Till I Fell In Love With You', 'Tryin' To Get To Heaven', 'Red River Shore' and 'Mississippi', near-as-dammit the whole album, over the next six days.†

Symptomatic of Dylan's inability to let go of an album he'd begun the previous July was the fact he returned to Teatro in March – after a

---

* The footage Bob Lanois shot does reside in the Tulsa archive, but is currently embargoed. I know not why.
† In the case of 'Cold Irons Bound', seven vocal tracks feature on the master multi. Yet, only 'Can't Wait' and 'Till I Fell In Love With You' on the LP have vocals *entirely* derived from the March overdub sessions.

brief tour of Japan paid the bills – to finish the record off. Even at this stage he refused to turn it loose. In fact, according to Howard, 'We were there for a month . . . Bob showed up every day in his pick-up truck . . . [He would] go down to the pool hall . . . and shoot a game of pool like it was nothing.'

Work on 'Mississippi' alone, still in contention for the album, took ten days, Dylan not just redoing the vocals but revisiting the words. Lanois recalls, 'He started turning up at the Teatro with lyrical amendments and entirely new stanzas that Howard and I worked in, couplets floating from song to song till they found their most potent home.' Actually, some of these belated rewrites on 'Mississippi' are a joy: 'Time is dragging on, I'm laying low/ Wonder what it's gonna take, wonder if I wanna really know,' and, 'My words aren't working, they're coming to an end/ Nothing's making any sense, I'm looking for a friend,' both cut to the chase, but still got chopped. At least Lanois found 'Bob's attention to mixing details . . . impressive. He would scrutinize the mixes and report back to the Teatro with razor-sharp observations. He also went on to overdub a few electric guitar parts; in fact, some of the solos are his.'

However, the album was a mess, not an artistic statement made in one clear moment, Dylan's determination to include all the songs he'd gerrymandered into shape at the death killing it by degrees. To include 'Highlands' at the expense of 'Mississippi' and 'Red River Shore' was an act of sabotage fully the equal of what he had done to *Infidels*, fourteen years earlier.

In fact, the album fit Dickinson's contemporary description of the sessions – 'sheer chaos for an hour and a half, and then eight minutes of beautiful music' – almost perfectly. The *eighteen* minutes worthy of comparison with, say, 'I And I' – 'Not Dark Yet', 'Standing In The Doorway', 'Tryin' To Get To Heaven' – were nowhere near enough to sustain a seventy-three minute artifact, seven seconds shorter than *Blonde on Blonde*.

During the concerted promotional push he gave the album on its release, Dylan talked about how 'all the stuff from the '20s and '30s and '40s and '50s has been reprocessed so it can fit onto a CD, [but] you don't get the impact that it had when you first heard it'. He pointed the finger at technology, 'Records today don't have impact, and that's a question of the sound of [the] technology . . . What we tried to do with [*Time Out of Mind*] is make a CD . . . which sounds like an old record.' It would take him until 2015 to accept the more obvious explanation, 'In the old days, maybe you'd hear "Matchbox" and "Prison Cell Blues." That would be all you would hear, so those songs would be prominent in your mind. But when you hear an onslaught of 100 more songs of Blind Lemon [Jefferson], then it's like, "Oh man! This is overkill!"' Ditto *Time Out of Mind*.

Never before had he released so much music with so few melodies, leaving a stockpile of better tunes behind. Yet again, he left an album waiting in the wings that could have done all he wanted, had he rescued enough actual live performances in the studio – at least two of them made in Oxnard – from the 'blundering transcriber' called Bob. By the end of March he was sick of it, having been in the thick of it for too long. As he told Gundersen pre-release, 'Up until I was sick, I was putting songs on, taking songs off. I didn't know what picture it was forming.' By that time he really was sick, life-threateningly sick; not just sick of lost love.

Winterlude #5

May–July 1997:
Can This Really Be The End?

Legendary folk and rock singer Bob Dylan is in the hospital after suffering chest pains the day after his 56th birthday and may be fighting for his life. A source close to the singer said last night that one of the tests being conducted would determine whether the problem is a potentially fatal fungal infection called histoplasmosis.

New York Post, May 29th, 1997.

*

If the premonitions of catastrophe had come thick and fast in the spring of 1966, nothing remotely similar preceded Bob's brush with death in the spring of 1997. Having spent the winter transforming lyrics of heartbreak into songs of mortality, he found out life really could be brief. In this case, he'd been wandering around bat caves in Missouri, not taking the Bonneville for a backwoods spin, but he proved equally reluctant to go see the doc.

Sounes, naturally, claimed the inside scoop: Dylan had fallen ill on his actual birthday, after which his stepdaughter, Maria, 'persuaded Bob to talk on the telephone with a doctor at the University of California at Los Angeles, [who] when Bob described his symptoms', suggested he go straight to hospital, which he supposedly did the following day, getting as far as Santa Monica's St John's.

The way Dylan described it to Gundersen – 'It was intolerable pain, where it affects your breathing every waking moment' – makes the above account sound most unlikely. He'd been hiding his pain, as he always did, for a few days, until finally it had become impossible to bear. At this point he told Van Morrison, who *needed* to know and who sent the first of many well-wishers' faxes on the 28th (followed the same day by Jack Nicholson).

It was Morrison with whom Dylan was due to begin a now-kaput European tour. Indeed, he later admitted, 'Those shows were like two days away, and . . . I didn't tell anybody that I was sick, even though I could not function, I could not walk.' Elliot Mintz told one of the five hundred callers the publicist was now obliged to field, 'He's cancelled his *tour*. And you know he's never cancelled a tour before.' Having wildly exaggerated the severity of the motorcycle accident, Dylan now downplayed the seriousness of this unwelcome reminder of his own mortality – unlike the *New York Post*, whose headline read, DYLAN COULD BE IN FIGHT FOR LIFE!

Only later did he admit, 'I [had been] in a lot of pain and couldn't get any correct readings on what was the matter with me until it was nearly too late . . . When I got out of the hospital, I could hardly walk around my yard. I had to stay in bed and sleep all the time.' He let English journalist Alan Jackson know he had remained 'on medication for a good long while afterwards, but . . . at some point . . . the sickness faded away.' Nothing was going to stop him from promoting his new album, not even the dying of the light.

Though almost no-one seemed to know where he was – not just which hospital, but the actual city – the 'get well' messages began to pile up. The day after Van and Jack's messages came similar faxes from Erik Andersen, Bono, Jackson Browne, John Lee Hooker, Sony's Don Inner, Sally Kirkland, Richard Rowe, Martin Sheen and Frank and Barbara Sinatra, all wishing him a speedy recovery. The last of these captured the general concern, 'Dear Bob, We're Betting on You.' (Ol' Blue Eyes would be dead within the year.) The following day, Eric Clapton and George Harrison both wished him well and told him to beware the darkness.

Soon the girlfriends, past and present, were starting to wonder why *they* couldn't get a message to him directly. According to Susan Ross, Jeff Rosen's response – when she called and said she knew he wasn't in New York, as the papers said – was predictably pragmatic, 'Let everyone think he's in New York.' Her true position on the slippery pole of faded passion now became apparent, prompting her to write, 'When you were hospitalized and didn't call, I realized you didn't feel any responsibility to let me know how and where you were.' And nor did he.

Likewise, Lee Shain – a decade on from a fortnight fling – seemed to think she might cut through the maze of misinformation. But when she finally got hold of Elliot Mintz, he told her, 'I have to be terribly guarded about what I say,' before admitting, 'We won't know for sure until the test comes in.' By the time they came back it had thankfully become apparent the fifty-something codger still had a couple more years in him.

For now, though, he wasn't taking any calls – not even from a concerned Cooky, who relied on their mutual friend Jerry to keep 'her informed as to when he was taken off the respirator, when he was able to talk on the phone, when he got out of the hospital, when the antibiotics weren't reaching the infection, and when he started regaining lost weight'. Jerry later told her 'how Bob was registered under names like Frank Smith and Harvey Wade, changing it every day to keep the press off the hospital'. For the first time, Bob had kept Cooky, of all people, at hand's length, even having Jerry tell *her* that he was hospitalized in New York, rather than Los Angeles. A change had come. Finally, they had an extended conversation, the essential contents of which she conveyed to trusty Bev:

> Shortly after he did get out of the hospital . . . Cooky herself was able to talk to him. He admitted to the difficulties he was having fighting off the infection. Low grade fevers kept popping up, so the doctors kept trying different antibiotics. This wreaked havoc on both ends of his digestive system . . . [His recovery] was [due to] the vigilance of his [daughters], that kept on [at] their dad to keep taking his meds. when he started to blow them off as no longer necessary. Complaining to Cooky, Bob was obviously most upset over how all the media had as good as declared him dead, and he was determined to prove them all wrong.

He hadn't played the new album in weeks, but felt he had the goods to make 'em sit up and listen. Indeed, *Time Out of Mind* was already on the Sony fast-track – hence, perhaps, chairman Don Ienner's concern – even if Cooky remained largely in the dark as to how much of its original inspiration had been triggered by *their* break-up. Without 'Dreamin' Of You' and the original, lovelorn 'Not Dark Yet', she could only respond to the album – when she heard it that August – like a fan, not a martyr to love lost.

She loved it and told him so, leaving a message on his answering machine, telling him how impressed she was. She also let him know he could call any time as she was now living alone, having finally severed all links with her lying, embezzling husband. There had been one message on this album of mortality and loss that spoke to her more than most of the others. It was the one its *auteur* referenced when he left a return message on her phone: 'Hey baby doll . . . I guess you're sick of . . .'

Part 6

Hung As A Thief

I profess to write not his Panegyrick, which must be all praise, but his Life.

James Boswell.

From a thief you . . . learn: (1) to work at night; (2) if one cannot gain what one wants in one night to try again the next night; (3) to love one's co-workers, just as thieves love each other; (4) to be willing to risk one's life, even for a little thing; (5) not to attach too much value to things, even though one has risked one's life for them – just as a thief will resell a stolen article for a fraction of its real value; (6) to withstand all kinds of beatings and tortures but to remain what you are; and (7) to believe that your work is worthwhile and not be willing to change it.

Dov Baer, the Mazid of Mezeritch.

His vagabond temperament and his unquiet spirit drove him [on] . . . never finding a place to repose in . . . Tortured by this predisposition always to seek the beyond, he ended up devoted exclusively to this way of thought, and lost himself there.

Obituary of Arthur Rimbaud by Louis Pierquin,
Courrier des Ardennes 29th November 1891.

[He] had been loved by several people, but few of these people loved, or even liked, each other. And yet all of them believed that their version of the man was the authentic one – it had to be because their love, which they knew to be authentic, made it so.

Ian Hamilton, *In Search of J.D. Salinger* (1988).

In my opinion, if I could write all my work again, I am convinced that I would do it better, which is the healthiest condition for an artist. That's why he keeps on working, trying again; he believes each time that this time he will do it, bring it off. Of course he won't, which is why this condition is healthy.

William Faulkner.

Actually, I'm not as cool or forgiving as I might have sounded.

Junichi Saga, *Confessions of a Yakuza* p158.

Most wretched men . . . learn in suffering what they teach in song.

Percy Bysshe Shelley.

The best songs don't get recorded, the best recordings don't get released, and the best releases don't get played.

Jim Dickinson, to Robert Gordon, *It Came From Memphis*.

I think [Dylan is] a grand and shining . . . immortal example of . . . the professional attitudinist . . . The man who develops that is, of course, cherished. But Dylan long ago abdicated that [position]. Dylan is a working musician who goes from town to town singing his songs. And for whatever reasons – and they're [entirely] his own – he has completely left the scene of fashion and influence. And my hat [goes] off to him.

Leonard Cohen, 1993.

If your dreams are fulfilled at twenty, what do you do with the rest of your life?

Bob Dylan, *The Philosophy of Modern Song*, p267.

6.1

1997–2001:
Ain't No Judy Garland

I'm not [someone] who's gonna die on stage in front of a thousand clowns.

> Bob Dylan, to Mikal Gilmore, Summer 1986.

No way am I [going] to become like an old actor fumbling in garbage cans outside the theatre of past triumphs.

> Bob Dylan, late 1990s.

The thing about being on the road is that you're not bogged down by anything. Not even bad news. You give pleasure to other people and you keep your grief to yourself.

> Bob Dylan, *The Philosophy of Modern Song* (2022).

I don't believe in writer's block.

> Michael Douglas, in *Wonder Boys*.

I often wonder what *Time Out of Mind* would've been like had it been [left] in Bob's hands.

> Cindy Cashdollar, 2010.

Lanois stripped [*Time Out of Mind*] down to where it's just an atmosphere of noise.

> Duke Robillard, 2010.

I was constantly thinking, 'Will any of these [new] songs stand up with what I'm playing night after night?'

> Bob Dylan, to Edna Gundersen, September 1997.

He gets lots of strange press about him being introverted. Maybe he is with other people, but . . . we kinda grew up together. I wanted to record some of his songs and I asked him how he would feel about that . . . and he said, 'Man, you don't seem to realize that you're my hero!'

Liam Clancy, *Rock'n'Reel* 1998.

A performer like myself wouldn't be around so long if all he was doing was singing words – there's more to it than that, much more.

Bob Dylan, 1997.

Who knows more [than Dylan] about being a wonder boy and the trap it can be, about the expectations and the fear of repeating yourself?

Curtis Hanson, director of *Wonder Boys*, 2000.

He's so self-consumed, he doesn't realize he's destroying you on the way. You're just in the line of fire.

Susan Ross, *Daily Mail Weekend*, 16th May 1998.

*

With the release of *Time Out of Mind*, things changed. While the peak years of the Never Ending Tour were already behind him, the album Dylan had worked on for so long finally reversed his commercial decline, even as his touring band entered yet another new phase. The recruitment of a more nuanced drummer in David Kemper, the previous August, was followed in April by the addition of guitarist Larry Campbell, at the expense of the long-suffering J.J. Jackson, changing the dynamics once and for all.

Both were here for the long haul, staying with Dylan through the end of 2001, and the release of TOOM's much-vaunted successor, '*Love and Theft*'. For the cocky Kemper, these were the salad days of latter-day Dylan:

I knew he had the greatest songs. I had seen Bob when he was at his peak, and I knew that he was in a slump. I felt, still, he can change things. I don't want to toot my horn but, man, as soon as I joined the band, his attitude changed. He started accepting dates that he felt like playing . . .

That was 1996 . . . He told me that he tried taking a break, and he real-ised that he was happiest when he was working . . . Of course . . . you may as well forget the arrangements of all of those songs, because they had very little to do with what we were going to do . . . His amp was right next to me, and you could just tell how he felt. He'd play a couple of strums, and go, 'One, two . . .' and you felt that little bit of swing in it, and off we'd go.

Campbell arrived with *Time Out of Mind* already complete, and quickly learnt to stay out of the way. Larry the lead guitarist realized the days of Dylan letting his band off the leash were long gone: 'You can't showboat. It's not a place to draw attention to your skills. It's not your place to detract in any way from the essence of what he's putting out . . . When we performed . . . we would do a bunch of traditional tunes . . . and *there* you felt like you had more license to play your instrument in a more permanent way. But with his songs . . . you knew on some level you shouldn't try to compete with his lyrics.'

Both newbies had time to find their feet before their new boss rolled out the new songs, Campbell contributing both fiddle and bouzouki as Dylan mixed up the medicine-show to keep himself interested. Indeed, his determination to endure was such that he returned to the road by the start of August, just three months after dipping his toe in the Styx. He felt renewed and ready to rock, but apparently not to roll, or so he told London's pressmen that October: 'My kind of stage show . . . there's nothing to compare it to out there. The influences are com-pletely different . . . Just American folk music and maybe rockabilly . . . from the '50s, but *no* rock'n'roll.'

The August shows even saw Dylan give a live debut to 'Blind Willie McTell' fourteen years after its composition, in a version later included on the first of a series of *Time Out of Mind* live E.P.s. If, as Maymudes later claimed, 'Bob lost a bit of his self-esteem when he sobered up, [and] became a little more introverted and less social,' he was throwing himself into the post-*TOOM* shows like a man looking to impress, even before he began plugging new product.

For now, that was Sony's job, and for once they seemed inclined to try. Unfortunately, as chairman Don Ienner ruefully observed in 2001, 'It used to be a cultural event when a great artist like Bob Dylan put out a new record. Not anymore. No matter how fantastic the music is, what you have to do now is create an aura around the record, so it seems like an event.' Though previews of *TOOM* to approved journalists were designed to turn the whisper of hype into a roaring success, Dylan's dalliance with death was doing more to whet appetites than anything the label could generate.

Dylan, meanwhile, held back from playing a single new song to the summer crowds, claiming, 'People don't think they can respond to a song that they haven't heard on a record. It didn't used to be that way.' The roar of appreciation that greeted 'Love Sick's live debut in Bournemouth on October 1st rather debunked this misconception, obliging Dylan to admit, three days later, 'It took me by surprise when they responded like they knew it . . . I'm under the impression that people aren't paying a great deal of attention to any record that's been [recently] released.'

It was hardly the only instance of Dylan blowing smoke and tilting mirrors in the bout of interviews he gave that fall, as he described a recording process 180 degrees removed from what really went down. According to Bob, 'The whole record [was recorded] live. That adds a certain ambience to everything'; also, 'There's no line that has to be there to get to another line.' There was one live track on the whole record, and how about, 'She wrote me a letter and she wrote it so kind', for a line that said nothing, a mere commonplace.

Even more ludicrous was his assertion that 'these songs were given to my record company . . . so they could see what I was recording and decide whether they wanted to release it . . . I don't think there were any demos on these songs. We went in and recorded them exactly the way you're hearing them.' Dylan had played Sony as much of *TOOM* as Orson Welles famously showed RKO of *Citizen Kane* before the final cut.* There were six weeks of demos Lanois was still playing to himself, wondering what happened.

Only in 2001 – when Dylan was trying to hype an album with a different recording aesthetic, but a near-identical musical conceit – did he start to 'dis' its 1997 predecessor, describing 'that album [as] a little *off*. . . and that memory overshadows any gratification about its acceptance.' It was also at this juncture that he had the temerity to lay the

---

* Welles's contract precluded the studio from even seeing the 'dailies' or a rough cut before he completed it.

blame squarely at Lanois's door, insisting he was 'extremely frustrated, because I couldn't get any of the uptempo songs that I wanted'. If he had written some, Danny boy would have recorded 'em. He also had the unmitigated gall to claim, 'They [sic] put on all kinds of effects and overdubs afterwards,' masking over his own culpability when it came to all that counterproductive post-production on an album he was now trying to write out of history by sheer force of will.

It was a new day, and a new Dylan – someone who imparted the truth, save when his lips were moving. Thus, '[Lanois] had his own way of looking at things, and in the end I had to reject this because I thought too highly of the . . . meaning behind the lyrics to bury them in some steamy cauldron of drum theory.' Only in 2006 did Dylan finally come up with an accurate description of the sessions, to the trusted Gundersen, 'It was just a mess. There was hardly any communication.'

By then, some of the musicians at the sessions had broken rank, like guitarist Duke Robillard, who was prepared to say: 'If somebody with ears that was trying to be respectful to all the music . . . remixed all those tracks, it would be an entirely different record . . . Lanois stripped it down to where it's just an atmosphere of noise. In fact, I recorded "Love Sick" myself because I was so pissed-off at the way it sounded [on *TOOM*]. I had a really cool tremolo guitar part for it. If I listen close, I can hear the faint echo of it leaking into somebody else's microphone.'

Dylan even placed the blame for the omission of 'Mississippi' at Lanois's door, telling Sheryl Crow it 'was something that [he] was going to put on his last record, but he didn't like the version . . . [which] was like a shuffle . . . He wanted to make it more uptempo.' Actually, Lanois had recorded it till his ears bled, and the version pulled to master was hardly 'a shuffle', although it did fit with Cindy Cashdollar's own encapsulation of all she heard, 'Everything was very slowed down and dark.' And that was down to Dylan.

At a July 2001 European press conference, a surprisingly expansive Dylan even made the observation, 'I've been criticised for not putting my best songs on certain albums, but it is because . . . it's not been recorded right.' By then, Sheryl Crow had made more of a mess of 'Mississippi' than Lanois had of the album that was missing 'Mississippi', recording it for *The Globe Sessions*. It rather proved the appositeness of something its author wrote in 1988, when not everything he put down was a lie:

> my songs are different & i don't expect others to make attempts to sing them because you have to get somewhat inside & behind them & its hard enough for me to do it sometimes . . . nobody breathes like me so they couldn't be expected to portray the meaning of a certain phrase in the correct way without bumping into other phrases & altering the mood, changing the understanding.

Lanois did not take the slings and arrows Dylan slung his way lying down, issuing a strong rebuttal in his 2010 memoir, insisting, 'Time Out of Mind drips blood, lyrically but also sonically . . . because the forefathers of the art form were all there, at least in my mind: Eno, Lee 'Scratch' Perry, even Arthur Alexander and Hendrix.' Evidently, it wasn't just Bob who'd been at the wacky baccy.

In fact, the producer confirmed as much on an extraordinary private recording (made for his ears only) during the post-production of the 1997 album, a twelve-minute version of 'Red River Shore' with a Lanois vocal superimposed, featuring lyrics like, 'The temperature's rising, Bob's getting mad'; 'Kemper's getting mad, but that's alright/ I'm way out of range,' and, 'We've been smoking all kinds of shit, but Tony [Garnier]'s straight/ He's watched them come and he's watched them go.'

In 2023, the world and his wife got to make up their own minds about 1997's 'Album of The Year', when an authorized Michael Brauer remix appeared as part of a five-disc TOOM-centric Bootleg Series. It may not have raised the dead, but it certainly returned Robillard and the rest of Bob's chosen few to the soundstage. Instrumentation once buried beneath all that 'drum theory' was given a Lazarene resurrection.

Yet in the here and now of its original 1997 release, Time Out of Mind had been greeted like the Second Coming, being nominated for the Grammy Album of The Year, an award Dylan scooped for the first time, after reminding everyone watching that his songs worked best live, performing a 'Love Sick' that breathed life into the song, while also exorcising the ghost of his last live Grammy performance and seven years of bad luck.

It would be live, before paying punters, over the next three years where Dylan would really have the last laugh on Lanois, debuting the *TOOM* songs in almost exact reverse order of merit – early debutant 'Not Dark Yet', excepted. By the turn of the century, he would perform all but the disposable 'Dirt Road Blues' to the teeming many, after informing Gundersen, 'I don't record a record and then go on tour and play it. But eventually the songs find their way into my stage show.'

As if to drive the point home that his songs were best heard live, his label issued a series of live E.P.s that by 2000 had given fans superior live reinventions of 'Love Sick', 'Cold Irons Bound', the Miami 'Can't Wait' remake, 'Million Miles', 'Highlands' and 'Make You Feel My Love' – not that a single one of these would appear on this biographer's version of the album.* The following July, Roman reporters were left in no doubt who he meant when lamenting 'working with slipshod producers or fakes or . . . nonentities, I have . . . allowed . . . thing[s] to happen [in the studio only] because I could get up on stage and rectify it . . . That's where all those [musical] elements come into play.'

Oddly enough, he waited until he had some real competition in concert before unleashing the better *TOOM* reinterpretations. Both 'Highlands' and 'Not Dark Yet' were introduced to their definitive live selves on a joint summer 1999 tour with Paul Simon; a full year after Dylan opened a May 1998 US Tour with Van Morrison and Joni Mitchell by performing spirited versions of five lesser *TOOM* songs at the warm-up show in Vancouver. Joni later claimed to have selected the set for him:

> I assumed that this was gonna be a writers' tour, so I picked a set for Bobby. And he did for me, too . . . He was there to greet me . . . It was the first one . . . and he was very excited, and he said, 'Oh, those chords, those chords – you've got to show me some of those chords. I love those chords that you play.' . . . I said, Bobby you don't want to learn these chords. First of all you have to learn tunings, and tunings are a pain in the butt. And you won't have nearly the fun that you're having now with your music.

---

* FYI, the seven-track 'Heylin-approved' LP comprises 'Mississippi', 'Red River Shore', 'Not Dark Yet', 'Standing In The Doorway', 'Tryin' To Get To Heaven' and Oxnard versions of 'Can't Wait' and 'Dreamin' Of You'.

The highlight of this brief triple-A-list tour, though, was a much older album-closer: Dylan doing a heartfelt fourth encore at the UCLA Pavilion of 'Restless Farewell' as a tribute to the recently departed Frank Sinatra, with whom Dylan had formed an unlikely bond after Sinatra's 80th birthday bash in 1995, when he had requested Dylan play that song and then called him out on his legendary 'wet fish' hand-shake, only being satisfied with Bob's third attempt, after which he said, '*Now* I feel like I've shook your hand.'

It was Joni who proved to be the reluctant crowd-pleaser on a mere eight-date-tour, and though Dylan continued touring with an on-fire Van, playing the UK in June and the west coast in September, it was the last time Joni got invited to act out. Part of the problem, according to Joni, was that she wasn't 'used to arenas. And my music was boun-cing off the walls. That had happened to me before in 1976, and there was no way that I could sing when it's bouncing around like that. I was just hearing echoes of myself . . . [Even] before we went out on tour [together], I went to a show of Bob's, and you couldn't hear the words . . . It was a mushy sound.'

Dylan's soundman, Ed 'Coach' Wynne, was originally her sound-man. Yet the lady would claim Dylan blamed 'Coach' for the poor sound and fired him. Not so. Nor did Dylan take umbrage at a good review Joni got in Chicago, as she later claimed, for the simple reason they never played there. She was simply not going over very well and Dylan quickly realized she was bringing nothing in the way of extra punters to the party with a fourteen-song set that was almost a what's what of latter-day 'misses', even as the *Time Out of Mind* songs con-tinued to go down well.

However, the soundman's days were indeed numbered, even if he did not leave until they got to Auckland in September, part of a brief Antipodean tour with Patti Smith. While there an altercation broke out between 'Coach' and Al Santos, who had been bawled out by Dylan about the sound and took it out on Ed, who walked out, never to return. He didn't need the headache, or the money, after ten years of trying to get the best possible sound for a man who consistently refused to invest in the best mikes or release the band from its musical straitjacket.

Foolishly, Dylan did nothing to persuade Coach to reverse his stance, and another stalwart of the Never Ending Tour's first decade was done gone. He joined guitar-tech César Díaz and snake-like sidekick Victor Maymudes, who had both resorted to acts of petty revenge to 'get back' at their former boss; in the former's case, according to Cooky, 'keeping one of Bob's favourite guitars in an ownership dispute over who'd actually paid for it. That César's disloyalty was sharply felt was evidenced when Bob ordered César's name taped over on all the remaining equipment.' Not smart.

Maymudes proved himself even more dissolute and dishonorable after he was banished to L.A. in spring 1995, having apparently, 'during the [previous year's] Florida run . . . [been] caught bedding the wife of one of the big promoters there, thus jeopardizing the gigs and future dealings. [For Dylan,] it was [the] last straw after he'd been sticking his nose in where he didn't have any business, setting up show arrangements and screwing things up.' Astonishingly, Dylan kept Victor on salary – thus demonstrating something George Harrison once said to Aronowitz: 'He doesn't judge people . . . I've seen him being very forgiving' – and invested in a coffee-shop in Santa Monica so that Maymudes could keep an eye on things and occasionally play chess in the back with his sponsor.

However, just to prove no good deed goes unpunished, when Dylan saw how much money the shop was losing and fired the manager, Victor's daughter, Maymudes sued him, claiming he was owed a pay-off after years of service. Worried about what might come out if the vexatious suit ever went to trial, Dylan reportedly paid him $75,000 in 1998 to settle the matter, before severing all contact with the ingrate.

Maymudes's response was entirely predictable. Without any literary skills or reliable memory, he started writing a proposal for a book he was convinced nobody but him could write, telling his son, 'I'm going to write the tell-all book! All the others only got ten per cent right, but I know the whole story.' Not on the evidence of his proposal, he didn't. Nor was he the only one touting a 'tell-all' at this time, believing that they – and they alone – could reveal the real Bob at last. Susan Ross was telling publishers:

> Since none of the previous authors have spent time with him or even knew him, they are hard-pressed to draw accurate conclusions about Dylan. Their information is so speculative and limited, at best, that even in the recent books, none of them mention (or know) that Dylan has

been married three times or has eight children. None of these authors know why . . . he married his wives, [or] whether they were pregnant at the time.

Dylan's failure to include the lady in the inner circle, or inform her of his whereabouts during his May 1997 stay in hospital, had convinced Ross she was never getting a World Series pennant from the man. She once again overplayed her hand, telling him she had been offered a huge sum of money to write a book about him. It prompted a response she found 'strange', 'I can't give you that kind of money.'

Having seen off gold-digger Ruth Tyrangiel back in November 1994, after she filed a palimony suit against him for $5 million in respect of property and an unspecified additional sum in respect of royalties, he was hardly about to fold at Ross's first gambit – as she should have known. When a March 1998 article in the *Sunday Mirror* by David Gardner – entitled, simply, 'Dylan's Secret Wives' – threatened to steal her thunder, and with no takers for what she claimed in her proposal to be the story of 'fifteen years' of 'tremendous intimacy and close-ness', Ross tried to up the ante by giving an interview to the *Daily Mail Weekend* magazine as he toured with Joni and Van. In it, she insisted 'he has been married secretly at different times to two of his backing singers – Clydie King and Carol Woods – by whom he has a total of three children, the youngest [being] a 12-year-old daughter, Narette.'

Ross had garnered the *wrong* 'name of his third wife one night at a bar from the drunken girlfriend of a record executive', after pumping her for information. She also discussed 'the female "cousins" that snuck into his hotel rooms, [and] about . . . his stubbornness, his temper, his lack of social graces.' What Ross left off her list of character traits was his keen sense of betrayal, insisting, 'I didn't betray him any more than he betrayed me in the past.' Intent on kicking this man she claimed to still love where it hurt, Ross talked about a 'framed painting by his daughter Anna on which she had cryptically written: "I'm so glad you finally became [a] good father."' Having broken another Dylan taboo – mentioning his children – Ross proceeded to insist 'that during the most intense phase of their relationship, Dylan – a heavy drinker – was impotent'.

Dylan metaphorically shrugged his shoulders. Asked about the Ross proposal by Gundersen, he said, 'I'm not going to read a book about myself . . . I would rather read about anybody else but me.'

Fortunately for him – and his mother* – he wouldn't need to read it, as the Ross account was neither credible, nor publishable. As for May-mudes's private pension plan, it turned out he didn't need one, dying of a cerebral aneurysm in January 2001, aged just 65. With only the material for a long article to hand, his son Jacob took thirteen years to complete *Another Side of Bob Dylan*, a pitifully thin attempt to tell Victor's side of the story.

By then, another potential memoirist and a more sympathetic one, Debbie Gold, had herself succumbed to a brain tumour, having discussed not its potential contents, just the methodology of her own rock'n'roll life with Dylan. She got no further than three short anecdotes, the last of which consisted of him telling her about a day in London in 1981 when the singer went out for a walk, alone:

'I had the best day!' he said. 'You did? What happened?' 'Well, I was feeling a little cooped up in this hotel room,' he began. 'It looked like such a nice afternoon, so I decided to take a walk. I put my sweatshirt on with the hood up.' (It was mid-July in London, but this was Bob's best attempt at disguising himself.) 'And I went out and just started walking.' 'By yourself?' I asked, incredulous. 'Yeah. First I went walking all through Piccadilly Circus, where of course there were thousands of people, and nobody noticed me. It was so great and so I just kept going. Then I walked down Baker Street and through Trafalgar Square [sic], and still, nobody said a word to me.' 'Wow, Bob, that's unbelievable. Must have felt great.' 'It did, and so I kept going. It was such a beautiful day too, so I walked thru Hyde Park. It was so peaceful. I saw so many people and nobody ever said a word to me. Finally, I was making my way back to Regent's Park and I ended up in the Regent's Park Zoo, just sitting quietly on a hill. It was so great I could hardly believe it and I didn't want the day to end. Finally, I noticed it must have been 5 P.M., because the zookeeper was politely asking everyone to leave. Eventually the whole place was empty, except for me. I was busy musing about the day when I was almost startled to find the zookeeper standing over me and he said, "It's closing time. I'm afraid you're going to have to leave now, Mr Dylan."'

---

* Supposedly, Dylan's comment to Ross on hearing of her plans was, 'God, Susan, my mother will read this, and she thinks I'm an angel.'

Gold and him had been close, real close, but twenty years after that 1981 debut of the man-in-a-hood, he seemed determined to keep it all inside, to observe and not be observed. Having been put on notice to only trust himself, he now began covering his tracks in earnest, leading to a determined separation from other, older friends at this time, none of whom had threatened to put pen to paper; childhood chums from Minnesota who used to catch an occasional show and talk about old times. Even that girl from the north country, Bonnie Beecher, found herself backstage at a show when he walked past her as if she didn't exist. Even though they had 'stayed friends for a really long time', Bonnie thought, 'I'm never doing that again . . . It's just too humiliating.' Nor was she alone. Maria Muldaur had heard several old friends complain, 'Oh, he walked right past me at this [or that] event.'

Sometimes, these former friends refused to admit those teen ties were now irrevocably sundered. In the Noughties, Louie Kemp had a major falling out with camp comrade Bobby, apparently over money (after losing most of his own fortune), yet told *Rolling Stone*'s Andy Greene in 2020, 'We're still friends. We're [just] not in touch like we used to be.' In fact, it had been nearly two decades since last they spoke, and when Kemp sent a signed copy of his whitewash of a memoir, *Dylan & Me* (2020), to the New York office, Dylan told them to send it back.

Not that Dylan was any better at keeping in touch with those he had known when he was a freewheelin' thief of fire. Al Kooper told *Goldmine* in 1994, 'There [have been] times when I thought he was heinous, and I didn't talk to him for seven years. [But] I may be one of the few from that era that he's still friendly with. He'll call up and ask my opinion of something, and then do exactly the opposite of what I say.' By the late Nineties, even those late-night phone calls had largely ground to a halt.

Sometimes, though, something reminded the accidental amnesiac of past times and he'd mysteriously appear on someone's stoop. as he did in 1997. Dana Gillespie had 'got a call from Dylan's UK agent . . . [to say] that Dylan had requested that I be the opening act on his British tour . . . Two days before the tour started, my doorbell rang, and there was Dylan himself standing on my doorstep. We spent the next four hours . . . drinking fennel tea while we swapped stories . . . and reminisced about the old days. I asked him how many children he'd got and he said he wasn't sure, but he thought seven or eight.'

He proceeded to describe the 'epiphany' he had 'when he toured with the Grateful Dead in 1987 . . . A few years later, he recounted parts of the story in . . . *Chronicles*.' A story is all it was. He had a million of them, on permanent shuffle. Earlier the same year, he had told a bunch of them to Mark Howard (and Daniel Lanois) during the post-production of *Time Out of Mind*:

> Bob would just go off and talk for literally two hours at a stretch. He told these stories about when he was living in New York and how he couldn't go home because there was a crowd of people in front of his house . . . When he wrote *Chronicles*, some of the same stories were in there, and I had the idea that a lot of these stories he'd had in his mind over the years.

Howard was as unaware that Dylan was in the early stages of writing an autobiography akin to Al Kooper's unreliable 1977 memoir, *Backstage Passes and Backstabbing Bastards*, as his ex-editor David Rosenthal, who wrote to him in November 1997 to say that he had moved to Simon & Schuster, and would 'love to talk about what project we might do next together . . . [because] I'm excited over the prospect of something grand.'

Dylan decided it was high time he got some things off his chest. The fifty-something grouch did just that, writing in April 1999 of how the Ark of the Covenant, the so-called True Cross and the relic of The Prophet had all been used 'to make war and rampage holy – in the name of the Lord'; how he considered the songs of Cole Porter 'light fluffy stuff, clever but pointless in a cruel world'; how most guitar-players 'learned wrong what they learned from Hendrix', and how Charlie Watts was the last jazz drummer to play rock'n'roll, and without Charlie there was 'no Stones, not even half-close'. He also wrote movingly about the impact Hank Williams and Elvis had on him growing up, in a period 'when the atom bomb was unleashed', as were Elvis, Jerry Lee Lewis, Carl Perkins, Little Richard, Fats Domino and Buddy Holly, all of whom 'came forth with power, truth and beauty', so much so that 'all of us who were there can still feel it'.

He had once wondered aloud to Hilburn as to whether 'people are remembering the right things about [Elvis's] music, rather than all the stuff that people wrote about him'. The thought had doubtless occurred, he might suffer the same fate himself, even as he considered just how scary it had been for the boy from Tupelo 'to gain so much and lose so much simultaneous[ly]'. All of the above singers were, to his mind, 'dead serious', and he fully 'intended to be the same'. He even wrote about Buddy Holly staring directly at him at the Duluth Armory two days before his death, a story he would take for a spin during his 1998 Grammy acceptance speech.

At this formative stage the book also ventured into some weirder diversions into history and myth. He described how 'the British [sic] broke away to form their own religion years ago . . . It's called the Church of England,' and the British Empire was 'the most beneficial thing to mankind', but they were still seen off by 'a bunch of ragtag Jews' seeking a homeland, because the latter had 'the soul of Belsen' in them.

He wasn't holding back, even when he got around to addressing his own history, proof he meant it when he said, 'I'm not a big fan of polite literature.' In a long section on his family's move to L.A. in 1973, he described Robbie Robertson as 'a strange bird' who 'tries to ride two horses going in two different directions', and David Geffen as 'a spunky little guy who talked a million miles a minute, and laughed a lot'. He also clocked that the two of them 'seemed to be pretty buddy-buddy', though 'neither one of them had [done] anything to endear themselves to me'. Another short prose section told the story of him and Barry Feinstein stopping in Colorado to see an evangelist preacher in action.

Originally, he fully intended to range wider and further, describing meetings with Robert Graves and Carl Sandburg in 1962 and 1964.* He also planned to write about how he first began to write songs. (His explanation was surprisingly straightforward, 'The way to start writing songs is to set words to an established melody.') There were other intriguing, envisaged sections, like 'family connections/ being in the right club/ nepotism and loyalty', scattered among papers lodged at Tulsa. As for the liberties he was already taking with his own convoluted chronology, he offered an explanation as early as April 1999, '1976 might as well be 2090 – it's all the same to me.'

---

* Dylan does mention meeting Graves, but only in passing, in the published *Chronicles*.

None of this material, though, would make the memoir he published in 2004, and nor would many such examples of refreshing
candidness. As he suggested on the release of *Chronicles*, 'I didn't go
strong on anybody.' In fact, he reined himself in to such an extent that
almost nothing from all this pre-millennium writing remained. Rather,
he started again, with an entirely different mindset in a century that
was no longer his to shape.

If having his own say about his past personae had always held a certain appeal, it was an itch he had only occasionally scratched. In 1985,
when talking about his career like never before, he told Scott Cohen, 'I
don't have any long great story to tell about when I was a kid that
would let anybody know how it is that I am what I am,' while informing Mikal Gilmore, 'I was once offered a great deal of money for an
autobiography, and I thought about it for a minute, then I decided I
wasn't ready . . . On my own I wouldn't think about these things . . .
When it's all said and done, the historians can figure it out.'

'Print the legend', though, was tattooed on his soul. The liberties he
took with each and every protest song he penned between 1962 and
1983 proved as much. Not that he *ever* intended to write a straight
memoir: not in 1963, when he said 'it's got all kinds of stuff in it which
just doesn't add up'; not in 1971, when he told Tony Glover, 'I got a lot
of stuff I want to tell . . . but I don't want to tell it the old cornball way.
A real writer knows how to hold it all up – he can then place the facts
wherever he feels like it'; and not in 1985, when he explained to Cameron Crowe that he had considered 'writ[ing] some stories the way
Kerouac did, about some of the people I know and knew, [and] change
the names'. Which is *exactly* the volume he would publish in 2004, a
book of stories. Tall stories.

In the late Nineties, though, he was still worried about the prospect
of an unflattering memoir by the spurned coming out for his mother
to read. He'd already ticked off Ross once for revealing private information to a mutual friend, telling her, 'If I wanted a reporter in my
midst, I'd have hired one.' And when the ever-enquiring Edna asked for
his thoughts on people who talk to biographers, he raved and drooled,
'All informers should be shot. A person should not rat on *anybody*.'

He gave a more temperate response to the London press at the *Time
Out of Mind* press conference, when he still feared Ross might find a
publisher, 'They usually interview people who know me or think they

know me or barely know me . . . It's like reading about somebody else that never existed.' Perhaps he had in mind the original 1991 edition of *Behind the Shades* – still in print and selling briskly in Britain – having told Cooky it was 'too personal, too probing', the greatest compliment this biographer ever received. Yet he seemed remarkably blasé about the prospect of Cooky writing her own version of what went down when the topic came up:

> **Sylvia Tribelhorn**: What are you afraid of? I'm not going to write anything mean or nasty.
> **Bob Dylan**: No, I know you wouldn't.
> **ST**: I'd just tell it like it is, just the straight truth.
> **BD**: I think you would, yeah.
> **ST**: Don't you think it would help your career? Make a splash?
> **BD**: Don't try it.
> **ST**: I'll let you proof read it. Oh, that's right, you won't be around. I'm going to outlive you.
> **BD**: Yeah, chances are.

She wouldn't outlive him, sadly succumbing to cancer in 2014. Nor would she ever deliver on her threat, though Dylan knew she had shared many a confidence with her best friend, a Bobcat of the first water. It seemed he was surrounded by 'spies'. How was a man of mystery to retain his own independence, a concern that continued to plague him in solitary moments. Yet he recognized that no artist – or public figure – 'can pay any mind to . . . how many books are written . . . if we want to exist and have a certain amount of free will about what we do,' a remark he made in 2001, after two new biographies had taken up the slack Susan and Victor left dangling.

At this juncture, Dylan was still hoping to be one of those 'people who died leaving a great unsolved mess behind, who left people for ages to do nothing but speculate'. Which is why he was a most reluctant participant in a project his manager, Jeff Rosen, had been working on throughout the late Nineties, a sort of video biograph for which he was picking up the tab. Even more annoyingly, when he sat down at a studio in Long Island City in January 2000 to be interviewed about his early years, he found Rosen had a copy of Heylin's *Dylan Day by Day* (1995), a book chock full of facts, to use while going 'over the questions, which were essentially factual, before each bit of filming'.

For five hours at a time, across four days, Dylan was grilled about a past he considered dead and gone, until they reached the motorcycle accident and he finally admitted he'd used it to get away from 'people like *you* . . . asking questions'. That delicious moment would feature in Martin Scorsese's 2005 Dylan documentary, *No Direction Home*, by which time Dylan had published his own false narrative, *Chronicles*. But not before he provided the theme song for a movie of a 400-page novel about a *wunderkind* looking to overcome a seven-year writer's block while his life of constant infidelity and professional frustrations was unravelling at a rate of knots.

The song in question, 'Things Have Changed', used the same voice as his last movie theme-tune, *Band of the Hand*, and the one he would adopt for his next movie, which he was already formulating. Here was a Pentecostal persona who believed 'the Bible is right', and 'the world will explode', even as he tries 'to get as far away from myself as I can', a line with a great deal more resonance for the songwriter than Michael Douglas's pot-smokin' Professor Tripp in Curtis Hanson's marvellously atmospheric *Wonder Boys*, prompting its director to offer the astute insight, 'The song also stands alone as Dylan's own caustic mid-life commentary on life at the turn of this new century.'*

This single line could well have triggered the whole song, Dylan scrawling this very phrase on the back of a boxing gym business card sometime early in 1999, shortly after he penned another couplet, 'Been lifted up to heaven, been cast down below / Never was the kind of person who knew how to say no,' encapsulating Michael Chabon's novel of the same name perfectly. Possibly part of a fragment that 'became' 'Things Have Changed' – containing as it does, 'Everything about today has just been one big lie', which may have become, 'All the truth in the world adds up to one big lie' – it was one of a number of stray lines offering a sign on the moviola as to his next album.†

---

* The 'Things Have Changed' promo video shifts between Dylan's and Douglas's guitar-totin' perspective.

† I am thinking of couplets like, 'Feel like falling in love with the first woman I meet / Putting her in a wheel barrow and wheeling her down the street,' and, 'Mr Jinx and Miss Lucy, they jumped in the lake / I'm not that eager to make a mistake.'

These were evidently the kind of half-formed ideas he was carrying in his head when he visited the director in the editing suite, during which Hanson 'told him the [Chabon] story and introduced him to the characters'. Only now did he complete 'Things Have Changed', propagating a worldview as dark as anything in his post-conversion canon. Hence, presumably why when he accepted the Oscar for Best Original Song in March 2001, he expressed his thanks to 'Curtis, who just kept at it and just encouraged me to do . . . a song which doesn't pussyfoot around or turn a blind eye to human nature.'

Hanson also co-opted three other Dylan songs that didn't 'pussyfoot around' for the soundtrack – 'Buckets Of Rain', 'Shooting Star' and 'Not Dark Yet'. But it was 'Things Have Changed' Dylan needed to get down on tape when the touring band convened one Manhattan afternoon in July 1999:

> **David Kemper**: Bob said, 'Tomorrow let's go in the studio, I got a song I want to record.' We went in and he played [us,] 'Things Have Changed'. And we did it with only an engineer, in New York . . . Bob produced it. We did two takes. The first was a New Orleans thing, and the second take was what you hear. And then Bob went back in, and he wanted to replace one word . . . And when you do a punch-in with Bob, that means the band all plays the song . . . You're recording Bob's vocal, plus all the leakage of the guitars and the drums in the vocal mike. So, when you hear it back, you don't hear any change . . . So, in about five hours, we learned it, recorded it, mixed it. And that was it.

Dylan's on-the-hoof methodology was not one the young engineer, Chris Shaw, had encountered while working with Booker T and the late Jeff Buckley. According to Shaw, Dylan had only really 'got very interested' in him taking over the console when 'he heard that I got my start doing Public Enemy records'. If they got 'Things Have Changed' in one afternoon, the real test would come when Dylan asked Shaw 'for a quick mix':

> So I did a quick rough mix to DAT. Bob listened and said everything was too clear, too easy to pick out every instrument and note. He wanted to 'mush' it up . . . [Dylan employed a trick of his own: running his vocal back through a guitar amplifier . . . Shaw placed an Electro-Harmonix

Graphic Fuzz box in the signal chain . . . Nodding in approval, Dylan reached over and pushed the percussion track up nearly all the way.] I thought, it's just a reference mix and ran the DAT again. A couple of days later Jeff Rosen, Bob's manager, called and asked me for the quarter-inch [tape] of the mix. I was stunned – it was just a rough mix, a very rough mix. Jeff said, 'Oh, you don't know Bob. That was the final mix.'

Whatever the sure-footed Shaw did, Dylan seemed to like it like that – as did the Academy of Motion Picture Arts and Sciences. The singer found himself belatedly nominated for an Oscar,* having already committed to another Antipodean tour in March 2001.

It meant he would have to film a 'safety' performance (in case the satellite link went down on the night) and his acceptance speech from a Melbourne studio. Unfortunately, when he arrived at the studio, he found an over-excited local production crew had spent the past four days programming the lights so that as soon as he started to play, they would interact with some complex camera moves. They obviously did not know their man. Four bars into the 'safety' version, the lights started to move. Six bars in, Dylan stopped playing and said, 'I'm not a disco act. Please change the lights.' The director came down from the control room, 'With all due respect, Bob, we just want to make you the star. We're all here to serve the song,' and got both barrels; he wasn't interested in being 'the star', his only concern was transmitting the song's meaning – so lose the lights and lose the camera moves. Capisce.

Though never one for awards, the nephew of a man who had owned four cinemas seemed genuinely delighted to receive an Oscar and a Golden Globe for this singular soft-shoe shuffle. The song even seemed to galvanize the performer in him, as he produced some of his best shows in recent years in 2000, especially in the acoustic intimacy of Anaheim and Portsmouth.† It also revived in Dylan a determination to

---

* The film was released just a week after the 2000 Oscar ceremony, meaning that the film's three nominees had to wait a full year for their nominations. Only Dylan won.
† The two shows in Anaheim in March were bootlegged on CD, as were the two shows in Portsmouth in September. Both are terrific. 'Things Have Changed' on the 2nd night in Portsmouth was released officially, and blows the studio version away.

make his own comedy masterpiece (*Wonder Boys* is, above all, darkly comedic), perhaps inspired by the success of his friend Eddie Gorodetsky's sitcom, *Dharma and Greg*.*

Jeff Rosen thought he knew just the right collaborator, Larry Charles, the co-creator of *Seinfeld*, the most successful US sitcom of the Nineties, and a distant cousin of his. Charles soon discovered, much to his delight, that the singer-songwriter 'was an inveterate movie watcher. He had a TV on the tour bus with a VCR slot in it, and they would get him stacks of VCR tapes and he would watch those, and at that particular period of his life he was watching a lot of Jerry Lewis . . . and he said to Jeff, "I'd really like to do . . . a comedy series." Jeff was, like, really?'

He was not the only one taken aback. The days of Dylan as the sharpest rapier wit on the planet had surely passed. Yet in the winter of 2000, there were rumours he was working on 'a film screenplay', and in May the *Hollywood Reporter* reported he'd agreed to do a one-hour TV special with HBO, to be created and developed by Larry Charles. It would be, apparently, 'a bit like a variety programme, mixing music and comedy'. True to form, by the time the *Reporter* secured its scoop, Dylan was already setting the project on fire:

Larry Charles: We used to write in a cubicle in the back by the boxing gym. He was chain-smoking in those days . . . The [HBO] project was him basically as kind of a Buster Keaton-cypher type of character, very stone faced, very detached, walking through this surreal comic landscape essentially, and using reference points from . . . his own songs . . . So, we were gonna go to HBO, and try to sell them the project. Jeff and I said to Bob, 'You know if you go to the meeting, we'll sell the project right in the room. They won't have the balls to say no to you.' He didn't want to do it, but reluctantly he finally agreed . . . He showed up to the meeting in full Western Villain regalia, black hat, black duster, black boots, black gloves, black shirt, a studded black shirt. He had bought the whole regalia, and the two of us strutted into HBO . . . There's Chris Albrecht, the president of HBO, waiting for us and he . . . point[s] to his wall and say[s], 'Look, I have my original Woodstock tickets right here,' and Bob [responded], 'Uh, I didn't play at Woodstock.' . . . After that, he

---

* Dylan himself would even make a rare cameo, in the episode, 'Play Lady Play'.

stared out the window for the entire meeting, and the vibe in the room
was extremely tense . . . He wouldn't even turn around to acknowledge
that the other people were there. Despite all that, they bought the project. [When] we walked out of the meeting . . . Bob seemed very pensive
and unhappy. I said, 'What's the matter?' And he [says], 'I don't want to
do it anymore . . . It's too slapstick.' Which is exactly what he wanted it
to be . . . I think he realized that the comedy thing was just too restrict-
ive for his creativity, it wouldn't be able to take into account all the
things that he had on his mind, which he [also] wanted to deal with.
[RP]

Maybe, just maybe, his was a sense of humour that no longer
synched with Clinton's America. After all, his reaction to a forensic
piece of satire at his expense in a 1994 issue of *SongTalk*, a magazine he
subscribed to and had been interviewed for in 1991, was so out of proportion as to make one question his sanity, let alone the thinness of his
wrinkly skin.

The article in question was written by Dan Burn, whom editor Paul
Zollo considered 'a brilliant songwriter, very funny', and had invited
'to do a humour[ous] column for the magazine . . . He wanted to write
a column on Dylan, in which he claimed that his mother wrote all of
his songs – except "Man Gave Names to All The Animals." And it was
an obvious joke. The way he wrote it, it was obviously meant to be
funny, but . . . Dylan, [who] was in Japan, [read] it, and got very upset.
He seemed more upset at me, 'cause I was the one that he knew, [refer-
ring to] this "limp Monsieur Zolo" [sic] making fun of his sainted
mother.' Zollo in no way exaggerates. The handwritten letter Dylan
intended to fax to the magazine began:

Greetings Gentlemen, does your house not have glass windows? Do
your journalists not have addresses and mothers? Do your family members not have names? Having a prefabricated laugh at the expense of my
own dear mother without provocation or cause is not my idea of gratitude for the interview which took up ten or more pages of your puerile
smokescreen periodical masquerading as songwriting litany! My mother
is not a public figure to be satirized and ridiculed . . . by some scurrilous
little wretch with a hard-on for comedy! . . . Seriously, Gentlemen, cancel my subscription, and put the spineless insolent scum who wrote

these words on notice . . . Trade him to the *National Lampoon* or cut off his hands, the seditious worm. As for your *Songtalk* rag, you know my opinion. Extinctus amabitur idem.*

It seems the po-faced Vineyard convert who flashed across *Saturday Night Live* in 1979 was alive and well, and touring Nippon. Thankfully, a night's sleep restored reason and the fax was never sent, perhaps because his still-in-favour sidekick Victor read it and hid it from him. Unfortunately, in 2015, Maymudes's son tried to auction the letter, and the prose equivalent of drunk dialling came back to haunt Dylan, some fifteen years since 'his sainted mother' had gone to meet her Maker after a long and fruitful life.

In her final interview, in June 1999, the beatific Beattie talked about how blessed she had been, and how the whole family, including the entire Dylan clan, would always 'celebrate Christmas, Thanksgiving [together]. We . . . see them all the time . . . When the phone rings and everyone's okay, I'm happy.' Which she was, right up until her death on January 25th, 2000, aged eighty-four.

Understandably absent from the following day's funeral was Rolling Thunder publicist, Chris O'Dell, who nonetheless summed up the lady who had given the world such a gifted son best in a 2009 memoir: 'I adored Beatty and often wondered how Bob could be related to her – she was such a joyful, silver-haired lady, so warm and affectionate, so social and uninhibited. He was the moon, it seemed, to her sun.' No-one, not even Miss O'Dell, could ever know what this loss meant to Dylan, save perhaps his brother David, to whom Bobby now turned in his singular sorrow:

Kevin Odegard: David might not have been fully acquainted with the hip-celebrity-rockstar invention known to the world as Bob Dylan, but he knows Bobby Zimmerman better than anyone on the planet. Bobby Zimmerman was always hiding there under the surface, accessible exclusively to his brother and mother. His invented persona was never the whole picture to them . . . Beattie's death shredded Bob . . . [meaning] David . . . is the one peer left in whom Bob has faith and trust.

---

* The Latin phrase, by Horace, roughly translates as: 'The same [hated] man will be loved after his death.'

Try as he might to put his feelings into song, Dylan struggled to express himself when death really was the end. The lyrics to the song he came up with, 'Everlasting Queen Of My Heart', read like something from Hank Williams's first folio. It begins by describing her as 'the only one who never done me wrong', going on to suggest she left him a book full of 'lines of truth . . . to always guide me', with 'hope and joy on every page'. The death of his mother had also served to remind him, 'Someday we must all stand in judgement.' If *she* had little to fear, her 'angel' of a son was perhaps starting to realize he might not be so lucky on that dreadful day. At least he sensed this valedictory did not come close to expressing the depths he felt, and it was quietly forgotten.

Actually, it was surplus to requirement, not just because he felt he already had enough for an album to reinforce the legend, but also real life was no longer a resource of which his new muse approved.* The mortality addressed on his 2001 album, *'Love and Theft'*, would be the kind that rained down from on high, arbitrary and pitiless, like the planes that ploughed into the World Trade Center on the day said album was released; a day etched on a world awakening to the reality that the most sacred of beliefs can be used 'to make war and rampage holy – in the name of the Lord'.

On a day when high water was everywhere in America, Dylan awoke to news of a very personal tragedy. Having only just learnt that the Beatle he loved best, George, was dying from cancer, he was now informed his childhood friend and lifelong inspiration, Larry Kegan, had died unexpectedly; according to one report while driving to the store to pick up a copy of his famous friend's latest, as proud as proud can be of all he had become. With the skies closed to planes, and a nation in collective mourning, Dylan couldn't even make his way to Minnesota to say goodbye to the friend whose teen dreams had been shattered on the sea shore, but who had lived a life without pity, a shining example to all who knew him.

Dylan had been gearing up for a US tour that would promote an album he was genuinely convinced was his best in more than a decade. Instead, he found himself alone with his thoughts, clinging to an

---

* 'Sometimes when songwriters write from their own lives, the results can be so specific, other people can't connect to them.' – *Philosophy of Modern Song* p151.

enduring faith. Fortunately, he continued to find his own 'religiosity and philosophy in the music – songs like "Let Me Rest On A Peaceful Mountain" or "I Saw The Light" – that's my religion. I don't adhere to rabbis, preachers, evangelists, all of that. I've learned more from the songs than I've learned from any of this kind of entity. The songs are my lexicon. I believe the songs.'

It was these very songs he had been playing since the turn of the century – songs like 'Halleluiah, I'm Ready To Go', 'This World Can't Stand Long' and 'Somebody Touched Me'. And another one from the lexicon would open the first fifteen shows on the rescheduled fall 2001 leg, directed at a nation in shock. That song – made famous by Larry Kegan's favourite country singer, Hank Williams – was Fred Rose's 'Wait For The Light To Shine'. Its message spoke to the country and to the ages:

> When the road is rocky and you're carrying the load
> > (Wait for the light to shine)
> If you find you're friendless on that weary lonesome road
> > (Wait for the light to shine).

6.2

January 2000 to July 2003:
Smoke'n'Mirrors

In any song I write, or any movie I'm in, I always become the character in it.

> Bob Dylan, *MacLean's* 20th March 1978.

These songs are not allegorical. I have given that up.

> Bob Dylan, to Edna Gundersen, September 1997.

It's [like] with my own songwriting. I overwrite something, then I chip away lines and phrases until I get to the real thing.

> Bob Dylan, *Wall Street Journal* 19th December 2022.

['*Love and Theft*'] is the way I really feel about things. It's not me dragging around a bottle of absinthe and coming up with Baudelairian poems.

> Bob Dylan, to Edna Gundersen, 10th September 2001.

He doesn't relate to himself as the powerful force we see.

> Larry Charles.

The thing about Bob is, he knows exactly what he wants. And . . . the people who have said that Bob is difficult are people who were trying to put what *they* wanted on the record.

> Chris Shaw, engineer on '*Love & Theft*'.

These so-called connoisseurs of Bob Dylan music – I don't feel they know a thing, or have an inkling of who I am and what I'm about.

> Bob Dylan, to Alan Jackson, 2001.

Since *Time Out of Mind*, he's more or less chosen to produce himself . . . But I personally think that self-production is a myth . . . I don't think he has really made a complete record since *Time Out of Mind* . . . He's denying himself the luxury of a relationship that can be good. He's obviously had problems with producers.

Jim Dickinson, to Damien Love.

My roots go back to the Thirties, not the Fifties.

Bob Dylan, to Jonathan Cott, 17th September 1978.

★

As the new millennia dawned without any sign of the world exploding, Dylan duly immersed himself in two projects that – thanks to his ongoing, unrelenting touring schedule – would take him three years to complete. Both were new departures in their own way. One would be an enormous commercial hit, received and reviewed as confirmation that he was back to his best; the other – something of a hidden gem in the man's *oeuvre* – was trashed mercilessly as an indulgence wholly unworthy of him. Once again, the critics managed to be King Solomon in reverse.

'*Love and Theft*', his twenty-fifth album of original songs, was the kind of foray into Anglo-Americana which seemed primarily intended to reaffirm 'genius steals'. Filching what was good, sometimes from himself, he gerrymandered an edifice which would 'only sound like a great album for a while'. It would be left to a page-bound poet, Michael McClure, to call him out on the one obvious flaw: '[These] lyrics are composed almost entirely of figures of speech. In the earlier works . . . – say *Blonde on Blonde* – there are no figures of speech, except just to connect the multi-layered, multi-dimensional imagery.'

Determined to prove he was not just 'very well read', but also knew his Americana inside out, Dylan set about plundering pop culture with elan. The references were as replete as they were recondite: in litera-ture, everything from *The Great Gatsby* via Junichi Saga's *Confessions of a Yakuza* (which was responsible for a whole verse of 'Po' Boy') to Mark Twain; in filmlore, everything from the Marx Brothers' *Room Ser-vice* to the noir of *The City Never Sleeps*; from the blues, self-conscious nods to Leroy Carr's 'Blues Before Sunrise', Charley Patton's 'High Water Everywhere' and Bukka White's 'Po' Boy'. The allusions, like the Russians, just kept a-coming.

He would also play cops'n'robbers with his first scripted film, *Masked and Anonymous* – which would not get even a limited cinema release until July 2003 – this time adding a great deal more humour to his withering worldview, having entrusted it to an accomplice he thought could do justice to his vision. (And did.) In director Larry Charles he had a willing cohort and a fan, who considered Dylan 'an *auteur* [who] has a very fluid sense of language, words and ideas. He doesn't impose any intentionality on them, any deliberate point of view . . . [Sure,] there's a lot of allusions and references and a lot of density to [*M&A*], but it's not necessary to be conscious of any of that to get something out of the movie.'

Dylan was strip-mining a medium the singer had never made his own, and no incursion from such an uppity upstart was ever going to be permitted by America's arbiters of what audiences watch. In a world where films were defined by the number of thumbs-up they got from a coupla couch potatoes, it never stood a chance.

Surprisingly, given that these respective releases would appear two years apart, both statements were conceived almost simultaneously and, initially, no single idea was definitively assigned to one or t'other. Larry Charles recalls, 'I had the privilege of going to the recording studio, and what happen[ed] is, a lot of lines that didn't wind up in *Masked and Anonymous*, wound up in *"Love and Theft"*, and vice versa.' One of these ended up in 'High Water' – the most gripping song on the 2001 album – but was initially offered to Charles:

> One day he came in with this line, 'I'm not a pig without a wig,' and I'm like, 'Look, Bob . . . I have to tell ya, even in a movie like this, this dense, weird movie, no-one's gonna understand that line.' And he said, 'What's so bad about being misunderstood?'

The line was not one of his. It came from an old nursery rhyme, 'As I Came To Bonner', he hadn't referenced on 1990's *under the red sky*. It was as if the person making *'Love and Theft'* was not Jack Frost – Dylan's *nom de plume* as its producer – but Jack Fate, his alter ego in the movie, a character described thus in the shooting script:

A cult musician – once a person on the radar of a popular culture – someone who had it all, but didn't care. Twenty years ago, he refused to cooperate with the powers that were and parlay his early success into a career. Instead, he has lived the past few decades in relative obscurity, playing honky tonks and bars, in and out of the county lock-up, content to be a wandering minstrel. Now, either his luck has changed or it's just run out.

Charles soon realized that what Dylan was doing with their script, 'he was [also] doing with the songs; he was collaging, and hoping . . . that in a subconscious way, meaning would emerge from the synthesis and juxtaposition of these disparate pieces.' It was a methodology common enough in film, but when it came to song, he was attempting something not many had tried, fewer still with any success – 'the juxtaposition of the old and the quaint and the old fashioned with the post-modern', as Charles put it.

If Dylan lifted some lines on *'Love and Theft'* from movies he loved, à la 1985's 'Seeing The Real You At Last', a lot more derived from traditional ballads and songs, as he drew from the font of Anglo-American song on a scale last seen in 1963. He now sought to do self-consciously what he used to do unconsciously, blend the traditional tropes and commonplaces of Anglo-Americana with a narrative distilled in his own imagination (and/or real life), imagining the joins would be invisible. But there was a randomness to some of his choices. Thus, 'The cuckoo is a pretty bird, she warbles as she flies,' opens one verse of 'High Water', without moving things along a single jot. It does not so much fly as plummet.

Dylan was no longer content to glean an idea from the lexicon and use it as a springboard – as he had done successfully as recently as 1997, with 'Tryin' To Get To Heaven' taking its initial impetus from an old baptist hymn ('The Old Ark's A-Moverin'). Likewise, 'Mississippi' had taken its burden from an old prison holler, 'Rosie', collected by John and Alan Lomax in the early Thirties: 'Ain' but de one thing I done wrong [x3]/ Stayed in Miss'ipppi jes a day too long/ Day too long, lawdy, day too long,'

If both songs had spiralled off in their own direction, borne aloft by Dylan's still-vivid imagination, by 2001 he was stitching together songs from 'knock knock jokes', gangster autobiographies, American literary classics and black-and-white movies, along with the usual common-place tropes of ballads and blues. Even the song that seemingly sent him down this beaten path, the unreleased 'The Time Will Come', was another patchwork quilt, rhyming the famous opening from 'In The Pines', 'The longest train . . . went down the Georgia line', with a Hollywood platitude, 'The most beautiful face I ever saw was just hiding a wicked mind'. When he admitted to being 'gone in the head, I speak well of the dead, I'm Alabama bound', it was three pretty non-sequiturs in a row. The punchline to the song, 'New things aren't true and true things aren't new,' sounds like a line from *The Magnificent Ambersons*. He was unapologetic, especially to Robert Hilburn:

> My songs are either based on old Protestant hymns or Carter Family songs or variations of the blues form . . . I'll take a song I know and simply start playing it in my head . . . People will think they are talking to me and I'm talking back, but . . . I'm listening to the song in my head. At a certain point, some of the words will change and I'll start writing a song. [2003]

The methodology suggested a certain dearth of inspiration from rock's greatest lyricist. He was no longer adapting the songs he heard in his head, the 'old Protestant hymns or Carter Family songs or variations of the blues form'; he was *stealing* chunks of them. And he knew his copyright law well enough to know there wasn't a damn thing anyone could do to stop him. He'd stood over the graves of the people whose songs he was stealin', and made sure they were dead. Embracing this conceit wholesale, he set about shuffling lines from song to song, as he had done on *Time Out of Mind*, and indeed from album to movie, despite telling Hilburn, 'It's important to keep the pieces until they are completely formed and glued together.'

All of which might give the impression *'Love and Theft'* was a work hastily cobbled together. Nothing could be further from the truth. Dylan worked long and hard on this construct, informing Gundersen as far back as April 1999 that he had kept the songs on the previous album 'for a while and wrote and rewrote them . . . [And] I'm taking that approach again.'

The effort he poured into these songs, written all over the world, suggested a connection to them he hadn't felt for a long time. He would write 'Moonlight' while staying at the Montgelas Palais, in Munich, presumably in the spring of 2000; 'Floater', originally 'Too Much To Ask', he handwrote on Nagoya hotel notepaper in March 2001; 'Highwater' came from an unspecified stay at New York's Essex House. This was no last-minute assemblage.

What Dylan was perhaps doing was trying to keep one step ahead of his peers by taking two steps back. Even when it failed to scale the heights, he remained unrepentant – because stubborn is as stubborn does – repeating the 'experiment' three more times in 2006, 2012 and 2020.

Initially, he needed to give his touring band a crash-course in the kind of Americana that would be the veritable bedrock of this 'new' aesthetic, having decided to record an album with his standing band for the first time in two decades:

> **David Kemper**: We'd go in a rehearsal hall, and we just would play for three days. And lots of times . . . we'd play only Dean Martin songs . . . We'd play 'em on the record player, we'd listen to 'Everybody Loves Somebody Some Time' and he'd sing it. [By] then . . . we could do a whole . . . gig playing those songs – but we never, ever played them. We just polished them up, and that was that. And he would do that with Johnny & Jack songs, Stanley Brothers songs . . . earlier American artists, too . . . [He'd] give us tapes of this real early stuff. And the next day in rehearsal, we'd run through them and learn to play them, [but] most of them we never replayed. And [then], the first day we went in to record 'Love and Theft', he said, 'Alright, the first song we're gonna start with is this song,' and he'd play it for us on the guitar, and then he'd say, 'I want you to do it in the style of this song.' And he'd play an early song. Like, he started with 'Summer Days' and he play[ed] a song called 'Rebecca' by Pete Johnson and Big Joe Turner. It became apparent that he'd been training us for over a year, to learn these old *styles*.

Dylan's regular deep-dives into pre-war Americana had already been well documented, as had his seeming aversion to modern pop music. In recent years he had even begun to display some of that love and knowledge onstage, while keeping much of it in reserve. Rehearsing for summer 1999 shows with Paul Simon, the rhymin' Simon remembers going 'through quite a menu [with Dylan], from deep folk stuff to the Everly Brothers to Johnny Cash to country to blues'. But little of this spilled onstage.

Once in a while, Dylan would give a CD to pedal-steel player Bucky Baxter – who would leave the band in 1999 after a series of warnings about his substance-abuse issues – 'It would be some black mandolin player from 1930, and he'd say, "Here, play like that."' He wasn't joking. As he once said, 'I think I liked the world better when talent scouts also sold furniture,' a cryptic reference to H.C. Speir, the man who discovered the likes of Tommy Johnson, Robert Johnson, Charley Patton and Son House.

In fact, he was in love with the idea – rather overstated in a series of recent historical studies from American universities, notably Eric Lott's 1993 study, *Love and Theft: Blackface Minstrelsy and the American Working Class* – that in the early recording era America was a melting pot of black-and-white musical styles. He bought into it to such an extent that he described Charlie Poole on a 2007 radio show as someone 'known as a country artist . . . but if you saw him live, you would hear a mixture of minstrel songs, Victorian ballads, humorous burlesque-type numbers, as well as old-timey country music.' Maybe. Maybe not.

Poole, of course, had the River Boys. Dylan did not, though he certainly could have picked musicians more steeped in these forms than his current touring band. Learning songs from CD-Rs only gets one so far. And yet clearly this is what Dylan was handing out. So, when he based 'Sugar Baby' on the traditional 'Lonesome Road', it was a very specific 'Lonesome Road': Gene Austin's superb 1928 recording. But Austin was no traditional singer. Almost a crooner, the expressive way he sings, 'Look up and seek your Maker/ 'Fore Gabriel blows his horn,' puts most of Dylan's sandpapered singing on *'Love and Theft'* in the shade.

The musicians, though, were sold on the idea. Kemper, for one, convinced himself all the influences 'on that record . . . comes from really early Americana, way back at the turn of the century . . . The songs that he would bring in would be these amazing examples of early Americana. Nobody . . . knows as much about American music as Bob Dylan . . . When we went in and recorded *"Love And Theft"* it was like, "Oh my God, he's been teaching us this music – not literally these songs, but these *styles*."'

So, when at the *L&T* sessions Dylan tried to get the right vibe for

'High Water', which had begun with a banjo/accordion arrangement, he tells the band, 'It's that Dock Boggs – country blues – "Pretty Polly" [feel] – that's what we need.' Try as they might, they didn't come close, even as a non-plussed Chris Shaw looked on:

> He's always trying to find the arrangement that works best with the sentiment he's trying to express. To that end, he might say, 'Well, I'm kinda hearing this like this old Billie Holiday song.' And so we'll start with that, the band will actually start playing that song, try to get that sound, and then he'll go, 'Okay, and this is how my song goes.' It's a weird process, and it's unique to him.

Actually, two tunes he lifted wholesale were post-war, 'Tweedle Dee & Tweedle Dum' ('Uncle John's Bongos') and 'Cry A While' ('Your Funeral, My Trial'). Even where tunes really were purloined from 'weird old America', Dylan treated the lyrics as almost interchangeable. The original bridge for 'Bye And Bye' – 'You gotta spare the defeated, you gotta speak to the crowd/ You gotta teach peace to people you conquer, gotta tame the proud,' a straight lift from Virgil's *Aeneid* – stuck out like Tom Thumb when it was switched to the equally derivative 'Lonesome Day Blues'.

Losses were inevitable, such was the scale of the changes Dylan made in the rewriting process.* And much of it happened during the sessions, as Augie Meyers duly noted: '[Dylan would] fool around for a while with a song, and then we'd cut it. And [then] he'd say, "I think I'm gonna write a couple more verses," sit down and write five more verses. Each verse had six or eight lines. It's complicated stuff, and he was doing it right there.'

Yet again, there came a point when he was no longer improving the songs, changing stuff for its own sake. This mid-life malady had already taken a toll on *Time Out of Mind*. One now feared for the future of America's finest lyricist. Previously, Dylan could be relied on to improve a song with almost every lyrical upgrade, even when – as is the case

---

* One of the better couplets in an earlier draft of 'Bye And Bye' reads, 'Every moment I'm not with you is a moment of despair/ Can't relax around anyone, there are thieves everywhere.'

with the LP versions of 'Jokerman' and 'Idiot Wind' – the re-recording lost more ground than it gained lyrically.

Even the symbolism employed in the new songs seemed at times arbitrary. If much has been made of names Dylan drops in a number of the L&T songs, the draft lyrics make it clear that most of the time he was just yanking chains. Two familiar figures from literature would be sacrificed in the rewriting of 'High Water' which carried on well into post-production. A reference to James Joyce, who 'left in the roaring rain/ Rode to Rosedale but they wouldn't let him off the train,' only featured in an early draft, while the intriguing couplet, 'Doctor Frankenstein's still up there at his castle on the hill/ The monster he created, he just [don't] know how to kill,' carried over to the sessions.

But to read significance into namedropping Big Joe Turner, Charles Darwin and George Lewes in the same song is to buy into Dylan's mind games. It also fails to explain how Lewes went from being a 'clergyman . . . talking to the clerk', to a stand-up comic telling racist jokes, while retaining the same portentous significance. It wasn't like Dylan hadn't thrown out random names before. Perhaps he was simply imagining famous figures being caught up in the 1927 Mississippi floods about which Patton ('High Water Everywhere'), Memphis Minnie ('When The Levee Breaks') and Bessie Smith ('Backwater Blues') wrote so memorably. Hence, the following deleted verse: 'Well, the tracks tore up at Vicksburg, Charles Darwin's house is gone/ River banks are swelling in the dreadful hours of dawn.'*

If so, it worked. 'High Water' is the most well-conceived song on the whole album. But it was subject to the same seemingly random changes as the rest. Another grade-A track, 'Sugar Baby', was another shape-shifter. Only the tune, already more than a century old, and its arrangement, seventy-three years young, remained the same. In a song that even in its final form hardly lauded womenfolk, he toned down some of its latent misogyny. Verse three of one draft reads, 'For years I lost sleep trying to get close to you/ Now I see there was nothing to get close to,' while an insert added to the second draft reads: 'Your charms have broken many a heart that has put its faith in you/ You got a way of tearing the world apart with words that ring so true.' Another

---

* Likewise, I believe Blind Willie Johnson, not Blind Willie McTell, to be the 'true' subject-matter of the 1983 song.

redundancy he ultimately red-penned was the clunky, 'Jim Dandy looking at his watch, and his watch is slow/ I haven't been sold out yet, if that's what you want to know.'

At least both songs warranted such care and attention, 'Sugar Babe' making for his best album-closer since 'Shooting Star'. But much of the record's residue was filler at best. At its worst, it verged on a black-faced parody of Lott's mythic melting-pot minstrelsy. He simply did not have the voice or the band to tackle such anachronistic styles. His ill-conceived decision to remove all other musical textures from the process, when his one consummate instrument – those torn and frayed vocal cords – had been shot to pieces from thirteen years of constant touring in arenas around the world, made for a gruelling listen at times.

Dylan anticipated the complaints, telling one interviewer, 'Soloing is not a big part of my records . . . Nobody buys them to hear solos. What I try to do [instead] is to make sure that the instrumental sections are . . . extensions of the overall feeling of the song.' It was a tacit admission he no longer cared to make records that bridged the genera-tions. *L&T* was an old man's record.

Occasionally, though, the playful Dylan of yore peaked through these post-modern clouds. On a draft version of 'Summer Days', he suggests, 'Mother taught me how to pray and I've learned to trust in God's grace.' Another allusion to his recent loss flits across an early 'Cry A While', 'I'm a long way from home/ Can't help feeling like a motherless child.'

He also was writing again about violent men ready to explode, not-ably on album-opener, 'Tweedle Dee & Tweedle Dum', which originally described Tweedle Dee as someone 'dressed in tweed, pipe in his mouth/ Speaks garbled Greek, fractured French/ Sleeping with a bullet-headed wrench.' It was another weak opener from a man who used to announce his albums with all the fanfare of Elijah's chariot. Intolerant of guitarists who liked to solo, he had also had enough of people who sat behind consoles and expressed *opinions*. This time no producer was going to tell him the world had no need of another two-note Dylan tune, original or not:

Chris Shaw: I'm not sure why Bob decided to start producing himself. Maybe [it was] because of the success he had with 'Things Have Changed', which he produced himself, and we did a couple of other things between that and 'Love and Theft', and I think he just realized he could do it himself. I don't think he ever really thinks he needs a producer, but this was the first time he had a chance to do it without a producer, and he just realized, 'I can do this myself. I know what I want.'

It had been a-long time coming. Augie Meyers, the one session-man recalled from Time Out of Mind, was surprised to find no producer: 'But I thought Bob did a great job producing it himself. He knew what he wanted to do. And he said it was a lot more comfortable. I mean, I think he enjoys making records, but he gets tired of all the hoopla, and everybody around him trying to put their two cents in.' Less surprised was Mark Howard, who concluded he decided, post-Lanois, 'I know my direction, and I don't want to have these conflicts with anybody.'

Dylan was certainly unapologetic: 'I felt like I've always produced my own records, except I just had someone there in the way . . . I knew this time it wouldn't be futile writing something I really love and . . . then gettin' in the studio and having it be . . . whacked around and come out with some kind of incoherent thing.' Even Chris Shaw, who did his best to accommodate Dylan's delusion that records sounded better in the Thirties, found himself treading on egg shells at times, especially when Dylan would launch into one of his tirades about technology:

He just hates how records sound today . . . The studio recording for him is sort of like a necessary evil . . . He just hates the time it takes. He's always talking about when he used to make albums: 'We did, like, four songs in one day' . . . On the last couple of albums, in the studio, he was always playing these old Carter Family albums, old Bob Wills records, and one of the things he's really enamoured with is the technology back then – you could only record with one or two microphones. You listen to a Carter Family record . . . he would talk about how immediate it sounds, how raw and vital it sounds . . . So, we're always trying to get that sound with modern techniques . . . His idea was just, basically, get the whole band in the room and get them playing.

Shaw's first history lesson came on 'the very first take of "Lonesome Day Blues" – the first track we did. We had the whole band playing in

the room, and there's a moment when it's the first time the band really
got their groove together, and Bob was just starting to sing it, and as
the song progresses, you can hear him getting really into and the band
really getting into it, the song builds up . . . The first two verses were
just Bob not really singing, because he wasn't sure if it was right yet.
But by that third verse he starts singing, and by the fifth he's just *really*
leaning into it. I distinctly remember that moment, standing in the
control room watching the band, everyone in the control room, the
hair on the back of the neck was standing up.'

If it seemed like a propitious start, the song still needed a tune – and
an arrangement that lifted it out of the 'just another gutbucket blues'
category. Dylan even admitted to the journalists who took a Roman
holiday that July, 'The tracks were not yet complete when we went
into the studio. I had a general idea in mind, but not their finished
form.' Chris Shaw soon discovered he would be 'constantly changing
it. He'll be like, "What key are we in?" "Oh, we're in G." "What
tempo?" "85 bpm, Bob." "Okay, well let's do it in C-minor, and let's
crank up the tempo to 104, and, Charlie, I want you on electric instead
of acoustic, Tony, I want you to play upright bass instead of electric,
I'm gonna switch to guitar, oh, and I want you playing lap-steel." . . .
As an engineer, you're suddenly racing to get all these sounds.' Fortunately, there were just eleven songs he had in mind to record. And
should they fail to get any, there was always someone else to blame:

> **Chris Shaw**: If he can't get a song completely recorded in a day, he
> thinks there's something wrong with (A) the band, (B) the song or (C)
> me [and/] or the studio. '*Love and Theft*', I think . . . we did twelve songs
> in twelve days, completed.

Actually, they did eleven songs in eleven days, and then took a
breather. That is, until as Kemper confirms, 'A friend of Bob's* passed
him a note, and he said, "Oh, yeah, I forgot about this: 'Mississippi'."
And then he [said], "Did you guys ever bring the version we did down
at the Lanois sessions . . . Let's listen to it." So, they put it up on the big
speakers.' It still sounded great, but Dylan thought it could sound a

---

* Presumably Jeff Rosen, who is credited as 'client' on all the studio sheets from Clinton Recording Studio.

whole lot better. They recut it in twenty-eight minutes. After just two takes, he turned to the others and said, 'That's a better track. That was a good idea to recut it. Yeah, great.'

The new 'Mississippi' had a tune, great lyrics and real momentum. It positively screamed album opener. But he had seemingly forgotten the art of sequencing, at around the same time he began to disregard the virtue of leaving well alone. Enamoured by the possibilities once-hated technology afforded, he was back at Power Station in 1983 with an engineer he trusted and a yen to rework all he'd wrought:

> **Chris Shaw**: On 'Love and Theft', he'd be like, 'Oh, I wanna re-write the second verse.' And he'd walk off, and ten minutes later come back, and say, Okay, and he'd sing something and I'd be, like, 'Jesus Christ, you just wrote that in ten minutes?' . . . There was a lot of editing done on 'Love and Theft'. Like, the song 'High Water', the verse order of that was changed quite a few times . . . He was like, 'Nah, maybe the third verse should come first. And maybe we should put that, there.' . . . On the [very] first day of mixing, he said, 'I wanna re-record the second verse again, change a couple of lines.' And I said, 'Okay, let me get a head-phone mix together so you can have something to sing to.' And he's, like, 'Nah, nah, I don't like wearing headphones.' So, I said, 'Okay, well, let me get a pair of speakers rigged up and you can sing to the speak-ers.' . . . 'Oh, I used to do that with Daniel. I dunno if I like doing that.' So . . . we put the whole band back in the room with him, and *the band* would wear headphones, and then . . . play along with the track.

As Shaw further explained to *Electronic Musician*, the band ended up playing 'along with the track at a lower volume while wearing head-phones, and . . . hav[ing the guitarist] sing the lead vocal he's hearing in the headphone, and Bob follows along in the room. Then I punch in for the line. It gets the same spill over from the band on the punched part of the vocal track.' So much for Kemper's later assertion that, 'He never overdubbed a line, or swapped a phrase.' But it rather undid a lot of the good work Shaw had undertaken to ensure live 'leakage is a big part of the sound'.

The master DAT Dylan compiled on May 19th, 2001 – which was still missing the as-yet-unrecorded 'Mississippi' – contained a version of 'Tweedle Dee' with two different verses; a version of 'Bye And Bye' with completely different lyrics; a 'Moonlight' with a different bridge, and a 'High Water' with two extra verses, one of which was a corker:

> Doctor Frankenstein's still up there at his castle on the hill
> If he ain't come down by now I guess he never will
> Livin' there in the underworld, I ain't sayin' it's wrong or right
> The sun is shining down like it's twelve o'clock at night.
> Like a nightmare up there/ High water everywhere.

But it was not the album he released. He thought its best song needed some trimming, when he could have just done the world a favour and put 'Lonesome Day Blues' and 'Summer Days' on a train that was cold irons bound. Cutting verses four and eight from 'High Water', he overdubbed vocals on two other verses. 'Tweedle Dee' also lost the one moment the narrator's mask slipped, 'Rain beatin' on the windowpane/ I got the cold shakes and a broken brain.' At least he dialled down on the clichés in 'Moonlight', which thankfully lost, 'My tears keep flowing to the sea/ Doctor, lawyer, Indian chief/ It takes a thief to catch a thief/ For whom the bell tolls for love, it tolls for you and me.' None of this was shape-shifting, though. It was tinkering.

As Katie Holmes's character tells Professor Tripp in *Wonder Boys*, 'You know, you always told us writers make choices . . .' Well, Dylan was making choices which only undermined the integrity of the whole. Nothing about the rewrites suggested they warranted such effort. But Dylan was convinced this was his first masterpiece of the 21st century, telling Mikal Gilmore, 'If it's a great album – which I hope it is – it's a great album because it deals with great themes . . . power, wealth, knowledge and salvation,' as if great themes = great work. Even more off-piste was a comment to Gundersen, 'The songs don't have any genetic history. Is it *Time Out of Mind* or *Oh Mercy*? . . . Probably not. I think of it more as a greatest hits album . . . without the hits.'

Fortunately for his 21st century career, he had a cabal of uncritical critics, and one label president, just champing at the bit to praise this new piece of product to the skies. To Gundersen's ears, 'The record . . . is an amazing throwback to early American music.' Don Ienner, head of a label that churned out more Capital-P-product than any other, insisted, 'A lot of people aren't being served by much of the music that they hear today, and this is the kind of music that people are hungry for.' Hilburn was more circumspect, if still convinced Dylan was 'revisit[ing] some of the . . . musical textures he heard on the radio as a youngster in Minnesota . . . rework[ing] them into striking contemporary pieces.'

Bucking all trends, save perhaps the freak success of the *O Brother, Where Art Thou?* soundtrack, in the weeks after 9/11, while other streams of pop culture temporarily dried up in the aftershock of the Twin Towers, the album seemed like a reassuringly recondite soundtrack for a stunned generation. It was enough to take the LP into *Billboard's* Top Five, his best US chart-placing since *Desire*. A couple of weeks later, asked for his thoughts on the momentous events of a day that had cast a shadow over *everything* – his forthcoming tour included – Dylan quoted Sun Tzu, of all people, 'If you know the enemy and know yourself, you need not fear the result of a hundred battles.'

It was not the last time he would reference *The Art of War*. In *Masked and Anonymous,* Jack Fate's half-brother Edmund quotes Sun Tzu as part of his vainglorious victory speech at film's end, 'Those who are victorious, win first, then go to war, while the defeated go to war first, and then seek to win.'* The version in the shooting script is, if anything, even more dictatorial:

As far as rights go, all people aren't entitled to the same rights. Freedom is only for people who can practise self-control . . . It is from within, amongst ourselves, from cupidity, corruption, disappointed ambition, and inordinate thirst for power that factions will be formed and liberty endangered. It is against such designs that we especially have to guard ourselves . . . We have the good of society at heart. We will bring back public display of games. We are going to empty the prisons. We will fill the football stadiums. We will have evil-doers from the prisons trampled by wild elephants, mauled by uncaged bears, pecked to death by screaming eagles . . .

The script, which Charles and Dylan had completed by May 21st, 2002, was littered with similar scattershot screeds. Indeed, the core of

---

* As per usual, Dylan delights in misquoting the source, '*Victorious warriors win first and then go to war, while defeated warriors go to war first and then seek to win.*'

the shooting script was a series of monologues Dylan gave to Larry Charles, hoping he might turn them into a film. He duly obliged. As Charles told Robert Polito in a wide-ranging discussion of the finished film:

> A lot of what he wrote [initially], you know [the] Andrew Jackson stuff, the biblical stuff about Ezekiel and the wheel, a lot of that stuff . . . was monologues . . . He would come in with these incredible monologues, [and] say, 'I wrote this last night,' and it would be . . . those great monologues, the John Goodman monologues, the Luke Wilson monologues, the Tom Friend monologues, the Jessica Lange monologues . . . which of course I wanted to shoot intact. I didn't want to change a word . . . So, a lot of the time . . . the rest of the scene . . . would be fashioned by me . . . around the monologue[s] . . . He would bring in these [almost] Biblical things folded into monologues . . . [They] suggested this Third World America, and we started to fashion [the film] around that idea.

The results were almost akin to the kind of worldview Dylan had planned to incorporate into the autobiography he had abandoned just as he was preparing his pitch to HBO, and had only recently picked up again, having accepted he might have 'the mind of the creator, but not the immortality nor the sense of wisdom', and so, 'has to work still to this day'.

Such were the smorgasbord of ideas he now regenerated and reworked, and which Charles wisely refrained from challenging him on. The film gave him an outlet for some particularly outlandish notions one or more of his Gemini selves held; all of which he could put into the mouths of actors as good as John Goodman, Val Kilmer, Jessica Lange and Jeff Bridges, loving the very idea of the anonymous *auteur*.

He even credited the script to Sergei Petrov and Rene Fontaine, adapted from a 'short story by Enrique Morales', a throwback to the *Eat the Document* proposal. The movie it most closely resembled, however, was the one he told Allen Ginsberg he was planning to do *after* 1978's *Renaldo & Clara*, 'It will be about Corruption, about Pride, about Vanity, and about Obsession.'

Fortunately for him, Charles had the contacts to make something happen and was enthralled enough by the idea of working with Dylan to take on board what his cousin said when he told him, 'Don't ever call him Dylan, just always call him Bob, 'cause he's Bob . . . Dylan is your issue to figure out. He doesn't care about that. He just wants to be Bob.'

When the singer put the kibosh on the HBO special, Charles told him, 'Look, I'm prepared to do whatever you want to make this work.' So, he and Charles 'started writing what became the *Masked and Anonymous* script, folding some of these [earlier] things into it . . . exchanging ideas, thoughts . . . without imposing any order on it . . . [just] letting the order and patterns emerge out of it naturally.' The one vestige of the TV special they retained was Dylan's abiding 'interest in puns and corny jokes . . . the kinds of jokes that Bob gets a kick out of, and at that time . . . his between song patter [at shows] was basically to do three or four of those.' Equally organic was the way the film's characters emerged out of the odd couple's initial discussions:

Larry Charles: He writes a lot on hotel stationary, especially in those days, I guess, but they were all torn into little pieces of paper with little things on them, little aphorisms, little lines of poetry, names of characters . . . I started picking through it and going, well Uncle Friendly, Uncle Sweetheart, well, this could be the name of a character, you know, Tom Friend, that's the name of a character; Jack Fate, that could be the name of a character, and here's a line that person could say, this person could say that, and he was, like, 'You can do that?' . . . Whatever he was interested in was [in] the movie, and we figured out a way to synthesize all those disparate elements.

All of this now coalesced into a story described in its synopsis as about 'a musician named Jack Fate and Fate's former manager, Uncle Sweetheart, a skimming, scamming, scheming cross between P.T. Barnum and Colonel Tom Parker; . . . of Nina Veronica, a TV producer who has seen it all and risks everything because she believes in Fate, or because she doesn't believe in anything at all; and of Bobby Cupid, the devoted acolyte and ex-roadie, whose entire life has been defined by Jack Fate's music . . . But mostly it's about Fate.' All of these figures, drawn from a Kerouacian version of real life, became Dylan's way of dealing with his own mythology head-on. It took Charles a little while to realize:

In *Masked and Anonymous*, Bob is able to say the things that as Bob Dylan he cannot say, but it can be done as Jack Fate . . . When Bob is talking about himself, he often refers to himself in the third person . . . Dylan is what we've imposed on him and he holds on to his Bob-ness, his human-ness in a way, his realness, because if he gets sucked into the Dylan part, that's the mythological part that everybody has kind of created, that is almost too gigantic a burden for him to carry.

Dylan was delighted to have another opportunity to send his own public persona up. And so, when Jessica Lange's character, Nina, says, 'Are his songs going to be recognizable? That's what I want to know,' he was sending up people like the man from Stuttgart. Likewise, in a discussion between Bobby Cupid and Uncle Sweetheart about 'Tryin' To Get To Heaven', the prosaic Cupid insists it's all 'about trying to get to heaven'. But Sweetheart knows better: 'No, it's not about that at all . . . The whole thing is about doing evil and killing your conscience if you can. It's not like those other songs of his. Those other ones about faithless women, booze, brothels, and the cruelty of society.'*

A natural satirist like Charles was delighted to discover that Dylan could be 'very irreverent in relation to his own work . . . A lot of these lines he would play with them and . . . push further and deeper and see if we can twist it around somehow.' The film also addressed the idea that any form of nostalgia is death to the creative mind, a point rein-forced for Charles by a most unlikely source, Dylan's eldest son, Jesse:

> I was talking about how on *'Love and Theft'* he doesn't really play harp and that I had been listening to 'Pledging My Time' on *Blonde on Blonde* and he does this avant-garde, Miles Davis sort of harp solo, and how brilliant that was. And Jesse says, 'From the day he walked out of that recording studio for *Blonde on Blonde*, he has never listened to that record again.' And that's the way he is . . . He can't get sucked into the nostal-gia of it.

The one thing Dylan continued to avoid throughout the entire col-laborative writing process was *explanations*. In fact, as Charles asserts,

---

* Dylan promptly replaced this apposite choice with 'Drifter's Escape', rather ruining the joke.

'We never, ever discussed what the meaning of anything was . . . I could tell just from being around him [that] . . . that was not something he was ever going to do. As he says at the end of the movie, "I stopped trying to figure things out a long time ago." . . . But he's [still] telling you, this is who people think I am, and this is who I am, and it's up to you to figure out [who's who].'

He was very much a *cinéaste* who had learnt his *métier* in New York's downtown arthouses. As Charles noted, 'Godard was a big influence . . . because he [also] made anti-movies.' Yet most direct celluloid references in the finished film came from Hollywood, specifically 'the shot at the end, where Bob is at the open bay doors and the light is shining and he's pushed out', which was lifted from John Ford's 1947 western, *The Fugitive*. The old Hollywood was his true milieu, even if he was again determined to make his own film outside the system, Charles saying at the time, 'This film is about as non-corporate as it gets . . . The financing comes from outside sources, the methodology is outside the system, and it's full of insiders willing to go outside of things and take some risks.'

Much to Charles delight, 'As soon as the word went out that Bob Dylan was going to make a movie, he couldn't stop people from wanting to get involved.' It was certainly a helluva cast of Hollywood insiders who agreed to take a busman's holiday: Luke Wilson, Penélope Cruz, Jeff Bridges, John Goodman, Jessica Lange. The only non-actors *in situ* were Eddie G and Dylan himself. Bridges, in particular, seemed delighted just to be there, 'It was a lot of fun. We did a lot of improvising [together] . . . We [even] played a tune that he sang on *Natural Born Killers*, "You Belong to Me" . . . He had such enthusiasm and openness, yet he had this wizened feeling, very wise and very young all at the same time.' Though he had still not developed an aptitude for learning his lines – lyrics, yes; lines, no – Charles pushed him to revel in the unique experience:

> The making of the movie pleased him. He enjoyed the process, he enjoyed the challenge, he enjoyed the interaction with the other actors . . . [I said] to Bob right at the beginning, 'Listen, we have twenty days to shoot this movie. If you go back to the trailer after each shot, each take, the crew is just not gonna care, but if I get you a comfortable chair and you sit on the set between takes . . . these people will die for

you.' . . . So, he sat on the set throughout the entire movie and never went to his trailer . . . I would walk onto the set and there would be Bob and Jeff Bridges and Jessica Lange just kinda hanging out and talking.

In complete contrast to *Renaldo & Clara* and *Eat the Document*, where *Masked and Anonymous* stumbled and fell was with its musical performances. Not the often inspiring foreign versions of Dylan songs that punctuate the film – from that magical opening sequence, set to a Japanese version of 'My Back Pages', to Sertab Erener's haunting 'One More Cup Of Coffee' at its denouement – but rather Dylan's pedestrian choice of songs performed himself, especially an excruciating 'Cold Irons Bound'. Dylan's preference for 'one mike, one camera' also did for him:

> **Larry Charles**: Bob had some very specific ideas about how he thought music should look, and what's gone wrong with music on film . . . We went back and looked at some things [he] liked a lot, like [the] old Johnny Cash shows, and even Ed Sullivan and The Grand Old Opry shows with Hank Williams and we found they basically used one camera, and [that] put you right there . . . An intimacy [was] created between the musician and the home audience.

The 'one camera' technique worked fine when the performance – whether it was Hank Williams or Fred Astaire (who pioneered this approach in his Thirties movies with Ginger Rogers) – was riveting. But with an artificial film-set, no live audience, a pedestrian band and a singer with a set-list more ill-conceived than a modern Joni Mitchell gig, all momentum was lost. Only a belting 'Battle Hymn Of The Republic' threatened to raise the tin roof.

Talk of some twenty-two songs filmed, including a terrific 'Ol' Joe Clark', merely annoyed fans, especially when the few DVD extras were as disappointing as the songs that made the final cut. That edit was just shy of two hours, even as Charles was telling reporters there was a longer version – ninety minutes longer – which was 'much more anarchic, much more chaotic . . . much more like the world that we were depicting at the beginning of the movie.'

That full version included a scene in which a song and dance man, Oscar Vogel, in blackface reminds Fate of his youth and the vanished past, as he relates the consequences of his own, unwise decision to speak out against 'the system': 'Your father was doing things that were wrong. His desire for retaliation and revenge was too strong . . . I was the only one in a position to say anything . . . I had the show . . . People choose to die in all kinds of ways . . . I opened my mouth.' Why the scene was cut is unclear, given the number of themes which it ticked.

It seems it wasn't just albums that could be dismantled in post-production; and it wasn't just CDs which, when they came out wrong, Dylan sought to disown. When *Masked and Anonymous* premiered at the Sundance Film Festival in January 2003, and was almost universally panned, he was quoted as saying, 'They took out so many scenes that were my favourites that I kind of lost heart with it.' Who, exactly, were '*they*'? And when caught outside the Hammerstein Ballroom in an August New York blackout just like the one that had inspired 'Visions Of Johanna', he was caught joking to fans that 'he'd heard the movie was pretty bad'.

He knew full well, it wasn't, having already warned Charles, before it was previewed and panned, 'that the critics wouldn't get this movie. But the audience would, if they had a chance to see it . . . It's just so easy to go, . . . "Oh it's a difficult movie. [Or,] how dare they make a movie."' He had seen it coming and he knew what he was talking about:

> **Larry Charles**: [Maybe] some of the critics . . . were so overwhelmed at first that they checked out, and they never got to engage with it and see all the levels and the layers and all the different things that were . . . in the[re] . . . This movie is . . . where Bob really confronts the media, [which may be] another reason why the media have been somewhat resistant to it . . . [It's] a movie that's intended to be savoured and revisited, like something you'd see in a museum or a poem you'd read in a book, rather than mass-market entertainment. [2004]

One of the film's main financier's, the BBC, had smartly hedged their bets, bundling the UK rights with those for a second, more 'factual' film, to which Dylan had made his own reluctant contribution the same month he had sat with the head of HBO and heard all about what it was like to be at Woodstock. The film in question would be 'directed' by the heavyweight filmmaker, Martin Scorsese, and it would tell the 'true' story of the rise of Bob Dylan.

Released in September 2005, *No Direction Home* would fully salvage the BBC's initial investment, having found a way to reuse the discarded footage from Dylan's first disastrous foray into film-making, the still-unreleased *Eat the Document*. By then, though, Dylan was too busy enjoying the new Criterion edition of Orson Welles's *F For Fake* mockumentary to pay Marty's latest any mind. Now *there* was a shining example of an *auteur* who knew how to make great films despite the system.

6.3

2001–2018:
Writings & Drawings

Autobiography is an unrivalled vehicle for telling the truth about other people.

Philip Guedalla.

Some people take a kind of pleasure in repudiating their own past. Some, whether they wish to or not, live long enough to become negations or caricatures.

Christopher Hitchens, *London Review of Books* 4th June 1998.

Only when one has lost all curiosity about the future has one reached the age to write an autobiography.

Evelyn Waugh, *A Little Learning* (1964).

It's not important to set the record straight. It's more important to keep myself together.

Bob Dylan, to Edna Gundersen, 21st September 1989.

My retrievable memory isn't as good as it should be.

Bob Dylan, to Robert Hilburn, 16th September 2001.

Finding a voice to write prose [in] is a whole other trip from finding a voice to write songs in, and you found a beauty.

Bruce Springsteen, in a letter to Dylan, after reading *Chronicles*.

I see beauty where other people don't.

Bob Dylan, to Ron Rosenbaum, November 1977.

Randy Anderson: Other interests besides writing or reading or playing music?
Bob Dylan: . . . I like to blast sculpture out of metal.

Minnesota Daily 17th February 1978.

My stuff don't hang in museums.

Bob Dylan, to Elliot Mintz, March 1991.

I'm not sure I'm as good a revisionist artist as da Vinci, Donatello or even Picasso . . . I definitely have a lot to learn.

Bob Dylan, 2012.

I might trade places with Picasso if I could, creatively speaking. I'd like to think I was the boss of my creative process, too, and I could just do anything I wanted whenever I wanted, and it would all be on a grand scale. But of course, that's not true.

Bob Dylan, 2015.

I think he gets rather annoyed by people trying to arrange things in order, placing him in a tradition, saying this is like that, if he doesn't see a relationship.

John Elderfield, ex-curator of MoMA.

★

Once again, we enter murky waters. By 2003, it had been forty years since Dylan wrote, on the back of an album-sleeve, that he was 'a thief of thoughts', and still the suspicion lingered that he was also a taker of liberties when it came to copyright law. But as long as he stuck to song, he remained ever sure-footed. He'd seen off many a claimant, most of them chancers, with nary a scratch. Even when a European website started documenting the extent of his melodic and lyrical lifts on *'Love and Theft'*, he easily laughed it off. Wasn't the album title a clue?

The one charge that wouldn't go away, though, was the sheer number of self-conscious lifts from *Confessions of a Yakuza*, a 1991 memoir of a Japanese gangster by Junichi Saga that had recently been translated into English. Perhaps not surprisingly, celluloid collaborator Larry Charles was quick to spring to his defence:

When people say, 'Oh this is from *Confessions of a Yakuza*,' I think he laughs, because he's taken a totally non-poetic sentence, perhaps out of the middle of a paragraph of *Confessions of a Yakuza*, and turned it into art . . . He's so well-read and . . . he can quote anything. He can quote The Bible, he can quote Rimbaud, he can quote Yeats . . . [In *Masked and Anonymous*,] a biblical reference might be followed by a reference to Shakespeare, which might be followed by a film-noir reference, just constantly . . . mixing and matching and seeing if they hold together.

It was a robust rejoinder, and in the case of their collaboration, a valid one. Dylan's catholic reading tastes had long been known. As Rolling Thunder bodyguard, Mike Evans, once noted, 'When he writes he doesn't have that much time, but when he doesn't, he reads *everything*.' What was disturbing about the multiple *Yakuza* lifts on '*Love and Theft*' was their sheer banality. Bereft of their original context, such verbal discordancy jarred long before the source was revealed. Coming from a man who could insert an image like 'near the wall' – a balladic commonplace with a very specific sexual subtext – into a song without even a well-informed listener noticing how he just added layers of meaning, it was a depressing fall from poetic grace.*

The use of *Yakuza* was no single lapse. It was a sea-change. When the 21st century Dylan stole – and he would do so on an industrial scale, knowingly and noddingly – he would do so on a grand scale. Starting with *Masked and Anonymous*, he began to also do it outside his comfort zone, in media he was not destined to make his own, with a nod and a wink that would eventually become as wearying as it was worrying. In song, where he had long ago mastered the rules the hard way, he was at least master of his own domain.

When *Chronicles* appeared in October 2004 – after initial reports in March 2003 suggested the book had been 'postponed indefinitely' – it became apparent to all but the more credulous reviewers that, far from getting 'carried away in the process', as he claimed, Dylan had found the experience akin to pulling teeth. He almost admitted as much to Alan Jackson, albeit not until 2008:

---

* The line is from 1975's 'Abandoned Love', 'One more time at midnight, near the wall . . .'

Writing any kind of book is a lonely thing. You cut yourself off from friends and family to find that necessarily quiet place in your mind. You have to disassociate and detach yourself from just about everything and everybody. I didn't like that part of it.

Backstage at Hammersmith Odeon in November 2003, he had told S&S staff, 'Once I started writing, I couldn't stop.' Actually, he was afraid if he did stop, he might never start again, informing Gundersen he'd completed entire sections in single sittings 'because if I stopped, I didn't want to have to go back and read it'. Perish the thought a first-time author might need to sometimes rewrite sections. Instead, he took a leaf from the magpie.

Hence, why entire unDylanesque phrases popped out of the pages of *Chronicles* from that very first reading – 'You knew he had ... achieved some great deed, praiseworthy and meritorious' [p63]; 'All movement ceases ... The slightest whisper seems sacrilege' [p96]; 'The afternoon sun was breaking, throwing a vague radiance to the earth' [p112]; 'I cast an embracing glance over the primordial landscape' [p167]; 'Wind whipped in the open doorway and ... was rumbling earthward' [p217]. All of these lines, it transpired, were verbatim lifts from Jack London's prose.

Alarm bells were ringing, not in the lawyers' offices – because London was out of copyright – but in the homes of Dylan's staunchest defenders as a *literary* genius. The inevitable online discussions seemed to tip off search-engine sleuths, who duly discovered he'd lifted entire phrases from a March 1961 issue of *Time*. (If they'd come from the same issue of *Newsweek* as Svedburg's 1963 'exposé', that would have been funny.) It all seemed to many, myself included, part of some elaborate, 89,000-word hoax.* At some point, he had changed tack and decided to write a memoir in which barely a paragraph was the unbelievable truth.

He was Casanova, he was Clifford Irving, he was Konrad Kujau,

---

* 'I don't eat something that's one third rat, one third cat and one third dog.' – *Chronicles* p102; 'They had turned Hanoi, the capital city, into the "brothel-studded Paris of the Orient."' – *Chronicles* p87; 'There'd be articles about . . . new modern-day phobias, all with fancy Latin names, like fear of flowers, fear of the dark, of height, fear of crossing bridges, of snakes, fear of getting old, fear of clouds.' – *Chronicles* p88; all from *Time* 31/3/61.

and/or the Orson Welles of *F For Fake*. But this would-be wizard wasn't about to let anyone peep behind the curtain. Instead, he was able to sit back and chortle at the critics as they lapped it up. And lap it up, they did. John Preston in *The Sunday Telegraph*, after apparently securing 'the first interview he has given to a British newspaper in twenty years',* gushed about how 'he devoured books – Rousseau's *Social Contract*, Machiavelli's *The Prince*, even the 19th-century Prussian General, Karl Clausewift's [sic] treatise on military strategy – cramming his head full of anything he could pick up'. For the young autodidact, this had presumably been just another sideline to selling dud oil stock and stealing songs in Gallup, New Mexico.

If the reviewers were slow to realize they had been sent up, Dylan's comment to Jonathan Lethem in 2006, 'The people who are writing reviews of this book, man, they know what the hell they're talking about,' surely tipped off even the last scoundrels from this confederacy of dunces. Yet *Chronicles* hadn't started out that way. He'd changed horses in mid-stream. And the burning question was, why? Was it because he was still not interested in looking back, preferring to look sideways through the glass darkly? Or could he simply not get back there, after spending so long behind walls others had erected around him?

The published *Chronicles* certainly wasn't the book talked up in the press release which broke the news of the million-dollar contract with Simon & Schuster in September 2001, or the one he described at the Rome press conference earlier that year, when asked, 'Have you ever been tempted to tell your own story?' His response – 'It'll be published shortly . . . as a book of articles . . . rather than . . . some kind of self-serving story of my particular past' – sounded like the Dylan we loved, cryptic to the ninth power.

Just two months later, as the deal was announced, the publisher was claiming these now-plural memoirs would 'be highly anecdotal, including just about everyone who was anyone on the New York folk scene of the early 60s, and . . . they will be impressionistic.' This hogwash was based on just forty pages editor David Rosenthal had seen, covering the early New York days he'd been itching to write about since 1963.

---

* In reality, it was three years since *The Times*'s previous cover-story interview with the man!

The rest of it didn't come so easily, even as he was soon claiming, 'I suddenly started remembering things . . . I got completely carried away in the process . . . I guess [you'd] call it novelistic writing.'*

At the same time, while promoting the patchwork audio artifact he'd just released, he was telling Gundersen the book would be at least partly his 'take on people who've had takes on me'. And to Mikal Gilmore, he suggested it had all come about because he'd been writing sleeve notes for expanded editions of three classic albums: *Freewheelin'*, *Blood on the Tracks* and *Oh Mercy*, none of which, needless to say, ever appeared. He also confided that he was 'collecting anecdotes about himself that other people have told and weaving them into the narrative'. Yet there were precious few from the early days to whom he spoke anymore, perhaps because, as Terri Thal had told his first biographer, 'He didn't relate to people too much. I think he was afraid to let anyone get to know him too well. I mean, if you're going to chuck your [whole] past every couple of years, you're not building on solid ground.'

All of which meant such anecdotes would have to be culled from published works, specifically the two new biographies published that year, both of which Dylan had already dismissed, telling Christoph Dallach in July, 'It's strange to read books about your own life. In your own memory things always present themselves differently to what others experienced. To me, these books are pure fiction.'

Coming from a man who intended to deliver a memoir closer to the Hitler Diaries than *Confessions of an Opium Eater*, it was another plume of smoke. As was his positively belligerent blast at these rival biographers, to that future biographer Hilburn, '[Even I] would[n't] . . . understand [my songs] if I believed everything that has been written about them by *imbeciles* who wouldn't know the first thing about writing songs.'

Mikal Gilmore, who had himself been interviewed for the better of the two new biographies, dared to ask him if 'any of these biographers stirred resentment from prying into . . . undisclosed aspects of your life?' Doing a particularly fine impression of J.D. Salinger, Dylan replied, 'A person [who] writes these kinds of books . . . has what they

---

* Certainly, the *Oh Mercy* section of *Chronicles* reads like an excerpt from a novel, say Lewis Shiner's *Glimpses*.

call a poetical lack of self,' a description one could certainly apply to Howard Sounes, who had phoned up Carolyn Dennis during his 'research' and, to her intense annoyance, when 'he could not get a word from me, just totally misinterpreted everything I said'.

Dennis had issued her own press statement making it clear there never was any cooperation on her part, or any 'multi-million dollar [divorce] settlement', as Sounes had asserted. Dylan simply dodged this particular bullet of bullshit, 'I've been married a bunch of times! I mean, I've never tried to hide that. I just don't advertise my life. I write songs, I play on stage, and I make records. That's it.' Not that he had any more time for the revised edition of the biography he once called 'too personal, too probing', responding to a question from Gilmore about his imbibing – evident throughout the *Knocked Out Loaded* sessions – by insisting, 'I don't know why people would associate drinking or not drinking with anything that I do, really.'

In reality, he'd been keeping tabs on what people said about him since the year dot – witness his reaction to a single line about Suze in the June 1963 *Little Sandy Review*. Britta Lee Shain's microcosmic memoir of the man 'and her' tells of how Dylan asked her to buy a copy of Joan Baez's 1987 autobiography, *And A Voice to Sing With*, saying, 'I wanna see what she put in there about me.'* Nor had he stopped reading about himself. Before starting in earnest on *Chronicles*, he admitted 'there had been other books about me and I'[ve] even read a couple . . . Some . . . were more accurate than others. But no one kn[ows] the full story, apart from me.'

However, this was also the man who once told Jim Keltner, while shooting a promo video for the Wilburys' second album, 'something [that] really . . . blew my mind – and I was gonna go tell Tom [Petty]. Bob stopped me and said, "Ya know you don't have to go say everything you know all at once to everybody all the time." ' Not so much *The Iceman Cometh* as *The Iceberg Hideth*.

The absent-minded Dylan was just another front lazy reporters, whether from *Time* or *The Times,* could buy into. After initially suggesting the book would be a response to others' presumptions, he was now

---

* The recently published *The Dylan Tapes* (University of Minnesota Press, 2022) reveals just how keen Dylan was to see what Scaduto had written about him *before* the book went to press.

insisting, 'I didn't feel like I had to counteract anything . . . [or] write an apology. I wasn't trying to explain anything to anybody.' And nor was he.

Instead, the budding memoirist drew on a prose style he'd experimented with in recent sleeve notes, jacket copy and faxed eulogies. Thus, in jacket copy for Peter Guralnick's *Last Train To Memphis* (1994), he described Elvis as 'the incendiary atomic musical firebrand loner who conquered the western world'; in a eulogy for George Harrison, he called him 'a giant, a great, great soul, with all the humanity, all the wit and humour, all the wisdom, the spirituality, the common sense of a man'; while the late Johnny Cash was someone 'blessed with a profound imagination, [who] used his gift to express all the various lost causes of the human soul'.

The apogee of such an approach could be found in his notes for a 2000 retrospective on Dion that aimed to capture the singer and his milieu in a couple of pithy phrases: 'Dion comes from a time when so-so singers couldn't cut it – they either never got heard or got exposed quick and got out of the way. To have it you really had to have it, no smoke and mirrors then – not a minute to spare – rough and ready – glorious and grand – grieving with heartache and feeling too much but still with the always "better not try it" attitude.'

Likewise, in *Chronicles*, we discover Karen Dalton was 'funky, lanky and sultry'; Ricky Nelson was 'a cross between a honky-tonk hero and a barn-dance fiddler'; Van Ronk 'sang like a soldier of fortune and sounded like he paid the price'; and Roy Orbison 'sounded like he was singing from an Olympian mountaintop' (or just plain ol' Mount Olympus, had the book been *copy-edited*) &c.

And when he said he was writing 'a book of articles', he wasn't joking. *Chronicles* read more like a taster for a memoir than a pukka self-portrait. It wasn't just short on veracity, it was bereft of narrative structure. Such seems to have been Dylan's intent – to avoid writing any 'kind of self-serving story of my particular past', i.e. a memoir. Of course, he'd always delighted in playing games, telling Cameron Crowe, ostensibly a *cineaste*, how he had worn glasses in *Pat Garrett & Billy the Kid* (1973) because he saw Dustin Hoffman 'do it in *Papillon*', a film that didn't come out until August 1974. Then there was the time he told the editor of *SongTalk*, 'Now that's a Byron line,' knowing full well it was a Shelley line. Each time, his lips were moving, talking to students of his work.

Whereas back in April 1966, he could ask Earl Leaf in all sincerity, 'If I laid nine put-ons and one truth on you, could you tell which is which?', in *Chronicles* it was all a put-on, it was all a lie. Not a single checkable story held water; not one anecdote couldn't be shot full of holes by any half-decent researcher. Far from being, as Jim DeRogatis suggested in his sceptical *Chicago Sun-Times* review, 'a ping-pong game between fiction and fact', *Chronicles* played ping-ping with fiction and myth-reinforcement, inspiring every fakir from Patti Smith (the National Book Award winner, *Just Kids*) to Q.R. Markham (the notorious *Assassin of Secrets*).* Many, too many, gave Dylan the benefit of the doubt.

Jonathan Lethem, an authentic purveyor of fine fiction, would claim in his enduring paean to plagiarism, 'The Ecstasy of Influence', 'Appropriation has always played a key role in Dylan's music,' having previously suggested, 'Dylan's sweeping simplifications of his own journey's story [are] outstandingly healthy ones. Puncturing myths, boycotting analysis and ignoring chronology are part of a . . . campaign not to be incarcerated within his own legend.' The second of these remarks would form part of Lethem's 2006 *Rolling Stone* interview with the ecstatically-influenced artist, almost the last time a Dylan interview was a conversation between equals.

Throughout the Nineties and Noughties, he had generally confined himself to doing interviews with Edna Gundersen at *USA Today* and Robert Hilburn at the *L.A. Times*, knowing they would observe the golden rule, explicated by Hilburn in a 1991 profile: 'Any talk about his former, 13-year marriage to Sara Lownds, or their four now-grown children is strictly off-limits.' In other words, the *interviewee* got to set the agenda.

Soon, the only interviews he would agree to do off-camera were with Bill Flanagan and Douglas Brinkley, members of his manager's inner circle, presumably because this pair had no problem with Dylan copy-editing himself – as he did most obviously in a 2017 interview with Flanagan, in which he insisted 'I *did* record ["Wagon Wheel"]. It's

---

* Dylan directly inspired the most blatant literary plagiarist of modern times. Bookseller Quentin Rowan wrote *Assassin of Secrets* (Little-Brown, 2011) under the pseudonym Q.R. Markham. It was hastily withdrawn when reviewers noticed it was a patchwork quilt of other spy thrillers. Rowan even named his own memoir of the great deception, *Never Say Goodbye* (2013), after a Dylan song.

on one of my old bootleg records. I recorded it with Roger McGuinn and Rita Coolidge and Booker T, at a movie studio in Hollywood,' information he simply wouldn't have recalled that easily, or that fully.

Two interviews he did do 'on-camera' at this time, one for 2015's *Lost Songs: The Basement Tapes Continued* – which professed to be about the basement tapes – and one for 2019's *Rolling Thunder Revue* – which professed to be about Rolling Thunder, but was one long, elaborate hoax – both took more liberties than Mr Valance. By then, the joins were not only showing, they were there for online sleuths to annotate. It prompted Dylan's most articulate response to the tide of accusations, to Bill Flanagan:

> There's always some precedent – most everything is a knock-off of something else . . . You'll see a newspaper clipping or a billboard sign, or a paragraph from an old Dickens novel, or you'll hear some line from another song, or something you might overhear somebody say just might be something in your mind that you didn't know you remembered. That will give you the point of approach . . . Once you get the idea, everything you see, read, taste or smell becomes an allusion to it . . . Try to create something original, you're in for a surprise. [2017]

If at the time of *'Love and Theft'*, *Confessions of Yakuza* generated the most online chatter, when it came to 2006's *Modern Times*, it would be the poems of the obscure Henry Timrod, a civil war poet, that set the *New York Times* off. Timrod had written lines as mawkish as, 'A round of precious hours . . . frailer than the flowers,' and, 'There is a wisdom that grows up in strife,' both of which Dylan appropriated for 'When The Deal Goes Down', one of the lesser songs on one of his lesser albums.* On the other hand, 'Ain't Talkin', a major work, took its cues from the somewhat more venerable Ovid, as well as The Stanley Brothers' 'Highway Of Regret', Matthew 22:39 and 'Wild Mountain Thyme'; confirmation he could still stitch a quilt in 4/4 time if he really wanted to.

But it was after his next non-soundtrack of original songs, 2012's *Tempest*, that he really found himself in the eye of a media storm about

---

* Dylan would still disingenuously suggest, 'No song you're listening to . . . is influencing it.'

plagiarism. This time, it had nothing to do with ecstatic influence. It had to do with lyrics – specifically, those of his earlier, homegrown classics, which had suddenly begun to appear on the manuscript market in suspiciously large numbers, often in surprisingly pristine form.

Previously, Dylan felt he had been blind-sided by collectors; wholly convinced that the 'little red notebook' which ended up in the Morgan Library was stolen goods; ditto, the Margolis & Moss manuscripts, which he told Cooky, privately, 'had been stolen from Albert Grossman's house by the woman who'd sold them to the rare book collectors in Santa Fe, claiming she'd had Grossman's permission to take whatever she wanted from the attic, when he was moving houses . . . [He was] infuriated by the notion of strangers . . . damaging his reputation by publishing inferior drafts.'

That significant collection of typescripts and handwritten lyrics had been on the market for a mere $12,000 back in 1990. However, by December 2010, real money had begun to enter the frame. A handwritten manuscript of 'The Times They Are A-Changin'' had just sold in auction at Sotheby's in New York for $422,500, having been described, somewhat foolishly, by the auctioneer as 'the original autograph lyrics', which it clearly was not. Everything about it was wrong, starting with the signature at the top. If the esteemed auction-house had asked an actual expert, alarm bells would have rung immediately, given that it was accompanied by 'an autograph fragment of the first five lines of the first verse of Dylan's "North Country Blues,"' a song Dylan had not only already written, but had already recorded when he wrote 'Times'.

Its provenance was also questionable. Kevin Krown – dead – to Eve McKenzie – dead – to (her son) Peter McKenzie, someone who had previously sold a cache of early lyrics to a wealthy New York collector without ever mentioning this gem.* When Peter tried to sell a '1965 set-list' with a fragment of 'Like A Rolling Stone' on the back, having failed to realize it was the set-list to the Halloween 1964 Philharmonic Hall show, he was busted.

Dylan was incensed, but nowhere near as incensed as the purchaser, who soon realized he'd been sold a dud. Legal threats flew thick and

---

* Peter had already been involved in a lawsuit over a 'signed' copy of *Freewheelin'* he sold to L.A. dealer, Jeff Gold.

fast, before Sotheby's refunded the money, though not before Dylan's office were dragged into the affair. Serendipitously, a real 'Times . . .' manuscript was discovered to have been published in facsimile in an obscure Bennington College literary journal, *Silo,* back in 1963. It looked nothing like the McKenzie ms. It *was* signed – wittily – at the bottom, 'me, Bob Dylan'.

But the real revelation – to Dylan, at least – was that a 'Times' manuscript was apparently 'worth' almost half a million dollars. Maybe it was time to clear out the garage. Suddenly, a cache of handwritten Dylan manuscripts of his most famous songs began to be traded for $$$ in the murky world of manuscript dealers; each of them authenticated as being in Dylan's hand – which they were – by his manager, Jeff Rosen. Their provenance, as such, was surely unimpeachable.

Nor were these Bob's 'foul papers'. Each of these manuscripts had variant verses, amendments, and marginalia, all in Dylan's unmistakeable 'early' scrawl. The first one to appear, 'Blowin' In The Wind', even had what appeared to be a fourth verse, which began, 'How many times have you heard someone say/ If I had his money, I'd do things my way/ But little do they know . . .' The lines were actually from the Hayes-Rhodes lyric, 'Satisfied Mind', a song he'd considered performing in the clubs in 1961 (a version of the lyrics in Dylan's early hand is in the Morgan Library). A more worrying aspect of the pencilled draft, though, was the stationery used, which came from the 51st St. Taft Hotel (where Jimmie Rodgers died), at a time when Dylan and Suze lived on Fourth Street.

Traded and re-traded privately, the manuscript created only a minimal stir, largely in Dylan circles. Likewise, an intriguing 'fair copy' two-page draft of 'Mr Tambourine Man' caused nary a ripple, so discreetly was it sold. Its handwriting was again affirmed as genuine. Again, it was on right-looking hotel notepaper. However, the hotel in question, The Royal Orleans, was not called by that name in February 1964, when Dylan visited the city and began to pen the song. Also, at the top of the manuscript was a snatch of 'Bob Dylan's 115th Dream', a song he was months away from writing. Something was happening, and Dylan did not seem to want anyone to know what it was.

A further ms. of 'It Ain't Me, Babe' was now offered for sale, this one on Greek hotel notepaper – unlike any of the substantial body of lyrics and poems we *know* he composed in, or took with him to, Greece in June 1964 (all housed at the Morgan). These included the first draft of the song on London Mayfair Hotel notepaper, which had already been published in the *Bob Dylan Scrapbook* (2005), and – unlike the 'Greek' version – had the extra verse he had sung at the Royal Festival Hall a fortnight earlier. It was almost as if these manuscripts were being manufactured to order. But how? The only person who could produce something this unequivocally 'authentic' looking was Dylan himself, and he sure didn't need the money.

With each manuscript that appeared, the questions only grew more plentiful, fuelling one nagging, disturbing doubt. Though unquestionably Dylan's work, validated by his right-hand man, these song manuscripts were also all *of a type*, yet purported to span a period of a dozen years when his penmanship changed drastically.

It wasn't just the penmanship that looked the same. The assorted headed notepapers all seemed to be from the right period, but were a little *off*; not the expected names.

'Lay Lady Lay' came on late-Sixties notepaper from an east coast lumber company. Was it mere coincidence that said notepaper was still being sold on eBay in the 2000s? 'Knockin' On Heaven's Door' came on TWA note paper, such as one might expect if he wrote it at an airport or on a plane to or from Durango. But that wasn't the case. And still, the identikit manuscripts kept eking their way into the world until, in spring 2014, the manuscript masquerade, if that is what it was, went into overdrive. A California-based dealer with links to the Halcyon Gallery in London had been given a list of handwritten lyrics he could purchase, authenticated manuscripts with just one degree of separation from Dylan himself. Every lyric on the list was on any collector's A-list.

Unbeknownst to the Dylan office, the dealer, Bernie Chase, now brought in an expert – a real expert – to evaluate the manuscripts not on the basis of the penmanship or provenance, but on whether they were *right*. Just the facts. He had concerns and he was looking to have them allayed. Having purchased three of Dylan's five or six greatest songs – 'A Hard Rain's A-Gonna Fall', 'Like A Rolling Stone' and 'Tangled Up In Blue' – he planned to put all three in a Sotheby's rock'n'roll memorabilia auction in June, which seemed certain to create the kind of stir the manuscript source had so far studiously avoided.

For once, the 'Hard Rain' manuscript was not on hotel notepaper. In almost all aspects, it looked right. Except it wasn't typed – as was the original version composed upstairs from The Gaslight. Nor did it have the line, 'I heard the sound of one person who cried he was human,' which he included at early performances.* Sotheby's, forewarned by the expert, erred on the side of caution, describing it as 'the final draft lyrics as recorded'. Again the draft topped its estimate, but only after Sotheby's – despite having access to the expert's report – chose to omit a crucial paragraph of his from its catalogue:

> More problematic is the quotation at the top of the first page of the manuscript, which is correctly identified as Jeremiah 1:5. It reads, 'Before I formed you in the womb I knew [and] approved of you.' This is indeed the correct chapter and verse, and the quote does seem to have a bearing on the song because the figure being addressed is 'a prophet to the nations,' much like the 'blue-eyed son' . . . [But] the specific source Dylan has used . . . is one the 21-year-old is unlikely to have drawn upon: the so-called Amplified Version of the Old Testament, a text only published in 1962.† The King James Bible was always Dylan's preferred translation throughout the sixties, and indeed up to his conversion . . . in 1979.

The 'Tangled Up In Blue' manuscript he'd purchased proved even more problematic because, irony of ironies, it was *unequivocally* a genuine working draft, with all the changes one would expect from a Dylan tweaking it line by line, in the moment. It also contained a very interesting final verse that turned the song on its head, à la the 1984 version:

---

* Once again, rich paper fetishists proved unable to discern historical import, when the genuine, original typed draft of 'Hard Rain', with unimpeachable provenance, turned up in auction the following year and failed to make reserve, which was less than the $485,000 this (much) later handwritten version got.

† The King James Version reads: 'Before I formed thee in the belly I knew thee, and before thou camest forth out of the womb I sanctified thee, and I ordained thee a prophet unto the nations.' The Amplified Version was published in parts. The relevant part was initially published in 1962, but the full Old Testament was not available until 1965. It seems unlikely a 21-year-old Dylan purchased this academic edition on publication.

All our yesterdays are gone
And tomorrow might as well be now
Some went to the mountain (top)
Some went down to the ground
Some of their names are written in flames
Some came falling down.
Me, I'm still on the road
Trying to stay out of the joint . . .

The problem this time was not the manuscript's provenance, but its marked similarity to the version he'd been performing that year in concert, incorporating elements of both the 1984 version ('radio blasting the news . . .') and the 1974 original, but indubitably *not* a product of the summer of '74 explosion. The expert's report was unambiguous. Even though the manuscript had already been assigned a lot number by Sotheby's, it was hastily withdrawn, leaving just 'Hard Rain' and that jewel of jewels, 'Like A Rolling Stone', in the catalogue. The latter was already causing quite a stir, the estimate price having been set at a staggering one to two million dollars.

It was a manuscript that dripped with Dylanesque doodles. Page one of the four-page ms., on Roger Smith Hotel notepaper,* contained a pair of goggles, a chicken, a hat and a deer's head(?) – as well as three unrelated song-titles: 'False Knight On The Road' (Child Ballad #3), 'Pony Blues', and 'Midnight Special'. On the second page, among the marginalia, was an alternate version of the second verse, 'You never listened to the man who could jump jive and wail/ Never believed him when he told you he had love for sale . . . now he looks into your eyes and says, do you want to make a deal?' And at the bottom of the third page Dylan riffed away on the refrain, 'How Does It Feel/ It Feels Real/ Does It Feel Real/ Shut up And Deal/ Get Down and Kneel.'

Enticing fare for anyone with a couple of mill. to spare. And all in Dylan's graphic hand! Come the day of the sale – June 23rd, 2014 – bids eventually cleared the estimate, peaking at a princely $2,045,000, the highest amount ever paid for a rock lyric, more than even the poetic genius of 'All You Need Is Love'. But the tsunami of press coverage and

---

* A respectable Washington hotel, it is difficult to see when Dylan could've visited it in the first half of June 1965.

the wide distribution of all four ms. pages online also meant the jig was up. In the wider world, people soon began to ask, did Dylan *only* keep drafts of his greatest songs? Where were the minor lyrics? Why were these manuscripts all of a type, right down to the headed notepaper? And why were they being sold in such a clandestine manner?

Once seeds of doubt had been sown, the flow of these manuscripts ceased as abruptly as they had started. Fortunately for Dylan, the real story never broke, even as he began exhibiting his latest artistic handi-work in the same London gallery where the Purchaser and the Expert had first discussed the possibility that he might be having an elaborate joke at the former's, the art world's and the media's expense.

One name that never came up in those discussions – or Dylan's own art-related conversations with ex-MoMA curator John Elderfield, who had been guiding him through the shark-infested art world – was that of the great Italian pre-surrealist painter de Chirico, whose *pittura metafisica* paintings from the 1910s had been such an influence on Surrealism.

However, de Chirico renounced his own direction around 1918, and began to develop a new neo-classical style, which neither the critics nor art patrons embraced. So, starting in the 1940s, infuriated by the art world's curt dismissal of his later work, de Chirico began to produce what became known as 'self-forgeries' of earlier work. Art dealers began to whisper that his bed must be six feet off the ground to hold all the 'early work' he kept 'discovering' beneath it.

If de Chirico remains perhaps the most notorious example of the self-forger, Dylan himself had recently picked up the gauntlet. In an introductory essay to a January 2013 catalogue for his latest art exhib-ition, called 'Step Inside The Hurricane', credited to B. Clavery but smacking of the same satirist who (co)wrote 'A Night With Bob Dylan' and rewrote the 1966 *Playboy* interview,* he directly referenced Marcel Duchamp's most famous '*objet trouvé*':

> He did not draw a moustache on the actual Mona Lisa . . . Rather, he modified an inexpensive mass-produced postcard. Revisionism is dependent on a shared cultural literacy within its audience. Without the knowledge that this is one of the most famous portraits in the world,

---

* John Elderfield certainly considered it Dylan's work, and Luc Sante disclaims any role in its composition.

this work would be no different than the defaced picture in a school yearbook of a particularly annoying teacher. Duchamp knew that . . . we would all understand the shift in context.

The exhibition in question was Dylan's second at Gagosian, New York's most prestigious commercial gallery, and it came with the provocative title, *Revisionist Art*. Revisionism was the concept around which he planned to hang his new exhibit, and be hung as a thief. It was one he co-opted from a 2008 spoof blog by a writer already on his radar, Luc Sante. In 'The Poetry of Ellery Queen', Sante had created a group calling itself The Resurrectionists, who were 'devoted to finding the poetry hidden in the works of the most prosaic authors . . . The Resurrectionists enjoyed waxing militant, calling for the abolition of "simple load-bearing literature, which trucks ideas from the factory and dumps them at your door" and the exposure of "functionaries who pretend to be writers."'

This delicious conceit was one Dylan was keen to run with, renaming Sante's fictional art-anarchists 'The Revisionists', and commissioning Sante to write an introduction to his latest catalogue. In it, Sante suggested, 'Revisionists have been around for as long as the vampire called "culture" has stalked the earth.' By then, Dylan had sent along some 'helpful' notes, to clarify the difference between Resurrectionists and Revisioninists: 'Revisionism is truer than the real thing. People think Coke is the real thing, but revisionism is the real thing . . . From Turner to Rockwell, to Michaelangelo to Picasso, to Renoir – all revisionists . . . Everything in the media is bullshit. Revisionism is truth; media isn't.' But the most telling observation he made to Sante was one neither Luc nor B. Clavery used, 'An artist does not claim rights, they assert them – they pounce on them. They create them and they destroy them.'

Dylan was about to do exactly that. The exhibition he had scheduled comprised a series of magazine covers which he'd parodied, hoping the result would be a sly commentary on popular culture, society and politics. It was advertised as *Revisionist Art: Thirty Works by Bob Dylan*, and included a January 2007 issue of *Architectural Digest* which had a scantily-clad woman flashing her wares in a beautiful home, and all because – or so the accompanying set of satirical notes suggested – Bob Guccione Jnr, former owner of *Penthouse*, had recently purchased *Architectural*

Digest. (He hadn't.) Seeing the pieces, the Gagosian grew worried about issues of copyright, imagined sleights and intellectual theft, i.e. the very issues Dylan had addressed in his pseudonymous introduction:

John Elderfield: As the images started to appear, the publication people said, 'We can't do this.' . . . Jeff [Rosen] talked to them. The gallery said, 'We need to have a disclaimer.' I think they got indemnification from Jeff. Anyhow, . . . we got computer images [first]. The first ones were really mild, and they started to get more *provocative* as they came through. Some of them are really [quite] unpleasant. As all this was going on, there was a discussion about what was going to be in the cata-logue. Bob agreed there would [need to] be an introduction, and then Bob said, 'I would like to have some commentary on the plates.' The introduction came in with a pseudonym, but [was] obviously written by Bob . . . We get this far and this thing doesn't have a title, and then Bob came up with some image of a broken statue for the cover. And then Jeff said, 'What about the back [cover]? Bob thinks it would be good if we had some blurbs.' And the gallery said, 'Well, who?' 'Don't worry about it. Bob will sort something out.' In the meantime, the exhibition had been open for a while, but the catalogue [had been] delayed because of the hurricane [that recently hit] New Jersey. Some of the [digital] pic-tures were still being printed as the exhibition was being hung . . . I think we had like a day and a half to hang them. I'd never seen them before, and we['re] think[ing], 'Holy shit! What is this?!' [With some of them,] it was like, 'Can we hide that somewhere?' . . . So, [the exhib-ition] opened, and . . . it had this really snotty review from Roberta Smith. So, the big blurb that came back [from Bob] was purportedly written by Robert A. Smith, and it began with Roberta's first paragraph and then it metamorphosed into this glowing review. And it was bril-liantly done. It began nastily and then ended up [saying] this is the greatest thing since sliced bread. Then the blurbs [were] beneath. My favourite was Al Gore – obviously written by Bob – 'Great, Bob. You've done it again.'* And . . . the Gagosian is going nuts – we'll get sued by

---

* The full Gore blurb reads: 'Hey, Bob, this is great stuff. Don't let the bastards get you down. If they recognized it immediately, they would have been doing it long before you.' The unoffended Gore would be among the first to congratulate Dylan when he won the Nobel Prize in 2016.

Roberta Smith – you can't put Al Gore [in] – I just said, 'Just do it!' And, of course, it was all fine.

The Roberta Smith review had run in the *New York Times* on December 13th, 2012, and was, indeed, scathing. Its final paragraph read, 'With the alterations ranging from obvious to juvenile to obscure, and the anonymous, deeply familiar format, <u>there is little incentive, visually or intellectually, to remain engaged. The line between naïveté and cynicism is sometimes very thin.</u>' Her (underlined) conclusion Dylan promptly inverted: 'This is an art show for the ages . . . The line between naïveté and cynicism is clearly blurred. I had a ball at this exhibition, unlike others that I have attended recently. I saw it in the morning and the rest of the day I was walking on air. See it at your own peril.'

He even ran his spoof rewrite underneath the *New York Times*'s own, copyrighted logo on the back cover. But where Dylan really turned Smith's review back in upon itself was when she accused him of 'tak[ing] the covers of old copies of *Time, Life, Rolling Stone, Playboy* and less prominent magazines and tinker[ing] with images, cover lines and much else, in what look like lame endeavors at satire'. Dylan, a.k.a. R. A. Smith, explicated – for perhaps the last time – his true artistic intent in creating such ruminative collages:

> Mr Dylan takes the covers of old copies of *Cosmopolitan, Reader's Digest, Field and Stream, Ladies' Home Journal*, and less prominent magazines, and tinkers with images, cover lines, and much else, in what looks like an attempt to redo the format. Almost all the works have an element of mystery in them. They are full of double meanings and are carefully plotted with several stories happening at once.

He had brilliantly turned Smith's review into yesterday's fake news. But why? Perhaps because he was still smarting from Ms Smith's snide slam of his 2011 Gagosian debut, *The Asian Series*, recalling how 'some of the images came from other photographers, including Cartier-Bresson, [and] a slight kerfuffle ensued, despite the rather routine appropriation involved'.*

---

* Again, Dylan tinkered with her words, changing 'appropriation' to 'approbation', and the photographer from Cartier-Bresson to the non-existent Irving Pendleton.

The implication that Dylan had simply 'traced' some photos had annoyed him greatly. Elderfield, too, thought 'the stuff about him copying stuff . . . is nonsensical. Because that is what artists *do*! It is just so ridiculous . . . Maybe [*The Asian Series*] were traced, [but] they are tightly conceived and in terms of the painting, it's not painting by numbers, they're really good, the colouration . . . But [that is why] the next thing he did for the Gagosian, it was [a case of], "Well, if you think I'm copying things, [now] I'm [really] copying things" – the magazine thing was very aggressively done . . . And the process was really something else. Very dark [and] deliberately provocative.' Further proof that Dylan retained a sense of humour about the art-world, and all the schmoozing and glad-handing it entailed, was provided at the opening to that first Gagosian exhibition, where he was introduced to the world-famous sculptor, Richard Serra:

John Elderfield: For the first one, Larry talked Bob into coming to the opening, sa[ying], 'The only way I'm gonna do it is if you come to the opening.' . . . He was in a private room, and then people can come and talk to him. It had its really funny moments. The funniest one was Richard Serra . . . this really tough, no-nonsense, abrasive guy. But he comes in to see Bob and he blushes . . . And Bob says, 'Pleased to meet you. What do you do?' 'I'm a sculptor.' 'Oh, I'm a sculptor. I drive around in my truck and collect scrap-metal.' And Richard says, 'So, do you weld it all together?' 'Yeah, I do that. What about you? Do you do that yourself?' 'Well, it's not like that, I have people who do that for me.' And Bob says, 'Well, you can do it yourself. I could show you how to do it.' There was something so priceless about it. The timing was so perfect. He didn't push it beyond the point he needed to, he just stopped there. He left Richard totally bewildered, whether he was being tugged along – which, of course, he was – or not.

The jester still had hold of the crown. But it had taken him a while to find his feet in this world of *Fake or Fortune*, or perhaps for him to really believe he had something to offer in this hall of mirrors. Back in 1994, when his book of sketches of mainly amply-endowed women, *Drawn Blank*, appeared, even the lovely Cooky had taunted him, 'One thing's for sure, your mother didn't breast-feed you enough.' When he offered her a signed copy, she asked, 'Why, am I in it?' Everyone, it seemed, was a critic.

It took until 2007 for Debbie Gold to convince him there was mucho denarii to be made in these choppy waters, introducing him to ideas of how to monetize his Art given to her by art-dealer friend, Raymond Foye, who in turn introduced him, via Rosen, to the ex-curator of the Museum of Modern Art, John Elderfield, a confirmed Dylan fan.

The first official Dylan exhibition was a classic example of testing the waters on the outskirts of town to assess the lie of the land, after the female curator of a provincial German gallery, Kunstsammlungen Chemnitz, had reached out to see if Dylan had any more drawings like the ones he had published in *Drawn Blank*. Having written in that collection's original introduction, 'These drawings are sketches for paintings that either never were painted [or] have yet to be painted,' he decided the time was ripe for turning the crude pencil drawings into digital colourized paintings of the same images and adding some newer work to the mix.*

The exhibition, which ran for three and a half months, was a triumph, transferring to the Halcyon Gallery in London in a scaled down version in June 2008, where the paintings sold for between £35,000 and £135,000 each. But where Dylan really started to coin it was when the Halcyon arranged for forty provincial British galleries to offer signed, 'limited-edition graphics', at two grand-plus a pop. Launched with a sixteen-page insert in *The Times*, on June 7th, 2008, featuring an exclusive interview by Alan Jackson, the entire run sold out on the day.

Dylan was now officially an Artist who didn't need to look back. But still he did, telling Jackson, 'I didn't really see the stuff that properly had an impact on me – Matisse, [André] Derain, Monet, Gauguin – till . . . I was in my twenties . . . The first exhibition I saw [at The Met] was of Gauguin paintings and I found I could stand in front of any one of them for as long as I'd sit at the movies, yet not get tired . . . I'd lose all sense of time.'

For once, much of what he said publicly was true, Suze Rotolo having only recently revealed his early love of art galleries in her 2008

---

* The story told at the time, which I find hard to believe, was that the original drawings had been misplaced.

memoir. Cooky, too, recalled how in May 1992, they 'toured the Norton Simon Museum of Art in Pasadena. Maybe Bob was looking to pick up some tips as he was still trying to keep his hands busy by constantly sketching, mostly unfamiliar faces.' She wished she had brought a camera to catch his poses as he studied these paintings. Dylan's Italian publisher had arranged for a private viewing of da Vinci's 'The Last Supper' when he was playing Milan, and now he had a contact at MoMA, he was able to get a private tour of the 2011 de Kooning exhibition. He left convinced the great man had come back, but hadn't come back all the way:

> **John Elderfield**: [When he saw] the de Kooning women paintings, he said, 'That's when de Kooning went electric.' I think he like[d] de Koonings's figurative work but I don't think he like[d] abstract painting at all. He genuinely liked the women paintings . . . But the later ones when he became abstract again, I think Bob just lost interest. But then, he want[ed] to come back and see the early Fifties women paintings again.

Suddenly, Dylan was talking about his *artistic* influences in interviews, informing Douglas Brinkley the following year, 'Jackson Pollock and Mark Rothko are good as far as Americans go, and I guess George Bellows and Thomas Hart Benton are okay. But this guy Rembrandt is one of my two favourite painters. I like his work because it's rough, crude and beautiful. Caravaggio's the other one. I'd probably go a hundred miles for a chance to see a Caravaggio painting or a Bernini sculpture. You know who I [also] like a lot . . . Turner, the English painter. [Because] Art is artillery.'

At one point, he had even told the Tate he'd be interested in 'curating' a Turner exhibition. The trail went cold after he realized there was more to being a curator than putting his name to the catalogue, and picking out a few paintings from the Tate's vast Turner archive.* Further evidence he had entered the big league came when he was approached by the curator at the Statens Museum in Copenhagen, Kasper Monrad, who flew to Santa Monica to meet the man, with John Elderfield there to run interference:

---

* The Tate director himself, Alex Farquharson, originally suggested Dylan consider 'doing' William Blake.

John Elderfield: Monrad says, 'I really enjoyed your exhibition in [Chemnitz].' Bob said, 'I'd be more interested in showing some new things, and preferably all new things.' And [then] Monrad says, 'I'd really like to have an area with some music.' Bob replies, 'I thought this was an art museum,' [to which] Monrad says, 'Well, you're a composer, a musician, people will expect it.' Bob says, 'I've learned over the years, you can't worry about what people expect.' I'm kicking Monrad under the table . . . Anyway, nothing was resolved. And then Bob made these narrative paintings which were different from what had been shown in [the] *Drawn Blank* [exhibit]. So Jeff calls and said, 'Bob wants you to go see these paintings, and to tell him what you think.' I forget where they were. They were the narrative pictures and a few landscapes. And I [told him], 'What I like to do with studio visits, is I like to find the painting I like the most, and I talk about what I like.' And Bob says, 'Can we start with what you really *don't* like, and then I'll know how to fix it?' So, I said [I] like[d] the figure compositions better.

Sure enough, the *Brazil Series*, which opened in Copenhagen in September 2010, largely stuck to 'figure compositions'. Although the original drawings seemed a tad more atmospheric than the resultant paintings, both paintings and prints sold briskly, as did the catalogue, even without any input from Dylan in terms of commentary or introduction. But when Gagosian entered the frame in 2011, Dylan was confronted by a gallery owner used to difficult, demanding artists, who still expected more input from him. He finally agreed to be interviewed by his favourite art expert:

John Elderfield: I think he was nervous about the New York one. Larry sweet-talked him into this . . . I was asked to do the catalogue. I didn't really want to do it again, so I told Jeff, who said, 'You can do an interview.' So that's what we did. I went [to L.A.] and we sat and talked. The deal was, I wasn't [allowed] to take notes, [or] to record anything. So I would go back to my hotel and write it all up. Over two visits. So, I sent it [to Bob], and got these responses to parts of it, 'This is what I meant,' and expanded it. Other [part]s, he would say, 'I don't want it in.' He talked a little about his childhood. And he didn't want *any* of that in. He was writing about growing up and the things he heard. It went through quite a [process].

If the September 2011 *Asian Series* opening at Gagosian was another success, almost all of the original art being sold there and then, the ensuing controversy over his photographic source/s sullied the waters, some critics making it seem like he was *xeroxing* his paintings. So that is precisely what he proceeded to do next, producing his one 21st century 'Positively 4th Street' moment, *Revisionist Art*.

Even the 'slight kerfuffle' over that delightfully Dylanesque catalogue failed to derail the juggernaut which was these near-annual Dylan art exhibitions. After the demanding Gagosian was kicked firmly into touch, the Halcyon became his preferred home, save for prestige 'retrospective' exhibitions in Shanghai (2019) and Miami (2021). He just no longer had any real interest in being a carney for his own Art career.

When Elderfield was asked to do another catalogue interview for the 2016 *Face Value* exhibition, he had a close encounter with a Dylan who 'was obviously not in the mood. I asked this [really] long question, and Bob just went, Nah. Could you elaborate on this? Nah. It was like squeezing a lemon. It [then] moved to e-mail, and I was getting pissed off. [Finally,] there was one thing he took out, and I just said [to] Jeff, if you take this out, I'm not gonna do it.' Dylan had lost an important sounding board just as the exhibitions were growing in scope, as was a general sense he was churning this stuff out.

The suspicion that Dylan was now producing work with his tongue firmly in his cheek, and a raised digit to the Art World behind his back, culminated in 2018 with *Mondo Scripto*, which opened at the Halcyon in October, accompanied by a catalogue that doubled as a doorstop. It seemed to many folk to be both a belated public admission that he could self-forge his own lyrics at will, and that he was as much at a loss to explain them as his fans.

The exhibition and 336-page catalogue comprised digitally-created, stylistically near-identical 'handwritten' drafts of some of Dylan's most famous and/or important songs, all with near-random line-breaks, accompanied by a drawing that was (presumably) meant in some way to convey the meaning of the song. The drawings were depressingly prosaic; a Napoleon 'in rags' for 'Like A Rolling Stone'; a dog barking in a street for 'One Too Many Mornings'. A two and a half page 'interview', conducted by Slim Pickens's cousin, took the place of an introduction to his rationale.

The lyrics did not even have the wordplay and/or attention to detail of the now circulated 2010-13 'self-forgeries'. The one flicker of creativity he brought to the project came when he rewrote no less than five of the *Blood on the Tracks* songs: 'Shelter From The Storm' (accompanied by a picture of a storm), 'If You See Her, Say Hello' (a set of Spanish stairs), 'You're Gonna Make Me Lonesome When You Go' (a row of trees), 'Simple Twist Of Fate' (a canal path) and 'Tangled Up In Blue' (a windscreen).*

These songs had always been both his most realized and his most amorphous love poems. All of them – save 'Lonesome' – he had returned to repeatedly in concert, though he was only performing 'Tangled Up In Blue' these days (despite the imminent release of the 'complete' New York 1974 sessions in the ongoing Bootleg Series). Some of the new rewrites were a little gratuitous. Others, though, showed signs of life:

> 'Still don't know what happened, don't know why or how/ And even if I did – nothing I can do about it now' ('If You See Her . . .');
>
> 'The play was over 'fore I knew it – my part was easy, I walked right through it/ There are things I never knew but now I know . . .' ('You're Gonna Make . . .');
>
> 'Stones in my passway, dust blowing in my eyes/ Boulders coming down the mountain, twenty times my size/ It's a pretty risky business and it comes in any form/ Come in, she said, I'll give you . . .' ('Shelter From The Storm').

But the exhibition only served to remind attendees of where his true gifts lay, even those who invested £1,500 for a 'limited edition print . . . presented in a bespoke linen-bound solander case accompanied by a linen-bound copy of the *Mondo Scripto* exhibition catalogue and a certificate of authenticity', personally delivered by a cash-cow.

A further reminder of those gifts and the era that produced them had recently been afforded fans by the second of Martin Scorsese's Dylan documentaries, *Rolling Thunder Revue: A Bob Dylan Story* (2019), which turned out to be Bob and Marty's first collaborative mockumentary.

---

* The only other lyrics he significantly rewrote were 'Gotta Serve Somebody' and 'Rainy Day Women', two songs he had long reinvented in concert.

The film left one participant almost speechless. Louie Kemp, now on the outside looking in, was reduced to watching it on Netflix. He thought it was 'like an interactive experience between the audience and the pranksters, [requiring] the audience to drill down and savour the real Rolling Thunder tour and spit out the pips inserted by the pranksters', a neat summation of the audience reaction at preview screenings in New York and London. As with Trump's election to president the previous year, 'WTF' about summed it up. Yet it seems the idea of a celluloid return to Rolling Thunder had been on Dylan's mind for a while. As far back as 1984, he told Bert Kleinman, 'I thought the Rolling Thunder shows were great. I think someday somebody should make a movie about them.'

If *Rolling Thunder Revue* was sending anything up, it was *No Direction Home*. This time the interviews were with people who weren't there, and were making it up as they were going along. As the man once said, 'Nothing is revealed.' This was not *Revisionist Art*, or even The Rutles, the mother of all musical mockumentaries, which also had its own uncredited collaborator, Dylan's old friend and fellow humourist, George Harrison. The one laugh-out-loud moment came early, when Dylan told the camera, 'I don't remember a damn thing.' The rest of the movie became a game of spot the spoof.

The few welcome exceptions were when the director allowed the white-faced Renaldo to take the stage and deliver blazing, cocaine-fuelled renditions of the Rolling Thunder set, a stark reminder of the artist formerly known as A Genius, who even when he looked back, wielded the flaming sword of truth (something Dylan duly acknowledged by quoting Oscar Wilde on camera, 'Man is least himself when he talks in his own person. Give him a *mask*, and he will tell you the *truth*').

Coming out at a time when the never-ending grind of touring had taken Dylan's primary art-form, performance, and turned it into a pleasant (if egregiously expensive) night out at best, the film was accompanied by a superlative 14-disc Sony set of rehearsals and complete 1975 shows (five of them). But Scorcese's *Rolling Thunder* suggested the man's restless mind was no longer aligned to an over-active imagination. Had the after-effects of too much Colombian marching powder finally taken its toll on them both?

Dylan, it seemed, had become his father's son, sitting in the back of the store, worrying about that day's receipts and whether he could con another customer into paying for his latest appliance on the never-never. Meanwhile, piling up in the store-room were boxes and boxes of a triple-LP of Frank Sinatra covers by a man whose voice was shot, and whose current band were journeymen.* What next? *What Is This Shit? – The Boxed-Set.*

---

* The best cross-cultural dig at Dylan's 2017 album, *Triplicate*, would come in a December 2017 episode of *The Simpsons*, where among a stack of albums is one called *Sinatra Ruins Dylan*.

6.4

2001–2017:
Columbia Recording Artist

Alan Jackson: Has it been disabling creatively to have people say your best work is behind you?
BD: Not really . . . For the most part I feel that way myself.

4th October 1997.

Meeting [him is like] holding a mirror to . . . the world and saying, 'Look!' [He's] just surprising you at all times, confounding you at all times . . . with the end result of cracking open your head, and [you] just seeing more deeply and more clearly.

Larry Charles, to Trevor Gibb, 2004.

Perhaps deep inside [Dylan']s Southern field-hand persona is a suburban sexagenarian pining for a quiet life in a residential cul-de-sac, dispensing advice over the fence to the next door neighbour on how to keep your lawn free of grass clippings.

Mark Steyn, 'Happy Birthday, Mister Bob', The National Post 24th May 2001.

After a certain point . . . it gets harder to . . . do something different.

Bob Dylan, to Edna Gundersen, August 2006.

Q: Do you ever think it would be a good idea to do new things, to follow new ways, to make a different kind of music?
Bob Dylan: No, I don't think so. The best thing is to continue in the same way.

Porto Alegre, Brazil, 13th August 1991.

An artist has got to be careful never to really arrive at a place where he thinks he's 'At Somewhere'. You always have to realize that you're constantly in the state of *becoming*. And as long as you can stay in that realm, you'll be all right.

Bob Dylan, January 2000.

He *always* keeps you on your toes, because you can never, ever, ever predict what he likes. Just when you think you know what he's going to do, he doesn't do it.

Chris Shaw, to Damien Love.

I listened to two [tracks] and I really couldn't go on. [But] I appreciate he doesn't give a fuck, [taking the Sinatra canon] on with barely a voice.

Joan Baez, *Mojo* 2019.

A lot of people around Bob don't tell him what they think . . . What do you do when no one will tell you the truth?

Johnny Rivers, c. 2005.

*

Before 2001 ended, Dylan had told Gundersen he may well record a live set at the fall shows,* and that 'a handful of partially sketched songs could yield a new album within two years'. Neither project came to pass. By 2006, for the first – and last – time, the gap between new Dylan albums had run to five long years. Was he done? Not by a long chalk, even as projects continued falling by the wayside. Three years later, Edna's replacement was noting how 'his mind is always crowded with future projects: a series of Brazil-inspired paintings, the next instalment of *Chronicles*, a TV special, an orchestra playing new arrangements of his timeless standards, and the composition of more song-poems for the ages, sometimes casually written on hotel letter-head.' Again, only the 'Brazil-inspired paintings' transpired, and those turned out *not* to be inspired by Brazil.

In both cases, he was coming off the high of delivering a new album

---

* The last dozen shows on the tour were all recorded from the desk. In the case of the last two shows, in Portland and Boston, soundchecks were also taped.

of original songs when he spoke. In each instance, he was three years or more away from recording another such album, which had become almost afterthoughts to the relentless touring. Even if the occasional song still came to him like a bull in a bull ring, it was a rare beast indeed that hung around long enough to force its way into the 'perennials' part of the set – unless it was another two-note jump blues. His most ambitious original composition in the sixteen years after 'Love and Theft' would never even get a live debut.

Post 9/11, the sets would change from career-overview plus covers-of-many-colours, to songs that were still within his limited vocal range – which meant his post-Oh Mercy canon and the odd folk or country standard. When he did tackle an 'It's Alright Ma', a 'Visions Of Johanna' and/or a 'She Belongs To Me' – and he would do all three memorably at a November 2006 show in Uniondale – the arrangement had to allow for his contracted range, a point perhaps lost on engineer Chris Shaw, who was at the show in question, before going backstage to say, 'Hey, I love the new version of "It's Alright Ma" – but do you ever play it like the original recording?' Dylan looked at him and said, 'Well, y'know, a record is just a recording of what you were doing that day. You don't wanna live the same day over and over again, now, do ya?'

In truth, the 2006 country-gentlemen shuffle-off-to-Buffalo arrangements simply reflected the fact that the 65-year-old Dylan hadn't taken a break from the road in twenty-one years. The people at the Nassau Coliseum that night just seemed happy to be there, as was a fellow time-traveller who caught a birthday show two years later, in Newfoundland:

> **Leonard Cohen**: Dylan has [his own] secret code with his audience. If someone came from the moon and watched it, they might wonder what was going on. In this particular case, he had his back to one half of the audience and was playing the organ, beautifully I might say, and just running through the songs. Some were hard to recognize. But nobody cared . . . Something else was going on, which was a celebration of some kind of genius that is so apparent and so clear and has touched people so deeply that all they need is some kind of symbolic unfolding . . . It doesn't have to be the songs.

Cohen was one of the very few for whom Dylan might have done a request in 2008. Generally, those days were long gone. Indeed, the reverse now seemed to be the case, as another song-scribbler witnessed. Paul 'Macca' McCartney reported, 'run[ning] into him . . . in an anorak in the corner of some airport lounge [and] a guy from his band said, "Mr Tambourine Man went down well tonight." So, Bob said, "Okay, take it out of the set." ' And when Dylan's most esteemed literary critic, Professor Christopher Ricks, visited him backstage at a New England show and enthused about 'The Lonesome Death Of Hattie Carroll', Dylan assured him, 'I won't be playing it tonight.' The following night in Lowell, having established Ricks was safely back home in Boston, he played it.

The sense that catching Dylan was to see an artist always confounding expectations remained, even as the set made its slow-train transition into a protracted reverie on his recent, limited palette of styles. Thankfully, he and his audience had long ago stopped worrying about what the critics thought. As Dylan bluntly told Brinkley, 'Critics might be uncomfortable with me [working so much]. Maybe they can't figure it out. But nobody in my particular audience feels that way about what I do.'

Fortunately, if people wanted to hear revelatory reinterpretations of his old songs, there was always Sony's born-again Bootleg Series, which kept up the flow of product in those inevitable fallow periods from a sixty-something artist with a lot on his mind. The Sony Corporation's response was to start putting out classic live shows from the Sixties and Seventies, methodically chronicling the live career of Columbia's most important Recording Artist.

Having swallowed CBS whole ten years earlier, Japanese giant Sony Music, in cahoots with Dylan's manager, Jeff Rosen, finally gave the moribund Bootleg Series a kick-start. In 1998, it issued the complete 'Royal Albert Hall 1966'. It followed up in 2002 with a two-disc anthology of the 1975 Rolling Thunder Tour; the oft-bootlegged Halloween concert in 2004, and a two-CD 'soundtrack' to the four-hour, two-part Scorsese documentary, *No Direction Home*, in 2005.

Amnesia or no amnesia, the Sony tape-library was by now (almost) catalogued, and as long as the checks kept being deposited, Dylan continued green-lighting an ongoing rape of the vaults, even as he studiously avoided referencing any of the belatedly-released jewels in concert,* or things he'd said during his Christian phase. When he decided to rework 'Change My Way Of Thinking' for a 2003 various artist tribute CD of his gospel songs, he was determined to render it unrecognisable, as his co-opted co-singer, Mavis Staples, looked on askance:

> He'd write a line and show it to me. Then he'd write another line and show me that. But I'd say, 'Bobby, you write so little.' He said he couldn't help it. When a person writes small like that, they're humble. He'd never heard that before. Then he came up with the line, 'I'm so hungry, I could eat a horse.' I said, 'Which one of us is gonna say that?' He said, we'd figure it out . . . We were in the studio until one in the morning. He kept rough mixing [while] he ordered out for Mexican food.

If most of the 'new' lines were older than he was, they were also further away from the original, apostolic inspiration. The recast song even made its way into the live set. Gone were the days when a new Dylan release shook the very foundations of modern song, even as he retained his capacity for making his label scratch their heads.

The album he began formulating in his head in 2005 would be to 'Love and Theft' what World Gone Wrong had been to Good As I Been To You, as he continued to collate sayings he overheard with ones he read and remembered, hoping to appropriate them and make his audience appreciate them. One Noughties notepad contains the following stray thoughts: 'I consider it an honour to be criticized'; 'Anybody can be a good enemy, not everyone makes a good friend'; and 'Fighting wars with other people's blood', as well as two notes reminding himself, 'I print my poems unsigned', and 'Got to overcome the world'.

The latter line could easily have sprung from the lips of the narrator in 'Ain't Talkin', the best of the songs he kept up his sleeve until 2006. A five-verse, handwritten draft on Mandarin Oriental notepaper dates from one of his stays in London, probably the one in November 2005 which saw him play five nights at the Brixton Academy, ten years after

---

* Unlike Van Morrison, who at their joint 1998 shows performed a number of fine reinterpretations of classic 'lost' songs finally released on his 1998 2-CD *The Philosopher's Stone*.

a triumphant three-night residency there. (He even knew where he was, encoring with The Clash's 'London Calling' on two nights.) For now, the narrator of 'Ain't Talkin' was a mean sonofabitch who believed 'people would have practically nothing to say to each other if there were no more lies to tell'. He really does seem to have it in for those who 'don't like to keep their word, don't have any sense of honor/ It's not like it was in the old days.' A man without pity, this narrator with no name had come not to change people's way of thinking, but to judge:

> You're a desperate man, my friend, you've a need to be (?governed)
> You've been an instrument of pleasure and your heart is surely flawed
> I might be mean and bad, shot a round at my dad, and I'm stubborn
> But you are a traitor, sir, and you are false to your God.

The last line of the above draft, 'When I'm through, you'll know that I was here,' could have been uttered by Clint Eastwood's character in 1992 Oscar winner, *Unforgiven*. Its narrator was on the warpath, and Tweedledum and Tweedledee – still not definitively removed from the live set – had better watch out. It was just as he reminded Gilmore in 2001, 'You're talking to a person that feels like he's walking around in the ruins of Pompeii.'

The 'Ain't Talkin' character was definitely a man 'still on the road, trying to stay out of the joint'. In a later draft, he even imagined being the kind of disillusioned lover who had loved and lost, having 'met her accidentally at a masked ball in Rome/ She was wearing a cloak, she was dressed like an imposter,' a cross between the topless-bar scene in 'Tangled Up In Blue' and Kubrick's *Eyes Wide Shut* (1999). Any lover's quest is quickly stripped from the song, though. This character knows 'a little trip down the primrose path', will inexorably lead to 'standing outside the gates of wrath'.*

If the sense of disillusion and dissolution seems real, he soon places himself in Christ's sandals in his moment of doubt, 'I often wonder how I bear the load.' Surprisingly, what keeps this murderous man going is his faith, originally expressed in the penultimate couplet, 'Just

---

* These lines survive to the *Tell-Tale Signs* alternate take, but not the album.

as sure as there's a sun and a heaven behind it/ All the troubles of this life must disappear.'

Indeed, references to faith pepper the song – in draft form, in out-take form (included on 2008's *Tell Tale Signs*) and, most overtly, on the album itself, where Dylan sings, 'I practice a faith that's been long abandoned/ Ain't no altars on this long and lonesome road.' Mistaken for a gardener 'in the mystic garden', he has to tell a weeping woman, 'There's no-one here, the gardener is gone,' surely a reference to Mary discovering Christ's empty tomb.

It seems Dylan had been leafing through the good book again. And as per usual, he had gone straight to the last book. The 2003 'Gonna Change My Way Of Thinking' had already reminded anyone uncon-vinced he was a believer, 'Jesus is coming back/ He's coming to gather his jewels.' A couple of *Modern Times*'s stronger songs also reference Judgment Day. A recast 'Rollin' And Tumblin'' includes some unidenti-fied soul insisting, 'I've been conjuring up all these long dead souls from their crumbling tombs.' This could hardly be anyone but He who will have possession over Judgement Day ('Death . . . delivered up the dead . . . and they were judged every man according to their works.'[Revelation 20:13]).

A further reference to the coming judgement appears in verse eight of 'Nettie Moore', as a judge beseeches everyone to 'lift up your eyes', an exhortation first found in Isaiah [51:6]: 'Lift up your eyes to the heav-ens, and look upon the earth beneath: for . . . the earth shall wax old like a garment, and they that dwell therein shall die in like manner: but my salvation shall be for ever.' Meanwhile, 'The Levee's Gonna Break' confirmed Dylan remained a pre-millennialist, as he prophesized, 'Few more years of hard work, then there'll be a thousand years of happiness.'

Another line in that song, 'Some people still sleepin', some people are wide awake,' surely alluded to Romans [13:11]: 'Now it is high time to awake out of sleep: for now is our salvation nearer than when we believed.' In neither case is the flood depicted some natural catas-trophe, but rather something of apocalyptic proportions, explicated by two verses he would cut from the song: 'Some people're stranded, they got nowhere to go/ Some people could tear your head off with what they already know,' and, 'The Son of Man, He got no place to lay his head/ Instead of killing people, He raises 'm from the dead.' The latter unambiguously references Jesus, who is alone in using the term 'the Son of Man', 'to describe his vocation and that of those . . . summoned to be with him.'*

Dylan thus built an album around three songs he had known since the Village days: Memphis Minnie's 'When The Levee Breaks' – a song found on *Blues Fell This Morning: Rare Recordings of Southern Blues Singers*, an album that according to a tell-tale scrawl across the top of the rear-sleeve of Rotolo's (recently auctioned) copy, was 'Made for and about Bob Dylan' – Hambone Willie's 'Roll And Tumble Blues', and Muddy Waters' 'Trouble No More'.

The trio were all reimagined for another century, becoming 'The Levee's Gonna Break', 'Rollin' And Tumblin'' and 'Someday Baby', with the narrator of a longer draft version of 'Rollin' And Tumblin'' becoming everyone from Odysseus ('Went into the underworld/ Talked with the dead and came back as a livin' man') via Shakespeare ('I played Hamlet in my younger days') to Casey Jones ('I was born by the railroad . . . Ears are ringin'/ Engine blowing off steam'), as well as a self-conscious version of himself: 'I'm a poet of a certain order – got a propensity for nocturnal themes.'

The released version was enough of a reinvention of the original, delivered with gusto to spare, to suggest Hambone Willie did not die in vain. But it was as nothing to the extraordinary version of 'Someday Baby' he recorded at the February 2006 Santa Monica sessions, as he wrestled with whether to stick to the Waters template or go rogue. For a brief, inspired moment, he decided originality had its virtues, though initially he taught the touring band to play the song the same Muddy way J.J. Jackson and crew had back in '92:

> **Chris Shaw**: On . . . *Modern Times*, Bob would sometimes come in with reference tracks, old songs, saying, 'I want the track to be like this.' So, on *Modern Times*, there's the Muddy Waters track [Trouble No More] that eventually became 'Someday Baby'. He'd come in and present these templates and use them as reference points . . . [But then,] there's the slow version of 'Someday Baby' . . . He was getting frustrated with the 'Muddy Waters' version not coming together and, after dinner I think, he walked back into the room and George Receli, his

---

* Moule, C. F. D. – *The Origin of Christology*. (Cambridge University Press, 1977).

drummer, was tapping out that groove, and Bob sat down at the piano, and all of a sudden, they came up with that version.

On the original 'rough mix', it is the piano that really drives the *Tell-Tale* version. Otherwise, it adheres to the same methodology as *'Love and Theft'*, the one Chris Shaw noted thus, 'Bob doesn't want anything getting in the way of a vocal. There should be no guitar riffs going on while he's singing, no soloing while he's singing, no fancy playing while he's singing.'

Nor was there. But this time the arrangement allowed Stu Kimball or Denny Freeman to 'try to put a little riff in there', even as Dylan's vocal *inhabits* the song, with entire verses that should have got the head's up but didn't,* including two personal favourites: 'You made me eat a ton of dust/ You're potentially dangerous, and not worthy of trust,' and 'Gonna blow out your mind, and make you pure/ I've taken about as much as I can endure.' Listen to the intonation on the last word of each line and tell me this guy can't sing. Freddie Mercury, eat your heart out on a plastic tray.

The other time on these sessions he produced something beguiling out of what began as a union state blues was the rather beautiful 'Nettie Moore'. Quite where Dylan found the 1857 parlour ballad, 'The Little White Cottage, Or Gentle Nettie Moore', from which he purloined a chorus absent from every handwritten draft of the song, is another head-scratcher. He again left 'Dr Frankenstein . . . up there at his castle on the hill', as he had five years earlier, but somehow made the whole thing blend, even if it was at the cost of a verse directed at Minnie the Moocher:

> Don't get the idea you can (just) mooch around
> Betta head for higher ground
> Albert's in the graveyard, Frankie's raising hell
> Nation's lost its soul, but nobody can tell.

The chorus completed the song, taking it somewhere that suggested he retained some of that ol' songcraft, not just an overweening yen to

---

* Of the eleven verses on the outtake, just five are replicated on the nine-verse album cut.

play gutbucket blues. He even admitted to Gundersen, '["Nettie Moore"] troubled me the most, because I wasn't sure I was getting it right. Finally, I could see . . . the song . . . was not just a bunch of random verses.'

It had been seventeen years since Dylan told Deevoy, 'The structure [of the blues] is so simple . . . you can say what you want to say in such an immediate kinda way,' and he still seemed to believe if one played blues with a feeling, that was good enough. Now, the likes of 'Thunder On The Mountain', 'Workingman's Blues' and 'Spirit On The Water' all offered more of the same, all being songs with interchangeable verses that suggested he'd been selected to captain Van Morrison's Grumpy Ol' Men XI. Occasional flashes of wit – including, 'I got grievances too many to list/ I thought I was free – I woke up right here/ Slave to an economist' ('Workingman's Blues') – failed to survive the pruning process, as Dylan crowbarred discordant themes into a series of songs none of which resolved into a contiguous whole.

Another odd decision which made the album seem like a series of disconnected pieces, separate and distinct, not a play-through experience, was the way the persona successfully crystallized in 'Ain't Talkin' was inserted ad hoc into other songs, even as Dylan dropped apposite couplets like, 'I been raised in the woods with the real wolves/ Never grieved yet over any past mistake', and, 'Gonna get me an army/ so[me] rough sons of bitches/ I'll recruit my army from out of the orphanages', from 'Workingman's Blues' and 'Thunder On The Mountain', respectively.

Meanwhile, a draft of 'Spirit on The Water' (on Wyndham Roanoke Airport notepaper) almost tipped its hat to 'Buckets Of Rain', before becoming something Marcus Aurelius might have said: 'Life is sad, filled with brutal tragic scenes/ Nobody ever gains anything by peaceful means.' All of these songs over-reached themselves in the quest for profundity, while failing to use any of the Devil's better tunes.

Variety being both the spice of life and of chart albums, Dylan would have been better served slipping onto the album a song he had recorded the previous June for a film soundtrack, 'Tell Ol' Bill' (a title culled from another traditional song he learnt back in 1961, completing the quartet), as well as one he was about to give Curtis Hanson for his latest box-office flop, *Lucky You*, the faintly fatalistic 'Huck's Tune'.

Both songs had tunes and a sensibility *simpatico* with *Modern Times*'s better moments, so could have provided a partial antidote to all those burdensome blues. Of course, if one believes what Dylan told Gundersen, he had completed fourteen or fifteen songs by September 2005, shelving those he considered 'lukewarm'. Presumably he made the call before he and the band convened at the Bardavon Opera House in Poughkeepsie on January 31st, 2006, for four days of rehearsals before recording commenced. The executive director of the Bardavon, Chris Silva, got to see Dylan distill matters down to just eight songs:

> It was a rehearsal [of] material for a new album he was gonna go into the studio with, the next week. He was playing all kinds of different things, from old blues to kick-ass rock'n'roll to Hawaiian-tinged music to Rudy Vallee . . . [He] was all business. He would show up, walk to the keyboard, work four or five hours straight. He was very low-key, in jeans . . . He was a working musician and he came to work. There was a lot of conversation back and forth, [like], 'Let's try this key. Let's try it faster. Let's try it slower. Hey, whadya think about this lick?' . . . He was certainly calling all the shots and . . . counting off every song . . . It was constant experimentation . . . He's not like, 'I got it. I know exactly what it is.' He's like, 'Let's experiment. Let's find it.' He never took a break . . . and when he was done, he just left the building.

At least, Dylan was looking after his voice, not wearing it down until it was sandpaper-thin by starting the year's touring before recording an album. He was upbeat about the sessions, too, while spending time with Debbie Gold at the turn of the year, the last time they would really hang out. He even agreed to let engineer Chris Shaw drag him into the 21st century with minimal kickin' and screamin':

> It was the very first album he had ever done using ProTools. That whole record was done digitally, and so everything was preserved, we have hours and hours and hours of all the outtakes, because we left the machine running twenty-four hours a day . . . And that's the reason *Modern Times* sounds so good: yeah, it was recorded using this new technology, ProTools, but we used an old desk, old microphones, old pre-amps . . . [even if] a couple of times during [the] *Modern Times* [sessions], the computer crashed, in the middle of a take . . . The sessions went a little slower, it took maybe a month . . . There were a lot of

different versions of each song he had to settle on, before he could decide where he wanted them to go, and I think he had this vision in his head that maybe he couldn't quite articulate to the band as quickly. So, it took a few times trying out ideas to get it to land where he wanted it to be. And I think there was a lot more lyric [re]writing he had to deal with. Bob never has a shortage of ideas where song lyrics are concerned.

The problem was not so much 'a shortage of ideas'. Rather, as Dylan admitted to his agony aunt Edna, 'I tend to overwrite stuff, and in the past, I probably would have left it all in. On this [album], I tried my best to edit myself.' Editing down rather than improving what he had – the new *modus operandi* – wasn't really working. It was like he thought of himself as a travelling songster shuffling verses between 'knife songs', semi-improvised collections of commonplace verses that articulated the blues a hundred years earlier.

The resultant album, not surprisingly, was viewed as more of the same by the critics – unaware he'd left off some better lines and his best studio vocal since 1989, 'Someday Baby'. Yet, such was the grip this idea of Dylan as a repository of Weird Ol' Americana now had on its target audience – a demographic most of whom bought records on the week of release – the album became Dylan's first number one in thirty years.

If the critical consensus suggested he had failed to redefine himself for the second time this century, at least he had a couple more jump blues his live set needed like JFK needed a hole in his head. By now, the Never Ending years of Touring had begun to blur into one, with the band bringing less and less to the party; which was not necessarily their fault. Stay in the shadows seemed to be the instruction coming from centre-stage, as Chris Shaw, for one, noted from the wings, 'If you go see Bob live, you'll see these little times when he might turn to the guitarist and give him the eye, like, "You're playing on top of me – don't do that."' It was The Bob Dylan Show, after all.

At least he wasn't shy of playing half the eight songs from his latest hit album, knowing there was zero chance of any of this number one album garnering any mainstream radioplay; not because he wasn't selling, but because US radio was going the way of the dodo. Dylan had been lamenting its slow decline since at least 1985, when he had asked

Denise Worrell rhetorically, 'How many radio stations [still] play Howlin' Wolf or Jimmy Reed or Muddy Waters?'*

The following year, he had told playwright-turned-therapist Sam
Shepard, 'I had lotsa . . . radio station dreams . . . [As] a kid, you stay up
late in bed, listening to the radio . . . That's when disc jockeys played
whatever they felt like . . . You'd hear a [song] like "Black Snake Moan"
or "Mississippi Flood," [and] you could see yourself waist-high in
muddy water.'† At a 1997 press conference, he longingly described how
'America was tied in with the radio when I grew up . . . The radio connected everybody like Orpheus. That's not so any more . . . I can't
stress the importance of that enough.'

On December 12th, 2005, sensing the hour was getting late, he did
something about it. XM – a digital-only radio station caught in a rat-
ings war it ultimately lost with Sirius – announced that day Dylan
would be their latest celebrity DJ. Starting in May, he would host fifty
weekly one-hour shows called *Theme Time Radio Hour*, each one with a
specific theme like 'Rain' or 'Money'.

Ever the publicist's teenage prayer, Dylan gave his one plug for the
first (of three) series (resulting in a hundred shows by April 2009), that
day: 'Songs and music have always inspired me. A lot of my own songs
have been played on the radio, but this is the first time I've ever been on
the other side of the mike.' Not that he was exactly 'on the other side
of the mike', all of his between-song chatter being edited in digitally,
supervised by producer Eddie Gorodetsky, after what XM's Lee Abrams
described as weekly 'conference call with Bob's team. Bob's not in on
the call – I don't think he does conference calls' – except with his
lawyers.

It seems Richard Serra's methodology *was* the way to go – come up
with suggested tracks, write (or remember) a few corny gags, occasionally write an *M&A*-like screed, and leave putting it together to his
'team'. If the result was a few gems for the Collected Wit and Wisdom
of Just Bob, most songs were culled from the 25,000-strong record collection of Eddie G – which in the mid-Nineties Dylan had paid to ship

---

* I'm not sure they ever did. Hence, The Animals selling coals to Newcastle.
† 'Singers that I would hear on the radio, I couldn't see what they looked like, so I
imagined what they looked like. What they were wearing. What their movements
were.' – Bob Dylan, AARP 2015.

lock, stock and non-smoking barrel from New York to L.A., when Eddie first went west in search of fame and fortune (both of which he found).

A mutual love of the blues in all its variegated forms encouraged Dylan to rhapsodize on-air about an artist like Skip James, 'who had a style that was celestially divine, sounded like it was coming from beyond the veil. Magic in the grooves . . . ghostly and other worldly, rare and unusual, mysterious and vague,' which sounds like a lost section from *Chronicles*. *TTRH* also gave him the opportunity to lament the loss of a collective commonalty of song for an hour a week. After playing George Jones and Melba Montgomery's 'Let's Invite Them Over', he went into a mini-rant about *his* kind of country music distinctly at odds with comments he'd made in Akron in 1980:

> Now I love country music, but I say 'What happened to it?' You hear a song like this and it's obvious it's about real people, and real emotions, and real problems, that's all. That's the country music we learned to love. Nowadays they want to sweep all the problems under the rug and pretend they don't exist. Well, guess what, folks – they do exist! And if you try and sweep 'em under the rug, they're just gonna pop up somewhere else. So, we might as well all just face it and listen to the old-style country music, the real country music. You know, about drinking and sleeping around. That's my kind of country music, and I hope yours!

For all his Luddite tendencies, he also let Eddie G.'s love of (and friendship with) fine modern singer-songwriters like Lucinda Williams, Laura Cantrell and Mary Gauthier leak into the *TTRH* grooves, along with an occasional rap track like Run DMC's 'My Adidas', which Dylan played only after venting about how rap had also gone down the drain:

> I remember buying this next record when it came out, down at St Mark's Records in New York . . . and it blew my mind. It was a powerful, exciting piece of music. Now when people listen to it, they think it's quaint and old-fashioned. They're already condescending to it and turning it into an 'oldie'. That's the problem – people don't always realize how powerful the innovators are . . . Rap records have gotten louder, more camouflaged, faster and dirtier, with a thousand samples . . . but it

doesn't mean that Run DMC should just be considered 'oldies'. They're important pieces of art, and art isn't looked at as something old or new, it's looked at as something that moves ya. And here's a record that moves me.

By April 2009, Dylan the DJ had shot his bolt, as he turned his focus to the other pillar of pre-war pop culture which had made America rich, and even great for a while: Hollywood films. He'd just told fellow film buff Doug Brinkley, 'I think America has produced the greatest films ever. No other country has ever come close. The great movies that came out of America in the studio system . . . were heroic and visionary, and inspired people in a way that no other country has ever done. If film is the ultimate art form, then you'll need to look no further than those films. Art has the ability to transform people's lives, and they did just that.'

Yet the film to which he now lent his name, his talent and an album's worth of songs had just been eaten alive by the very studio system he was lauding. *My Own Love Song*, Olivier Dahan's first movie since *La Vie en Rose* won an Oscar, starred A-listers Renée Zellweger and Forest Whitaker. About a singer-songwriter (Zellweger) in a wheelchair from a debilitating accident, suffering an equally crippling writer's block having given up her son for adoption, she travels across country to see him take communion. Dahan's new road movie made *Easy Rider* feel like a light romcom, yet when he asked Dylan if he'd be interested in doing the whole soundtrack, he leapt at the chance:

[Dahan] was so audacious! Usually you get asked to do, like, one song . . . at the end of the movie. But ten songs? Dahan wanted to put these songs throughout the movie and find different reasons for them. I just kind of gave the guy the benefit of the doubt that he knew what he was doing. I always liked . . . those black-and-white movies where Veronica Lake all of a sudden out of nowhere is singing in a nightclub . . . They don't put that kind of thing in movies anymore. Now it's come down to just an end-title song – which has nothing to do with the movie. [2009]

Disappointingly, even before *My Own Love Song* had been edited, the word 'difficult' was being applied to it, and fearing another *Pat Garrett*,

Dylan decided to jump the gun, releasing *Together Through Life* as his latest album in April 2009, just two and a half years after *Modern Times*, and a full year before the movie which inspired it made its US debut at the Tribeca Film Festival.

Devoid of context, and without 'soundtrack' appearing anywhere in the packaging, the album's ten songs – even 'Life Is Hard', which he wrote specifically for Zellweger to sing at her son's communion, and about which Dahan later wrote, 'The whole movie came together in that song' – was a ragbag of ideas doused in a ubiquitous accordion, and lyrics co-written with Dead lyricist, Robert Hunter, though no-one seems to know when. The almost total absence of any manuscript versions in the Tulsa archive suggests they were written in one stint, probably at Hunter's home in Mill Valley.*

It was Dylan's most lightweight album of originals since *New Morning*. This time no-one was saying, 'We've Got Dylan Back Again'. The one 'Sign On The Window' moment was 'Forgetful Heart', a song with depths not entirely excavated in the studio but later strip-mined in performance, a highlight of many a latter-day NET show. Having captured the kind of 'love sick' amnesia Zellweger's character exemplified, Dahan used it over the opening scene to express her sense of bottomless loss, mirrored in lines like, 'Without you it's so hard to live/ Can't take much more/ Why can't we love like we did before?'

Just as *Modern Times* had seemed impervious to the few critical slings and arrows sent its way, so the mixed reviews for *Together Through Life* failed to stop it becoming his second number one of the Noughties, proof it really does all come 'round again. It seemed the man was still a legend, just not to a bubblehead with a badge named Kristie Buble, who only a matter of weeks after the man had a *Number One* album on the *Billboard* charts, detained him for wandering around Freehold, New Jersey, and peering into the windows of vacant homes on July 23rd, 2009, apparently now a crime in post-Patriot Act America. Where was Guthrie's mighty pen when it was needed?

For those who thought Dylan a harsh critic of all that America had become since 9/11, nothing more perfectly encapsulated how right he had been when he told Brinkley, three months earlier, 'It's . . .

---

* Perhaps they even re-examined some of the song-ideas left over from their mid-Nineties writing stint.

unnerving . . . to see so many young people walking around with cell-phones and iPods in their ears, so wrapped up in media and video games. It robs them of their self-identity. It's a shame to see them so tuned out to real life.'

Ms Buble was a fully paid-up member of this particularly blank gen-eration. A decade before America decided Black Lives Matter, this badge-wielding bimbo with no concept of civil rights decided that a man who stood on the same stage as Martin Luther King when King proclaimed he had a dream, 'Free at last!', was a threat to the body pol-itic and needed taking in. Of her own free will, she then told *Esquire* magazine all about the day she arrested Bob Dylan for walking the streets of New Jersey on his own:

> I just happened to be there and stopped him, asking, you know, normal questions. 'What are you doing here? What's your name?' He said, 'I'm Bob Dylan. I'm on tour.' And I thought, 'No, that doesn't seem right.' . . . He's saying these things that are normal indicators of liars. 'I'm Bob Dylan.' Okay, what's your real name? And he told me his real name – his real, real name . . . I think [he said] Zimmerman. And I'm like, that's not right. He has two names! . . . I just put him in the car and said, 'Okay, where are you staying, Bob?' kind of sarcastically, messing with him a little bit. 'Where's your hotel, where might you be staying, where are your friends?' And he says, 'Oh, it's this hotel out by the ocean,' . . . He talked a lot [in the car]. I wasn't even paying attention to some of the things he was saying, because in my head I was wondering . . . 'What am I going to tell the [mental] hospital?' He's just blabbering in the back, 'Just take me over there, I'll give you tickets to my show, you can see me play.' . . . It didn't actually occur to me to ask him, 'Sing me a song.' . . . I think he named a couple of songs. But I wouldn't have known any of the songs . . . It was just a suspicious thing . . . Even if he didn't say he was Bob Dylan, I would have thought something was off . . . He said, 'I have houses all over the place. I don't live in one place. I travel so much, I have a house in London, I have a house in California.' . . . He looks like a homeless person, and he's saying he's rich, he has all these houses, and he's walking around in the rain in a rain jacket . . . soaking wet . . . rain boots on, sweat pants, and a jacket. He said that he saw a house with a for-sale sign, and he was looking to possibly buy this house. I said, 'Nor-mal people go through a real estate agent. Why were you walking

around the back of the house?' He was [saying], 'I don't know, I just wanted to check it out.' . . . As soon as we got to the hotel, and I pulled the police car in . . . his manager came running out to us and flipped out . . . He grabbed Bob out of the car and said, 'Don't talk to them anymore, come with me.' I was like, 'Sorry! Sorry, Bob! I didn't mean to not believe you.' . . . The manager wouldn't let me have anything to do with him. And I go, 'Whoa, we're still the cops, give us some form of ID or we're going to come on your bus.' And he says, 'You don't have a warrant, [you can't] come on this bus!' . . . [I] tried to look in the bus . . . The manager wasn't allowing [me] anywhere near it . . . I don't even know how [the story] got out . . . The biggest newspaper in New York . . . made it seem like I was some dumb girl who didn't know who he was.

Making Buble out to be 'some dumb girl' was hardly a stretch, but the bigger picture – the patent Idiocracy which produces cops like her – was lost in the newsworthiness of the situation. Obscured was a straight line from the Patriot Act, to Dylan being detained for no reason, to George Floyd's brutal 2020 murder by a white policeman in Dylan's home state, all the inevitable outcome of a country which seems overly proud of a constitution hastily concocted on the back of a second-hand copy of John Locke's *Second Treatise on Government*, resulting in jumped-up traffic wardens getting to carry guns and bully citizens.

Thankfully, Dylan remained calm throughout his own run-in with the modern law-enforcer. He may even have got a kick out of the situation. As he told Marc Rowland back in 1978, 'I'm more comfortable in a place with a person who wouldn't know who I was,' and Gundersen in 1997, 'I don't want to be a celebrity . . . It short-circuits your creative powers when people come up and interrupt your train of thought.' If most of the time being recognized was a pain, such was not always the case. As Cooky once recalled:

Often in the car he would automatically duck down from sight . . . When [I] teased him about what would happen if he didn't hide, like, so what if someone looked over and saw him at a stop light, he sat up . . . Other times he'd just wander around in public completely naturally, in and out of stores. Such was the case in Malibu, where he wasn't [usually] bothered.

A family man, he continued trying to protect those related to him, who had in no way signed up for the impositions of others on *him*. Particularly during the period when he was still denying the existence of a second (or third) family, he deemed this important. So, when an amateur filmmaker, who in the late Eighties had shot a film about Dylan's Minnesotan roots and interviewed almost all of his Dinkytown contemporaries, followed him one day to the beach, he met a Dylan who didn't take kindly to being stalked:

Markus Wittman: [In the early Nineties, my friend John and I] decided to go take a ride up the coast and do a drive-by of Dylan's house . . . Right before we got to Dylan's property line, a white van emerged from Dylan's property and cut directly in front of us . . . From my driver seat angle, I can see Dylan's face in his oversized side view mirror . . . There really was nothing I could do, but follow Dylan . . . Once we got to the bottom of the hill . . . Dylan is picking up and dropping speed and makes a couple of erratic lane changes. I tell John, I'm gonna pass him and just drive on. [But] as I'm doing so, Dylan does a u-turn . . . pulling over to park . . . I decided to . . . head back to see if maybe we could talk to [him] . . . I apologized for intruding and said that we . . . didn't want to bother him, but we're fans and could I trouble him for an autograph. Dylan . . . looked up at me, squinted really, and . . . said, 'Nah' . . . He then looked away towards the back of the van. I noticed a very young black girl standing up in the passenger front seat. She was skinny, cute, maybe between 4-5 years old. I waved back at her . . . I told him that I made a documentary about him as my senior thesis at U.C. Berkeley and would he like me to give him a copy? . . . I dropped some names . . . Old friends like Dave Morton, Dave Whitaker, Bonnie Beecher . . . I asked again if he wanted a copy of the documentary. 'Nah.' . . . Dylan kept looking towards the back of his van. I was convinced there must be a woman in the back . . . He made John and I so uncomfortable we left him alone pretty quick . . . It was kind of brilliant, the way he got rid of us.

If there was a woman in the van, it would have been Carolyn Dennis. The young child was, of course, Desiree. As Dennis herself has said, 'He loves humanity . . . but he wants his space and doesn't respect those who do not [give him it].' His reward for protecting his nearest and dearest has been, as his ex-bodyguard once put it, '[People] always want to know about how weird Bob is . . . Look, the man works hard, takes care of his extended family and a lot of other people too. What more can you ask from a person?'

Of course, if he wanted to stop people from thinking he was border-line nuts, he perhaps should have reconsidered releasing his second new album of 2009, an LP that made *Self Portrait* seem like *Blonde on Blonde*. Released in October 2009, *Christmas in the Heart* was Dylan's *Metal Machine Music*. The best excuses his apologists could come up with were: a) lots of people make Christmas albums which are almost as bad, and b) he was giving the money to a homeless charity.

It was certainly no spur of the moment decision. He'd given Christ-mas songs a test-run at the *Infidels* sessions, and at a couple of Fall 2001 soundchecks recorded for a planned live album. But the least said about the 2009 album, the better. So, let us move swiftly on, stopping merely to note that he got torn apart critically for *Revisionist Art*, but *Christmas in the Heart* got a free pass. (I know which one made me laugh, and which made me wince.)

This was product, pure and simple, from an artist who increasingly did what he wanted, and no longer listened to others. As his old friend Louie Kemp lamented, 'There are people around who tell you the truth and there are people who say, "Yes sir." You gotta have people who speak up. Arthur [Rosato] would speak up if [he] didn't agree with something or have a suggestion . . . And [Bob] listened – back then.' The subtext: he no longer did.

Now, he merely wished to live outside the law, a persona Larry Charles for one thought suited him, '[He has] a kind of Buster Keaton quality to him[self] almost . . . but at the same time he's a cowboy, he kicks Jeff Bridges['s character] in the balls . . . he's ready to cut his throat. You know, he's a badass.' It was during this period he became adept at quoting Sun Tzu's *Art of War* and, in one unexpected jotting, telling the government, 'If [you] can't protect me, then let me protect myself,' the kind of statement he was hopefully qualifying to Jonathan Lethem by suggesting, 'A lot of us don't have the murderous instinct, but we wouldn't mind having the license to kill.'

Such would be the backdrop to his fourth 21st century album of ori-ginal songs, *Tempest*, released in September 2012, and potentially his strongest album in fifteen years. This time he had a surfeit of songs – including one called 'Can't Do a Thing With You' he didn't do anything with, and another called 'Girl With A Rose Tatoo', which became 'Long And Wasted Years.' Both contained a surfeit of verses the younger Dylan would have pruned to make the resultant album a play-through experience.

Now, or so he would proclaim, 'I just let the lyrics go, and when I was singing them, they seemed to have an ancient presence.' In the case of the title-track, this 'ancient presence' seemed to have inspired him to write a fourteen-minute Gothic romance about the sinking of the *Titanic*. Two other songs, 'Tin Angel' and 'Roll On John', ran to over nine minutes. As a result, the ten-song album ran to over sixty-eight minutes.

Once again, less would have been more. A forty-five minute album could comfortably accommodate all he really had to say, and allowed him to jettison the turgid 'Early Roman Kings' (which, naturally, became the one song he was still playing in 2021) and the overlong 'Tempest', plus apply some judicious editing to the others – though *not* to the seven-minute 'Scarlet Town' or the nine-minute 'Tin Angel', both of which cracked a code he'd spent the past two decades trying to decipher – once again claiming 'the only true valid death you can feel today' for his own. In both cases, he was having fun with traditional tropes, incorporating the malignant spirit first given rein on *'Love and Theft'*.

At nine minutes, 'Tin Angel' was hardly hiding its light under a bushel. Yet it seemed to pass most commentators by. Here was the kinda song he'd been trying to capture since he opened the door on tradition again in the mid-Nineties. A brilliant distillation of the hoariest of murder ballads in the Child canon – 'Gypsy Davey', 'Matty Groves', 'Love Henry' (to give them their American names) – it pulled off a trick that had eluded Burns and Scott, one he'd been trying to realize since he debuted Elizabeth Cotton's 'Shake Sugaree' in 1995. As he told listeners of TTRH, before playing Cotton's original, 'Listen to this and you think it's a traditional song, but it's not – Elizabeth wrote it.'

'Tin Angel' seamlessly inhabited the ballad world he'd long considered 'in mythological terms: the myth of the younger sister, the myth of the false bride, the myth of the two brothers . . . [I] think of those stories . . . as myths.' Producing his most multi-layered lyric in years by using commonplaces that were centuries old, Dylan applied some frosted icing by naming it 'Tin Angel', a title that appears in none of the handwritten drafts in Tulsa, but had once been an early, juvenile Joni Mitchell song.

Mitchell, after years of begrudgingly accepting she was probably destined to live in the man's shadow, had shown her other side now in an April 2010 interview in the one daily Dylan took, the *L.A. Times*: 'Bob is not authentic at all. He's a plagiarist, and his name and voice are fake. Everything about Bob is a deception. We are like night and day, he and I.' Unlike most of Joni's close friends, who already feared for her sanity, Dylan did not rise to the bait. He merely filed the slur away while he sketched out on Marriott notepaper the first half of his first epic ballad since 'Danville Girl' to contain the whole world:

> 1. It was late last night when the boss came home
> To a desolate mansion [and a] deserted throne
> He called for his lady, the curtains were drawn
> The stable was empty, his lady was gone . . .

Biff – bang – wallop – the listener is hurled headlong into a maelstrom of murderous balladry – the song form most suited to, and mined, by America's purveyors of tradition. But who is carrying a weapon? In a thirteen-page draft on Crowne Plaza notepaper, we encounter a certain Henry Lee. The absent lady who 'last night . . . slept in a feather bed/ Black snake burning [around] her head,' is tonight 'floating on the bou[n]dless sea/ Sleeping in the arms of Henry Lee.' Her husband demands to know of his servant, what happened:

> [2.] Servant met him at [the] door
> Said, 'Your baby's gone, she['s] here no more.'
> 'How can it be, explain it to me, tell me, man
> Get to the point as quick as you can.'
> 'Henry Lee, chief of the clan,
> Came riding thru the wood, took her by the hand.'

With the idea for the whole song having come to him in outline, as only the best of them used to do, he concerned himself initially with the set-up, not the denouement. The 'chief of the clan' at this stage may have had a more daemonic identity, Dylan suggesting 'the devil

[is] avoid[ing] him', while someone is 'pay[ing] the ransom' for a 'Bride of Heaven'. He soon decides to instead complete the story of 'Gypsy Davey',* which in its 'Johnny Faa' original ended with the gypsies being hung, but in most latter-day variants has the lady living the life of a gypsy, while her former Lord broods.

Dylan's Lord determines to hunt them down, whatever the cost. Even when he comes to 'the threshold of oak and stone', with his men having all deserted him, he rides on alone, until he comes 'to the place where they bust out your brains'. Once there, 'He crawled on his belly, put his ear to the wall/ One way or another he's [gonna] put an end to it [all].' He already knows how Child murder ballads and Shakespeare tragedies invariably end: with everyone dead. He cares not, 'He turned [to put] on his helmet and his cross-hand sword/ He cursed his fate. He denied his Lord.' And in so doing, he seals his Fate, even if the denouement, as unforgiving as the *Unforgiven,* would only be revealed on the recorded version.

In the old days, Dylan would have made the song the centrepiece of one side of a carefully conceived, two-sided, forty-minute album. On the other side would have been 'Scarlet Town'. Familiar as the mythical setting for 'Barbara Allen', here it more resembled the scene in Todd Haynes's Dylan 'biopic' *I'm Not There (2007),* where the 'Alias' Dylan, played by Richard Gere, rides into town to find 'old, weird America, so sadly and sweetly on the brink'.† Right from 'Scarlet Town's earliest draft, characters from traditional ballads like 'Barbara Allen' and 'Dives And Lazarus' find themselves trapped in a landscape even bloodier and more biblical than tradition:

> Scarlet Town in the month of May
> Sweet William on his deathbed lay
> Bleeding from the mouth, face up in the bed
> His lovesick harlot heaping prayers on his head.
> Lazarus crouching outside the gate
> Couldn't care less about church 'n' state . . .

---

* As Reverend Sabine Baring-Gould, author of 'Onward, Christian Soldiers', had famously done before him.
† Apparently, this scene with Jim James's performance of 'Goin' To Acapulco' was Dylan's favourite.

In Scarlet Town save your breath
The price for speaking the truth is death . . .
They shut the factories (alt: shot the priest), closed the school
In Scarlet Town the devil rules . . .

Dylan seemed particularly keen to play this song live to see how it felt, debuting it on the first fall 2012 show, in Manitoba. The rest of the album – the unperformed 'Tin Angel' and 'Tempest' excepted – would take their own sweet time joining it. In the case of 'Tempest', it simply fell well short of its better-conceived cousins. The idea, which had been germinating for a while, had a certain promise. As he told the London press in 1997, '[You'll] find twenty songs about the sinking of the *Titanic*, each one of them gives you a different point of view and each one of them is heartfelt.' Dylan now decided to combine them into a single song, which starts promisingly enough, on Holiday Inn notepaper:

> 2. I think of Edith P[iaf] as sometimes I go to sleep
> I think of all [her] songs, melted in the deep . . .
>
> 3. Count Dracula was sleeping/ in a chamber dead inside
> His bloodless heart was beating/ His bed began to slide
> He put [on] his Armor/ And sharpened all his knives
> Wild eyed boys and farmers/ went fleeing for their lives . . .

It wasn't a premise that needed to be milked to death, and at fourteen meandering minutes, it was. Even Dylan probably suspected he'd lose the audience if he played it live, and he never did. In fact, despite the largely kind reviews and another Top Three album, after 'Scarlet Town's October 5th debut, he didn't play another *Tempest* song until November 7th, when 'Early Roman Kings' found its bolted-on berth. Something was holding him back.

When he *did* start to slip the other songs into the set, the shows got better, and the songs came alive. A single 2012 performance of 'Pay In Blood', the best vocal on the album and the other song reflective of the man at his very best, treated fans to another instalment in the Man With No Name saga. 'Soon After Midnight' soon followed, and by the following Spring, he was playing these four songs every night.

But something had changed, a seismical shift. Without fanfare, indeed without comment, the Never Ending Tour had come to an end after a quarter of a century and 2,480 shows. Starting on April 5th, 2013 in Buffalo Dylan began the Never Changing Tour, with set-lists largely set in stone and formalised arrangements the order of the day. The only exception would be a pair of mid-November 2013 shows in Rome where he ripped up the set-list for the last time – just to prove he could.

At least he was now promoting new product with verve and vim, having re-signed to Sony for another ten years. This time, unbeknownst to his hardcore fans, he was committing himself to the official plundering of the simple years with annual instalments of The Bootleg Series.

Further releases in the previously sporadic series now acquired the power of legal writ. Schedule B of the 2013 contract outlined no less than fourteen 'approved' future projects including the 1993 Supper Club shows (already bootlegged in their entirety); 'complete' releases of *The Basement Tapes* 'with hours of extra unreleased material' and the New York *Blood on the Tracks* sessions; a live Never Ending Tour set, 'possibly including crowd-sourced material from fans sending in their favourite live moments';* a *Time Out of Mind* set, 'possibly including rare in-studio footage shot by Daniel Lanois's brother';† and an 'Early Years' set which has still to be released, tantalisingly set to include 'radio shows [plural] in Chicago'.‡ Also on the list – last, but not least – was 'Gospel-Themed Concert Tour 1979-81' – 'including footage of the performance[s]'.

Sure enough, between 2013 and 2018, Sony released the cream of the above crop from their and Dylan's various vaults, releasing a revisionist set of the *Self Portrait* and *New Morning* sessions (*Another Self Portrait*); a 6-CD set of *The Basement Tapes* that finally swept up most of the rogue Red Room recordings and – thanks to archivist Glenn Korman, who found a 10" compilation-reel of post-*JWH* recordings Hudson had

---

* Perhaps an open admission they don't have the necessary knowledge of these shows to compile such a set 'in-house'. No such set has appeared or been mooted subsequently. It would be a mammoth task.

† It finally appeared in 2023, minus any of the now-embargoed video footage.

‡ Dylan only ever did two, one in January 1961 – still uncirculated, and as far as I'm aware unsourced, though we now know it definitely happened – and the April 1963 Studs Terkel show.

mislaid – giving the world proper dubs of 'Wild Wolf', 'Bourbon Street' and 'All-American Boy'; a complete record of four September days at the New York *BoTT* sessions (*More Blood, More Tracks*), minus studio chatter and the first minute and a half of the first take on day one; a complete, if insultingly expensive 18-disc boxed-set (*The Cutting Edge*) of Dylan's entire 1965-66 studio canon, minus the odd expletive; and, perhaps most welcome of all, an 8-CD + DVD boxed-set of the Gospel Years (*Trouble No More*) that gave fans complete shows from Toronto 1980 and London 1981, and rehearsal takes and live one-offs of songs as important as 'No Man Righteous', 'Makin' A Liar', 'Yonder Comes Sin', 'Caribbean Wind', 'The Groom's Still Waiting' and an inspired, seven-minute Clover out-take of 'Dead Man, Dead Man'.

Lavishly packaged and invariably released in time for Christmas, the revived Bootleg Series put some of the most important music from half a century of recorded song into the public domain, at the exact same time as Dylan himself was recording and releasing some of the worst music of his career, paying homage to one of its greats, Ol' Blue Eyes, in a series of albums that became progressively more painful to bear or hear.

Yet the first of them, *Shadows in the Night*, released February 3rd, 2015, was greeted like there was a logic to an exercise that, if it was ever going to happen, should have happened thirty years earlier. Actually, two of its songs *had* been captured in the Eighties when Dylan still had 'a voice'. The Farm Aid 1985 version of 'That Lucky Old Sun' may be his greatest-ever live cover, even if the idiots at the Nashville Network managed to omit it from their TV broadcast, preferring to interview the long-forgotten Alabama. Meanwhile, 'Some Enchanted Evening' was laid down one inspired evening in New Orleans during the *Oh Mercy* sessions, and could have moved mountains if he'd ever completed it, as he did 'We Three'.

He told Malcolm Burn at the time, after Burn bravely asked him 'who were [his] great influences, especially when it comes to phrasing', 'My two favourite singers are Frank Sinatra and Al Jolson.' He described the tone of Sinatra's voice, shortly before Frank's death in 1998, as 'like a cello', and claimed he and Don Was 'wanted to record [an octogenarian] Sinatra doing Hank Williams songs', which was almost as bad an idea as the septuagenarian Dylan doing songs Sinatra had made his own, not once but thrice.

How ironic that Dylan should, in the one interview he gave to promote *Shadows in the Night*, talk about these being 'the same songs that rock'n'roll came to destroy – music hall, tangos, pop songs from the '40s, fox-trots, rumbas, Irving Berlin, Gershwin, Harold Arlen, Hammerstein . . . It's hard for modern singers to connect with that kind of music.' It was even harder for the audience of said modern singer to connect with what he now perpetrated.

What was equally dispiriting was his refusal to tackle anything outside the Sinatra canon after performing a perfectly creditable cover of Charles Aznavour's 'The Times We've Known' at some Noughties NET shows, and recording a lovely 'Return To Me', a song usually identified with Dean Martin, for the third series of *The Sopranos*. It was almost like he was consciously disavowing his own place in the pantheon, as he had seemed to do in conversation with Elliot Mintz in 1991, when he still had things to say:

> There's too many other people that have done far superior things than me, in the same field . . . None of my songs are that good . . . Hoagie Carmichael songs are much better than mine, so are George Gershwin's and Irving Berlin . . . Hank Williams' songs are *all* better than mine.

But he held off recording any of these songs, leaving it to that most unlikely crooner, former r&b singer Rod Stewart, to smother them with a voice which – after corrective surgery – was in even worse shape than Dylan's. Nonetheless, Stewart's 2002 album, *It Had to Be You*, was a big seller. And still Dylan held off, telling Gundersen, 'I can't get away with singing cover songs like Rod Stewart. Nobody's going to buy it . . . [But] I love those songs.' Only after Stewart followed up with three more volumes, did Dylan's mind turn to showing Rod how they really should be done:

> All through the years, I've heard these songs being recorded by other people and I've always wanted to do that. And I wondered if anybody else saw it the way I did. I was looking forward to hearing Rod [Stewart]'s records of standards. I thought if anybody could bring something different to these songs, Rod certainly could. But the records were disappointing . . . You can always tell if somebody's heart and soul is into something, and I didn't think Rod was into it in that way. It sounds

like so many records where the vocals are overdubbed . . . These kind of songs don't come off well if you use modern recording techniques . . . I could only record these songs one way, and that was live on the floor with a very small number of mikes. No headphones, no overdubs, no vocal booth, no separate tracking . . . I rehearsed the band all last fall . . . We [play]ed a whole bunch of things on the stage, with no microphones, so we could play at the right volume. By the time we went in to make this record, it was almost like we'd done it already.

When his old friend, Eric Clapton, cut one of his all-time favourites, wartime jazz standard 'Autumn Leaves', a song Sinatra didn't record until 1957, Dylan kept back what he thought of Clapton's version until he did it 'justice' himself – as he evidently thought he had on *Shadows in the Night* – before publicly chastising Clapton for failing 'to decide what's real about it and what's not . . . He sings the song, and then he plays the guitar for ten minutes, and then he sings the song again. He might even play the guitar again . . . But . . . he sings the song twice, both the same way . . . It's not exactly getting to the heart of what "Autumn Leaves" is about.' MusiCares, here he comes.

He was certainly putting his head on the block by daring to enter this alien domain. Fortunately for him, the English-speaking world's cabal of rock critics now collectively lost their marbles, including the previously sane Michael Simmons who, in his five-star review in *Mojo*, concluded, 'There have been moments when one wondered whether Dylan would ever carry a tune again. Then something like *Shadows in the Night* arrives, and we remember that he is the king of the confounded expectation . . . The audible regret on opener 'I'm A Fool To Want You' is heartbreaking – *Blood on the Tracks* condensed in under five minutes.' My, oh my. Meanwhile, the temporarily cloth-eared Neil McCormick wrote in the *Daily Telegraph* that the album contained 'the best singing from Dylan in 25 years'.

In which parallel universe does either statement hold up? Was Dylan now officially 'critic-proof'? The album duly debuted at number one on the UK album charts, fifty years (almost to the week) after *Freewheelin'* hit the top spot, and changed the parameters of Pop forever.

Not that anyone who bought that album in 1965 recognized the figure people paid good money to see at shows in Europe the autumn of 2015, surely the nadir of Dylan's career as a live performer. Most nights he busked his way through seven American songbook standards (five of them from the latest platter), nine songs from his post-*TOOM* canon and just three songs that a casual fan might know, or expect to hear: 'Blowin' In The Wind', 'She Belongs To Me' and 'Tangled Up In Blue'. It was a gruelling experience for many, and even in the theatres he was now playing, there was a restless, antsy feeling from the not-so-cheap seats that greeted this unenchanting evening-out fare.

Worryingly, even before the deflated audiences at those 2015 shows had shuffled off into the shadowy night, and the credulous critics had put their quivering quills away, Dylan was talking about the fact that he had actually recorded 'about thirty songs, and these ten [just] fall together to create a certain kind of drama'. There would be more. More and more. The man was determined to push his luck, and show Rod he knew more examples from the American songbook than even an L.A.-based UK tax exile who lived a life without a dull moment, save when recording albums. *Fallen Angels* followed a year later, and did no-one, least of all Dylan, any favours, before he delivered the *coup de grâce*, a triple-LP called *Triplicate* that finally denuded the vaults of all the Sinatra songs he had stockpiled.

It peaked at a chastening thirty-seven on the US charts. Enough is enough, his fan base belly-ached. By now, not even Mr McCormick was quite so sanguine about this tsunami of shellac from a man who once wrote songs that defined people's lives. The headline to McCormick's *Triplicate* review said it all, 'Bob Dylan should stop crooning and get back to writing songs.' Fortunately, that's exactly what he now did.

2015–2021:
My Echo, My Shadow And Me, Too

Q: [What do you think about being] nominated for the Nobel Prize for Literature?
Bob Dylan: I don't know what it even is. I know it's [some] high, elevated honour.

London press conference 4th October 1997.

The Nobel [Prize] is a ticket to one's own funeral. No one has ever done anything after he got it.

T.S. Eliot, on winning it.

I can forgive Alfred Nobel for having invented dynamite, but only a fiend in human form could have invented the Nobel Prize.

George Bernard Shaw.

They give the Nobel Prize to too many second-raters for me to get excited about it. Besides, I'd have to go to Sweden and dress up and make a speech. Is the Nobel Prize worth all that? Hell, no.

Raymond Chandler, 1949.

What do I hear in my ear
                    approaching my 70th year –
Echoes of popular tunes, old rhymes . . .

'Popular Tunes', Allen Ginsberg, 1996.

If I can't please everybody, I only might as well please myself.

Dylan's handwritten inscription to Jonathan Cott's
copy of *Writings & Drawings*, 1978.

He [still] doesn't know that he's the best . . . If he finds out he's the best, he might quit . . . [So] I treat him like he's one of the guys. Because if you look up to him . . . he won't respect you anymore.

Roger McGuinn, 1975.

GC: Which of your albums is your favourite one?
BD: The one I still have to do!

Gino Castaldo, 23rd June 1993.

People think they know me from my songs . . . [but] you'd have to be a madman to [try to] figure out the characteristics of the person who wrote all those songs.

Bob Dylan, to Joe Smith, *Off The Record*.

If I'm here at eighty, I'll be doing the same thing.

Bob Dylan, to Mikal Gilmore, Summer 1986.

*

Anyone who knows him well can attest that, even in the 21st century, Dylan remains a man of fierce opinions, outwardly phlegmatic, but bubbling under with ire at the shape of things. And starting in 2001, that undercurrent occasionally washed up in print, usually expressed either as a distaste for the modern world or, more specifically, modern music. At his most gregarious press conference ever, in the summer of 2001, he singled out the main culprit – mass media:

We are living in a time when the media has taken over everything. What can a writer think or write about, that you don't see every day in a news-paper or on television? . . . When Rimbaud, William Blake, Shelley or Byron were writing . . . they were free to explore their minds . . . There's nobody like Kafka who . . . writes something without wanting some-body to read it . . . We live in a world of fantasy where Disney has conquered [all].

When one of the attendees that day in Rome, Christoph Dallach, pressed him on when he last 'liked a movie', he admitted to preferring movies from 'the time of which I [also] liked the music, the twenties, thirties and forties . . . I can rather identify with the thoughts and characters from that time.'

Having dismissed 'modern records' to Jonathan Lethem in 2006 as 'atrocious . . . no definition of nothing, no vocal . . . just like – static,' he took time out from cueing up the Mississippi Sheiks' 'Blood In My Eyes' on his radio show in 2008, to remind listeners, 'It is important to remember that [the Sheiks] . . . went somewhere to record it, and went many places to perform it. That's how they got life experience to write and record more songs . . . What's the next generation gonna write about? Sitting home alone?'

By 2015, his savage indictments of modern life had cast America in the role of Sodom and Gomorrah: 'People's lives today are filled on so many levels with . . . ambition, greed and selfishness . . . We don't see the people that [such] vice destroys. We just see the glamour of it on a daily basis – everywhere we look, from billboard signs to movies, to newspapers, to magazines. We see the destruction of human life and the mockery of it, everywhere we look.'

So, it should have come as no surprise when, after an afternoon at the boxing gym he leased, the gloves came off at a February 2015 charity event, where he was the guest of honour. When Dylan stepped up to the podium at the annual MusiCares gathering of gladhanders, the ghost of the ECLC dinner flickered fleetingly as Dylan decided to 'tell it right like it is', producing a long checklist of scores to settle with his verbal Sten gun:

> I didn't really care what Leiber and Stoller thought of my songs. They didn't like 'em, but Doc Pomus did . . . I never liked their songs, either. 'Yakety yak, don't talk back.' 'Charlie Brown is a clown', 'Baby I'm a hog for you'. Novelty songs. They weren't saying anything *serious*. Doc's songs, they were better. 'This Magic Moment', 'Lonely Avenue', 'Save The Last Dance For Me'. Those songs broke my heart . . . Ahmet Ertegun didn't think much of my songs, but Sam Phillips did . . . Merle Haggard didn't even think much of my songs . . . Buck Owens did, and he recorded some of my early songs . . . 'Together Again'? That's Buck Owens, and that trumps anything coming out of Bakersfield . . . The Byrds, the Turtles, Sonny & Cher – they made some of my songs Top 10 hits but . . . their versions of songs were like commercials . . . Critics have been giving me a hard time since Day One. Critics say, I can't

sing . . . Why don't critics say that same thing about Tom Waits? Critics say, my voice is shot . . . Why don't they say those things about Leonard Cohen? . . . Critics say, I can't carry a tune and I talk my way through a song . . . I've never heard that said about Lou Reed. Why does he get to go scot-free? . . . [They say I] slur my words, got no diction. Have you people ever listened to Charley Patton or Robert Johnson, Muddy Waters? . . . I was at a boxing match a few years ago seeing Floyd Mayweather fight a Puerto Rican guy. And . . . it was time for our national anthem. And a very popular soul-singing sister was chosen to sing. She sang every note that exists, and some that don't exist . . . [But] Sam Cooke said . . . 'Voices ought not to be measured by how pretty they are. Instead, they matter only if they convince you that they are telling the truth.'

On and on he went, as cameras rolled and the suits squirmed. But this time he wasn't drunk, and he wasn't just letting words fall to the floor; he'd prepped for a full fortnight beforehand. This was how he felt, and he wasn't about to apologize, or offer to cover the shortfall on contributions from the evening. An old friend from the ECLC era was left non-plussed:

Barry Kornfeld: He did this speech at MusiCares and he used it for payback. I thought, 'Bob Dylan doesn't need to pay anyone back!' And I realized all he ever does is complain about everybody forcing him to do what he didn't want to do, when in actual fact I've never known anybody who was [more] able to call the shots.

Some gave him the benefit of the doubt. An attendant Jackson Browne insisted, 'The point he was making was really interesting . . . He was trying to say where he came from.' What the speech really proved was that his critical faculties were intact, and he was gnarled enough and great enough to no longer care whose feathers he ruffled.

He had generally directed such comments previously at those who were beyond the veil, suggesting that *Rolling Stone* readers interested in what Johnny Cash was about, 'should listen to Johnny on his Sun records and reject all that notorious low-grade stuff he did in his later years, [which] can't hold a candlelight to the frightening depth of the man that you hear on his early records'. He made a similar – and similarly astute – observation about Skip James on his *TTRH* radio show, warning listeners, 'If you listen to the records he made in the Sixties, when they rediscovered him, you['ll] find that there's something missing. And what's missing is that interconnected thread of the structure of the songs.'

One suspects the real target he had in his MusiCares sights was not the likes of Merle Haggard – who was apparently genuinely hurt by Dylan's remarks – or the Teflon-coated Lou Reed, it was his 'auld enemy', the critics, specifically the reviewers of a record he'd released four days earlier:

> I just released an album of standards, all the songs usually done by Michael Buble, Harry Connick Jr . . . But the reviews of their records are different than the reviews of my record . . . They've got to look under every stone when it comes to me . . . Critics have made a career out of accusing me of having a career of confounding expectations. Really? Because that's all I do.

As far as he was concerned, the critics could go hang themselves. So could all academics, even those in Swedish cloisters, as an eighteen-strong committee set about determining if he deserved more than just a doctorate from Princeton, a Presidential Medal of Freedom and the Legion d'Honneur. The impetus for giving him the 'ultimate' literary accolade was coming from the very places Dylan once compared with old-people's homes, save that more people died in colleges. A groundswell had been growing since the mid-Nineties, when Allen Ginsberg tried in vain to petition the Nobel committee to give the award to the greatest bard of modern times. In 2013, the Einstein Forum in Potsdam held an entire conference asking if Dylan should be awarded the Nobel Prize in Literature.*

And yet, as of October 13th, 2016, the favourite to win that year's $900,000 prize was Japanese novelist, Haruki Murakami. Dylan remained a long shot, at least two fences further back than Italian

---

* As one of those who read a paper in Potsdam, pointing out it was high time an oral poet won this prestigious prize, I was informed the papers were being sent to the Nobel committee. I can only presume mine tipped the balance.

scholar Claudio Magris or Syrian poet, Adonis. At the Dylan office in New York, it was a normal day. Then, all hell broke loose, with Jeff Rosen obliged to break the news to a mystified Dylan, even as the literary world to a man had to decide which side of this desultory philippic barricade they were on.

Will Self took a leaf from Michael Gray's Potsdam polemic,* insisting, 'It cheapens Dylan to be associated at all with a prize founded on an explosives and armaments fortune, and more often awarded to a Buggins whose turn it is than a world-class creative artist,' before expressing the forlorn hope Dylan would follow Sartre's lead and refuse it. He could certainly afford to do so, being by far the richest recipient ever, having made almost as much dosh blowing up people's expectations as Mr Nobel had made, blowing people up.

Others who lined up on Dylan's side included potential future Nobel recipients, Salman Rushdie ('Dylan is the brilliant inheritor of the bardic tradition. Great choice.') and Philip Pullman, alongside Stephen King and Leonard Cohen, who nailed his last great *bon mot* to the mast in a speech he gave that evening, suggesting it was 'like pinning a medal on Mount Everest for being the highest mountain'.[†]

The best that the carpers could muster was Scottish novelist Irvine Welsh, who was claiming to be a Dylan fan, while calling it 'an ill-conceived nostalgia award wrenched from the rancid prostates of senile, gibbering hippies', a poor piece of invective when put alongside 'Positively 4th Street', placing Welsh squarely with Sean O'Casey and other pissed-off performing fleas passed over for literary prizes.

Dylan's response – the sound of silence – was entirely in keeping, from a man who once said, 'I don't know if I call myself a poet or not . . . because I come in on such a back door.' Even when the

---

* 'Don't Give Dylan The Nobel Prize In Literature', in *Outtakes on Bob Dylan* (Route, 2021) pp251-257.

† 'We live in a time of great lyricist-songwriters – Leonard Cohen, Paul Simon, Joni Mitchell, Tom Waits – but Dylan towers over everyone. His words have been an inspiration to me all my life ever since I first heard a Dylan album at school and I am delighted by his Nobel win. The frontiers of literature keep widening, and it's exciting that the Nobel Prize recognises that. I intend to spend the day playing "Mr Tambourine Man", "Love Minus Zero – No Limit", "Like a Rolling Stone", "Idiot Wind", "Jokerman", "Tangled Up In Blue" and "It's A Hard Rain's Gonna Fall".' – Salman Rushdie. Cohen himself died three weeks later, aged eighty-two.

committee pointed out that for him to collect the substantial cheque – Victoria's Secret-like money, minus the eye candy – he would have to deliver a lecture, he stonewalled, adding fuel to the fire of known origin his nomination had sparked.

Instead, he asked Patti Smith to go to Stockholm in his place, promising her a slap-up meal, and an opportunity to sing 'A Hard Rain's A-Gonna Fall' for the first time in twenty-five years, and then recorded a lecture for the committee which he delivered when he was next passing through Sweden on June 5th, 2017. By then, it was exam time. So, like any good student, he cribbed most of his essay's contents from second-hand sources any university library carried. Initially, though, he talked convincingly about his songcraft, and how he stumbled upon that way he had with words; a reminder to the committee he was a poet of performance, not the page:

> Somebody I'd never seen before handed me a Leadbelly record with the song 'Cottonfields' on it. And that record changed my life, right then and there . . . I wanted to learn this music and meet the people who played it. Eventually, I did . . . learn to play those songs. They were different than the radio songs that I'd been listening to all along . . . I had a natural feeling for the ancient ballads and country blues, but everything else I had to learn from scratch . . . By listening to all the early folk artists and singing the songs yourself, you pick up the vernacular . . . You know that Stagger Lee was a bad man and that Frankie was a good girl. You know that Washington is a bourgeois town, and you've heard the deep-pitched voice of John the Revelator, and you saw the Titanic sink in a boggy creek . . . You've seen the lusty Lord Donald stick a knife in his wife, and a lot of your comrades have been wrapped in white linen . . . I could make it all connect and move with the current of the day. When I started writing my own songs, the folk lingo was the only vocabulary that I knew . . . Songs are alive in the land of the living. But songs are unlike literature. They're meant to be sung, not read, [as] the words in Shakespeare's plays were meant to be acted on the stage . . . I hope some of you get the chance to listen to these lyrics the way they were intended to be heard: in concert.

It was a theme he had thought long and hard about, even writing a section for *Chronicles* he later cut, remembering the occasion when

Steve Allen read the lyrics out to 'Be-Bop-A-Lula' like it was poetry, a gag Peter Sellers copied with 'A Hard Day's Night'. Dylan dismissed the Allen gag for failing to 'get anywhere near giv[ing] away any secrets, for the hidden message is in the way the singer sings the song'.

But Dylan found his college drop-out essay was a couple of thousand words short of the necessary word-count. His solution was to analyze three seemingly random works by Herman Melville, Homer and Erich Maria Remarque, prompting *The Times* to sarcastically remark, 'With the deadline fast approaching to deliver his Nobel Prize in Literature lecture, Bob Dylan did what a[ny] harassed student would do. The singer plagiarised portions of his winner's speech from SparkNotes.'

Of the three works he decided to scrutinize, *Moby Dick* was the only one he previously claimed to know, telling Neil Hickey in 1976, 'Melville is somebody I can identify with, because of how he looked at life,' as well as confirming to Randy Anderson in 1978 he had indeed read *Moby Dick*.

His descriptions of *All Quiet on the Western Front* and *The Odyssey*, on the other hand, were much like his recollection of *The Gunfighter* in 'New Danville Girl', slightly off. Thus, 'When Odysseus in *The Odyssey* visits the famed warrior Achilles in the underworld – Achilles, who traded a long life full of peace and contentment for a short one full of honour and glory – tells Odysseus it was all a mistake. "I just died, that's all." ' Neither Achilles nor Homer would ever have said anything quite so prosaic.*

If Dylan seemed content to wind academics up, pocket the cheque and get back on the road, he had already pocketed a far larger cheque that year, an eye-watering $22 million, for pandering to another set of would-be scholars who really gave him the hump: Dylan 'scholars'. He had previously 'voiced his disdain for those [Dylan] completists who wish to see every scrap of paper he has written on or hear every studio outtake that he has rejected', to *Times* journalist, Alan Jackson.† It now

---

* 'Don't give me consolation about death, glorious Odysseus. I'd rather be above earth and labour for someone else, a man with no land of his own and little livelihood, than be king over all the lifeless dead.'
† The $22 million payment was not Dylan's entire largesse. The *New York Times* reported, 'The full archive was appraised at more than $60 million, with the bulk of it

turned out that the person he hated most – the most fastidious Dylan archivist of them all – was himself.

His own written archive, which had been purchased by the Tulsa-based George Kaiser Foundation (GKF), turned out to be staggering in both scope and size. According to the report in the *New York Times* of the 2016 sale, it ran to some six thousand items, a conservative estimate I'd say. Yet there was a secret its powerful purchaser 'ain't gonna tell' the *New York Times*, *Rolling Stone* or the *Washington Post*, all of whom sent reporters to the scene of the crime. Although the items these papers were allowed to partially reproduce were largely pre-accident – already published versions of 'Chimes Of Freedom' and 'Subterranean Homesick Blues', and a partial, typewritten 'Like A Rolling Stone', which vied with a couple of pages from the *Blood on the Tracks* notebooks – no-one reported the elephant in the room: they had acquired almost nothing – save for a wealth of *Tarantula* typescripts – from before 1967, when Dylan's new lawyer-manager, Naomi Saltzman, began nagging him to save his detritus.

The sum total of 'classics from the 1960s [that] appear in coffee-stained fragments', as the *New York Times* enticingly (and misleadingly) described the hoard, amounted to less than a dozen typescripts and manuscripts; mainly the ones Sally Grossman tried to sell at Christie's in 2011 but was forced to turn over to the Dylan office. What the GKF *had* acquired was all the pre-accident studio sessions, save the three that had been lost, one each from *Freewheelin'*, *BIABH* and *Blonde on Blonde*. Unfortunately for them, the Dylan office were in the process of putting *all* that material out in a series of copyright collections designed to legally protect unreleased material that was more than fifty years old, which under current EU law would otherwise fall into the public domain, thus rendering that part of the GKF acquisitions worthless to them *and* Sony.

Also entirely absent were any letters from Dylan, who in the early years had been an inveterate letter writer, though it was fascinating to see that he had kept letters from the likes of Johnny Cash and Joan Baez dating as far back as 1964. And though the GKF were talking about digitizing 'hundreds of original master tapes . . . down to the

given as a donation; [which] may allow Mr Dylan to claim a large charitable donation for tax purposes.'

level of their individual instrumental tracks, or stems', without the multitrack sheets that went with them and a way of listening to them other than a computer console, such work would be almost entirely useless to anyone but a studio engineer.

For now, the really salivating stuff lay in the notebooks, the hotel stationary, the Post-it notes and typescripts Dylan had kept from *John Wesley Harding* on. Taken in toto they confirmed his working methods were more meticulous, and far more crafted than anyone had previously imagined. Accidentally like a poet, he stood revealed – as he had when reporter Lynne Allen secured Dylan's last pre-conversion interview in December 1978, and noted, 'a small notebook peek[ing] out of one of the pockets. What appeared to be chicken scratchings made their way across the open page. "I'm always writing something," he explained.' But not everything had been saved – not by a long chalk – as one of his few girlfriends to realize the importance of this material once complained:

> Cooky commonly observed him leave bits of the constant stream of notes coming off his pens everywhere he went, notepads, slips of paper and napkins. If she brought them to his attention, he'd tell her to just throw them away. She'd object that she couldn't, and make him do it himself, which gave her the urge to dive for the waste basket. He tried explaining how keeping too many dead-ends just cluttered up his life. So that if he finds something he'd jotted down earlier that didn't mean anything to him, he throws it away, rather than try to make something out of it, because there were just too many of those kinds of thoughts, and the volume would be too much to deal with. He said he can't force meaning into pieces that refuse to develop.

After the Dylan office finally began to box things up, now was the time to cash in. The *New York Times*'s Ben Sisario surmised that 'the astronomical sums paid at auction for some of his early manuscripts, [including] a handwritten copy of "Like a Rolling Stone" [sic] sold for more than $2 million at Sotheby's in 2014,' had partly triggered this fire sale. What he failed to notice was the absence of any similar-looking manuscripts in the collection. It led Dylan via Rosen to hire in-house archivist, Michael Chaiken, and retain legendary wheeler-dealer, Glenn Horowitz, to catalogue what was real and what was not.

The choice of Horowitz was telling. Fellow high-end dealer and author, Rick Gekowski, has written, 'This [idea of the] flexibility of value once led New York's Glenn Horowitz, the most successful contemporary dealer in modern literary books and manuscripts, to claim that the value of a book is "transactional": it is worth what you can get a buyer to pay for it.'* And not just books. Horowitz was a man with a happy knack for hyping material of 'historical import' to achieve his primary goal: getting as much money (and therefore as much commission) as he could. Issues of accessibility and academic rigour could take care of themselves. Or not. If Horowitz believed value was 'transactional', Jeff Gold, a self-publicising L.A. dealer in records and memorabilia, a figure known to Rosen, was a willing disciple. What he wasn't was either a scholar or a qualified archivist. Yet this is who the office entrusted with producing a rather shoddy Finding Aid.

Between this unholy pair, the material was hastily assessed and catalogued for the 'Finding Aid'. Nobody – but nobody – had notated how the material had been originally grouped, or where exactly it had been found when the great excavation was undertaken, thanks to the secrecy in which the whole operation was shrouded. The loss of context would prove irretrievable, and may well have sent the likes of the Ransom Collection in Austin and California's Stanton University – both of whom expressed an interest – scurrying to the hills. Instead, the hills of Oklahoma were where the archive was bound, and a dedicated center devoted to Dylan, and him alone, next to the Guthrie Center.

At least the GKF would have a good five years after its acquisition to build up its collection, acquiring some much-needed artifactal items – bootlegs, rare records, booklegs &c. – and key pre-accident material that was starting to wash up in the auction houses of New York and London; material the GKF otherwise could not access.

They had just missed out on an important cache of song typescripts from the September 1965 'guitar-case', auctioned in December 2013 along with Dylan's guitar and jacket from Newport 1965. Bizarrely, the GKF ended up acquiring the jacket, an item of interest only to leather fetishists, instead. Likewise, when the original typescript of 'A Hard

---

* Horowitz's laissez-faire attitude to provenance has recently come back to bite him with The Eagles issuing a suit in 2022 against him, and two other dealers, over some lyric manuscripts. Apparently, they're worth money.

Rain's A-Gonna Fall' was auctioned in London in 2015, they didn't even bid on an item that didn't even meet reserve. What *was* going on?

It seemed the GKF were content to talk up what they had – which was certainly the mother of all hoards of Dylan mss. – and to hope that all those US collectors Dylan professed to despise would leave their collections to the Center in their wills, or take the tax write-off. Only one thing they got wrong: many, if not most, of the extensive Dylan archives in private hands lay *outside* America, and no-one in Tulsa was putting out feelers to see if the GKF – down to its last $7 billion – could acquire, or cherry-pick, these. As such, while the Center finally opened its doors in May 2022, with much fanfare, as a genuinely world-class repository of Dylan manuscripts and audio-visual recordings, its transition into a Folger-like institution for Dylan *and* his contemporaries remains some way off.

On the plus side, they had acquired the official archive of a living, breathing artist. There was soon more material coming down the pike. When a series of fires on the Malibu coastline jumped Highway One and burnt next door neighbour Rick Rubin's house to a crisp, Dylan instituted a hasty trawl of some overlooked outhouses, shipping the contents to Tulsa, post-haste. And though the post-2001 session-tapes have yet to be transferred or digitized, manuscripts of the songs from *Modern Times* and *Tempest* (though not *Together Through Life*) were among the original cache of papers.

As of 2020, there was also a whole set of new Dylan lyrics and session-tapes which at some point will hopefully be heading to Tulsa, because Dylan had a new album and – if the advance word was anything to go by – it was a doozie. The few specks of rumour that had escaped were promising. Chris Shaw was back as engineer, extracting every ounce of texture from Dylan's well-trammelled voice. And they'd recorded more than enough for a single album. But as of March 2020, and the end of the world as we know it, that was all anyone was saying.

It was on March 27th – as the world entered its darkest days since World War II, an almost complete global lockdown to stem the tide of a Covid virus the Chinese had allowed to fester until it was primed to spread unchecked, on or about Chinese New Year 2020 – Dylan posted across social media a simple message, 'This is an unreleased song we recorded a while back that you might find interesting . . . God be with you.'

The song in question, a downloadable, sixteen-minute, half-sung, half-spoken screed on the assassination of JFK, took its title from a line in *Hamlet* (or a February 1964 Margaret Rutherford movie, if you prefer). The first original lyric he'd published since collecting his Nobel award, it had more in common with Grub Street than the Jacobethan scribes of Shoreditch:

> You got me dizzy, Miss Lizzy, you filled me with lead
> That magic bullet of yours has gone to my head
> I'm just a patsy like Patsy Cline
> Never shot anyone from in front or behind
> Got blood in my eye, got blood in my ear
> I'm never gonna make it to the new frontier . . .

Nonetheless, the subject-matter, combined with the fact that everyone was sat at home wondering what to do with themselves, seemed to trigger a conspiracy-fest the world had not seen since the Seventies, as people read more into the song than it warranted. As *The Times* helpfully explained, 'One thing is clear – Bob Dylan does not buy the sole gunman theory,' seemingly unaware that the *majority* of Americans polled ten years after Dallas didn't believe that fairy tale, or that Dylan had instinctively rejected it the day after the deed. Someone noted that a 2012 exhibition of his paintings had featured one of Lee Harvey Oswald and another of *his* murderer, Jack Ruby; the song-title, it was discovered, was the name of a rare, early pamphlet on the assassination. And so on.

Didn't people have anything better to do with their time? They did not. Within a week the track had been downloaded – legally – three million times in America alone, and Dylan had his first US number-one single, despite the lack of physical sales and a track length that precluded any single format known to man. At least it confirmed he had an album in the works, even if such a sprawling song would tilt any LP-length artifact off its axis, especially one which, when it appeared, three months later, opened with 'I Contain Multitudes', which took its cue from a Walt Whitman poem Dylan had referenced in his 2019 *Rolling Thunder Revue* mockumentary, claiming, 'We still remember those lines today. Today's poets don't reach into the public consciousness that way.' (Maybe there's a reason.)

When the attendant artifact did appear, after 'I Contain Multitudes' was also drip-fed to downloaders, it seemed to some, Dylan scholar Michael Gray included, that, 'Dylan's songs once gave us clear yet creative narratives . . . Now it feels as if what we get is fragments from the ruminative thrashing of his mind.' Out of sync. with his target audience, though, Gray found his own critical voice drowned in the tide of triumphalism that greeted the June 19th, 2020 release of *Rough and Rowdy Ways*.

The Guardian's Alexis Petridis set the tone, insisting contrary to all evidence that, 'What sets *Rough and Rowdy Ways* apart from *Tempest* or 2006's *Modern Times* is the sheer consistency of the songwriting.' Arrant nonsense. The new album almost exactly mirrored its two predecessors in its random sequencing, its self-conscious shuffling between 12-bar dreck and five-star Dylan, and the ongoing inability of the seventy-something genius to *edit* himself. The inclusion of 'Murder Most Foul' at the end of what was already a 54-minute album made for an artifact that single-handedly justified the invention of the skip function.

The main thing the album had going for it – aside from two nailed-on classics, the neo-gothic 'My Own Version Of You', the unearthly 'Key West', plus the close-but-no-cigar 'Black Rider' – was that it came from 'a man of 79 with mortality on his mind', as *The Times*'s Will Hodgkinson sought to remind us.

Hodgkinson thankfully had the ears to single out 'Key West', a nine-minute masterpiece the subject-matter of which remains as great a mystery as the Bermuda Triangle, for some fully-warranted praise. For once, it was possible to believe Dylan had no more idea what this song was about than his fans. It was like one of those songs he described to AARP in 2015, that 'just play . . . in my mind until an idea comes from out of nowhere, and it's usually the key to the whole song. It's the idea that matters. The idea is floating around long before me.' The lyrics certainly suggested it had very little to do with the town at Mile Marker Nought. Even at seventy-nine, he had found a way to invade this listener's every locked-down waking hour with wondering what he meant when he sang, 'Key West is fine and fair / If you lost your mind, you will find it there,' or even,' I play both sides against the middle / Trying to pick up that pirate radio signal / I heard the news, I heard your last request . . .' In the end, all he can tell us is that 'Key West is on the horizon line'.

The other gem he'd been keeping close to his chest was 'My Own Version Of You', which finally made a song out of the 'Dr Franken-stein' verse he'd tried inserting into at least three songs previously. It was worth the wait. What a song, what a hoot! If Kitty Empire, a fully signed-up Me Too-er, considered 'Dylan's Frankenbride . . . some ghoulish fantasy of a woman without aesthetics of her own, much less a mind,' those of us with the wit to see him raise the ante on *Young Frankenstein* made it far enough in to notice the imprecation in the last line of the song:

> One strike of lightning is all that I need
> And a blast of electricity that runs at top speed
> Shimmy your ribs, I'll stick in the knife
> Gonna jumpstart my creation to life
> I wanna bring someone to life, turn back the years
> Do it with laughter, and do it with tears.

But even as his 39th studio album peaked at number two Stateside and number one in Blighty, he still remained stuck at home, working on more artifacts for his next Art exhibition, *Retrospectum,* due to open in Miami in November 2021, which would include newly-painted images of 'Times Square', 'Florida Keys', 'Night Time St Louis', 'Rainy Night in Grand Forks' and 'Sycamore Street', presumably all painted from memory.

Meanwhile, such was his desperation to get back to playing that he conceived the idea of recording a whole series of private 'live' concerts to be streamed on pay-per-view. 'Cept, this being Dylan, the whole project was bathed in secrecy and what should have been a straightforward performance – like many other house-bound contemporaries who broad-cast front-room gigs in lockdown, initially for free, but soon to payees – became bathed in mystery, even to the musicians brought in to play:

Tim Pierce: We did get a list of songs before we went in . . . This was four musicians in the round, no drums, no keyboards . . . no selfies, no photos, no Facebook, no recording. We drove to an undisclosed loca-tion. It was very early, Sixties-style recording, live off the floor . . . We were in a circle and Bob was facing us. His track was the only track that was isolated. So, you had to play to the microphones. We would play back and constantly adjust. I was brought in to play acoustic guitar, to strum and be the timekeeper. Bob would show us ideas on the guitar but he would not play guitar on these tracks. Greg Leisz would be next to me, playing mandolin. If he needed to be louder, he would simply move his chair forward. Don [Was] was playing upright. We had a couple of other musicians join us. T-Bone Burnett played some electric guitar. Jeff Taylor, from the Time Jumpers in Nashville, a multi-instrumentalist, played accordion. So, we['d] be given a list of songs, say five songs, for a particular session. These were Bob classics . . . He would spring new ones on us constantly. I remember learning one of the songs on my iPhone with headphones [on], while he was starting the song . . . We['d be] changing keys all the time. He's done this for so long, it's just instant [for him]. Whatever version of a song he does at a given time is a snapshot. I [also] had the privilege of watching him write lyrics in front of me . . . We were all sitting around between songs, and he [felt he] had to change some things. He just starts writing, rhyming stream-of-consciousness [lines], and . . . it starts to flow, [until] at a certain point he says, 'I don't know where this stuff comes from.'

The nineteen sessions Pierce apparently undertook occupied two whole months, ending around Dylan's 80th birthday, when he and his colleagues were replaced by a band Ira Ingber had been asked to assemble, which included Greg Sutton from the 1984 band. Dylan was convinced he had found a new way to get his music across. But, as ever these days, he could not let it be. Even with dozens of songs in the can, he hit upon the oddball idea of getting another band in to mime over these recordings in a so-called smoky bar, all filmed in black and white. With Veronica Lake nowhere to be seen, Dylan mimed his own vocals for a one-hour streamed broadcast he christened *Shadow Kingdom: The Early Songs of Bob Dylan*.*

The resultant broadcast, on July 18th, 2021, comprised thirteen songs (permed from at least four dozen reportedly recorded), three of which – 'When I Paint My Masterpiece', 'Watching The River Flow' and 'To Be Alone With You', all from the first amnesia – were given

---

* He called it this despite failing to feature a single song from before he went electric, and including a 1989 cut, 'What Was It You Wanted?'.

Mondo Scripto-style rewrites. The last of these, in particular, was a very different reimagining. Seemingly set in some kinda lockdown, it gave a whole new meaning to the song's title. Other than that, the lack of any arresting visuals – thanks to the whole thing being shot in pillow-soft-focus – made one wonder how this was a substitute for the live performances he professed to crave, and to which he announced he was returning just as the disappointing returns on *Shadow Kingdom* put the kibosh on further instalments.

Dylan was done with new-fangled film reels. It was time he got back to the country, as the high waters finally receded. He was ready to present his rough and rowdy sound to a post-Covid constituency, beginning on November 2nd, 2021 with a show in Milwaukee that only Americans could attend. The bumbling Biden still hadn't signed off on letting fans from countries with working vaccine programmes and much lower case-numbers attend, in case they infected the 35% of Americans who of their own free will preferred to die from a virus which had not one but three proven vaccines available.

It was the most eagerly awaited Dylan show in decades, perhaps since the last time he opened a tour in Milwaukee in 1981. But Dylan himself didn't want anyone to *know* what deal went down. When *Rolling Stone* agreed to pick up the tab for their resident Bobcat, Andy Greene, to report on this first show, Dylan's publicist, Larry Jenkins, told him his employer would rather he didn't review the show, and vaguely hinted at retribution if he did. Greene pointed out that he'd booked a hotel and a flight, and if need be, he'd buy a ticket outside. Hell or highwater, he was coming.

Given that the entire show was going to be posted on the Interweb by morning, one wonders which part of the modern world Dylan imagined he could still control. He had nothing to fear, anyway. The review from Greene was ultra-positive as Dylan debuted no less than eight new originals, including the eagerly awaited 'Key West', and by the following night in Chicago was performing all three of the *Shadow Kingdom* rewrites.

The fans who had wondered if they would ever hear the new songs live embraced the latest incarnation, and when Dylan announced three shows in New York at the end of the month, after someone had explained to Biden in single syllables why it was time to let world travellers in again, the world and his wife turned up at the 1,800-seater

Beacon Theatre, site of his historic 1989, 1990 and 1995 residencies, to share one final homecoming.

We'd got Dylan back again, and even though he looked a little unsteady on his pins, the voice was remarkably strong for an octogenarian. When someone on the Sunday (21st) shouted for 'Pretty Boy Floyd', he told them they were at the wrong show; they should be at *Springsteen on Broadway*, another dig perhaps at the very notion Bruce might be the natural inheritor of Woody's mantle.

The Saturday New York show, chockfull of Music Biz types, coincided with the sixtieth anniversary of Dylan's first ever Columbia studio session, a dozen blocks away from the Beacon. Though one could hardly claim it was like he'd never been away, even for those who had previously endured the eight-year 'amnesia' and/or that five-year Eighties hiatus, it proved to be more than worth the wait.

The sheer commitment this old man, with a history of chronic back trouble, brought to each night's performance, playing for a hundred minutes yet never letting the intensity drop, and the warm applause that greeted each and every new song, proved that although the world outside may be decidedly broken, the compact between this consummate artist and his audience never would be, not as long as there was another joint he could head for, another song he could sing when he got there. Already, his booking agent was pencilling in shows to fill 2022, including another residency at the London Palladium.

It is a long way from Highway One to Route One, from Point Dume to Key West, but he remains determined to play every pissant pit stop along the way. 'Twas ever so. The tour has even been billed, somewhat optimistically, as the *Rough and Rowdy Ways World-Wide Tour / 2021-24*. As he'd told MTV back in 1986, when the media fondly imagined pop videos might replace live performance:

> I'll be doing this for as long as I'm around. And all the people I admired, they've all done it all the way to the end, too. It's all I do.

Postlude

How Much Longer?

He's a very ordinary person; he's full of compassion; he has no ego. People don't really know him.

Beattie Zimmerman, 1990.

All of my deep relationships are concerned with my work. My work is my life.

Bob Dylan, to Barbara Kerr, February 1978.

I can talk about [Bob Dylan], but my dad belongs to me and four [sic] other people.

Jakob Dylan, 2005.

I wake and I'm one person, and when I go to sleep I know for certain I'm somebody else. I don't know who I am most of the time.

Bob Dylan, to David Gates, September 1997.

The[se fans] think they know me because I've written some song that happens to bother them in a certain way . . . That's got nothing to do with me . . . I think I could prove that in any court!

Bob Dylan, to Christopher Sykes, 17th October 1986.

The truth is there's not much that they can really pry into now. I've got walls up all over the place.

Bob Dylan, to Robert Hilburn, 30th October 1983.

Q: What would you do if you met yourself in the street?
Bob Dylan: I'd probably cross the street.

Verona press conference 29th May 1984.

Q: What does Bob Dylan think of Bob Dylan?
Bob Dylan: Bob Dylan doesn't ever think about Bob Dylan.

Sydney press conference 10th February 1986.

Bill Flanagan: Every time I turn on PBS, they're running another documentary about folk music in the sixties, and all sorts of people from that scene are talking about you like you were best friends. Does that bug you?
BD: I don't know, maybe we *were* best friends.

2017.

Here was a fantastically talented cat, who was a pathological liar with an identity crisis . . . [But] whatever he said offstage, onstage he told the truth.

Dave Van Ronk, 1970.

I don't remember a damn thing.

Bob Dylan, to Martin Scorsese, 2017.

He forgets what he wants to forget, but if he wants to remember something, he'll remember forever.

Joan Baez, to Anthony Scaduto, 1970.

★

Of the handful of true geniuses who bestride 20th century Pop Culture, Dylan certainly intends to emulate the 70-year-old Orson Welles and the 93-year old P.G. Wodehouse, both of whom were found slumped over a typewriter or notebook, still working on something new, when their time came. As he asked Doug Brinkley rhetorically during one of their ad hoc conversations in the past decade, when the subject of retirement came up, 'Are you still gonna be writing on your death-bed?'

But where Orson Welles's last night on earth surely departs from Dylan's preferred brief is in what he was doing before he came home and started shaping another never-to-be-completed screenplay: he was on the *Merv Griffin Show*, sharing a sofa with his latest, semi-authorized biographer, Barbara Leaming, talking up her gossipy skim-read, and loving the opportunity to talk some more about his favourite subject:

himself, having lived a life full of struggle and strife, with three very different wives and a string of mistresses, but one refreshingly free of scandal. For that, he had to thank a Chicago cop who one night in the early 1940s warned him that there was an underage girl in his hotel room, and a photographer at the ready; he was being set-up by the Hearst organization for daring to create a fictional version of their beloved leader, in Charles Foster Kane.

If Welles had a lucky escape, Dylan, who has certainly given his libido as much free rein as Orson ever did, got to eighty only having to deal with cops who didn't know who he was. But in August 2021, having hit the big 8-0 three months earlier, words he'd uttered in jest in his 2003 film, *Masked and Anonymous*, came back to haunt him:

> You can make heroes out of bums and villains out of good, upstanding people with the stroke of your pen. You've got the right to slander anybody, assassinate anybody's character. You can tell any kind of story you want, and you never have to reveal your sources. It's called freedom of the press.

He now found himself, suddenly and unexpectedly, on the end of a lawsuit from a plainly damaged woman – ironically, with the same initials as Our Lord – alleging that he had sexually abused her back in April or May 1965, when she was aged just twelve. It was hardly his m.o., and the complete lack of corroborative evidence damned only her, but Dylan knew his Benjamin Franklin, 'It takes many good deeds to build a good reputation, only one bad one to lose it.' To his eternal credit, he realized, joke or no joke, he needed to take this absurd allegation seriously and threw the full weight of his legal team behind refuting the allegations.

The mass media soon clicked into gear, and in their post-PC way displayed zero interest in balanced reporting. The BBC – the one broadcast organization *legally* bound by its charter to present unbiased news – ran a three-minute item on its *One O'Clock News* on the day Ms Carara filed papers, reiterating the charges in detail before deigning to note, 'Mr Dylan denies the allegations.'* Meanwhile, the

---

* When the case was finally dropped by Dylan's accuser, in July 2022, the BBC failed to even report it.

Somerset-based 'world's leading authority' sat waiting for the phone to ring, before being contacted by three *American* media outlets, *Variety*, *Rolling Stone* and *Huffington Post*.

Two days later, the BBC website finally noticed that said authority's 1995 chronology of Dylan's career, *Dylan Day by Day*, cast serious doubt on the woman's claims. It had evidently taken their twenty-something researcher that long to get off that 'news resource', Twitter, and discover Dylan was overseas for almost the entire period, flirting with some of the most desirable, womanly women on the planet: Marianne Faithfull, Nico, Dana Gillespie, Joan Baez, Sara Lownds, even Sally Grossman, all of them besotted with him.

And then there was the question of Dylan's private attitude to those who preyed on young girls. Back in 1993, when allegations relating to Michael Jackson's disturbing interest in underage boys'n'girls first arose, Cooky tried to give 'Wacko Jacko' the benefit of the doubt. Dylan flew into a rage, making it plain he considered the pop star's alleged actions wholly beyond the pale. At around the same time he began writing a song he never finished, about a dirty man who preyed on young girls, one couplet of which was as unequivocal as could be, 'If it'd been my daughter he took up to his house and fed her cocoa/ He'd've had his brains rubbed out.'

Surely, given the vast body of 'confessional' work from the man, if Dylan had ever been that way inclined, there'd be a hint, a flicker, a subtext somewhere in his lyrics, published or unpublished. After all, Van Morrison wrote a series of songs in the first four years of his recording career with lyrics apparently referring to 14-year-old girls: 'Hey Girl', 'Mighty Like A Rose', 'Cyprus Avenue', and 'Little Girl', in the commercially released recording of which he audibly shouted 'I want to fuck you!'

Had not Dylan spent almost his whole life dealing with people who read too much into his lyrics? As he once bemoaned to his favourite promotions man, 'The problem is, when people meet me, they think they're meeting the lyrics. I know how heavy the songs are, but they're the songs. I'm me.' Another of the true popular geniuses, Fred Astaire, nursed a similar complaint about women wanting to dance with him, expecting him to be the romantic lead he played in his films.

How many times did Dylan need to say, as he did in 1997 to David Gates – sent by *Newsweek*, the first major national weekly to libel him back in 1963 – 'I'm not the songs. It's like somebody expecting

Shakespeare to be Hamlet, or Goethe to be Faust.' Actually, as a per-forming artist, the line was bound to be a little more blurred, as he fully admitted to a lady reporter in 1978, 'It's a fine line between where I am [in a song] and where I'm projecting – . . . what I'm familiar with, [and] what I know to be the truth.'

At some point, others' interpretations of what his songs *mean* had perforce become as water off a drake's back. As Faridi McFree told me, 'He never seemed to be upset by people's interpretations, no matter how avant-garde they were.' He got a kick out of some of 'em, just not when they didn't even listen to the words, as his new accuser Ms Car-ara self-evidently had not, writing privately to a Dylan fan who had herself been abused as a child, referencing the line about Dylan marry-ing a twelve-year old prostitute in 'Key West'. Save that it was the narrator who was twelve years old, *she* was a prostitute, and the moon was a balloon.

Having informed Randy Anderson, twenty-four years earlier, 'At dif-ferent times you confront people who . . . are only seeing . . . whatever they're choosing to see,' he had little choice but to confront Carara, and by proxy, a whole legal system which convicted, on the word of a woman who stood to gain $12 million if she was believed, a very rich pugilist of rape without forensic evidence or a single eyewitness. Thankfully, Dylan has the money to fight – which was presumably the motivation of his accuser and her lawyer (a character straight out of a John Grisham novel), forlornly hoping other teary-eyed tramps might come forth to corroborate his predatory paedophilia. Fat chance.

And still those armoured trucks kept rolling up to Point Dume. One can only imagine what went through the mind, such as it was, of Dylan's accuser when she read that he'd sold his song publishing for 'an estimated $300 million', the previous December. Actually, the figure was more like half a billion, but hey, who's counting? Dylan clearly was, because he promptly almost doubled his money by selling future rights from catalogue sales to Sony Music.

He was rolling in the stuff, having learnt the hard way, money talks. That ongoing education also meant his attitude revolved a full 180 degrees. After telling Kurt Loder during their September 1987 drinking session, 'They'd like to use my tunes for different beer companies and perfumes and automobiles . . . But, shit, I didn't write them for that reason,' twenty years later he was telling trustworthy Edna, 'It matters not to me which commercials or movies or TV shows [my songs] are [used] in.'

By then, he'd been selling song-rights to advertisers for a decade or more, amused by fans who had risen up in arms on 'his' behalf when a Canadian bank used 'The Times They Are A-Changin' – a song he said, on the day he wrote it, 'It seems to be what people want.' Dylan found the whole furore hilarious, chuckling to Cooky, 'Wait till they see the other two [ads].' By the time he opened up to Edna, he was under no illusions as to what made the world go round: 'So much has been done to me and to my work, and it's been exploited on such grandiose levels with no thought of me, that you get to a point where you don't care anymore. Anything that comes your way is better than somebody taking it their way.'

It was an attitude he shared with P.G. Wodehouse, who like Dylan (and Robert Graves's Claudius) had learnt the hard way, trust no-one. Ripped off by his first American collaborator and his first American agent, 'Plum' – to his friends – learnt to know the numbers and demand top-dollar advances at every turn, and to never, ever undersell oneself. Ditto, Dylan.

If Dylan officially became a billionaire in 2021, the year also brought him a(nother) disappointing development. He was being sued by the widow of one of his most cherished collaborators, Jacques Levy. The woman he'd introduced to Jacques, Claudia, wanted seven million dollars, convinced she was entitled to some of the proceeds from the sale of *his* publishing. The outcome of the case was never in doubt, but it certainly affirmed that no good deed goes unpunished. Contrary to the stereotype, Dylan had generously given her late husband 40% of the publishing on songs they co-wrote when 25% (for half the lyrics) would have been the norm. As for Claudia, she had evidently forgotten, as Cooky had not, 'He never forgets a betrayal.'

Hence, the moment when Dylan confronted Elliott Landy, who had been his preferred photographer for a few years in Woodstock, at Bill Clinton's January 1993 inauguration, about a nude photo of his baby daughter, Anna, that had recently appeared in a German-only photobook. A plainly drunk Dylan poked the photographer, saying, 'That's my daughter!' while Elliot Mintz looked on aghast. Landy was left in no doubt that any bridge between him and Bob had been definitively burnt to the ground.

How Just Bob reconciles his own lack of forgiveness with his professed Christian beliefs and the teachings of Christ on the Mount as regards the turning of the cheek, his alter-ego isn't about to explain. He has rarely ever explained his own beliefs, even in private – or at least not since 1979-80, when the Vineyard Fellowship temporarily melted the sceptical part of his mind.

The one time he tried to explain his worldview to that good Catholic girl, Cooky, he told her 'believing in God isn't enough; that you had to go through Jesus to get to God, "To live your life in Jesus." "Jesus being like a holy man?" "He's more than a holy man. He was sent here for a *purpose*." "But what exactly does it mean to accept Jesus as your saviour? What effect does that have?" . . . [Still, he refused to be] pinned down . . . falling back on the necessity of studying The Bible . . . He would sometimes make statements from one end of the religious spectrum and then later from the opposite . . . He seemed able to reconcile for himself both Jewish and Christian beliefs at the same time.'

Keats called it negative capability. Dylan calls his inner duality 'my twin, that enemy within'. Perhaps he had no choice but to referee his own internal struggle. The world he inhabited made it necessary, just as experience made him at times nostalgic for a wild and wicked youth. As he told Al Kooper in 1986, between lines, 'God, I miss the Sixties.' He could even joke about the separation of Self to a journalist at a mid-Nineties press conference who asked him if, by the mid-Eighties, he had forgotten 'who you were when you were young?'

Dylan rifled back, 'I had forgotten about that [person] *long* before that.' But he hadn't, he didn't, forget. When he saw Cooky in the audience at a 2006 show in Foggia, nine years after they last spoke, he immediately started throwing looks and playing to her, making her laugh out loud. She had always known he had a memory like a vice, having once used the expression, 'Rich peoples' sand in the suitcase is just as coarse and yellow as any other sand,' only for him to remind her she'd said it once before, years earlier.

Even now, at business meetings, his recall of detail astounds others. Of course, he'd prefer people to think his memory is shot, and not realize it is just another smokescreen emanating from behind the shades. When he asked his ex-publicist, Chris O'Dell, in 1986, 'Did I ever look like that? Was I ever really that person?' he knew the answer. It just wasn't one he was about to share with Martin Scorsese in a 2019 recreation of the tour Dylan and Dell shared. Let 'em all think he doesn't 'remember a damn thing'.

As his long-time art director, Geoff Gans, noted, after his boss looked longingly at a set of Doug Gilbert photos from Woodstock 1964, 'Bob really liked [the fact] you can see the furniture, which . . . really dates the time. He also liked [seeing] photos of him sitting around with a bunch of people, because they weren't just focused on him.'

That is what it had been like ever since – people focused only on *him*. And yet the way he used to sing Don Gibson's 'I'd Be A Legend In My Time', back in 1989, suggests he sometimes enjoys toying with the notion, 'If heartaches brought fame . . . I'd be a legend in my time.' Anyone who fondly imagines he has no interest in Fame is a fool. He's as much of a sucker for stories of and by the famous as any Mr Jones, as evidenced by a story Wilton Morley told me. (For who, dear reader, wouldn't give their right n-t to have been in Morley's shoes the night in 1986 when he was seated with Lauren Bacall – 'Betty' to her friends – and Bob in the bar of the Sebel Town House in Sydney?)

That evening Wilton was with two members 'of a very exclusive club, . . . the 20th Century American Icons Club. Bacall was married to one of its members, Humphrey Bogart, and engaged to another, Frank Sinatra. [But] what Bob really wants to know, this hot January [sic] night, is how did Bogart handle being a member of the club. Betty is patient: "Well Bob, you see Bogart wasn't really Bogart when he was alive. [He] became Bogart after he died." . . . But Bob presses her, and the conversation takes a surreal turn. [He wants to know:] "When is a legend *really* a legend?" '

However much the singer yearned to know the answer that evening, the more pressing question – at this remove, anyway – is how do you cope with people who treat you as a legend? Do you lock yourself in your room and write, while your wife throws extravagant parties downstairs to people who bore you to tears, like Wodehouse did in later life, or do you find a way to amuse yourself, to have a little fun?

If Dylan the whippersnapper, with his verbal rapier ever at the ready, used to do exactly that in his wild mercury years, he has done it less frequently as the years passed. But even in the early Nineties, Susan Ross would see him sometimes lie 'for sport, just to see how much he can confuse and baffle an unwitting subject'. The ongoing quest for artistic elbow-room has required him to insist, 'The people that listen to me . . . hear what I'm doing, but where I come from is a place they might not know, and that's what forms my music,' which is his own special way of saying, 'You think you know me well, but you don't know me.'

As he started to make it all but impossible for anyone outside the vetted and verified interviewers of choice to speak to him on the record, he also started to distance himself from the work, increasingly inclined to write about figures far removed from his daily life, in situations he can only have picked up from his prodigious reading. Removing the first person from almost all of his 21st century songs has made every original album a mixed bag. Still, he remains convinced it suits him well.

What is perhaps odder is the distance he has allowed to grow between him and fellow musicians, when even in the Nineties, as Cooky noted, 'Nothing rated above hanging with the guys playing music.' Robben Ford, who played on Dylan's last play-through album of original songs in 1990, tells of a joint tour Dylan did with Phil Lesh in 2000, 'We were out on the road together for two and a half *months*. And Dylan wouldn't allow people near him at all. You just couldn't go *near* the guy. You couldn't be in the hallway if he was walking down the hall.' Even Jim Keltner, his greatest timekeeper, admits, 'He's never been to my house in fifty years.'

The explanation may be simple. He gets on best with those who learnt early on to stop digging; like the man who saved his career at Columbia and introduced him to a grown-up audience, Johnny Cash, who told his own biographer, 'I never did try to dig into his personal life and he didn't try to dig into mine. If he's aloof and hard to get to, I can understand why. So many people take advantage of him.'

A friend of the Devil and other angels flying too close to the ground, Dylan has known Milton's Paradise and Dante's Inferno. He'd still prefer the immortality of not dying to that of his work living on after him, but he knows f'sure the sands of time are running out.

If he could – and perhaps he can – he might cast his memory back to the summer of 1986, when he was sitting around at a session for a car-crash of an album (*Knocked Out Loaded*), from which few expected his recording career to recover. He was envisaging a time when he had used up every grain of sand allotted. But he still wasn't about to make it any easier for the man sat across from him, Mikal Gilmore, to make sense of the picture he would – some decades later, he hoped – leave behind:

> That day's gonna come when there aren't gonna be any more [of my] records, and then people [like you] . . . are gonna have to look at it all. And I don't know what the picture will be . . . I can't help you in that area.

★ ★ ★

The biographer at work . . . is like the professional burglar, breaking into a house, rifling through certain drawers that he has good reason to think contain the jewelry and money, and triumphantly bearing his loot away. The voyeurism and busybodyism that impel writers and readers of biography alike are obscured by an apparatus of scholarship designed to give the enterprise an appearance of banklike blandness and solidity . . . The transgressive nature of biography is rarely acknowledged.

Janet Malcolm, The Silent Woman *(1993).*

Notes On Sources

Below are the primary resources for *Far Away From Myself*. Where a quote has the following code, . . . [] . . ., it indicates that it is a composite of two (or more) quotes from the same person. To save time, space and energy, the various biographical sources, below, have each been given a capital-letter code – e.g. [AA] – to indicate where it has been used in the relevant chapter/s. I have included both official and unofficial publications of Dylan's own words, as many of his more important poems and unpublished lyrics were book-legged in the 1970s and 1980s. The *Some Other Kinds of Songs* bookleg has now been incorporated into Olof Björner's *About Bob Dylan* website, seemingly with permission or at least the tacit consent of the copyright-holder.

The manuscripts listed below pertain to material which exists outside the official Dylan archive in Tulsa, the resources of which remain vast and, as yet, not fully catalogued. Of the Dylan fanzines, a vital resource for Dylan researchers for well nigh forty years, just the two asterisked – both based in the UK – remain current. Finally, a note of thanks to the various contributors to the 'Reference resources' section for blazing a trail, in most cases unaware that the Internet would place most or all of their work into the public domain without attribution or recognition, for the Internet 'experts' (an oxymoron) to misuse. As they say, no good deeds go unpunished.

Please note: The considerable collection of Dylan manuscripts housed at the Gilcrease Museum in Tulsa were, when I inspected them, divided into approximately 130 boxes, containing a variable number of individual folders. Because the material, when it was acquired by the George Kaiser Foundation back in 2016, had been given a somewhat scattershot arrangement – the exigencies of history having been sacrificed in favour of confidentiality – the numbering system given to it was often arbitrary and at odds with the internal evidence.

The Covid crisis has enabled the Bob Dylan Archive to recatalogue all this material, led by the indefatigable Mark Davidson. But it means that the Box and Folder numbering system I used during my on-site research no longer applies, and therefore citing the Box and Folder numbers I used would be both confusing and pointless. Suffice to say, if an unpublished quote is not sourced in the following notes, it is from Tulsa. Once again, I gratefully acknowledge the archive's ongoing help and support in bringing this project to fruition.

Biographical portraits and oral histories:
Aronowitz, Al – *Bob Dylan and The Beatles* (1st Books, 2003) [AA]
Baez, Joan – *And A Voice To Sing With: A Memoir* (Summit Books, 1987) [JB]
Balfour, Victoria – *Rock Wives* (William Morrow, 1986) [VB]
Barker, Derek – *Too Much of Nothing* (Red Planet, 2018) [DB]
Barker, Derek – *Isis: A Bob Dylan Anthology* (Helter-Skelter, 2001) [Isis Anthology]
Bell, Ian – *Once Upon A Time: The Lives of Bob Dylan* (Mainstream, 2012) [IB]
Berger, Glenn – *Never Say No To A Rock Star* (Schaffner Press, 2016) [GB]

Bicker, Stewart P. [a.k.a. Patrick Webster] – *Friends & Other Strangers: Bob Dylan In Other People's Words* (pp, 1985) [F&OS]

Boni, Claude-Angèle – *Stuck Inside of Mobile (with a rhapsody for Bob Dylan)* (pp) [CAB]

Brooks, Harvey (w/ Frank Beacham) – *View From The Bottom* (Tangible Press, 2020) [HB]

Bayer-Sager, Carole – *They're Playing Our Song* (Simon & Schuster, 2016)

Cohen, John – *Here and Gone* (Steidl, 2014) [CBS]

Colby, Paul (w/ Martin Fitzpatrick) – *The Bitter End: Hanging Out at America's Nightclub* (Cooper Square Press, 2002) [PC]

Cornyn, Stan – *Exploding* (Harper Entertainment, 2002) [SC]

Davis, Clive (w/ James Willwerth) – *Clive: Inside The Record Business* (Ballantine Books, 1976) [CD]

Dylan, Bob – *Chronicles Volume One* (Simon & Schuster, 2004) [CHR]

Eliot, Marc – *Rockonomics: The Money Behind The Music* (Omnibus Press, 1989) [ME]

Everett, Rupert – *Red Carpets & Other Banana Skins* (Petit Merde, 2006) [RE]

Foulk, Ray – *Stealing Dylan From Woodstock* (Medina Publishing, 2015) [RF]

Gans, Terry – *Surviving In A Ruthless World: Bob Dylan's Voyage To Infidels* (Red Planet, 2020) [TG]

Gillespie, Dana (w/ David Shasha) – *Weren't Born A Man* (Hawksmoor, 2020)

Gottlieb, Robert – *Avid Reader: A Life* (Farrar, Straus and Giroux, 2016)

Greenfield, Robert – *Bill Graham Presents* (Da Capo, 2004) [BGP]

Griffin, Sid – *Million Dollar Bash: Bob Dylan, The Band and the Basement Tapes* (revised ed., Jawbone, 2014) [M$B]

Griffin, Sid – *Shelter From The Storm: Bob Dylan's Rolling Thunder Years* (Jawbone, 2010) [SG]

Hajdu, David – *Positively 4th Street: The Lives and Times of Joan Baez, Bob Dylan, Mimi & Richard Fariña* (Farrar, Straus & Giroux, 2001) [DH]

Harrison, George – *I Me Mine: An Autobiography* (Pocket Books, 1981) [GH]

Helm, Levon (w/ Stephen Davis) – *This Wheel's On Fire: Levon Helm and the Story of The Band* (William Morrow, 1993) [LH]

Heylin, Clinton – *Dylan Behind The Shades: 20th Anniversary Edition* (Faber & Faber, 2011) [BTS]

Heylin, Clinton – *Trouble In Mind: Bob Dylan's Gospel Years* (Route, 2017) [TIM]

Heylin, Clinton – *No One Else Could Play That Tune* (Route, 2018) [NOE]

Hilburn, Robert – *Johnny Cash; The Life* (W&N, 2013) [RH]

Hoskyns, Barney – *Small Town Talk* (Faber & Faber, 2016) [STT]

Idle, Eric – *Always Look On The Bright Side of Life* (W&N, 2019) [EI]

Kemp, Louie – *Dylan & Me: 50 Years of Adventures* (Westrose Press, 2019) [LK]

Lanois, Daniel – *Soul Mining: A Musical Life* (Faber & Faber, 2010) [DL]

MacKay, Kathleen – *Bob Dylan: Intimate Insights* (Omnibus Press, 2007) [KM]

McLagan, Ian – *All The Rage: A Rock & Roll Odyssey* (Sidgwick & Jackson, 1998) [IM]

Marshall, Scott – *Bob Dylan: A Spiritual Life* (WND Books, 2017) [SM]

Martin, Robert – *Dix Jours Avec Bob Dylan* [pp, 2018] [DJABD]

Martyn, Beverley – *Sweet Honesty: The Beverley Martyn Story* (Grosvenor House, 2011) [BM]

Maymudes, Victor (w/ Jacob Maymudes) – *Another Side of Bob Dylan* (St. Martin's Press, 2014) [VM]

O'Dell, Chris – *Miss O'Dell: My Hard Days and Long Nights . . .* (Touchstone, 2009) [COD]

Odegard, Kevin (w/ Andy Gill) – *A Simple Twist of Fate: Bob Dylan and The Making of Blood On The Tracks* (Da Capo, 2005) [KO]

Ostrow, Stuart – *Present At The Creation* (Applause Books, 2005) [SO]

Regan, Ken – *All Access: The Rock 'n' Roll Photography of . . .* (Insight Editions, 2011) [KR]

Robertson, Robbie – *Testimony* (Crown Archetype, 2016) [RR]

Rotolo, Suze – *A Freewheelin' Time* (Aurum, 2008) [SR]

Sagal, Katey – *Grace Notes: My Recollections* (Gallery Books, 2017) [KS]

Scaduto, Anthony – *Bob Dylan* (W. H. Allen, 1972) [AS]

Scaduto, Anthony (w/ Stephanie Trudeau) – *The Dylan Tapes* (Univ. of Minnesota Press, 2022) [TDT]

Schatzberg, Jerry – *Dylan* (ACC Art Books, 2018) [JS]

Schumacher, Michael – *There But For Fortune: The Life of Phil Ochs* (Hyperion, 1996) [MS]

Seydor, Paul – *The Authentic Death & Contentious Afterlife of Pat Garrett and Billy The Kid* (North-western University Press, 2015) [PS]

Shain, Britta Lee – *Seeing The Real You At Last: Life & Love on the Road with Bob Dylan* (Jawbone, 2016) [BLS]

Shelton, Robert – *No Direction Home* (New English Library, 1986) [RS]

Shepard, Sam – *Rolling Thunder Logbook* (Viking, 1977) [RTL]

Sloman, Larry – *On The Road with Bob Dylan* (Bantam Books, 1978) [OTRBD]

Spitz, Bob – *Dylan: A Biography* (McGraw-Hill, 1989) [BS]

Sounes, Howard – *Down The Highway: The Life of Bob Dylan* (Grove Press, 2001) [HS]

Taplin, Jonathan – *The Magic Years: Scenes From A Rock-and-Roll Life* (Heyday, 2021) [JT]

Thompson, Toby: *Positively Main Street* (Coward-McCann, 1971) [TT]

Van Zandt, Steve – *Unrequited Infatuations: A Memoir* (White Rabbit, 2021) [SVZ]

Weberman, A.J. – *My Life In Garbology* (Stonehill, 1980) [AJW]

Weissman, Dick – *Which Side Are You On?* (Continuum, 2006) [DW]

Wexler, Jerry (w/ David Ritz) – *Rhythm and The Blues* (Knopf, 1993) [JW]

Williams, Paul – *What Happened?* (Entwistle Books, 1980)[PW]

Yaffe, David – *Reckless Daughter: A Profile of Joni Mitchell* (Macmillan, 2017) [DY]

Dylan's own published works:

Dylan, Bob – *Tarantula* (Macmillan, 1971)

Dylan, Bob – *Writings & Drawings* (Knopf, 1973)

Dylan, Bob – *Lyrics 1962–1985* (Knopf, 1985)

Dylan, Bob – *Some Other Kinds of Songs* (bookleg, 1987)

Dylan, Bob – *Whaaat? The Original Playboy Interview* (bookleg, 1988)

Dylan, Bob (ed. John Tuttle) – *In His Own Write: Personal Sketches Vol. 2* (bookleg, 1990)

Dylan, Bob (ed. John Tuttle) – *In His Own Write: Personal Sketches Vol. 3* (bookleg, 1992)

Dylan, Bob – *Drawn Blank* (Random House, 1994)

Dylan, Bob – *The Drawn Blank Series* (Prestel, 2008)

Dylan, Bob – *The Brazil Series* (Prestel, 2010)

Dylan, Bob – *The Asia Series* (Gagosian Gallery, 2011)

Dylan, Bob – *Revisionist Art: Thirty Works by Bob Dylan* (Abrams, 2013)

Dylan, Bob – *The Lyrics* (annotated edition, edited by Christopher Ricks) (Simon & Schuster, 2014)

Dylan, Bob – *The Beaten Path* (Halcyòn, 2016)

Dylan, Bob – *The Nobel Lecture* (Simon & Schuster 2017)

Dylan, Bob – *Mondo Scripto* (Halcyon, 2018)

Dylan, Bob – *The Philosophy of Modern Song* (Simon & Schuster, 2022)

Reference resources:

Anon. ('Artur') – *Every Mind Polluting Word: Assorted Dylan Utterances* (online)

Cable, Paul – *Bob Dylan: His Unreleased Recordings* (Dark Star, 1978)

Dundas, Glen – *Tangled Up In Tapes* (pp, various editions 1987–99)

Dunn, Tim – *The Bob Dylan Copyright Files 1962–2007* (AuthorHouse, 2008)

Heylin, Clinton – *Bob Dylan: The Recording Sessions 1960–94* (St Martin's Press, 1995)

Heylin, Clinton – *Bob Dylan Day By Day 1941–1995* (Schirmer Books, 1996)

Krogsgaard, Michael – 'Bob Dylan: The Recording Sessions', published initially in *The Telegraph* and *The Bridge*; now available (still uncorrected) online

Maus, Christoph (w/ Alan Fraser) – *Bob Dylan Worldwide: An Anthology of Original Album, Singles & EP Releases 1961–81* (Maus of Music, 2016)

'Rolling Stone' (eds.) – *Rolling Stone: Cover To Cover 1967–2007* (Bondi, DVD-ROMx4)

Roques, Dominique – *The Great White Answers: The Bob Dylan Bootleg Records* (pp, 1980)

Useful websites:
About Bob Dylan
Expecting Rain
Flagging Down The Double E's
Rocksbackpages.com
Searching For A Gem

Dylan fanzines:
The Bridge – 75 issues (to date)
Isis – (218 issues)
The Telegraph (56 issues)
Dignity (31 issues)
Look Back (32 issues)
On The Tracks (25 issues)
Judas! (19 issues)
Homer The Slut (11 issues)
Zimmerman Blues (10 issues)
Who Threw The Glass (8 issues)
Endless Road (7 issues)
Occasionally (5 issues)

Useful Dylan anthologies:
Cott, Jonathan – *Bob Dylan: The Essential Interviews* (Simon & Schuster, 2006)
McGregor, Craig (ed.) – *Bob Dylan: A Retrospective* (Morrow, 1972)
Percival, Dave (ed.) – *The Dust of Rumour* (pp, 1985)
Percival, Dave (ed.) – *This Wasn't Written In Tin Pan Alley* (pp, 1989)

Other books used as resources:
Aronowitz, Al – 'A Family Album' [*Age of Rock* ed. Eisen, Vintage 1969]
Avery, Kevin (ed.) – *Everything Is An Afterthought: The Life and Writings of Paul Nelson* (Fantagraphics Books, 2011)
Banauch, Eugen (ed.) – *Refractions of Bob Dylan* (Manchester University Press, 2015)
Barker, Derek – 'The Story of The Hurricane' [*Isis: A Bob Dylan Anthology*, Helter-Skelter 2001]
Dawson, Jim & Propes, Steve – *What Was The First Rock'n'Roll Record* (Faber & Faber, 1992)
Fariña, Richard – 'A Generation Singing Out', in *Long Time Coming and A Long Time Gone* (Random House, 1969)
Flanagan, Bill – *Written In My Soul: Rock's Great Songwriters Talk About Creating Their Music* (Contemporary Books, 1986)
Rick Gekoski – *Guarded By Dragons: Encounters with Rare Books and Rare People* (Constable, 2021)
Gray, Michael & Bauldie, John (ed.) – *All Across The Telegraph: A Bob Dylan Handbook* (Sidgwick & Jackson, 1987)
Gray, Michael – 'Rough and Rowdy Ways', in *Outtakes On Bob Dylan* (Route, 2021)
Heylin, Clinton – *Rain Unravelled Tales: A Rumourography* (omnibus edition) (pp, 1985)
Heylin, Clinton – *Revolution In The Air: The Songs of Bob Dylan 1957–73* (Constable, 2009)
Heylin, Clinton – *Still On The Road: The Songs of Bob Dylan 1974-2009* (Constable, 2010)
Lethem, Jonathan – *The Ecstasy of Influence* (Doubleday, 2011)
MacLeish, Archibald – *The Letters of . . .* (Houghton-Mifflin, 1983)

Marcus, Greil – *Invisible Republic* (Picador, 1997)

Miles – *Bob Dylan In His Own Words* (Omnibus Press, 1978)

O'Brien, Lucy – *Annie Lennox: Sweet Dreams Are Made of This* (St Martin's Press, 1993) [LB]

Pat Garrett & Billy The Kid press book

Pickering, Stephen – *Dylan: A Commemoration* (pp, 1971)

Reineke, Hank – *Ramblin' Jack Elliott: The Never-Ending Highway* (Scarecrow Press, 2009)

Seay, Davin & Neely, Mary – *Stairway To Heaven* (Ballantine Books, 1986)

Sheehy, Colleen J. & Swiss, Thomas (eds.) – *Highway 61 Revisited: Bob Dylan's Road From Minnesota To The World* (University of Minnesota Press, 2009)

Williams, Paul – 'One Year Later' and 'Blood on the Tracks', in *Watching The River Flow* (Omnibus Press, 1996)

Wurlitzer, Rudy – *Pat Garrett and Billy The Kid* (Signet, 1973)

Zollo, Paul – *Songwriters On Songwriting* (Da Capo Press, 1997)

Interviews with others [with chapter references]:

[CH] = Clinton Heylin

[TWM] = *The Wicked Messenger* [Ian Woodward's Newsletter, 1980-2009]

Kenny Aaronson [CH]		5.5; 5.6;
Josh Abbey	(i) [TG]	5.1;
	(ii) [CH]	5.2; 5.4;
Howard Alk [*Take One* 3/78]		4.2;
Colin Allen [*The Telegraph* #28]		5.2;
Dave Alvin	(i) [transcript from Peter Doggett]	5.4;
	(ii) [pleasekillme.com 13/12/20]	5.4;
Dave Amram [CH]		3.3; 3.4; 3.6;
Al Aronowitz [Isis Anthology]		3.2;
Mary Alice Artes [SM]		4.4;
Joan Baez	(i) [*Mojo* 6/19]	4.2; 6.4;
	(ii) [*Rolling Stone* 15/1/76]	4.3;
	(iii) [TDT]	Postlude;
Arthur Baker [*Uncut* 6/21]		5.2;
Bucky Baxter	(i) [TWM #4369]	6.2;
Barry Beckett [*The Bridge* #37]		4.5;
Bonnie Beecher [HS]		6.1;
Glenn Berger [CH]		3.8;
Ellen Bernstein [CH]		3.7; 3.8; 4.3; 5.3;
Joel Bernstein [CH]		4.2; 4.3;
Ronee Blakley	(i) [OTRBD]	4.3;
	(ii) [*Mojo* 5/11]	5.5;
Rich Blakin [CH]		3.8;
Michael Bloomfield	(i) [*Hit Parader* 6/68]	3.1; 3.5;
	(ii) [OTRBD]	3.8; 4.3;
Michael Bolton [*Rolling Stone* 18/11/19]		5.8;
Bono [*NME* 19+26/12/87]		5.4;
Terry Botwick [SM]		4.5;
Farir Bouhafa [*Rolling Stone* 28/8/75]		4.2;
Pattie Boyd [CH]		3.3; 3.4; 4.4;
Jeff Bridges	(i) [*Mojo* 5/11]	6.2;
	(ii) [TWM #5562]	6.2;
Dave Bromberg	(i) [*Rolling Stone* 26/11/70]	3.5;

	(ii) [*Melody Maker* 10/7/71]	3.5;
	(iii) [*Uncut* 9/13]	3.5; 5.8;
	(iv) [WBAI 2007]	5.8;
	(v) [TWM #6178]	5.8;
Charlie Brown III	(i) [KO]	3.8;
	(ii) [*Rolling Stone* 21/11/74]	3.8;
Tony Brown [CH]		3.8;
Jackson Browne [*Uncut* 6/21]		6.5;
Kristie Buble [*Esquire* 23/1/14]		6.4;
John Bucklen [*On The Tracks* #8]		3.1;
Stephanie Buffington [CH]		4.2;
Malcolm Burn [*Uncut* online 2008]		5.6;
T-Bone Burnett [*Mojo* 6/19]		4.1;
Larry Campbell	(i) [STT]	3.3;
	(ii) [*Dylan Review* #3]	6.1;
Bill Carruthers [*South Bay Daily Breeze* 15/6/69]		3.4;
Martin Carthy [*The Telegraph* #42]		4.4;
Johnny Cash [Robert Hilburn]		3.3; Postlude;
Roseanne Cash [KM]		5.7;
Cindy Cashdollar [*Mojo* 07/10]		5.8; 6.1;
Larry Charles	(i) [Trevor Gibb]	5.6; 6.2; 6.3; 6.4;
	(ii) [Robert Polito]	6.1; 6.2; 6.4;
	(iii) [TWM #5312]	6.2;
	(iv) [TWM #5324]	6.2;
Liam Clancy	(i) [HS]	3.1;
	(ii) [TWM #4137]	5.7;
	(iii) [KM]	5.7;
	(iv) [*Rock'n'Reel* 1998]	6.1;
Tom Clancy [TDT]		3.4;
Alan Clark [*The Telegraph* #25]		5.1;
Wendy Clarke [*Barbara Rubin & The Exploding NY Underground* DVD]		3.5;
Al Clayton [*Uncut* 9/13]		3.4;
James Coburn [TCM 1987 interview]		3.6;
John Cohen	(i) [*Uncut* 9/13]	3.4;
	(ii) [*The Times* 26/8/13]	3.5;
Leonard Cohen	(i) [*Maclean's* 12/6/08]	6.4;
Chris Colley [RF]		3.4; 3.5;
Dick Cooper [SM]		4.6;
Ron Cornelius [*Melody Maker* 1/5/71]		3.4; 3.5;
Marshall Crenshaw [*Isis* #88]		5.5;
Richard Crooks [KO]		3.8;
Billy Cross [HS]		4.4;
Sheryl Crow	(i) [*Q* 10/98]	6.1;
	(ii) [*The Times* 9/98]	6.1;
Olivier Dahan [*Isis* #218]		6.4;
Charlie Daniels	(i) [*Melody Maker* 2/8/69]	3.3;
	(ii) [HS]	3.5;
Rick Danko	(i) [STT]	3.2;
	(ii) [*Woodstock Times* 3/85]	3.2;

Gordon Dawson [*The Telegraph* #37]   3.6;

Carolyn Dennis [Scott Marshall transcript]   4.4; 5.3; 6.4;

César Díaz [CH]   5.5; 5.7;

Jim Dickinson   (i) [*Uncut* online 2008]   5.8; 6.2;

   (ii) [*Perfect Sound Forever* 1997]   5.8;

   (iii) [*On The Tracks* #12]   5.8;

Bruce Dorfman   (i) [STT]   3.1; 3.3; 3.5;

   (ii) [HS]   3.3;

Pete Drake [*Guitar Player* 1973]   3.2;

Tim Drummond   (i) [*Rolling Stone* 29/8/74]   3.8;

   (ii) [*Rolling Stone* 19/6/14]   3.8; 4.6;

   (iii) [Scott Marshall transcript]   4.6;

Bill Dwyer [*The Gospel Years* DVD]   4.5;

Jakob Dylan [*New York Times* 10/5/05]   3.8; 4.5; Postlude;

Sara Dylan   (i) [OTRBD]   3.4; 4.1;

   (ii) [*Rolling Stone* 15/1/76]   4.1;

John Elderfield [CH]   6.3;

Ramblin' Jack Elliott   (i) [TDT]   3.3;

   (ii) [HS]   4.2;

Paul Emond [*Christianity Today* 1983]   4.5;

Mike Evans [OTRBD]   6.3;

Dan Fiala [*The Bridge* #52]   4.3; 4.7;

Jerry Fielding [*The Telegraph* #37]   3.6;

Robben Ford   (i) [*Uncut* online 2008]   5.7;

   (ii) [*Mojo* 5/11]   Postlude;

Ronnie Foulk [*The Times* 2/9/69]   3.4;

Raymond Foye [CH]   4.6; 5.8;

Rob Fraboni   (i) [*Recording Engineer* 3-4/74]   3.7;

   (ii) [CH]   3.7; 3.8;

Kinky Friedman [*Mojo* 6/19]   4.2;

Geoff Gans [Gilbert photobook]   Postlude;

Jerry Garcia   (i) [*Rolling Stone* 7/12/72]   3.6;

   (ii) [*Melody Maker* 13/5/89]   5.5;

Bruce Gary [CH]   4.8;

David Geffen [*Melody Maker* 8/12/73]   3.7;

Rosemary Gerrette [AS]   3.1;

Mikal Gilmore [CH]   5.4;

Allen Ginsberg   (i) [*World Journal Tribune* 14/10/66]   3.1;

   (ii) [F&OS]   3.2; 4.2; 5.1;

   (iii) [*Melody Maker* 18/3/72]   3.6;

   (iv) [*Rolling Stone* 15/1/76]   4.2;

   (v) [*Melody Maker* 3/1/81]   4.6;

   (vi) [*The Telegraph* #20]   Winterlude #4;

Debbie Gold [CH]   5.1; 5.2; 5.8;

Barry Goldberg [*Crawdaddy* 7/74]   3.7;

Robert Gottlieb [*Crawdaddy* 9/73]   3.6;

Susan Green [CH]   3.6; 4.2;

Sally Grossman [*The Observer* 2/11/14]   3.2;

Kenn Gulliksen [*Buzz* 11/80]   4.5;

Curtis Hanson [*Wonder Boys* DVD]   6.1;

Emmylou Harris [*Occasionally #5*]		4.1;
Jo Ann Harris [HS]		4.4;
George Harrison	(i) [F&OS]	3.6;
	(ii) [MTV 1988]	5.5;
	(iii) [AA]	6.1;
Don Heffington	(i) [CH]	5.2;
	(ii) [*Mojo* 5/11]	5.2;
Bruce Heiman [Scott Marshall transcript]		4.6;
Levon Helm [LH]		3.3
Robert Hilburn [CH]		4.6; 4.7;
Mark Howard	(i) [*Uncut* online 2008]	5.6; 5.8; 6.1; 6.2;
	(ii) [*Mojo* 5/11]	5.8;
Mel Howard	(i) [OTRBD]	4.1; 4.3;
	(ii) [*The Telegraph* #46]	4.2;
Garth Hudson	(i) [*Musician* 7/87]	3.2;
	(ii) [HS]	3.2;
Scott Huffstetler [*On The Tracks* #23]		4.5;
Don Ienner [*L.A. Times* 29/1/01]		6.1;
Ira Ingber [CH]		5.2; 5.4;
Markus Innocenti [CH]		5.3; 5.4;
Maurice Jacox [CH]		5.2;
Larry Johnson [CH – *Isis* #94]		4.1; 4.2;
Bob Johnston	(i) [STT]	3.2;
	(ii) [RH]	3.3;
	(iii) [*Rolling Stone* 22/7/71]	3.5;
	(iv) [*Melody Maker* 19/9/71]	3.5;
	(v) [*Uncut* 3/14]	3.5;
Rabbi Kasriel Kastel [*Christianity Today* 1983]		Winterlude #4;
Sue Kawalerski [CH]		3.6;
Dave Kelly	(i) [*Isis* #22]	4.5; 4.6;
	(ii) [SM]	4.5; Winterlude #4
Jim Keltner	(i) [*Uncut* 6/21]	3.6;
	(ii) [CH]	3.7; 4.6; 4.7; 4.8; 5.7;
	(iii) [*Uncut* online 2008]	5.8;
	(iv) [*Mojo* 5/11]	6.3;
Louie Kemp	(i) [CH]	3.7; 4.1; Winterlude #4; 6.3; 6.4;
	(ii) [Andy Greene – *Rolling Stone* online 2020]	Winterlude #4; 6.1;
David Kemper	(i) [*Uncut* online 2008]	5.8; 6.1; 6.2;
	(ii) [TWM #6397]	6.2;
Doug Kershaw [*South Bay Daily Breeze* 15/6/69]		3.4;
Louis Killen [*The Electric Muse*]		3.4;
Al Kooper	(i) [*Melody Maker* 12/12/70]	3.5;
	(ii) [*Uncut* 9/13]	3.5;
	(iii) [CH]	3.5; 5.4;
	(iv) [*Goldmine* 1994/RBP]	6.1;
Mark Knopfler [BTS]		5.1;

Kris Kristofferson	(i) [*Rolling Stone* 15/3/73]	3.5;
	(ii) [*Rolling Stone* 24/5/73]	3.6;
	(iii) [*Rolling Stone* 23/2/78]	3.6;
	(iv) [*Creem* 7/73]	3.6;
	(v) [KM]	3.7;
Barry Kornfeld	(i) [The Dylan Tapes]	3.4;
	(ii) [CH]	3.8; 5.1; 6.5;
Elliott Landy [*The Telegraph* #56]		3.3;
Daniel Lanois	(i) [*NME* 7/10/89]	5.6;
	(ii) [*Request* 10/89]	5.6;
	(iii) [TWM6424]	5.8;
	(iv) [*Uncut* online 2008]	5.6; 5.8;
Claudia Levy	(i) [*Mojo* 6/19]	3.8; 4.2; 5.8;
	(ii) [*Flagging Down The Double E's* 11/2020]	4.1;
Jacques Levy	(i) [Isis Anthology]	4.1;
	(ii) [*Melody Maker* 24/1/76]	4.1;
	(iii) [OTRBD]	4.1;
Judy Lewis [RF]		3.4;
David Lindley [*Uncut* 6/21]		5.7;
Stan Lynch	(i) [*Rolling Stone* 17+31/7/86]	5.3;
	(ii) [*The Telegraph* #25]	5.5;
David Mansfield [CH]		4.1; 4.2; 4.3; 4.4;
Richard Manuel [*Woodstock Times* 3/85]		3.2;
Bob Markel [*The Telegraph* #52]		3.5;
Tony Marsico [*The Bridge* #12]		5.1;
Richard Marquand [*The Telegraph* #28]		5.4;
Paul Martinson [Odegard interview tape]		3.8;
Paul McCartney [TWM #5647]		6.4;
Michael McClure [HS]		3.3;
Charlie McCoy	(i) [BS]	3.2;
	(ii) [*Uncut* 9/13]	3.5;
Regina McCrary	(i) [*On The Tracks* #18]	4.6;
	(ii) [*On The Tracks* #23]	4.6;
Faridi McFree	(i) [DB]	3.5;
	(ii) [CH]	4.2; 4.3; Postlude;
Roger McGuinn	(i) [*Rolling Stone* 29/10/70]	3.5;
	(ii) [*Melody Maker* 8/5/71]	3.6;
	(iii) [OTRBD]	3.7; 4.1; 4.5; 6.5;
Maria McKee [*The Telegraph* #27]		5.2;
Augie Meyers [*Mojo* 2010]		5.8; 6.2;
Bette Midler [*Rolling Stone* 20/11/82]		4.1;
Joni Mitchell	(i) [*South Bay Daily Breeze* 15/6/69]	3.4;
	(ii) [*Rolling Stone* 26/7/79]	3.7;
	(iii) [DY]	3.8; 4.1; 4.2; 6.1;
	(iv) [Grammy Interview 3/97]	4.6;
	(v) [*Rolling Stone* 30/5/91]	5.5; 5.7;
	(vi) [*Mojo* 12/94]	5.7;
	(vii) [*Mojo* 8/98]	6.1;
	(viii) [*L.A. Times* 22/4/10]	6.4;
Marvin Mitchelson [TWM #543]		4.2;

Wilton Morley [CH]   5.3; Postlude;
Van Morrison [STT]   3.4; 3.5;
Nana Mouskouri [*Sunday Express* 21/9/14]   3.7;
Roland Moussa [CH]   4.1;
Maria Muldaur [KM]   3.4; 5.3; 6.1;
Larry Myers   (i) [*On The Tracks* #4]   4.5;
                       (ii) [*The Bridge* #47]   4.5; 4.6;
Graham Nash   (i) [CH]   3.3;
                       (ii) [*Uncut* 4/09]   3.4;
Paul Nelson [CH]   5.4;
Stevie Nicks [*Boston Globe* 17/6/94]   5.4;
Carlos Nuno [*The Bridge* #30]   3.6;
Kevin Odegard [CH]   3.8; 6.1;
Odetta [HS]   3.1;
David Oppenheim   (i) 'I Could Have Kidnapped Bob Dylan' [*FTA* #2]   Winterlude #3;
                       (ii) Online interview 11/18   Winterlude #3;
Spooner Oldham [*On The Tracks* #17]   4.6;
Roy Orbison [*The Telegraph* #32]   5.5;
Tom Paxton [DB]   3.4;
Alan Pasqua [*Searching For A Gem* website]   4.3; 4.4;
D.A. Pennebaker   (i) [*Who Threw The Glass* #4]   3.1;
                       (ii) [*Melody Maker* 17/6/72]   3.1; 3.2;
                       (iii) [*Gadfly* 4/99]   3.1; 3.2; 3.3;
Tom Petty   (i) [*The Leeds* 11/88]   5.5;
                       (ii) [*Mojo* 2006]   5.4; 5.7;
Tim Pierce [YouTube 2021]   6.5;
Chuck Plotkin [Damien Love online post 2017]   4.5; 4.7; 4.8;
John Prine [*Illinois Entertainer* 11/81]   3.6;
Charlie Quintana [*The Telegraph* #37]   5.1;
Phil Ramone   (i) [*Melody Maker* 9/3/74]   3.8;
                       (ii) [KO]   3.8;
Paul Rappaport [CH]   3.8; 4.7; 4.8; 5.3-5.5;
                                                                     Postlude;

Scarlet Rivera [CH]   4.1; 4.2;
Johnny Rivers [KM]   6.4;
Robbie Robertson   (i) [*The Times* 13/2/21]   3.2;
                       (ii) [*The Observer* 2/11/14]   3.2;
                       (iii) [MsB]   3.2;
                       (iv) [*Crawdaddy* 3/76]   3.2; 3.7;
                       (v) [*NME* 17/6/78]   3.2;
                       (vi) [F&OS]   3.2;
                       (vii) [*Melody Maker* 7/10/72]   3.6;
                       (viii) [OTRBD]   4.1;
Duke Robillard   (i) [*Mojo* 2010]   5.8; 6.1;
                       (ii) [*Louisville Eccentric Observer* 1999]   5.8;
                       (ii) [TWM #6401]   5.8;
Mick Ronson [*NME* 15/12/79]   4.1;
Arthur Rosato   (i) [DB]   4.2; 4.3;
                       (ii) [CH]   3.7; 4.2; 4.5-4.8; 5.1;
                                                                     5.4;

Susan Ross [*Daily Mail* 16/5/98]		5.3; 6.1
Suze Rotolo [VB]		3.8;
Pete Rowan [CH]		3.8;
Mason Ruffner [*Uncut* online 2008]		5.6;
Leon Russell [KM]		3.6;
Micajah Ryan [*Uncut* online 2008]		5.8;
Ed Sanders [STT]		3.3;
Jerry Schatzberg [JS]		3.6;
Paul Schrader [TWM #696]		5.2;
Mike Scott [BTS]		5.4;
Toby Scott [CH]		4.8;
Joel Selvin [CH]		4.6;
Charlie Sexton [BTS]		5.1;
Chris Shaw	(i) [*Uncut* online 2008]	5.5; 6.1; 6.2; 6.4;
	(ii) [*Electronic Musician* 2009]	6.1; 6.2;
Sam Shepard [*Rolling Stone* 18/12/86]		5.2;
Chris Silva [TWM #5942]		6.4;
Paul Simon [*Rolling Stone* 20/7/72]		3.4;
Larry Sloman [*Isis* #104]		4.1; 5.1;
G.E. Smith [*Mojo* 5/11]		5.5;
Iain Smith [*The Telegraph* #28]		5.4;
Patti Smith [*The Telegraph* #32]		4.1;
Steven Soles	(i) [Jon Kanis interview tape]	4.2;
	(ii) [HS]	4.2;
J.D. Souther [TWM #6415]		5.8;
Neil Spencer [CH]		4.8;
Helena Springs [*Endless Road* #7]		4.3; 4.5; 4.6;
Mavis Staples [TWM #5231]		6.4;
Dave Stewart	(i) [*Uncut* 6/21]	5.2; 5.4;
	(ii) [LB]	5.4;
Rob Stoner	(i) [CH]	4.1; 4.2; 4.3;
	(ii) [RBP]	4.1;
Noel Stookey [KM]		3.2;
Fred Tackett	(i) [*The Bridge* #4]	4.5; 4.6; 4.7; 4.8;
	(ii) [Scott Marshall transcript]	4.6; 4.7;
	(iii) [Damien Love online post 2017]	4.7; 4.8;
Jonathan Taplin [BGP]		3.7; 4.2;
Benmont Tench	(i) [Damien Love online 2017]	4.8;
	(ii) [*Uncut* 6/21]	5.5;
Terri Thal	(i) [TDT]	3.4; 6.3;
	(ii) [*New York Times* 26/11/71]	3.4;
Dr Thaler [HS]		Prelude;
Linda Thompson [CH]		5.4;
Dave C. Towbin [DB]		3.7;
Happy Traum	(i) [STT]	3.2;
	(ii) [F&OS]	3.3;
	(iii) [*Guitar World* 1999/ RBP]	3.6;
Dave Van Ronk [TDT]		3.4; Postlude;
Bill Walker [HS]		3.5;
David Was [*The Telegraph* #44]		5.7;

Don Was	(i) [*Isis* #92]	5.5; 5.7; 5.8;
	(ii) [*Uncut* online 2008]	5.6; 5.7;
Paul Wasserman	(i) [BGP]	3.7;
	(ii) [*The Bridge* #49]	4.5; 4.6; 5.3;
Winston Watson [CH]		5.7;
Bob Weir [*Melody Maker* 13/5/89]		5.5;
Eric Weissberg	(i) [KO]	3.8;
	(ii) [*Rolling Stone* 21/11/74]	3.8;
Jerry Wexler	(i) [JW]	4.5;
	(ii) [*The Gospel Years* DVD]	4.5;
	(iii) [TWM #708]	4.5;
	(iv) [*Rolling Stone* 27/11/80]	4.6;
Dan White [*The Mix* 11/92]		5.8;
Stephen Wilson [CH]		3.1; 3.8;
Markus Wittman [CH]		6.4;
Ron Wood [*The Telegraph* #33]		4.2; 5.2; 5.3;
Tony Wright [*The Telegraph* #43]		4.6;
Rudy Wurlitzer	(i) [*The Believer* 5/13]	3.6;
	(ii) [Sam Davies 2001]	3.7;
Howie Wyeth [CH]		4.1; 4.2; 4.3;
Beattie Zimmerman	(i) [TT]	3.2; 3.3;
	(ii) [Isis Anthology]	3.3;
	(iii) [OTRBD]	4.1;
	(iv) [TWM #4315]	Winterlude #4;
Paul Zollo [CH]		6.1;

Bob Dylan interviews quoted:
26/4/63 – Studs Terkel [WFMT, Chicago]
27/4/65 – Maureen Cleave [*Don't Look Back* outtakes, Tulsa archive]
10/65 – The 'Original' *Playboy* interview, w/ Nat Hentoff [*Whaaat!*]
8/4/66 – Earl Leaf [*Teen* 7/66]
10/5/66 – Michael Braun [*Eat The Document* outtakes, Tulsa archive]
6/5/67 – Michael Iachetta [*New York Daily News* 8/5/67]
6+7/68 – John Cohen & Happy Traum [*Sing Out!* 10/68]
3/69 – Hubert Saal [*Newsweek* 4/4/69]
8/69 – Ian Brady [*Top Pops* 30/8/69]
26/6/69 – Jann Wenner [*Rolling Stone* 29/11/69]
27/8/69 – Isle of Wight press conference [transcript]
1/71 – Anthony Scaduto [*The Dylan Tapes*]
3/71 – Tony Glover [R.R. auction catalog + online version 19/11/20]
21/5/71 – Robert Shelton [*No Direction Home*]
12/1/74 – Ben Fong-Torres [*Knockin' on Dylan's Door*]
3/75 – Mary Travers [KNX-FM 26/4/75]
10/75 – Jim Jerome [*People Weekly* 10/11/75]
10-12/75 – Larry Sloman [*On The Road With Bob Dylan*]
8/76 – Neil Hickey [*TV Guide* 11/9/76]
28-31/10/77 – Allen Ginsberg [*The Telegraph* #33]
30/10/77 – Pierre Cotrell [*The Telegraph* #33]
11/77 – Ron Rosenbaum [*Playboy* 3/78]
12/77 – John Rockwell [*New York Times* 8/1/78]

12/77 – Jonathan Cott [*Rolling Stone* 23/2/78]

1/78 – Gregg Kilday [*L.A. Times* 22/1/78]

1/78 – Randy Anderson [*The Minnesota Daily* 17/2/78]

1978 – [*Photoplay* 9/78]

2/78 – Philip Fleishman [*MacLean's* 20/3/78]

2/78 – Barbara Kerr [*Toronto Sun* 26-29/3/78]

12/3/78 – Craig McGregor [*NME* 22/4/78]

14/3/78 – Helen Thomas [*The Age* 3/78]

1/4/78 – Karen Hughes [*Rock Express* #4]

5/78 – Robert Hilburn [*L.A. Times* 28/5/78]

20/6/78 – Robert Shelton [*Melody Maker* 29/7/78]

15/9/78 – Matt Damsker [*Talkin' Bob Dylan* 1978]

17/9/78 – Jonathan Cott [*Rolling Stone* 16/11/78]

23/9/78 – Marc Rowland [*Talkin' Bob Dylan* 1978]

6-15/11/78 – Pete Oppel [*Dallas Morning News* 18-23/11/78]

12/78 – Lynne Allen [*Trouser Press* #39]

7/12/79 – Bruce Heiman [KMEX-FM]

15/5/80 – Pat Crosby [KDKA-TV]

21/5/80 – Karen Hughes [*Occasionally* #4]

19/11/80 – Robert Hilburn [*L.A. Times* 23/11/80]

12/6/81 – Yves Bigot [Radio Europe One 22+23/6/81]

12/6/81 – Paul Gambaccini ['Rock On', BBC Radio One 20/6/81]

2/7/81 – Dave Herman [WNEW-FM 27/7/81]

13/7/81 Travemünde press conference [transcript]

20+21/7/81 – Neil Spencer [*NME* 15/8/81]

5/7/83 – Martin Keller [*NME* 6/8/83]

10/83 – Robert Hilburn [*L.A. Times* 30/10/83]

3/84 – Kurt Loder [*Rolling Stone* 21/6/84 + transcript]

29/5/84 – Verona press conference [*Talkin' Bob Dylan* 1984]

13/6/84 – Robert Hilburn [*L.A. Times* 5/8/84]

27/6/84 – Mick Brown [*Sunday Times* 1/7/84]

7/7/84 Martha Quinn [MTV]

8/7/84 – Bono [*Hot Press* 26/8/84]

30/7/84 – Bert Kleinman & Artie Mogull [Westwood One network]

3/85 – Bill Flanagan 3/85 [*Written In My Soul*]

17/6/85 – Bob Coburn [Rockline FM]

8-9/85 – Cameron Crowe [*Biograph*]

19/9/85 – Bob Brown [20/20 ABC-TV]

9/85 – Scott Cohen [*Spin* 12/85]

9/85 – Scott Cohen [*Interview* 2/86]

9/85 – Mikal Gilmore [*L.A. Herald-Examiner* 13/10/85]

11/85 – David Fricke [*Rolling Stone* 5/12/85]

11/85 – Robert Hilburn [*L.A. Times* 17/11/85]

11/85 – Denise Worrell [*Time* 25/11/85 + *Icons*]

11/85 – Charles Kaiser [*Boston Review* 4/86]

22/11/85 – Andy Kershaw [*OGWT*, BBC-2 11/85]

1/86 – Toby Creswell [*Rolling Stone* – Australia ed. 16/1/86 + transcript]

10/2/86 – Sydney press conference [transcript]

22/2/86 – Maurice Parker [ABC-TV, Australia]

10/3/86 – ??? [MTV 7/4/86]

5/86 – Mikal Gilmore [*Rolling Stone* 17+31/7/86]

21/5/86 – Bob Fass [WBAI-FM 21/5/86]

8/86 – Sam Shepard [*Esquire* 9/86]

14/6/86 – Jon Bream [*Minneapolis Star & Tribune* 22/6/86]

17/7/86 – David Hepworth [*Q* #1]

17/8/86 – Hearts of Fire press conference [transcript]

17/10/86 – Christopher Sykes [*The Telegraph* #30]

18/10/86 – Christopher Sykes ['*Getting To Dylan*', Omnibus BBC-2 10/87]

6/9/87 – Robert Hilburn [*L.A. Times* 9/87]

7/9/87 – Kurt Loder [*Rolling Stone* 5/11/87 + transcript]

5/8/88 – Kathryn Baker [*The Stars & Stripes* 7/9/88]

?1988 – Joe Smith [*Off The Record*]

6/89 – [*El Diario Vasco* 18/6/89]

9/89 – Edna Gundersen [*USA Today* 21/9/89]

21/10/89 – Adrian Deevoy [*Q* #39]

31/8/90 – Edna Gundersen [*USA Today* 9/90]

3/91 – Elliot Mintz [Westwood One network 5/91]

4/4/91 – Paul Zollo [*SongTalk* Vol. 2 #16]

8/91 – [*Porto Alegre* 13/8/91 – trans. *The Telegraph* #41]

4-5/11/91 – Robert Hilburn [*L.A. Times* 9/2/92]

13/3/92 – Stuart Coupe [*Time Off* 27/3/92]

8/93 – Greg Kot [*Chicago Tribune* 8/93]

23/6/93 – Gino Castaldo [*La Repubblica* 24/6/93]

4/94 – Ellen Futterman [*St Louis Post-Dispatch* 7/4/94]

5/95 – Edna Gundersen [*USA Today* 5-7/5/95]

8/97 – Edna Gundersen [*USA Today* 28/8/97]

9/97 – Edna Gundersen [*USA Today* 29/9/97]

9/97 – Jon Pareles [*New York Times* 28/9/97]

9/97 – David Gates [*Newsweek* 6/10/97]

4/10/97 – London press conference [transcript]

4/10/97 – Alan Jackson [*The Times* 15/11/97]

11/97 – Robert Hilburn [*L.A. Times* 14/12/97]

4/99 – Edna Gundersen [*On The Tracks* #17]

1/00 – Jeff Rosen [*No Direction Home* DVD]

23/7/01 – Rome press conference [transcript/ *Isis* #99]

23/7/01 – Alan Jackson [*The Times* 8/9/01]

23/7/01 – Christoph Gallach [*Der Spiegel* 9/01]

8/01 – David Fricke [*Rolling Stone* 27/9/01]

9/01 – Christopher Farley [*Time* 17/9/01]

9/01 – Edna Gundersen [*USA Today* 10/9/01]

9/01 – Robert Hilburn [*L.A. Times* 16/9/01]

25/9/01 – Mikal Gilmore [*Rolling Stone* 6/12/01]

23/1/03 – Sundance Film Festival [misc. press reports]

10/11/03 – Robert Hilburn [*L.A. Times* 4/4/04]

9/04 – David Gates [*Newsweek* 4/10/04]

9/04 – John Preston [*Sunday Telegraph* 26/9/04]

9/04 – Edna Gundersen [*USA Today* 4/10/04]

26/10/04 – Austin Scaggs [*Rolling Stone* online 17/11/04]

19/11/04 – Ed Bradley [*60 Minutes* 5/12/04]

12/12/05 – *Theme Time Radio Hour* press release [TWM #5918]

8/06 – Edna Gundersen [*USA Today* 28/8/06]

8/06 – Jonathan Lethem [*Rolling Stone* online 21/8/06]

5/08 – Alan Jackson [*The Times* 6/6/08]

5/09 – Douglas Brinkley [*Rolling Stone* 14/5/09]

1/15 – Bob Love [*AARP* 2-3/15]

22/3/17 – Bill Flanagan [online transcript]

2019 – Martin Scorsese [*Rolling Thunder Revue* DVD]

5/20 – Douglas Brinkley [*New York Times* 12/6/20]

11/22 – Jeff Slate [*Wall Street Journal* 19/12/22]

Other manuscript material & unpublished resources:
  Primary sources (i.e. referenced in multiple chapters):
– Recording Contracts with Columbia Records: 1/7/67, 1/8/74, 1/2/78, 1/7/82, 18/1/88, 6/12/90, 21/12/93 (all courtesy of Naomi Saltzman); Contract w/ MGM Records 1/67, never executed (deposited in Sony archives); Agreement for new contract 29/11/71, never executed (deposited in the official Bob Dylan Archive, Tulsa); CBS Contract for *The Basement Tapes* 1/6/75 (from auction of signed copy thereof); Schedule B of 2012 Sony recording contract (from private source).
– CBS memos c. 1966-78 including memos dated 28/3/68; 2/69; 6/73; 9/73; 7/74; 2/12/76; 9/9/77; and 1/78.
– Tape Identification Data for Dylan's Columbia studio reels 1967–2001 (with the exception of *Pat Garrett & Billy The Kid* sessions).
– American Federation of Musicians Sheets for *Self-Portrait* (from Country Music Hall of Fame), Planet Waves (from Tulsa archive) & *Blood on the Tracks* sessions (from AFM, NYC).
– Court papers, Kingston; Bob Dylan. Grossman, Albert: Estate Papers, filed at county court offices, Kingston, NY, specifically as pertaining to 'The Management Agreement', 'The Witmark Agreement' and '1970 Settlement Agreement'.
– 'Cooky: A Memoir', an 80,000 typescript by 'Cooky' Tribelhorn's friend, Bev Martin, written posthumously; drawing on 30 notebooks of verbatim contemporary conversations from the 1990s.
– A series of Dylan manuscripts, all put up for sale in the 2010s, privately or by auction (Courtesy of the Halcyon Gallery):
(i) 'Blowin' In The Wind' ms., on Taft Hotel notepaper, purportedly 1962
(ii) 'Mr Tambourine Man' ms., on Royal Orleans Hotel notepaper, two pages, purportedly 1964
(iii) 'It Ain't Me Babe' ms., on headed Greek hotel notepaper, purportedly 1964
(iv) 'Lay Lady Lay' ms., on Atlantic Lumber Company notepaper, purportedly 1969
(v) 'Knockin' On Heaven's Door' ms., on TWA headed paper, colour copy, purportedly 1973
(vi) 'Like A Rolling Stone' ms.; on Roger Smith Hotel notepaper, four pages, purportedly 1965
(vii) 'A Hard Rain's A-Gonna Fall' ms., handwritten, two pages, purportedly 1962.

  Secondary sources (i.e. referenced in a single chapter):
– *Book of Dreams*, Dylan's 1974 tour diary, Morgan Library, New York (transcript, courtesy of Michelle Engert)
– 'I'm Not There' typescript, reproduced in *The Telegraph* #24
– Typed letter to Lawrence Ferlinghetti, 28/4/64, Bancroft Library, Berkeley. Reproduced in *Words Fill My Head*
– Macmillan memo from Bob Markel 12/8/66; pertaining to cancellation of Tarantula publication (courtesy of Bob Bettendorf)
– Letters to Marcia Foreman from Geno Foreman c. 1966 (courtesy of Marcia Foreman)
– Tiny Tim's 1967 diary (courtesy of Justin Martell)
– Barney Hoskyns – *Small Town Talk* [proof]

– Scott Marshall – *A Spiritual Life* [proof]
– The Stuart Ostrow Papers, New York Public Library (Lincoln Center Performance Arts Division)
– Handwritten lyric on acetate sleeve, spring 1970 (courtesy of Mitch Blank)
– 'Shirley's Room', unfinished lyric, circa August 1970 [auction catalogue]
– The 'Little Red Notebook', c. summer 1974, Morgan Library [almost reproduced in facsimile in deluxe edition of *More Blood, More Tracks* (2018)]
– Patti Smith – online posting 5/21
– Typescript of Allen Ginsberg's tour diary 11/75 (courtesy of Allen Ginsberg)
– 'I Threw It To The Wind' – Faridi McFree's 1990 proposal for a memoir.
– Auctioned outline for a Carolyn Dennis memoir (courtesy of Arie De Reus)
– *Trouble No More* Deluxe edition
– Letter to fellow Christian from Toronto, 4/80
– Doc Pomus essay 27/7/84 (courtesy of Sharyn Felder)
– Susan Ross proposal
– Online auction catalogue 2017 [Margie Rogerson]
– Gypsy Fire [*Expecting Rain* website]
– Wilton Morley's account of 2/86 (courtesy of Wilton Morley)
– Letter to author from Markus Innocenti 8/12/88
– Dylan's handwritten *Oh Mercy* sequence 2/5/89 (courtesy of Arie De Reus)
– Postcard to Susan Ross 24/10/92
– Jerry Garcia eulogy 1995
– Jimi Hendrix exhibition 1988
– Debbie Gold proposal
– Dylan's letter to *SongTalk* 1994, Sotheby's, London, catalogue 29/9/15
– 1994-95 lyrical scraps, on cardex, in pencil, Sotheby's, London, catalogue 29/9/15
– *Masked & Anonymous* shooting script & synopsis (courtesy of Andy Muir)
– George Harrison eulogy 11/01
– Johnny Cash eulogy 12/9/03
– 'The Times They Are A-Changin', Sotheby's catalogue 12/10
– Facsimile of draft of 'The Times They Are A-Changin', *Silo* 12/63
– 'A Hard Rain's A-Gonna Fall', typescript, hand-corrected 10/62, reproduced in Sotheby's, London, auction catalogue 29/9/15
– 'It Ain't Me Babe' ms., Mayfair notepaper [reproduced in *Bob Dylan Scrapbook*]
– 'Tangled Up In Blue' ms., c. 2013 (courtesy of Bernie Chase)
– E-mailed notes provided for Luc Sante's essay in *Revisionist Art* (courtesy of Lucy Sante)
– Dylan's inscription to Jonathan Cott's copy of *Writings & Drawings*, 1978 (courtesy of Raymond Foye)
– Tulsa Finding Aid (courtesy of Jeff Rosen)

Audio-video sources
  Video:
Getting To Dylan, Omnibus, BBC-2, 10/87
Bruce Springsteen's and Bob Dylan's speeches at Rock'n'Roll Hall of Fame 1/88
Dylan's Oscar speech 3/01
Lost Songs – The Basement Tapes Continued DVD (Eagle Vision, 2015)
The Gunfighter DVD (20th Century Fox, 2006)
Wonder Boys [inc. special features] DVD (Universal Pictures, 2001)
Rolling Thunder Revue DVD (Criterion, 2019)
Barbara Rubin & The Exploding NY Underground DVD (Juno Films, 2019)

Audio:

(i) In concert recordings:

'Señor' rap, Savannah, Georgia 8/12/78

– Soundboard recordings from the Gospel Tour November 1979 to May 1980:

Warfield soundboards 2, 15+16/11/79; Santa Monica Civic soundboards 18+19/11/79; Tempe soundboards 25+26/11/79; San Diego 27+28/11/79 soundboards; interviews w/ Albuquerque audience members 5/12/79; Albuquerque soundboard 6/12/79; Tucson soundboard 8/12/79; Seattle soundboard 12/1/80; Omaha soundboard 25/1/80; Birmingham soundboards 2+3/2/80; Rundown rehearsals 9-11/4/80; Toronto soundboards 17-20/4/80; Montreal soundboards 22-25/4/80; Albany soundboards 27+28/4/80; Syracuse soundboards 4+5/5/80; Hartford soundboards 7+8/5/80; Providence soundboards 11+12/5/80; Pittsburgh soundboards 14-16/5/80; Akron soundboards 17+18/5/80

– Soundboard recordings from Fall 1980 to Fall 1981:

Warfield Theatre soundboards 12+15/11/80; Paramount Portland soundboard 3/12/80; Clarkston soundboard tape 12/6/81; Earl's Court soundboards 26-30/6/81; Meadowlands soundboard 27/10/81

– 'License To Kill' rap, Sydney 12/2/86

– 'Tomorrow Is A Long Time', O'Keefe Center, Toronto 2/6/90

– Maria McKee at 'Dylan tribute concert', L.A., 2008

(ii) Rehearsals, studio tapes & misc. recordings:

Dylan & Tiny Tim, Woodstock home session 2/67

John Wesley Harding session-tapes 17/10/67 + 6/11/67

'All American Boy' and 'All You Have To Do Is Dream', from source reels

Nashville Skyline session-tapes 13-14/2/69

Dylan/Cash session-tape 17/2/69

Nashville session-tape 3/5/69

Studio B, New York session-tapes 3-5/3/70

Studio B, New York complete session-tape 1/5/70

Planet Waves session-tapes and multitrack masters 11/73

A&R, New York session-tapes 16-19/9/74

Paul Martinson interview by Kevin Odegard

Craig McGregor/Dylan interview tape 12/3/78 (courtesy of Zac Dadic)

'Isis' work-tape, Jacques Levy's apartment 10/7/75

CBS Studios session-tape 14/7/75

CBS Studios session-tapes 28-31/7/75

CBS Studios session-tape 24/10/75

Bette Midler session-tape 10/75

'Luke Train' tape, Harry Smith & Phil Ochs 10/75

'Street-Legal piano tape' 26/12/77

Japanese rehearsal-tape 22/2/78

Power Station session-tapes 11-29/4/83

'Sweetheart Like You', alternate take 18/4/83

'How Many Days' 29/4/83

'Union Sundown', alternate take 2/5/83

Plugz rehearsal tape, Malibu 3/84

'Political World', complete version 3+4/89

Chicago sessions w/ Dave Bromberg 7/92

World Gone Wrong session-tapes, Malibu 1993

Time Out of Mind overdub sessions, Teatro, Oxnard, Ca. 3/97

'Red River Shore' with Daniel Lanois vocal, 1997
'Someday Baby', *Tell-Tale Signs* version, 2006
Theme Time Radio Hour, 100 one-hour broadcasts 2007-2009
MusiCares speech 7/2/15
Dylan's Nobel lecture 5/6/17

FAR AWAY FROM MYSELF: CHAPTER BREAKDOWN

Three Distinctly Different Amnesiacs (a.k.a. I Forgot To Remember To Forget)

Prelude – July 29th, 1966: Bound Upon The Wheel
Relevant published sources
Ren Grevatt – *Melody Maker* 13/8/66.

Dylan quotes
Michael Iachetta 5/67; Isle of Wight press conference 8/69; Craig McGregor 3/78; Sam Shepard 8/86.

Interviews with others
Sally Grossman; Dr Thaler.

3.1 – July 1966 to May 1967: There Must Be Some Way Out Of Here
Biographical Sources
DH; RR; BTS; STT; AA; CHR; CD; ME; AS; HS.

Other relevant published sources
Richard Fariña – 'A Generation Singing Out'; Phil Ochs – *Broadside* 10/65; 'Letters' – *Disc* 27/5/67; John Bauldie – 'Ceilings, Basements & Evening Things Up' [*The Telegraph* #20].

Dylan quotes
Nat Hentoff 10/65; Michael Iachetta 5/67; John Cohen 6-7/68; Ian Brady 8/69; Jann Wenner 6/69; Robert Shelton 5/71; Ben Fong-Torres 1/74; Kurt Loder 3/84; Sam Shepard 8/86; Jeff Rosen 1/00.

Interviews with others
Michael Bloomfield; John Bucklen; Liam Clancy; Bruce Dorfman; Rosemary Gerrette; Allen Ginsberg; Odetta; D.A. Pennebaker; Stephen Wilson.

Tulsa
'Stand Back From The Fire'; 'The Return Of The Wicked Messenger'; 'The Whistle Is Blowing'; 'Try A Little Muscatel'; 'Eskimo Woman'; 'Card Shark'; 'Santa Cruz'; 'The Bank Teller'; *Something Is Happening*; *Eat The Document* outtakes.

3.2 – February to December 1967: A Bunch Of Basement Noise
Biographical Sources
RR; SR; BTS; IB; AA; SST; F&OS; HS; TT.

Other relevant published sources
'A Family Album' – Al Aronowitz; *Random Notes* 9/3/68; John Bauldie – 'Ceilings, Basements & Evening Things Up' [*The Telegraph* #20]; Clinton Heylin – 'Lo and Behold! The Complete Story of the Basement Tapes' [*Uncut* 12/14].

Dylan quotes
John Cohen 6-7/68; Mary Travers 3/75; Matt Damsker 9/78; Pete Oppel 11/78; Cameron Crowe 9/85; Kurt Loder 9/87.

Interviews with others
Al Aronowitz; Rick Danko; Pete Drake; Allen Ginsberg; Sally Grossman; Garth Hudson; Bob Johnston; Richard Manuel; Charlie McCoy; D.A. Pennebaker; Robbie Robertson; Noel Stookey; Happy Traum; Beattie Zimmerman.

Tulsa
Eat The Document notes; 'You Can Change Your Name'; 'I Dreamed I Saw St Augustine'; 'As I Went Out One Morning'; 'I Am The Lonesome Hobo'; 'Dear Landlord'.

3.3 – October 1967 to February 1969: When The Lights Went Out
Biographical Sources
AA; CD; RR; JT; DW; GH; STT; BTS; HS; AS; TT.

Other relevant published sources
Ellen Willis – Woody Guthrie Memorial review [*Cheetah* 3/68]; Al Aronowitz – *John Wesley Harding* review [*Saturday Evening Post* 2/68].

Dylan quotes
John Cohen 6-7/68; Hubert Saal 3/69; Ian Brady 8/69; Matt Damsker 9/78; Jonathan Cott 9/78; John Preston 9/04; Bob Love 1/15.

Interviews with others
Dave Amram; Pattie Boyd; Larry Campbell; Johnny Cash; Charlie Daniels; Bruce Dorfman; Ramblin' Jack Elliott; Levon Helm; Bob Johnston; Elliott Landy; Michael McClure; Graham Nash; D.A. Pennebaker; Ed Sanders; Happy Traum; Beattie Zimmerman.

Tulsa
Eat The Document notes; 'Dump Truck'; 'Miss Lucy'; 'Take A Little Trip With Me'; 'I Am That Wicked Messenger'; 'I Gave It All Away' (a.k.a. 'I Threw It All Away'); 'Wanted Man'.

3.4 – March 1969 to February 1970: Town & Country
Biographical Sources
AA; BTS; VM; JC; BM; STT; RF; RR; CHR; SO; AS; DB.

Other relevant published sources
Bill Reed – 'Bob Dylan's Nashville Sessions', *Rolling Stone* 16/4/70; Carol Botwin – *South Bay Daily Breeze* 15/6/69; *Melody Maker* 23/8/69; *The Sun* 26/8/69; *The Times* 2/9/69; *Random Notes* 15/11/69; Bob Finkbine – *Scottsdale Progress* 3/5/86.

Dylan quotes
Michael Braun 5/66; Jann Wenner 6/69; Ian Brady 8/69; *The Sun* 8/69; Isle of Wight press conference 8/69; Larry Sloman 11/75; Travemünde press conference 7/81; *El Diario Vasco* 6/89; Ed Bradley 11/04.

Interviews with others
Dave Amram; Pattie Boyd; Bill Carruthers; Tom Clancy; Al Clayton; John Cohen; Chris Colley; Ron Cornelius; Sara Dylan; Ronnie Foulk; Doug Kershaw; Louis Killen; Barry Kornfeld; Judy

Lewis; Van Morrison; Maria Muldaur; Graham Nash; Tom Paxton; Paul Simon; Terri Thal; Dave Van Ronk.

Tulsa
Letter from Izzy Young to Dylan, 1968; 'I remember as if it was yesterday . . .'; 'Interview'; 'The Ballad of Jabez Stone'; Braun 5/66.

3.5 – March 1970 to March 1971: A Different Village
Biographical Sources
AA; CHR; CD; BS; STT; HB; RF; HS; DB; BTS.

Other relevant published sources
Greil Marcus – 'Self Portrait #25' [*Rolling Stone* 8/6/70]; *Random Notes* 16/4/70; Anthony Scaduto – *New York Times* 26/11/71; *Bitches Brew* Deluxe Edition; The Letters of Archibald MacLeish [TWM #489].

Dylan quotes
Ian Brady 8/69; Anthony Scaduto 1/71; Larry Sloman 11/75; Travemünde press conference 7/81; Cameron Crowe 9/85.

Interviews with others
Michael Bloomfield; David Bromberg; Wendy Clarke; John Cohen; Chris Colley; Ron Cornelius; Charlie Daniels; Bruce Dorfman; Bob Johnston; Al Kooper; Kris Kristofferson; Bob Markel; Charlie McCoy; Faridi McFree; Roger McGuinn; Van Morrison; Bill Walker.

Tulsa
Porky Morgan; 'Becky and Albert'; *New Morning* b+w video 6/70.

3.6 – January 1971 to February 1973: Escaping On The Run
Biographical Sources
PC; LK; RR; BLS; CD; CHR; AS; AJW; PS.

Other relevant published sources
Bob Finkbine – *Scottsdale Progress* 3/5/86; Bob Finkbine – 'Dylan's Idaho Sojourn', *Scottsdale Progress* 1986; *Random Notes* 8/7/71; *Random Notes* 2/3/72; Anthony Scaduto – *New York Times* 26/11/71; *Random Notes* 7/12/72; *Random Notes* 10/5/73; *Rolling Stone* 15/3/73; Dave Marsh – *Creem* 7/73; *Pat Garrett & Billy The Kid* press book; Rudy Wurlitzer – *Pat Garrett & Billy The Kid* screenplay; Clinton Heylin – 'The True Story of Pat Garrett & Billy The Kid' [*The Telegraph* #37].

Dylan quotes
Scaduto 1/71; Tony Glover 3/71; Neil Hickey 8/76; John Rockwell 12/77; Jonathan Cott 12/77; Jonathan Cott 9/78; Pete Oppel 11/78; Randy Anderson 1/78; Cameron Crowe 9/85; David Hepworth 7/86; Elliot Mintz 3/91.

Interviews with others
Dave Amram; Stephanie Buffington; James Coburn; John Cohen; Gordon Dawson; Jerry Fielding; Robert Gottlieb; George Harrison; Sue Kawalerski; Jim Keltner; Kris Kristofferson; Roger McGuinn; Carlos Nuno; John Prine; Robbie Robertson; Leon Russell; Jerry Schatzberg; Happy Traum; Rudy Wurlitzer.

Tulsa
Autobiographical writings, late 90s; *Writings & Drawings* ms.; 1971 recording contract; CBS memo 6/73; letters from Baez, Mary Martin and Tony Glover; 'Stubborn Child'; Blue Rock session-tape 16/3/71.

3.7 – March 1973 to February 1974: Bobby, You're So Far Away From Home
Biographical Sources
PS; CD; RR; JT; SC; LK; BTS; OTRBD; DB.

Other relevant published sources
Jean Carroll's diary of *PG&BTK* shoot – *Rocky Mountain Magazine* 1982; Jon Landau – *Pat Garrett* soundtrack LP review [*Rolling Stone* 30/8/73]; Michael Watts on release of *Dylan* LP [*Melody Maker* 5/11/73+8/12/73]; Nick Kent – *Planet Waves* review NME 9/2/74.

Dylan quotes
Barbara Kerr 2/78; Craig McGregor 3/78; Robert Hilburn 11/80; Cameron Crowe 9/85; Adrian Deevoy 10/89.

Interviews with others
Ellen Bernstein; Rob Fraboni; David Geffen; Barry Goldberg; Jim Keltner; Louie Kemp; Kris Kristofferson; Roger McGuinn; Joni Mitchell; Nana Mouskouri; Robbie Robertson; Arthur Rosato; Dave C. Towbin; Rudy Wurlitzer.

Tulsa
Letter from Joe Santora to David Braun re *Dylan* 1/74; Autobiographical writings, late 90s; 'Ruling Kisses'; 'Whirlwind'; *Planet Waves* draft sleeve-notes; 'Tough Mama'; 'Wedding Song, Medicine Song'; 'On A Night Like This'; 'Don't Want No Married Woman'; 'Hero Blues' soundboard tapes Chicago 3+4/1/74.

3.8 – March 1974 to January 1975: Into Dealing With Slaves
Biographical Sources
MS; LK; GB; RR; OTRBD; KO.

Other relevant published sources
Glenn Berger – *Esquire* 17/9/14; *Billboard* 17/8/74; Earl Wilson – syndicated gossip column 22/6/74; *Melody Maker* 7/9/74; Larry Sloman – *Rolling Stone* 21/11/74; Paul Nelson, Greil Marcus and Jon Landau reviews of *Blood on the Tracks* [*Rolling Stone* 13/3/75]; Nick Kent – *Blood on the Tracks* review NME 25/1/75; Michael Gray – *Blood on the Tracks* review *Let It Rock* 4/75; *Random Notes* 13/2/75; Paul Williams – *Blood on the Tracks* review [*Watching The River Flow*]; Chris Weber – *Insider* 3/75; Sam Sussman – 'The Silent Type' (*Harper's*, 4/21).

Dylan quotes
Ron Rosenbaum 11/77; Craig McGregor 3/78; Jonathan Cott 9/78; Pete Oppel 11/78; Lynne Allen 12/78; Bill Flanagan 3/85; Cameron Crowe 9/85; Toby Creswell 1/86; Elliot Mintz 3/91.

Interviews with others
Glenn Berger; Ellen Bernstein; Rich Blakin; Michael Bloomfield; Charlie Brown III; Tony Brown; Claudia Carr; Richard Crooks; Tim Drummond; Jakob Dylan; Rob Fraboni; Barry Kornfeld; Paul Martinson; Joni Mitchell; Kevin Odegard; Phil Ramone; Paul Rappaport; Suze Rotolo; Pete Rowan; Eric Weissberg; Stephen Wilson.

Tulsa
'Tangled Up In Blue'; 'Idiot Wind'; 'You're Gonna Make Me Miss You When You Go'; 'You Were Good To Me'; 'The Pouring Down Rain'; 'Little Tiger (Night In The Dark Swamp)'; 'Up To Me'; 'Simple Twist Of Fate'; 'Parting Shot'; 'It's Breakin' Me Up'; 'Ain't It Funny'; 'Lily, Rosemary And The Jack Of Hearts'; 'There Ain't Gonna Be Any Next Time'; 'Shelter From The Storm'; 'Bell-tower Blues'; 'Death Is Inside Of Me'; 'If You See Her, Say Hello'; 'Meet Me In the Morning'.

Winterlude #3 – May 1975: Lost In France
Dylan quotes
Jim Jerome 10/75.

Other relevant published sources
David Oppenheim – 'I Could Have Kidnapped Bob Dylan' [*Fourth Time Around #2*]; David Oppenheim interview 11/18; Robert Martin – *Dix Jours Avec Bob Dylan* [*Ten Days With Bob Dylan*].

4.1 – June to December 1975: Rolling With The Thunder
Biographical Sources
KR; RR; PC; OTRBD; RTL; COD; JB; BTS; DY.

Other relevant published sources
Jim Jerome – *People Weekly* 10/11/75; Nat Hentoff – 'Is It Rolling Zeus?' [*Rolling Stone* 26/1/76]; Derek Barker – 'The Story of The Hurricane' [*Isis* #91]; Michael Simmons – 'The Greatest Show on Earth' [*Mojo* 6/19].

Dylan quotes
Jim Jerome 10/75; Larry Sloman 10-12/75; Craig McGregor 3/78; Lynne Allen 12/78; Bill Flanagan 3/85.

Interviews with others
T-Bone Burnett; Sara Dylan; Emmylou Harris; Ronnie Hawkins; Mel Howard; Larry Johnson; Louie Kemp; Claudia Levy; Jacques Levy; David Mansfield; Roger McGuinn; Bette Midler; Joni Mitchell; Roland Moussa; Scarlet Rivera; Robbie Robertson; Mick Ronson; Larry Sloman; Patti Smith; Rob Stoner; Howie Wyeth; Beattie Zimmerman.

Tulsa
'Hurricane'; 'Abandoned Love'; draft sleeve-notes for *Desire*; 'Sara'; *Renaldo & Clara* production notes.

4.2 – January 1976 to March 1977: Gulf Coast Highway
Biographical Sources
JB; RR; JT; VM; OTRBD; DH; BTS; DY; DB.

Dylan quotes
Gregg Kilday 1/78; Barbara Kerr 2/78; Craig McGregor 3/78; Robert Hilburn 5/78; Pete Oppel 11/78; Yves Bigot 6/81.

Interviews with others
Joan Baez; Joel Bernstein; Farir Brouhafa; Stephanie Buffington; Ramblin' Jack Elliott; Kinky Friedman; Allen Ginsberg; Susan Green; Mel Howard; Larry Johnson; Claudia Levy; David Mansfield; Faridi McFree; Joni Mitchell; Marvin Mitchelson; Scarlet Rivera; Arthur Rosato; Steven Soles; Rob Stoner; Ron Wood; Howie Wyeth.

Tulsa
'Cold'; 'Possessive Eyes'; 'Cross The Line'; 'Let Me Taste It, Crystal Queen'; Lakeland 18/4/76 soundboard tape; 'Lily, Rosemary And The Jack Of Hearts' rehearsal tape 5/76;

4.3 – March 1977 to June 1978: Her Version Of Jealousy
Biographical Sources
KS; BTS.

Other relevant published sources
Dylan's blurb to Peter Guralnick's *Last Train To Memphis*.

Dylan quotes
Ron Rosenbaum 11/77; Allen Ginsberg 10/77; John Rockwell 12/77; Barbara Kerr 2/78; *Photoplay* 9/1978; Philip Fleishman 2/78; Craig McGregor 3/78; Helen Thomas 3/78; Robert Hilburn 5/78; Jonathan Cott 9/78; Marc Rowland 9/78; Kurt Loder 3/84.

Interviews with others
Joan Baez; Ellen Bernstein; Joel Bernstein; Ronee Blakley; Michael Bloomfield; Jakob Dylan; Dan Fiala; Mel Howard; David Mansfield; Faridi McFree; Joni Mitchell; Alan Pasqua; Arthur Rosato; Helena Springs; Rob Stoner; Howie Wyeth.

Tulsa
'Let Me Taste It, Crystal Queen'; 'Possessive Eyes'; 'No Time To Think'; 'Spellbound Magician'; 'Changing Of The Guards'; 'We'd Better Talk This Over'; 'Where Are You Tonight?'; 'Señor'; 'New Pony'; 'Long Time Train'; 'Baby Stop Crying'; 'Tell Me The Truth One Time'; Rundown rehearsal tapes 2+4/1/78; Five-song 'blues' copyright tape 1/78; *Street-Legal* rehearsal tapes 13-21/4/78; 'Where Are You Tonight?' alternate take.

4.4 – June 1978 to January 1979: More Than Flesh & Blood Can Bear
Biographical Sources
TIM; SM; HS.

Other relevant published sources
Richard Williams – 'De-evolution and Dylan', *Melody Maker* 11/11/78.

Dylan quotes
Ron Rosenbaum 11/77; Pierre Cotrell 10/77; Jonathan Cott 12/77; Barbara Kerr 2/78; Craig McGregor 3/78; Karen Hughes 4/78; Robert Hilburn 5/78; Robert Shelton 6/78; Matt Damsker 9/78; Marc Rowland 9/78; Robert Hilburn 11/80; Dave Herman 7/81; Kurt Loder 3/84; Bill Flanagan 3/85; Cameron Crowe 9/85; Edna Gundersen 9/97; Jon Pareles 9/97.

Interviews with others
Mary Alice Artes; Pattie Boyd; Martin Carthy; Billy Cross; Carolyn Dennis; Jo Ann Harris; David Mansfield; Alan Pasqua.

Tulsa
'Without You'; 'More Than Flesh And Blood'; 'Marching Out Of Time'; 'Slow Train'; 'Gonna Change My Way Of Thinking'; Tour rehearsals 28+30/8/78; Largo soundcheck 5/10/78; 'Legionnaire's Disease', Kalamazoo soundcheck 13/10/78; 'Take It Or Leave It', Terre Haute soundcheck 14/10/78; 'This A-Way, That A-Way', Savannah soundcheck 8/12/78.

4.5 – January to October 1979: In The Lion's Den
Biographical Sources
TIM; BTS; SM; EI; OTRBD.

Other relevant published sources
Jann Wenner – *Slow Train Coming* review [*Rolling Stone* 20/9/79]; Clinton Heylin – 'Saved! Bob Dylan's Conversion To Christianity' Pt 1 [*The Telegraph* #28]; Michael Simmons – 'The Missionary Position' [*Mojo* 12/17].

Dylan quotes
Ron Rosenbaum 11/77; Matt Damsker 9/78; Lynne Allen 12/78; Robert Hilburn 11/80; Bono 7/84; Bob Coburn 6/85; Scott Cohen 9/85.

Interviews with others
Barry Beckett; Terry Botwick; Bill Dwyer; Kenn Gulliksen; Scott Huffstetler; Dave Kelly; Roger McGuinn; Joni Mitchell; Larry Myers; Chuck Plotkin; Arthur Rosato; Helena Springs; Fred Tackett; Paul Wasserman; Jerry Wexler.

Tulsa
'When You Gonna Wake Up'; 'Ain't Too Proud To Repent'; 'Gonna Change My Way Of Thinking'; 'Precious Angel'; Letter from Allen Ginsberg 5/79; 'When He Returns'; 'Saving Grace'; 'Solid Rock'.

4.6 – November 1979 to May 1980: A Man With A Message
Biographical Sources
TIM; BTS; SM; PW.

Other relevant published sources
Gail S. Tagashire – *San Jose Mercury News* 11/79; Robert Hilburn – Warfield review [*L.A. Times* 3/11/79]; Leslie Goldberg – Warfield review [*San Francisco Bay Guardian* 11/79]; *Arizona Republic* 26/11/79; Patrick MacDonald – *Seattle Times* 1/80; Karen Hughes – *Village Voice* 5/80; Clinton Heylin – 'Saved! Bob Dylan's Conversion To Christianity' Pts 2-3 [*The Telegraph* # 29-30].

Dylan quotes
Bruce Heiman 12/79; Pat Crosby 5/80; Martin Keller 7/83; Scott Cohen 9/85; Cameron Crowe 9/85; Denise Worrell 11/85; Kathryn Baker 8/88; Elliot Mintz 3/91.

Interviews with others
Dick Cooper; Tim Drummond; Raymond Foye; Allen Ginsberg; Bruce Heiman; Robert Hilburn; Dave Kelly; Jim Keltner; Regina McCrary; Spooner Oldham; Arthur Rosato; Joel Selvin; Helena Springs; Fred Tackett; Paul Wasserman; Jerry Wexler; Tony Wright.

Tulsa
'Cover Down (Pray It Through)'; '(Oh Yeah) You Know Me'; 'Talk About What He Did For Me';

4.7 – June 1980 to April 1981: A Voice In The Wilderness
Biographical Sources
TIM; BTS; SM.

Other relevant published sources
Kurt Loder – *Saved* review [*Rolling Stone* 18/9/80]; Michael Oldfield – Mark Knopfler interview [*Melody Maker* 15/11/80]; 'One Year Later' – Paul Williams [*Watching The River Flow*].

Dylan quotes
Jim Jerome 10/75; Neil Hickey 8/76; Barbara Kerr 2/78; Robert Hilburn 11/80; Yves Bigot 6/81; Bill Flanagan 3/85; Cameron Crowe 9/85; David Gates 9/97.

Interviews with others
Dan Fiala; Robert Hilburn; Jim Keltner; Chuck Plotkin; Paul Rappaport; Arthur Rosato; Fred Tackett.

Tulsa
'Cover Down Pray Thru'; 'Ain't Gonna Go To Hell'; 'Yonder Comes Sin'; 'Makin' A Liar'; 'The Groom's Still Waiting At The Altar'; 'Caribbean Wind'; 'Somebody's Child'; 'Wild About You Babe'; 'Let's Keep It Between Us'; 'Dead Man, Dead Man'; 'Need A Woman'; 'Property Of Jesus'; 'Angelina'.

4.8 – May to December 1981: Stepping Back Into The Arena

Biographical Sources
TIM; BTS; SM; HS.

Other relevant published sources
Paul Nelson – *Shot of Love* review [*Rolling Stone* 15/10/81].

Dylan quotes
Larry Sloman 10/75; Helen Thomas 3/78; Pete Oppel 11/78]; Lynne Allen 12/78; Paul Gambaccini 6/81; Dave Herman 7/81; Neil Spencer 7/81; Martin Keller 7/83; Bob Fass 5/86.

Interviews with others
Bruce Gary; Jim Keltner; Chuck Plotkin; Paul Rappaport; Arthur Rosato; Toby Scott; Fred Tackett; Benmont Tench.

Tulsa
'Trouble'; 'I Play To The Crowd That Jesus Played To'.

Winterlude #4 – 1982: Disappearing Off The Grid
Biographical Sources
LK.

Dylan quotes
Martin Keller 7/83.

Interviews with others
Allen Ginsberg; Rabbi Kasriel Kastel; Dave Kelly; Louie Kemp; Beattie Zimmerman.

5.1 – January 1983 to April 1984: King Snake Will Crawl
Biographical Sources
AA; HS; TG; BTS.

Dylan quotes
Maureen Cleave 4/65; Randy Anderson 1/78; Matt Damsker 9/78; Neil Spencer 7/81; Martin Keller 7/83; Robert Hilburn 10/83; Kurt Loder 3/84; Robert Hilburn 6/84; Mick Brown 6/84; Bill Flanagan 3/85; Mikal Gilmore 9/85; Scott Cohen 9/85; Paul Zollo 4/91; Austin Scaggs 10/04; Bob Love 1/15.

Interviews with others
Josh Abbey; Alan Clark; Allen Ginsberg; Debbie Gold; Barry Kornfeld; Mark Knopfler; Tony Marsico; Charlie Quintana; Arthur Rosato; Charlie Sexton; Larry Sloman.

Tulsa
'Prison Guard'; 'Jokerman'; 'Man Of Peace'; 'Neighborhood Bully'; 'License To Kill'; 'I And I'; 'Blind Willie McTell'; 'Someone's Got A Hold Of My Heart'; 'Tell Me'; 'Too Late'; 'Foot Of Pride'.

5.2 – March 1984 to June 1985: I'll Go Along With This Charade
Biographical Sources
IM; TG; JB; BLS; BTS; SVZ; CHR.

Dylan quotes
Karen Hughes 4/78; Kurt Loder 3/84; Verona press conference 5/84; Martha Quinn 7/84; Bill Flanagan 3/85; Cameron Crowe 9/85; Christopher Sykes 10/86; Paul Zollo 4/91.

Interviews with others
Josh Abbey; Colin Allen; Arthur Baker; Debbie Gold; Don Heffington; Ira Ingber; Maurice Jacox; Maria McKee; Paul Schrader; Sam Shepard; Dave Stewart; Benmont Tench; Ron Wood.

Tulsa
'New Danville Girl'; 'I'll Remember You'; 'Trust Yourself'; 'The Queen Of Rock'n'Roll'; 'Maybe Someday'; 'Emotionally Yours'; 'Where Is This God?'; 'When The Night Comes Falling From The Sky'; Cherokee Studios, LA 6+14/12/84; Cherokee Studios, LA 5/2/85; 'Dark Eyes' session, Power Station 3/85.

5.3 – 1983–87: There Ain't No Limit To The Trouble Women Bring
Biographical Sources
BLS; CAB; HS; COD; SM.

Other relevant published sources
Sam Sussman – 'The Silent Type' (*Harper's*, 4/21); Nick Kent – *Vox* 10/90.

Dylan quotes
Ron Rosenbaum 11/77; Philip Fleishman 2/78; Karen Hughes 4/78; Dave Herman 7/81; Mick Brown 6/84; Bill Flanagan 3/85; Scott Cohen 9/85; Cameron Crowe 9/85; Charles Kaiser 11/85; Sam Shepard 8/86; Kurt Loder 9/87; Kathryn Baker 8/88.

Interviews with others
Ellen Bernstein; Carolyn Dennis; Markus Innocenti; Stan Lynch; Maria Muldaur; Paul Rappaport; Susan Ross; Paul Wasserman; Ron Wood.

5.4 – July 1985 to June 1987: Meet Me In The Bottom
Biographical Sources

HS; RG; RE; BGP; BLS; CHR; CBS; BTS.

Other relevant published sources
Mikal Gilmore – *Rolling Stone* 17+31/7/86.

Dylan quotes
Bert Kleinman 7/84; Bob Brown 9/85; Mikal Gilmore 9/85; Scott Cohen 9/85; Denise Worrell 11/85; Robert Hilburn 11/85; Andy Kershaw 11/85; David Fricke 11/85; Maurice Parker 2/86; David Hepworth 7/86; *Hearts of Fire* press conference 9/86; Adrian Deevoy 10/89; Bob Love 1/15.

Interviews with others
Josh Abbey; Dave Alvin; Bono; Mikal Gilmore; Ira Ingber; Markus Innocenti; Al Kooper; Richard Marquand; Paul Nelson; Tom Petty; Paul Rappaport; Arthur Rosato; Mike Scott; Iain Smith; Dave Stewart; Linda Thompson.

Tulsa
'Band Of The Hand'; 'Under Your Spell'; 'Driftin' Too Far From Shore'; 'To Fall In Love With You'; Skyline Sessions 28/4-16/5/86.

5.5 – June 1987 to December 1988: Struck By Lightning
Biographical Sources
TT; DG; BLS; VM; CHR; DL; BTS.

Dylan quotes
Robert Hilburn 5/78; Dave Herman 7/81; Bono 7/84; Bill Flanagan 3/85; Dave Fricke 11/85; Denise Worrell 11/85; Toby Cresswell 1/86; Mikal Gilmore 5/86; Jon Bream 6/86; Robert Hilburn 9/87; Kurt Loder 9/87; Kathryn Baker 8/88; Edna Gundersen 9/89; Adrian Deevoy 10/89; Edna Gundersen 8/90; Paul Zollo 4/91; Robert Hilburn 11/91; Stuart Coupe 3/92; London press conference 10/97; Christopher Farley 7/01; Mikal Gilmore 9/01.

Interviews with others
Kenny Aaronson; Ronee Blakley; Marshall Crenshaw; César Díaz; Jerry Garcia; George Harrison; Stan Lynch; Joni Mitchell; Roy Orbison; Tom Petty; Paul Rappaport; Chris Shaw; G.E. Smith; Fred Tackett; Benmont Tench; Don Was; Bob Weir.

Tulsa
'I Have Prayed For Liberty'; 'Dignity'; 'Silence Is Golden'; 'Blackbeard Was A Woman'; 'Mr Moneybags'; 'If Jesus Walked The Streets Today'; 'You Are My Destiny'.

5.6 – January 1988 to December 1989: The Quality Of Mercy
Biographical Sources
BLS; DL; CHR; BTS; VM.

Other relevant published sources
David Hepworth – Q 10/86; *Look Back* #14.

Dylan quotes
Karen Hughes 4/78; Cameron Crowe 9/85; Scott Cohen 9/85; Denise Worrell 11/85; Toby Cresswell 1/86; Sydney press conference 2/86; Edna Gundersen 9/89; Paul Zollo 4/91.

Interviews with others
Kenny Aaronson; Malcolm Burn; Larry Charles; Mark Howard; Daniel Lanois; Mason Ruffner; Don Was.

Tulsa
'Series Of Dreams'; 'Most Of The Time'; 'Ring Them Bells'; 'TV Talkin' Song'; 'Born In Time'; 'Man In The Long Black Coat'; *Oh Mercy* sessions March 1989.

5.7 – January 1990 to August 1994: The Contingency Of Assholes
Biographical Sources
VM; HS; KM; BTS.

Other relevant published sources
Dylan Letter – *Sister2Sister* 7/90; Valentine message – *Arizona Republic* 14/2/93.

Dylan quotes
Marc Rowland 9/78; Adrian Deevoy 10/89; Paul Zollo 4/91; Elliot Mintz 3/91; Robert Hilburn 11/91; Stuart Coupe 3/92; Ellen Futterman 4/94; Edna Gundersen 5/95; Jon Pareles 9/97; Alan Jackson 10/97; Mikal Gilmore 9/01; Edna Gundersen 9/01; Jonathan Lethem 8/06.

Interviews with others
Roseanne Cash; Liam Clancy; César Díaz; Robben Ford; Jim Keltner; David Lindley; Joni Mitchell; Tom Petty; David Was; Don Was; Winston Watson.

Tulsa
'Handy Dandy'; 'Ten Thousand Men'; 'TV Talkin' Song'; 'Under The Red Sky'; 'Unbelievable'; 'Not Dark Yet', alternate take 1/97.

5.8 – June 1992 to March 1997: Meeting The Criteria
Biographical Sources
DL; CHR.

Other relevant published sources
Greil Marcus – *Invisible Republic*; Dawson & Propes – *What Was The First Rock'n'Roll Record*.

Dylan quotes
Ron Rosenbaum 11/77; Toby Cresswell 1/86; Kathryn Baker 8/88; Greg Kot 8/93; Edna Gundersen 5/95; Jon Pareles 9/97; Robert Hilburn 9/97; Edna Gundersen 9/97; London press conference 10/97; Alan Jackson 10/97; Edna Gundersen 9/01; Mikal Gilmore 9/01; Bob Love 1/15.

Interviews with others
Michael Bolton; Dave Bromberg; Cindy Cashdollar; Jim Dickinson; Raymond Foye; Debbie Gold; Mark Howard; Jim Keltner; David Kemper; Daniel Lanois; Claudia Levy; Augie Meyers; Duke Robillard; Micajah Ryan; J.D. Souther; Don Was; Dan White.

Tulsa
Draft version of *World Gone Wrong* sleeve-notes, 1993; 'All I Ever Loved Is You'; 'Not Dark Yet'; 'Trying To Get To Heaven'; 'Not Dark Yet' Teatro demo 10/96; Criteria sessions 1/97.

Winterlude #5 – May-July 1997: Can This Really Be The End?
Biographical Sources
BLS.

Other relevant published sources
New York Post 29/5/97.

Dylan quotes
Alan Jackson 10/97; Edna Gundersen 9/01.

6.1 – 1997–2001: Ain't No Judy Garland
Biographical Sources
VM; DL; DG; COD; HS; AA; DY; KM.

Other relevant published sources
TWM #4659; TWM #4315.

Dylan quotes
Studs Terkel 4/63; Tony Glover 3/71; Cameron Crowe 9/85; Scott Cohen 9/85; Mikal Gilmore 9/85; Mikal Gilmore 5/86; Robert Hilburn 11/97; Edna Gundersen 9/97; Jon Pareles 9/97]; London press conference 10/97; Edna Gundersen 4/99; Jeff Rosen 1/00; Rome press conference 7/01; Alan Jackson 7/01; David Fricke 8/01; Mikal Gilmore 9/01; Edna Gundersen 9/01; David Gates 9/04; Edna Gundersen 8/06.

Interviews with others
Bonnie Beecher; Larry Campbell; Cindy Cashdollar; Larry Charles; Liam Clancy; Sheryl Crow; Curtis Hanson; Don Ienner; George Harrison; Mark Howard; Louie Kemp; David Kemper; Al Kooper; Joni Mitchell; Maria Muldaur; Kevin Odegard; Duke Robillard; Susan Ross; Chris Shaw; Paul Zollo.

Tulsa
Autobiographical materials, late 1990s; 'Things Have Changed'; 'Everlasting Queen Of My Heart'.

6.2 – January 2000 to July 2003: Smoke'n'Mirrors
Biographical Sources
HS; BTS.

Dylan quotes
Allen Ginsberg 10/77; Philip Fleishman 2/78; Jonathan Cott 9/78; Edna Gundersen 9/97; Edna Gundersen 5/99; Rome press conference 7/01; Edna Gundersen 9/01; Mikal Gilmore 9/01; Sundance Film Festival 1/03; Robert Hilburn 11/03; Jonathan Lethem 8/06; Alan Jackson 5/08; Douglas Brinkley 5/09.

Interviews with others
Bucky Baxter; Jeff Bridges; Larry Charles; Jim Dickinson; Mark Howard; David Kemper; Augie Meyers; Chris Shaw.

Tulsa
'The Time Will Come'; 'Bye And Bye'; 'High Water'; 'Sugar Babe'; 'Summer Days'; 'Cry A While'; 'Tweedle Dee & Tweedle Dum'; Clinton Recording Studio session-tapes 5/01; 'High

Water', 'Tweedle Dee & Tweedle Dum' and 'Moonlight', on pre-overdub master for *'Love and Theft'* ?11/5/01.

6.3 – 2001–2018: Writings & Drawings
Biographical Sources
CHR; HS; BLS; BTS.

Other relevant published sources
Roberta Smith – *New York Times* 13/12/12; *Ecstasy of Influence* – Jonathan Lethem; 'Songs With Echoes' – *New York Times* 14/9/06; 'The Times They Are A-Changin', Sotheby's catalogue 12/10; 'The Poetry of Ellery Queen' – Luc Sante [2008 blog].

Dylan quotes
Earl Leaf 4/66; Ron Rosenbaum 11/77; Randy Anderson 1/78; Bob Coburn 6/85; Cameron Crowe 9/85; Edna Gundersen 9/89; Elliot Mintz 3/91; Paul Zollo 4/91; Robert Hilburn 11/91; Rome press conference 7/01; Christoph Gallach 7/01; Mikal Gilmore 9/01; Edna Gundersen 9/01; Robert Hilburn 9/01; John Preston 9/04; Jonathan Lethem 8/06; Alan Jackson 5/08; Douglas Brinkley 5/09; Bob Love 1/15; Bill Flanagan 3/17.

Interviews with others
Larry Charles; John Elderfield; Mike Evans; Jim Keltner; Louie Kemp; Terri Thal.

Tulsa
Letter from Bruce Springsteen to Bob Dylan, 2004.

6.4 – 2001-2017: Columbia Recording Artist
Biographical Sources
BTS; SM.

Other relevant published sources
Michael Simmons – review of *Shadows In The Night* [*Mojo* 2/15]; Neil McCormick – review of *Shadows In The Night* [*Daily Telegraph* 23/1/15]; Neil McCormick – review of *Triplicate* [*Daily Telegraph* 30/3/17].

Dylan quotes
Randy Anderson 1/78; Marc Rowland 9/78; Denise Worrell 11/85; Sam Shepard 8/86; Elliot Mintz 3/91; *Porto Alegre* 8/91; Edna Gundersen 9/97; David Gates 9/97; London press conference 10/97; Jeff Rosen 1/00; Alan Jackson 7/01; Edna Gundersen 9/01; Mikal Gilmore 9/01; Edna Gundersen 8/06; Jonathan Lethem 8/06; *Theme Time Radio Hour* press release 12/05; Douglas Brinkley 5/09; Bob Love 1/15.

Interviews with others
Joan Baez; Kristie Buble; Larry Charles; Leonard Cohen; Olivier Dahan; Carolyn Dennis; Louie Kemp; Paul McCartney; Joni Mitchell; Johnny Rivers; Chris Shaw; Chris Silva; Mavis Staples; Markus Wittman.

Tulsa
'Ain't Talkin'; 'Rollin' And Tumblin'; 'The Levee's Gonna Break'; 'Nettie Moore'; 'Workingman's Blues'; 'Thunder On The Mountain'; 'Spirit On The Water'; 'Tin Angel'; 'Scarlet Town'; 'Tempest'.

6.5 – 2015–2021: My Echo, My Shadow And Me, Too
Other relevant published sources
Ben Sisario – 'Bob Dylan's Secret Archive', *New York Times* 2/3/16; 'Popular Tunes' – Allen Gins-
berg, 1996; Irvine Welsh, Will Self + Salman Rushdie – social media postings on Dylan winning
Nobel Prize 13/10/16; Adam Sherwin – 'Bob Dylan "plagiarised" Nobel Prize for Literature lec-
ture using online student study aid' [*i-Paper* 15/6/17]; Michael Gray on *Rough and Rowdy Ways*
[*Outtakes on Bob Dylan*] Kitty Empire – review of *Rough and Rowdy Ways* (*Observer* 21/6/20).

Dylan quotes
Neil Hickey 8/76; Randy Anderson 1/78; Lynne Allen 12/78; Bob Brown 9/85; MTV 3/86; Mikal
Gilmore 5/86; Joe Smith ?1988; Gino Castaldo 6/93; London press conference 10/97; Rome press
conference 7/01; Christoph Gallach 7/01; Jonathan Lethem 8/06]; Alan Jackson 5/08; Douglas
Brinkley 5/09; Bob Love 1/15.

Interviews with others
Jackson Browne; Barry Kornfeld; Roger McGuinn; Tim Pierce.

Postlude – 2022: How Much Longer?
Dylan quotes
Barbara Kerr 2/78; Philip Fleishman 2/78; Lynne Allen 12/78; Robert Hilburn 10/83; Verona
press conference 5/84; Sydney press conference 2/86; Mikal Gilmore 5/86; Chris O'Dell 1986;
Christopher Sykes 10/86; Kurt Loder 9/87; David Gates 9/97; Edna Gundersen 8/06; Bill Flana-
gan 3/17; Martin Scorsese 2017.

Interviews with others
Joan Baez; Johnny Cash; Jakob Dylan; Robben Ford; Geoff Gans; Faridi McFree; Wilton Morley;
Chris O'Dell; Paul Rappaport; Dave Van Ronk.

Acknowledgements

Well, what a long, strange trip this has been. I left New York in mid-March 2020 on the last flight to Dublin before Trump closed the air-space, and began writing the first section of this book on touching down. It was delivered on June 22nd, 2022, eight days early, and then Little, Brown took five months to decide it was too long to publish, without commenting on a single word. I had told them eight months earlier it would be 300,000 words, and it was 299,764 words.

So, the fact that you are reading this is in no way thanks to Little, Brown.

To have delivered eight days early in mid-pandemic was only possible because of Jeff Rosen and his ever-efficient sidekick, Parker Fishel, at the Dylan office, who didn't just smooth the way to letting me quote from Tulsa's plentiful treasures, but facilitated me hearing the things I needed to hear when a trip to Tulsa was not an option. Thanks, guys.

Glenn Korman, the ex-head of Sony Archives in New York and the most knowledgeable of archivists, again served as my very own (unpaid) go-to audio engineer/commentator when I needed someone to translate the secrets of multitracks, tape boxes and studio protocols. The work of his wife, Katie, on the *Time Out of Mind* multitracks must also be acknowledged, along with various favours extended by Tom Tierney, Rob Santos and Jeroen Vandermeer at Sony.

As the volume where the Tulsa Bob Dylan Archives really comes into its own, my next fulsome set of thanks must go to its then-curator, Michael Chaiken, its director, Mark Davidson, and the George Kaiser Foundation for the generous way it facilitated my work at the coalface when the archive was still under semi-secret wraps at the Gilcrease Museum. Thanks, too, to Steve Higgins for enabling my last trip to Tulsa, at the time of the opening of the Bob Dylan Center in May 2022.

Many real titans of Dylan research from all around the world were once again responsive to my endless queries. A big thank you to Mitch Blank, Zac Dadic, Dave Dingle (RIP), Glen Dundas, Terry Gans, Rod MacBeath, Bill Pagell, Arie De Reus and Ian Woodward. Thanks, too, to Bob Bettendorf, Jonathan Cott, Peter Doggett, Robert Hilburn, Barney Hoskyns, Lucy Sante and Neil Spencer for sharing a precious few secret things that had been hidden from the world.

In New York, I was able to call on expertise, insights and kindnesses willingly offered by Steve Berkowitz, Lenny Kaye, Lee Ranaldo, Paul Rappaport, and Jeremy Tepper; as well as the generosity of Mike Decapite, Nick Hill, Bob Strano and David Thomas. Others who opened doors and suggested avenues include Frank Beacham, Joel Bernstein, Paul Burch, Scott Curran, Erik Flannagan, Fred Goodman, Peter Hale, Jan Haust, Sam Jones, Reid Kopel, Arthur Rosato, Mark Satlof, Steve Shepherd, Rani Singh, Jonathan Taplin and Marcus Whitman.

If the many, many sharers of thoughts and anecdotes from across the simple years are too numerous to mention individually, I'd like to give a special, heartfelt mention this time around to Josh Abbey, Ellen Bernstein, Glen Berger, Pattie Boyd, Harvey Brooks, John Elderfield, Marcia Foreman, Rob Fraboni, Dana Gillespie, Ira Ingber, Marcus Innocenti (and Eddie Arno), Louie

Kemp, Barry Kornfeld, Graham Nash, Kevin Odegard, Ron Radosh, Pete Rowan and Steve Wilson.

My main helpers on the manuscript trail were Richard Austin, Bernie Chase, Ed Kozinski, Bobby Livingston, and that lovable rogue, Peter McKenzie. I'd also like to express a deep sense of gratitude to Peter Doggett, Sharyn Felder (overseer of the Doc Pomus archive), Marcia Foreman, Allen Ginsberg, Scott Marshall, Justin Martell (overseer of Tiny Tim's papers), Bev Martin, Wilton Morley, Stuart Ostrow, Robert Polito and Bruce Springsteen for permission to quote from unpublished correspondence, papers, and interviews. It shows a true generosity of spirit in this age of fibreglass.

For allowing me to use some fabulous photos the world has not seen I extend warm thanks to Arie De Reus, Barry Ollman, Ellen Bernstein, Dave Tulsky and Sue Kawalerski. For doing some digging on my behalf into some of the more legal issues that bubble beneath the surface of a life like this, thanks go to the two Raymonds, Foye and Landry, and to John Pelosi and Bruce Scavuzzo. And profusest of thanks go to two editors who actually *edit*, Jörg Hensgen at Bodley Head, who kept the faith when others preferred the Judas role, and Ian and Isabel Daley, the best copy-editors in the business.

Finally, I'd like to express my abiding affection for three ladies who won't see another day, but who lit up both mine and my subject's lives: Faridi McFree, Debbie Gold and 'Cooky' Tribelhorn. Others who have fallen along the way, but remain in my thoughts, include Peter Stone Brown, Cesar Diaz, Bruce Gary, Allen Ginsberg, Don Heffington, Paul Nelson and Paul Williams. I miss you all.

In fact, if it wasn't for the astonishingly competent, hard-working people at the Beth Israel cardiology unit in lower Manhattan, I might have been joining you before my own last thoughts on Bobby D saw the light of day. I dedicate this doorstopper of a volume to all the doctors, nurses and ambulance crews there. Because of them – and unlike the Invisible Man – I'm still here. Rave on, and fear not the dying of the light.

Clinton Heylin, March 2023

Index